The Arab-Israeli Dilemma

Contemporary Issues in the Middle East

Fred J. Khouri, professor of Political Science at Villanova University, Villanova, Pennsylvania, has devoted approximately thirty years of study to the Arab-Israeli and other Middle Eastern problems. During extensive travels throughout the Middle East between 1958 and 1984, American-born Professor Khouri did considerable on-the-spot research in the area, and he held many frank off-the-record discussions with many top leaders and others, including American diplomats, in the Middle East and with key U.S. and UN officials involved with Middle Eastern affairs. He was a visiting professor at the American University of Beirut (AUB) from 1961 to 1964 while on leave from Villanova University. He is the author of a monograph (*The Arab States and the UN*, 1954) and helped write *Towards Peace in the Middle East: A Report of a Study Group* (Brookings, 1975). He contributed chapters or essays to eight books: *To Make War or to Make Peace* (1969); *Politics of International Crises* (1970); *Peoples and Politics in the Middle East* (1971); *The Elusive Peace in the Middle East* (1975); *Dictionary of American History* (1976); *UN Reform and Reconstructuring* (1978); *Lebanon in Crisis: Participants and Issues* (1979); *The Middle East in the 1980s: Problems and Prospects* (1983). In addition, his articles have appeared in many journals: *The Middle East Journal; Journal of South Asian and Middle Eastern Affairs; American-Arab Affairs; The Review of Politics; New Outlook* (Tel Aviv); *Transaction; Middle East International* (London); *Asia; Middle East Forum; Arab Perspectives*. He holds a B.A., M.A., and Ph. D. from Columbia University. He is an associate editor of the *Journal of South Asian and Middle Eastern Affairs*.

The Arab-Israeli Dilemma

Third Edition

1985

FRED J. KHOURI

Villanova University

SYRACUSE UNIVERSITY PRESS

Library of Congress Cataloging in Publication Data

Khouri, Fred John.
    The Arab-Israeli dilemma.

    1. Jewish-Arab relations—1917–   —History.
I. Title.
            DS119.7.K48 1976   327.5694'017'4927   68-20483
    ISBN 0-8156-2339-9 (cloth)   0-8156-2340-2 (paper)

Manufactured in the United States of America

Preface to the Third Edition

Since the first edition of this book was published in 1968, many important changes have taken place, and the Arab-Israel dilemma has, if anything, become more complicated, more dangerous to peace in the Middle East and the world, and more difficult to resolve than ever before. Unfortunately, deeply rooted misunderstanding, distrust, and animosity, as well as widespread disagreements over the facts and principles involved, and the pressures and constraints caused by domestic politics, have continued to hinder efforts to deal effectively with the overall problem. Moreover, all parties, including the United States, have too frequently ignored the lessons of history, repeated the same costly mistakes made in the past, and pursued policies which generally have done more to undermine than to promote their own long-term best interests. Consequently, despite many well-meaning, but often faulty and irresolute, efforts made to resolve the Arab-Israeli conflict, we are in early 1985 no closer to—and probably further away from—lasting peace and stability in the Middle East than we were in 1968.

To attain as deep, complete, and accurate an understanding as possible of all aspects of and points of view on the overall Arab-Israeli problem, I have spent approximately thirty years (1) studying the principal primary and secondary sources—ranging from UN records to memoirs of key policy makers; (2) doing considerable on-the-spot research throughout the Middle East; and (3) making extensive use of the invaluable information and insight gained over a period of many years from teaching, lecturing, and traveling in many Arab states and Israel. I have especially benefited from holding frequent and frank off-the-record discussions with many top leaders and other high officials, scholars, writers, and others from various walks of life in the area and with key American and UN officials, diplomats, and specialists on the Middle East. This unique background has enabled me to write a comprehensive, scholarly, highly documented study of the overall Arab-Israeli problem from its earliest beginning in history to the present day.

Ever since majoring in International Relations at Columbia University in the late 1930s and serving in the Air Corps in World War II, I have been deeply concerned about the cause of world peace. Moreover, after specializing in Middle Eastern affairs after the war, I became convinced that only through repudiating brute force as an instrument for resolving disputes and increasing the authority and effectiveness of the UN and international law can human beings have any real hope of ever achieving true and lasting security and peace and avoiding in the future catastrophic wars whether in the Middle East or elsewhere in the world. I also became convinced that ignorance and misunderstanding on the part of most leaders and peoples in the world, including our own, have been the principal causes of most conflicts and have created the most formidable obstacles to lasting peace. Until these causes and obstacles can be adequately overcome, the Middle East and the world in general will continue to be plagued by unending insecurity, instability, strife, and, inevitably, more armed conflicts. That is why ever since the end of World War II my life's aim has been to do everything I could—especially through my teaching and writing—to help break through the wall of ignorance, misunderstanding, and mistrust which has throughout history obstructed our efforts to find enlightened, peaceful means for resolving international disputes and promoting the rule of law.

Since Arab-Israeli relations, like all international relations, are not determined by impersonal states but by human beings who alone are able to act and react, I have frequently given great emphasis to the attitudes and feelings of the Arabs and Israelis and to those policies and actions which have contributed significantly to creating and intensifying Arab-Israeli mistrust, fear, and hostility. In short, by presenting the Arab-Israeli dilemma in all of its major dimensions, including the human one, and by using as many eminent and authoritative sources as possible to effectively document and substantiate the accuracy and cogency of the materials and analyses presented, I have tried to bring to light the most pertinent facts and principles involved and to analyze and evaluate as fully, candidly, and objectively as possible the views, policies, and actions of the contending parties, as well as the roles played by the major powers, in the hope of promoting among their leaders and peoples that deeper and clearer understanding of the realities of the situation in the Middle East and of the enlightened and determined steps that must be taken by all the parties, especially the United States, to bring about a just peace—for only a peace based on justice can, by removing the causes of war, endure and serve the real, long-term best interests of all of those directly or indirectly involved in the Arab-Israeli conflict.

There are so many to whom I am deeply indebted for assistance in preparing this and earlier editions of my book that it will be impossible to name them all. However, I wish to express my appreciation to the Reverend John M. Driscoll (president) and the Reverend Lawrence C. Gallen (vice-president) and other Villanova University officials for encouraging and facilitating my research activities here and abroad. I am also grateful to my sister Margaret for her invaluable help with all three editions.

FRED J. KHOURI

Villanova, Pennsylvania
March 25, 1985

Contents

The Arab-Israeli Dilemma

CHAPTER I

The Historical Background of Palestine Through World War I

ORIGIN OF JEWISH AND ARAB TIES TO PALESTINE

Over a period of many centuries, Arabs and Jews have developed deep historical roots in Palestine and strong emotional attachments to it. In the nineteenth century, out of these entangled roots and attachments there emerged two nationalisms—Arab nationalism and political Zionism —both laying claim to the same land. It was the confrontation of two incompatible nationalisms that produced the troublesome "Palestine question" of earlier years, the bitter Arab-Israeli antagonisms, disputes, and wars of more recent years, and the dangerous Arab-Israeli dilemma challenging the world today.

The Jews had their first contact with their "promised land" about 1800 B.C., when Abraham led his Bedouin followers to the outskirts of the Palestine area, much of which was controlled by the Canaanites. Later, Abraham's descendants migrated to Egypt, where they multiplied and lived for several centuries before Moses led them out again. The Jews returned to Palestine around the twelfth century B.C., but they remained weak and divided until Saul united them into one kingdom. Saul's successor, David, extended the country's borders, and his son Solomon built the First Temple in the city of Jerusalem during the tenth century. This first united kingdom, which lasted less than two hundred years before dissolving into the kingdoms of Judah and Israel, provided the religious and emotional basis for Jewish interest in Palestine and Zionist claims to the area.

In 721 B.C. the Assyrians invaded the northern kingdom of Israel and destroyed part of it. The small southern kingdom of Judah continued to exist until the Babylonians attacked Jerusalem in 586 B.C., destroyed the First Temple, and scattered the people. Fifty years later Persia captured Babylonia and permitted some Jews to return to Palestine. A second temple was built in the early part of the sixth century B.C. Subse-

1

quently Alexander the Great, the Ptolemies of Egypt, and leaders of the Syrian-Greek state to the north ruled all or part of the area. The Maccabean revolt in 168 B.C. against Antiochus' efforts to enforce Hellenism resulted in a century of Jewish dominance which ended with the Roman conquest about 63 B.C. Two major Jewish revolts in A.D. 70 and A.D. 135 led to the leveling of the Second Temple, the destruction of Jerusalem, and the expulsion of all Jews from Jerusalem "forever." Few Jews remained in the Palestine region after that date.

Palestine as the birthplace of Christianity became politically significant with the conversion to Christianity of the Emperor Constantine who moved his capital from Rome to Constantinople. When the Empire divided in A.D. 395, Palestine became part of the Eastern, or Byzantine, Empire. In the fifth and sixth centuries, small and scattered Jewish settlements lived among the Christian majority. Palestine was briefly lost to the Persians but reconquered by Byzantium in 628. Around 634 it was lost again, and for good, to the Arabs during the caliphate of Omar, successor of the prophet Muhammad.

In the early part of the seventh century Muhammad's teachings of Islam had united the tribes of the Arabs, another Semitic people inhabiting the Arabian peninsula. Following his death in A.D. 632, Muhammad's followers conquered a vast empire and spread their religion, their culture, and their language, Arabic, from Spain to Indonesia over some four centuries. While Europe slumbered during the Dark Ages, Arab power and civilization flourished, providing the basis for the revived pride and national aspirations of the Arabs in the twentieth century.

The Christian inhabitants of Palestine, mostly descendants of the original Canaanites, became Arabized—as did the small Jewish communities. Most of these Christians also became Muslim, though a small but important minority kept up what are among the oldest sects in Christianity. In A.D. 691, with the building of the Mosque of Omar, called the Dome of the Rock, near the spot in Jerusalem where Muhammad was believed to have ascended briefly to heaven, Jerusalem became the third city sacred to the Muslims—after Mecca and Medina. Arab rule in the Palestine area ended in 1071. Although from that date parts or all of Palestine fell under the control of the Seljuk Turks (1071–1099), the Crusaders (twelfth and thirteenth centuries), the Tartars and Mongols (1244–1260), the Mamlukes of Egypt (1260–1517), and the Ottoman Turks (1517 to World War I), the majority of the inhabitants remained Arab and Muslim.

As the world's third monotheistic religion, Islam shared many historical and religious traditions with Judaism and Christianity. Muhammad had been greatly influenced by the teachings of the prophets and

Jesus. His followers revered the prophets and Jesus, and they were instructed by Muhammad to respect the "peoples of the book." Since Muslims regulated all aspects of their lives in accordance with the principles of their faith, they usually did not deny a similar right to those who remained Jews and Christians. Given considerable autonomy, these religious communities made and enforced their own religious, judicial, and social rules, and paid taxes in exchange for state protection and exemption from military service. Actually, heterodox Christian sects found more freedom within the tolerance of Islamic rule than they had under the established Byzantine church. Christians and Jews held important posts under the various Arab caliphs. The Ottoman Turks continued to maintain separate religious communities called millets. All in all, from the beginning of the Diaspora (the dispersion of the Jews), Jewish communities enjoyed a freer life in Muslim Asia than in Christian Europe.

ZIONIST MOVEMENT AND BALFOUR DECLARATION

The hope of returning one day to the Promised Land of the Old Testament never died among the Jews. In fact, for two thousand years Jewish prayers and rituals were built around the theme of the eventual coming of the Messiah to unite the Jews in Israel and rule over them.

Until the latter part of the nineteenth century, Jewish interest in Palestine was basically religious and humanitarian. Most who settled there with the financial help of wealthy European Jews did so largely on religious grounds. In the latter part of the nineteenth century, however, some European Jews began to take a political interest in Palestine. In Western Europe they had greatly improved their social and political status, and the process of assimilation was well advanced among them. But in the undemocratic semi-feudal systems characteristic of Eastern Europe, Jews had long been considered a separate and alien ethnic group, many of them still living in ghettos. The Jews in these countries were divided in their reactions to this categorizing. Most Jews were resigned to it, while some sought to alter their inferior status by pressing for social and political reforms. However, the intensification of anti-Semitism in Russia in the 1880's, at a time when nationalism was on the rise in Europe, finally led a number of them to the conclusion that a just and lasting solution to the problem of the Jews could never be achieved until the Jews attained their own national home in which they could administer their own affairs and determine their own destiny. The concept of a Jewish nationalism was first expounded by Leon Pinsker, a Russian Jew, in 1882. However, it was Theodor Herzl, an Austrian Jew and journalist, who provided political Zionism with its most effective leadership.

In response to Herzl's book, *The Jewish State,* and his other efforts, the First Zionist Congress met in 1897 in Basle, Switzerland, and created the World Zionist Organization. Most of the delegates were from Eastern Europe, and many desired ultimately to set up a Jewish state, but caution and practical considerations caused the Congress to pass a resolution favoring only a "home in Palestine" for the Jewish people. Herzl first endeavored, without success, to obtain permission from the Ottoman government to establish a Jewish charter company for the settlement of Jews in Palestine. In 1903, pogroms of Russian Jews and the feeling that anti-Semitism could never be fully eradicated led him to seek British aid in acquiring a "homeland," and Britain offered the East African Protectorate (later Kenya and often erroneously referred to as Uganda).[1] Herzl was willing to accept this, at least as a temporary measure, but the Russian Zionist majority in the Seventh Zionist Congress refused to consider an alternative to Palestine.

Although Herzl thought in terms of mass migration of Jews to Palestine, he apparently did not consider the matter of future Arab-Jewish relations important. He seemed to feel that since the Arabs allegedly would benefit economically from the Jewish settlements, they would not object to the Jews' taking control. In fact, it was not until after 1908 that a few leading Zionists began to be aware of an Arab problem.[2]

Initially, the Zionist organization was strongest among the Jews of Eastern Europe where most Jews of the world lived and persecution was greatest. Although the Zionist movement spread slowly to Western Europe and the United States, mainly as a result of the large-scale migration of Eastern European Jews to those areas, opposition to political Zionism developed there and remained firm for many years. Many Orthodox Jews objected to the political aspects of Zionism because they believed that a return to Zion should be brought about only by divine intervention, as indicated in the Torah, and not by a temporal, political movement. Other Jews opposed the nationalist aspects because they felt Judaism was a religion, not a nationality, and that the mission of Judaism, being universal and religious, could best be performed in Diaspora. Many also feared that the existence of Jewish nationalism would complicate the status of Jews in countries outside any Jewish state. Marxist Jews considered Zionism a reactionary bourgeois movement. All these objections notwithstanding, the world Zionist movement gained momentum. Jewish settlements in Palestine increased, and by the outbreak of World War I, there were some 80,000 Jews there.

Dr. Chaim Weizmann, a distinguished British chemist, and Nahum Sokolow, Russian member of the Zionist executive, led the efforts in Britain to achieve Zionist goals in Palestine. Starting as early as

1906, Weizmann began communicating with such important British leaders as Lords Balfour and Milner, Lloyd George, Sir Mark Sykes, and the editor of the influential *Manchester Guardian*. These acquaintances were to prove most helpful, especially in 1917, when Weizmann began to press the British government for specific action to implement the Zionist program. At that point, Weizmann's main opposition came from prominent anti-Zionist Jews in Britain who feared that the demands for nationality rights in Palestine for the Jewish people would be incompatible with the desire of Jews elsewhere in the world for equal rights as citizens of the nations in which they lived.

The spring of 1917 brought developments which advanced the Zionist cause. In March the Kerensky government put a number of Jews into key positions in the new Russian duma. Britain hoped that by placating the advocates of Zionism, she could encourage the Russian Jewish leaders to keep Russia in the war. After the United States entered the conflict, Britain was concerned about the continued apathy toward the war of a major section of American Jewry. When the German government began to solicit the support of German and world Jewry, Britain felt the urgent need to outbid Germany and to sow internal disaffection among the Jews in the Central powers so as to weaken the enemy. Encouraged by Zionist arguments that a Jewish-dominated Palestine would strengthen Britain's strategic position in the Middle East, some British officials gave increasing consideration to developing Palestine as a major outpost which covered the approaches to the Suez Canal. In addition, Britain hoped to use Zionist support to help block the internationalization of Palestine, as required by the secret Sykes-Picot Agreement with France, and thereby to obtain Palestine for Britain alone.

Christians in Great Britain and the United States, particularly Protestants, were swayed on this issue by emotional and religious considerations. Concerned over the difficult situation of Jews in continental Europe, they lent sympathetic ears to the Zionist argument that providing Jews with their own home would alleviate their suffering. Steeped in the stories of the Old Testament, they thought of their Holy Land in terms of the homeland of Jehovah's chosen people, not in terms of the long-resident Muslim Arab communities, let alone their fellow Christians belonging to sects dating back to the time of Christ.

As a result of these various factors, on November 2, 1917, British Foreign Secretary Arthur Balfour wrote an official letter to a private British subject, Lord Lionel Walter Rothschild. Several texts had been prepared before the final one, which came to be known as the Balfour Declaration, was adopted by the British government. An earlier text approved by the Prime Minister and the Foreign Office stated, "Palestine shall be reconstituted as the National Home of the Jewish people." The final text, however, referred merely to "the establishment in Palestine of a National Home for the Jewish people." This was further qualified by the statement that "nothing shall be done which may prejudice the civic and religious rights of the existing non-Jewish communities or the rights and political status enjoyed by Jews in any other country." Weizmann blamed the opposition of Edwin Montagu, an anti-Zionist Jew in the British cabinet, for the substantial weakening of the final declaration. Britain obtained the hesitant support of the United States for the declaration before she formally committed herself. Later, France and Italy vaguely proclaimed their backing of the Zionist program without specifically mentioning the Balfour Declaration itself.[3]

Although the Balfour Declaration was not a legally binding document, did not give the Zionists all they wanted, and was not as specific as they would have liked, it nevertheless strengthened their cause immeasurably. Actually, the Zionists, at least in their more formal demands, had been careful to avoid specifically requesting a Jewish state—despite the fact that a state was indeed their ultimate goal. Zionist leaders were willing to take one step at a time and achieve their objective piecemeal; they were even willing to make tactical retreats when necessary. These policies and tactics paid off in 1917, and they were to pay off later as well.

ARAB NATIONALIST MOVEMENT AND BRITISH WARTIME PROMISES

In the nineteenth century, French and American missionary and educational activities in the Levant provided the stimulus of new ideas and encouraged the study of Arab history and language. This awakened the interest and pride of the Arab in his heritage, thus giving birth to Arab nationalism. At first, this nationalism was basically cultural and affected only a handful of Syrian and Lebanese intellectuals. With time, however, it became more politically oriented and involved an increasing number of people, both Christians and Muslims, as it spread to other Arab areas. During the despotic rule of the Ottoman Sultan Abdul Hamid, Arab nationalism had to work underground. Although the Young Turk revolt in 1908 aroused hopes among the Arab nationalists for greater autonomy, they quickly found that the Young Turks were as opposed to Arab aspirations as had been the sultan overthrown by the Young Turks.

At the outbreak of World War I, Arab nationalists thought they had a choice of two courses: to cast their lot with the Turks in the hope of achieving autonomy and some self-government as an ultimate reward, or to support the Allies in the hope of acquiring complete independence.

Turkish ruthlessness in dealing with Arab nationalists soon drove even the moderate Arabs into the anti-Turkish camp. Once the Ottoman Empire joined the Central powers in the war, Britain quickly saw the advantages of an Arab revolt. Not only would it weaken Turkey militarily by depriving her of Arab manpower, but Arab forces could be used to augment the Allied armies in the Near East. Arab backing could also help prevent the Sultan's proclamation of a *jihad* (holy war) by all Muslims against the Allies, and prevent it from having any dangerous repercussions in the Arab world and in India. Furthermore, Britain now felt the need of creating an independent Arab state or federation to serve in place of the Ottoman Empire as a bulwark for her lifeline to India.

While the main intellectual centers of Arab nationalism were located in the principal cities of the Levant, the most effective military leadership arose in the Hejaz section of the Arab Peninsula. Firm Ottoman control over the Levant had effectively throttled the nationalist movement there, but Turkish control in Arabia was generally so weak that a nationalist revolt could develop with little interference. Despite the fact that Sharif Hussein of the Hejaz trusted the British implicitly, other more skeptical Arabs, particularly in Syria and Mesopotamia, were wary of them. These Arabs felt that they should not join the Allies until Britain made satisfactory promises to the Arabs. Syrian nationalists agreed to accept Hussein as their spokesman in any negotiations with Britain, provided he espoused their political platform, commonly known as the Damascus Protocol, as the essential condition for an alliance. Hussein accepted the terms of the Protocol, and they were incorporated in his negotiations with the British.

The Arab demands and British concessions were contained in an exchange of ten letters [4] between the Sharif and Sir Henry McMahon, British high commissioner of Egypt. Hussein's first note on July 14, 1915, presented the main Arab demands. He requested British recognition of Arab independence in an area bounded on the north by a line from Mersin-Adana to the Persian frontier, on the east by Persia and the Persian Gulf, on the south by the Indian Ocean, and on the west by the Red and Mediterranean seas. Only Aden was excluded. In his letters of October 24 and December 13, 1915, Sir Henry agreed "to recognize and uphold the independence of the Arabs in all the regions lying within the frontiers proposed by the Sharif of Mecca" with certain exceptions, none of which appeared, at least to the Arabs, to include the Palestine area. The British excluded the "districts of Mersin and Alexandretta and portions of Syria lying to the west of the districts of Damascus, Homs, Hama, and Aleppo," all of which "lie well to the north of Palestine." [5] Britain's position was that she had to give more careful consideration to Arab requests for the districts of Aleppo and Beirut because of the interests there of her ally, France. Britain also referred to the need for special administrative arrangements for the Baghdad and Basra vilayets. Britain went on to promise not "to conclude any peace whatsoever of which the freedom of the Arab peoples . . . does not form an essential condition." Hussein accepted the exclusion of the districts of Mersin-Adana and agreed to a temporary British occupation of the vilayets of Baghdad and Basra. He rejected the other modifications, but agreed not to press these matters until the end of the war in order not to impair the war effort. He had such faith in British integrity that he felt sure that Britain would not betray the Arabs when the war was over.

On the strength of McMahon's assurances, the Arab revolt began on June 5, 1916. While the Arabs did not play a large role in the overall war picture, their revolt was of great military value because it diverted a considerable number of Turkish reinforcements and supplies to the Hejaz, protected the right flank of the British armies as they advanced through Palestine, removed any danger of the establishment of a German submarine base on the Red Sea, and prevented the proclamation of a *jihad* by the Sultan from having any serious consequences in Allied-controlled areas. As the effects of the revolt spread northward through the Levant in the summer of 1918, the whole countryside began to rise against the Turks, thus aiding the advancing Allied forces.[6]

Meanwhile, on May 16, 1916, the French and British governments signed the secret Sykes-Picot Agreement which divided many Arab-inhabited territories into French- and British-administered areas as well as zones of influence and provided for the internationalization of Palestine. This agreement clearly conflicted with the McMahon promises to Hussein. But Hussein did not learn of the treaty until a year and a half later when Russia's revolutionary government published this and other secret war agreements in December, 1917. Early in 1918, Sir Reginald Wingate, the newly appointed high commissioner of Egypt, sent Hussein two telegrams which reaffirmed Britain's former pledges to the Arabs, held that the Sykes-Picot Agreement was not a formal treaty, and concluded that in any case Russia's exit from the war "had long ago created an altogether different situation." The telegrams, which deliberately misrepresented the facts, were apparently designed to reassure Hussein, and they achieved their purpose in that he continued to trust Britain.[7]

Hussein's confidence in the British survived even the publication of the Balfour Declaration on November 2, 1917. This time Britain sent Commander David George Hogarth to explain the declaration to Hussein. Again, the facts were deliberately distorted to placate Hussein. Although the declaration stated merely that "nothing shall be done which may prejudice the civil and religious rights" of the Palestine Arabs, Hogarth told Hussein that the "Jewish settlements in Palestine would only be allowed insofar as would be consistent with the political and economic freedom of the Arab population." Hogarth's term "political and economic freedom" was much stronger and more favorable to the Arabs than "civil and religious rights," the words used in the declaration itself. Hogarth also assured Hussein that Britain was "determined that the Arab race shall be given full opportunity of once again forming a nation in the world." Hussein not only accepted Hogarth's explanation, but he revealed his freedom from religious prejudice by expressing a willingness to welcome Jews who wished to settle in Palestine or in any other Arab territory as long as these areas remained under Arab control. On March 23, 1918, an article in his official publication *Al-Qibla,* Mecca called upon the Palestine Arabs to welcome the Jews as brethren and to cooperate with them for the common welfare. Moreover, in March, 1918, a Zionist commission headed by Dr. Chaim Weizmann went to Cairo and Palestine to try to allay Arab fears. Weizmann denied the allegation that Zionism sought political power. Although this statement misrepresented the true goal of most of the leading Zionists, for a while it did lessen Arab concern.[8]

As late as June, 1918, active recruiting was carried out in Palestine for the Sharifian army, "the recruits being given to understand," as the British government was to admit in 1930, "that they were fighting in a national cause to liberate their country from the Turks." On June 16, 1918, in response to a formal inquiry by seven Arab spokesmen from various parts of the Ottoman Empire, then residing in Cairo, the British government again formally and publicly assured the Arabs that it would abide by its earlier pledges. Concerning the Arab territories (including Palestine) that had already been liberated by Allied arms, the British policy would be "that the future government of those territories should be based upon the principles of the consent of the governed." The declaration made to the seven Arabs contained neither territorial reservations nor any other limitations based on the Sykes-Picot Agreement or the Balfour Declaration. The British made no effort to refute the conclusion drawn by the seven Arab spokesmen that Britain was "not free to dispose of Palestine without regard for the wishes and interests of the inhabitants of Palestine." [9]

In October, 1918, Arab doubts about British intentions began to rise again, and Arab unrest grew. On November 8, an official communiqué containing the text of a statement of policy representing the aims of the British and French governments in the liberated Arab areas was given to the press and posted on village bulletin boards throughout the Levant, including the Palestine area. The communiqué stated:

> The goal envisaged by France and Great Britain in prosecuting in the East the war . . . is the complete and final liberation of the peoples who have for so long been oppressed by the Turks, and the setting up of national governments and administrations that shall derive their authority from the free exercise of the initiative and choice of the indigenous populations.

The two countries would assist in setting up "indigenous governments and administrations in Syria and Mesopotamia." This statement did much to quiet Arab unrest, especially since France was also a party to it and since the Arabs considered Palestine to be an integral part of Syria. The Sykes-Picot Agreement and even the Balfour Declaration now seemed to be less dangerous to the Arab cause. Wilson's Fourteen Points, widely publicized in the Middle East, gave additional emphasis to the principle of the right of national self-determination. This further strengthened the hopes of the Arabs that they would be able to achieve their nationalist goals in Palestine as elsewhere.[10]

On the basis of these statements and promises made to the Arabs, as even a British royal commission admitted in 1930, "the real impression left upon the Arabs generally was that the British were going to set up an independent Arab state which would include Palestine." [11] Britain's failure to publish until 1939 the full correspondence with the Arabs during World War I helped to conceal the strongest evidence providing some support for Arab claims; this seriously handicapped the presentation of the Arab case in England and before the world for many critical years. The Arabs themselves shared the responsibility for the suppression of these important documents by their failure to publish them in English and other major languages in order to explain and justify their own cause more effectively in the international propaganda campaign that was to develop over Palestine.

PARIS PEACE CONFERENCE AND ITS AFTERMATH

The Zionist delegation at the 1919 Paris Peace Conference included prominent and capable persons from various countries. Well versed in Western diplomacy and psychology, they received a friendly, sympathetic reception from the delegates of the Allied states. This was to give them a major advantage over the Arab delegation.

At the time of the conference, Zionist claims to Palestine rested on the British wartime promise to the Jews as contained in the Balfour

Declaration, as well as on the various historic, religious, and humanitarian "rights" mentioned earlier. Zionists further contended that a Jewish Palestine could give new hope and inspiration to Jews everywhere and that Jewish capital and practical abilities could help develop the backward Palestine area for the benefit of the Arabs, too.

The Zionist delegates asked the conference, in effect, to (1) include the Balfour Declaration in the peace treaty; (2) disregard, since the Jews then represented only 10 per cent of the population of Palestine, the principle of the right of self-determination, at least until the Jews became a majority there; (3) oppose making Palestine into either an Arab state or an internationalized one, but to set it up as a British mandate; (4) provide for unlimited Jewish immigration into Palestine and "close settlement" by Jews on the land there; and (5) provide for the establishment of a Jewish Council for Palestine, representing the Jews in Palestine and elsewhere, with legal status and considerable powers. The Zionists continued to use the term Jewish "national home" rather than "state."

The Zionists did not obtain all their demands at the Paris Conference, but they put themselves in a strong position for achieving greater success when the Palestine Mandate was established.

The Arab case could be summarized as follows. The Arabs had a more valid claim to Palestine than did the Jews. A continuous occupation of Palestine from the seventh to the twentieth century provided a stronger historic right than one based only on a much shorter occupation that ended some two thousand years ago. The world would be thrown into chaos, legally and politically, if every group were permitted to lay claim to an area that its ancestors had possessed at one time in history. If claims based on religion had any real validity, the Christians and the Muslims could also assert their rights to Palestine. It was contended that even on religious grounds, the land of Palestine was not promised to the Jews exclusively; the Old Testament promise of a return was fulfilled by the return of the Jews from Babylon when the Second Temple was built; and in any case, the return was to come by divine guidance and intervention, not by human, political action. Furthermore, one group could not be legally or morally bound by the religious beliefs of or by the promises made to another group. As for humanitarian considerations, the Christian world was attempting to right an unhappy situation created by Christian intolerance—at Arab expense alone. The Arabs did not oppose the Jews as a religious entity, and they did not object to the immigration of Jews into Palestine as long as they came without political motives. Besides, it was neither just nor democratic to allow a minority to overrule the wishes and interests of the large majority. Since the Balfour Declaration was merely a promise made by a British official to a private British subject, it had no legally binding validity under international law. In contrast, the British pledges to the Arabs had been made through formal agreements between sovereign states.

T. E. Lawrence, British leader of the Arab revolt, helped the Arab delegation which was led by Amir Feisal, son of Sharif Hussein, but the delegation was at a serious disadvantage because it lacked men of world stature with experience in Western affairs, diplomacy, and psychology. As a result, the Arab case was not presented effectively at the Peace Conference. Amir Feisal urged backing for Arab unity and independence as promised by the British; the Arabs would temporarily accept "the effective superposition of a great trustee" so long as provision was made for a "representative local administration." In late 1918 and early 1919 Feisal was actually more concerned about French than Zionist aspirations in the Near East. He even hoped that Zionist support could be used against France, but by this time Feisal had lost touch with Arab nationalist feeling, especially in Palestine. These factors helped induce him to sign an agreement with Weizmann on January 3, 1919, welcoming Jewish immigration to Palestine. However, he specifically made this agreement dependent upon the fulfillment of the wartime pledges of the British regarding Arab independence. When Britain did not fulfill her promises, the Arabs contended that this agreement had no further validity. On March 3, 1919, Feisal wrote a letter to Felix Frankfurter referring to the Arabs and Jews as cousins and stating that there was room for both in "Syria." At the same time, Feisal made it clear that the Arabs would not accept a Jewish state as such but only a possible Jewish province in a larger Arab state.[12]

The Paris Peace Conference, in writing Articles 20 and 22 of the League of Nations Covenant, further encouraged Arab hopes regarding Palestine. Article 22, paragraph 4 stated that certain communities taken from the Ottoman Empire had

> reached a stage of development where their existence as independent nations can be provisionally recognized, subject to the rendering of administrative advice and assistance by a Mandatory until such time as they are able to stand alone. The wishes of these communities must be a principal consideration in the selection of the Mandatory.

To the Arabs, the mandate system was to be an attempt at a partial fulfillment of Allied, and especially Wilsonian, promises that an Allied victory would foster the principles of independence, self-determination, and democracy based upon the will of the people. To the Arabs, all these principles supported the cause of the majority—namely, themselves—in Palestine. Article 20, moreover, stating that the League members agreed "that this covenant is accepted as abrogating all obligations or understandings *inter se* which are inconsistent with the terms thereof," appeared to the Arabs to render null and void both the Sykes-Picot Agreement and the Balfour Declaration, since these were inconsistent with the League Covenant. In August, 1919, even Lord Balfour admitted the existence of such an inconsistency when he conceded that

> the contradiction between the letter of the Covenant and the policy of the Allies is even more flagrant in the case of the "independent nation" of Palestine than in that of the "independent nation" of Syria. For in Palestine we do not propose even to go through the form of consulting the wishes of the present inhabitants of the country.[13]

With the approval of the Supreme Council at the Paris Peace Conference, President Wilson sent Dr. Henry C. King, president of Oberlin College, and Charles Crane, a businessman, to the Middle East for a report on the situation there. The King-Crane Commission found that an overwhelming number of Palestine Arabs wanted Palestine to remain part of Syria with Feisal as the head of state. If a mandate were established, the Arabs insisted that it include Palestine as well as Syria and that it be temporary, with either the United States or Britain as the mandatory power. The commission also warned against "the extreme Zionist programme for Palestine of unlimited immigration of Jews, looking finally to making Palestine a Jewish state." Although the commission felt that some of the aspirations and plans of the Zionists were praiseworthy, it concluded that the Zionist proposals as a whole would be unfair to the Arab majority and would require the use of military force to be implemented. The commission recommended that Palestine be kept as part of Syria and that only a limited part of the Zionist program be carried out.[14] The King-Crane report was not only to be ignored by the Peace Conference, but it was not even made public until 1922. Since this document gave more support to the Arab case than to the Zionist one, the conference's failure to consider the report or to publish it before the Palestine Mandate was set up by the League of Nations had the practical effect of aiding the Zionist cause and depriving the Arabs of favorable documentary evidence.

CONCLUSION

The British government seriously underestimated both the extent and the implications of the rise of Arab nationalism in and over Palestine and the determination of the Zionists to realize their goal of a Jewish state. In addition, it ignored the warnings made as early as 1918 by a number of official observers and experts that Britain's conflicting promises and policies would ultimately lead to strife between Arabs and Jews and to endless troubles for Britain in Palestine. Some suggested that one way of resolving Britain's conflicting promises to the Arabs and Jews would be to establish one large Arab federation with a Jewish national home being set up in the Palestine part of this federation. Since the Jews then in Palestine represented only about 10 per cent of the total population, and since there was little assurance that the Jews could ever become an actual majority in Palestine, this proposed solution, if effectively pressed by Britain, might very well have been acceptable to many Zionists, as well as to many Arabs. This early period—before major problems and vested interests had had a chance to take root and when the Zionists were still calling for only a national home, not a sovereign state, and Arab opposition to Jewish immigration was just beginning to develop—was the most opportune time for Britain to have sought some fair and practical way of reconciling her conflicting commitments. By failing to take advantage of this singular moment in history to devise a consistent, farsighted program for Palestine, the British helped to create future dilemmas.[15]

Over the years, most Zionist leaders ignored the admonitions of various specialists on the Middle East, including those who were Zionist and pro-Zionist. As early as 1913, the director of the Palestine Office of the Zionist Organization warned,

> We have before us the task, which in no wise can be evaded, of creating peaceful and friendly relations between the Jews and the Arabs. In this respect we have to catch up a great deal that we have neglected, and to rectify errors that we have committed. It is, of course, quite useless to content ourselves with merely assuring the Arabs we are coming into the country as their friends. We must prove this by our deeds.[16]

Later, various Zionist sympathizers such as Mark Sykes and Colonel R. Meinertzhagen, also urged the Zionists to realize that the success of their cause depended upon an "understanding with the Arabs, whose national aspirations must . . . be reconciled and linked with their own," that the Jews must show patience and moderation in dealing with the Arabs if Arab hostility were to be broken down, and that Arab opposition "may possibly be averted if the Jews through a policy of peaceful penetration, without the blaring of trumpets and without special privileges such as Dr. Weizmann and other official Zionists desire, attain by their own merits a position of supremacy in the land." [17] This friendly counsel notwithstanding, many Zionists, including well-educated and politically mature Western Jews, continued to display a serious lack of understanding of the existence and intensity of Arab national pride. Rather than seeking to foster the Arab friendship and cooperation so essential to the peaceful achievement of Zionist goals from the very beginning, short-sighted Zionist tactics and lack of consideration for Arab feelings and interests whipped up Arab fears and opposition.

As for the Arabs, because they had lived for centuries in the backward Ottoman Empire, most of them found themselves, at the end of World War I, lacking in political experience and ill-prepared to compete with the political acumen of the Zionists. Even their leaders were insufficiently aware of the dynamics and subtleties of international diplomacy and ignorant of how to present their case effectively. In fact, they were unable to realize that their conflict with Zionist political aspirations would be greatly determined by events and developments far removed from Palestine. As a result, they failed to make adequately serious and determined efforts in the field of international propaganda to defend the Palestine Arab cause. Furthermore, they neither correctly evaluated the determination and ability of the Zionists to achieve their own goals nor developed a policy which would have realistically dealt with the growing schism between Arabs and Jews in Palestine.

In short, the conflicting pledges and indecision of the British, the impatience of the Zionists to achieve their goals in complete disregard for the feelings and interests of the Palestine Arabs, and the political immaturity of the Arabs themselves at this critical stage in the history of Palestine helped to launch the chain of events which produced the Arab-Israeli dilemma confronting the world today.

CHAPTER II

The Palestine Mandate, 1922–1948

Although by the end of World War I a few seeds of the future Arab-Israeli conflict had already been sown, far more serious ones were to take root during the mandate period itself. During the years immediately after World War I, when the split between the Arabs and the Jews over Palestine was still in its embryonic stage, the possibility remained that determined, farsighted efforts could still build a bridge between the two communities. But neither the British nor the Arabs and Zionists were willing to make the required efforts and concessions. As the years went by, Arab and Zionist attitudes and actions became increasingly antagonistic and irreconcilable, while British policies frequently did more to aggravate the deteriorating situation than to ameliorate it.

The Palestine Mandate, as Britain received it in 1920, included Transjordan, but Transjordan, despite strong Zionist objections, was made into a separate mandate in 1922. At that point Palestine came into being as a distinct political unit.

Initially the Balfour Declaration was only a vaguely worded promise made in a letter to Lord Rothschild. However, when the Palestine Mandate Agreement between Britain and the League of Nations was signed with the Balfour Declaration incorporated into it, the Zionists acquired their first internationally binding pledge of support; consequently, their political claims to Palestine were greatly strengthened. In fact the mandatory agreement was framed largely in the interest of the Jews. For example, it provided for (1) the incorporation of the whole of the Balfour Declaration; (2) the recognition of the "historical connection of the Jewish people with Palestine"; (3) the establishment of a Jewish agency to be "recognized as a public body for the purpose of advising and cooperating with the Administration of Palestine in such economic, social, and other matters as may affect the establishment of the Jewish population in Palestine"; (4) the facilitation of Jewish immigration and the "close settlement by Jews on the land," provided that the mandatory insures "that the rights and position of other sections of the population are not prejudiced"; (5) the right of each community to maintain its own schools; and (6) the use of Hebrew, as well as Arabic and English, as official languages.[1] Both Britain and the League of Nations apparently believed that building a Jewish "national home" (a term still left vague and undefined) and protecting Arab rights and position were not incompatible objectives. They were convinced that the whole population of Palestine would so benefit from the material prosperity which Jewish immigration and money were expected to bring to the country that the Arabs would ultimately accept the new situation. It soon became apparent, however, that Britain and the League had failed to anticipate the determination of the Zionists and both the rapid growth and the effects of Arab nationalism. In addition, they failed to realize that for the Palestine Arabs, national goals were far more important than any potential economic advantages.

While the Zionists were delighted with the mandatory agreement, the Arabs were embittered because they considered its provisions unjust, undemocratic, and contrary to all promises which had been made to them. They denied the mandate's legal validity on the grounds that, contrary to the terms of the League Covenant, Palestine was not "provisionally recognized" as independent and the wishes of the inhabitants were not the "principal consideration in the selection of the mandatory" power as required by the Covenant. The Arabs were especially aroused because, whereas numerous articles of the mandatory agreement referred to the Jewish community by name, the Arabs, 90 per cent of the population, were referred to merely as "the other sections" of the population.

Apparently aiming at a unitary state, in 1920 the first high commissioner, Sir Herbert Samuel, set up an advisory council, including ten British officials, four Muslim and three Christian Arabs, and three Jews. It was an interim body designed to suggest legislation, but it was dissolved in February, 1923. A proposed twenty-three-member legislative council was never formed because the Arab leaders, opposed to any action which might imply recognition of the mandate's validity, and unhappy about the fact that the Arabs would have only ten seats on the council, withheld their participation. The advisory council was reestablished, but nationalistic pressures forced its Arab members to withdraw from it. Not until 1935–36 was a legislative council proposed again, but without success. Since no locally acceptable constitutional system could be agreed upon, neither the Arabs nor the Jews participated directly in governing Palestine, which continued to be ruled by Britain through a high commissioner.[2]

DEVELOPMENTS WITHIN THE JEWISH AND ARAB COMMUNITIES

Despite the mandate's failure to provide specifically for an independent Jewish state, the Zionists regarded this as its main purpose. Zionist leaders wanted to retain the mandate until large-scale immigration could put Jews in the majority. Only then would the Zionists press for an independent Palestine. That is the reason why unrestricted immigration was so vital to the Zionists and, at the same time, so objectionable to the Arabs; it also explains why the immigration issue became the most basic source of friction between the Arabs and the Jews.

At the end of World War I, there were only about 55,000 Jews in Palestine, and though Jewish immigration was steadily promoted by Zionist organizations, there were some years prior to 1933 in which the moderate annual quota established by the mandate was far from filled. Nazi persecution after 1933, however, brought an upswing in the number of Jews (mostly from Central and Eastern Europe) entering Palestine both legally and illegally. By 1939 the Jewish community had reached 450,000—about 30 per cent of the total.

Between 1919 and 1936, $400 million was invested by Jews in Palestine. As a result new industries were set up and Arab land was purchased by the Jewish National Fund. The total amount of Jewish-owned land increased from 594,000 dunums (1 dunum = ¼ acre) in 1922 to 1,533,000 dunums in 1939.[3] Some of this acreage had been what Britain considered state-owned land (on the basis of Ottoman land registries) which the fund "rented" for nominal sums under ninety-nine-year leases. Other land was bought from absentee owners living in Syria and Lebanon who had been isolated from their properties by the British and French mandate boundaries. Arab tenants and workers were evicted from all this acreage. The land bought by the Jewish National Fund became the inalienable property of the Jewish people. It could not be resold to Arabs, nor could any Arab be employed on it.

During the mandate the Jews in Palestine enjoyed many formidable advantages over the Arabs. For example, the mandate provided for a Jewish Agency empowered to serve as the official spokesman of world Jewry in connection with Jewish immigration, agricultural, educational, and other interests in Palestine. The Palestine Jews developed their own communal organization, composed of an elected assembly and general council and an administrative apparatus, which soon assumed expanding quasi-governmental functions. The experience gained from this considerable degree of self-government was to be very valuable to the Jews when the time came to set up their own government. Since most of the Jewish immigrants entering Palestine during these years came from relatively advanced countries in Europe, they were better educated and possessed greater political and economic maturity than did their Arab neighbors. Moreover, without centuries-old traditions to hinder them or vested interests and class divisions to combat—as was the case with the Palestine Arabs—the Palestine Jews could make quick progress in developing an up-to-date economic, social, and political system. In addition, more and more Jewish communities over the world pooled their many talents and extensive resources and applied their great influence—which often reached into all levels of Western public opinion, into the highest places in some Western governments, and into the League of Nations itself—to aid the Zionist cause in Palestine.

Just at the time when most Jews in various countries were uniting to support the Zionist cause in Palestine, the Arab world found itself split into many political units—mandates, protectorates, and "independent" states. In the Middle East, France acquired Syria and Lebanon as mandates. Britain became the mandatory power for Iraq, Transjordan, and Palestine, retained colonies and protectorates along the southern and eastern edges of the Arabian peninsula, and maintained her "special relations" with Egypt. Only the Hejaz and the Nejd (later Saudi Arabia) and Yemen were allowed to become independent states as a result of World War I.

The Arabs who found themselves in Palestine continued to suffer the consequences of having lived in the backward Ottoman Empire for centuries. Unlike the Jews, they did not have a constant stream of educated and politically and technologically advanced fellow-Arabs immigrating into Palestine with large amounts of capital. Thus, being as far in arrears as most Arabs found themselves in 1919, it would have taken them a long time to overcome all their deficiencies, even under the most auspicious of circumstances—but circumstances during the mandatory period proved far from ideal for the Arabs.

The British grant of considerable autonomy to the various religious groups, along the lines of the old Turkish millet system, worked against the development of a closely knit, organized Arab community. Separate Muslim, Christian, and Druze communities administered their own cultural, educational, religious, and certain judicial affairs. While nearly all Arabs agreed on opposition to Zionism, political differences arose between the communities over other issues. In 1921–22 the mandate set up and provided funds for a supreme Muslim council with the British-sponsored al-Haj Muhammad Amin al-Husseini, the Grand Mufti of Jerusalem, as its lifetime head. Nevertheless, disagreements cropped up even among Arab Muslims. A relatively bitter struggle developed between the Husseini faction and the more moderate faction led by Raghib

Nashashibi, mayor of Jerusalem, who opposed the Husseini policy of noncooperation with the mandate authorities. However, during periods of crisis, as when in 1936–37 an Arab general strike took place and an Arab revolt broke out, the various groups managed to work together, but genuine Arab unity rarely lasted for any length of time. Because the Arab community failed to organize itself politically as effectively as the Jewish, it was unable to obtain adequate political experience, particularly on the national level, and this was to have harmful consequences for them in the critical period after World War II. Moreover, after the Arab revolt broke out, Britain arrested most of the members of the Arab Higher Committee and forced the Grand Mufti and others to flee the country, leaving the Arab community deprived of many of its most popular leaders.

By 1936 the Arab population had increased by 67 per cent over the previous two decades to about a million—primarily as the result of a high birth rate. A small group of Muslims constituted the wealthy land-owning families, with a growing number joining the embryonic middle class made up mostly of the 95,000 Christians (Roman Catholic, Greek Orthodox, Syrian Catholic, and Protestant) who lived chiefly in the towns. Though the mandatory authority did introduce modern government services, it provided little money for public education. Attendance by girls as well as boys at privately supported Christian and Muslim schools (with Christian schools registering some Muslims also) rose steadily over the years, but there were never enough schools to accept all applicants. The 1931 census revealed literacy rates of 57.7 per cent for Christians, and 14.5 per cent for Muslims, with the rates rising everywhere—but again, not fast enough, particularly in contrast to the higher Jewish literacy rate.[4]

Unlike members of the Jewish community, the Arabs achieved little unity and produced few effective leaders. Whereas the Zionist leaders remained relatively flexible in their strategy and policies in the hope of making piecemeal progress toward their ultimate goal, the Arab leaders lacked the political experience and foresight to realize the long-range value of making occasional and essential tactical retreats. While the Zionists were cultivating the Western press, public, and government officials and organizing local Zionist groups throughout the world so they could more readily marshal world-wide support for their cause, the Arabs did not become fully aware of the importance of such activities until 1936. By this time they had lost so much ground to the Zionists on the international scene that they were never able to catch up.

The only significant headway made by the Palestine Arabs was among their fellow Arabs in adjacent areas. Arab nationalism, already on the rise throughout the Middle East, found in the Zionist threat a rallying point for Arab nationalists everywhere. In 1936, the independent Arab governments began to lend growing support to the Palestine Arab cause. This was to have some practical value, particularly since Britain was anxious to retain the friendship of the Arab states. In fact, in 1939, Britain gave formal recognition to the right of these Arab countries to intercede on behalf of the Palestine Arabs.

BRITISH VACILLATION BEFORE WORLD WAR II

Britain had not only trapped herself with conflicting promises to Arabs and Jews, but despite repeated warnings, she added immeasurably to her future woes by continuous indecision and vacillation in her Palestine policy. For instance, by seeming to grant the requests of each side, Britain encouraged Arabs and Zionists to increase their discordant demands and to seek ways of extracting further concessions. In result, the Arabs frequently refused to cooperate with the Palestine administration and even at times resorted to violence. The Zionists, in turn, applied direct pressure on British officials through influential Jews and others holding high positions in and outside the British government. Once started, these pressures and counter-pressures tended to foster more British indecision and more futile statements aimed at placating both sides simultaneously. Britain tended to wait until the situation in Palestine had become relatively serious before she took any action, and she then found it more difficult than ever to deal effectively with the resulting problems. As Arab efforts moved into the international arena, where the Zionists had been actively working all along, the Palestine question grew even more complicated as it became relevant to larger world issues.

Arab opposition to the Balfour Declaration and to Zionist political activities in Palestine resulted in outbreaks of violence in 1920 and 1922 and the dispatch of an Arab delegation to London in early 1922 to advise the British government about the depth of Arab resentment over Zionist political ambitions. On July 1, 1922, even before the Palestine Mandate had actually come into formal existence, Arab pressures led the British government to issue a new statement of policy, known as the Churchill Memorandum, after the Colonial Secretary. Although this statement assured the Jews that Britain did not intend to depart from the Balfour Declaration, most of it was directed toward calming Arab apprehensions. The statement denied that "the disappearance or the subordination of the Arabic population, language or culture in Palestine" was contemplated and defined the promise of a Jewish national home as

> not the imposition of a Jewish nationality upon the inhabitants of Palestine as a whole, but rather the further development of the existing Jewish community . . . in order that it may become a centre in which the Jewish people as a whole may take, on grounds of religion and race, an interest and pride.

The statement declared that Jewish immigration would be limited by the economic capacity of the country so that the "immigrants should not deprive any section . . . of their employment." It also quoted that part of a resolution passed by the Zionist Congress in 1921 claiming that the Zionists intended the "Jewish people to live with the Arab people on terms of unity and mutual respect, and together with them to make the common home into a flourishing community, the upbuilding of which may assure to each of its peoples an undisturbed national develop-ment." [5] Despite these favorable features, the Arabs were not satisfied with the statement of policy, especially as it was to be interpreted and carried out in Palestine.

The Zionists considered the memorandum to be a "serious whittling down" of the Balfour Declaration; they accepted it, however, because Britain made clear that the confirmation of the mandate would be con-ditioned on such an acceptance and because British officials presented off-the-record assurances and interpretations of the statement of policy which mollified the Zionists.[6]

Another outbreak of violence in the Holy Land in 1929 brought about the dispatch of the Shaw and Hope-Simpson Royal Commissions in 1929 and 1930. These commissions, as well as later ones, agreed that the basic cause of the troubled situation was the intensifying conflict between the nationalist efforts and aspirations of the Arabs and the Zionists in Palestine. The commissions reported that the following factors also contributed greatly to Arab unrest:

> 1) The Arabs feared that continued Jewish immigration and land purchases would ultimately make them a minority in what they considered to be their own country. Moreover, the Arabs re-sented bitterly the many Jewish immigrants who came into Pales-tine not only sporting a superior air but also showing little or no concern for the Arabs and Arab interests. The Arabs saw Zionist demands growing step by step—largely at Arab expense—and they did not know when or where these demands and gains would end.

> 2) The Arabs were concerned about being economically, as well as politically, dominated by the Jews. The more the Zionists stressed their economic, financial, and technical superiority over

the Arabs, the greater this fear became. The Arabs complained that, although the Zionists were claiming to bring great material benefits to the Arabs, the Zionists not only excluded Arabs from their farm lands "forever," but Zionist industries frowned on the hiring of Arab workers. The Arabs felt that, whatever material benefits some Arabs derived, these were only incidental and at the expense of the displacement of many other Arabs from the land. Furthermore, the Arabs feared that large-scale Jewish immigration would create unemployment in the future.

3) The Arabs felt that they suffered a serious disadvantage whenever the political battlefield shifted from Palestine to London, where the Zionists were far better equipped than the Arabs to press their case before the British government and public. As a result, the Arabs began seriously to question the ability or willingness of the British government to carry out its promises. They observed how, time and again, when a royal commission made a recommendation favorable to the Arabs, Zionist influence in Parliament and the press forced the government to modify the recommendation in favor of the Zionists. Lacking confidence in the British government and lacking what they considered to be an adequate peaceful means for attaining their goals, many Palestine Arabs were led to believe that the use of force was the only practical means left to them. Since these tactics, on occasion, had led to more favorable British statements, if not actions, the Arabs were encouraged to continue resorting to violence.

The reports of the Shaw and Hope-Simpson Commissions submitted in 1930 upheld many of the Arab claims and fears. After blaming the economic crisis and Arab unemployment in the 1927–29 period on excessive Jewish immigration, they urged more stringent restrictions on Jewish immigration and land purchases. They warned that the exclusion of Arab labor from Zionist agricultural settlements and most Zionist industries caused bitterness among the Arabs and endangered peaceful Arab-Jewish relations.[7]

In October, 1930, the British government issued a new policy statement, which was based largely on the conclusions and recommendations contained in the reports of the two royal commissions. The Zionists were so aroused over this statement that they launched a major campaign against the policy in Parliament and before the public in Britain and the dominions. As a result of these pressures, Prime Minister J. Ramsay MacDonald wrote an open letter to Dr. Weizmann which explained away many, though not all, of those features of the policy statement most objectionable to the Zionists. The letter denied that the mandatory was considering the prohibition of either Jewish immigration or land acquisition. Disturbed over what they called the "black letter," the Arabs became increasingly distrustful of Britain's desire and ability, in the face of powerful Zionist objections, to carry out any of these recommendations or of earlier official promises that favored the Arabs.[8]

As a result of the failure of large-scale immigration to materialize in the late twenties and the growing fear that fewer Jews than anticipated would come to Palestine, Zionist leaders by the early thirties changed from their earlier demand for a Jewish-dominated Palestine to one providing for complete parity between Arabs and Jews, regardless of either group's numerical strength. Starting in 1933, however, the mushrooming of anti-Semitism in Central Europe in the wake of Hitler's rise to power suddenly compelled increasing numbers of Jews to flee. The Zionists developed an underground network in Europe to persuade young Jews to go to Palestine rather than elsewhere and then helped spirit them there. Restrictive immigration policies in the United States and other Western countries forced most Jewish refugees to seek refuge in Palestine anyway. Though moved by the plight of the persecuted European Jews, non-Zionist Jews and Christians (with a few notable exceptions) were unwilling to open the doors of their own nations to the hapless Nazi victims and began to support the Zionist program for large-scale immigration into Palestine; thus Zionist policy was able to revert back to the concept of a Jewish-dominated Palestine, and Zionist pressures on the British government were intensified.

The Palestine Arabs became so alarmed at the tremendous increase in Jewish immigration and land purchases that the various political factions, despite their previous frictions and antagonisms, began to close ranks to oppose this new development. In April, 1936, all major groups, including Muslims and Christians, formed a Supreme Arab Committee, later known as the Arab Higher Committee. A widely supported general strike was called to force Britain to follow policies supporting Arab "rights." The tension and hostility which mounted rapidly between the Arab and Jewish communities led to acts of violence on both sides.

At this time, a number of other international developments began to affect the Palestine question. Burgeoning nationalism throughout the Arab world brought about a sharp upsurge of interest in and activities on behalf of the Palestine Arabs by many Arabs outside the Holy Land. Volunteers and armaments came from neighboring Arab states. Local committees for the defense of Palestine and parliamentary defense committees, organized in various Arab countries, held international conferences to muster support for the Palestine Arabs. In 1936, the monarchs of Saudi Arabia, Iraq, Transjordan, and Yemen jointly intervened to bring the Palestine strike to an end. This step was important for it was the first time that outside Arab leaders took such major, united action on an issue involving Palestine. In addition, the Germans and Italians started propaganda efforts to whip up Arab feelings against Britain in and over Palestine. These developments added new dimensions and complexities to the Palestine dilemma.

After the outbreak of a large-scale Arab rebellion in 1936, Britain sent yet another royal commission to Palestine. The commission reported that the underlying cause of Arab unrest continued to be the desire of the Arabs for national independence and their hatred and fear of the Jewish national home. For the first time an official report described the promises made to the Jews and the Arabs as irreconcilable and the mandate itself as unworkable. The commission warned that the only hope of giving some satisfaction to both parties and of providing at least a chance of ultimate peace was to end the mandate and partition the country into separate Jewish and Arab states, with Britain retaining control over several enclaves in order to insure uninterrupted access for all to the holy places. Having accepted the commission's recommendations, Britain created another commission to draw up a detailed plan for partitioning Palestine.[9]

The partition proposal gave rise to a sharp difference of opinion among the Jews, especially between the Zionists and non-Zionists in the Jewish Agency. Dr. Weizmann and David Ben-Gurion, chairman of the Agency's executive, led the group which was willing to accept partition. They argued that under existing circumstances it would be wise to accept a smaller state than originally desired as the most practical way of attaining both early self-rule and the right of unrestricted Jewish immigration. In 1937, the Zionist Congress agreed to accept the principle of partition, but only on the condition that the Jews receive a sufficiently large area.

The Palestine Arabs objected strongly to the idea of partition. The Arabs, intensifying their agitation against Jewish land purchases and immigration, increased their acts of violence against the British. The mandatory administration reacted vigorously to these moves. The Arab Higher Committee was declared unlawful, and many of the Arab leaders were arrested, deported, or forced, like the Mufti, to flee Palestine. The death penalty was imposed on numerous Arabs who carried bombs or other unlicensed weapons. These actions scattered the Palestine Arab leadership, killed many of the most zealous of the Arab nationalists, and stripped the Arabs of their weapons. At the same time the British actually assisted in the training and arming of the Jewish defense forces.

Until Nazi Germany and Fascist Italy began to threaten British interests in the Middle East, the Zionists were in a strong position vis-à-vis the Arabs over Palestine. With Zionists and/or their friends holding important posts in the British government, the League Mandates Commission, and the League Council and with powerful propaganda facilities at their disposal in many countries, the Zionists were able to promote their interests effectively. On the other hand, except for the practice of violence, which was being forcibly eliminated, and feeble propaganda activities belatedly initiated in 1936, the Palestine Arabs had only the moral support of the few independent Arab states. Nevertheless, once the Nazis threatened the Middle East, the situation changed radically in favor of the Arabs. Since the Germans and the Italians began to court the Arabs and since the Jews had no choice but to stand with the West, the British now found it necessary to placate the Arabs.

The royal commission created to draw up a detailed partition plan found that the Arabs were completely opposed to partition and even the Jews were relatively unenthusiastic about the idea. The commission concluded that since it would be impossible to divide Palestine in a just manner acceptable to both communities, partitioning Palestine would be unworkable. Influenced by the commission's pessimistic views, the British government decided, in November, 1938, to invite representatives of the Palestine Arabs, the Arab states, and the Jewish Agency to London in March, 1939, to discuss a solution acceptable to all parties.

Members of the Arab Higher Committee and the opposition Nashashibi faction made up the Palestine Arab delegation to the London conference. While Britain had invited representatives from Egypt, Iraq, Transjordan, Saudi Arabia, and Yemen partly in the hope that they might provide a moderating influence on the Palestine Arabs, the invitation was also significant in that it constituted the first official recognition by the outside world of the reality of pan-Arab feeling, the deep concern of the Arab world for the fate of Palestine, and the right of all Arabs to be consulted on the Palestine question. This move, plus the steadily growing Nazi threat, tended to strengthen the bargaining position of the Arabs at the conference.

Since the Arabs and the Zionists continued to press for incompatible goals, the London conference ended in failure. Britain then issued a White Paper which provided that (1) Britain would continue to rule Palestine for a ten-year period. If the Arabs and Jews were able to work together satisfactorily during this period, they would be given an increasing role in the Palestine government, and Palestine would be established as an independent state within ten years. Otherwise, independence would be postponed. (2) Seventy-five thousand Jewish immigrants would be allowed to enter Palestine over a five-year period. Any immigration after that would be subject to the acquiescence of the Arabs. (3) Stringent restrictions would be placed on land sales to Jews in certain areas and complete prohibition in other areas.[10]

Arab reaction to the British decision varied. The government of Transjordan and the moderate Nashashibi faction, which were reconciled to the need of some compromise and held that Britain had made many concessions to Arab views, praised the new British policy; the Arab Higher Committee, however, rejected it. The Committee and others opposed the continuation of large-scale Jewish immigration for five more years. Remembering how British promises and proposals favorable to the Arabs in the past had been reversed under Zionist pressures, this latter group remained extremely distrustful of Britain and her policy statements. Such an inflexible attitude was also encouraged by the strong bargaining position maintained by the Arabs then as a result of the taut world situation.

The Zionists assailed the White Paper. They accused Britain of a breach of mandate and warned that they would never accept Palestine as an Arab state with the Jews as a permanent minority. Mass demonstrations were held against the new British policy, and Jewish quasi-military forces were strengthened. Extremist Palestine Jewish groups, who gained many adherents from those who had become increasingly convinced that violence would now be the most effective weapon against the new policy, began launching terroristic attacks on the Palestine government. The Jewish Agency not only refused to help the British round up the terrorists, but it stepped up its support of illegal immigration into Palestine. Britain found that she had alienated the Jews without having won over the strongest Arab factions in Palestine. The Jews were further angered by land transfer regulations issued in February, 1940, to curtail the sale of Arab-owned lands to Jews.

PALESTINE DURING AND AFTER WORLD WAR II

During World War II Jewish efforts were aimed both at helping defeat the Nazis and at bolstering the Zionist military and political position in and outside Palestine. It was recognized that active participation by many Jews in the war would strengthen the Zionist cause before the British government and world public opinion. Many Zionist leaders, believing that the Jews would ultimately be compelled to fight the Arabs if not also the British to attain their national home, realized the great value of making thousands of men with military training and experience available after the war to the Haganah, the military arm of the Jewish Agency. By early 1944, the Zionists had helped the British induct some

43,000 Palestine Jews into military service; most of them had been screened by the Jewish Agency, and many already belonged to the Haganah. As a result of Jewish pressures in Britain, the dominions, and the United States, Britain finally agreed, in late 1944, to set up a separate Jewish Brigade Group in her Army. The smuggling of arms and illegal immigrants (especially young men) into Palestine had begun before 1939, but it continued throughout the war and intensified after 1943. Between 1939 and 1943 close to 20,000 illegal immigrants were added to the 19,000 legal ones.[11] Some new villages were hurriedly organized in sections of the Holy Land never before inhabited by Jews in order to provide a basis for claiming these areas in the event that partition proposals were revived. Other villages were set up primarily for strategic purposes.

Not all Zionist wartime acts helped the Western cause. The small but dangerous Stern Gang (a fanatical group which had broken away from the somewhat less extremist Irgun Zvai Leumi) not only continued its violent attacks on the mandatory government for some time after the war had begun but sought the help of Fascist Italy against the hated British. Terroristic forays generally stopped during the bleakest days of the fighting in North Africa when Palestine was threatened. However, the situation changed greatly once the Nazi threat to the Middle East receded and an ultimate Western victory in Europe seemed assured. For the Zionists, the war against the Axis powers then became secondary to their own cause. In the beginning of 1944, the Irgun and the Stern Gang resumed their harassing attacks against the Palestine administration despite the facts that victory against Japan still seemed to require a long, costly effort and that even the European phase of the war was far from won. Many moderate Palestine Jews frequently gave indirect, if not direct, backing to these extremist groups, while the Haganah stole munitions from British military establishments.[12]

At the same time, the Zionists were intensifying their propaganda campaign outside Palestine. In Britain a parliamentary Palestine committee with important contacts and membership promoted the Zionist cause in both houses of Parliament. Local committees were organized in various cities in Britain and the dominions to influence views of the people there. Special efforts were made to court the major political parties. In their statements and platforms, the Liberal and Labor parties strongly endorsed the Zionist program, and the Labor party went so far as to advocate that the Palestine Arabs be encouraged to leave Palestine so as to provide more room for Jewish immigrants—a proposal which only a few of the extremist Zionist "maximalists" had ever dared to present. The Zionist cause was given another boost when Winston Churchill, who had backed some Zionist views, took over the reins of government from Neville Chamberlain. By September, 1943, Colonial Secretary Oliver Stanley quietly began to revive the idea of partitioning Palestine. In November, 1944, Churchill privately informed Weizmann of the decision of the British Cabinet Committee on Palestine to grant ultimately full Jewish sovereignty in a divided Palestine. During this same period, the British government continued to reassure the Arabs that it was standing by the 1939 White Paper so as not to antagonize them while the war was still on.[13]

With the radical decrease in the number and influence of Jews in Central and Eastern Europe, the Jewish population in the United States became the largest and most influential of the Jewish communities. Before Hitler came to power most American Jews had been indifferent or opposed to Zionism. But after Hitler had begun his savage persecutions, a large number of Jews, many with relatives in the critical areas, joined or backed the Zionist movement. With a swelling membership, the American Zionist Emergency Council established state and regional branches over the nation subdivided into a myriad of local committees. Through an endless stream of books, pamphlets, letters to the editor, mass meetings, and every other conceivable means of communication, the Zionists effectively won the support of many ordinary Americans disturbed by Jewish suffering in Europe, of Protestants influenced by the Old Testament and historic Jewish connections with Palestine, and of liberals who applauded the Zionists' progressive policies. As a result of these developments, in 1942 and 1943, thirty-three state legislatures passed pro-Zionist resolutions. A pro-Zionist congressional resolution in 1944 was only temporarily delayed in passage—and that was because of the military exigencies of the war. In the presidential campaign of 1944, both political parties and their candidates, Franklin D. Roosevelt and Thomas E. Dewey, strongly backed the Zionist program. The fact that more than four-fifths of the influential American Jewish population lived in a handful of politically important states was not ignored by the party organizers who tried to outbid each other for Jewish political support.

Up to World War II, the Zionists had deliberately avoided asking for a Jewish state and had requested merely a national home. But during the early war years, with increasing evidence of Nazi persecution of the Jews, Zionist opinion in Palestine and the West began to shift. A conference in May, 1942, called by the American Emergency Committee for Zionist Affairs, with six hundred delegates participating, adopted the Biltmore Program, which concluded with the following:

> The Conference declares that the new world order that will follow victory cannot be established on foundations of peace, justice, and equality, unless the problem of Jewish homelessness is finally

solved. The Conference urges that the gates of Palestine be opened, that the Jewish Agency be vested with control of immigration into Palestine and with the necessary authority for upbuilding the country, including the development of its unoccupied and uncultivated lands; and that Palestine be established as a Jewish Commonwealth integrated in the structure of the new democratic world. Then and only then will the age-old wrong to the Jewish people be righted.[14]

Ben-Gurion's campaign within the Palestine Mandate to support the Biltmore Program was so successful that in the 1944 elections for the fourth elected assembly of the Jewish community, his Mapai party obtained 66 per cent of the votes cast.

But Jewish opinion was not monolithic, regardless of how much the Zionists wished to make it appear so. The Biltmore Program was opposed by the religious fundamentalists within the Agudat Israel who believed that their promised homeland should be redeemed by God and not by man, by the extreme revisionist groups who wanted Transjordan too, by some Jewish Marxists, and by a number of non-Zionist Jews who feared that the drive toward a Jewish nation and Jewish nationhood would lead to harmful consequences. In 1942 Judah Magnes, president of Hebrew University, along with Martin Buber, distinguished philosopher, and Henrietta Szold, American-born founder of Hadassah, organized the Ihud or union party which supported the goal of a binational state in Palestine.

In the United States, ninety-nine reform rabbis established the American Council for Judaism which maintained that the Jews, as a religious group, were nationals of the countries in which they lived; the Council rejected the effort to establish a national Jewish state in Palestine or anywhere else as a "philosophy of defeatism." Its Statement of Principles included the following:

> In the light of our universalistic interpretation of Jewish history and destiny, and also because of our concern for the welfare and status of the Jewish people living in other parts of the world, we are unable to subscribe to or support the political emphasis now paramount in the Zionistic program. We cannot but believe that Jewish nationalism tends to confuse our fellow men about our place and function in society and also divert our attention from our historic role to live as a religious community wherever we may dwell.[15]

The Council advocated a democratic political solution for Palestine in which all, regardless of race or faith, would be treated equally.

Once the war had started, Britain sought to placate the Palestine Arabs by strictly enforcing the immigration and land provisions of the 1939 White Paper. She encouraged the exiled Arab nationalist leaders to return to Palestine with the promise of dropping all charges against them if they did not participate in any political activities. Many of these leaders agreed to return; the Mufti, however, still strongly distrustful of the British, refused to come back. To avoid capture, he fled from one Middle Eastern country to another, keeping out of reach of advancing Western forces. He finally found it necessary to flee into Nazi-controlled territory. Partly in the belief that the Axis powers would win the war—and it would therefore be wise to befriend them—and partly in the belief that "the enemy of my enemy is my friend," the Mufti, naively accepting at face value Hitler's promise to respect Arab independence if he won the war, sought German help against the British. Fortunately for the Allied cause as well as the Arab, the Mufti's efforts had little practical effect in Palestine or the Arab world as a whole. During the critical war years, no significant Arab disturbance took place in Palestine. Moderate Arabs who warmly backed the Allies had come to consider the 1939 White Paper as a British policy pledge, and they were generally ready to accept it. By 1943, about 8,000 Palestine Arabs had joined the British military forces in one capacity or another.

In the early war years, Arab-Jewish relations in Palestine improved slightly. Arabs and Jews served together on various governmental war advisory boards and committees. Unfortunately, the Palestine government did not take advantage of this rare opportunity to exploit a potential area of Arab-Jewish cooperation, as it also failed to give adequate encouragement to the moderate Palestine Arabs. Thus, when the Fascist threat subsided and Zionist pressures on the British again increased, the Palestine Arabs, fearing yet another change of British policy more favorable to the Jews, grew restless once more.

Due to constant factional bickering and the absence of effective leadership, the initiative in Palestine Arab politics passed increasingly in the later war years to the heads of the Arab states. This trend was accelerated after March, 1945, when the Arab League was created partly as a result of the common Arab fear of the growing Zionist threat to Palestine. (The Arab League Pact had a special section which allowed Palestinians to participate to some extent in League meetings in the expectation that Palestine would ultimately become independent and a full-fledged member of the League.) Arab governments, individually and collectively, began to apply diplomatic pressures on behalf of the Palestine Arabs. For instance, in April, 1945, King Ibn Saud elicited a promise from President Roosevelt that he would consider Arab interests and views in any final settlement of the Palestine issue.[16] In September, 1945, Arab League Secretary-General Abdur Rahman Azzam Pasha went to London to enlist the support of British officials on the Arab position on Palestine. On October 12, 1945, the Washington, D.C., legations of Iraq, Syria, Lebanon, and Egypt, in a joint memorandum to the Secretary of State, warned him that peace in the Near East would be jeopardized if a Zionist state were established. Arab League members, finally recognizing the importance of propaganda and noting with dismay the successful achievements of the Zionists in this field, decided in the summer of 1945 to launch an extensive propaganda campaign of their own in certain key Western countries. Arab information offices were set up in Washington and London, various pamphlets in English and the fortnightly *Arab News Bulletin* were published, and several Arab-Americans were recruited to present Arab views in the United States. These Arab measures proved relatively ineffective because (1) in contrast to the growing nationalism of many of the five million Jews of the United States, the approximately one-half million Americans of Arab origin, who were primarily Christians from Syria and Lebanon, became truly a part of American life maintaining only tenuous relations with Arabs in the Middle East; (2) Zionist propaganda over the years had already conditioned a large part of public opinion in the West, and Arab efforts were too weak and too late; and (3) the Arabs were unable to match two major advantages held by the Zionists—a well-publicized humanitarian issue and the powerful support of numerous Jewish organizations and individuals, including many with far greater knowledge and experience than the Arabs in Western psychology and propaganda techniques and many in key positions in various fields within their respective nations.

The end of the war in Europe revealed for the first time the extent and brutality of the slaughter of the Jews. The Palestine Jews, more determined than ever before to provide a haven and a national home for all Jews, intensified their terrorism and illegal immigration. World Jewry, in turn, began applying all kinds of pressures on Britain and the United States for a repudiation of the 1939 White Paper, for permission for the migration of all Jewish survivors in Europe to Palestine rather than to other countries, and for an agreement to establish a Jewish state.[17]

The victory of the British Labor party in the July, 1945, elections raised Zionist hopes because it had consistently backed the Zionist cause, but when the Labor party was forced to assume full responsibility for its policies, it found, as had the Churchill government, that it could not deal with the Palestine question independently of Britain's other problems and obligations in the Middle East and elsewhere. The British economy was near prostration, and Britain was in debt even to the Arab states. British officials were becoming increasingly worried about Soviet moves in the Middle East. Many government advisers warned that Britain had to maintain good relations with the Arabs if she wished to protect her vital interests in the area. Besides, a special subcommittee set up by the Labor government to study the Palestine question concluded that without active American support Britain could not hope to carry out a pro-Zionist program. Thus the Labor Party, much to its embarrassment, soon discovered that it could not fulfill its pledges to the Zionists.

American public opinion had been so effectively influenced by Zionist propaganda that the Palestine issue had become more enmeshed in party politics than ever before. Only those officials in the State and War Departments who were aware of the strategic and economic importance of the Middle East expressed any concern about Arab feelings towards the United States. They warned that the Soviet Union was already trying to extend her influence into the Middle East and that the long-range interests of the United States in that area depended upon the pursuit of friendly relations with the Arabs. President Harry Truman's experts advised him that only with military force could a Jewish state be established in the face of any determined Arab opposition. He formally assured the Arab leaders that he would abide by the promises made to them by his predecessor, Franklin D. Roosevelt. Nevertheless, he was so influenced by the plight of Nazi victims and Jewish political pressures that he decided to disregard the recommendations of his own experts and the official promises made to the Arabs. Giving strong support to Zionist goals, he encouraged Britain to allow 100,000 Jews to enter Palestine without delay.[18] Since Congress and the American public were clamoring for a rapid demobilization of the armed forces and against any new United States military commitments, Truman found it necessary to reject Britain's request that the United States share the financial and military burdens involved in the enforcement of actions leading to large-scale migrations of Jews to Palestine. British officials were understandably annoyed when the American government continued to insist that Britain adopt American policies without the United States herself assuming any responsibility for the implementation of those policies.

The Zionists welcomed Truman's statements, but the Arabs were angered by them. The Arabs wanted to know why Americans were forcing open the gates of tiny Palestine to Jewish refugees when they were so unwilling to open the doors of their own spacious country despite the fact that the United States could have absorbed far more refugees more quickly and efficiently than any country in the world.

Arab doubts about American sincerity increased when they observed that even many American Jews, fearful that an influx of foreign Jews would aggravate anti-Semitism in the United States, discouraged any liberalization of the country's immigration laws. (A notable exception to this position was taken by the American Council for Judaism, which lobbied for opening American doors to Hitler's victims.) [19]

In October, 1945, Britain finally succeeded in obtaining Truman's acceptance of her suggestion that the two countries undertake a joint study of the Palestine problem. An Anglo-American Committee of Inquiry, composed of six Englishmen and six Americans, was set up. The committee visited Jewish refugee camps in Europe as well as Palestine itself. Extensive testimony was presented by the Arabs, by the Zionists, and by Palestine's anti-Zionists, notably Judah Magnes and Martin Buber. The committee report (Cmd. 6808), released on May 1, 1946, drew the following conclusions:

> 1) Even though most European Jews wished to go to Palestine, Palestine did not have enough room for all of them. The United States and other nations were urged to open their doors to some of the displaced persons.
>
> 2) One hundred thousand permits should be issued in 1946 for entry into Palestine.
>
> 3) Although the Jews had an historical connection with Palestine and a Jewish National Home was a reality, Palestine was holy to three religions and should therefore be neither Arab nor Jewish. It should, instead, be binational with equal representation for both groups in a democratic government.
>
> 4) Since independence could not be achieved by peaceful means, Palestine should become a trust area under the UN. The primary duty of the Trustee would be to prepare the two communities for ultimate independence on a binational basis.
>
> 5) Future immigration must be based on a compromise agreement between the two communities. Land transfer regulations and the Jewish National Fund practice of employing only Jews on Jewish-owned land must be terminated.

With the 1946 congressional elections close at hand, President Truman accepted those parts of the recommendations which were favorable to the Zionists and reserved judgment on the rest. The Zionists applauded Truman's selection, while the Arabs bitterly attacked it. Britain, on the other hand, insisted that the committee report had to be considered and carried out as a whole. Even then, Britain contended that she could not admit one hundred thousand refugees into Palestine until the illegal Jewish armies had been disbanded, all Jewish arms had been surrendered, and the Jewish Agency had agreed to cooperate with the Palestine administration's efforts to suppress acts of terrorism.

While some moderate Zionists conceded that the Anglo-American Committee's report had some favorable points, others, led by David Ben-Gurion, objected to all of it. In fact, Ben-Gurion had already asserted before the committee that in his eyes "statehood was now more necessary than the 100,000 refugees." [20] American Zionists criticized the U.S. State Department and its Middle East experts. To meet an increase in Jewish acts of violence in Palestine, the mandatory government began to arrest many Jewish leaders and to take firm measures against the Jewish Agency; so the American Zionists and their supporters threatened to press for a congressional rejection of a proposed United States loan desperately needed by Britain. British officials were thus forced to suspend their disciplinary action against the Palestine Jews. Nevertheless, following further outrages, such as the bombing of the King David Hotel with heavy loss of life, Britain resumed repressive policies. As a result of these developments, the position of the Zionist moderates weakened while that of the extremists grew stronger, and Anglo-Jewish relations rapidly deteriorated.

Arab-Western relations also worsened as the Arabs became increasingly aroused over the developments in Palestine. At an unusual meeting in Inchass, Egypt, on May 27 and 28, the heads of state of Egypt, Transjordan, Saudi Arabia, and Yemen agreed on a statement warning Britain and the United States that "although the Arabs wanted their friendship, that friendship would depend on whether the two democracies would or would not transgress upon the rights of the Palestine Arabs." [21] At an extraordinary session held in Bludan, Syria, in June, 1946, the Arab League Council (1) set up a special committee to supervise all activities relating to Palestine; (2) recommended further action to strengthen the boycott of Zionist goods, to prevent the sale of Arab land in Palestine, and to increase Arab propaganda efforts in the West; and (3) sent notes to Britain and the United States in which it opposed the proposals of the Anglo-American Committee, complained that the United States had no legal justification for intervening in Palestine affairs, and asked Britain to negotiate with the Arabs in accordance with the UN Charter before the next session of the UN General Assembly. Secret decisions were also agreed upon at Bludan as to what future military and economic action would be taken, if necessary, in defense of Arab rights in Palestine.

At this critical point the Soviet Union, taking advantage of the excellent opportunity to further her own interests in the Middle East at the expense of the West, began to curry Arab favor. Soviet newspapers criticized the Anglo-American Committee for bypassing the Arab states and the UN and attacked Zionism as an agent of British imperialism.

In July, 1946, American and British experts, led by Henry F. Grady (deputy to the Secretary of State) and Herbert S. Morrison (lord president of the Council and leader of the House of Commons), attempted to carry out the recommendations of the Anglo-American Committee. They agreed on a plan to convert the mandate into a British trusteeship. Under the trusteeship, Palestine would be divided into a Jewish province, an Arab province, and a purely British-administered area composed of the districts of Jerusalem and the Negev. This could lead ultimately either to a unitary or binational state or to partition. In the interim, Britain would control foreign affairs, defense, and other major fields. If the scheme were accepted and if the United States agreed to share in the financial costs that would be involved, 100,000 Jews would be admitted into Palestine in the first year. After that, the number of immigrants to be admitted would be determined by the economic absorptive capacity of the country. This proposal, known as the Morrison-Grady Plan, was rejected by President Truman.[22]

Vehement Zionist opposition to the Morrison-Grady Plan led to more acts of violence and to a new Anglo-Zionist crisis. Meanwhile, the Jewish Agency formally agreed, in a secret resolution, to abandon its previous demand for all of Palestine and to accept a sovereign Jewish state in a partitioned Palestine provided that this state include Galilee, the coastal plain, and the Negev, and also that it have full control over immigration and economic policies. The American and British governments were quietly informed of this new resolution.

LONDON CONFERENCE ON PALESTINE

In a final, desperate attempt to resolve the Palestine problem through direct negotiations with the parties concerned, on July 25, 1946, Britain invited the Arab governments, the Arab Higher Committee for Palestine, and the Jewish Agency to attend a conference beginning in September in London. While the Arab states accepted the invitation, the Arab Higher Committee rejected it because Britain would not allow the Mufti to participate. The Jewish Agency also refused to attend because Britain would not accept its conditions, namely, that its partition plan be discussed and that it be permitted to include among its delegates some Jewish leaders then being held in custody in Palestine.

The Arabs submitted their own plan providing for the creation of an independent, unitary Palestine state which would put an end to further

Jewish immigration, protect both Jewish minority rights and the holy places, and conclude a treaty of alliance with Britain. The conference was unable to make any real progress, however, because, among other reasons, it lacked delegates from one of the contending parties and it was held at a very inopportune time.

American congressional and state election campaigns were moving into full swing. Because of the close election races in the key state of New York, with its large Jewish population, President Truman (Democrat), against the advice of his State Department officials,[23] and Governor Thomas E. Dewey (Republican), a candidate for reelection, felt it politically expedient to come out strongly behind the Zionist program for statehood and for immediate large-scale Jewish immigration into Palestine. Once again the Arabs protested strongly that Truman was acting contrary to the American pledges made to them in the past.[24] British officials complained that the President's political campaign speeches had undermined the chances of success of informal talks they were conducting with Jewish representatives. Although both the Arab and British charges were denied, Truman's and Dewey's pro-Zionist positions naturally encouraged the Zionists to hold fast to their maximum demands and to refuse to make any significant concessions. Realizing that the situation was unfavorable, Britain decided in October to adjourn the conference temporarily.

The second phase of the London conference was postponed until January, 1947, in the hope that the Twenty-second Zionist Congress, meeting in the middle of December, would finally authorize the Jewish Agency to be represented at the conference. But the activists dominated the congress, and the Zionist position hardened. Resolutions were passed accepting nothing less than a Jewish state, although a partition solution would be considered if it were favorable enough. While Jewish Agency representatives once again met with British officials informally, the Agency continued to boycott the conference itself. On the other hand, the Arab League had finally prevailed upon the Arab Higher Committee to send delegates of its own to London. However, with the Mufti now back in full control of the Arab Higher Committee, the Palestine Arab position had also stiffened against the acceptance of any partition scheme.

Failing to obtain Arab-Jewish agreement on any major issue, the British government submitted its own final proposal. This provided that after becoming a trusteeship for a maximum period of five years, Palestine would form a unified state with cantons. Over a two-year period, 100,000 Jews would be admitted into Palestine, but the Arabs would ultimately be given a voice in determining future immigration policy.

Since both the Arabs and the Zionists rejected this latest proposal, the British, on April 12, 1947, formally requested the Secretary-General of the UN to summon a special session of the General Assembly for the purpose of constituting and instructing a special committee to prepare for the consideration of the Palestine question at the next regular session of the General Assembly.

The Labor party's foreign secretary, Ernest Bevin, placed more blame on the Zionists than on the Arabs for the failure to reach a common agreement on the future of Palestine. He accused the Jews of being more unreasonable than the Arabs, proclaimed that the Arabs had strong arguments in their favor, and rejected partition as a realistic or practical solution. He thereby raised Arab hopes while alienating the Zionists. Many Jewish nationalists became increasingly convinced that only through intensifying their acts of violence against the Palestine administration and through working harder than ever before to obtain still more active American official support for their cause could the Jews finally hope to achieve their cherished goals in Palestine.

Between the end of World War I and 1947, Arab-Jewish, Anglo-Jewish, and Arab-Western relations seriously deteriorated, and the Palestine question became increasingly explosive and difficult to deal with. Britain, the United States, the Arabs, and the Jews shared varying degrees of responsibility for the development of this tragic situation.

The dilemma in which Britain found herself in 1947 was largely the result of her own past errors of omission and commission. By vacillating in word and deed, by often allowing competing and extremist pressures to alter her policies, by avoiding unpopular and difficult decisions and enforcement actions, and by trying to please all sides at the same time, Britain was only postponing the day of reckoning and making the ultimate solution that much harder to find and implement. At no time after the mandate was established could the Palestine issue have been solved without resorting to some force against at least the extremists of one party or another in the Holy Land. Moreover, Britain had been advised repeatedly by her experts that the longer she delayed the formulation of a definite, consistent, and realistic policy—and showing both parties that she intended to carry out that policy regardless of internal and external pressures—the greater would be the force ultimately required to do so because Arab and Jewish nationalisms and ambitions, as well as intransigence, were bound to grow in scope and intensity. Having gained at least verbal concessions from Britain through the use of violence in the past, both Arabs and Jews were encouraged to continue employing similar drastic measures. Also, with the intensification of Zionist and Arab lobbying and propaganda efforts in various countries and with the rise of Fascist and, later, Soviet ambitions and activities in the Middle East, the Palestine question became more deeply enmeshed in larger and more dangerous world conflicts, thus adding further dimensions to an already difficult and complicated problem.

Many British policies implemented in Palestine tended to aggravate matters. Not only did Britain fail to make any determined attempt to bring Arabs and Jews closer together, but many of her policies actually tended to perpetuate and even to widen the personal, economic, and political gulfs existing between the two peoples. Britain also failed to create any forum in which the leaders of the different communities could exchange views, work out their disagreements, or establish those personal ties of respect and understanding which are so necessary to the proper functioning of any multinational political unit.

During World War II the United States found herself increasingly involved in Middle Eastern affairs. Yet she failed to formulate a sound, over-all, long-range policy for this area. Instead, she improvised her promises and policies to meet the pressing internal and external needs of the moment. Just as the British had done during World War I, Presidents Roosevelt and Truman made contradictory promises to Arabs and Jews. These divergent promises not only led to one policy dilemma after another, but they added seriously to the complications surrounding the Palestine problem.

Had the United States been willing to cooperate fully and dispassionately with Britain in finding a reasonable compromise solution, in effectively backing the Arab and Jewish moderates willing to accept such a compromise, and in taking the measures necessary to implement it, a workable solution might have been found and implemented at a minimum cost. Instead, by allowing partisan pressures and politics to determine national policy, the United States simply encouraged the extremists on both sides and weakened her ability to influence the situation favorably. On the one hand, the Arabs had been so antagonized by the pro-Zionist position of American officials that they became more reluctant than ever before to accept any American advice or intervention in the Palestine dispute. On the other hand, the Zionists had become so confident of American support that they did not feel any need to lessen their own more extreme demands. Moreover, while the United States insisted on playing a major role in arriving at a settlement of the Palestine problem, she refused to accept any share of the burden of enforcement action. The British were so irritated by the unfairness of this attitude that they also proved reluctant to accept American advice. Thus, on the whole,

United States policies and actions during these crucial years tended to harden the position of both the Arabs and the Zionists, making it more difficult than ever to find a peaceful settlement of the Palestine issue.

The Arabs made many costly mistakes in the period after World War I. Most Palestine Arab leaders often took negative and intransigent positions, and, by insisting upon getting everything, they ended up with practically nothing. They failed to give adequate consideration to the advice of those officials in the independent Arab states who had more experience in international affairs and who were more moderate, realistic, and flexible than the leaders of the Palestine Arabs. For example, the Palestine Arabs, by frequently refusing to appear before investigating commissions or by refusing to attend conferences, lost many valuable opportunities for presenting and pressing their case before the Western peoples and governments in whose hands the fate of Palestine ultimately lay. When the Arabs finally awakened to the need for challenging Zionist propaganda on the international scene, their efforts to put their case before the world turned out to be too little and too late. In addition, while the overwhelming majority of the Palestine Arabs remained fully loyal to the West in World War II, the Mufti's support of the Nazis, even though given primarily in the misguided belief that it would somehow help the Arabs and his own position, made his leadership of the Palestine Arabs after the war a serious handicap in winning public and governmental support for their cause in the Western countries where feelings against Hitler remained intense.

Within Palestine the Arabs allowed petty, personal, and factional rivalries and ambitions to stand in the way of genuine Arab unity, and they failed to rally around their more perceptive leaders. Their refusal to accept an Arab Agency, which Britain had once suggested, left them without a practical and legal instrument for protecting their interests before the mandatory government. Such an agency could also have provided a more formal, effective means for coordinating the views, policies, and actions of the Christian and Muslin Arabs and for providing machinery to promote experience in self-government—an experience which would have been invaluable in those critical days before the termination of the mandate. Furthermore, unlike the Jews, the Palestine Arabs made no serious efforts to plan ahead and work for the day when they might have to fight to save their homeland. For instance, they did little to rebuild their forces, train their men in modern warfare, acquire sufficient modern arms, and seek more able military and political leadership. Thus, they were extremely ill-prepared militarily and politically when the struggle for Palestine reached its climax.

The Arabs also failed to realize in time how strongly the Zionists felt about their own cause and how determined they were to achieve their own goals. The Arabs misunderstood and underestimated the growth and intensity of Jewish nationalism as much as the Zionists misunderstood and underestimated the rise of Arab nationalism. The Arabs, in addition, made inadequate attempts to help close the widening rift between the Arab and Jewish communities. Considering the size and importance of the Jewish community already established in Palestine, some kind of understanding between the two communities would have been essential to peace and order even in an Arab-dominated Palestine.

Over the years many Jews, both Zionist and non-Zionist, had emphasized the vital need to work for Arab-Jewish understanding, and they had warned that the Arabs would peacefully accept the Jews only when given evidence of Jewish friendship and desire to live with the Arabs on the basis of equality and mutual respect. For example, Dr. Judah Magnes, a leading exponent of a binationalist solution, repeatedly advised that "the way of Arab-Jewish understanding is the longer but the one effective way, if there is to be peace and development in Palestine." [25] Even Ben-Gurion had stated in 1931 that the Arab "right to live in Palestine, develop it and win national autonomy is as incontrovertible as is ours to independence. The two can be realized. We must in our work in Palestine respect Arab rights." He also had opposed handling the Arabs as "adversaries" and had backed a "policy of rapprochement and mutual understanding towards the Palestine Arabs." [26] Chaim Weizmann told the Fourteenth Zionist Congress that

> Palestine must be built up without violating the legitimate interests of the Arabs—not a hair of their heads shall be touched. . . . [The Zionist Congress] has to learn the truth that Palestine is not Rhodesia and that 600,000 Arabs live there who . . . have exactly the same right to their homes as we have to our National Home.[27]

Unfortunately, the Zionists, including Ben-Gurion and Weizmann, largely ignored even their own admonitions about the need to encourage Jewish-Arab cooperation. While objecting to becoming a permanent minority in an Arab-dominated Palestine, the Zionists gave little heed to the fact that the Arabs would be equally opposed to becoming a minority in a Jewish-dominated state. Since the Arabs had constituted the majority of the population for centuries and since their cooperation was essential to the peaceful establishment of a Jewish nation, in the final analysis it was the responsibility of the Zionists to present their case in a way that would not antagonize the Arabs. Instead, the Zionists failed to treat the Arabs as equals, to cultivate better relations with them, or to consider objectively and realistically how the problem of the Arabs in a future Jewish state could be justly and pacifically resolved.

Many Zionist policies actually alarmed rather than reassured the

Arabs and widened the breach between the two communities. For example, the Zionists made all land purchased from the Arabs inalienable property of the Jewish people and forever exempt from resale to the Arabs. All the tenant farmers were forced to leave Jewish land. The Zionists sought to keep Arab workers out of their industries and labor unions. Zionist leaders mistakenly and unrealistically believed that somehow most Arabs would be so grateful for their improved economic well-being as a result of Jewish financial and economic development of the country that they would readily relinquish their nationalist feelings and goals and meekly accept their fate in a Jewish-dominated state. Moreover, not only had Jewish immigration and restrictive land and hiring policies helped bring about economic hardship for many of those Arabs forced off the land or otherwise unemployed, but, as the Shaw Royal Commission pointed out, even those Arabs who did happen to benefit materially as a result of the influx of Jewish capital could not feel grateful since the benefits they received were merely "incidental to the main purpose of the [Jewish] enterprise" and "unintended features of a policy which they disliked." [28]

Other Zionist actions had accentuated the cultural disparity between the two communities. The Jews had established their own educational system and had promoted only their own culture and language, Hebrew. Setting up their own political structure, they had managed their own affairs independently of their Arab neighbors. They did not develop any effective contacts or means of cooperating with the Arabs. As a result, the Jews began to think and act as a completely separate entity. Because they were able to attain a more advanced level of education and a higher standard of living than the Arabs, many Jews tended to consider and treat the Arabs as inferiors. This development in particular had serious repercussions: it increased Arab bitterness; it hardened their determination not to be subjected to Jewish rule; and it widened still further the already dangerous psychological and emotional gaps between the two communities.

CHAPTER III

The Palestine Question Before
the United Nations

Though Britain hoped to obtain UN assistance in finding some workable solution to the Palestine problem, it was not originally her intention to surrender her power of decision completely. Nevertheless, once the UN became deeply involved, Britain decided to leave the entire issue in its hands. At the time the fledgling world organization accepted the issue, no one could have foreseen how difficult and time consuming the problem would be or how decisive a role the UN would ultimately play.

UN Special Committee on Palestine (UNSCOP)

At the first Special Session in May, 1947, the Arabs failed in their efforts (1) to include on the session's agenda an item calling for the abrogation of the mandate and the proclamation of Palestine's independence; (2) to oppose the creation of another committee of inquiry on Palestine; and (3) to provide that the main term of reference of any investigatory body be the early independence of Palestine. Only Afghanistan and Turkey gave unqualified backing to the Arab position, while India, Iran, Haiti, Cuba, and El Salvador gave some support. Zionist spokesmen were allowed to present their case before the Political Committee of the General Assembly despite Arab objections to the Zionists' nongovernmental status, and quite a few UN members, including the United States, Poland, South Africa, Chile, and Colombia, expressed agreement with many of the Zionist contentions. By the middle of May, the Soviet Union, hoping to gain some political advantages from increased tension and strife in the Middle East and from the early departure of Britain from Palestine, began to alter her traditionally anti-Zionist position. On May 14, 1947, the Soviet delegate told the General Assembly that although his government preferred that Palestine be made into a single, Arab-Jewish state, it would be willing to consider the partition of Palestine if a binational state proved impossible. Shortly after this the Russian press stopped publishing anti-Zionist material.

On May 15, after lengthy debates, the General Assembly adopted a resolution authorizing an eleven-nation Special Committee on Palestine to investigate all questions and issues relevant to the Palestine problem and to make recommendations to the UN by September, 1947. Representatives from Australia, Canada, Czechoslovakia, Guatemala, India, Iran, the Netherlands, Peru, Sweden, Uruguay, and Yugoslavia were appointed members of this committee.

Between May 26 and August 31, 1947, UNSCOP held numerous public and private meetings, primarily in New York, Jerusalem, Beirut, and Geneva. It studied reports, held hearings of persons and groups concerned with Palestine, made field trips in Palestine and some of the Arab states, and visited Jewish refugee camps in Europe. Tension in Palestine remained high even in the period during which UNSCOP was there. Jewish terrorist and illegal immigration activities continued without interruption. The Zionists sent the ship *Exodus* with 4,550 illegal Jewish immigrants to Palestine while UNSCOP was investigating there—in order to embarrass the British and play on the emotions of the committee members. Three of the ship's passengers were killed and many others injured while resisting British efforts to prevent their disembarkation. Britain ultimately forced the remainder of these particular Jewish refugees to return to Germany.[1] This whole affair proved to be of considerable propaganda value for the Zionist cause. UNSCOP also became involved in the case of three Jewish terrorists condemned to death by a British court, and it passed a resolution expressing concern about the possible unfavorable repercussions that the executions might have on its work.

In their statements before UNSCOP, Zionist representatives emphasized Jewish religious, historical, and legal "rights" to Palestine. By this time world Zionist enrollment had doubled from one million in 1939 to well over two million in 1946. The relative number of Jews who had become members of the organization had trebled from 6.2 to 19.6 per cent. Countries with Zionist branches rose from fifty to sixty-three, and the United States replaced Poland as the Zionist center, with nearly half the world's membership.[2] The Zionists insisted that their situation was unique and that only a Jewish state could resolve the problems of Jewish homelessness, insecurity, and persecution. At first, they asked that the whole of Palestine be made into a Jewish state as soon as large-scale immigration enabled the Jews to attain a majority. Later, however, they reluctantly agreed to accept a partition as a solution if the Jewish state were given enough territory to sustain one or two million more Jewish immigrants. While admitting that partition would represent an injustice to the Palestine Arabs, they held that it would be a "lesser injustice" than denying the Jews a country. They contended that the Arabs would benefit materially from the existence of a Jewish nation possessing considerable capital and technical know-how. It was charged that Arab opposition to Zionist goals came primarily from the Arab *effendis* and feudal lords, not from the masses of the people. Some Jewish representatives, like Ben-Gurion, even claimed that the main conflict was between the Jews and the British, not between the Jews and the Arabs, and that the Arabs and Jews would be able to live in "peace and cooperation" within a Jewish state. Both Ben-Gurion and Moshe Shertok (later Sharett) even spoke of working for an Arab-Jewish alliance and possibly for a confederation or limited federation with the Arab states. Various spokesmen warned UNSCOP that "tension and explosive situations" would "continue" and there would be no "permanent stability" in Palestine until the Jewish "craving for their own state was satisfied." [3]

Other than the Communists, the main Jewish opponents of the Zionist program within Palestine were *Ihud* and the League for Jewish-Arab Rapprochement and Cooperation in Palestine. Both advocated a binational state with equal political rights for the two communities regardless of their size, as well as continued Jewish immigration. These groups blamed Britain primarily for the failure to foster Arab-Jewish cooperation and friendship.[4] Dr. Magnes, *Ihud's* leader, warned that partition would merely create a future irredenta and war. He contended that

> upon the basis of experience of the past twenty-five years . . . Arab-Jewish cooperation has never been made the chief objective of major policy, either by the mandatory government, by the Jewish Agency, or by those representing the Arabs. We regard this as the great sin of omission which has been committed throughout all the years. Arab-Jewish relationship is the main political problem which one has to face. . . . This is the kernel of the problem.[5]

In the United States the anti-Zionist case was strongly presented by the American Council for Judaism.

The Palestine Arab Higher Committee, as well as other Palestine Arab groups, refused to cooperate in any way with UNSCOP on the grounds that UNSCOP's membership was weighted in favor of the Zionists and that there was no need for further investigation of the Palestine situation because the natural rights of the Arabs were so self-evident. The Higher Committee even organized a one-day general strike in the Palestine Arab community on the arrival of UNSCOP in Palestine. The Arab League, the Arab governments, and others tried unsuccessfully to persuade the Higher Committee to change its negative attitude, which they considered to be "poor propaganda" and harmful to the Arab cause. In order to compensate for the shortsighted behavior of the Palestine Arabs, official delegates from Egypt, Iraq, Lebanon, Saudi Arabia, Syria, and Yemen met with UNSCOP twice in Lebanon. They stressed the following points: (1) because the Arabs had been for centuries and still remained the overwhelming majority of the population of Palestine, their historic and democratic right to Palestine was more valid than that of the Jews; (2) all Arabs, not merely a few feudal lords, were opposed to Zionism as a political force, but not to Jews as a people nor to Judaism as a religion; (3) until the rise of political Zionism, Arabs and Jews lived together on a friendly basis; (4) the Arabs feared that large-scale Jewish immigration and Zionist ambitions would lead a future Jewish state to seek political and economic expansion at the expense of the neighboring Arab countries; (5) the Palestine problem was not an economic one; (6) the Jewish argument that the Arabs were backward and needed Jewish help represented merely a revival of the nineteenth-century concept of the "white man's burden," which had been used as an excuse by imperialistic nations desiring to annex so-called backward areas, and the proper remedy would be to help the Palestine Arabs raise their own standard of living and not to penalize them by taking away their land forever; (7) the Jewish refugee question was a humanitarian one which all countries should aid in solving, or in any case, the Palestine Arabs should not be forced to suffer for Hitler's crimes by having to bear alone the entire burden of the Jewish refugees; (8) Judaism was not the only religion which had ties with the Holy Land; and (9) because the Arabs could not remain indifferent to the Zionist threat, they would resort to violence, if necessary, as a "legitimate right of self-defense." [6]

It had been obvious from the beginning that there would be divergent views among the members of UNSCOP. The Indian member clearly and quickly revealed his pro-Arab views, while the representatives from Uruguay and Guatemala made no effort to conceal their strongly pro-Zionist bias. Nevertheless, in the final report[7] there was unanimous agreement on eleven basic recommendations, including that: (1) the Palestine Mandate should be terminated as soon as possible and the country given ultimate independence; (2) provision should be made for protecting the holy places; (3) steps should be taken to preserve the economic unity of Palestine; and (4) "any solution for Palestine cannot be considered as a solution of the Jewish problem in general," and the General Assembly should help solve the Jewish refugee question by international action so as to "alleviate . . . the plight of the Palestine problem."

The UNSCOP report then contained two suggestions for a Palestine settlement. A majority of UNSCOP proposed a plan of partition with an economic union. Palestine was to be divided into an Arab state, a Jewish state, and an independent Jerusalem under a UN trusteeship. The Jewish state would contain approximately 498,000 Jews and 497,000 Arabs, including Bedouins. The Arab state, made up largely of the less richly endowed portions of Palestine, would have some 10,000 Jews and 725,000 non-Jews, while Jerusalem was to hold 100,000 Jews and 105,000 non-Jews. The two states were to become independent after a transitional period of two years, beginning September 1, 1947, with Britain retaining control under UN auspices during this period. One hundred and fifty thousand Jewish immigrants were to be allowed to enter Palestine during the first two years and subsequently 60,000 would be able to enter annually. An economic union was to be set up and to be administered by a joint economic board consisting of members selected by each state and by the UN Economic and Social Council. The majority did not indicate how, in the charged atmosphere then existing between the Arabs and Jews, a workable economic unity was to be achieved within a politically divided Palestine and how any potential armed opposition to its proposal would be dealt with by the UN.

A minority plan, proposed by India, Iran, and Yugoslavia, provided that after a three-year transitional period, a federal union consisting of autonomous Arab and Jewish "states" would be set up. Immigration would be allowed for three years only to the extent to which the country could absorb the immigrants without undue hardship to the inhabitants. Although it warned of the consequences to the peace of the area if partition were forced upon the Arabs, the minority, like the majority, apparently believed that a UN decision, if it were the "right" one, would not be forcibly contested. In any case, no provision was made for dealing with any violent opposition that might arise.

Australia signed neither plan on the reasonable ground that the task of UNSCOP was not to back any specific proposal but to present various alternative solutions with their good and bad features and then leave the final decision to the General Assembly.

Both Arabs and Zionists reacted quickly to the UNSCOP report when it was made public early in September, 1947. The Arabs denounced both the majority and minority proposals, organized general strikes and demonstrations against them, and threatened armed opposition if efforts were made to implement either. In a meeting in Zurich, Switzerland, the Zionist General Council found the federal scheme "wholly unacceptable," but it expressed some satisfaction with the majority partition recommendation. However, since the Zionist General Council felt that the majority plan allocated too little territory to the Jews, it decided to reserve final judgment until after the General Assembly had acted in order to determine how big a slice of Palestine the Jews would ultimately get. Both parties were aware that the UNSCOP majority proposal represented a victory for the Zionists and a defeat for the Arabs, for it immeasurably strengthened the Zionist position before the United Nations. In fact, the closeness of the final vote in the General Assembly for the partition resolution showed that, had the majority of UNSCOP not recommended partition, the Zionist cause would probably have suffered defeat at the hands of the General Assembly. Although the Arab position had been weakened, the Arabs still had high hopes of being able to prevent the majority proposal from being accepted by the UN.

PARTITION PASSES THE GENERAL ASSEMBLY

The Second Session of the General Assembly, convening in September, 1947, had before it "The Question of Palestine" submitted by Britain, the UNSCOP report, and a joint proposal from Iraq and Saudi Arabia for "The Termination of the Mandate over Palestine and the Recognition of Its Independence." Ordinarily, the General Assembly referred all political items on its agenda to the First Committee, but this time it set up an *Ad Hoc* Committee on Palestine to handle these three items. This special committee not only invited the Palestine Arab Higher Committee and the Jewish Agency to send representatives to its deliberations, but it also established three subcommittees.

Subcommittee I, composed of nine pro-partition states (including the United States and the Soviet Union), was delegated the task of drawing up a detailed plan on the basis of the UNSCOP majority proposal. Because the Jewish Agency accepted, while the Higher Committee rejected, the subcommittee's invitations to send representatives to attend its meetings, its deliberations and its final report were completely one-sided.

Subcommittee II, composed of five Arab states, pro-Arab Pakistan and Afghanistan, and neutral Colombia, was requested to draw up a scheme on the basis of the proposal of Iraq and Saudi Arabia for a single, unified Palestine. The Arab members and Colombia complained that the two subcommittees represented only two extreme points of view and suggested that uncommitted states be added to both groups in order to increase the chances of finding some middle ground which could provide some basis for a compromise agreement. When Australia's Dr. Herbert V. Evatt, chairman of the *Ad Hoc* Committee, ignored these complaints and suggestions, Colombia resigned from Subcommittee II, leaving it composed of Arab and pro-Arab members only.

Although Subcommittee III, composed of Dr. Evatt and the delegates from Siam and Iceland, was set up to conciliate the two opposing sides, it hardly functioned at all. A number of states, including France and Colombia, strongly criticized this subcommittee because it did not try, seriously, to carry out its responsibilities. No group was created to study either the UNSCOP minority recommendation for a federal state of Palestine or any other possible compromise solution. Thus, the General Assembly ultimately found itself having to make a momentous decision on the future of Palestine on the basis of only two subcommittee proposals representing two diametrically opposed positions.

In the UN debates, the Arabs reiterated their fears of Zionism and accused the UNSCOP majority partition scheme of being grossly unfair and undemocratic. They protested that while the Jews represented only a minority of the population and owned only a small fraction of the land, they would be allotted the "best part" of Palestine, including nearly all the citrus land (then equally divided between Arab and Jewish ownership), 80 per cent of the cereal area (mostly Arab owned), and 40 per cent of Arab industry. They complained that the UNSCOP plan would leave "practically as many Arabs as Jews in the proposed Jewish state." They asked how was it possible to "recognize the right of half a million Jews, most of them still nationals of foreign countries, to self-determination, while refusing it" to the half million Arabs left under Jewish political domination. They denied the legal and moral right of the UN to partition Palestine against the wishes of the majority of the inhabitants. They contended that the General Assembly had the power only to make recommendations which had no legal binding force.[8] The Arabs also warned that the UN would be creating even "graver problems" if it tried to carry out partition; they would resist it by force, if necessary, under the right of self-defense. In the debates, the Arabs received considerable backing for their views only from Pakistan and some support from India, Afghanistan, Iran, China, Cuba, Turkey, El Salvador, Belgium, Colombia, and Mexico. Arab draft resolutions proposing the setting up of a unitary state of Palestine with protection for minority rights and the holy places and the termination of official help to immigrants going to Palestine were easily defeated. Actually, the main efforts of the Arabs and their closest supporters were aimed not so much at getting their own proposals accepted (for they knew that there was little chance of this happening) but at defeating partition. The Arabs did have better results with a draft resolution which asked the World Court to determine the legal competence of the UN to "enforce or recommend the enforcement of . . . any plan of partition which is contrary to the wishes, or adopted without the consent, of the inhabitants of Palestine." This particular resolution failed by only one vote.[9]

While the Zionists did not have the advantage of membership in the

UN, as did six Arab states with the consequent right to submit draft resolutions and to vote, Jewish Agency representatives were allowed to present their views before both Subcommittee I and the *Ad Hoc* Committee. They reiterated their historical, legal, and political claims to Palestine. They strongly opposed a unitary state on the grounds that: (1) the Jews would then remain a helpless minority in Palestine, as elsewhere; (2) "a highly democratic minority would be forced down to the economic and social level of an Arab majority, whereas under partition the Arab minority would benefit from contact with the progressive majority"; and (3) there would be no place for Jewish refugees to go, whereas partition "could provide a complete solution to the problem." These representatives held that even though partition called for "heavy sacrifices" by the Jews, they would accept the UNSCOP majority recommendation as the "indispensable minimum," subject to further discussions on the constitutional and territorial provisions. They claimed that if the UN did nothing, a clash would "unavoidably" result upon the withdrawal of the mandatory power, and this clash would be "graver" than any that might take place over the enforcement of partition. They belittled Arab determination to oppose partition by force, while they cautioned that the Arabs would have "no easy task" in trying to control "nearly 700,000 Jews" in an Arab Palestine. In any case, they assured the UN, they were not frightened by Arab threats and would be able to defend themselves and their state in a partitioned Palestine. They warned that they would fight alone, if necessary, to achieve their state. The partition plan and many Zionist views were given strong backing by Guatemala, Uruguay, South Africa, Poland, Czechoslovakia, Sweden, the United States and, after October 13, the Soviet Union.[10]

The Soviet Union did not definitely endorse partition until October 13. Prior to this date, the Arabs exercised restraint in dealing with various Soviet proposals and actions on a number of agenda items before the General Assembly in the hope that Russia would oppose both the Zionists and the United States. On October 13, however, the Soviet delegate made a major speech providing solid support for the concept of partition. Russian leaders had apparently become convinced that they had more to gain than to lose from the partitioning of Palestine because it could (1) drive out British control and influence and increase anti-Western feeling generally in the Middle East, thus making it easier for the Russians to make some headway there; (2) bring about a highly nationalistic, anti-British Jewish state containing many thousands of refugees from Soviet-dominated areas in Eastern Europe; (3) cause a general increase in tension and unrest in the Middle East which would hurt the West and enable the Communists to exploit the situation;

(4) compel the Security Council, where Russia had a veto, to deal with the Palestine dispute; and (5) require the UN to dispatch an international force, possibly including Russian troops, into Palestine.[11]

Once they lost all hope for a change in Soviet policy, the Arab delegates began to take an increasingly anti-Soviet position. They even sought to win converts from the West by warning that (1) Russia was seeking to gain a foothold by sending thousands of Communists in the guise of Jewish refugees into Palestine; (2) partition would establish a precedent which would encourage the Russians to promote the setting up of Communist-dominated states in such places as Azerbaijan and Kurdistan; and (3) only the Communists would profit from a strife-ridden, anti-Western Middle East.[12]

As a result of conflicting points of view and pressures within the United States, the official American position on partition tended to be somewhat uncertain and unclear in the early weeks of the General Assembly session, but eventually the United States came out solidly in support of partition. On the one side, the Joint Chiefs of Staff and the State Department advised against supporting partition for fear that it would endanger Western political and strategic interests in the Middle East by alienating the Arabs and promoting the growth of Russian influence in the area and that it would also threaten access to the vast Arab oil resources so vital to America's allies in Europe. The State Department reminded President Truman of Roosevelt's earlier promise to the Arabs that the United States would consult with them before any final decisions were made over Palestine. The military advised the President of America's inability, at that particular time, to send more than purely token military forces to Palestine if serious trouble broke out there.[13]

On the other side, Truman's religious and humanitarian feelings had already influenced him to adopt a "generally sympathetic attitude toward Jewish aspirations." [14] He felt sorry for the Jewish refugees and believed that a Jewish state would relieve their sufferings. He also agreed with the Zionist contention that a Jewish country could help improve the economic well-being of the Arabs throughout the Middle East. Despite warnings to the contrary from American diplomatic and military experts and from the Arabs, Truman believed that partition was a "practicable" solution that could be achieved "without bloodshed." [15] Not only Jewish leaders, but many Americans and most of the press tended to discount Arab threats of violence against any partition scheme.[16]

Tremendous political and personal pressures were put to bear on Truman in support of partition. At this stage, the vast lobbying and propaganda facilities built up by the Zionists over the years came into action. An enormous amount of Zionist literature was distributed throughout the country. Numerous conferences and meetings were organized. Special efforts were made to influence key leaders in the fields of the arts, education, religion, and politics.[17] As a result of these efforts, an overwhelming majority of Americans, having been repeatedly exposed over the years to effective Zionist propaganda and knowing little or nothing about the concerns of the State Department and the military with the broader political and security interests of the United States in the Middle East, were strongly pro-partition. American politicians, including Truman, found it difficult to ignore these pressures and popular attitudes. Only a few men, such as Secretary of the Navy James Forrestal, recognizing the dangers to American interests that could arise from allowing partisan politics to determine major aspects of American foreign policy, attempted unsuccessfully to keep the Palestine question out of politics. Arab propaganda efforts, on the other hand, were too feeble to affect the situation in any way.[18]

While the Arabs largely limited their propaganda activities outside of the Middle East to the United States and Britain, the Zionists vigorously pressed their own propaganda in many European and Latin American countries, South Africa, and elsewhere. In Palestine, the attitude of most Arab leaders towards the foreign press was usually hostile and suspicious, and Arab public relations services were very inadequate. The Jewish Agency's press department, on the other hand, placed every possible facility at the service of visiting newspaper reporters and others in order to insure that Zionist views were favorably presented before world public opinion. In short, the Zionists during this critical period were doing a far more effective job than the Arabs in achieving a favorable opinion from millions of people in many parts of the world.[19]

When British officials first submitted the Palestine question to the UN in February, 1947, they indicated that this move did not necessarily imply their intention to relinquish the Palestine Mandate. By the early part of the Second Session of the General Assembly, however, these officials had a change of mind. As a result of Britain's economic, financial, and military weakness, they finally decided to give up India, to terminate their military and political commitments to Greece, and to move their military bases in the Middle East to Kenya in East Africa. Because these developments reduced the strategic importance of Palestine and because Britain's difficulties in the Holy Land seemed practically insoluble and unending, British leaders concluded that Palestine was no longer worth holding. Once this decision was made, Britain informed the UN that she accepted UNSCOP's recommendation to end the mandate as soon as possible. She warned, however, that although she would gladly accept any solution agreed to by both contending parties, she would not assume the responsibility for imposing any General Assembly proposal which, if opposed by one side or the other, would require the use of military force. She also warned the UN of the risk involved if the partition scheme were accepted without any adequate consideration being given by the world organization to the problem of implementation. Throughout each of the General Assembly debates, Britain generally played an inactive role and even abstained in all the votes taken on the various draft resolutions submitted.

The Arabs were pleased with this British position because they believed that even if the General Assembly did ultimately adopt a partition resolution, it could not be enforced without active British cooperation—and Britain had publicly and officially committed herself not to help enforce any decision objected to by either side. This British attitude and the strongly pro-Zionist stands taken by both the United States and the Soviet Union lessened the chances of achieving a compromise solution to the Palestine problem because they tended to strengthen the beliefs of both Arabs and Zionists that they could achieve their goals without having to make any concessions.

An unusual feature of Subcommittee I was the fact that Russia and the United States found themselves on the same side of a major political issue. Both actively supported partition, although they did differ on certain details involving its implementation. For example, Russia wanted the mandate to be terminated and British troops withdrawn as quickly as possible. She also insisted that the Security Council be given the task of carrying out and enforcing, with troops from the major powers if necessary, any General Assembly partition resolution. The United States, opposing any procedure which might open the gates to increased Soviet influence in Palestine, preferred that Britain administer the mandate for the UN in the transition period.

The final report of Subcommittee I provided for an amended version of the UNSCOP majority proposal for partition and economic union with an international regime for Jerusalem. The main changes included increasing the powers of the joint economic board and shifting the boundaries slightly to reduce the number of Arabs left in the Jewish state. The proposed Arab state was to encompass the central and eastern part of Palestine from the Valley of Esdraelon down to Beersheba, western Galilee, Jaffa, and narrow strips of land along the coast from north of Gaza down to the Egyptian frontier and then along the Egyptian frontier to about halfway to Aqaba. This area of about 4,500 square miles contained 800,000 non-Jews and 10,000 Jews. The proposed Jewish state was to include eastern Galilee and the Valley of Esdraelon, a coastal strip of land from Haifa to below Tel Aviv, and the major part of the

Negev down to the Gulf of Aqaba. This area of approximately 5,500 square miles contained close to 500,000 Jews and well over 400,000 Arabs. A commission was to be set up to administer Palestine during the transitional period from the end of the mandate until full independence was achieved by both states. Although to be elected by the General Assembly, this commission would operate under the guidance of the Security Council. The subcommittee plan itself was to be amended before final passage. The more important changes included the following: (1) the boundaries were altered slightly in favor of the Arab state at Beersheba and along the Egyptian border; (2) the joint economic board was given increased power to provide greater assistance and protection to the Arab state; and (3) the Security Council was given more specific authority to implement partition.

On November 25, 1947, the *Ad Hoc* Committee passed the amended partition resolution by a vote of twenty-five to thirteen, with seventeen abstentions—which was well above the simple majority needed in the committee, but one vote short of the two-thirds vote required for final passage by the General Assembly in plenary session. Afghanistan, Cuba, India, Iran, Pakistan, Siam, and Turkey joined the six Arab members in voting against the resolution. Britain, France, China, Argentina, Belgium, Colombia, El Salvador, Ethiopia, Greece, Haiti, Honduras, Liberia, Luxembourg, Mexico, the Netherlands, New Zealand, and Yugoslavia abstained. The remainder of the UN members, including the Soviet bloc, the United States, and most of the Latin American and all of the Scandinavian countries voted for the resolution.

On the morning of November 26, when the General Assembly began to debate the partition resolution passed by its *Ad Hoc* Committee, the Arab delegates were optimistic about the final outcome. Siam's vote against partition was lost as a result of the withdrawal of the credentials of the Siamese delegation by a new revolutionary government which had taken over power in that country, but the Haitian delegate, who had abstained in the committee, and the Philippine delegate, who had been absent during the committee voting, openly indicated that they would vote against partition in the General Assembly. The Arabs thought they were assured of the final backing of Greece and Liberia, too, while they still had high hopes of winning even Colombia's support. Thus, by the afternoon of Wednesday, November 26, the Arabs were confident that if a vote were taken that same day as they had anticipated, they could muster at least sixteen votes against partition while their opponents could not obtain the necessary thirty-two votes.

Later that day, the Arabs became gravely concerned when Dr. Oswald Aranha, president of the Assembly, implied that he was going to cancel the planned evening session and ask for an adjournment at the conclusion of the afternoon session until Friday, November 28— the day after the American Thanksgiving. The Arabs implored Aranha not to cancel the evening session for they knew that many delegations which had not supported partition were under great pressure to change their votes. The Arabs feared that if these pressures were allowed to continue for two more days they could face defeat. Despite the fact that the Arab and pro-Arab delegates expressed a willingness to remove their names from the list of speakers so the Assembly could complete its discussions and take a vote that evening, Aranha insisted on submitting his proposal for an adjournment to the Assembly. The proposal was carried by the close vote of twenty-four to twenty-one.

Between Wednesday evening and Friday, both sides intensified their pressures on various delegations and their governments. Some Arabs and pro-Arabs appealed to the delegates of a number of the smaller countries, including several Latin American states, to either vote against partition or at least abstain.[20] The United States and the Zionists led the lobbying efforts of the pro-partition forces. The delegates, as well as the home governments, of Haiti, Liberia, Ethiopia, China, the Philippines, and Greece were swamped with telegrams, telephone calls, letters, and visitations from many sources, including the White House, congressmen, other government officials, and prominent persons from a number of business corporations and other fields of endeavor. As a result of these tremendous official and nonofficial pressures, Haiti, Liberia, and the Philippines finally agreed to vote for partition.[21] With the Siamese delegation still without credentials, these voting changes assured the two-thirds vote required for the partition resolution.

When the General Assembly convened again on Friday, Arab, French, and Colombian delegates charged that the *Ad Hoc* Committee and Subcommittee III had failed to make adequate efforts to bridge at least part of the gap existing between the contending parties. The Arabs, facing certain defeat in case of an early vote, desperately fought for more time in the hope that they could somehow find a way to prevent the acceptance of the partition resolution. They insisted that a "reconciliation" between the Arabs and Jews was "still possible" and urged the UN to try a "conciliatory approach" even if this took a little more time before trying to push partition against determined and, if necessary, violent opposition.[22] Believing that the situation was too serious to allow the opportunity for a peaceful settlement to "slip away," the French delegate requested and won a twenty-four-hour delay in the partition vote to allow one final attempt to obtain an agreement between the Arabs and Jews. Meeting privately that evening, the Arab delegates worked out and presented to the Assembly the next day a proposal for an independent, democratic, federal state divided into Jewish and Arab cantons with provisions for protecting and supervising the holy places. This plan was similar to the one recommended by the UNSCOP minority which the Arabs had turned down and which the Assembly had not seriously examined in the past. Realizing that the new suggestion was not going to save their situation, the Arabs expressed a willingness to consider other alternative proposals and asked the Assembly to adjourn for an extended period to allow more time for efforts at conciliation and compromise. An Iranian motion requesting an adjournment until January 15, 1948, in order to give the *Ad Hoc* Committee time to study the Palestine question anew was not even submitted for a vote because the President of the Assembly ruled that the partition resolution had to be voted on before the Iranian motion.[23]

The partition resolution then passed by a vote of thirty-three to thirteen with ten abstentions. Compared with the results in the *Ad Hoc* Committee, the pro-partition forces, although they lost the vote of Chile, which abstained, had gained the backing of Belgium, France, Haiti, Liberia, Luxembourg, the Netherlands, New Zealand, Paraguay, and the Philippines. Some countries such as Haiti, Liberia, and the Philippines had changed their votes because of outside pressure. Several states, including Belgium, the Netherlands and New Zealand, frankly admitted that while they did not think that partition was a good solution, they voted for it because a bad solution was better than none at all. A few states, such as Canada, were equally unenthusiastic about partition, but they were finally swayed to support it by the fact that the United States and the Soviet Union agreed on a major political issue, and they believed that such a rare phenomenon should not be destroyed.[24] France's vote was influenced partly by this reasoning and partly by the hope that partition would somehow help her reestablish her prestige in the Middle East through her probable presence in the organization charged with administering an internationalized Jerusalem. These various factors and considerations were significant in changing enough votes to enable the partition resolution to pass. The Arabs, on the other hand, had lost the vote of Siam and gained only the support of Greece. Of the thirteen negative votes only Cuba and Greece were non-Asiatic states.

Although the UN resolution provided that the members of the Palestine Commission responsible for the implementation of partition should be elected by the General Assembly, the President of the Assembly actually appointed Bolivia, Czechoslovakia, Denmark, Panama, and the Philippines to this body.

REACTIONS TO THE PARTITION RESOLUTION

Arabs everywhere bitterly attacked the partition resolution. The various Palestine Arab factions, closing their ranks in the face of this new threat, called for a general strike in protest. Not only did Arab officials warn that they would refuse to recognize the validity of the resolution, but the Arab League Council, after a meeting held in December, 1947, announced that the Arabs would take whatever measures necessary to insure that it would never be implemented. While the council also decided against sending the military forces of the Arab states into Palestine, it agreed to help recruit volunteers to be sent to assist the Palestine Arabs. Actually, many Arabs were confident that this resolution would suffer the same fate as many others which had remained unenforced year after year. Nevertheless, the passage of the partition resolution resulted in a major loss of UN prestige in the Arab world.

The United States received the lion's share of blame from the Arabs for the passage of the partition resolution as well as for many of the Arab difficulties in Palestine. The Arabs charged that American money, arms, and other aid had helped increase the size and strength of the Jewish community in Palestine to such an extent that an effective demand for independence had finally become possible. Furthermore, many Arabs saw in a Jewish state backed by considerable American financial and political support the rise of a new American imperialism to replace expiring British imperialism in Palestine. Before World War II the United States had been held in high esteem by the Arabs because American activities in the Middle East had, up to then, been largely confined to humanitarian, religious, and educational fields. After the war, however, American prestige and influence in the Arab world declined rapidly as a result of the major role played by the United States government and citizens on behalf of the Zionist cause.

Britain's "passivity" during the General Assembly session was rated by the Arabs "almost as culpable as the positive activities of the United States," [25] and her position among the Arabs began to weaken seriously; nevertheless, some Arabs still hoped to regain British support. Though the Arab League closed the Arab Information Offices in the United States, it kept the London office open in the belief that there was yet a chance to influence the British public in favor of the Arab cause.

The Arabs were stunned by the unexpected change in the Soviet attitude towards Zionism. Recognizing the vital role played by the Soviet bloc in bringing about the passage of the partition resolution, Russia also became the object of bitter Arab attacks. Even though Russia continued to proclaim her friendship for the Arabs, Soviet prestige and even the influence of the Arab Communist parties received a serious blow.

Most Jews were overjoyed at the passage of the partition resolution for they considered it to have given them vital legal and political bases for their state. They were especially grateful to the Untied States and Russia for the essential roles they played in obtaining the two-thirds vote and held the UN itself in high esteem. The very passage of the UN resolution helped to unite many diverse Jewish groups behind partition. Even various binationalist factions and the anti-Zionist American Council for Judaism, although still theoretically opposed to the principle of partition, agreed to accept partition as the will of the world community expressed through the UN.

But not all Jews were happy with the resolution. Many were con cerned because the UN had not made any serious provisions for enforcing partition against possible violent Arab opposition. Extremist groups, like the Irgun, proclaimed that "the partition of the Homeland" was "illegal" and would "never be recognized. . . . Eretz Israel will be restored to the people of Israel. All of it. And forever." Irgun also warned that partition would not mean peace and asked the Jews to "take up the offensive" not merely to repel any possible Arab attacks but also to enable the Zionists to seize all of Palestine.[26]

Even while the UN was still debating the Palestine question, the Jewish Agency and the National Council Executives (who acted as the cabinet for the Elected Assembly, the Palestine Jewish community's quasi-parliament) began making arrangements for the defense of Palestine Jews in the event of armed Arab resistance to a Jewish state and for the maintenance of essential government services after the British departure. The political plans included drafting a constitution and a legal code for a Jewish state, establishing a school for diplomatic and administrative personnel, canvassing Arab, British, and Jewish civil servants to determine their willingness to serve a future Jewish government, and making all other preparations necessary for the effective transfer of governmental authority. The Elected Assembly decreed total mobilization of Jewish manpower. The Haganah began to be converted from an underground force into a regular army, and its units were deployed along the Syrian frontier where the Arab military threat appeared to be greatest. All possible efforts were made to increase Jewish immigration, legally and illegally, because more Jews in Palestine meant more military manpower to draw from. At this stage, humanitarian motives for immigration became completely secondary. Obviously, from the humanitarian point of view, Jewish refugees would have been far safer staying in the refugee camps in Europe than coming to tense and dangerous Palestine. Extraordinary endeavors were made to bring in those younger refugees who would be most useful in case of war. Jewish as well as non-Jewish veterans of Allied armies—pilots, engineers, naval experts, and the like —were hastily recruited. Arms and military equipment were desperately sought from various sources. New Jewish villages in strategic areas were hurriedly set up. In brief, while the shortsighted Arabs were doing little to prepare themselves for taking over and running their hoped-for state, the Jews both inside and outside of Palestine were making far more determined and effective preparations.[27]

The passage of the partition resolution on November 29, 1947, led to demonstrations and a general strike by the Palestine Arabs and celebrations by the Jews. In Jerusalem, Haifa, Tel Aviv, Jaffa, and similar areas where Arabs and Jews lived in close proximity, fighting between the two communities broke out; this was to spread and become more serious with time. Charges and countercharges developed, with each side blaming the other for precipitating the disorders and each side accusing the British of helping its opponent.[28] The chaos that ensued was ideal for the extremists in both camps, who were frequently able to take the law into their own hands with relative impunity. The British generally tried to maintain order in the territories they still controlled, but they were not always successful. Since both Arabs and Jews attempted to seize control of the areas being vacated in stages by British troops as a result of a British decision to evacuate Palestine completely by May 15, 1948, armed clashes between the opposing sides were inevitable. Outrages were committed by both Arabs and Jews. Between December 1, 1947, and February 1, 1948, according to a UN report, there were 2,778 casualties, including 1,462 Arabs, 1,106 Jews, and 181 Britishers.[29]

The General Assembly resolution had placed primary responsibility for implementing the partition on the Palestine Commission, which was to work under the guidance and with the assistance of the Security Council. The commission invited the Arab Higher Committee, the Jewish Agency, and the mandatory power to designate representatives to assist and consult with it. Only the Higher Committee refused the invitation on the grounds that it did not recognize the validity of the UN resolution and that it opposed partition. The Jewish Agency was naturally anxious to cooperate with the commission's efforts to set up a Jewish state. Although Britain sent a representative as requested, she refused to take any active part in implementing the partition since it was opposed by one of the parties. Britain even announced that she would not share her control with the commission before she left on May 15 and that she would not allow the commission to enter Palestine before May 1, allegedly because of fear for the safety of the members of the commission. Without Arab and British cooperation, the commission faced a formidable task in trying to carry out its responsibilities for arranging a transfer of authority from the British, establishing Arab and Jewish militias and provisional councils, delimiting the frontiers, and preparing for the economic unity of the two proposed states. Actually, the commission members never left New York. They sent a representative to the strife-torn country, but he was able to accomplish little.

Unmindful of the rapid deterioration of the situation in Palestine, the Security Council was dilatory in fulfilling its obligations under the partition resolution. Not until February 24, 1948, did it seriously take up the Palestine question by discussing the First Special Report (A/AC 21/9) of the Palestine Commission which accused the Arabs of trying to alter the UN partition resolution "by force" and asked the Security Council to provide the commission with armed assistance in discharging its responsibilities and preventing bloodshed once British troops had fully evacuated Palestine.

Because fighting had intensified between Arabs and Jews in Palestine, because Arab states were showing increasing signs of determination to resist partition by force, and because Britain had finally convinced American officials that she really did not intend to take any part in the enforcement of partition, the United States became much less confident than she had been in November that partition would not be seriously challenged. State Department and military officials grew anxious about the rise of Arab hostility and the Arab threats of interference with the westward flow of oil. By January 21, 1948, the State Department's planning staff had drawn up a paper concluding that partition was not workable, the United States was not committed to back it if force were required for its implementation, and the United States should take steps to secure the withdrawal of the partition proposal. The military advised the president that from 80,000 to 160,000 troops would be needed to implement partition, while the employment by the United States of more than one division in Palestine would make partial mobilization necessary. Especially with the development of the Czechoslovak crisis in February, the sudden mushrooming of the Cold War, and the increasingly obvious desire of the Russians to push their influence into the Middle East, American officials became greatly concerned about the dangerous consequences to Western interests which could come from antagonizing the strategically important Arab world and from pushing a solution that would require for its implementation the employment in Palestine of an international force which might have to include Soviet troops. President Truman, however, was also faced with strong pressures from Zionist and pro-Zionist sources, including some of his own personal aides, to continue his support for partition.

For a time the military and diplomatic advisers seemed to have won the day. On February 24, the American delegate told the Security Council that its first duty was "directed to keep the peace and not enforce partition." On March 19, the United States took the position that General Assembly resolutions were merely recommendations and that if the partition resolution were not put into effect by the end of the mandate on May 15, the UN would no longer have any administrative and governmental responsibility for Palestine unless further action were taken by the General Assembly. Moreover, since the Security Council was not prepared to enforce partition, the UN should set up a "temporary trusteeship for Palestine" under the Trusteeship Council in order "to maintain the peace and to afford the Jews and Arabs of Palestine . . . further opportunity to reach an agreement regarding the future government of that country." On April 1, the Security Council passed an American resolution calling a special session of the General Assembly to "consider further the question of the future government of Palestine." Later in April two other resolutions were also adopted, one calling for a cessation of hostilities and the establishment of a truce in Palestine and the other for setting up a Truce Commission consisting of the American, French, and Belgian consuls in Jerusalem to check on the observance of any truce that might be agreed upon.[30]

The Arabs were cautiously pleased with the new American position. Arab delegates to the UN and the Arab League Political Committee expressed their willingness to consider the trusteeship proposal and to accept a truce in Palestine. But the Arab Higher Committee was less receptive to the trusteeship idea than were the Arab governments. While the Higher Committee did not oppose the truce resolutions, it informed the Security Council that as long as Jewish immigration continued and the Zionists were proceeding with their plans to set up a Jewish state, the Palestine Arabs would not stop fighting.

Jewish representatives emphasized their unalterable opposition to the trusteeship proposal and their expectation that the UN would implement the partition resolution, by force if necessary. They warned that once the mandate ended on May 15, a provisional Jewish government would begin to function whether the UN changed its resolution or not. The Zionists were angered by the new American attitude, which they considered a betrayal of their cause. Zionist propaganda and pressure activities were intensified in an effort to regain American support for partition. The Jewish Agency agreed to accept a truce if all foreign

Arab "volunteers" were withdrawn from Palestine, further Arab incursions were prevented, unrestricted Jewish immigration were allowed to continue, and the truce did not delay the achievement of independence. Britain was accused of conniving with Arab efforts to infiltrate Palestine, selling military equipment to the Arabs, and withholding it from the Zionists.

The Soviet Union and the Ukraine were the only members of the Security Council who remained unwavering in their support of partition. The Arabs were especially aroused by the anti-Arab statements and amendment proposals made by the Soviet bloc delegates. UN Secretary-General Trygve Lie also opposed the American trusteeship proposal and insisted that the UN carry out its partition resolution, if necessary by means of an international police force. He threatened to resign if this resolution were disavowed.[31]

On April 20, the Second Special Session of the General Assembly began to discuss an American "working paper" which proposed the setting up of a temporary trusteeship with the UN as the administering authority acting through the Trusteeship Council and an appointed governor-general. As the Soviet Union had never occupied her seat on the Trusteeship Council, this proposal appeared to be aimed at denying her any significant role in the governing of Palestine during this transitional period. On April 27, however, Russia, in order to block such a development, sent her first representative to sit with the Trusteeship Council.

Initially, Arab reaction to the American "working paper" was reserved. By the latter part of April, however, the Arabs began to worry about the lack of progress in the General Assembly discussions and to fear that some states were purposely trying to delay action on the trusteeship scheme so that the mandate would end on May 15 with the November 29, 1947, partition resolution still in force. Thus, although they disliked certain features of the "working paper," the Arabs felt impelled, as time fled by, to accept the trusteeship plan as the most practical means of killing partition. At this juncture the Arabs expressed greater readiness to compromise than did the Zionists.

Pakistan, Greece, China, India, Iran, Siam, and Turkey continued their opposition to partition, while Britain cautioned that its implementation would require force. Some states which had reluctantly voted for the November 29, 1947, resolution now expressed dissatisfaction or serious objection. For example, Panama considered partition to be a "mistake" which should be rectified. Belgium felt that the attitude of the Security Council had virtually invalidated the decision of November 29, 1947. France wondered whether the Assembly should persist in supporting a plan which could provoke a war.[32]

Realizing how fortunate they were to have the partition resolution passed in the first place and how increasing numbers of UN members who had voted for this resolution were beginning to regret their votes, the Zionists worked desperately to kill the trusteeship proposal and to keep the partition resolution intact, at least until the mandate ended on May 15. Whereas American-Soviet agreement helped the Zionists obtain the partition resolution in November, now American-Soviet disagreement aided them in blocking the trusteeship plan. In any case, Zionist spokesmen warned that they would fight, if necessary, to oppose the setting up of a trusteeship and to establish a Jewish state on May 15. Only Australia, New Zealand, Uruguay, Guatemala, South Africa, and the Soviet bloc persisted in their strong support for the Zionist position on partition.

As May 15 approached, the United States finally abandoned the trusteeship idea, partly because the Zionists made clear that it could be implemented only by force and partly because, late in April, President Truman had transferred the supervision of Palestine affairs from Loy W. Henderson, a career Foreign Service officer and long a Zionist target, to Major General J. H. Hilldring, an ardent pro-Zionist. On May 14, since most members had lost their enthusiasm for the trusteeship scheme and the May 15 deadline was almost at hand, the First Committee of the General Assembly hastily accepted an amended American resolution which stated that: (1) a mediator was to be selected by the Big Five powers; (2) he was to use his good offices with the authorities and communities in Palestine to arrange for the operation of essential public services, to assure protection of the holy places, and to promote the peaceful adjustment of the Palestine situation; (3) the life of the Palestine Commission was ended; and (4) all governments and organizations should cooperate in effecting the Security Council's truce resolutions.

The General Assembly met in plenary session at 5 P.M. Eastern Standard Time on May 14, just one hour before the mandate was to end in Palestine, to act on the First Committee's resolution. Before the Assembly had convened, the Jewish Agency announced that the new State of Israel had formally come into existence that day at 10 A.M. Eastern Standard Time. Shortly after the Assembly convened, news reached the press and UN delegates that President Truman had given full diplomatic recognition to Israel sixteen minutes after the official proclamation was made in Tel Aviv. He had neither consulted with the State Department nor informed the American delegates to the UN before taking this action. Truman's decision was a purely personal one made largely as a result of strong pro-Zionist pressures on him and of his desire to take this step before the Russians did. (The Soviet Union gave full recognition to Israel on May 17.) The General Assembly then belatedly adopted the First Committee's resolution providing for a mediator by a vote of thirty-one to seven with sixteen abstentions. Cuba, Yugoslavia, and the Soviet bloc voted against it, while the Arab states were among the abstainers.

While the Jews were overjoyed at this major act of American support, the Arabs were furious. Soviet policy had been consistently propartition for months, and the Arabs had been given no reason to expect a change. The United States, however, had seemed to be moving away from partition for some time, and this had raised Arab hopes. This sudden, unexpected reversal of American policy evoked greater bitterness against the United States than ever before. Now the Arabs were convinced that the United States had been deliberately deceiving everyone all along about her true intentions so that the mandate would end before any anti-partition resolution could pass the Assembly. This conviction further weakened the position of the United States in the Arab world.

CONCLUSION

Unfortunately neither the UN nor any member nation had made a serious and determined attempt to bridge the dangerously wide gap that had developed between the Arabs and the Jews. After all, whether Palestine was to be a binational or partitioned state, hundreds of thousands of Arabs and Jews would still have had to learn to live with each other harmoniously. Thus, every effort should have been made to bring the two communities closer together—difficult and slow as the process would naturally have been—for this was the only procedure with at least some chance, in the long run, of providing a reasonably firm basis for a peaceful and permanent solution. By failing to promote conciliation adequately, the UN ultimately was to find that not only would its partition resolution not be peacefully accepted, but it had merely exchanged a major Palestine problem for an even bigger, more complex, and more perilous Arab-Israeli dilemma which has created more critical situations for the UN and has taken up far more of its time than any other single world issue. What had once been a relatively local dispute among the Arabs, the Jews, and the British was soon to develop into a matter of worldwide concern and to become distressingly involved in the expanding Cold War.

Both Britain and the United States must share heavily the responsibility for the failure to resolve the Palestine question peacefully and conclusively, as well as for the serious difficulties that arose because of this failure. The two powers had considerable means for pressing the Arabs and Jews into taking a more moderate and compromising position. What they lacked really was the will.

Britain had endured much over a long period of time while trying to retain control of Palestine. Once she realized that her efforts would prove fruitless, it was probably natural that she should desire to relieve herself of all further responsibility by withdrawing as quickly as possible. The pro-partition states were unfair in their complaints about Britain's unwillingness to assume the primary burden for enforcing a plan to which she had repeatedly objected, especially since not one of the pro-partition governments was willing to contribute its fair share of the forces and money that would be required. Nevertheless, the precipitous and ill-advised manner in which Britain abandoned Palestine was unworthy of a great nation and harmful, in the long run, to her own best interests, for this action helped to undermine her own prestige and influence in the Middle East as well as to make widespread strife and armed conflict in Palestine inevitable.

The United States allowed popular emotions and partisan politics rather than a calm, informed appraisal of long-range national interests to determine American foreign policy. Thus she did more to aggravate than relieve the troubled situation and more to weaken than strengthen her own position in the Middle East. Just as British policy encouraged the Arabs in their belief that they could take over all of Palestine once the British left without having to yield anything to their opponents, so Truman's strongly pro-Zionist attitude encouraged the Zionists to feel that they could achieve most of their goals without making significant concessions. In short both Britain and the United States helped to increase the intransigence of the two sides and, as a result, lessened the chances of finding any meaningful and acceptable compromise solution. In addition, although the United States insisted upon the right to play a major role in deciding the future of Palestine, she was unwilling to accept her share of the responsibility for any enforcement action.

Arab bitterness over the UN partition resolution is understandable. The resolution sought to give the larger and more desirable areas to the minority, against the wishes of the majority, to enable the Jews to set up their own state. It was also natural that the Arabs would blame the United States, Britain, and Russia for the passage of this resolution. Yet, the Arabs themselves were not without considerable responsibility for their own unhappy situation. The Arabs in general, and the Palestine Arabs in particular, showed a lack of constructive political sense. On the whole, the Zionists had proved to be much more skilful, realistic, flexible, and farsighted in the handling of their cause than had the Arabs. The Arabs, naively relying merely on the justness of their case to achieve their goals, failed to realize in time that in the realm of practical politics, justness alone does not assure success. Consequently, they did far too little to compete with Zionist propaganda activities in many parts of the world. They neglected to learn the lesson of history that sometimes one step backward may be necessary in order, ultimately, to take two steps forward. Until it was too late, they refused to offer any significant concessions which might have won them some of the support of the many UN members who were not completely satisfied with partition as the proper solution. Most of these members finally voted for the partition resolution solely because they saw no other acceptable alternative course of action available and because they believed that the Jews had been more reasonable and cooperative than the Arabs. For instance, the delegate of the Netherlands, who had abstained in the November, 1947, voting in the *Ad Hoc* Committee of the General Assembly on account of the many serious drawbacks to partition, stated before voting for the resolution in the General Assembly:

> We found the Arabs, whose case we had considered to be a very strong one, to be in a weaker position than the Jews, partly because their attitude of non-cooperation deprived them of many opportunities to influence the course of events.[33]

Had the Arabs, over the years, presented their case more effectively before the world and had they been as willing to seek and accept compromise solutions in the earlier stages of the Second and Special Sessions of the General Assembly as they were in the last few days of each session when their situation had become desperate, the results might not have been so disastrous for them. By adamantly insisting on all or nothing, they ended up with practically nothing.

While the Zionists planned thoroughly and farsightedly in some respects, they were surprisingly careless and shortsighted in other ways. They failed to realize that winning the backing of many foreign governments and the UN could, in the long run, be less important than winning the support and understanding of the Arabs inside and outside of Palestine, for the Jews in any Jewish state would constantly be faced with the necessity of living with an Arab minority within their country and with the many millions of Arabs in the surrounding areas. By ignoring the rights and feelings of the Arabs and by looking down upon them as inferiors, the Zionists had made the Arabs even more vehemently opposed to a Jewish nation and seriously lessened the chances that a peaceful solution to the Palestine issue could be found and that the Arabs and Jews could learn to live in harmony with each other. Had the Zionists seriously tried to befriend rather than belittle the Arabs and to make reasonable concessions to satisfy, in part, Arab pride and national aspirations, they would have gained a more limited immediate victory in 1947 and 1948, but they probably could also have avoided much of the heavy price they have paid and will continue to pay as a result of the Palestine War, the weakened position of the Jews in the Arab world generally, and the dangerous rise in Arab bitterness and hostility towards the very existence of Israel.

CHAPTER IV

The Palestine War and United Nations Truces

The initial fighting between Palestine Arabs and Jews which began shortly after the UN General Assembly passed the partition resolution on November 29, 1947, was localized and limited. Later, however, it increased in scope and intensity until on May 15, 1948, with the complete withdrawal of British units, a full-fledged war broke out.

The progressive withdrawal of British troops and administrative facilities in the early months of 1948 triggered the fighting because it left a series of political and military vacuums which each side was determined to fill first, but this method of evacuation put the Arabs at a special disadvantage. The Jewish community had possessed its own quasi-governmental institutions over the years, had established its own health, social, and other essential public services, and, well in advance, had devised detailed plans and had trained personnel specifically for taking over and managing the affairs of its projected state; thus it was far better prepared than the Arab community to step in and effectively administer the portions of Palestine already occupied by it in the wake of the British withdrawal. The Palestine Arabs, on the other hand, had failed to set up their own quasi-governmental organizations, to gain experience in self-government, or to make any significant preparations for administering areas they hoped to take over. Not only had some of their abler leaders been prevented from returning to Palestine from their forced exile abroad, but large numbers of the middle class, including many local business and political leaders, began to flee Palestine as soon as fighting broke out in December, 1947. By April, as a result of these developments, plus a partial breakdown in many essential services, a number of Jewish military victories, real and imagined atrocity stories, and Jewish psychological warfare aimed at encouraging the Arabs either to surrender or flee, large numbers of Arabs lost their self-confidence and were gripped with fear about their future. Consequently, by May 15, about 200,000 Arabs had already fled their homes in panic.[1]

In general, the poorly trained, poorly organized, and poorly led Palestine Arab fighters did not prove effective. Except for several half-hearted local attempts to seize some of the more isolated Jewish settlements, they were largely content to blockade roads leading to Jewish villages in the hope of starving them into submission. Starting in December, 1947, individual volunteers from the neighboring Arab countries began to trickle into Palestine to aid the Palestine Arabs. Between January and March, 1948, three organized groups of volunteers trained in Syria entered Palestine. Altogether, some 5,000 to 7,000 armed Arab irregulars, most of whom were led by the incompetent Fawzi al-Kaukji, infiltrated Palestine to bolster the Palestine Arab forces. Aided by this "Arab Liberation Army," the Palestine Arabs were finally able to launch a limited offensive in February and March, but with little success.

The Palestine Jews, although constituting only one-third of the population, possessed a far larger, better trained, and better led military force than the Palestine Arabs. Yet until early April, the shortage of war equipment compelled the Jewish military units to remain relatively inactive and largely on the defensive. The arrival of a big shipment of arms from Czechoslovakia late in March finally enabled them to assume the offensive in April. From early April until the end of the mandate on May 15, the Jews were able to seize many important towns and areas from the Arabs, who now found themselves in an increasingly desperate military position. Since most Jews were not satisfied with the amount of territory allotted to them by the UN partition resolution, they readily took advantage of the opportunity to extend the borders of their future state.

Up to this point, the Arab governments had hoped that the Palestine Arabs, with the aid of a few thousand armed and trained "volunteers," would be able to take over control of Palestine without the intervention of regular Arab armies. But the fighting in April and May revealed that the Jewish forces were too strong and too determined for the Palestine Arabs to contain, much less defeat. The Arab masses, aroused over the increasingly grave plight of the Palestine Arab military situation and the flight of tens of thousands of Palestine Arabs, began to press their governments to take more active measures on behalf of the Palestine Arab cause. In a meeting on April 16, the Arab League Political Committee decided to make plans for possible armed intervention, and the Arab chiefs of staff met later in the month to deal further with this matter. Nevertheless, certain Arab states, including Egypt, waited until the last minute before definitely committing themselves to take part in such a military intervention. The Arab situation at this time was not helped by the existence of various dynastic rivalries and by the serious differences that had developed between some Arab states, particularly Egypt and Transjordan, over the military and political goals to be achieved in

Palestine. Egypt insisted that the Arab armies which entered Palestine should remain there only long enough to liberate the country and then turn it over to the Palestine Arabs to run as they wished. But King Abdullah of Transjordan (son of Sharif Hussein) did not intend to make a merely temporary entry into Palestine; he wished to achieve his long-standing dream of ruling a "Greater Syria," composed of Transjordan, Syria, Palestine, and at least part of Lebanon.

Jewish leaders in Palestine sought to exploit these inter-Arab differences in order to avoid having to face all the Arab armies at the same time. Believing that they had a better chance of making a deal with King Abdullah than with any other Arab leader, the Jewish authorities sent a secret mission headed by Mrs. Golda Myerson (later to become Golda Meir) to see him shortly before the mandate came to an end in an effort to keep at least Jordan's highly regarded Arab Legion out of the impending battle. Even though King Abdullah apparently preferred a political to a military solution for Palestine as long as he could make significant territorial gains there, popular pressures throughout the whole Arab world against any agreements with the Jews were too strong for him to ignore; so the secret peace mission failed.[2]

INITIAL ARAB AND JEWISH FORCES

On May 15, 1948, the five Arab states most directly involved in the Palestine crisis maintained a total of some 70,000 to 80,000 troops of varying qualities. Partly because there was a need to keep some soldiers within their own borders to maintain internal peace and order and partly because the Arab governments had gravely underestimated Jewish strength and determination while grossly overestimating their own military capabilities, the Arab states dispatched only about 20,000 to 25,000 troops to help the "Arab Liberation Army" and the armed Palestine Arabs. These included approximately 8,000 to 10,000 Egyptians, 2,000 to 4,000 Iraqis, 4,000 to 5,000 Jordanians, 3,000 to 4,000 Syrians, 1,000 to 2,000 Lebanese, and token units from Saudi Arabia and Yemen. Except for Transjordan's Arab Legion, most of the Arab troops were poorly trained and led, inexperienced in modern warfare, and fighting far from home. The Arab armies lacked the technicians and specialists so greatly needed in modern warfare. Furthermore, because of jealousies and rivalries, the Arab leaders could not agree either on an effective unified military command or on an over-all military policy. Each separate army fought on its own front without seriously coordinating military strategy or even exchanging vital military information with the others. While only Egypt, Iraq, and Syria possessed significant air power, they assigned too few of their planes to the battle, and their airfields were far from the combat areas. Egypt alone had a navy of any dimensions, and even this was a tiny one. The Palestine Arabs themselves proved to be of limited military value once the Palestine War broke out. Lacking competent military and political leadership and adequate military equipment, overwhelmed by Jewish successes, and fearful of a repetition of the April Deir Yaseen massacre at the hands of the Jewish extremists, the Palestine Arabs—especially those who became refugees—were at times more of a military liability than an asset.[3]

Although initially the Arabs were better armed than the Israelis, Arab stocks of military equipment, especially ammunition, had never been adequate for war. In the past, Britain had refrained from providing the Egyptian, Iraqi, and Transjordanian forces with substantial amounts of spare parts and ammunition for the British-made military weapons they held, to prevent their possible use against herself and to keep those governments that much more dependent upon British good will. Starting in February, 1948, Britain ceased accepting any more new orders for Arab munitions, and shortly after the Palestine War began, she joined other UN members in an arms embargo aimed at the Arab states and Israel. Lacking an adequate stock of ammunition for their largely British-style weapons, the main Arab armies were ill prepared for any protracted war. Besides, much of the available military equipment was obsolete, and some of it proved defective. In the absence of adequate roads between the various Arab armies and the different war fronts, it became difficult to assure sufficient military liaison between them and to shift troops from one front to another as needed. The Arab supply lines were frequently long, and the Arabs' maintenance and supply services were inefficient.[4]

The Jewish Agency had ordered a partial mobilization of Jewish manpower as early as November, 1947, and a complete mobilization on May 2, 1948. On May 15, the Haganah, made up of 60,000 to 70,000 trained members, became the backbone of the Israeli army. Some 20,000 to 25,000 had served in various Western military forces during World War II and had thus gained invaluable experience in modern warfare. Extensive women's auxiliary services had been organized to save as many able-bodied men as possible for combat. The extremist Irgun and Stern Gang maintained several thousand armed fighters of their own who operated independently of the Haganah until all Israeli forces were fully integrated in late June. Different authorities have estimated the total number of persons in the Israeli armed services on May 15 as from 35,000 to 80,000.[5] Moreover, Israel added greatly to her manpower in two ways: (1) some 30,000 new immigrants, selected carefully with the war effort in mind, entered Israel between May 15 and August 9, 1948;

(2) foreign volunteers, especially from among those Jews and non-Jews who had military and technical skills most urgently needed by the Israeli armed services, were encouraged to come to Israel. Harry Sacher, a British writer and Zionist, estimated that these volunteers came from fifty-two different countries and ultimately made up 18 per cent of the Israeli armed forces. The official *Israel Digest* stated that "these volunteers formed the nucleus of the Israel Air Force, Navy, Tank Corps and radar units." [6]

Initially, the principal weakness of the Jewish forces was lack of arms. Even before World War II, the Jews had begun to acquire weapons, primarily small arms, legally and illegally. During and shortly after the war these activities were intensified, and an extensive arms purchasing organization with agents in the United States and Europe bought much surplus equipment. Because it was too risky for the Jews to smuggle in this war material while Britain remained in control of Palestine, the purchased munitions were stored in Europe pending the day when they could be shipped safely to Palestine. Shortly before the mandate ended, about thirty shiploads of men, food, and munitions left European and other ports for Israel. On the night of May 14–15, some of these ships entered Israeli ports, and their cargoes were unloaded and rushed to the battle fronts. Moreover, by quickly converting ordinary industries into war industries, the technically proficient Jews were soon able to manufacture and/or improvise large numbers of armored cars, mortars, and other vitally needed items. (Neither the Palestine Arabs nor the other Arabs possessed the facilities or skills to produce any of their own military equipment in this way.) As a result of all of these endeavors, Israel was quickly able to surmount her deficiency in weapons, and thus suffered less from the UN-imposed arms embargo than did the Arabs.

When the war broke out, Israel was faced with a number of weaknesses other than that involving the lack of arms. The Israeli military forces, not yet fully united and organized, sometimes worked at cross purposes. The new government had to overcome many political and administrative problems, including the need to enforce its own authority over all Israeli factions. Moreover, Israel controlled such a small, narrow area that there was little room for retreat and maneuver.

But Israel had a number of major factors in her favor. While the Jews were fighting on interior lines close to their bases of supplies and benefited from a relatively good network of roads, the Arabs frequently had to move men and supplies for long distances over poor or nonexistent roads. Thus, the Israelis were better able than the Arabs to shift their troops quickly from one front to another for defensive or offensive purposes. With no long lines of communication to defend and with many old men, women, and children performing everything but combat duty, almost every Israeli soldier could be employed with maximum effect in the front lines. Moreover, the Israelis, realizing that the fate of their cherished state was gravely threatened and there was little if any room for retreat, often fought with great courage and tenacity. They also benefited greatly from their able political and military leadership, from a highly effective intelligence system which over the years had provided Israeli officers with the detailed data and information so essential to successful military planning, and from the vast financial help that poured in from Jews in the United States and other Western countries. Long before May 15, the Israelis had established new settlements at various strategically important places and provided these, as well as the older settlements, with trained men and some of the scarce military equipment. All of these factors were eventually to play a decisive role in enabling the Israelis to win the Palestine War.

PALESTINE WAR, 1948

Immediately after the mandate ended on May 15, the Arab states dispatched part of their armed forces into Palestine in order to save the country for her Arab inhabitants. One Egyptian column moved up along the coast to within twenty miles of Tel Aviv, while another advanced via Beersheba to the southern suburbs of Jerusalem. The Arab Legion entered Palestine from the east to occupy the Old City of Jerusalem, plus adjacent areas. Iraqi troops were sent in to bolster or take over from Arab Legion contingents on the central front west and northwest of Jerusalem. Syrian units crossed into northeastern Palestine, while a small Lebanese force entered from the north to join the "Arab Liberation Army" fighting in the Galilee sector. In the beginning, the Arab armies generally assumed the offensive and seemed to be making reasonable progress, at least in occupying areas which had, in the main, been assigned to the Palestine Arabs by the UN partition resolution. The Israelis were largely on the defensive while they desperately sought to build up, equip, and reorganize their military forces.

During this critical period, Israel also turned to the UN Security Council for help. The United States, the Soviet Union, and UN Secretary-General Trygve Lie backed Israel's charge that the Arabs had started an aggression contrary to the UN Charter. Trygve Lie urged the Security Council and key UN members to take whatever action necessary, including sanctions, against the Arabs. Both the Soviet Union and the United States submitted draft resolutions which declared that the situation in Palestine was a threat to peace under Chapter VII of the Charter (entitled "Action with Respect to Threats to Peace, Breaches of the Peace, and Acts of Aggression"), ordered a cease-fire within thirty-six hours, and threatened sanctions against the party which refused to comply. No resolution based upon Chapter VII had ever been adopted before this time. Only on three prior occasions had draft resolutions been introduced which even cited this chapter. Because only Colombia, France, the Soviet Union, and the United States favored any reference to Chapter VII, the American resolution (S/749) had to be amended in such a way as to delete all mention of this chapter before it could pass on May 22. In its final, milder form, the resolution called upon

> all governments and authorities, without prejudice to the rights, claims and position of the parties concerned, to abstain from any hostile military action in Palestine, and to that end to issue a cease-fire order to become effective in thirty-six hours.

The Arab delegates not only attacked Israel, Russia, and the United States, but they also defended their own actions. They argued as follows: The partition resolution had been terminated when the General Assembly dissolved the Palestine Commission, which had been set up to implement the resolution. Britain's surrender of the mandate, therefore, had released Palestine to her inhabitants, who had the right to determine their own future. The Arab League, a "regional arrangement under Article 52 of the Charter," had first tried to settle the Palestine problem peacefully. Since this effort had failed, the question of security in the area became the primary responsibility of this regional organization, which had been invited by the people of Palestine to help them defend themselves against Zionist "aggression" and to restore order in the country. Jewish "atrocities" had caused "over a quarter of a million" Palestine Arabs to flee from their homes. Moreover, the Zionists had "aggressive" and imperialistic intentions in the Middle East which threatened all Arab states; thus, Arab armed intervention in Palestine was both necessary and "lawful."

The first task of the Security Council was to determine the actual and legal status of Palestine because if Israel was not legally a state, then the Arabs could not have committed aggression. In any case, Palestine was now an independent Arab state and so recognized by the Arab governments. Therefore, the Security Council could no longer interfere in her internal affairs. China was the only member of the Security Council which gave broad support to the Arabs, while several others, including Britain, did agree with some Arab contentions. In fact, a British proposal asking for a "further clarification of . . . [the legal] status" of Palestine failed to pass by only one vote.[7]

In a meeting on May 25, the Arab League Political Committee agreed to accept a cease-fire only if the Security Council prohibited Jewish immigration and Israel's importation of war materials on the ground that otherwise a truce would merely aid the Jews in strengthening their position. Since these conditions were unacceptable to Israel, the Arab League refused to accept a truce. Israel, seriously pressed by the Arab armies and desperately needing more time to absorb the men and arms flowing in, readily agreed to accept a cease-fire.

On May 29, the Security Council passed a British draft resolution (S/795) which had been amended at the insistence of the United States to meet certain Israeli objections. In its final form this resolution provided that: (1) all parties were to issue a cease-fire order for four weeks; (2) a cessation of hostilities would not "prejudice the rights, claims and position of either Arabs or Jews"; (3) no government or authority was to introduce fighting personnel or war material into either Palestine or the Arab states; (4) the UN mediator, Count Folke Bernadotte, and the Truce Commission were to supervise the observance of the truce; (5) all parties were to communicate their acceptance by June 1; and (6) action under Chapter VII would be considered if the resolution were rejected or violated.

Many Arabs, especially those on the Palestine Arab Higher Committee, opposed accepting a truce for fear that a truce would break the momentum of the Arab attack, threaten the delicate unity among the Arab governments, and generally benefit the Israelis far more than the Arabs. On the surface, military developments seemed to be moving along favorably for the Arabs. Israel generally had been on the defensive, except in the northern sector. The Arab forces had occupied a large part of Palestine, had the Israelis practically under siege in the New City section of Jerusalem, and had driven west of Jerusalem to within ten miles of the Mediterranean Sea, threatening to cut Israel in half. Arab morale and hopes were high. Because Arab newspapers, especially in Egypt, had been exaggerating Arab victories, the Arab masses were expecting a quick, decisive Arab victory.

The Arab military situation, however, was not as bright as it appeared. The areas occupied by the Arab armies were largely those inhabited by Palestine Arabs, while the principal Israeli centers of population and power and the main Israeli lines of defense remained intact. Numerous Israeli settlements behind the Arab lines, particularly in the south, remained unconquered and thus posed threats to the Arab lines of communication. The forces committed by the Arab governments were too small in number and lacked competent leadership and adequate reserves. Only Transjordan had committed the bulk of her military manpower to the Palestine War from the start. Arab lines of communication, especially for the Iraqi and Egyptian forces, were greatly extended, and Arab supply and communication facilities were becoming increasingly ineffective. For example, Iraqi units, partly because they had outrun their supply columns, had become relatively inactive even though they were in the best geographical position to threaten the most vital Israeli cities and lines of communication. With insufficient reserves of military equipment and supplies, with no effective services to repair and maintain their equipment, and with the UN arms embargo coming into full effect, the Arabs began to run dangerously low on ammunition, parts, and other essential war materials. Consequently, their only hope of defeating the larger and better trained and led Israeli forces, which were growing far more rapidly in size and power than those of the Arabs, was to commit more troops, unify their plans and leadership, and press their attacks energetically and intelligently in order to overrun the Jewish state before it had had time to arm, augment, and organize its military forces. Obviously, a truce would, under these circumstances, be far more helpful to the Israelis than to the Arabs.[8]

Even though Israel's main defense lines remained intact, morale continued to be high, and arms and manpower were pouring in from abroad, the over-all position of Israel was still precarious. Israel's hard-pressed soldiers had suffered several defeats, and they retained the initiative only against Kaukji's irregulars in the north. Food and other supplies were urgently needed by Israeli units in Jerusalem. Israel's armed forces were divided, with the Irgun and the Stern Gang fighters operating independently of the Haganah. Reporters Jon and David Kimche described the situation:

> The fledgling [Israeli] army was on the point of collapse. . . . Unless the army could complete its reorganization, increase its numbers, and secure more arms and equipment, it could not hope to hold out much longer.[9]

Even David Ben-Gurion admitted that the situation verged, at times, on the "catastrophic." Moreover, domestic problems had to be dealt with and the civil administration had to be more firmly established and its authority more widely accepted. The Israelis, therefore, greatly welcomed a truce because it gave them a badly needed breathing space.[10]

As a result of strong diplomatic and political pressures from the United States, Britain, and other countries and of increasing agitation in the Security Council for a stronger cease-fire resolution which would include a direct threat of sanctions against the party which refused to halt its military operations, the Arabs finally agreed to abide by the

Security Council resolution calling for a four-week truce. After some delay brought about by differences between the Arabs and Israelis over the interpretation of the resolution's provisions involving the question of Jewish immigration, the Mediator was finally able to set June 11 as the day the truce would begin. The Mediator interpreted this disputed section to mean that during the truce Israel could admit immigrants of military age but should not train or mobilize them. He also held that "no military advantage" was to "accrue to either side." Despite Soviet protests, the Mediator asked Belgium, France, and the United States (but not Russia) to supply military observers who would help supervise the truce.[11]

The truce resolution forbade the introduction of new military equipment and manpower into the area. Nevertheless, both sides disregarded these restrictions, and it soon became obvious that Israel was disregarding them to far better advantage than the Arabs.

Aided by Jewish money and organizations, especially in the United States, the Zionist world-wide arms purchasing organization established a regular arms airlift with Czechoslovakia, smuggled flying fortresses and fighter-bombers from the United States and Britain, and bought tanks on their way to the scrap yard. Israel continued to recruit foreign volunteers with especially needed military skills and experience and to push the immigration of young Jews. By the end of the truce Israeli forces were estimated by various authorities to have grown to anywhere from 60,000 to 100,000 men.[12] At this point Israel also found herself "for the first time reasonably well armed, having aircraft, armor, some artillery and ample small arms and ammunition." "A small but formidable Israeli air force was in being. . . . Small ships and coastal craft had been acquired and the nucleus of an Israeli navy was soon apparent." [13]

The Arabs managed to add some strength to their own armies in Palestine. But only Egypt and Iraq were able to build up the size of their military units to any significant degree. It has been estimated that the total number of Arab troops in Palestine was raised during the first truce from about 25,000 to between 35,000 and 45,000,[14] compared to the 60,000 to 100,000 soldiers then available to Israel. The Arabs were far less successful than the Israelis in their efforts to add to their military equipment and ammunition supplies. Thus, when the war resumed, the Arabs found their forces in Palestine to be smaller and more poorly armed than those of the Israelis.[15]

While the Israelis were able to attain greater political unity during the truce period, the Arabs achieved the opposite result. During the heat of the first phase of the war, the Arabs had been able to maintain at least a semblance of unity. Once the truce came into effect, however, former rivalries and suspicions, especially between King Abdullah, on the one hand, and Egypt and the Mufti, on the other, were revived and even intensified. The fact that Abdullah had not given up his desire to annex at least a part of Palestine, whereas the Egyptians, the Arab Higher Committee, and other Arabs continued to work for the setting up of a separate Arab government for all of Palestine under the Mufti, further deepened existing disagreements over Arab political goals in Palestine.

Soon after the cease-fire went into effect on June 11, the Mediator undertook exploratory discussions with Arab and Israeli representatives on the future of Palestine. On June 28, he submitted tentative proposals to them for a permanent settlement of the Palestine dispute: A Palestine Union, embracing Transjordan and Palestine, was to be set up and divided into two autonomous units, one Arab and the other Jewish. While each unit was to control its own domestic affairs, over-all cooperation on economic and defense problems was to be achieved through a central council. The partition resolution boundaries were altered to give the Arabs the Negev, Ramleh, and Lydda, whereas the Israelis were to get western Galilee. Haifa was to become a free port. Jerusalem was to be placed under Arab control, but it was to have a special UN status to guarantee access to the holy places. Persons who had been displaced by the fighting would be granted the right to return to their homes and recover their property.

Despite the fact that the terms of the Bernadotte Plan were more favorable to the Arabs than was the original partition resolution, most Arabs quickly rejected them. The Arabs then presented a counter-proposal which provided for a unitary Palestine state. The Israelis condemned Bernadotte's proposals on the grounds that they encouraged false Arab hopes, wounded Jewish feelings, and contradicted the partition resolution which had given to Israel an "irreducible minimum" part of Palestine. In fact, Israel even began to consider that the partition boundaries no longer provided her with adequate security against possible Arab "aggression" and did not give adequate consideration to the gains Israel had achieved in "repelling" the Arab attack.[16]

Having failed to make progress toward attaining a final settlement of the Palestine issue, the Mediator urgently sought a prolongation of the truce to prevent a renewal of fighting and to provide more time for further mediation efforts. On July 7, in response to the Mediator's urgings, the Security Council passed a British draft resolution (S/867) which appealed "to the interested parties to accept in principle the prolongation of the truce for such period as may be decided upon in consultation with the Mediator."

Israel, still needing more time to complete the build-up of her military forces, was willing to accept a limited continuation of the truce. Because a presidential election campaign was then moving into full swing in the United States with both major political parties again trying to outbid each other in backing Israel, the Israelis naturally concluded that they could extract the maximum amount of American support before the November elections. That is why Israel wanted either to obtain a favorable peace settlement or to be allowed to use her rapidly growing military power to seize more territory without outside interference before election day.[17]

Many Arab leaders, particularly in Iraq, Lebanon, Saudi Arabia, and Transjordan, were personally ready to accept a prolongation of the truce as they were under strong external pressure and had begun to realize that the military balance of power had started to turn in favor of Israel during the truce period. Other Arab leaders, however, especially those in Syria and on the Arab Higher Committee, backed a resumption of fighting. The Arab masses, misled by official Arab propaganda into believing that the Arab armies had won many major battles and that Israel was on the verge of collapse, clamored for a renewal of the war and for the expected victory. Fearing either to reveal the true military situation or to stand against the persistent demands of the masses, Arab officials formally rejected a continuation of the truce—and Arab-Jewish warfare was resumed.

Because Arab military power had seriously declined in comparison to that of Israel during the truce period, the Arab armies concentrated more on defensive than offensive action once fighting broke out again. The Arab military position was further weakened as a result of (1) a big influx of refugees who tended to interfere with military lines of communication and to make added demands on the Arab economies and administrative machinery, already overtaxed by the war; and (2) an increase in inter-Arab friction and rivalry which reduced still further the already limited military cooperation between the various armies. Not only did the Arab governments refrain from unifying their military leadership and planning, but most of them failed to inform their allies as to the size and capacity of their forces, their war strategy, and the true military situation on their respective fronts. At one time King Abdullah even had to withdraw a number of his combat units from their positions facing Israeli troops and to send them back to Transjordan in order to deal with internal disturbances reportedly created by the pro-Mufti elements of his population.

During the truce, Israel had firmly established her political authority throughout the country; she had substantially increased, trained, reor-

ganized, and unified her forces under a single command and outstripped
the Arabs in the race to acquire military equipment. Once the truce
ended, Israel for the first time was in a position to take the offensive on
several fronts simultaneously.

The main fighting took place on the strategically vital central front.
Israeli troops seized Ramleh and Lydda, with its valuable airport, plus
some adjacent Arab villages. But the Arab Legion, although greatly out-
numbered and lacking air support, continued to hold both the Old City
section of Jerusalem and strategically important Latrun on the main road
between Jerusalem and Tel Aviv. Israel's most successful offensive was
against the incompetent Kaukji and his followers in central Galilee,
where she occupied a considerable Arab area, including Nazareth. The
second round of fighting went in favor of the Israelis, who seized some
780 square miles of territory from the Arabs on nearly all fronts. Yet
Israel's gains during the ten days of combat were "limited" in that the
main Arab armies in the field, though hard pressed, remained "relatively
intact." Moreover, the Arabs continued to hold parts of Galilee, nearly
all of eastern Palestine, and most of the Negev. Syrian units, after throwing back an Israeli offensive south of Lake Huleh, actually gained some
ground at the expense of the Israelis.[18]

Partly as a result of the Mediator's appeal to the Security Council to
take action to bring about another cease-fire in Palestine and partly as a
result of Israel's request that the Arabs be condemned as aggressors and
threatened with UN sanctions, the United States submitted a draft resolution (S/890) which (1) blamed the Arabs for the failure to arrive at
a truce; (2) ordered a permanent cease-fire in three days; (3) threatened the use of sanctions if the cease-fire injunction were ignored; (4)
ordered an unconditional cease-fire in Jerusalem within twenty-four
hours and the demilitarization of the city; and (5) made the Mediator
responsible for supervising the observance of the truce. This resolution
passed the Security Council on July 15 by a vote of seven to one (Syria)
with Argentina, the Soviet Union, and the Ukraine abstaining. The first
truce in Palestine resulted from negotiations, conducted by the Mediator
with the parties concerned, but the second, permanent truce was ordered
by the Security Council directly, and the actual terms were laid down
without the need of further consultations with the Arabs and Israelis.

Since the rapidly improving Israeli army had been making good
progress against Arab forces on a number of fronts, Israeli military
leaders, as well as many other Israelis, opposed calling a second halt to
the fighting because they were anxious to seize more Arab territory.
Nevertheless, bowing before strong pressures from the United States and
other countries, the Israeli government reluctantly agreed to accept a
truce if the Arabs did.

Some of the Arab leaders, especially the Mufti and Syrian and Iraqi officials, objected to a second cease-fire. Powerful pressures from Britain and the United States and the threats of applying UN sanctions, however, forced the Arabs to agree to it.

MEDIATION EFFORTS AND THE GENERAL ASSEMBLY

In a report (A/648) to the General Assembly on September 16, 1948, Count Bernadotte described the existing Palestine situation as follows: Both sides retained an "uncompromising position" and were in no mood to make any fundamental concessions. The Arabs, while ready to maintain the truce, rejected "any suggestion of acceptance or recognition of the Jewish state" because they considered the Jews to be "interlopers and aggressors." Greatly concerned about the mounting distress among the large number of Arab refugees, the Arabs "considered the solution of this problem fundamental to the settlement of the Palestine question." The Arabs also harbored "grave fears" that a Jewish state which allowed unrestricted immigration would not want "to stay within its defined boundaries," but would try to expand.

As a consequence of recent victories, the Jewish "attitude had stiffened," they had become "less receptive to mediation," and "Jewish demands in the [final peace] settlement would probably be more ambitious" than ever before. In fact, while insisting upon the implementation of those parts of the UN partition resolution which remained favorable to her, Israel rejected the other parts which she no longer wanted. Because Israel felt that she could use her superior military power as an effective bargaining lever to obtain better terms than those provided by the partition resolution, Israel preferred to bypass the UN and the Mediator and to insist upon direct peace negotiations with the Arabs. The Israelis, moreover, refused to allow the Arab refugees to return until a peace agreement had been reached, on the ground that the refugees could threaten Israel's security as long as a state of war continued.

Presenting his personal views, Bernadotte criticized Israel for trying to bypass the UN, and he urged her, "in the interest of promoting friendly relations" with her Arab neighbors, to define her immigration policy in such a way as "to take carefully into consideration the basis of Arab fears and to consider measures and policies designed to allay them." He felt it would be unjust if the "innocent" Arab refugee "victims" of the conflict were denied the right to return to their homes while Jewish immigrants poured into Palestine. On the other hand, the Mediator warned the Arabs that the Jewish state had become a fact which could be eliminated only by means of force. Therefore, they must "resign themselves" to the presence of Israel or pursue the "reckless course of defying the United Nations." Any Arab hope for a unitary state for Palestine was now "unrealistic."

The Mediator then presented to the UN a modified version of his earlier proposal as his recommendation for the settlement of the Palestine question. He suggested that (1) a special conciliation commission be set up to help the parties to supplant the existing truce with either an armistice or a formal peace agreement; (2) the partition boundaries be modified so that the Arabs would receive the Negev, Ramleh, and Lydda, while the Israelis would obtain the Galilee area, and Haifa would become a free port; (3) the Arab section of Palestine not become an independent state but be annexed to Transjordan; (4) Jerusalem be placed under UN control; and (5) the Arab refugees be allowed to return to their homes.

Britain quickly endorsed Bernadotte's proposals since they closely coincided with many of her own views. In fact, Britain submitted to the autumn session of the General Assembly a draft resolution (A/C.1/394) which provided for the creation of a conciliation commission to aid the parties in reaching a final settlement based upon the Mediator's suggestions.

When, late in September, American Secretary of State George Marshall also fully endorsed the new Bernadotte Plan, it appeared that the two major Western powers had at last found a basis for agreeing on a Palestine policy. Because a closely contested presidential campaign was then in full swing, however, and American Zionists and pro-Zionists had vehemently attacked the new plan, President Truman announced on October 24 that the United States would not approve any change in the 1947 partition resolution unless it was acceptable to Israel. This action dealt a death blow both to the Bernadotte Plan and to the recently established Anglo-American agreement on Palestine's future.[19]

Australia, Canada, Colombia, Guatemala, Uruguay, Venezuela, and the Soviet bloc joined Israel as well as the United States after October 24 in opposing the Mediator's proposals. Russia supported Israel's position to the extent of submitting a draft resolution (A/C.1/401) which required the immediate withdrawal of all Arab troops from Palestine. Israel especially objected to Bernadotte's recommendations concerning the territorial changes and the annexation of all Arab parts of Palestine by Transjordan. She complained about the inability of the UN to assure Israel's security and to prevent Arab truce violations. Many Israelis, including high officials, began to accuse the Mediator and the UN truce observers of being partial to the Arabs and/or ineffectual, while Jewish extremists actually advocated the complete ousting of all UN personnel from Israeli-controlled areas.[20]

Anti-UN feeling reached a climax on September 17 when some Sternists killed Bernadotte in Jerusalem. Israel's position in the UN was greatly weakened, at least temporarily, as a result of her failure to express adequate regret for this crime and to make sufficiently serious efforts to apprehend and punish the culprits. Ralph Bunche, who took over as acting mediator, soon found himself subject to frequent verbal attacks by many Israelis and their supporters. Despite the fact that the prestige of the UN in Israel had seriously declined, Israel still wanted to become a member of the world organization. Israel expressed a desire for peace with the Arabs to be achieved preferably through direct negotiations and not through UN mediation.

All Arab states but Transjordan strongly criticized the Bernadotte Plan and the British draft resolution, and all bitterly attacked the Russian proposal as being anti-Arab and pro-Israel. Egypt, Syria, and Saudi Arabia, fearing the political consequences of a significant increase in the power and prestige of the ambitious King Abdullah, vigorously opposed the Mediator's suggestion that Transjordan annex the Arab portions of Palestine. Led by these three Arab states, the Arab League, despite Transjordan's protests, established on September 20 an "All-Palestine Government," with headquarters in Gaza, which all Arab governments except Transjordan ultimately recognized as the official spokesman for all Palestinians. Abdullah's reply to this move was to assemble some Palestine Arab leaders in Jerusalem on December 1, 1948, and to obtain a resolution from this meeting which called for the annexation of Arab Palestine by Transjordan. (Although Abdullah's cabinet quickly approved this request, he delayed formally annexing the areas he controlled until April, 1950, when the dangerous effects of such a move on his position among his own people and among all Arabs had significantly decreased.)

The Arabs expressed a willingness both to accept a conciliation commission if it were not associated with partition and to negotiate with any UN organ, but not with the Israelis, on the problem of peace in Palestine. They also contended that they would be willing to consider a solution which provided for a federal state of Palestine, but they would not accept any plan which required them to accept an independent Jewish state. The Arabs complained that Israel, by continuing to import military manpower and equipment from abroad, was violating the terms of the truces which forbade any activities which would alter the military *status quo.* They reiterated their fears that continued unlimited Jewish immigration would provide the excuse and the means for future aggression and expansion at Arab expense. To support this contention, Arab spokesmen repeatedly quoted from a *Time* magazine interview with Ben-Gurion, published in the August 16, 1948 issue. Ben-Gurion had said, "I can quite imagine a Jewish state of ten million." When asked if that many could be accommodated within the United Nations partition boundaries of Israel, Ben-Gurion had replied, "I doubt it. . . . We would not have taken on this war merely for the purpose of enjoying this tiny state." The Arabs also insisted that the Arab refugees be allowed to return home without delay. Only Pakistan, Burma, Cuba, and Liberia supported Arab views in the General Assembly debates. The Arabs received considerably wider backing, however, for a Syrian draft resolution (A/C.1/405) which requested an advisory opinion from the World Court on the competence of the UN to partition Palestine. This proposal was defeated by a vote of twenty-one to twenty-one with four abstentions.

On December 4, 1948, the First Committee of the General Assembly passed most of the British draft resolution (A/C.1/394/Rev.2) by a close vote of twenty-five to twenty-one with nine abstentions. A strange combination of pro-Arab and pro-Israel members defeated paragraph five of the resolution which endorsed the Mediator's proposal that Transjordan annex the Arab areas of Palestine. The Arab and Soviet blocs, plus some pro-Arab states, voted against the whole resolution, while Britain and the United States led the states voting for it. The Soviet Union objected primarily because it proposed moving away from the original partition plan, while the Arabs opposed it because it still provided for partition. Failing to obtain the two-thirds vote required for final passage in the General Assembly, the resolution was amended still further before it ultimately passed its final test on December 11 by a vote of thirty-five to fifteen with eight abstentions.

The resolution [194 (III)] provided for the setting up of a UN Conciliation Commission consisting of representatives from France, Turkey, and the United States. This commission was to assume all the functions previously assigned to the Mediator, as well as (1) to take steps to assist the parties in achieving a peace settlement either through the commission's auspices or by direct negotiations; (2) to present to the next session of the General Assembly detailed proposals for a permanent international regime for Jerusalem; (3) to seek arrangements to facilitate the economic development of the area; and (4) to facilitate the repatriation, resettlement, and economic and social rehabilitation of the refugees. The Security Council was asked to take steps to insure the demilitarization of Jerusalem.

TRUCE VIOLATIONS AND THE SECURITY COUNCIL

The second truce was an uneasy one, especially in the Jerusalem area. In the middle of September, 1948, the Mediator reported, "There have been daily incidents of a localized character; and there have been numerous breaches of the terms of the truce by both sides." Not only had the Arabs and Israelis indulged in sniping and looting, but they had strengthened their military positions contrary to the terms of the truces. (According to different sources, by October, 1948, Arab forces in Palestine had grown to about 50,000 to 55,000, while the Israeli forces had increased, mostly as a result of the arrival of tens of thousands of immigrants and large numbers of foreign volunteers, to from 75,000 to 120,000. Also, Israel, receiving shipments of war materials "daily," was able to do a far better job of acquiring more arms than the Arabs.[21]) In reporting on the fighting and truce violations in the Jerusalem area, the Mediator and the Truce Commission held that "the Jews have been generally speaking, though not on all occasions, the more aggressive party since the renewal of the truce." [22]

Prompted by reports of truce violations, the Security Council, on August 19, 1948, passed a joint American, British, and French draft resolution (S/981) which: (1) made each party responsible for the "actions of both regular and irregular forces"; (2) obligated each party "to prevent acts of violating the truce" and to punish violators; and (3) forbade any party from breaking the truce on the ground of reprisals or from gaining "military or political advantage through truce violations."

Relatively localized incidents gave way to a serious outbreak of fighting in the middle of October. The Israelis had become increasingly disillusioned and unhappy with the UN. Not only were they bitter because the world organization had done so little to help them materially once the Arab armies had intervened in Palestine, but they began to feel that the UN, its resolutions, and its agents in Palestine prevented them from achieving more favorable boundaries. They repeatedly accused Bernadotte and, after his death, Ralph Bunche, as well as the Truce Supervision Organization and its observers, of being partial to the Arabs. Consequently, the Israeli government and people began to give less and less consideration to the UN in their actions and to believe that they had much to gain from the use of "force and *fait accompli*." Israeli army officers pressed the government to use Israel's superior military power to seize more areas of Palestine, and many Israelis "talked confidently . . . of a state of ten million not necessarily confined to the present boundaries." Israeli leaders requested the Security Council to set an "early time limit" for the truce in order to assure that, if Israel were unable to obtain a favorable peace settlement with the Arabs quickly, she could at least satisfy her territorial ambitions through the use of her superior military power. Ben-Gurion, for example, made it clear that: (1) "even if the truce would have been fully observed by the Arab countries we would not have accepted it for an indefinite period"; (2) "the fate of Israel would be determined in Palestine either in battle or in peace negotiations between the Arabs and Israelis and not in the United Nations conference rooms"; and (3) Israel would force the Arab armies out of Palestine if the UN failed to accomplish this itself.[23]

In the second week of September, 1948, Israeli military leaders obtained Ben-Gurion's approval, despite the opposition of Foreign Minister Moshe Sharett, to attack Arab Legion positions on the central front in order to gain more territory in that strategically vital area. Israeli officials then "began to feed the foreign press with reports that the Arabs were ready to launch an assault on Jerusalem." However, the assassination of Count Bernadotte in Jerusalem on September 17 and the resulting world-wide indignation compelled Israel to postpone her planned action against Transjordanian forces.[24]

Israeli military leaders then turned their attention from Jerusalem to the southern front. The Bernadotte Plan, proposing that the Arabs be given the Negev instead of Galilee, was submitted to the General Assembly in September. Many Israelis, opposed to losing the Negev, began to feel that their government should seize that area and present the world with a *fait accompli* before the UN had a chance to decide its fate. In October, the "clamor" in Israel "for a resumption of hostilities," for " 'delivering one more knock' against the Egyptians," and for seizing all of the Negev increased.[25] A number of other major factors influenced Israel's final decision. The 1948 American presidential election campaign was reaching a climax. The Israelis realized that the best time to act would be before the election took place early in November, when there would be the least probability of a strong and hostile American reaction to any Israeli attack. The Soviet Union had indicated that she would not seriously consider applying sanctions against Israel. Moreover, because of increasing inter-Arab rivalry and distrust, especially between Egypt and Transjordan, the Israelis were encouraged to believe that they could concentrate their best military units for an attack on the southern front without having to worry that the Arab Legion (the only other Arab force that caused the Israelis any concern) would enter the fray. By this time, the Israelis had become convinced that Egypt was their principal enemy. So Israeli military officers urged Ben-Gurion to attack on the Egyptian front. Knowing that Ben-Gurion was also greatly interested in acquiring the Arab-held Old City section of Jerusalem, these officers pointed out that, once the Israeli army had occupied the Negev, it could readily attack the Old City from the rear. Even though Foreign Minister Sharett warned that any Israeli aggression could seriously harm Israel's international standing, Ben-Gurion ordered his military leaders to begin preparations for an invasion of the Negev.[26]

As early as September 8, Israeli units, disregarding provisions of the second truce, had occupied a series of strategic hills covering the road from Faluja to Beersheba in the Negev. On September 29 Israelis occupied Mahaz, another key position, and held it against an Egyptian attempt to retake it. Israel began to infiltrate men and military equipment through gaps in the Egyptian lines and to send others by air to the surrounded Israeli settlements in the south.[27] Even though Israel started to accuse Egypt of making assaults on strategic heights and of preparing for large-scale aggressive action, Israel was silent about requesting that UN observers check on these accusations.[28] According to the acting mediator, Ralph Bunche, under the truce agreement Israel had the right to send nonmilitary supplies by land convoy and, in an emergency, by airplane to her isolated settlements in the Negev, but only under UN supervision. Bunche reported that during this period Israel "had refused to allow United Nations supervision" of either road or air convoys, had sent airplanes and land convoys to her settlements contrary to the terms of the truce agreement, had "refused permission" to UN observers to enter any Israeli airfield, and had "limited" the movements of these observers in other critical areas as well.[29] Thus, Israel, while in the process of surreptitiously concentrating 15,000 of her best troops and much of her heavy military equipment on the Egyptian front, waited for the Egyptians to be goaded into producing an incident which she could use as a "pretext" for accusing Egypt of being the real aggressor and for justifying her own planned attack.[30] The hoped-for incident occurred on October 14 when Egypt, refusing to allow any more land convoys through her lines until all unsupervised air flights by Israel had stopped, forcibly sought to prevent the next Israeli convoy from passing through. Using this Egyptian action as an excuse, Israel then unleashed a major offensive, known as "Operation Ten Plagues." Mr. Bunche, charging Israel with a "serious breach of the truce," stated:

> It would seem clear that the [Israeli] military action of the last few days has been on a scale which could only be undertaken after considerable preparation, and could scarcely be explained as a simple retaliatory action for an attack on a convoy.[31]

Many factors helped to assure the success of Israel's invasion. She had able leaders, a daring plan of operations, war-hardened and well-trained manpower, sufficient transport and armor to provide mobility and striking power, adequate weapons and armaments, a small but effective navy, and air superiority in the fighting zone. She also benefited immeasurably from Arab disunity because this enabled her to deplete her forces on other fronts and to concentrate the major portion of her striking power against one Arab foe. The Egyptian and Sudanese soldiers attached to the Egyptian army did not lack "courage" and generally "fought bravely . . . , especially on defense"; but the 15,000 men in the Egyptian army were committed to a static defense on a long and shallow front, and they lacked reserves, mobility, good leadership, dependable equipment, and an adequate transportation and communications system. In addition, while the Egyptians, lulled into a false sense of security because of the existence of a "permanent truce," had not effectively prepared themselves to meet any major Israeli assault, the Israelis, picking their own time and place for an invasion, had the advantage of both surprise and superiority of weapons and manpower at the specific points chosen for their attacks.[32]

The Israelis made substantial gains of territory against stiff resistance in the areas east of Gaza and south of Jerusalem. They surrounded a large unit composed of Egyptian and Sudanese soldiers, as well as 3,000 Arab civilians, at Faluja. Bunche ordered Israel to halt her forces and to withdraw them behind the October 14 lines, but she refused to comply. In fact, on October 17, an Israeli foreign office spokesman stated that Israel "stands by its claim to the whole of the Negev." Only strong opposition from some of his cabinet colleagues prevented Prime Minister Ben-Gurion from ordering his victorious army in the Negev to turn north and seize the Old City of Jerusalem and the area eastward to the Jordan River.[33]

While Egyptian forces were being defeated, the Egyptian leaders tried to keep the full truth about the serious military situation from their own people and from their allies. When Egypt finally asked the other Arab states to assist her hard-pressed troops, response came only from King Abdullah, who sent a small unit of 350 men to head off an Israeli group moving toward Hebron south of Jerusalem, and from Kaukji's irregulars, who made a minor diversionary attack in the Galilee sector. The Transjordanian unit did help save some territory for the Arabs in the Hebron-Jerusalem area, but it was not large or prompt enough to be of much practical help to the Egyptians. Kaukji's action was also too small and too late. Ignoring the fact that by neglecting to inform their allies in time about the gravity of their military position they had been partly responsible for the delay of other Arab forces to respond to their request for aid, the Egyptians angrily accused the other Arabs of deliberately failing to come to their rescue. This development accentuated inter-Arab distrust and hard feelings and dealt Arab unity yet another major blow, thus weakening even more the ability of the Arabs to face the Israelis on the battlefield and giving even greater encouragement to the Israelis to take advantage of this opportunity to defeat their Arab enemies one at a time and expand their frontiers in many directions.

The Security Council met in the middle of October to consider reports from the Chairman of the Palestine Truce Commission and from the Acting Mediator concerning truce violations in general and the outbreak of hostilities in the Negev in particular. The Truce Commission Chairman accused Israeli leaders of trying to weaken the authority of the UN by disregarding the Truce Commission, of refusing to agree to neutral zones between the fighting forces, and of wanting to incorporate Jerusalem into Israel. Ralph Bunche, in turn, criticized both Arabs and Israelis for violating the truce, blamed Israel for failing to control and punish the extremists responsible for killing Count Bernadotte, and charged Israel with having committed the most serious breach of the second truce by her attack in the Negev. He also urged the Security Council to take action to enforce the truce and to encourage the opposing sides to negotiate a peace settlement either directly or through UN intermediaries. Because Israel's Negev truce violation was on "a scale beyond anything else seen heretofore" and because it was "the first time either party" had "flatly refused UN Truce Observers' orders to yield positions captured by a breach of the truce," Bunche and other UN officials considered the Negev crisis as a test of the world organization's ability to enforce its will. Therefore, the Acting Mediator requested the Security Council's help in bringing about an immediate cease-fire and the withdrawal of Israeli forces from any position not occupied at the time of the outbreak of fighting on October 14.[34]

An Anglo-Chinese draft resolution (S/1032) was unanimously passed on October 9. The resolution noted with concern Israel's failure to report on the assassination of Bernadotte and requested her to submit such a report as soon as possible. It also reminded both sides of their obligations under the July 15 and August 19, 1948, resolutions to maintain a cease-fire and to cooperate with UN observers and truce officials. On the basis of this resolution, Bunche once again ordered a cease-fire and a withdrawal of armed forces to their October 14 positions.

On October 28 Britain and China introduced another draft resolution (S/1059) which: (1) stated that no party was either to use retaliation as an excuse for breaking the truce or to gain any advantage from violations of the truce; (2) endorsed Bunche's orders regarding the withdrawal of forces to the positions held on October 14; and (3) appointed a committee to examine and report on the measures which would be appropriate to take under UN Charter article 41, which provided for nonmilitary types of sanctions if any side failed to comply with these orders. The Arabs, accusing Israel of flagrantly violating both truces, supported this resolution.

Israel, backed by Russia and the Ukraine, strongly opposed the second Anglo-Chinese proposal. She claimed that Egypt had broken the truce first and was responsible for subsequent events. Agreeing to a cease-fire, she refused to withdraw her troops as demanded until direct Arab-Israeli peace negotiations had been brought about. Israeli military officers "scored" the UN for halting the fighting when it was going so well for Israel, while other high-ranking Israelis once again accused UN, as well as International Red Cross, officials of being pro-Arab.[35] Confident in her own superior power and aware of the unwillingness of either the Soviet Union or the United States to enforce any UN sanctions against her, Israel not only felt she could safely disregard UN orders but was encouraged to continue to use force in order to gain more territory and to coerce the Arabs into suing for peace on her terms. Ben-Gurion bluntly stated that Israel would not surrender any part of the Negev "unless we are physically" compelled to do so and that "we do not require the help of the United Nations or the agreement of the Egyptians." [36] Even after the cease-fire went into effect, Israeli military attacks and interferences with UN observer movements continued in the Negev despite the protests of UN officials. Israel also rushed plans to colonize the areas seized both as a security factor and as a means of strengthening her claims to the whole Negev. Whereas Israel had strenuously objected to earlier Egyptian efforts to interfere with the supplying of the isolated Israeli settlements containing both military and civilian personnel, Israel now refused, despite the repeated requests of UN officials, to allow Egypt to send food and other nonmilitary supplies, even under strict UN supervision, to the isolated Egyptian troops and the Palestinian civilians trapped in Faluja.[37]

At first, the American delegation to the UN, headed by Secretary of State George Marshall, supported the second Anglo-Chinese draft resolution even though it threatened possible sanctions against Israel. However, at this time the hotly contested 1948 presidential campaign was nearing its end, and President Truman found it increasingly profitable politically to strengthen his support of Israel. As a result, without consulting the State Department, Truman suddenly ordered his UN delegates to terminate their backing of the resolution.[38] Influenced by the American desire to postpone any action on the resolution until after election day, a Canadian proposal to set up a subcommittee to arrive at a compromise on the Negev question was adopted by the Security Council on October 29.

The subcommittee proposal (S/1064), which differed only slightly from the original Anglo-Chinese draft resolution, was finally taken up and passed on November 4 by a vote of nine (including Syria, the only Arab state then on the Security Council) to one (Ukraine) with Russia abstaining. Although the resolution which passed continued to retain among its provisions a threat of sanctions against the party which failed to comply with its terms, both the United States and the Soviet Union made it obvious that they would not support the application of any strong measures against Israel. As a result, Israel was once again encouraged to disregard UN orders.

While the Security Council was still discussing the Negev situation, fighting broke out in western Galilee. Both Israeli and Kaukji units had transgressed truce lines through localized actions like Kaukji's small diversionary raid to help the hard-pressed Egyptian army in the Negev. Tension had also developed over Kaukji's interferences with Israel's supply lines and over Israeli forays into Lebanese territory north of Lake Huleh. Nevertheless, the incidents, on the whole, remained relatively localized and minor until October 28, when Israel started a major, well-planned offensive aimed at seizing all of western Galilee.[39] Encouraged by their easy success in the Negev, by Arab military weakness and disunity, by the pro-Israeli positions of Russia and the United States, and by the American presidential election campaign then in full swing, they decided to take advantage of these favorable circumstances to expand to the north, as well as to the south. Once again Israel, prior to unleashing her own attack, accused the Kaukji forces of assaulting Israeli positions, but she also refused to allow UN observers to investigate her charges and to enter her own front line areas where her military build-up was taking place. After the Israeli attack had begun, Bunche ordered Israel to return her troops to their original positions. He complained that Israeli soldiers were "looting" Arab villages. Nevertheless, the Israeli army continued its offensive actions until it had occupied the rest of western Galilee and some fifteen villages in southern Lebanon and had "created a new influx of refugees into Lebanon." [40]

Israel's military victory in the north was complete. Kaukji had only about 5,000 poorly trained fighters under his inferior leadership, and Lebanese units in the area were small and ineffective. Having already defeated Egyptian forces in the south and no longer fearing any serious Arab attack from any other direction, Israel again was able to concentrate much of her best manpower and equipment, including her airpower, against a single foe much weaker than she and virtually without air support. Only Syria tried to help her fellow Arabs, but the small battalion she could spare for this diversionary venture was badly mauled by superior Israeli forces. Some Palestinian Druze fought with the Israelis during the Galilee campaign, while others sided with the Arabs.

Early in November the Security Council began to discuss the Galilee situation. The Acting Mediator stressed that Israel should abide by his orders for an Israeli troop withdrawal from new positions seized in the Galilee offensive. He also suggested that the Security Council encourage the Arabs and Israelis to replace the truce with an armistice as the best way to prevent further fighting and the next logical step toward an ultimate peace settlement. In compliance with Bunche's recommendations, Belgium, Canada, and France submitted a joint draft resolution (S/1079) calling upon all parties to seek armistice agreements through negotiations conducted either directly or through the Acting Mediator. Without prejudice to the Acting Mediator's order of withdrawal of Israeli forces in the Negev to the October 14 lines, the resolution further provided for the delineation of permanent cease-fire lines beyond which the troops of both sides were not to go and for such withdrawal and reduction of armed forces as would insure the maintenance of the armistice during the transition to permanent peace. This resolution passed the Security Council on November 16 with eight favorable votes and with Syria and the two Soviet states abstaining.

Continuing her generally anti-Arab stand, the Soviet Union submitted her own proposal (S/1075) calling not merely for an armistice but for final peace as well. It received the favorable votes of only the two Soviet states.

The Arabs vigorously opposed the Soviet proposal in its entirety, while they objected to parts of the joint draft resolution. They complained that the joint draft resolution would impose an armistice on the parties before the implementation of previous UN decisions, such as the November 29, 1947, partition and the November 4, 1948, Negev withdrawal resolutions. Taking a somewhat more conciliatory stand than Syria, Egypt held that she would welcome negotiations with representatives of the UN but not with the Israelis. At this stage, the Arabs began to reveal the beginning of a change in their attitude toward the original 1947 partition resolution. Although in principle most Arabs continued to oppose this resolution and UN interferences in Palestine, as time passed, Arab officials, aware that Israel now possessed superior military strength, grew increasingly anxious to have the UN compel Israel to live up to the truces and to withdraw her troops from areas not given to her by the partition resolution. This would at least represent a gain for the Arabs over the existing unfavorable situation. For example, in December, 1948, the Arabs requested that the Security Council discuss ways for implementing prior UN resolutions, including that of November, 1947, but without success.

Israel preferred the Russian proposal to the joint draft resolution because she wanted peace negotiations to be conducted directly between the parties concerned without having to go through an armistice stage.

She wished to avoid involving the UN in order to ignore those prior UN decisions which might hinder her territorial ambitions, and she could more rapidly use her strong bargaining position resulting from her superior military power in any negotiations with the Arabs.[41] The continued pro-Israeli stand of the Russians delighted the Israelis and helped to promote friendlier relations than ever before between the two countries. Soviet prestige in the Arab world at that time sank to a record low.[42]

Late in December, after the UN General Assembly had adjourned, Security Council delegates, returning to New York after meetings in Paris, were on the high seas, and Christians everywhere were preoccupied with the Christmas season, Ben-Gurion felt that the time was "ripe once more for action." [43] So on December 22 the Israelis, reported to be in "no mood to wait for either world opinion or the UN to solve their problem," convinced that they could "win much more on the battlefield than at the peace table," and believing that "possession is nine points of the law," [44] once again launched a major offensive ("Operation Ayin") against Egyptian forces in the Negev. Since Israel had refused to allow even UN-supervised convoys to supply the basic needs of the thousands of encircled Arab soldiers and civilians in Faluja, the Egyptians were "goaded to attack to relieve" the suffering of the trapped people in order to give Israel the "excuse to apply Operation Ayin." [45] Israel also sought to justify her action by claiming that Egypt had committed a series of "provocations," the presence of Egyptians in the Negev was a "threat" to her security, and Egypt had failed to abide by the November 16 Security Council resolution calling for armistice negotiations.[46]

Repudiating Israel's official justifications for her military offensive, the Acting Mediator reported (S/1152) to the Security Council on December 27 that he had "no knowledge of any incidents which could be claimed as a provocation for the fighting in the Negev." He complained that despite the UN resolutions and his orders to the contrary, Israeli forces "had not withdrawn from localities occupied since 14 October," "the establishment of UN observer posts in the Negev had not been permitted," food and medical supplies "had not been permitted through Israeli lines to the encircled Egyptians at Faluja" even in UN supervised convoys, and the Egyptians had "not been permitted to withdraw from Faluja in compliance with the 13 November plan for the implementation of the 4 November resolution of the Security Council." Bunche also stated that after conferring with Egyptian leaders he was "convinced" that they would be willing to enter armistice negotiations as required by the November 14 resolution if Israeli authorities changed their "intransigent attitude . . . on the situation in Faluja" sufficiently so that the Egyptian units there could withdraw. UN officials also found, as reported by the *New York Times* on December 25, 1948, that as Egypt moved closer and closer to accepting armistice negotiations on the basis of the November 4 and November 16 Security Council resolutions, Israel kept "raising the ante" for she had apparently resolved to take what she could by military means before agreeing to start negotiations with Egypt.

Israeli troops, once again victorious, were able to push into Sinai on December 28. Although Egypt refused to invoke her 1936 alliance with Britain, Britain threatened to use her military power to compel the Israelis to withdraw from Egyptian territory. Anglo-Israeli relations became even more strained when Israeli pilots shot down five British planes during the Negev campaign. The American government, worried about this explosive situation, brought strong pressures to bear on Israel to remove her units from Sinai. The United States also worked to stop the serious deterioration in Anglo-Israeli relations.[47]

During the fighting, Egypt formally urged the other Arab states to come to her aid, and the Arab League called on the Arab governments to resume the war against Israel on the ground that Israel had gravely violated the UN truce. While Lebanon, Saudi Arabia, and Yemen promised to act upon Egypt's appeal, they were located too far from the battle area and/or too weak militarily to do much. King Abdullah did not bother to answer Egypt's note. Iraq wanted to provide some help, but Abdullah, controlling much of Iraq's supply lines, refused to cooperate. Iraqi artillery did open fire on several Israeli positions, but this turned out to be the only diversionary effort made by any of the Arabs. Feeling unjustly let down by their allies, the Egyptians became so bitter that they considered entering upon separate negotiations with Israel to extricate themselves from their dangerous military position.[48]

The second Israeli invasion of the Negev caused the Security Council to meet on December 28 to take up the new crisis and the charges made against Israel by the Arabs and the Acting Mediator. The Arabs complained that Israel was not living up to the truces and the November 4 resolution and the Security Council was not implementing its own decisions. They further claimed that they did not disapprove of the November 16 resolution, but they insisted that since the November 4 resolution had been passed first, it should be enforced first.[49]

Britain, supporting many Arab contentions, submitted a draft resolution (S/1163) calling upon the governments concerned to order an immediate cease-fire in the Negev and to withdraw without further delay to positions held by each side prior to October 14. After the addition of an Egyptian amendment (which called upon the parties "to allow and facilitate the complete supervision of the truce by the UN observers") and a French amendment (which called upon the parties "to implement without further delay the resolution of November 16," as well as the one of November 4), the revised British draft was passed on December 29 by a vote of eight (including Syria) to zero with the United States and the two Soviet members abstaining. Israel opposed the original British proposal. She also repeatedly attacked the Acting Mediator for placing the blame for the major truce difficulties on Israel instead of on the Arabs. Only the Soviet Union sided fully with Israel.

Armistice Negotiations

Early in January, 1949, Egypt decided to enter armistice negotiations with Israel. This unpleasant and unpopular decision was forced upon Egypt by a number of factors. Egypt's military position had become so critical that a continuation of hostilities would probably bring about the loss both of more men and of that narrow stretch of Palestinian territory extending along the Mediterranean coast from the old Egyptian frontier to a few miles north of the town of Gaza (later to be known as the Gaza Strip) which remained under Egyptian control after the December fighting. Between the strong anti-British feeling among the people and the established Egyptian position that the 1936 treaty of alliance with Britain was no longer valid, Egypt felt that she could not appeal to Britain for military assistance. Having been convinced that their Arab allies had deserted them in their hour of need, the Egyptians no longer considered it necessary to consult with or wait for the other Arab governments before acting. The British and American governments had also added their pressures on the Egyptian government to accept an armistice.

Even though not all of the objectives of her military offensive had yet been achieved, Israel finally and somewhat reluctantly agreed to a cease-fire and armistice negotiations in response to the exhortations of both the UN and the United States.

After a formal UN cease-fire went into effect on January 7, Egyptian and Israeli delegations began armistice talks on January 12 on the island of Rhodes with Ralph Bunche in the role of a mediator. At first, Dr. Bunche discussed every substantive item separately with each side. Then informal meetings were arranged between the heads of the two delegations. When discussions reached an advanced stage on an item, joint formal meetings of the two delegations were held. This was the first time the two parties had ever come together at the same table to negotiate directly. Major differences existed between the Israelis and the Egyptians. For example, while Egypt originally insisted that Israel withdraw her forces to the military positions occupied before October 14, Israel demanded that Egypt should remove all of her troops from whatever parts of Palestine they still occupied. After considerable and skilful efforts by the Acting Mediator, most of the differences were overcome, and a compromise General Armistice Agreement was finally signed on February 24, 1949.

Lebanon quickly followed Egypt's lead in seeking an armistice. Because Lebanon was militarily the weakest of the Arab states and because some Lebanese, particularly certain Christians, had not been too enthusiastic about the war with Israel from the beginning, the Lebanese government was quite ready to replace the undependable truce with an armistice once one of the larger Arab states had set a precedent on this issue. Thus, on January 16, Israeli and Lebanese representatives met at Ras an-Naqura on the former Lebanese-Palestine border to initiate exploratory talks. Israel's unwillingness to evacuate strategic positions on Lebanese territory near the Syrian border until Syria was also willing to accept an armistice caused a delay in the progress of these talks. Once Syria agreed on March 21 to negotiate with Israel, the Israeli-Lebanese armistice agreement was quickly concluded on March 23.

Transjordan consented to armistice negotiations on February 8. However, since Israel was still anxious to acquire the whole of the Palestine area south of the Dead Sea in order to gain more land and to obtain an outlet to the Gulf of Aqaba, she sought to delay the negotiations as long as possible.[50] As early as June, 1948, Arab Legion units had occupied two former Palestine police posts south of the Dead Sea. Soon after Egyptian forces were compelled to retreat on the central and western Negev fronts as a result of the Israeli offensive in October, Israeli units occupied the lower end of the Dead Sea and pushed southward until they met and fought a skirmish with Arab Legion troops on December 1 about forty-five miles from the Dead Sea. Even after Israeli-Transjordanian armistice negotiations began on March 4, Israel ordered her forces to continue their advance. Only after her troops had reached the Gulf of Aqaba on March 10 did Israel, on March 11, sign a "complete and enduring" cease-fire with Transjordan. Although the cease-fire forbade any further military movements beyond positions held on March 11, Israeli units kept pressing ahead and seizing more territory. Arab and UN officials accused Israel of breaking both the second truce and the March 11 cease-fire agreement. UN reports also indicated that as a result of the Israeli advance numerous Arabs had fled the area occupied by Israel. King Abdullah, fearing that Israel would use her superior military power to invade and seize Transjordanian territory in the Gulf of Aqaba region as well, invoked his treaty of alliance with Britain and appealed to the UN to halt Israel's illegal advances. Britain responded by sending some British military units to southwestern Transjordan, but it was made clear that these would be used to defend Transjordanian territory only. The UN dispatched observers to check on the situation, but nothing was done to compel Israel to withdraw from the occupied sections.[51]

Encouraged by her military triumphs, her great military superiority, and UN inaction, Israel now turned her attention to the central front and the Iraqi and Transjordanian forces located there. Once again in an attempt to create a justification for a planned military action, Israeli officials began to accuse Iraqi "irregulars" of making raids on Israeli territory and to warn that Israel might be compelled to take necessary action to protect herself.[52] Despite these charges, Israel did not request UN observers to check on the alleged Iraqi violations. On March 21, when it was reported that Arab Legion units would replace Iraqi troops withdrawing from positions on the central front, Israel insisted that this move would be contrary to the truce and that she would not permit it to take place.[53]

Realizing that his army was too weak to face Israel's much larger and better armed military forces, King Abdullah quietly contacted Israeli officials through a private emissary in the hope of averting a major Israeli attack. In a secret meeting with Abdullah, Israeli representatives Reuven Shiloah and Colonel Moshe Dayan informed the King that Israel would agree to the replacement of Iraqi units by the Arab Legion only if he agreed to cede to Israel an important belt of land averaging about two miles in width along a fifty-five mile section of the central front where Arab-controlled territory bulged so far west and northwest of Jerusalem that it nearly cut Israel into two sections. This area also contained a number of strategically valuable mountain positions and much good farming land. The Israelis warned that the alternative to this cession of land was the renewal of military hostilities. Reluctant to pay this heavy price, Abdullah turned to Britain and the United States in the hope of obtaining their support in preventing an Israeli attack. Once he learned that neither of the Western countries was willing to intervene, he felt compelled to accept Israel's demands.[54] Thus, only after Israel had seized the southeastern part of Palestine down to the Gulf of Aqaba and had obtained the strategically and economically important belt of land in central Palestine did she finally sign an armistice with Transjordan on April 3. The Arab Legion then took over Iraqi-held positions on the central front except in the areas ceded to Israel. One major consequence of this cession of territory and the secret negotiations which preceded it was the intensification of bitterness among many Arab nationalists against Abdullah, who was accused of having betrayed the Arab cause. Another important result was that a number of Arab villages found themselves separated from most of their farming land without adequate means for supporting their inhabitants.[55]

Since the Syrians had felt more intensely about the Palestine issue than most other Arabs and had not yet experienced large-scale military defeats, they were reluctant to negotiate with the enemy. However, Syrian leaders, recognizing that they were far too weak to stand up to Israel alone, realized that it would be foolhardy to try to fight on against hopeless odds. Although armistice talks began on April 4 in tents on the frontier, two developments delayed their progress. On April 5 an Israeli force seized a point one-fourth of a mile inside of Syria northeast of Lake Huleh. Syria refused to continue the proceedings until Israel bowed before a strong demand from the Acting Mediator to withdraw her force. Another delay was caused by Israel's opposition to the retention by Syria of three small bits of Palestinian territory still under Syrian military control. This problem was resolved only by Bunche's proposal that these areas, along with a tiny piece of adjacent land controlled by Israel, be included in a demilitarized zone not subject to the sovereignty of either side but supervised by the chairman of the proposed Israeli-Syrian Mixed Armistice Commission. While a permanent cease-fire came into force on April 13, the armistice agreement itself was not finally signed until July 20.[56]

Since Saudi Arabia's small token force had been under Egyptian command and had not held a separate front, Saudi Arabia contended that there was no need for negotiating an armistice treaty with Israel. Although Iraq had taken an active part in the war, she withdrew her forces from Palestine and returned them to Iraq so there was no longer any physical contact between Israel and Iraq. Iraq's refusal to hold armistice talks with Israel thus did not produce any serious consequences. Moreover, because Arab Legion units had taken over the positions in Palestine formerly held by the Iraqis, it was felt that the Israeli-Transjordan armistice agreement sufficiently covered the resultant situation.

CONCLUSION

A thorough understanding of the Palestine War period is important not only because many of the facts of this period have been frequently distorted, overlooked, or oversimplified, but also because the events which took place then have greatly influenced later developments within the Arab world and Israel, as well as between the Arab states and Israel.

Within their countries, the Arab military defeats dealt such a blow to Arab pride and self-confidence that they created major instability and unrest. Increasing numbers of educated Arabs, including young army officers, began to reappraise Arab political, economic, and social ways of life in their search for the basic causes of Arab weaknesses. While most Arabs continued to blame others, especially the United States and Britain, for their plight, the more discerning Arabs began to acknowledge that the deficiencies of the Arabs themselves were greatly responsible for their own misfortune. These Arabs frankly criticized their inefficient, corrupt, and inept political leadership, their backward economic and social systems, their complacent, self-deluded, and undisciplined fellow countrymen, and the deplorable lack of unity among the Arab peoples and governments. This mounting discontent with existing conditions led to the rise of movements which clamored for major and revolutionary economic, social, and political reforms and for increased Arab unity in order to provide the essential bases for the development of Arab power and prestige and for the improvement of the living standards of the masses. In Syria, for example, the Palestine War fiasco brought about considerable agitation against the existing regime, especially among army officers and those who advocated greater Arab unity. In fact, in December, 1948, major anti-government riots forced the cabinet to resign and by the end of March, 1949, a segment of the army had taken over control through a military coup. In Transjordan, the monarchy found itself plagued with serious unrest among the Palestinians, who now made up two-thirds of the population of the country. Because of his secret dealings with the Israelis and other unpopular activities, King Abdullah was accused of being a traitor to the Arab cause, and on July 20, 1951, he was assassinated by a Palestinian refugee in Jerusalem. The Egyptian government, which had suffered the most humiliating defeat of all during the Palestine War, found itself faced with serious dissension. In July, 1952, a group of young officers, led by Colonel Gamal Abdel Nasser and aroused by their injured pride and their hatred for the corrupt and inefficient government of King Farouk, overthrew the monarchy. Military control was established over Egypt. The Palestine War also widened the breach between many states and groups within the Arab world—especially between Jordan and Egypt and between those supporting local nationalism (as in Lebanon, Jordan, and Syria) and those pressing for greater Arab unity.

The war not only assured the existence of a Jewish state, but it also enabled this state to extend its boundaries well beyond those provided for by the UN partition resolution. This increased size created room for more Jewish immigrants and greater physical security. The military victory intensified an already strong Israeli nationalism and inflated still more the Israeli sense of superiority vis-à-vis the Arabs. Over the years, too, numerous Israelis, having survived horrible persecutions under the Nazis and feeling that the world owed them something for their suffering, had grown increasingly hard and dedicated to the achievement of their ends regardless of the methods used. This tendency was reflected in the increase of terroristic acts after World War II and in the change in leadership from the moderate, gradualist Chaim Weizmann to the volatile, impatient, and more belligerently minded David Ben-Gurion. In addition, the fact that the Israelis had to resort to war to achieve their state brought about a significant growth in the influence of the military mentality in the internal and external affairs of the new nation and encouraged Israelis to demand the continued use of force in order to attain their other goals as well. This cynicism, supreme devotion to self-interest, and propensity to use armed power made Israelis impatient with and, at times, even contemptuous of the UN, its agencies, and its personnel.[57] Although the UN did not actually enforce its partition resolution and the Israelis had to fight to save their state, the fact remains that too few Israelis gave adequate credit to the essential role of the UN in furnishing, through its resolutions, both the legal basis for Israel's existence and the desperately needed breathing spell provided by the first truce. While it is understandable that the Israelis would become bitter because the UN failed to enforce partition against the Arabs in the early days, similar failures on the part of the world organization to execute many later resolutions against Israel did not produce quite such drastic and lasting anti-UN feeling among the Arabs. Anti-UN sentiments in Israel were also engendered by the realization that the international organization and its resolutions had become, after the first truce, serious obstacles to Israel's expanding territorial ambitions. Besides, many Israelis had become so hypersensitive to criticism that they began to consider anyone not wholly with them as against them. This naturally led them to attack, without real justification, the objectivity of the Acting Mediator and other UN officials in the area and to disregard UN decisions.[58] Israel actually won her biggest military victories and attained her largest territorial gains during the second truce and in violation of both that truce and such Security Council resolutions as those of August 19 and November 4, 1948.

Certain aspects of Israel's military achievements were to have a deleterious effect upon Arab-Israeli relations. On the one hand, the extent of their war victory caused such a great increase in the pride and self-confidence of the Israelis that they became less willing to make those concessions which were needed if there was to be any hope for reconciliation with the Arabs. On the other hand, the extent of the Arab defeat brought about such a blow to the pride and self-reliance of the Arabs that they became more opposed than ever to acknowledging the existence of the enemy who had so deeply humiliated them. In the long run, a lesser Israeli victory, even a military stalemate, would have netted Israel less territory but might have provided a better and more practical basis for meaningful and lasting Arab-Israeli peace.

By tending to belittle Arab courage, character, and way of life, to gloat unduly, and even to inflate the extent of their victory,[59] the Israelis and their supporters merely helped intensify Arab bitterness and foster the conviction among many Arabs that they could regain their self-respect only by proving themselves successful in a future battle.

While the Arabs generally placed primary blame on Britain and the United States for the creation of Israel, they largely ignored the key role played by the Soviet Union, which proved to be more consistently, if not also more strongly, pro-Israel than even the United States. Without Soviet support in November, 1947, the original partition resolution would have failed to pass. In addition, continued Soviet backing in the UN during the critical months after partition was passed and the timely sale of Communist bloc weapons to Israel when she desperately needed them proved most decisive to the success of Israel's cause and most damaging to Arab interests in Palestine.

Neither the UN nor its most powerful members played as constructive a role during the crucial period as they could and should have played. By failing to enforce its resolutions, first largely against the Arabs and later mainly against the Israelis, the UN weakened its own prestige and ability to influence events in Palestine and encouraged the opposing parties to disregard the world organization when they chose. As for the major powers, they were reluctant to apply the pressures available to them in order to discourage the use of force by either side and to uphold the authority of and insure greater respect for the UN. As a result, Arab-Israeli hostility was not reduced, their differences were not resolved, and as future events were to demonstrate, the cause of peace was not served during this critical period.

CHAPTER V

Jerusalem—City of Peace and Source of Conflict

Over the centuries, Jerusalem had become a Holy City for three major religions, a fact which led to many serious clashes through the years, like those between the Romans and the Jews in A.D. 70 and in A.D. 135, and between Christians and Muslims in the wake of the Crusades. So much friction had developed between different Christian groups over the control of certain Christian shrines that peace was achieved only through a compromise providing that a neutral Muslim family supervise these shrines. However, under Ottoman rule, religious and political rivalries over Jerusalem remained relatively quiescent.

With the defeat of Turkey in World War I and the rise of Arab and Jewish nationalisms, potentially dangerous rivalries began to develop over Jerusalem and Palestine as a whole. Some efforts were made to deal with this new situation. For instance, the League of Nations mandatory agreement for Palestine provided special protection for the rights of all religions in Jerusalem. In 1936, the Peel Commission suggested not only the partition of Palestine but also the retention of an enclave, including Jerusalem and Bethlehem, under a separate British mandate in order to insure the preservation of this area's unique religious status. For a similar reason the Morrison-Grady Plan, devised to implement the proposals of the 1946 Anglo-American Committee on Palestine, also provided for continued British control over Jerusalem. Thus, it was not surprising that the UN Special Committee on Palestine (UNSCOP), in its majority report submitted to the General Assembly in 1947, recommended the internationalization of Jerusalem as the best means for protecting the interests of all religious groups in the Holy City.

At the Second Session of the General Assembly, all Arabs strongly opposed the draft resolution submitted to carry out UNSCOP's proposals to partition Palestine and to establish a *corpus separatum* for Jerusalem because they considered Palestine and Jerusalem to be integral parts of the Arab world. They advocated, instead, that Palestine be made into a

102

unitary state which would be legally obligated to safeguard the rights of all religions throughout the Holy Land. In their view, no special status was needed for Jerusalem.

Originally anxious to have Jerusalem included in the proposed Jewish state, the Zionists finally and reluctantly accepted the draft resolution's provision for internationalization because they realized that without it the resolution might fail to attract enough votes, especially from the Roman Catholic countries, to enable it to pass the General Assembly.[1] At this stage, the Zionists were immediately concerned more with obtaining UN support for the creation of a Jewish nation than with the extent of its boundaries.

As passed on November 29, 1947, the partition resolution [181(II)] instructed the Trusteeship Council to prepare a statute for an internationalized Jerusalem. In February and early March, 1948, the Trusteeship Council adopted various parts of a draft statute (T.118/Rev.2) which provided for a governor with broad executive authority, a legislative council made up of equal numbers of Arabs and Jews, and some safeguards for human rights and the holy places. On March 10, 1948, however, a final vote on the statute as a whole was delayed because the Security Council had called a special session of the General Assembly to reconsider the over-all Palestine question with the possibility that the partition resolution might be dropped altogether.

When the General Assembly met, it found itself with a rapidly deteriorating situation in Jerusalem as well as in Palestine generally. After quickly passing a French resolution asking the Trusteeship Council to work out emergency plans for establishing a truce in the Holy City, the Assembly took up an American proposal calling for a provisional trusteeship for Palestine in order to give the Palestine Arabs and Jews time to agree on the future form of state and government. But early in May, with the life of the mandate rapidly drawing to a close, the United States decided to discard the trusteeship plan.

During the Palestine War, Israel seized the western, New City section of Jerusalem. Transjordan, in turn, occupied the much smaller eastern sector, including what was known as the Old City which contained most of the holy places. The Israeli-Transjordanian Armistice Agreement accepted the *de facto* holdings of each party in Jerusalem without any reference to internationalization.

Despite these developments, however, considerable support for the setting up of a *corpus separatum* for Jerusalem continued to exist both within and outside the UN. The Pope, in encyclicals of May 1 and October 24, 1948, vigorously backed internationalization—and the Vatican's views had considerable influence on the positions taken by

many Catholic members of the UN. A number of officials in the Orthodox and Armenian churches indicated that they also remained in favor
of internationalization. Moreover, many states which had been the
strongest and most consistent proponents of the partition resolution,
such as Australia and the Soviet bloc, continued to insist upon the fulfillment of those resolution provisions dealing with the Holy City.[2]

As a result of these pressures, on December 11, 1948, the General
Assembly reaffirmed its support for internationalization in Resolution
194(III) setting up a Conciliation Commission for Palestine. Among
other things, the commission was instructed to draw up "detailed proposals for a permanent regime for the Jerusalem area."

After investigating the existing situation and ascertaining the views of
the parties most directly concerned, the Conciliation Commission submitted recommendations (A/973) which represented a major departure
from the actual terms of the partition resolution. Instead of an international regime for Jerusalem, the commission proposed the division of
the city into two sections, one Arab and the other Jewish. Not only would
virtually all of the normal powers of government be left in the hands of
the Arabs and the Jews in their respective zones, but these zones could
be placed under the over-all political control of Jordan and Israel. A UN
commissioner for Jerusalem would be appointed, but his powers would
be largely limited to insuring the protection of the holy places and to
supervising the demilitarization and neutralization of the city. A general
council, composed of equal numbers of Arabs and Jews, would be set up
to act as a coordinating body, but not as a legislative one, for the two
communities.

CHANGES IN ISRAELI AND ARAB POSITIONS

Before the Palestine War, Zionist leaders had reluctantly agreed to
relinquish their claim to Jerusalem. After occupying the larger part of the
city, however, their position changed. Israel contended that armed Arab
opposition to the partition resolution and the failure of the UN to come
to her aid during the fighting had created a new situation allowing the
Jews to regain "their rights to Jerusalem." They also held that although
the Holy City was greatly revered throughout the entire world, "such
universal veneration should not overshadow the special interests of the
Jewish people, which regarded Jerusalem as the symbol of past glory."
They opposed placing the 100,000 Jews living in Jerusalem under "foreign control" for only Israel could "assure" them of adequate security
and could properly "provide for the needs and growth . . . of Jewish
Jerusalem." They warned that "the sanctity of the holy places would not
be served by surrounding them with a turbulent and resentful disen-

franchised population determined to regain the liberty and union they had recently achieved at the cost of great sacrifices." Israeli officials argued that full internationalization was not necessary to protect the holy places because Israel was willing to "guarantee" their "sanctity." Israel was prepared to accept only very limited UN supervision over the few sacred shrines under her jurisdiction. She even rejected the milder Conciliation Commission proposal on the grounds that it was "impractical" and provided "too much interference" with Israel's sovereignty.[3] Members of the extremist Herut Party even threatened to reorganize themselves once again as the Irgun to remove any UN commissioner who might be sent to Jerusalem.[4] Starting in March, 1949, Israel, despite urgent Arab protests to the UN, began moving many governmental agencies to Jerusalem in order to serve notice that she considered it to be an integral, permanent part of the country.[5]

When in the spring of 1949 the General Assembly began to discuss Israel's request to be admitted as a member of the UN, Israeli officials found themselves in a delicate situation which forced them to make equivocal statements concerning Jerusalem and other Palestine issues. The Arabs and delegates from Roman Catholic countries pressed Israel to give some prior assurance that after being admitted into the UN she would actually abide by all UN resolutions, particularly those providing for the right of the Arab refugees to return to their homes and the internationalization of Jerusalem. Recognizing that many Latin American, Asiatic, and European delegates were hesitant about accepting Israel's membership without some reassuring statement, the Israeli representative formally declared that his government would pursue "no policies on any question which were inconsistent with . . . the resolutions of the Assembly and the Security Council." [6]

Although many delegates would have preferred a more detailed and explicit statement, they finally expressed a willingness to accept the one presented as sufficient evidence of Israel's intention to carry out the earlier resolutions. Since the Colombian delegate felt that there were "still some doubts on the matter," he directly addressed the Israeli delegation and received "formal assurance in writing that Israel would not oppose the internationalization of Jerusalem. In view of that guarantee, Colombia . . . supported Israel's request for admission." [7] The resolution [273 (III)] admitting Israel, which finally passed on May 11, 1949, specifically recalled the "resolutions of 29 November 1947 and 11 December 1948" and took "note of the declarations and explanations made by the representative of the Government of Israel before the *Ad Hoc* Political Committee in respect of the implementation of the said resolutions." But shortly after becoming a member of the UN, Israel once again made clear that she would oppose the internationalization of the Holy City.[8]

Until early 1949, the Arabs objected to both the partition of Palestine and the establishment of a *corpus separatum* for Jerusalem. Nevertheless, the facts that Israel had won the Palestine War, that she had conquered large areas beyond those allocated by the General Assembly to the Jewish state, and that she maintained a military superiority over the Arabs caused most Arab governments to change their views about the partition resolution. The Arabs were not—and for quite some time to come could not hope to become—powerful enough to destroy Israel and to attain the desired goal of an Arab Palestine. Alone they could not even force Israel to give up those territories occupied by her which had been originally assigned either to the Arab part of Palestine or to the internationalized Holy City. From a realistic point of view, the Arabs, at least for the near future, had more to gain than to lose from a UN enforcement of the partition resolution, for this would compel the Israelis to give up a large part of their country, including the portion of Jerusalem occupied by them. Not only would this make for a smaller and weaker Israel, but it would also enable large numbers of Arab refugees to return to their homes in the sectors evacuated by Israel. Many Arab officials came to the conclusion, therefore, that under the circumstances they would benefit more from having Jerusalem internationalized than from having most of the city under Israeli control for an indefinite period. In view of these considerations, all Arab states except Transjordan decided to support those resolutions calling for internationalization. They opposed the Conciliation Commission's proposals because they disregarded the provisions for internationalization as specified in these resolutions. They also strongly protested the transfer of Israeli government agencies to Jerusalem and demanded their withdrawal. Some Arab governments even started urging the UN to use force, if necessary, to implement its decision on the Holy City.[9]

Transjordan disagreed with her fellow Arab states on this issue. The Palestine War gave King Abdullah his first real opportunity to take a limited step towards achieving his goal of a Greater Syria. As a result of the war, Abdullah's troops occupied large sections of eastern and central Palestine, and he quickly made clear his intention to add these territories to his domain. Most of Abdullah's Arab neighbors, however, feared his ambitions and opposed his plans. Under Egypt's leadership, an All-Palestine government was organized in the Gaza Strip, September 20, 1948, and it was recognized by every Arab League member but Transjordan as the "government" of all of Palestine, including the areas occupied by Israel. In a meeting in March, 1950, the Arab League denounced Transjordan's efforts to annex part of Palestine and threatened her with expulsion. Arab nationalists, already distrustful of Abdullah because of his earlier dealings with Israel, became even more aroused when they learned about his latest secret peace talks with the enemy. While Abdullah found it necessary to terminate his negotiations with Israel, he had his Parliament give final approval on April 24, 1950, to his earlier actions to annex eastern Palestine (December 1, 1948) and to change the name of the country from Transjordan to the Hashemite Kingdom of Jordan (April 26, 1949). Recognizing the strategic, political, and religious importance of the Old City, Abdullah was reluctant to give it up; therefore Jordan informed the General Assembly that "no form of internationalization . . . would serve any purpose, as the holy places under Jordan's protection . . . were safe and secure without the necessity for a special regime." Jordan stated that she would be willing formally to guarantee full freedom of worship in and ready access to the holy places. Nevertheless, at least unofficially, Jordan did not close the door completely against the possibility of a future change in her position. The *Times* of London reported on November 21, 1949, that Abdullah had told its correspondent that he would consider withdrawing from the Old City if and when Israel gave up those areas allotted to the Arab state by the 1947 partition resolution.[10]

THE UN TRIES AGAIN, 1949–1950

The General Assembly found itself faced once again with the Jerusalem question at its Fourth Session. The United States, Britain, and Turkey, whose representatives made up the membership of the Conciliation Commission for Palestine, urged the Assembly to accept the commission's proposal. But most UN members—particularly the Arab states (Jordan was not yet a member of the UN), many Roman Catholic countries, and the Soviet bloc—continued to insist upon full internationalization. Russia's position was partly influenced by her hope that she could somehow increase her influence in the Middle East through her participation as a big power both in UN supervisory activities over an internationalized Holy City and in any enforcement measures that might prove necessary to implement internationalization. Israel and Jordan opposed both the commission's and the partition resolution's plans for Jerusalem. Despite the warnings of Jordanian officials that they would "oppose the execution of whatever is decided contrary to" Jordan's "rightful wishes" and of Ben-Gurion that the "Jews will sacrifice themselves for Jerusalem no less than Englishmen for London," on December 9, 1949, the General Assembly voted thirty-eight to fourteen for Resolution 303 (IV), which requested the Trusteeship Council to draw up a statute for an internationalized Jerusalem and to assure its implementation.[11]

Israel not only voted against this resolution, but she accelerated her efforts to move government ministries and other agencies from Tel Aviv to Jerusalem in order to make it her capital in fact as well as in name before the UN had a chance to implement its decisions. She ignored both a "firm note" from the United States cautioning her not to do anything that would prejudice the enforcement of internationalization [12] and a Trusteeship Council resolution (T/L.3/Rev.1) expressing "concern" over Israel's actions and inviting her to "revoke" them and to "abstain from any action liable to hinder the implementation" of the December 9 resolution. On December 26, 1949, Israel's parliament, the Knesset, began to hold sessions in Jerusalem. On January 23, 1950, it approved a proclamation announcing that Jerusalem had been the capital of Israel from the first day of her independence. All the ministries except the Foreign Ministry were immediately moved from Tel Aviv, and in July, 1953, it too was transferred.[13]

Most Arabs considered the passage of Resolution 303(IV) a victory for their side. Nevertheless, they were greatly distressed over Israel's endeavors to establish Jerusalem as her capital and over the UN's failure to make any serious effort to prevent this. They urged the UN to use force, if necessary, not only against Israel, but also against Jordan in order to implement its decision on Jerusalem.[14]

On December 19, 1949, the Trusteeship Council passed a resolution (T/426) asking its president, Roger Garreau, to ascertain the views of the interested parties and prepare a working paper for a draft statute. In a report (T/457) made in January, 1950, President Garreau suggested that only a tiny area containing the major holy places should be internationalized under UN control. The rest of the city would be divided into Arab and Jewish zones, to be placed under the sovereignty of Jordan and Israel, respectively.

Both Israel and the Arab states criticized Garreau's proposal. Israel objected to the loss of sovereignty over any portion, no matter how small, of the New City; Jordan remained opposed to any change in the *status quo*. Most Arabs supported a Chinese proposal (T/L.15) asking the Trusteeship Council to "proceed immediately with the completion of the preparation of the statute in accordance with the terms" of the December 9, 1949, resolution. This resolution passed on February 10, 1950, without a dissenting vote.[15]

In result, the Trusteeship Council returned to the consideration of the draft statute it had first formulated in the early part of 1948. On April 4, 1950, the council adopted an amended version of this earlier proposal. The new statute provided for the setting up of a *corpus separatum* under UN control for all of Jerusalem and a part of the surrounding area. The council would appoint a governor, with broad executive powers, and a supreme court. A legislative council, with both elected and appointed members, was to have authority over local matters. Jerusalem would be demilitarized and neutralized. The holy places, "human rights," and "fundamental freedoms" were to be protected. Although most Arab states urged that this statute be put into effect immediately, Article 41 stipulated that it would come into force "at a date to be determined by a resolution of the Trusteeship Council." [16]

Before putting the statute into effect, however, the Trusteeship Council decided to contact Israel and Jordan to see how much cooperation could be expected from them. Jordan ignored the council's communication, while Israel merely submitted a counterproposal providing only for the functional internationalization of the holy places. Realizing the practical difficulties that would be involved in trying to implement the new statute in the face of Israel's and Jordan's opposition, the Trusteeship Council referred the whole matter back to the General Assembly.[17]

Thus, at its Fifth Session, the General Assembly found itself again dealing with the Jerusalem problem. By this time it had become increasingly obvious to many governments that the actions and attitudes of Israel and Jordan had created far more serious obstacles in the way of carrying out the UN decisions involving Jerusalem than was originally anticipated when these decisions were actually made. Recognizing this, a number of UN members who had previously backed internationalization began to lose hope that it could be brought about under existing circumstances and to seek some other solution more acceptable to the Israelis and Jordanians. For instance, as early as April, 1950, Russia announced the withdrawal of her backing for internationalization on the ground that it had now become clearer that the UN General Assembly resolution did not satisfy the Arab and Jewish populations of either Jerusalem or Palestine as a whole. After this date, the important votes of the Soviet bloc were to be cast against, rather than for, all proposals espousing the cause of internationalization. In December, 1950, the only draft resolutions which received serious consideration in the General Assembly were those which took this new situation into consideration. A Swedish proposal (A/AC.38/L.63) provided for a limited functional, rather than territorial, internationalization. A Belgian resolution (A/AC.38/L.71) asked the Trusteeship Council to select four persons "to study . . . the conditions of a settlement capable of ensuring the effective protection, under the supervision of the UN, of the holy places." While only the Belgian resolution succeeded in obtaining the simple majority vote required in the *Ad Hoc* Political Committee, even this failed to receive the two-thirds vote needed for final passage. Thus, the General Assembly ended its Fifth Session without taking any new action either to enforce or to change previous decisions. In fact, although in succeeding years some of the Arab and Roman Catholic members occasionally reminded the Assembly that the existing resolutions on Jerusalem were not being carried out,[18] the Jerusalem question was not seriously considered again by the General Assembly until after the Arab-Israeli war in June, 1967.

DEVELOPMENTS OUTSIDE THE UN

The Western powers criticized Israel when she transferred her Foreign Ministry to Jerusalem. They not only refused to move their own diplomatic establishments from Tel Aviv, but for a time they even avoided transacting formal business in Jerusalem. Nonetheless, on a few occasions Western diplomats did meet informally with Israeli officials in hotels or at private social gatherings in the New City. Secretary of State John Foster Dulles' public disapproval of the Israeli action was hailed by many Arabs as a sign of a welcome decrease in the American government's pro-Israel bias.[19]

In December, 1953, however, the Soviet Union instructed her new envoy to Israel to present his credentials in a formal call on the Israeli President in Jerusalem. This action was unexpected since for some time the Soviet Union had been taking a relatively pro-Arab and anti-Israeli position in the Security Council during discussions of various complaints about armistice violations in the latter part of 1953. This step naturally pleased the Israelis while it surprised and angered the Arabs, who charged the Russians with "flouting" UN resolutions. Despite Arab protests, Chile, Yugoslavia, and Bulgaria quickly followed Russia's example.[20]

In early November, 1954, the British and American governments, after consulting with each other and with French officials, also decided to instruct their new ambassadors to Israel to present their credentials in Jerusalem. Although both governments insisted that this decision did not presage any change in their positions regarding the continued validity of the UN resolutions on Jerusalem, the Arabs, through diplomatic channels, strongly protested this move. The Arabs were further disturbed when many other countries were encouraged to follow a similar procedure. Some nations, including Guatemala, Venezuela, the Netherlands, and Uruguay, even transferred their entire diplomatic establishments from Tel Aviv to Jerusalem.[21]

Jordan, opposed to any form of internationalization, took various measures to indicate her intention to retain sovereign control over the Old City. On January 2, 1951, King Abdullah appointed a custodian of the holy places with cabinet rank. On July 27, 1953, the Jordanian cabinet met formally in the Old City for the first time, and it decided to hold some sessions of parliament and to set up a few central government offices there. In 1959, the Council of Ministers proclaimed the Old City to be Jordan's second capital, while King Hussein, Abdullah's grandson, began spending some time there each year. Despite these moves, Jordan refrained from actually making Jerusalem her first capital and even from transferring any major portion of the central government from Amman, probably in part because the Old City was in a dangerously exposed position.[22]

Developments since the early 1950's gave little encouragement to those Arabs who persisted in their demand that the UN should enforce its resolutions involving Jerusalem. They did what they could to keep an active interest alive among the dwindling number of non-Arab states, primarily Roman Catholic, who continued to favor internationalization. Recognizing the important influence exerted by the Popes on many Roman Catholic countries, these Arabs increased their efforts to cultivate the support of the Vatican. From as far back as 1946, the Arabs had been seeking to promote closer ties with the Holy See. In the summer of 1946, a Palestine Arab delegation visited Pope Pius XII to present the Arab position on the Palestine question. In 1947, Lebanon and Egypt became the first Arab nations to exchange diplomatic representatives with the Vatican. During 1947 and 1948, the Arabs and Roman Catholics held conflicting views on the fate of Jerusalem, but when in 1949 most Arabs decided for the first time to accept the principle of internationalization, it was possible for the Arabs and the Holy See to develop closer ties. The Arabs, through both normal diplomatic channels and special missions, took advantage of these closer ties to seek the Vatican's backing for their views on all aspects of the Palestine problem. The Popes, in turn, were anxious to maintain good relations with the Arab world. Appreciating Arab sensitivity, the Popes were careful to avoid any action which might imply recognition of Israel. For instance, when in December, 1963, Pope Paul VI indicated his intention to make a pilgrimage to the Holy Land, he carefully referred to the Israeli part as "Palestine." To quiet Arab fears he stated that his trip to Nazareth in Israel was not to be interpreted as an act of recognition.[23]

The Jerusalem issue was brought more actively to the fore again on August 30, 1966, when Israel dedicated her new, $7,000,000 Knesset building in the Israeli-held sector of Jerusalem before 5,000 guests, including parliamentary delegates from forty-one nations. By repeatedly referring to the permanence and symbolic importance of the new structure, Israeli speakers at the dedication made it clear once again that they intended Jerusalem to remain their capital forever. The Arabs branded Israel's move as an "aggression" and a violation of existing UN resolutions and sent vigorous protests to the UN. Some Arab League officials urged that the situation called for a "more pronounced joint Arab presence in Arab Jerusalem." The Palestine Liberation Organization, officially recognized since 1964 by the Arab League and most Arab governments as the spokesman for all Palestinians, pressed King Hussein to declare Jerusalem an "Arab city" and to make it the capital of Jordan. But Hussein refused to act on these proposals and thereby further antagonized the leaders of the Palestine Liberation Organization and other opponents within the Arab world.[24]

ISRAELI TAKEOVER OF ALL JERUSALEM, JUNE, 1967

Israel's decisive military victory over the Arab states in early June, 1967 (see Chapter VIII), brought under her control all the Jordanian territory west of the Jordan River. But the part of this area that evoked the greatest emotional response from the Israeli Jews was the Old City of Jerusalem. For the first time since 1948 they could pray at the Wailing Wall, and they rushed there by the thousands. Although the Wailing Wall, which many Jews believe was once part of the Second Temple, has no formal place in Jewish religious teachings, it is revered as the symbol of the history and unity of the Jewish people. To many religiously oriented Jews, praying at the Wall is an important act of devotion. To facilitate the gathering of large numbers of Jews before the Wall, the Israeli government gave several hundred Arabs living close to it twenty-four hours to leave before bulldozers cleared the area.[25]

The tremendous outpouring of emotion unleashed by their occupation of the Old City had a major impact upon the Israeli populace and officials. Many Israelis began to believe that the "recovery" of all Jerusalem was a fulfillment of religious prophecies, and they insisted that the Holy City should be completely reunited under Israeli sovereignty. Claiming that no other people had as strong an attachment to any city as theirs to Jerusalem, they cited their religious oath: "If I forget thee O Jerusalem, let my right hand forget its cunning, let my tongue cleave to the roof of my mouth, if I remember thee not, if I set not Jerusalem above my chiefest joy." Defense Minister Moshe Dayan and other political leaders added their powerful influence in favor of retaining the Old City.

The United States, supported by Britain, urged the Israelis not to act hastily and to wait at least for a "better time" before formally annexing the Jordanian part of Jerusalem. She warned that any precipitous action would weaken Israel's position before the Fifth Emergency Special Session of the UN General Assembly then discussing various draft resolutions requesting an Israeli withdrawal from all conquered areas. Hasty action would foreclose any possibility for an eventual reconciliation with moderate King Hussein and would seriously lessen the chances of ever arriving at a durable Arab-Israeli peace settlement. Some American officials sought to convince Israel that an internationalized Old City could serve both as a point of contact and trade between Arabs and Israelis and as a political and economic "decompression chamber." A number of American officials held that because the United States had frequently opposed any forceful territorial aggrandizement in the Middle East, the American government was obligated to resist any Israeli annexations.[26]

Soon after the end of the fighting in early June, the Vatican reasserted its traditional position on the Jerusalem question. On June 23, the Holy See circulated a note at the UN in which it called for the setting up of an international regime for Jerusalem to safeguard free access by all religious faiths to the holy places. The note was studied with special interest by the Latin American and other delegations representing countries with large majorities of Roman Catholics.[27]

By the latter part of June the Israeli government had decided to disregard the urgings of the United States and Britain and the views of the Vatican and to annex the Old City quickly. Israel wished to present the world with still another *fait accompli* before Western and UN pressures had an opportunity to intensify further.[28] Israel also wished to make it absolutely clear that insofar as she was concerned, Jerusalem's future would no longer be considered a negotiable issue. In arriving at this decision, the Israeli government was influenced not only by the clamor of its own people but also by the fact that the Old City had considerable value politically, strategically, and economically because of its great appeal to foreign tourists.[29] On June 27, the Knesset hurriedly passed without debate a law enabling the Minister of the Interior to proclaim Jerusalem a single city under Israeli administration. At the same time the Knesset approved a measure which provided for the protection of the holy places against desecration and guaranteed freedom of access to them by all religious groups. The next day the government formally united the two sections of the Holy City and extended its borders to include Kallandia Airport and Mount Scopus to the north and northwest, the Mount of Olives to the east, and several villages to the south.[30]

Israel's action was criticized by many states. Even President Lyndon B. Johnson and his top advisers, while they might not have objected if Israel had annexed only some of the residential areas in the Old City, expressed their annoyance because Israel had disregarded their urgings not to flout world public opinion and to wait for a more favorable occasion before moving to annex the Old City. In a formal statement, the American government deplored Israel's hasty and unilateral move and declared that it would not recognize its validity.[31] Britain, France, and many Roman Catholic countries also expressed their strong disapproval, while the Arabs and their friends condemned Israel and demanded that the UN take effective action against her.[32] In response to these criticisms and demands, Pakistan introduced a draft resolution (A/L.527) before the General Assembly. The draft considered Israel's annexation to be invalid, called upon her to rescind all measures taken to alter the city's status, and asked UN Secretary-General U Thant to report on the implementation of the resolution within a week. The overwhelming opposition in the UN to Israel's action in Jerusalem was clearly indicated by the fact that the Pakistani resolution [2253(ES-V)] passed easily on July 4. Ninety-nine countries—including the Arab and Soviet blocs, Britain, France, and a number of other Western nations—voted in favor of the resolution. No negative vote was cast. The United States and nineteen other UN members abstained, while Israel did not participate in the voting.

In an official letter to the UN, Israel promised to work out arrangements with the world's religious bodies to insure the universal character of the holy places and free access to them, but she gave no indication that she would rescind her action in Jerusalem.[33] In fact, Israeli officials quickly made it clear that they would not give up the Old City regardless of what resolutions the General Assembly passed.[34]

Many UN delegations, revealing growing anger and impatience, sharply condemned Israel's attitude. The Jerusalem issue became one of the few aspects of the general Arab-Israeli problem resulting in broad agreement within the UN and even causing delegates who were normally friendly to Israel to criticize her refusal to abide by the will of the world community. A number of Western countries, like Britain and France, urged Israel to relinquish her claim to the Old City until the ultimate status of Jerusalem could be determined in a future general peace settlement. Many delegates warned Israel that her action would further aggravate tension in an area already fraught with considerable danger. The United States reiterated that she would not recognize or accept the measures taken by Israel, but the U.S. refused to apply any effective pressures on Israel to annul her decree unifying Jerusalem "without obtaining something from the Arabs" in return.[35]

The Arabs accused Israel of defying the General Assembly, of holding the UN and world public opinion in contempt, and of "desecrating" mosques in occupied areas. They insisted that they would never accept the loss of the Old City or the other territories seized by Israel. The Communist bloc, non-Arab Muslim nations, and a number of nonaligned states supported the Arab views on Jerusalem. On July 12, Pakistan, joined later by eight other Asian and African countries, introduced another draft resolution (A/L.528) proposing that the General Assembly (1) deplore the failure of Israel to implement the resolution passed on July 4; (2) reiterate its call to Israel to rescind all measures taken and to desist from any further action to change the status of Jerusalem; (3) request the Secretary-General to report on the Jerusalem situation and on the implementation of this resolution; and (4) ask the Security Council to take all necessary measures to insure the implementation of this resolution.

Realizing that the Jerusalem issue was hurting her position before the UN and the world and desiring to defeat the Pakistani draft, Israel quickly initiated major and urgent efforts to reach an agreement with the Pope and other Christian leaders which would appease the anxieties of the delegates from Roman Catholic and other Christian nations before the General Assembly voted on the Pakistani resolution. Israeli representatives met with officials of the Vatican, the World Council of Churches, and other Christian groups, as well as with Latin American and other Christian delegations to the UN. Israel offered an arrangement whereby she would retain sovereignty over Jerusalem, but the holy sites would be given an extraterritorial and "universal" status and would be supervised and administered by the religious communities themselves. Israel offered to give quasi-diplomatic standing to the official church delegations stationed in Jerusalem and expressed a willingness to work out the final details with representatives of the various religious organizations. In particular, Israel sought to convince the religious leaders that their interests in the Holy Land could be adequately protected without internationalizing Jerusalem, that an international regime would not be a practical solution, and that peace in Jerusalem and the safety of the holy places would more likely be assured by a unified city administration than a divided one.

Israel was apparently able to make considerable headway with a number of Protestant and Greek Orthodox leaders soon after the end of the June War. But Russian Orthodox, Coptic, and a few Greek Orthodox and Protestant leaders refused to accept Israel's views. In early July, 1967, Israeli sources claimed that they had convinced the Vatican to alter its position as well. At that time, however, the Vatican did not confirm this, and there were indications that it was still seeking other views on the subject before deciding upon a final policy.[36] In a statement made on December 22, 1967, the Pope appeared to indicate that he had moved away from his long-term objective of full internationalization of Jerusalem. According to the *New York Times,* December 23, 1967, the Pope was reported to have spoken of the need for an "institution of an international character, with special regard for the historical and religious physiognomy of Jerusalem" to safeguard and guarantee access to the holy places.

Israel sought, but without much success, to win over the Muslim officials who remained in the areas she had wrested from the Arabs. Muslim authorities elsewhere, such as Inamullah Khan, secretary-general of the World Muslim Congress, proclaimed they would never accept Israel's physical control of their religious shrines. Some Muslims, especially in the Arab world, rejected suggestions that the Old City itself be internationalized. Others even called upon all followers of Muhammad to join in the struggle to recover Jerusalem and the Islamic holy places located there.

Despite Israel's efforts to prevent its passage, the second Pakistani resolution was adopted on July 14, again by an overwhelming majority of ninety-nine to zero with eighteen abstentions. Before the voting took place, however, Pakistan, in order to win as much support as possible for her proposal, withdrew that operative paragraph which, by requesting the Security Council to insure that the resolution would be implemented, posed the most serious threat to Israel's position. Pakistan declared, nonetheless, that if the Israelis disregarded the resolution, she was prepared to join with other member states in demanding Security Council enforcement action. Israel again did not participate in the voting on the grounds that the resolution was "inaccurate" about the factual situation and that it ignored the "affirmative aspects" of Israel's unification of the Holy City. The United States, holding that the Jerusalem question should not be considered in complete isolation from other Arab-Israeli problems, abstained once more. But she joined Britain, France, Canada, and others in urging Israel to keep the Jerusalem issue open so that its final status could be included in any further negotiations for an over-all peace settlement.

Soon after the General Assembly passed the second Pakistani resolution [2254 (ES-V)], Israel found herself facing mounting difficulties with the Arabs in the Old City. For several weeks after the Israeli military victory, the Arabs in the occupied west bank passively accepted their unhappy fate because they remained stunned and frightened by their disastrous defeat and did not see any practical alternative to co-operating with the Israeli authorities. Victors and losers mingled freely in Jerusalem and appeared to be getting along surprisingly well. But by the middle of July the shock of defeat had worn off. The Palestine Liberation Organization and newer organizations began to form resist-ance groups in occupied areas, and radio programs from Amman and other Arab capitals began appealing to the west-bank residents not to cooperate with the Israeli government. The hopes and morale of Arab residents were raised by the passage of the two General Assembly reso-lutions calling upon Israel to rescind her annexation measures and by the assurances given by King Hussein and other Arab leaders that they would never accept Israel's control of the Old City and other conquered territories. About the middle of July, clandestine Arab groups began to distribute leaflets warning their fellow Arabs against collaborating with the "enemy." In the latter part of July, twenty-five Muslim leaders in Jerusalem signed a public statement denouncing the legality of Israel's absorption of Jordanian territory and challenging the authority of the Israeli Ministry of Religious Affairs to deal with Muslim religious activi-ties. In response to this act of defiance, Israel banished to other parts of the west-bank four of the Arab political leaders who had signed the statement. The Mayor of the Old City and his seven-man city council refused individual invitations to join Israeli officials in an enlarged coun-cil for Jerusalem and stated that they would not be a party to the Israeli annexation. On August 7, in response to the circulation of pamphlets by a new organization called the Committee for the Defense of Arab Jerusalem, all 2,000 Arab business establishments closed down, and an Arab bus company ceased all operations in a one-day general strike. The strike coincided with a visit by Nils-Goran Gussing, UN Secretary-General U Thant's personal envoy on the refugee problems arising from the June War. Israeli officials took punitive action by taking away the bus company's franchise and by closing four Arab stores for ten days. A second, but apparently unorganized, attempt at a general strike on Au-gust 21—the day that U Thant's personal representative in Jerusalem, Ambassador Ernesto A. Thalmann,[37] of Switzerland, first arrived in the Holy City—did not succeed. Underground Arab groups continued to operate, and radio programs from neighboring Arab states continued to incite resistance to Israel's rule of the conquered areas. Consequently, Arab unrest and opposition persisted.

Israel, in turn, began to employ increasingly tougher punitive actions and to seek out and arrest the leaders of the Arab resistance movements to discourage further acts of defiance and disobedience. Concurrently, she pressed ahead with her own plans to absorb the Old City fully. She sought ways to revive its economy and rewrote school textbooks to eliminate all anti-Israel materials before Arab schools reopened in the fall of 1967. Israeli officials initiated plans to resettle Jews in the former Jewish Quarter of the Old City.

CONCLUSION

Since the UN General Assembly had not altered or repealed Resolution 303 (IV) of December 19, 1949, providing for the internationalization of the Holy City, this resolution formally continued to exist. However, despite the repeated urgings of some Arab and Roman Catholic states, as well as the Vatican, the General Assembly never seriously tried to implement its decision.

Jordan, like Israel, had frequently proclaimed that she would not relinquish authority over her part of Jerusalem, but she did not display equal dedication to this end. On several occasions a few Jordanian officials had privately expressed a willingness (as King Abdullah had done in November, 1949) to consider the possibility of having to give up the Old City some day, but only as part of an acceptable over-all settlement of the Arab-Israeli problem.[38]

By occupying and annexing the Old City in June, 1967, Israel radically altered the *de facto* situation, but she did not eliminate or finally resolve the Jerusalem question. The Arab governments refused to resign themselves to the loss of the Old City and other conquered areas. In passing by overwhelming majorities two resolutions calling upon Israel to rescind her annexation of the Old City, the General Assembly clearly indicated that it considered Israel's action illegal. Even the United States, the only large power that had not voted for these resolutions, regarded Israel's move as invalid. In short, neither the Arabs nor the UN considered the Jerusalem issue closed.

If Israel could persuade major Christian leaders to accept her sovereignty over all sectors of Jerusalem and could make formal arrangements with them concerning the religious shrines, then opposition to Israel's absorption of the Old City would probably decline in most Christian areas. Even then, of course, some friction between Israel and Christian organizations could still arise as a result of Israel's strong disapproval of missionary activities and the likelihood that, in dealing with the religious officials and communities in the Old City, Israeli authorities would prove to be less accommodating than the Jordanians had been.[39] Moreover, Israel would find it far more difficult, if not actually impossible, to secure the acquiescence of those Christians, such as the Copts, the Maronites, and the Greek Orthodox, who live in the Arab world.

Even if Israel were able to win over all the major Christian groups, she would still be confronted with resistance from hundreds of millions of Muslims in the non-Arab, as well as the Arab, countries. Because the Prophet, the Koran, and the most sacred Muslim shrines and major centers for religious education are all associated with the Arab world, large numbers of non-Arab Muslims and their governments sympathize deeply with the Arabs. Before the June War, Muslims did not have to enter Israeli territory to visit their shrines in that part of Jerusalem controlled by Jordan. Now that these shrines are under the jurisdiction of Israel, Arab citizens, Muslim or Christian (there are between two and three million Christians in Egypt and Lebanon alone), would be generally unable to visit them, at least until the Arab governments formally recognize Israel. Moreover, since most non-Arab Muslim states had not extended diplomatic recognition to Israel, tens of millions of their nationals would also find it difficult, if not impossible, to visit an Israeli-dominated Jerusalem. Consequently, the greatest dissatisfaction with Israel's annexation of the Old City and the most powerful pressures in favor of an Israeli withdrawal would continue to come from Muslim countries—the very same countries who are Israel's closest neighbors.

Another source of potential trouble between Israel and the Muslims was the fact that Jewish and Muslim shrines in the Old City overlap. For instance, it is widely believed that at least part of the Haram al-Sharif compound, which includes the Muslims' revered Dome of the Rock and the Aqsa Mosque, is built on the site of the Jewish Second Temple, which was demolished in A.D. 70, and is adjacent to the Wailing Wall. This kind of overlapping precipitated serious incidents between the Arab Muslims and the Jews during the Palestine Mandate period. Before 1948, some Muslims feared that the Jews wished to destroy Muslim religious properties which might be deemed necessary in order to rebuild the Second Temple. As soon as Israel had occupied the Old City, this fear was revived and even intensified. The Muslims became very concerned when, on August 15, 1967, the Chief Chaplain of the Israeli Army held a service within the Haram al-Sharif compound and sought to hold another one a few days later in the plaza between the mosques in order, as he announced, to lay claim to part of the compound for the Jews. When the highly aroused Muslim community began to organize a demonstration in protest, Israeli authorities canceled plans for the second service, fearing that it might lead to a clash between the two religious communities.[40] In the emotion-charged atmosphere it would remain extremely difficult to prevent future disputes and conflicts from arising as a consequence of this overlapping.

In addition, friction would continue to develop over Israeli efforts to extend her social practices, traditions, and laws to the Arab residents of the Old City, whose traditions, values, and social concepts are substantially different from those of the Israelis. Conservative Arabs criticized the "immodest" dress and behavior of the Israelis visiting the Old City. Arab governments and Muslim officials accused Israel of denying freedom of worship to the Muslims in Jerusalem and elsewhere, of censoring prayer sermons, of interfering in the affairs of the *Sharia* (religious law) Courts, of preparing to subject Muslims to Israeli civil laws which "conflict with" Islamic laws, and of demolishing mosques and other properties owned by Muslim religious organizations without their consent.[41]

Because of the many religious, national, social, and economic differences between the conquered Arabs and the Israelis, Israel was not finding it easy to integrate the Arabs of the Old City into an Israeli-dominated Jerusalem. Underground Arab organizations and radios from the neighboring Arab states urged these Arabs not to accept Israeli rule as a permanent fact of life and to resist the imposition of Israeli authority. Even Israeli officials came to realize that it would take much effort and a long time before they could really unify the Arabs and Jews of Jerusalem. By their actions and attitudes, most Arabs of the Old City, as well as the Arab governments, clearly indicated that they did not consider the Jerusalem issue resolved.

The hostile and unaccommodating stand of the Arab countries provided the greatest threat of all to Israel's efforts to "solve" the Jerusalem question to her own liking. All Arab governments insisted that they intended at the very least to regain all the territories seized by Israel in June, 1967. Some gave particular stress to the restoration of Arab control over the Old City because of its special religious and emotional significance to the Arabs and to all Muslims and because, as one Arab put it, the Israelis "have made a martyr out of Jerusalem and given the Arabs a cause." [42] Even moderate King Hussein, who would normally have been far readier than other Arab leaders to consider a final settlement with Israel, frequently stressed that, unless the Old City, as well as other parts of the west bank, were returned to Jordan, the war with Israel would inevitably be renewed some day.[43] In the past, Jordan had gained political influence and prestige from her control of the strategically and religiously important Old City, and she had earned much desperately needed foreign exchange from the many tourists who visited the holy places. Thus, Hussein's ability to come to some terms with Israel, as well as his country's chances for economic and political survival, could well depend upon whether the Old City and other west-bank areas would be ultimately returned. But, unfortunately for both Jordan and for the hopes for peace, the Israelis firmly decided that the Old City was their most cherished territorial acquisition and that regardless of the costs they would absolutely refuse to give it up. To make this perfectly clear, of all the Arab areas seized in June, 1967, they quickly and formally annexed only the Jordanian sector of Jerusalem.

The Arab leaders united in their demand for an Israeli withdrawal from the Old City and in their objection to the proposals made for internationalizing only this part. In the months following their defeat, the Arab governments had to reappraise their whole situation, and because of the gravity and complexity of their problem, many of their future policies and actions were shrouded with uncertainty. Thus, some Arab leaders remained unsure as to whether they should revive their former demands for the internationalization of all Jerusalem. With Israel in complete control of the entire city, such a solution could have considerable appeal to the Arabs, especially since only Israel would have to do any withdrawing. Even Jordan would probably prefer internationalization to Israel's continued sovereignty over the Holy City.

There remained widespread opposition in the UN to Israel's annexation of the Old City and considerable support for some kind of international regime. Some officials, like President Charles de Gaulle, felt that neither a divided nor a united city, but only an internationalized one, could permanently remove the Jerusalem issue as a source of international and interreligious contention. Nevertheless, there was also an awareness of the tremendous practical difficulties standing in the way of establishing an international regime. A number of governments began to think in terms of a compromise solution which would provide some international status and protection for the holy places themselves, no matter who had actual sovereignty over the whole city. Yet, they had to face the fact that the UN was still on record in favor of internationalization and in strong opposition to Israel's annexation of the Old City.

From the beginning it should have been clear that the Jerusalem question was emotionally and politically tied to, and could not be resolved in complete isolation from, other major Arab-Israeli issues. Nevertheless, for many years prior to the June War, when the Arabs and Israelis shared the city, the Jerusalem controversy had come to play a far less important role than did the refugee, water, and border problems in aggravating Arab-Israeli feelings and in obstructing the path to peace. Israel's wresting of the Old City from the Arabs and laying claim to the whole city, however, suddenly brought the Jerusalem question to the fore once again and made it one of the most dangerous bones of contention between the opposing parties. In the light of emotional and political conditions in both the Arab world and Israel, it is difficult to see how the Arab governments could dare to make peace with Israel without the return of the Old City or how the Israeli government could dare to relinquish voluntarily any part of Jerusalem. The June War and Israel's annexation of the Old City did not finally settle the Jerusalem issue. On the contrary, these events in many ways complicated and magnified the problem—and made the Holy City a major, potential cause for another Arab-Israeli war.

CHAPTER VI

The Arab Refugees

The Palestine War uprooted hundreds of thousands of Palestine Arabs, Christian as well as Muslim, and turned most of them into bitter, resentful, and restless refugees living in crowded camps near the borders of Israel. Over the years the number of refugees steadily rose, their bitterness and discontent intensified, and their political influence increased and spread throughout the Arab world. Then came the June, 1967, war. The defeat of the Arabs and the extensive territorial acquisitions of the Israelis in some ways radically altered—but did not improve —the refugee situation. By suddenly bringing hundreds of thousands of Palestine refugees under Israeli control, by driving many thousands from their homes and camps once again, and by forcing tens of thousands of Syrians, Jordanians, and Egyptians to join the ranks of the refugees for the first time, Israel's military victory added formidable new dimensions and complications to the already perplexing refugee problem.

Arab Exodus, 1948

Immediately after the UN General Assembly passed the partition resolution on November 29, 1947, serious clashes broke out between the Arab and Jewish communities in Palestine. Fearfully recalling the bloody communal skirmishes which took place during the Arab revolt in the 1930's, some 30,000 upper- and middle-class Arabs left Palestine for safer areas. The loss of so many key people soon led to a serious breakdown in economic, communications, and administrative services and in political leadership in numerous Palestine Arab communities. As the fighting spread and intensified, many more thousands of frightened Arabs fled their homes to escape areas of combat and to seek food and other necessities of life. After April 1, 1948, the Arab exodus accelerated as a result of several successful Jewish military offensives into Arab-inhabited territories and terroristic attacks by the Irgun and the Stern Gang against Arab civilians, like the massacre of 250 men, women, and children in the village of Deir Yaseen, to spread panic among the

Arabs and to cause them to flee whenever Jewish forces approached. Even before the armies from the neighboring Arab states moved into Palestine when the mandate ended on May 15, 1948, approximately 200,000 Palestine Arabs had already become refugees.[1]

After May 15, many Arabs in combat areas fled their villages. Israelis claimed that their leaders had ordered them to leave until they could return with the victorious Arab armies. The Arabs denied this and held that Palestine Arabs had been urged to remain in their villages.[2]

The Arab exodus accelerated after the first truce ended and the Israeli army assumed the offensive on most fronts and penetrated deeply into many Arab-inhabited areas. At that time the Israeli authorities used both military force and psychological warfare to compel as many Arabs as possible to leave their homes because this would: (1) lessen the danger of Arab espionage and threats to Israeli lines of communication; (2) provide desperately needed land and buildings for the Jewish immigrants pouring in; (3) weaken the neighboring Arab states and interfere with their military efforts by forcing them to cope with a vast and unexpected refugee problem which their relatively primitive economy and administrative machinery, already overtaxed by the war, were ill-equipped to handle; and (4) give Israel a "trump card" which could be used in future political bargaining. From the Lydda-Ramleh section alone some 60,000 Arabs were ordered by the Israelis to leave on such short notice that they were able to take few if any of their possessions. Moreover, many of them suffered greatly from the lack of food and water, from the extreme heat, and from exhaustion during their long trek to Transjordanian-held territory. Evacuated Arab villages undesirable for Jewish habitation were destroyed by the Israelis so that the former inhabitants would be less likely to try to return. As UN Mediator Count Folke Bernadotte informed the UN, by the end of the second military phase of the war, "Almost the whole of the Arab population [had] fled or [been] expelled from the area under Jewish occupation." [3]

During the second and permanent truce period, illegal Israeli military offensives caused many more thousands of Arabs to leave their homes. UN officials reported the following: (1) as a result of the Israeli attacks in the Negev in October, 1948, about 30,000 Arabs fled to Transjordan alone, not counting those who escaped to Egyptian-controlled territory; (2) additional thousands abandoned their homes during another Israeli offensive in the Negev in December; (3) a "new influx of refugees into Lebanon" was created by the Israeli occupation of western Galilee in October, 1948, and by the "systematic" and "extensive looting" and the destruction of Arab villages there; and (4) "numerous refugees" entered Transjordan when Israeli troops seized the area north of the Gulf of Aqaba in March, 1949.[4]

Even after the armistice agreements were concluded in 1949, additional thousands of Arabs were expelled from Israeli-controlled territory. For example, in the fall of 1950 and the summer of 1953, large numbers of Arabs, especially Bedouins, were compelled to flee into Egypt, while in 1951 many Arab inhabitants of the Israeli-Syrian Demilitarized Zone were forced to leave their homes.[5]

EARLY UN EFFORTS

During the spring and summer of 1948, the neighboring Arab states made great efforts to help the Palestine refugees, but the refugees' enormous and continuing needs soon overwhelmed their meager resources. They then appealed to the UN Mediator and to the UN itself for help.

The gravity of the situation led Count Bernadotte to take interim relief measures pending action by the UN General Assembly. Emergency aid in the form of food and other essential supplies was provided at his request by a number of governments and private agencies. A relief program was instituted under the control of a UN Director of Disaster Relief assisted by the World Health Organization and other agencies associated with the UN. Bernadotte also tried to alleviate the situation by asking Israel to repatriate some of the refugees. Although he assured her that the refugees seeking repatriation would be carefully screened by UN officials to eliminate potential security risks, Israel refused his request on the ground that she could not take such a perilous action while a state of war continued. Bernadotte, disappointed with Israel's response, reported to the UN:

> It is . . . undeniable that no settlement can be just and complete if recognition is not accorded to the rights of the Arab refugee to return to the home from which he has been dislodged by the hazards and strategy of the armed conflict. . . . The exodus resulted from the panic created by the fighting in their communities, by rumors concerning real or alleged acts of terrorism, or expulsion. It would be an offense against the principles of elemental justice if those innocent victims of the conflict were denied the right to return to their homes while Jewish immigrants flow into Palestine.

He also contended that because of "large-scale looting, pillaging and plundering and of instances of destruction of villages without military necessity," Israel's liability to "restore private property to its Arab owners and to indemnify those owners of property wantonly destroyed" was "clear." [6]

In response to the appeals of the Mediator and, to some extent, of the Arabs as well, the General Assembly passed two important resolutions during its Third Session. The first [212(III)], passed unanimously on November 19, 1948, attempted to deal with the humanitarian aspect of the refugee question. It instructed the UN Secretary-General to appoint a Director of UN Relief for Palestine Refugees (UNRPR) and to advance up to $5,000,000 immediately from the UN Working Capital Fund for starting relief operations as quickly as possible. It also urged all members to contribute $32,000,000 to a special fund to provide for relief operations until August 31, 1949. The second resolution [194(III)], passed on December 11, established a Conciliation Commission and instructed it to "take steps to assist the Governments and authorities concerned to achieve a final peace settlement of all questions outstanding between them," and to "facilitate the repatriation, resettlement and economic and social rehabilitation of the refugees and the payment of compensation" to them. A key section of this resolution was contained in paragraph 11:

> Resolves that the refugees wishing to return to their homes and live in peace with their neighbours should be permitted to do so at the earliest practicable date, and that compensation should be paid for the property of those choosing not to return and for the loss or damage to property which, under the principles of international law or in equity, should be made by the Governments or authorities responsible.

Although the Arab states voted against this latter resolution and continued to oppose the November 29, 1947, partition resolution, within a few months they started to change their position. By early 1949, increasing numbers of Arab officials began to realize that, at least for the immediate future, the enforcement of the refugee and territorial provisions of these two resolutions would give them far more than they could actually hope to attain on their own because of their military weakness vis-à-vis Israel. In fact, the Arabs soon became the strongest advocates of UN implementation of the refugee and territorial provisions of these resolutions.

UNRPR assumed responsibility for organizing a comprehensive but temporary relief program and acted as an over-all coordinating and planning body. Actual operational activities were entrusted to the International Committee of the Red Cross, the League of Red Cross Societies, and the American Friends Service Committee. The World Health Organization, the Food and Agricultural Organization, and other UN specialized agencies contributed supplies, experienced personnel, and other services.

The Conciliation Commission (composed of representatives from France, Turkey, and the United States) began its activities with high hopes. It soon discovered, however, that the views of the Arabs and Israelis were so irreconcilable that a final solution of their differences would be considerably harder to achieve than was originally anticipated. Convinced from their own studies that the refugee problem was the most pressing and basic of all, the members of the commission tried for some months to resolve it in accordance with the provisions of paragraph 11 of Resolution 194(III). The commission believed that a solution of the refugee question would help not only to relieve human suffering, but also to open the way to progress in dealing with other points in dispute.

The Arab states insisted that the refugee issue had to be dealt with satisfactorily before they would seriously discuss other matters. Israel's initial position was that the return of the refugees was contingent upon the establishment of formal peace; otherwise the repatriated refugees could pose a threat to her security. But it was not long before Israel began to oppose the whole idea of repatriation and to insist that even if a peace agreement were reached, the "real solution" of the refugee question would have to be based upon the resettlement of all the refugees in the Arab states.[7] Actually, as early as June 16, 1948, Prime Minister Ben-Gurion took the position before his cabinet that "no Arab refugee should be admitted back." [8] As Kenneth Bilby, reporter for the *New York Herald Tribune,* indicated, "At the beginning the Israeli government actually led public opinion" in opposing repatriation, although later it was to use "as justification [for its policy] the possibility that it would be overthrown through popular indignation if it agreed to a large return of the refugees." He also wrote that Israel had been encouraging large numbers of Jewish immigrants to enter Israel as quickly as possible partly to use them as an "argument" as to why Israel "could not allow the Arabs to return—the policy of *fait accompli."* [9]

By the spring of 1949, Western and UN officials began to grow impatient with Israel's refusal to abide by the repatriation provision in Resolution 194(III). The American government exerted increasing pressure on Israel in the hope of influencing her to accept the return of at least 200,000 to 300,000 refugees. In a strong note to Ben-Gurion on May 29, 1949, President Truman expressed his "deep disappointment at the failure" of Israel to make any concessions on the refugee issue, "interpreted Israel's attitude as dangerous to peace," insisted that "tangible refugee concessions should be made now as an essential preliminary to any prospect for a general settlement," and threatened that "the United States would reconsider its attitude toward Israel." [10]

Under these and other pressures, the Israeli government finally decided to modify its position slightly. In June, Israel expressed a willingness to accept the return of the refugees in the Gaza Strip if her sovereign rights to this area were acknowledged by the Arabs and if international aid were given to help resettle the refugees in Israel. This proposal proved generally unacceptable to the Arabs, the Conciliation Commission, and even to the American government. Later, pressed again by the United States, Israel offered to take 100,000 refugees, but only if she could settle them where they would not endanger her security and would best fit into her plans for economic development and if the Arabs would agree to a general peace settlement at the same time. Neither the Arabs nor the UN and the United States found this offer adequate. Besides, strong opposition to it quickly developed in Israel for by this time most Israelis were opposed to the repatriation of any refugees. Influenced by this growing internal opposition, Israeli officials hurriedly withdrew their new offer and sought to reassure their people that they would stand fast against the principle of repatriation.[11]

Late in the summer of 1949, the United States made another effort to resolve the refugee issue. American officials expressed their belief that the Arabs would negotiate a peace settlement if Israel were willing to take back a substantial number of refugees and to surrender Galilee and the southern section of the Negev in exchange for the Gaza Strip. President Truman personally pressed Israel to accept these terms, but without success.[12]

By the latter part of the summer, the Conciliation Commission was able to report only a few minor achievements. Jordan and Syria had formally informed the commission that they would receive those refugees who did not want to be repatriated. (Lebanon and Egypt had contended that they were already too overpopulated to be able to absorb any significant number of the refugees.) The Arabs and Israelis had agreed to set up a mixed committee of experts to deal with the matter of refugees' blocked bank accounts in Israel. Induced by the commission, Israel agreed to repatriate a limited number of refugees under a "reunion of families" plan. To quiet internal opposition to this move, it was stressed that the complete reunion of some families would help eliminate one major cause for Arab infiltration into Israel, alleviate the deteriorating economic conditions of those Arab families in Israel cut off from their breadwinners, and restore the normal family life so necessary to make loyal citizens of the Arabs still residing in Israel.[13]

Having failed to make any important headway in solving the refugee question by political means, the Conciliation Commission decided in late August, 1949, to try an economic approach. It set up an Economic

Survey Mission with Gordon Clapp, formerly of the Tennessee Valley Authority (TVA), as chairman. The mission was instructed to

> examine the economic situation arising from the recent hostilities in the Near East and ... recommend to the Conciliation Commission means of overcoming resultant economic dislocations, of reintegrating the refugees into the economic life of the area, and of creating the economic conditions which will be conducive to the establishment of permanent peace.

In the meantime, the commission suspended further attempts at settling the refugee issue until the mission could present its report.[14]

Initially, the members of the Economic Survey Mission had hoped that, after some study, they would be able to recommend the construction of several large-scale projects which could ultimately integrate most refugees into the economic life of the area. They soon discovered, however, that there were "many obstacles," especially political and emotional ones, to economic development. Any comprehensive scheme for developing the Jordan River system would require political cooperation between Israel and the Arab states, illustrating, as Gordon Clapp put it, the "inseparability of political and engineering planning of a major water resource." [15] Since neither side was prepared to provide the necessary cooperation, the mission warned that

> the region is not ready, the projects are not ready, the people and governments are not ready for large-scale development of the region's basic river systems or major undeveloped areas. To press forward on such a course is to pursue folly and frustration and thereby delay sound economic growth.

Because of the "realities" of the situation, the mission members proposed that stress should be placed on creating a series of "pilot demonstration projects," including small irrigation works, roadbuilding, and small dams, in the hope that these would provide immediate employment for some of the refugees and useful experience for those administering the program and would set the stage for larger projects. They recommended that the General Assembly set up a special agency and supply it with $49,000,000 to carry out a relief and works program for an eighteen-month period. The Arab states were asked to contribute an additional $6,000,000 in the form of materials, tools, and equipment.[16]

On December 8, 1949, the General Assembly passed Resolution 302(IV) (introduced by the United States, Britain, France, and Turkey to put the mission's recommendations into effect) without a single negative vote and with only the Soviet bloc and South Africa abstaining. This resolution reaffirmed paragraph 11 of Resolution 194(III), established a UN Relief and Works Agency for Palestine Refugees (UNRWA), and authorized it to spend up to $54,900,000 on a relief and works program during an eighteen-month period. While accusing Israel of using the refugees as a "political pawn" for achieving "political advantages and territorial gains" and criticizing the UN for failing to enforce earlier resolutions, the Arabs nevertheless supported Resolution 302(IV) because it would provide relief and economic assistance to the refugees without prejudicing their right to repatriation. Israel, while voting for the resolution and conceding the need to provide temporary relief and to promote works projects, continued to blame the Arabs for the refugee situation and to insist that she would not allow the return of the refugees. At this time, Poland led the Soviet bloc and several other states in backing some of Israel's views on the repatriation issue. On the other hand, Pakistan, Britain, France, and many other countries upheld the right of the refugees to return to their homes and urged Israel to abide by the UN decision on this subject.[17]

UN officials soon discovered that the Arab governments were still hesitant about cooperating with efforts to organize a large-scale development program, but this attitude changed after a meeting of the Arab League Council in June, 1950. The council issued a statement which advised its members to accept major projects as long as the UN could assure them that the rights of the refugees to repatriation and compensation would not be jeopardized by such a step. By late July, 1950, Egypt, Jordan, Lebanon, and Syria began consultations with UNRWA on works projects. By the end of the summer the Conciliation Commission was able to report that it had

> received the impression that these [Arab] governments are inclining more and more to the view that the problem cannot be fully solved by the return of the refugees to their homes; and that consequently the settlement—either temporary or permanent—of a considerable number of refugees in the Arab countries must also be contemplated in order to achieve a complete and final solution of the problem.[18]

UNRWA and the Conciliation Commission also found that the Palestine refugees "invariably displayed an extremely emotional and deep-seated desire to return to their homes." The average refugee was "tired of his present condition," was "resentful of his plight," and blamed his troubles on the UN and the Western powers. In spite of the fact that the Arab is a "confirmed individualist," and is not readily willing to follow those advocating a change in his traditional way of life, subversive groups were able to exploit his misery for "political and other ends." In fact, the refugee situation had become so grave that it constituted "a serious threat to the peace and stability" of the area. The UN was warned that it had no choice but to continue providing money for a relief and works program if it hoped to prevent conditions from deteriorating still further. The UN was advised that because of the lack of resources, few major projects were possible within the four Arab host states. As a consequence, only part of the refugee population could ever hope to be resettled within the host countries even if all the potential development projects were actually completed.[19]

In December, 1950, the General Assembly readily passed two resolutions dealing with the refugee question. The first resolution [393(V)], based upon the recommendations of UNRWA, authorized the spending of $20,000,000 for relief and set up a $30,000,000 "re-integration fund" to be utilized for works projects "without prejudice to the provisions of paragraph 11 of General Assembly resolution 194(III)." The second resolution [394(V)] asked the Arabs and Israelis to engage without delay in either direct or indirect discussions under the auspices of the Conciliation Commission or independently in an endeavor to resolve all questions in dispute. It also directed the commission to establish a Refugee Office which would work out arrangements for the implementation of paragraph 11 of Resolution 194(III) and would continue consultations with the Arabs and Israelis regarding measures to be taken for the protection of the refugees' property and other interests.

Despite the passage of the second resolution, by the early part of 1951 the Conciliation Commission reached the conclusion that there was little hope of making any headway in resolving any major Arab-Israeli problem in the immediate future. It therefore decided for the time being, to suspend all efforts aimed at conciliation and to concentrate, instead, on those few matters of limited scope which held out a possibility of success. Thus, the commission worked to attain agreement on the release of the refugees' blocked bank accounts in Israel and began to examine the technical and legal phases of the compensation issue. This was done in belief that "every positive result obtained in specific aspects of the refugee problem [would] bring it nearer to the fulfillment of" its main task of ultimately bringing about a final settlement of the refugee and other disputes.[20]

In August, 1951, the United States persuaded the Conciliation Commission to make one more attempt to find a solution to the refugee question. The commission, in turn, persuaded Israel and the Arab states to send special representatives to meet with it in Paris in September.

The commission contended that circumstances had changed so much since 1948 that it was now unrealistic to try to repatriate all Arab refugees. It suggested that Israel should agree to repatriate "specified numbers of Arab refugees in categories which can be integrated into the economy of the State of Israel and who wish to return to live in peace with their neighbors." The remainder would be resettled in the Arab world. Israel would pay to those not repatriated a "global sum based upon the evaluation arrived at by the Commission's Refugee Office" and upon "Israel's ability to pay." Both sides would agree to a mutual release of all blocked accounts and to a mutual cancellation of all war damage claims. The refugees would be informed of actual conditions existing in Israel to help them decide whether to request repatriation or not.[21]

Both the Arabs and the Israelis promptly opposed the commission's new proposals. The Arabs accused the commission of trying to sabotage existing UN resolutions and of "exceeding its mandate in submitting proposals which had already been subject to [UN] decisions." The Israelis, in turn, were more opposed than ever to any repatriation as a result of the development of a major exodus of Jews from Iraq and other Arab countries. Israel claimed that a virtual exchange of populations had taken place and that the sudden influx of several hundred thousand Jews from the Arab world and elsewhere into her small land area had made it "unrealistic," if not impossible, for her to repatriate any of the refugees. The passage in early 1951 of an Iraqi law which set up a Custodian of Jewish Property with power to control the properties of the departed Iraqi Jews and the fact that these Jews had organized themselves into a powerful pressure group within Israel caused Israeli officials to take a still harder attitude on the compensation issue as well. Israel now made it clear that in any future negotiations on the subject of refugee compensation she would hold the Arab governments responsible for paying for Jewish properties abandoned in Iraq and other Arab countries.[22]

To add to the Conciliation Commission's difficulties, the Paris Conference was held at an unpropitious time. As will be seen in the next chapter, the Lake Huleh dispute between Israel and Syria in the spring of 1951 and the bristling differences between Israel and Egypt over Egyptian restrictions on the shipping of Israeli goods through the Suez Canal had dragged Arab-Israeli relations to their lowest level since the Palestine War. The influence of the Western powers in the Middle East was further undermined by the increasingly strained relations between Britain and several Arab states, the development of the Iranian oil crisis, and the rapid growth of anti-West feeling. Thus, from the beginning the chances of any real success at Paris were very slim indeed. Although negotiations dragged on for some time, the commission finally realized that the situation was hopeless and terminated the conference.

Having failed to make any progress on a political level, the commission concentrated its efforts once more on the less formidable aspects of the refugee problem. It finally succeeded in obtaining Arab-Israeli agreement to the setting up of mixed committees to deal with refugee blocked accounts in Israel. At first, these committees made little progress, but after the relatively moderate Moshe Sharett replaced Ben-Gurion as prime minister in November, 1953, Israel and some of the Arab states were able to come to terms on this matter. By June 30, 1960, £2,790,045 of Arab refugee accounts had been released, and more funds were freed later. The Conciliation Commission also succeeded in obtaining the release of Arab safe deposits blocked in Israel and, with the cooperation of Israel and the Arab states, started to make some headway in the technical work of identifying immovable refugee properties in Israel and of placing specific values on some of them. However, the commission was unable to obtain any positive action or commitment from Israel on the question of compensation. Israel insisted she would not reveal her detailed plans for compensation until other Palestine issues, such as those involving final peace and the end of the Arab economic blockade, had been settled. Furthermore, the Israeli government had formally taken over all Arab refugee properties and was using them for its own needs. It would not allow the commission any voice in their administration or final disposition. Until the late 1950's, the commission was obliged to restrict its work almost wholly to technical aspects of the refugee question, and neither the Arabs nor other members of the UN seriously sought to revive the commission's efforts at general conciliation.[23]

UN RELIEF AND WORKS AGENCY (UNRWA)

When it was established in December, 1949, UNRWA was given funds and authority to carry on relief and works projects for only eighteen months because there was then great expectation that the refugee and other Arab-Israeli problems would soon be solved by final peace treaties. Although no significant progress was made in dealing with any of the major Arab-Israeli disputes, on December 2, 1950, the UN General Assembly hopefully extended UNRWA's mandate for only one year. But by the summer of 1951, the Director of UNRWA concluded that the refugee question remained as formidable as ever and that it would require far more time and money to resolve than was originally anticipated. He recommended that the General Assembly approve a three-year program involving the expenditure of $50,000,000 for relief and $200,000,000 for development projects. Refugee participation in this program was not to prejudice their rights to repatriation or compensation.

Despite the warnings of the UN Economic Survey Mission that to press forward with large-scale projects before the Arabs and Israelis were psychologically and politically prepared for such a step would merely result in "folly and frustration," most UN members, impatient with the lack of progress being made, believed that an economic solution to the refugee issue was worth the search. On January 26, 1952, the General Assembly passed Resolution 513 (VI) which, in line with the recommendations of UNRWA's Director, provided for a three-year $250,000,000 relief and works program.

Armed with this new, longer mandate, UNRWA did what it could to reintegrate the refugees within the three-year time limit. By 1954, it was able to report that some progress had been made. For instance, Iraq had admitted and assumed full responsibility for approximately 5,000 refugees, and Libya had expressed a willingness to absorb about 6,000 more. Israel had agreed to take care of the 19,000 Arab refugees located within her borders. The Jordanian government had offered full citizenship to all Palestinians in Jordan, although it was unable to provide work for most of the refugees. Syria had allowed the refugees living within her territory to seek employment on the same basis as her own citizens. UNRWA had begun a vocational training program for a small number of the refugees, who easily found employment after they had attained new skills. UNRWA had started providing loans to some of the more able refugees so that they could set up small business enterprises and become self-supporting. Moreover, in 1953, several agreements had been concluded with Syria, Jordan, and Egypt to develop various projects, including one to draw water from the Yarmouk River to irrigate the lower Jordan River valley and another to irrigate a part of the Sinai Peninsula with water from the Nile River. An expenditure of about $110,000,000 on these projects was envisaged, and it was anticipated that through them 150,000 to 200,000 refugees could eventually become self-supporting. Partly as a consequence of these favorable developments and especially as a result of the continued belief in the potential value of works projects, on December 4, 1954, the General Assembly passed Resolution 818(IX), which decided, "without prejudice to the rights of the refugees to repatriation or compensation," to extend the mandate of UNRWA for another five years and to "maintain the rehabilitation fund of $200 million." [24]

At the same time UNRWA indicated a little progress made in some areas, it also reported that the refugee problem remained as large and explosive as ever. By 1953 there were still 872,000 refugees depending upon relief.[25]

This number of refugees was increasing rapidly because the birth rate greatly exceeded the death rate and because many of the refugees previously capable of caring for their personal needs from their own resources now found these resources depleted. UNRWA considered that the food, clothing, and housing conditions of the refugees remained "inadequate." For instance, UNRWA was spending an average of only ten cents a day on each refugee for food, shelter, welfare, health care, and education. While many thousands of names were illegally on the refugee registration rolls (primarily in Jordan), many other thousands of needy refugees (especially children born in Jordan in more recent years) were denied relief aid largely because of the lack of funds. In addition, UNRWA estimated that there were more than 300,000 hardship cases among the Palestinians who were not eligible, for one reason or another, to receive UNRWA help. These included, among others, the following: (1) 165,000 "economic refugees"—Palestinians no longer able to earn a living since their farm lands were in Israel while their homes remained in Jordan; (2) 60,000 natives of the Gaza Strip who lost their means of livelihood as a result of Israel's acquisition of areas which formerly had provided them with work and markets; and (3) 7,000 Azazme Bedouins forcibly expelled from Israel in 1950. UNRWA repeatedly, though unsuccessfully, appealed to the UN to supply it with more funds so that it could give at least some assistance to these destitute Palestinians.[26]

By 1953 UNRWA also found it "increasingly clear that the economic, political and social obstacles to rehabilitation were much more serious than had been anticipated." That is why it had been so difficult to resettle or repatriate any significant number of the refugees. For example, by June, 1955, only $18,743,150 of the proposed $200,-000,000 reintegration fund had been expended, mostly on small-scale projects, and relatively few refugees had been made self-supporting in the process. The major obstacles which confronted UNRWA were: (1) the availability of only meager physical resources in the area; (2) the lack of skills and training among the refugees; (3) the attitude of the refugees and its influence upon the Arab governments; (4) the unfavorable political conditions in the Middle East; and (5) the lack of adequate UNRWA funds.[27]

Among the four Arab host states where nearly all of the refugees lived, Jordan (with over half the refugees), Egypt (with nearly one-fourth of the refugees living in the crowded Gaza Strip), and Lebanon (with more than one-tenth of the refugees) were poor in natural resources and already overpopulated. Only Syria (with another tenth of the refugees) was reasonably well endowed with land and water resources, but she had a rapidly growing population of which many had little or no land for their own needs. Moreover, the Arab world lacked natural resources, except for oil, and contained only about the same amount of arable land as may be found in the state of Iowa. Aside from the proposed Sinai and Yarmouk-Jordan River projects, UNRWA reported that there appeared "to be no practical possibilities for major rehabilitation projects in the areas in which the largest numbers of the refugees" were living. Even if these two large-scale projects were carried out, they would ultimately take care of a "maximum of 200,000 refugees"—or not very many more than the anticipated increase in the refugee population during the period required to complete the projects. Since most of the refugees would have to cross national boundaries or demarcation lines before they could find sufficient land and jobs to enable them to become self-supporting, UNRWA urged the UN to initiate an economic development program for the Middle East as a whole. UNRWA warned, however, that the Arab governments would hesitate to hand over to the refugees, rather than to their own underprivileged citizens, the best parcels of land as they became available through costly and time-consuming development projects. Any early, extensive refugee resettlement would obviously require large numbers of these poverty-stricken native inhabitants to forego any significant improvement in their own economic well-being for many years because their own basic needs and those of the refugees could not be satisfied at the same time.[28]

Refugee reintegration was also being hindered by the fact that most of the refugees lacked any specialized skills or education. In 1948–49, about 20 per cent of all the adult refugees had some particular skills or professions useful in the host countries. These fortunate individuals had no difficulty in becoming self-supporting. The other 80 per cent, either farmers or untrained workers, were unable to find employment because they were living in areas already saturated with farmers and laborers. Over the years UNRWA was able to provide a vocational or university education for only a relatively small number of refugees, who were then able to find jobs in many parts of the Arab world because of its great need for specialists of all kinds. UNRWA warned that merely supplying economic aid to further the development of the Arab states would not be enough, for "the same technological process that brings higher total employment also brings a decrease in the relative need" for the unskilled worker. Thus, even if the refugees were allowed to cross international boundaries, unless they were first provided with some kind of special training, they would be "virtually unemployable in the kind of market that accompanies an era of technological progress" and would "constitute more of a drag than an asset to the economy" of the country that accepted them.[29]

The attitude of the refugees produced yet another obstacle. UNRWA reports repeatedly emphasized that the refugees' desire to return to their homes had not only "not diminished," but that it had actually been "strengthened and encouraged by the General Assembly's resolutions on repatriation." Although most refugees wished to become self-supporting —as indicated by an increased interest in vocational training and individual self-support programs—a "large majority" of them considered that participation in works projects was "tantamount to renunciation of the rights" to repatriation or compensation. The degree of the refugees' resistance usually depended upon the nature, location, and size of the projects. The larger the project and the further away it was from "Palestine," the greater was the opposition to it and the fear of accepting it. So the refugees accepted small-scale projects and grants to set up local business enterprises in areas close to Israel while they strongly objected to any schemes which might have been proposed for northern Syria and Iraq even though these regions contained far greater resources and economic potentialities. At times, some of the refugees hesitated seeking employment or self-support loans, fearing that, if their jobs or business enterprises did not last, they might be unable to regain their ration cards when they needed them again. For many years, the refugees expressed their hostility towards the UN (which they held primarily responsible for their wretched plight) through attacks on UNRWA's property and personnel and through occasional failure to cooperate with UNRWA's activities. Such emotional reactions proved harmful to the interests of the refugees for they merely weakened the ability of UNRWA to help them.

Various unfavorable political developments in the Middle East during the middle 1950's added further complications to the already difficult refugee situation. For example, serious border clashes, raids, and counterraids and a mounting arms race in 1955 and 1956 brought about a dangerous deterioration in Arab-Israeli feelings and relations which, in turn, made both sides less willing than ever to yield in any way on the refugee issue.[30]

Israel's adamant stand was also strengthened by certain internal and external developments during this period. In the July, 1955, Knesset elections, such activist groups as the Herut Party made substantial gains at the expense of the moderate parties. The election results reflected the growth of strong nationalist and anti-Arab feelings among the Israeli people. In November, 1955, Ben-Gurion took over from the moderate Moshe Sharett as prime minister, although Sharett remained as foreign minister. When Golda Meir, an advocate of a tough policy towards the Arabs, replaced Sharett as foreign minister in the middle of 1956, his moderating influence was completely removed from the scene.

A number of external factors also encouraged Israel to refuse to make any concessions on the refugee question. The purchase by Egypt of large amounts of modern weapons from the Soviet bloc and the moves made in 1955 and 1956 to bring about closer political and military ties between some of the Arab states heightened Israel's fear and hostility. While the Eisenhower administration had initially sought to take a more neutral stand on Arab-Israeli issues than had President Truman's administration, during the middle 1950's many influential members of Congress and Jewish groups throughout the United States intensified their endeavors on behalf of Israel because her security seemed to be threatened. This tended to nullify President Eisenhower's efforts at neutrality. Moreover, although Franco-Israeli relations had not been especially warm in the earlier years, by the fall of 1956 France had become an unofficial ally of Israel, her primary supplier of modern military equipment, and her staunchest political and diplomatic defender inside and outside the UN. The new, close Franco-Israeli ties and the increasingly anti-Israeli position of the Russians helped to strengthen the potential ability of the West to apply effective pressures on Israel; yet Western governments, partly as a result of the powerful political influence of pro-Israeli groups and individuals, usually made no serious effort to apply the pressures at their disposal. Consequently, Israel felt confident that she could safely refuse to make any concessions or to abide by the UN resolutions involving the refugees.

The increase of governmental instability within some Arab countries and of friction between a number of Arab governments added to political complications. By the middle 1950's the conservative, pro-Western Iraqi monarchy faced growing internal unrest. After the fall of Colonel Adib al-Shishakli's dictatorship in 1954 and until she joined Egypt in the UAR in 1958, Syria was plagued with deep political divisions within the country and the army. Weak party coalitions in the Parliament found it difficult to stay in office. In Lebanon, the split between the Muslims and the Christians and between the Lebanese nationalists and the Arab nationalists became graver than ever. Jordanian King Hussein's pro-Western policies added so greatly to the discontent among the Palestinians within his country that between 1955 and 1958 he faced a number of threats and riots. Only in Egypt, under Colonel Nasser, did governmental stability remain generally unshaken.

Also in the middle 1950's there was a great rise in inter-Arab frictions and rivalries for leadership within the Arab world. The most momentous split was that which developed between the conservative, pro-Western Iraqi monarchy, at times backed by Hussein, and Egypt's progressive, neutralist Nasser regime, frequently supported by Syria. These rivalries became so bitter on several occasions that some efforts were made by one country to overthrow the government of another—as when Saudi Arabia and Egypt worked to overthrow King Hussein late in 1955. Generally speaking, the weaker the internal position an Arab leader held and/or the more intense the rivalry he faced with other Arab leaders, the more afraid he was to disregard popular emotions and pressures and the stronger the anti-Israeli stand he felt that he had to take, at least publicly. As a result of these developments, Arab officials usually felt it politically imperative to support all the refugee demands, and they found it very difficult to make any concessions on Arab-Israeli questions.

In addition, the Arab refugees, having won the sympathetic and active support of the Arab masses, were able to apply effective pressures on most of the host governments. Refugee influence was especially strong in Jordan (where the refugees constituted one-third of the population, while other Palestinians made up another third), Syria, and Lebanon. The refugees under Egyptian control were unable to exert any significant influence on the Egyptian government and people because they were kept almost completely confined to the Gaza Strip. As large numbers of the refugees moved into other parts of the Arab world, they tended to spread their intense feelings of bitterness and frustration beyond the host countries. The *New York Times* reported on December 8, 1957, that the scattering of the refugees had also caused the spread of the "power, ability and cold fury of the Palestinian exiles" with their "one goal— revenge." The ordinary Arab citizen might someday have forgotten the disgrace of the Palestine War, but "with the goading Palestinian in his midst . . . , he can never forget." The Director of UNRWA warned that

> the passage of time has not improved the prospects for a settlement of the problem and the longer the refugee problem remains unsolved, the more dangerous would be the consequences for the countries of the Near East. . . . It is no exaggeration to state that every aspect of life and human endeavor in the Near East is conditioned and complicated by the Palestine refugee problem. Its psychological, political and social repercussions are of no less significance than its economic and humanitarian aspects. . . . Unless the refugees are given the choice between repatriation and com-

pensation provided for in Resolution 194(III), or unless some other solution acceptable to all parties is found, it would be unrealistic for the General Assembly to believe that decisive progress can be accomplished by UNRWA towards the "reintegration of the refugees into the economic life of the Near East, either by repatriation or resettlement." [31]

The intrusion of the Cold War into the Middle East also added to existing political difficulties. Having failed to make any significant headway in promoting her own ambitions in the area through the backing of Israel, the Soviet Union began, in the early 1950's, to curry favor among the Arabs at the expense of Israel. The Western powers had alienated many Arabs by (1) their promotion of the Baghdad Pact; (2) the tactless manner in which the United States rejected Egypt's request for aid in building the Aswan Dam; (3) the strong economic and political measures taken against Egypt after she nationalized the Suez Canal Company; and (4) the military attack on the Suez Canal by Britain and France. The Russians skilfully exploited these Western blunders and played up to the rising tide of Arab nationalism in order to undermine further the position of the West in the Middle East and to facilitate the spread of their own influence in that area. Moreover, Russia's willingness to provide the Arabs with arms and political support tended to make them feel that there was no real need to soften their anti-Israeli position. These developments weakened the ability of the West to apply effective pressures on the Arabs in order to obtain concessions on the refugee issue. They also enabled the Soviet Union to promote not only stronger anti-Western feelings among the Arabs, but also greater Arab-Israeli hostility. At the same time, the Soviet Union gave neither the refugees nor the Arab governments any good reason to be grateful for her policies on the refugee question. Until the summer of 1967 the Soviet bloc governments never contributed any funds either directly or through UNRWA to help the refugees and frequently opposed Arab attempts to have the UN General Assembly order the Conciliation Commission to enforce UN resolutions dealing with refugee repatriation and compensation. Especially in the earlier years, Communist agitators occasionally sought to incite the refugees to riot and create disturbances, thus aggravating the internal security problems of the host governments.

UNRWA's efforts to bring about the reintegration of the refugees into the life of the area were also hampered by a serious lack of money. Although in its resolution of January 26, 1952, the General Assembly had authorized the establishment of a $200,000,000 rehabilitation fund,

UNRWA reported in 1956 that it had received only $37,000,000 of this amount. Approximately $18,700,000 of this sum had been spent, and the balance was kept as essential working capital. Because of the shortage of money, after 1955 UNRWA was unable to make any significant progress in promoting large-scale development schemes. It had to concentrate on smaller, self-help projects and on providing a limited number of individual grants. From 1956 to 1958, UNRWA was in such financial straits that it had to restrict expenditures on educational activities and to use money from the rehabilitation fund for essential relief purposes. As early as 1955 the UNRWA Director warned that even if political and other impediments to progress could be removed, it would still be necessary to provide far more than $200,000,000 and would take many years of effort to bring about the rehabilitation of the refugees because the economic obstacles had proved to be "much more serious than had been anticipated." Regardless of whether major development projects were actually carried out in the host states, about "two-thirds" of the refugees would still have to "cross a demarcation line or a national boundary, in one direction or another," to find employment. Even then, suitable work would have to be created. Therefore, only by means of a costly and long-range economic development program for the entire Middle East could there be any hope of successfully reintegrating the refugees into the area's economic life, either by resettlement or repatriation, without adversely affecting the economic well-being of the indigenous inhabitants.

Although UNRWA's financial position improved slightly after 1958, it still lacked sufficient funds for any major projects, so it concentrated its efforts on expanding vocational training and other forms of higher education. In this way it was anticipated that at least some of the younger refugees would be provided with sufficient training which would enable them to find useful work wherever they might ultimately live. When John H. Davis became UNRWA's director, he initiated a determined and relatively successful campaign to obtain funds for vocational and higher educational purposes from private individuals and groups, as well as from various governments. By the early 1960's, because UNRWA was able to give increasing numbers of the refugees higher education or vocational training, and also because some Arab countries were beginning to make substantial economic progress, more and more of the younger refugees were finding it possible to improve their standard of living.

In response to the occasional recommendations made by various states to terminate UN aid to the refugees, the UNRWA Director repeatedly warned of the "most serious human and political repercussions" which would develop if relief aid were ended prematurely or even drastically reduced. In the final analysis,

> UNRWA was one of the prices—and perhaps the cheapest— that the international community was paying for not having been able to solve with equity the political problems of the refugees. . . . UNRWA's work was surely well worth what it cost. If its existence was not of itself sufficient to solve the refugee problem, it nevertheless helped to maintain a more favorable climate for its [ultimate] solution. It was essential [therefore] to extend UNRWA's mandate until such time as the forces which would shape the future of the Middle East made it possible to solve the problem of the Palestine refugees.[32]

FURTHER U.S. AND UN EFFORTS

Impelled in the early 1950's by growing pressures from an impatient Congress to find some quick formula for solving the refugee problem, the American government decided in 1953 to seek an economic solution largely on its own initiative. In October, 1953, President Eisenhower sent a mission, headed by Eric Johnston, to press for Arab and Israeli acceptance of a regional development scheme for the entire Jordan River system worked out by the Charles T. Main engineering firm on behalf of the Tennessee Valley Authority which, in turn, had been acting on behalf of UNRWA. It was hoped that the carrying out of the Main Plan with considerable American financial aid would not only make it possible to resettle most of the refugees but would also promote sufficient Arab-Israeli contacts to provide a possible basis for a final political settlement between the parties. Unfortunately, Johnston's trip took place at an unpropitious time. Border strife, especially between Israel on the one hand and Jordan and Syria on the other, had seriously increased in scope and intensity. In fact, on October 14, Israel made a major "reprisal" raid on the Jordanian village of Qibya in which fifty-three Jordanians were killed.[33]

After Johnston had made several other trips to the Middle East in 1954 and 1955, considerable Arab-Israeli accord was reached on a number of technical aspects involved in the Johnston Plan (a modified version of the Main Plan). Nevertheless, major psychological and political obstacles continued to prevent any final agreement. The Arabs, distrustful of Israel and concerned about the political capital she might make of any direct Arab relations with her, insisted that all contacts be handled through the UN and that the UN supervise all phases of the project. Israel, however, opposed any UN involvement on the ground that this would result in an infringement of her sovereignty. Arab officials feared that by signing a formal convention with Israel they would be accused by their own people of having given implied political recognition to the state of Israel. Even Israel might then publicly proclaim such an action as being tantamount to recognition. The large-scale Israeli attack on the Gaza Strip on February 28, 1955, further raids and counterraids by both sides, and the sale of Soviet bloc arms to Egypt added to Arab-Israeli fears and lessened still more the chances for a successful agreement. In addition, American involvement in the Baghdad Pact, American failure to sell arms to Egypt, and other actions which antagonized the Arabs seriously weakened Johnston's position in the Arab world.

By August, 1955, after having carefully examined the whole Arab-Israeli situation over a period of months, most of the high State Department officials finally began to agree with those Middle East specialists both inside and outside the government who had been contending that there could be "no permanent solution to the refugee problem until there [was] a more favorable political atmosphere leading to a workable peace settlement between the Arab states and Israel" and that this problem could not be solved by economic means alone because of "the depth of the emotions and the character of the issues involved on both sides." [34] Secretary of State John Foster Dulles also concluded that some outside intervention was needed to break the existing political deadlock. Thus, in a speech on August 26, he openly sought to commit American policy to a "new course." He suggested that the Arabs and Israelis make such adjustments in their positions as would make it possible "to convert armistice lines of danger into boundary lines of safety." He expressed American willingness to guarantee any new boundaries that might be mutually agreed upon. He also recommended that the refugee dispute be solved through "the resettling and, to such an extent as may be feasible, repatriation" of the refugees. Israel would pay "compensation . . . due . . . to the refugees" with the help of an "international loan" in which the United States would be a "substantial" participant. [35]

With Britain's active cooperation, the American government pressed the Arabs and Israelis to accept Dulles' proposals as the basis for a final peace settlement. But neither the Arab nor the Israeli leaders were ready to accept them, especially since increasingly serious border clashes in late 1955 and early 1956 had brought Arab-Israeli relations close to a breaking point. In fact, only strong UN intervention in the spring of 1956 prevented the outbreak of large-scale fighting. Even though the UN succeeded in lessening the threat of war for several months, the situation deteriorated again by the middle of the summer. By the latter part of

October, Egypt and Israel were at war. These adverse developments naturally did not promote that favorable political atmosphere so essential to the achieving of any agreement on the refugee and other Arab-Israeli disputes. Thus, although for a long time after August, 1955, Dulles continued to urge the Arabs and the Israelis to accept his proposals, his efforts proved in vain.

At the Twelfth Session of the General Assembly late in 1957, a number of UN members, including the United States, expressed their impatience at the lack of progress in resolving the refugee question by threatening to withhold further financial support from UNRWA. The American action was undoubtedly prompted by the insistence of increasing numbers of congressmen—especially those who usually backed Israel's views—that they could not be expected to continue indefinitely to vote for large annual appropriations for UNRWA. Some legislators began to call for either a quick solution of the refugee question or an early termination of the UNRWA program. At the same time, State Department officials warned that "there was clearly no acceptable alternative to the extension of UNRWA" because its disappearance would result in "serious internal security problems for all the Arab host governments" and would cause a "blow to the general stability of the Near East, adversely affecting the security of Israel" and the best interests of the United States. They also cautioned that even reducing UNRWA's funds would arouse Arab emotions and aggravate political conditions in the area, and this would merely add to the difficulties involved and delay a final solution of the refugee and other Arab-Israeli differences.[36]

By the Thirteenth Session of the General Assembly, American and other UN delegates began to agree openly with UNRWA's Director that under the circumstances, UNRWA's work was "well worth what it cost." Yet many UN members continued to look for some kind of final solution to the refugee dilemma. Thus, in the fall of 1958 the General Assembly formally asked the UN Secretary-General to make a new study of the whole situation and submit his suggestions. In his 1959 report (A/4121), Secretary-General Dag Hammarskjold emphasized once again that the unfavorable psychological and political conditions provided the main obstacles and that until these were somehow overcome there could be little hope of making any significant progress in finding a solution to the refugee question. Nevertheless, he recommended the early initiation of a large-scale and long-range economic development program for the whole Middle East to raise the already low standard of living of the indigenous populations and, when circumstances permitted, to integrate the refugees through resettlement and repatriation. He advised that such a program would require a vast amount of money (from $1.5 to $2 billion by 1965 alone), extensive technical assistance, and many years of determined effort.

It was soon evident that the Arabs and Israelis were still far from ready to agree to and cooperate with any area-wide development scheme and that the large sums of money required would not be forthcoming. While Israel was pleased with much of the Secretary-General's report, the Arabs complained that he had placed too much stress on the economic aspects of the problem and too little stress on the refugees' rights to repatriation. Refugee leaders became so aroused over the report that they met in Lebanon and agreed, for the first time, to combine all of the different refugee groups into one organization, the Palestine Arab Congress. Finally united, even though it was to be for only a short period of time, the refugees were in a more powerful position to insist that the Arab governments reject the Secretary-General's proposals and take an even more determined stand on the principle of repatriation.[37]

After the failure of UNRWA and the Secretary-General to find a solution, some UN members decided to revive the diplomatic activities of the UN Conciliation Commission. The outcome was Resolution 1456(XIV), which the General Assembly passed on December 9, 1959. This resolution not only continued UNRWA's mandate for another three years, but it noted

> with deep regret that repatriation or compensation of the refugees, as provided for in paragraph 11 of ... Resolution 194(III), has not been effected, and that no substantial progress has been made in the programme endorsed in paragraph 2 of Resolution 513(VI) for the reintegration of the refugees either by repatriation or re-settlement and that, therefore, the situation of the refugees continues to be a matter of serious concern.

It also requested that the Conciliation Commission "make further efforts to secure the implementation of paragraph 11." This resolution, actively backed by the Arab members and the United States and opposed mainly by Israel, passed by a vote of eighty to zero with only Israel abstaining.[38]

The United States not only continued her practice of giving energetic diplomatic support to the commission, but she also involved herself even more directly in the situation. President John F. Kennedy addressed personal appeals to the leaders in the area. In an effort to allay Arab fears about the United States' attitude towards the existing UN resolutions, the President wrote special letters to a number of Arab leaders in May, 1961. In these letters he stated unequivocally that this Government's position is anchored and will continue to be anchored in the firm bedrock of support for General Assembly recommendations concerning the refugees and of action and impartial concern that these resolutions be implemented in a way most beneficial to the refugees.[39]

But all these renewed activities failed to produce any favorable results.

Finally, in desperation the commission decided to try a different approach. On August 21, 1961, it appointed Dr. Joseph E. Johnson, president of the Carnegie Endowment for International Peace, as its special representative to explore with Arab and Israeli officials practical means for dealing with the refugee problem. After months of study and private discussions, Dr. Johnson began to sound out the contending parties on certain tentative proposals: (1) each refugee would be given an opportunity, free from all external pressures, to express whether he preferred repatriation or resettlement; (2) Israel's legitimate security interests would be safeguarded by allowing her, subject to UN review, to reject individual Arabs as security risks; (3) both repatriation and resettlement would be handled on a gradual, "step-by-step process" and would be undertaken simultaneously; (4) a special fund, to which Israel would be expected to make a substantial contribution, would be set up to pay compensation for Arab properties left in Israel, as well as to provide financial help to assist the resettled refugees to become self-supporting; and (5) the UN would play a vital role in supervising all aspects and stages of the program.[40]

Both the Arabs states and Israel criticized the Johnson Plan. While the more moderate Arabs were not especially hostile to Johnson's suggestions, the extremist Arabs, led by many of the refugee leaders, complained that the suggestions placed too much emphasis on resettlement and too little on repatriation. They contended that the UN should stop trying to find solutions more acceptable to Israel and start concentrating on the enforcement of existing resolutions. Because of these strong pressures, even moderate Arab leaders felt it necessary to oppose the Johnson Plan, at least publicly. The Israelis, in turn, objected to any recommendations that included the principle of repatriation and insisted they could not accept any proposed solution for the refugee question except as part of a final peace settlement.[41]

Despite the failure of the Johnson Mission, on December 3, 1963, the UN General Assembly, by a vote of eighty-two to one (Israel) with fourteen abstentions, passed Resolution 1912(XVIII), which once again called upon the Conciliation Commission "to continue its efforts for the implementation of paragraph 11 of Resolution 194(III)." The United

States, however, prevailed upon the commission to give her a chance to cope with the matter through normal diplomatic channels. Thus, for many months American diplomats had a series of "quiet talks" with the parties concerned. Although these talks were reported to have been "useful," they too proved unsuccessful.[42]

By the early 1960's the position of the commission had been seriously weakened. Since Israel objected to the implementation of paragraph 11 of Resolution 194(III), she opposed the revival of the commission's nontechnical activities and advocated that the life of the commission be ended. While the Arabs had for many years been staunch supporters of the commission and especially of its mandate to carry out paragraph 11, they had never been happy with its composition. They had complained that France and the United States (two of the three members) were too pro-Israel to be impartial. Starting in 1961, they insisted that the commission's membership must either be enlarged or changed. Some Arabs even contended that no useful purpose would be served by keeping the commission in existence. Most Arabs, however, did not press this point too far for they feared that such a step might undermine those resolutions which they favored. In any case, by the early 1960's the Arabs had lost much of the enthusiasm which they had once held for the commission, and this made them less ready to cooperate with it.[43]

Realizing there was little immediate chance of obtaining any effective UN action on the repatriation issue, the Arabs began to press for the attainment of more limited objectives. Starting in 1960, they submitted to the General Assembly draft resolutions which called upon the UN to appoint a custodian to protect Arab refugee property in Israel, to collect the income from it, and to turn it over to the refugees. The Arabs argued that this would not only be fair to the refugees, but it would cut UNRWA's relief costs. Israel, maintaining that the UN had no competence to take over the administration of any property under her sovereign control and warning that she would not permit any custodian to function on her territory, vigorously opposed this new Arab move.[44]

Israel endorsed and encouraged certain draft resolutions which some of her friends from Africa, Latin America, and Europe had started to present to the General Assembly in the latter part of 1961. These resolutions proposed that the Arab and Israeli governments enter into direct negotiations to resolve the refugee and all other major problems. While Israel considered such resolutions "realistic," the Arabs claimed that by deliberately ignoring and even countermanding the repatriation and compensation provisions of earlier General Assembly decisions, these new proposals were contrived to help only Israel. The Arabs also insisted that if they ever did agree to negotiate, they would do so only under UN auspices and on the basis of existing resolutions. Since Israel had repeatedly refused to repatriate any refugees, to accept any significant boundary changes, or to allow the internationalization of Jerusalem, the Arabs argued that no useful purpose would be served by negotiations anyway.[45]

The United States took the lead in opposing both types of resolutions. She argued that by introducing new controversies and by further aggravating Arab-Israeli relations, the resolutions would make it still more difficult to find a solution to the refugee question. Since many other UN members agreed with the United States' point of view, neither the resolutions approved by the Arabs nor those backed by the Israelis could muster a sufficient number of votes for passage.

By this time most UN members had finally become convinced that the political climate in the Middle East was and would remain so unfavorable that it would not only be futile, but perhaps even harmful, to continue pressing for a definitive solution of the refugee problem before the Arabs and Israelis were psychologically prepared for such a step. Consequently, the Conciliation Commission was allowed to confine its activities once again to such technical matters as completing the release of blocked bank accounts, finishing its evaluation of all refugee properties in Israel, and preparing an index of the names of the owners. This was done in the hope that progress in these more limited areas would provide additional funds to some of the refugees, facilitate any future compensation operations, and possibly create a better atmosphere for future conciliation efforts. UNRWA's mandate was continued not only for humanitarian reasons, but also because it was realized that, as the New Zealand delegate to the UN stated, "If the Assembly were not prepared to act in the political field, it should at least act to ensure that the conditions of the refugees did not aggravate the political difficulties." [46]

In the meantime, the total number of refugees was growing by more than 30,000 each year. Moreover, according to a report (A/5813) by UNRWA in 1964, because the refugees lived in areas of limited economic opportunities, only about 10 to 20 per cent of them were able to become reasonably self-supporting. Between 40 and 50 per cent continued to be "destitute or nearly destitute," and 30 to 40 per cent, though partially self-supporting, remained in need of substantial outside aid. A large "hard core" of refugees continued to live "in poverty and dependence on the charity of their fellow men for the indefinite future." This was especially true for "most of the refugees . . . living in the Gaza Strip, a substantial part of those living in Jordan, and a significant number of those in other host states."

Although, prior to the June War, the General Assembly had adopted annually and by overwhelming majorities a series of resolutions which reiterated the right of the refugees to repatriation or compensation, neither the UN nor the major powers had ever revealed any serious intention of using those means available to them for their implementation. Even while voting for these resolutions a number of the larger Western states had nevertheless contended that the refugee dispute was basically between Israel and the Arab countries and that in the final analysis it was really up to them, not the UN, to solve it. This attitude, causing great disappointment among the Arabs, had encouraged the Israelis to hold fast to their refusal to repatriate and compensate the refugees according to the provisions of UN decisions. Thus the UN and its members, as well as the Arabs and the Israelis, proved unprepared to take the measures necessary to break the existing deadlock on the refugee issue.

JUNE WAR

Israel's swift victory in June, 1967—which enabled her to occupy the Gaza Strip, the Sinai Peninsula, the Golan Heights in southwestern Syria, and all of Jordan west of the Jordan River—created a brand-new refugee problem at the same time that it greatly altered some aspects of the old one. During and after the fighting more than 100,000 refugees from the Palestine War and over 200,000 Jordanians, Syrians, and Egyptians living in the conquered areas fled to Arab-controlled territories, while Israel suddenly found herself in command of lands containing nearly one-half of all the Palestine War refugees.

UN Secretary-General U Thant's report (S/8124) of August 18, 1967, stated that more than 100,000 Palestine refugees and more than 200,000 other Arab residents had been displaced as a result of the June War. He noted that the densely populated Gaza Strip had suffered considerably more civilian casualties and property damage than any other area. Since the strip had been quickly cut off and captured by the Israeli troops, few of the inhabitants had the opportunity or means to flee. Most refugees who crossed into Egypt proper had come from towns and villages in the Sinai Peninsula. Most of the Arabs newly displaced from Jordan's west bank had come from the Jericho, Nablus, and Hebron districts. For months after the war, hundreds continued to cross to the east bank daily. Many Arabs who had remained in the occupied west bank, but who were displaced through the destruction of their homes and villages, were compelled to seek shelter in other towns.

Many of the same factors that contributed to the Palestine Arab exodus of 1948 caused the exodus of June, 1967. Large numbers fled from sheer panic generated by the fighting and/or their fear that they might suffer physical harm at the hands of the victorious Israelis. Many departed for financial and economic reasons, including civil servants, pensioners, and others dependent on remittances from their breadwinners working in Kuwait and other Arab countries. The serious postwar unemployment and food shortages in some occupied sectors compelled many others to leave their homes in search of food and jobs. Some left to be reunited with other members of their families or because they were strongly opposed to living under Israeli rule. In addition, there were considerable numbers of Arabs who abandoned their homes because the Israelis, by one means or another, encouraged them to go. Some American and UN officials indicated that during the war and for several weeks after the fighting ended, Israel, despite formal denials, followed "a selective pattern of expulsion"—"encouraging Arab residents to leave certain areas, warning residents in other areas that they could not return if they left, and telling those in still other areas such as Jerusalem that they could remain if they wanted to." [47] Israel appeared determined to push out particularly those Arabs living in parts of the Old City of Jerusalem (such as the old Jewish Quarter and the area around the Wailing Wall), in some of the refugee camps on the west bank (such as those near Jericho), and in frontier villages in western Jordan and southwestern Syria which had strategic value or had been suspected of having harbored and assisted Arab commando groups. Many reports indicated that in order to promote and expedite the exodus in some places, Israel had applied psychological and economic pressures and, on occasion, even more direct measures. In certain towns, loudspeakers urged or ordered people to leave within a very short period of time. Elsewhere, rumors were initiated or Israeli soldiers fired their guns, knocked on doors, and searched the same houses for arms, night after night, to create uneasiness and even panic. In various west-bank areas, Israeli authorities pointedly made buses and trucks available, day after day, to transport Arabs to the Jordan River. Journalists reported Israeli troops firing in the air along the west bank of the Jordan River to "spur" the refugees to cross over into Jordanian-controlled territory. On June 26, 1967, the *New York Times* reported, "According to unimpeachable sources, the Israelis are driving Arabs out of occupied south Syria." Some Arabs accused Israel of deliberately allowing food shortages to develop in order to induce the Arab inhabitants to leave. Israeli denials notwithstanding, many UN and other neutral sources claimed that a number of border villages had been either partly or wholly leveled to punish those who had helped *al-Fatah* commandos and to discourage the evicted Arabs from trying to return. In an effort to diminish the unfavorable propaganda and political effects of the widely publicized charges that Israel was forcibly expelling many Arabs, Israeli authorities began to require those Arabs who were leaving to sign documents indicating they were leaving of their own free will.[48]

During the first few weeks after the end of the war, Israel not only encouraged many Arabs to leave, but she generally refused to allow any except a small handful of hardship cases to return. Defense Minister Moshe Dayan and other high Israeli officials frankly admitted that they were happy to see the Arabs go and did not "want them to come back."[49] To many Israelis, the fewer the Arabs who remained, the easier it would be for their government to administer and, ultimately, to annex conquered areas and possibly even to settle new Jewish immigrants on them. Those Israelis who advocated the permanent retention of the strategically important, but also greatly overpopulated, Gaza Strip probably felt that it would help facilitate the resettlement of most inhabitants of the Gaza area on the west bank if the latter's population had first been thinned out. Then, too, there was a major conflict between Israel's demographic and territorial interests. As Moshe Dayan contended, since Israel was a small country of "two and one-half million Jews" with nearly 300,000 Israeli Arabs, she could not readily and safely absorb all the 1.5 million "hostile" Arabs living in the conquered sections at the outbreak of the June War. Lastly, some Israelis felt that the new Arab refugees could be used as a bargaining weapon to force King Hussein to the peace table.[50]

The United States, concerned on both humanitarian and political grounds, cautioned Israel against evicting Arabs from the west bank and joined Britain, France, and other countries in urging her to readmit the "maximum number" possible. Western officials were particularly worried that an inflexible Israeli stand on the refugee question would strengthen the hand of the Arab militants, making it much more difficult to reach an agreement on permanent frontiers and to bring even moderate Hussein to the conference table.[51]

The Arab states complained that Israel was looting Arab properties and forcibly expelling large numbers of Arabs from the conquered areas. They insisted that Israel be compelled to withdraw from the "illegally" seized Arab lands and that the new refugees be allowed to return to their homes forthwith. Although the Syrian and Egyptian leaders did not openly urge their own displaced citizens to return while Israel remained in the occupied territories, King Hussein appealed to the Arab inhabitants still on the west bank not to sell their properties but to stay in their homes. He pressed those who had already left to try to return. Not only could the badly shattered economy of the east-bank area not absorb the influx of tens of thousands of people, but Hussein also feared that Israel would not want to give up the west bank and Jordan would have considerably greater difficulty in regaining it if most of its Arab population left.[52]

In response to this situation Argentina, Brazil, and Ethiopia, after consulting other countries, introduced a joint draft resolution (S/7968/Rev. 3) before the Security Council then attempting to deal with the Middle East crisis. This draft (1) reminded the Arab and Israeli governments they should respect the "humanitarian principles governing the treatment of war prisoners and the protection of civil persons in time of war"; (2) called upon Israel "to ensure the safety, welfare and security of the inhabitants of the areas where military operations have taken place and to facilitate the return of those inhabitants who have fled the areas since the outbreak of hostilities"; and (3) requested the UN Secretary-General "to follow the effective implementation" of the resolution and to report to the Security Council concerning its "compliance." This resolution [237(1967)], welcomed by the Arabs and warmly supported by Britain and France, was unanimously adopted on June 14.

By the latter part of June, since the Arab exodus continued at a rapid pace, particularly from the west bank, and since Israel was allowing very few of the displaced Arabs to return despite the provisions of Security Council Resolution 237(1967), the Arab states pressed the General Assembly, which had convened in an Emergency Special Session to deal with the Middle East crisis, to take effective action against Israel. Not only was the Arab request backed by many Afro-Asian nations, but even Britain and France strongly urged the Assembly to deal quickly with the worsening refugee situation. Consequently, on July 1, Sweden introduced a draft resolution (A/L.526) on behalf of twenty-three delegations. This draft (1) pressed for efforts to alleviate "the suffering inflicted on civilians and prisoners of war"; (2) appealed to all states, organizations, and individuals to make special contributions to UNRWA and other relief organizations; (3) again called upon Israel to facilitate the return of the refugees; and (4) asked the UN Secretary-General to investigate conditions in the area and to report back on them. On July 4 this resolution [2252(ES-V)] passed by a vote of 116 to zero with two abstentions. In order to carry out his responsibilities under this resolution and Resolution 237(1967) passed by the Security Council, UN Secretary-General U Thant appointed Nils-Goran Gussing, a Swede, as his personal representative to investigate the status of the refugees and war prisoners in the Middle East and report back to him.

Nils-Goran Gussing reported (A/6797) to the UN General Assembly on October 2, 1967. Besides providing refugee statistical data supplied to him mostly by UNRWA and information about conditions in the occupied areas furnished to some extent by Israel, he also noted: (1) the Jordanian, Egyptian, and Syrian governments had stated that they wanted the newly displaced Arabs to return to their former homes; (2) many of the new refugees said they wanted to be repatriated; (3) many of those made homeless by the June War and its aftermath would face considerable hardship once cold weather set in because of the lack of adequate housing for them; and (4) in some areas the Israelis had looted and had used psychological techniques to encourage Arabs to leave their towns and villages.

In the meantime, as a result of increasing pressures from the UN and Western governments and the urgings of Foreign Minister Abba Eban, the Israeli cabinet on July 2, by a very slim majority and despite the vigorous objections of Moshe Dayan and others, decided to permit west-bank (but not Syrian and Egyptian) refugees to return under certain conditions. Those desiring readmission were given from July 10 to August 10 to fill out application forms which Israel would provide and which the International Red Cross would submit to the displaced persons involved. Not only would the applicants have to furnish documentary proof of prior residence on the west bank, but even though Red Cross officials urged that no other requirements be established, Israel insisted that they must also obtain health and customs clearance and be given a security check. In addition, only those refugees who had left before July 5 would be eligible to apply for readmission.[53]

King Hussein and other Jordanian officials declared that it was the "national and sacred duty" of the refugees to return in order to relieve the overburdened and shaky economy on the east bank and to "upset the enemy's plans" to annex the west bank and to settle new Jewish immigrants there. They promised to give money and food to those who agreed to go back, and they warned that they would cut off economic aid from those who failed to apply for readmission. They also sought to assure the refugees that, somehow, control of the Jordanian territory now occupied by Israel would be regained.[54]

It was originally anticipated that all administrative arrangements for the repatriation of the Arab refugees would be quickly completed so they could start returning to their homes by mid-July. However, differences arose between Jordan and Israel over the application forms to be used. Jordan wanted only Red Cross forms to be used, while the forms which Israel furnished were made out in the name of the State of Israel. It took weeks before both sides finally agreed on a form which included the names of the Red Cross, Jordan, and Israel. (Meanwhile, Israel allowed the immediate return of a few hundred hardship cases, while some displaced persons were secretly crossing back to the west bank.) Because of the delay in launching the new program, Israel extended the deadline for the return of the refugees to August 31. The first group of approved applicants did not actually cross over to the west bank until August 18. At the end of August, the Red Cross announced that of the 170,000 refugees who had filled out the required forms, 130,000 applications had been submitted to Israel; yet, by the August 31 deadline, Israel had approved only 21,000 of these applications and only 14,000 persons had actually been able to return to their homes. At the year's end several thousand Arabs, mostly from the Gaza Strip, were still crossing to the east bank each month.[55]

The very narrow margin by which the Israeli cabinet had originally agreed to readmit some of the refugees indicated the existence of strong opposition to this program. In the early part of August, this opposition grew rapidly as a result of certain undiplomatic statements made by important Jordanian officials. On August 7, the Jordanian Finance Minister, who was also the Chairman of the Higher Committee for Refugees, said, "Every refugee should return . . . to help his brothers to continue their political action and remain a thorn in the flesh of the aggressor until the crisis has been solved." [56] Israel began to accuse the Jordanian government of initiating a campaign of "vituperative and direct incitement" which could only create "serious obstacles" to the return of the refugees. At an Israeli cabinet meeting called on August 13, a slim majority defeated a motion to cancel the entire readmission arrangement. Nevertheless, the cabinet decided to make tougher security checks and to keep down the number of refugees repatriated. On August 19, the *New York Times* reported, "Israeli officials have made no secret of their intention to suppress the flow of refugees. They said that this decision had been made as a result of the Jordanian campaign." Israel refused to authorize new crossing points, took her time in approving applications and in submitting them to the Red Cross and Jordanian authorities, refused to extend the repatriation deadline beyond August 31, and became highly selective in determining which displaced persons would be allowed to return. According to the *New York Times,* September 1, 1967, besides barring known agitators and convicted criminals, "None of the old refugees from the 1948 fighting who were quartered in the camps" around Jericho and no "more than a handful of those who fled from the Jordanian sector of Jerusalem were allowed . . . to return" because most of them were considered to be "potential security threats." "An Israeli source said: 'Our first consideration was to bring back those who were an active part of the economy of the west bank. There was no hurry to fill up the Jericho camps again with people who never contributed anything to the welfare of this area.' " Special consideration was given to hardship cases, involving primarily reunion of families, and to refugees who owned property.[57]

Israel was widely criticized for setting an early deadline for the repatriation program, especially since it became increasingly obvious that only a small number of refugees would be authorized to return before August 31. The Arabs accused Israel of deliberately restricting the number of refugees to be readmitted in order to "accommodate" more Jewish immigrants. They also contended that, since the Security Council and General Assembly resolutions had not authorized any deadline, Israel had no legal right to set one arbitrarily. The United States, Britain, and other Western countries strongly pressed Israel to admit as many refugees as possible for both humanitarian and political reasons. Again they warned Israel that her "hard line" on the refugee issue would seriously interfere with any quiet diplomatic efforts aimed at opening the way for an eventual Arab acceptance of Israel. U Thant also appealed to Israel to extend the deadline, not only as a humanitarian gesture, but also to insure that Israel fully complied with UN resolutions.[58]

On August 30, the Israeli government, yielding somewhat to these various pressures, decided to permit all those refugees whose applications had already been favorably acted upon to return after August 31. Since 14,000 of the 21,000 approved applicants had crossed to the west bank before the cutoff date, only 7,000 were affected by this decision. At the same time, the government also agreed to permit the reunification of some families after August 31, but formal requests for these had to originate with relatives living on the west bank. Notwithstanding the fact that the United States and other countries expressed dissatisfaction with this very limited modification of the deadline, Israel refused to liberalize her policies further. Israel insisted that Jordan must agree to negotiate directly with her on the refugee issue before she would consider reviving the repatriation arrangement. Some Israeli officials felt they should even use the question of the remaining large number of refugees from the west bank as an inducement to bring Jordan to the peace table.[59]

Although by the end of August, 1967, at least 113,000 of the refugees from the 1948 war had fled to neighboring Arab states, nearly 550,000 of the approximately 1,350,000 UNRWA-registered refugees remained under Israeli rule. Consequently, Israel found herself deeply and directly involved for the first time in the old refugee problem. As a result of this new situation, a number of Israeli officials began to contend that (1) it was more than ever in Israel's best interests to take the initiative in trying to solve the refugee problem since it was one of the major obstacles in the path of improving relations with the Arabs and also one of the major propaganda weapons held by the Arabs; and (2) some progress could finally be made in dealing with the issue by Israel alone without waiting for a final settlement with the Arabs. Moreover, it was recognized that to have any chance of success, any resettlement program would require large-scale financial help from the United States and other countries, the cooperation of most of the refugees and their leaders in the occupied areas, and continued Israeli control over these sectors. Despite the many uncertainties obviously involved, in the early part of July Israel set up a committee to work out plans for the rehabilitation and resettlement of the refugees in the Gaza Strip and the west bank. By the latter part of August, the Israeli government had apparently decided to initiate some limited steps towards refugee resettlement without waiting for the committee's report. Arabs from the Gaza Strip were encouraged to visit the west bank in the hope that most of them would decide either to stay there or to cross over to the east bank and never return. During this early period, about 500 Gaza residents were leaving for the west bank each day with Israeli government assistance, and many of them were continuing on to Jordanian-held territory. Even as late as the middle of January, according to the *New York Times,* January 17, 1968, Israeli officials were admitting that "perhaps 200 Gaza Strip residents" were leaving "every day" for the Jordanian eastern sector and that "the truth is we want them to go" and "we made it easy because there are too many here." [60]

In the meantime, while the vast, new refugee problem remained largely unresolved, UNRWA, the Food and Agricultural Organization, other international agencies and governments, and a number of private relief agencies provided food, medicine, tents, and other necessities to the newly displaced Arabs, as well as to the thousands remaining in the occupied areas who were in dire need because of the serious economic dislocations which had developed after the end of the war. Many Palestine refugees from the 1948 war who had become self-supporting found themselves in desperate straits. Many others who had supplemented UNRWA provisions with odd jobs discovered that such jobs were no longer available. Taking into account the greater than usual needs of the refugees, UNRWA began to give extra rations to many of them. UNRWA urgently sought and received special donations of money and supplies from the United States, Sweden, Canada, Britain, and other countries to cover additional demands on its resources. Many of these same countries—and others such as Russia and most of the Arab states —gave considerable financial aid directly to Jordan, Syria, and Egypt, who also used their own resources to help their own displaced citizens.

In spite of all these efforts, large numbers of the new refugees, particularly in Jordan, remained for many months without adequate housing, sanitation, and other essential facilities.

Fortunately, UNRWA, with its experienced personnel and administrative facilities and machinery largely intact, was able to function without any serious interruptions, although for a while its work was seriously handicapped by the lack of funds. UNRWA even managed to provide emergency rations and other essentials to many Arabs who found themselves refugees for the first time. Under a special arrangement with Israel, UNRWA continued operating in the occupied areas as well. UNRWA officials made it clear, however, that the arrangement was "concerned solely with the continuation of [its] humanitarian task" and did not imply any recognition of Israel's claims to the conquered territories. With nearly 550,000 refugees from the 1948 war under her control, it was obviously to Israel's advantage to permit the agency to continue its relief activities on her side of the cease-fire lines.[61]

The Twenty-second Session of the UN General Assembly took up the refugee question in December, 1967. On December 11, UNRWA Commissioner-General Laurence Michelmore provided the Assembly with "an up-to-date report" (A/SPC./121) on the refugee situation:

(1) By December, 1967, "110,000 Palestinians formerly registered with UNRWA on the West Bank [of Jordan] . . . and 15,000 refugees from the Gaza Strip" had joined "332,000 UNRWA refugees living on the East Bank"; (2) "120,000 other West Bank residents" had become displaced for the first time; (3) "the Jordan Government" had "indicated that some 200 or 300 persons" were "daily crossing the River Jordan from west to east, the majority of them now coming from the Gaza Strip"; (4) 16,000 Palestine refugees and 100,000 Syrians had fled from the Golan Heights sector; (5) the UAR now estimated "the total number of persons who were displaced from areas occupied by Israel . . . to be 60,000 to 70,000," 10,000 to 11,000 of whom were from the Gaza Strip; (6) the "new refugees may number 350,000 or 400,000," many of whom were "facing the coming winter in the misery and discomfort of the temporary tented camps or in the even more precarious conditions outside the camps"; (7) "some progress" was being made in "rectifying the ration rolls in East Jordan"; (8) there were approximately 270,000 Palestine refugees in the Gaza Strip and 270,000 in the west-bank area; (9) Syria, Jordan, Egypt, and Israel were cooperating with UNRWA in providing aid to the

refugees in their respective territories; and (10) "perhaps as many as 300,000 [Egyptians are] said to have moved from the West Bank of the Suez Canal to locations further to the west."

The Commissioner-General urged that the Palestine refugees "be allowed to return to their previous places of residence," where UNRWA had "shelter, health centres, schools and other factilities" and could "give them more adequate assistance." He held that since education was the key to opportunity for the younger generation of refugees, he would "devote as much as possible of any special contributions . . . to improving and expanding [UNRWA's] educational services." There was continuing need to provide food for the refugees. The ration ceiling that had been established for financial reasons in the past allowed "only two-thirds of the registered refugees" to receive food rations, which amounted to 1,500 calories at the cost of four cents a day. There were "284,000 children" whose claims have been "deferred because of the ration ceilings."

Laurence Michelmore requested $47,500,000 for 1968. This amount would be for "normal activities and emergency services, but not including the expansion of education and training services for which [UNRWA] may receive specially earmarked contributions." This amount would not provide for the "needs of all the persons displaced during 1967." At a conference held on December 6, thirty-three governments pledged only $26,300,000. While the Commissioner-General expected more pledges to come in later, he still feared that UNRWA would be more than $7,000,000 short of the required amount. He requested guidance from the General Assembly as to whether it wished UNRWA (1) to "maintain its existing services [to the Palestine refugees] during 1968 on the same basis" as in the past; (2) "to continue in 1968 giving help . . . to new groups of beneficiaries [newly displaced Arabs] in urgent need"; and (3) "to expand and improve its existing education and training services." He strongly pressed the Assembly to furnish UNRWA "with secure and adequate sources of funds."

Three proposals were submitted in the General Assembly in response to the Commissioner-General's report. An American draft (A/SPC/L.155): (1) recalled all prior resolutions dealing with the refugee issue; (2) noted "with deep regret that repatriation or compensation of the refugees as provided for in paragraph 11 of General Assembly Resolution 194(III) has not been effected"; (3) directed UNRWA to continue its efforts to rectify relief rolls; (4) noted "with regret that the UN Conciliation Commission for Palestine was unable to find means to achieve progress on the implementation of paragraph

11," and requested it "to exert continued efforts towards the implementation thereof"; (5) directed "attention to the continuing critical financial position" of UNRWA; and (6) called "upon all Governments as a matter of urgency to make the most generous efforts possible to meet" UNRWA's financial needs.

An eighteen-power proposal (A/SPC/L.156): (1) reaffirmed Assembly Resolution 2252(ES-V) of July 4, 1967 calling upon Israel "to ensure the safety, welfare and security of the inhabitants of the areas where military operations have taken place and to facilitate the return of those inhabitants who have fled the areas since the outbreak of hostilities"; (2) endorsed the efforts of UNRWA "to provide humanitarian assistance, as far as practicable, on an emergency basis and as a temporary measure, to other persons in the area who are at present displaced and are in serious need of immediate assistance"; and (3) appealed to "all Governments, as well as organizations and individuals, to make special contributions for the above purposes" to UNRWA and to other "inter-governmental and non-governmental organizations concerned."

Afghanistan, India, Malaysia, Pakistan, and Somalia introduced a draft (A/SPC/L.157) which requested the UN Secretary-General to appoint a "Custodian . . . to protect and administer Arab property, assets, and property rights in Israel and to receive income derived therefrom on behalf of the rightful owners."

Israel again insisted that the refugee problem could be solved only "in the broad context of peace." She offered a general outline of a plan in which she proposed that "consultations should immediately be initiated between Israel and the Arab host countries, together with the main contributing countries, to negotiate a five-year plan for the rehabilitation of the refugees and their final integration into the economic life of the region." She would contribute to a "re-integration and compensation fund to provide the financial means for a solution of the refugee problem in all its aspects." In addition, she stated that she had already contributed one million Israeli pounds directly to UNRWA and another million pounds in services to the Arab refugees under her control. Israeli officials vehemently opposed the proposal for setting up of a custodian and made it clear that they would "certainly not accept such an arrangement." They expressed a willingness to consider repatriating a limited number of newly displaced persons "on compassionate grounds." [62]

The Arabs, in turn, pressed the General Assembly to enforce those resolutions calling for the repatriation or compensation of the Palestine refugees and for the return of those Arabs who had fled their homes since the June War. They complained that Israel was not only not complying with UN decisions but was continuing to "expel" large numbers

of Arabs and was seeking more Jewish immigrants to resettle the conquered areas to facilitate their annexation. Moreover, they warned that
there could be no peaceful solution to the Arab-Israeli problem until
there had been a "just" settlement of the refugee question. Israel's five-
year plan was rejected on the grounds that it was too vague, would
require direct negotiations, and was meant to "bury" the refugee issue
and not to solve it. Arab delegates strongly backed the idea of establishing a custodian and firmly maintained that the refugee problem was "not
negotiable but must be settled according to the wishes of the refugees
themselves" and to UN resolutions.[63]

An overwhelming preponderance of UN members, including the
United States, came out once again in favor of the principles of repatriation or compensation for the Palestine refugees and of the right of the
newly displaced Arabs to return to their homes as soon as possible.
Many delegates warmly praised the efforts of UNRWA and expressed
their belief that it was vital that UNRWA continue to provide essential
services to both the "old" and the "new" refugees. Consequently, both
the American resolution [2341A(XXII)] and the eighteen-power resolution [2341B(XXII)] passed both the Special Political Committee and
the General Assembly with ease. The former was adopted by a vote of
ninety-eight to none with three abstentions, and the latter by a vote of
105 to none, with no abstentions. The five-power draft providing for a
custodian passed the Special Political Committee by a vote of forty-two
(including all the Arab and Communist countries, most Asiatic and
eight African nations, and Spain) to thirty-eight (including all Anglo-
Saxon and most Western European members and ten African and ten
Latin American states), with twenty-four abstentions. However, realizing that their proposal would not be able to muster the required two-
thirds vote, the sponsors of the five-power draft did not press for a vote
on it before the General Assembly.[64]

By these actions the Assembly kept alive its earlier decisions and
the principles expressed in them and reaffirmed its support of UNRWA
and the Conciliation Commission for Palestine. Nevertheless, it failed to
come to grips with the basic issues involved in the refugee dispute. As
a result, the future of the old and the new refugees remained shrouded
in uncertainty for it depended on many imponderables. Would Israel—
or would she not—give back to the Arabs some or all of the seized territories? Would she encourage more Arabs to leave their homes? Would
she liberalize her repatriation policies? Would the Arabs cooperate fully
with UNRWA and all UN efforts to promote refugee resettlement, as
well as repatriation? Would the Arabs, as well as the Israelis, refrain
from using the refugees for political purposes? Would the UN Security

Council, the General Assembly, and the major powers try to implement UN resolutions? Would Arab-Israeli relations improve sufficiently to make a final peace settlement possible?

While the answers to these questions would be long in coming, some facts about the situation had clearly emerged. The third Arab-Israeli war did not bring the refugee problem closer to a solution; it served only to alter the problem and compound its complexity. Moreover, while nearly all UN members supported the principles of repatriation or compensation for the refugees from the 1948 war and wanted Israel to allow the early return of the newly displaced Arabs, these members remained unprepared to take those measures which would be necessary to break the existing deadlock, and there was no indication that any one of the parties, whether directly or indirectly involved, would be ready in the foreseeable future to alter its position significantly. It was likely, therefore, that both old and new refugees would continue to live under adverse conditions and suffer greatly from disillusionment and frustration, that the intensity of Arab-Israeli hostility would not subside, and that the refugee problem would continue to constitute one of the most formidable obstacles to an Arab-Israeli peace settlement.

ANALYSIS OF ISRAELI AND ARAB POSITIONS

Israel Before the June War

Israel's basic contentions on the original refugee issue were the following: (1) the Arabs alone caused the problem and theirs alone was the responsibility for resolving it; (2) instead of helping the refugees, the Arab governments were deliberately using the refugees for political ends, were pressuring them into opposing resettlement, and were keeping the refugee issue alive to employ it as a weapon against Israel; (3) the Arab world was sufficiently large and rich in resources to absorb all of the refugees easily; (4) the refugees would be happier if they settled in Arab countries where they would be with their own people; and (5) Israel was unable to accept repatriation because of the lack of space, the continued existence of a state of war with the Arabs, and the serious social, political, and security consequences which would arise for her. Thus, Israel insisted that all refugees be resettled within the Arab world. Israel would agree to discuss the matter of compensation under the following conditions: (1) a final peace agreement had first to be reached; (2) "in fixing the level of compensation, it would be necessary to take into account . . . property left behind by Israeli citizens" in the "Jewish quarter of the Old City of Jerusalem," various villages in the "Jerusalem and Hebron districts," Iraq, and other Arab countries, as well as the cost of the "economic warfare against Israel carried on by the [Arab] states"; (3) international financial assistance would be "forthcoming"; and (4) the payment of a "global sum" would end all further obligations to the refugees. Israel had also indicated that she might some day be willing to revive the reunion-of-families scheme to a limited extent.[65]

Actually, Israel shared responsibility with the Arabs and others for the refugee problem. Initially such extremist groups as Irgun and the Stern Gang and then later the Israeli government itself deliberately expelled large numbers of Arabs from the areas occupied by Israeli forces. Even after the armistice agreement had come into operation, Israel compelled additional thousands of Palestine Arabs to leave. A number of Israeli officials conceded that many Arabs had fled their homes because it was the natural reaction of any human being to try to "escape from the horrors of war" and that the refugees were, on the whole, innocent "victims" for "whom none could feel anything but compassion." [66]

There was some validity in the Israeli claim that Arab officials had played politics with the refugee problem. Nevertheless, there were other factors to be considered. First and foremost was the fact that the refugees themselves had turned their plight into a major political issue throughout the Arab world with the result that no Arab leader could possibly ignore it. Besides, Israel had played her own share of politics with the Arab refugees. She had not hesitated to use the refugees as a lever to bring the Arabs to the peace table and to obtain more territory in return for repatriating some of the refugees. Also, both the Zionist organization and Israel had frequently used Jewish refugees from Europe for political ends.

Israel had charged that had it not been for the selfish motives and propaganda efforts of the Arab governments, the refugees would long ago have been willing to give up repatriation and accept resettlement. While many Arab leaders had at one time or another sought to exploit refugee feelings for their own interests, it would be wrong to conclude that they had created and kept alive feelings which would not otherwise have developed and persisted. UN experts in close contact with the refugees repeatedly emphasized that the overwhelming majority from the beginning and on their own initiative desired and insisted upon a return to their homes and that this desire had remained "unabated" over the years. In fact, it probably would have been more accurate to state that the position of the Arab governments on the repatriation issue had been determined far more by the feelings and pressures of the refugees (backed by the Arab masses who greatly sympathized with them) than by any other factor. Especially whenever and wherever there had been a close struggle for power between competing leaders within individual Arab states and/or between different Arab countries, those leaders had usually felt it necessary to try to outbid each other for popular favor by claiming to be a great champion of the refugee cause.

Since for 2,000 years the Jews had been able to keep alive their hope of returning to Israel, it should not have been difficult for them to understand the Arab refugees' unquenchable yearning to return to their homes, many of which were still within actual sight. Year after year nearly all UN members, including at times even Israel herself, had voted for UN resolutions which provided for the right of repatriation, resolutions which had further encouraged and strengthened the "natural longing" of the refugees to return. So the Arab governments could not reasonably have been expected to insist unilaterally that the refugees give up this very right which the UN had reiterated year after year by nearly unanimous votes.

UNRWA officials denied Israel's contention that the Arab governments had done little or nothing to provide material aid to the refugees. UNRWA's report (A/5813) for the year ending June 30, 1964, stated:

> Over the years, the governments of the four host countries have shown a deep concern in the well-being of the refugees. They have also given substantial direct help to the refugee community in the form of educational, health, administrative and other services and the provision of building sites, water and security protection. The aggregate cost of such direct help reported by the host Governments since 1948 exceeds $66 million; during the year under review its cost, as reported by the governments and summarized in table 27 of annex I, was $6,575,000.[67]

Table 25 in this report showed that from May 1, 1950, to December 31, 1964, the Arab states contributed $12,000,000 to UNRWA. For many years assistance had also been given to several hundred thousand Palestinians ("economic refugees" in Jordan, natives of the Gaza Strip, and others) who had lost their livelihood as a result of the Palestine War but who were not eligible for UNRWA's relief aid. UNRWA further noted that the host nations had also "carried a burden no less real or costly, even though less tangible, in the form of the complex political and social problems that stem from the presence of refugees within their boundaries."[68] Actually, because the refugees had often created serious social, political, and security difficulties and had depressed wages in many areas, with a resultant loss to indigenous workers, many Arab officials would have been relieved of a major burden had the refugee question been satisfactorily resolved.

Israel had greatly exaggerated the actual wealth and absorptive capacity of the Arab world and oversimplified the whole resettlement problem. Despite its large size, the Arab part of the Middle East is mostly poor in resources, and it suffers from overpopulation. Even the more favorably endowed countries would find it difficult to turn over unexploited lands to the refugees when they were already planning to use these lands for improving the economic lot of millions of their own underprivileged citizens. Only a large-scale economic development program for the whole Middle East could have made possible the integration of all of the refugees into the economic life of the area without, at the same time, seriously impairing the economic interests of the indigenous populations. To complete such a scheme would have required many years and billions of dollars of outside aid—and there was no indication as to where such vast sums of money would have come from.

There was another important consideration which was often overlooked. Although the Palestinians were Arabs, it did not follow that they would have been equally happy to settle anywhere within the Arab world. Not only had they developed a strong Palestine national consciousness, but they would have found the economic, social, and political situation in many Arab states, as well as the customs and spoken Arabic dialect, considerably different from their own. Actually, in the fields of economic and political development, the refugees had more in common with most Israelis than with Arabs who lived in such places as Yemen and Oman. If the refugees had been given a completely free choice, they would naturally have wished to live within an Arab state of Palestine. If denied this choice, they would then have probably preferred to settle among those Arabs with whom they had the most in common. These Arabs resided in Lebanon (already over-crowded and afflicted with a delicate political balance between Christians and Muslims), Jordan (also seriously over-crowded), Syria, and Israel. The resettlement of large numbers of the better educated and more politically sophisticated Palestinians in the less advanced sections of the Arab world would undoubtedly have given rise to major social, political, and even security problems and would have aroused serious resentment and opposition on the part of the native inhabitants.

Israel's assertion that she was too small to absorb many Arab refugees was not wholly valid because, at the same time, she also claimed she could absorb several million more Jewish immigrants without the need for expanding her borders. To be more accurate and consistent her position should have been that she did not have enough room for both the Arab refugees and for all the Jews who might ultimately want to settle in Israel.

It was obvious that the repatriation of large numbers of Arab refugees would have created serious economic, social, and political difficulties for Israel. Because of her relatively advanced economy, Israel could have absorbed more newcomers, whether Arabs or Jews, more readily than the Arab states with less developed economies. Especially in the earlier years, Israel would actually have benefited from having experienced refugee farmers to help increase her agricultural production. It could also have been contended that in some ways Israel had faced a more formidable task in integrating large numbers of very backward Jewish immigrants from Asia and North Africa than in integrating the considerably better educated and more advanced Palestine Arabs.

Israel was justified in being concerned about the possibly harmful effects to her security of any large-scale refugee repatriation. Nevertheless, she tended to stress only the security risks involved in repatriation while failing to weigh sufficiently the potential risks that would have been involved in allowing the refugee deadlock to persist. Most authorities agreed that Israel's acceptance of repatriation would not inevitably have brought about, as Israelis frequently had contended, a sudden mass movement into Israel of one million hostile refugees determined to undermine her social and political structure and her security. As a staff study made for the United States Senate Foreign Relations Committee in 1960 stated, most experts

> generally believed that relatively few of them [refugees]—probably less than 10 per cent—would exercise the right [of repatriation]. As the Israelis themselves so often suggest, the Moslem refugees would be disinclined to return to a land utterly transformed by the predominance of its Jewish culture and Jewish government . . . [since repatriation would be on a gradual basis], the experts also suggest that in all probability the pool of those refugees awaiting repatriation under the quota would dry up in a few years. The theory is that the majority of the returnees, drawn back by nostalgic pull, would find the homeland strange, its ways alien, its society less than cordial. Some would leave again. This sense of disillusionment would in turn be communicated to the other refugees, many of whom would then be discouraged from returning.[69]

A number of Israelis concurred with this conclusion. For example, one well-informed Israeli maintained that "not more than 10 per cent of them [Arab refugees] would return," while another stated:

> American, Israeli and independent specialists are quite close in agreeing that given the choice of settling in an Arab country, of

emigrating abroad or returning to "Zionist" Israel, only a small proportion of the refugees would opt for return. A considerable part of those who did return might desire to leave afterwards.[70]

The pertinent UN resolutions already stipulated that only those who agreed to live in peace with their neighbors could return. The UN agency set up to supervise any repatriation would naturally have been empowered to screen carefully all refugees choosing repatriation and to refuse it to those who could become troublemakers. Obviously, if any significant number of those returning refugees had shown signs of disloyalty in the early stages of repatriation, they could have been expelled from Israel. Moreover, they would have jeopardized the chances of repatriation for other refugees because Israel could then have used this development as a justification for refusing to admit any more refugees and because many UN members would have sympathized with Israel's refusal under those circumstances. Most experts believed that the greater part of those likely to choose repatriation would have been the ones with family ties in Israel. Not only would these refugees not have wished to cause any trouble which might compromise the position of their relatives living in Israel, but these relatives would have had good reasons for wanting to help their repatriated kin integrate successfully. Besides, a full reunion of Arab families in Israel would have enabled Israeli Arabs to overcome any existing discontent and divided loyalty. Israel's acceptance of repatriation might also have opened the way to a security guarantee from the United States and Britain. (Both Western nations had offered to guarantee the security of Israel if the Arabs and Israelis came to terms on the refugee and other issues in dispute.[71]) According to some of her own officials, Israel had been able to integrate safely over 200,000 Israeli Arabs, including thousands of refugees admitted in earlier years under the reunion-of-families scheme, and these had actually been "contributing to the development of Israel."[72] Consequently, had proper precautions been taken, there would have been good reason to believe that Israel could also have safely integrated more Arabs.

UN officials and other specialists reported that the unresolved refugee problem was one of the main causes for border incidents resulting from refugee attempts to visit relatives in Israel or give vent to their hatred of Israel. It was these refugees who exerted the most persistent pressure against any Arab peace with Israel and who would continue to do so—at least until their "rights" had been reasonably satisfied. In the long run, Israel's security would depend far more upon the growth of general stability in the Middle East and the development of more normal relations with her Arab neighbors than upon the actual number of Arabs living within her borders.

The presence of more Arabs in Israel could have had its advantages, as well as disadvantages. In the course of time, the repatriated Arabs could have helped provide an essential bridge between Israel and the Arab world. Israelis had to learn to live in harmony and equality with as large a number of Arabs as possible within Israel before they could ever have hoped to live in peace and friendship with the many millions of Arabs surrounding her. As a State Department specialist cautioned, it "is [not] in the interest of Israel that a generation is growing up in isolation from the people and culture of the area where Israel must live." [73] Besides, the Arab governments would have found it more difficult to contemplate invading Israel if large numbers of reasonably contented Arabs were living there and if an attack with modern weapons would have endangered the lives of hundreds of thousands of Israeli Arabs.

Israel's refusal to abide by those General Assembly resolutions providing for refugee repatriation helped to weaken the authority of the UN, upon whose future strength Israel's security, like that of all small states, would ultimately depend. Israel's refusal also encouraged the Arabs to ignore those UN resolutions which favored Israel.

Israel had apparently believed that, if the *status quo* lasted long enough, the UN would eventually lose interest in taking further action on the refugee issue, the Arab refugees and governments would ultimately give up all hope of attaining any repatriation, and a *de facto* resettlement of all the refugees would then take place. In this way, the refugee dispute would disappear from the scene and Israel would be spared having to take back any refugees. This line of reasoning ignored the facts that the refugees could never be fully integrated in the four host states and that the refugees and the Arab masses would have vehemently opposed either large-scale resettlement projects in the host countries or major movements of refugees into other non-host countries until Israel had at least agreed to implement the repatriation and compensation provisions of UN resolutions.

In the final analysis, there would have been some danger for Israel no matter what course of action she had decided to follow. In any case, Israel would not have been the only one to take risks and make sacrifices by agreeing to repatriation. The refugees and the Arab countries would also have faced some risks and sacrifices. Neither the repatriated nor the resettled refugees could have been sure that they would have been welcomed and treated with full equality and consideration in the areas where they would have ultimately lived. The Arab governments would have been saddled with new economic, social, political, and security problems of their own in the resettling process. As a Senate Foreign Relations Committee staff study concluded, if the pertinent UN resolutions were implemented,

> the Israelis, in the judgment of most disinterested authorities on the subject, would have to make the greatest *diplomatic* concession. . . . The Arabs, on the other hand, would have to make the greatest *practical* concession. . . . The burden of such a solution to the refugee problem, as envisaged by those most familiar with it, would fall on the Arab states [because some nine-tenths of the refugees would end up being resettled within the Arab world]. Less affluent than Israel, far less well along in their economic development, the possibility of serious economic dislocations would be greatest for them.[74]

Israel correctly charged that the Arab governments had not been adequately frank with the refugees and their own people on all phases of the refugee issue. At the same time, Israeli officials could also have been accused of failing to be sufficiently frank with their own citizens. Unfortunately, over the years only a few Israelis (such as Professor Martin Buber and those supporting the liberal Israeli magazine, *New Outlook*) and Israeli organizations (such as the Ihud Association) had sought to present all sides and aspects of the refugee issue to the Israeli public.[75] Consequently, most Israelis had not yet realized that it would have been impossible to resolve the refugee question until Israel, as well as the Arabs, had shown greater readiness to make significant concessions and that as long as the refugee problem remained alive, Arab hatred of Israel would persist and the Arabs would refuse to make peace with her, as later events were to demonstrate.

The Arabs Before the June War

Before June, 1967, Arab contentions were, in brief, as follows: (1) Israel, the UN, and the major Western nations were primarily responsible for creating the refugee problem, and it was up to them to solve it fairly; (2) the refugee issue was the most pressing dispute of all between the Arabs and the Israelis, and no progress could be made in dealing with other differences until the refugee question had been equitably resolved; (3) since the refugee situation was deeply affected by political and humanitarian considerations, it could not be cleared up by economic means alone; (4) large-scale works projects might ultimately impair, if not completely eliminate, those refugee rights provided for in UN resolutions; (5) continued unlimited Jewish immigration into Israel would harden Israeli opposition to repatriation, enable Israel to build up her military power substantially—thus further threatening Arab security—and compel Israel to expand her boundaries at the expense of the Arabs; (6) the UN should employ every means at its disposal to implement those resolutions which provided for refugee repatriation and compensation; (7) until the UN enforced these resolutions, the world organization would be obligated to take care of the basic needs of the refugees through UNRWA; and (8) if the UN would set up an agency to take custody over refugee property in Israel and pay the refugees the income derived from it, the world organization could help the refugees and lessen its own financial burden.

The Arabs—if only because of their own ineptness, overconfidence, and lack of flexibility—shared responsibility for the refugee situation with Israel and others. The shortsighted Palestine Arab leaders failed to prepare their own people either to be victorious in any armed struggle with the Zionists or to live with Zionist aspirations. Shortly after the passage of the UN partition resolution in November, 1947, many frightened and selfish Palestine Arab leaders fled at the first sign of trouble, leaving their people disorganized and an easy prey to rumors and fears. The armed Arab intervention on May 15, 1948, precipitated such widespread and large-scale fighting throughout Palestine that many other Arabs fled their homes to avoid the dangers of warfare. Moreover, this intervention had been so badly planned and executed that it had led to a humiliating defeat which prevented most of the refugees from returning to their homes. The Arabs had, therefore, helped to create the refugee problem.

Most UN members finally agreed with the Arabs that because of the many basic psychological and political obstacles involved, the refugee situation could never be cleared up by economic means alone. At the same time, the Arabs had not sufficiently acknowledged that it never could be fully resolved without major efforts in the economic field as well. They had not revealed adequate interest in large-scale development schemes, mainly because they had been worried that the more they cooperated with any works project and the more successful it proved to be, the more endangered refugee rights would have become and the more powerful the pressures would have grown in the UN for the abandonment of all further UN responsibility for the refugees. On the basis of numerous statements made in the UN General Assembly over the years, the Arabs had become increasingly concerned that most UN members would readily have taken advantage of the first opportunity to bring an end to further UN involvement in the refugee situation. As a result, the Arab governments had strongly objected to taking over even part of UNRWA's activities—such as in the field of education as some

UN officials had advocated—because of the potential danger that such a step might set a precedent and start a trend they could not have stopped. Only Israel's acceptance of the principles of repatriation and compensation could have removed these Arab apprehensions and encouraged the Arabs to approve large-scale projects for refugee resettlement.

Whereas Israel exaggerated the economic, social, political, and security problems which would have been created by repatriation, the Arabs tended to minimize them. Integrating a large number of Arab refugees, most of whom were lacking in useful skills and were harboring bitter feelings towards Israel, would undoubtedly have caused major difficulties for Israel. Although Arab delegates to the UN occasionally sought to reassure Israel that the return of the refugees would not actually endanger her security, many other Arabs, particularly refugee leaders and other extremists, as well as moderates who had felt the need to placate the refugees and their more ardent supporters, frequently made bellicose statements which had not allayed Israel's natural fears for her safety. Moreover, Israel had been understandably concerned because several Arab states (particularly Syria, Iraq, and the UAR) had been giving military training to thousands of refugees who were to form the nucleus of the Palestine Liberation Army, according to the plans made by the Arab chiefs of state in a 1964 summit meeting. The Arabs should have been aware that the more belligerent they appeared, the more difficult it would be to persuade the Israelis to accept repatriation and the easier it would be for Israel to convince the UN that she was entitled on security grounds to deny the return of any of the refugees. The Arabs also should have given greater consideration to the fact that the refugee question could not be resolved in complete isolation from other Arab-Israeli issues.

Since the overwhelming majority of UN members had repeatedly voted for resolutions reaffirming paragraph 11 of Resolution 194(III), the Arabs stood on strong legal and moral grounds whenever they called upon the UN to carry out the terms of this paragraph. But they weakened their position whenever they stressed only those parts of the resolution which they favored and when they tried to demand more than it actually provided for. For instance, although some Arab governments had formally agreed to accept those refugees who did not wish to be repatriated, too frequently Arab officials, fearful of antagonizing the refugees and their supporters, emphasized only the principle of repatriation, largely ignoring the provision for resettlement in paragraph 11. By taking this position, these officials not only supplied a strong basis for Israel's charge that the Arabs were deliberately seeking a mass return of the refugees in order to undermine Israel's security, but they also made it far more difficult to obtain support within the UN for the implementation of the repatriation and compensation provisions of UN resolutions. In addition, Arab leaders generally neglected to mention the fact that paragraph 11 specifically stated that only those refugees "wishing to . . . live in peace with their neighbors should be permitted" to return to their homes in Israel. To have done otherwise would have precipitated serious outcries among the refugees and other Arabs. Nevertheless, this neglect tended to lesson still further the chances that the UN would have eventually enforced the principles of repatriation and compensation as desired by the Arabs because few UN members would have been willing to press Israel to accept repatriation if any significant danger to Israel's security would have resulted.

Thus, for the long-range best interests of the refugees and their own citizens, Arab leaders, despite the major difficulties and even potential personal risks involved, should have clearly and unequivocally agreed to abide by all parts of paragraph 11, informed the refugees of the full meaning and implications of this paragraph, and expressed their readiness, within the reasonable limits of their own national resources and with essential outside help, to resettle those refugees who wished to remain within the Arab world.

The Arab governments did not serve their cause over the years by their failure to cooperate in every possible way with UNRWA, whose dedicated officials had been making major efforts and sacrifices to help the unfortunate refugees. By the late 1950's UNRWA did begin to report that: (1) Arab cooperation had greatly improved and UNRWA's differences with the Arab governments had substantially lessened; (2) some disputes had been inevitable under the existing complex and difficult circumstances; and (3) some misunderstandings had probably been due to mistakes made by UNRWA itself.[76] Nevertheless, the Arabs should never have overlooked the fact that they were the principal losers every time UNRWA's services were hindered.

Israel After the June War

After the June War Israel continued to oppose the repatriation of any Palestine refugees remaining in Arab-held territories, insisted that the refugee problem could be resolved only as part of a final peace settlement, and refused to allow the return of those Palestine refugees who had left their homes or camps in southwestern Syria, the west bank of Jordan, and the Gaza Strip during and after the June conflict. Even the preliminary suggestions made by Israeli officials for rehabilitating those refugees now living under Israeli rule were based on their resettlement primarily in the occupied west-bank area, which, some

Israelis urged, should be made into an autonomous Arab state under Israel's control—and not in Israel proper.

Israel's victory in the June War brought about major alterations in the over-all refugee situation and confronted her with three somewhat different, although closely related, refugee issues resulting from: (1) the movement of thousands of Arabs from one part of the occupied zone to another; (2) the acquisition of territories with nearly 550,000 refugees; and (3) the exodus of more than 300,000 Arabs from the conquered areas.

The first issue developed when some thousands of Arabs, especially from the old Jewish quarter of Jerusalem and from villages located near the former Jordanian-Israeli demarcation lines, fled to other sections of the west bank. While some moved in with friends and relatives or temporarily occupied properties abandoned by other Arabs, large numbers of them were unable to find adequate accommodations. The depressed economic conditions prevented most from finding work or other means of support. Because of this and inadequate housing, many fled onward to the east bank. Israel allowed some of these Arabs to return to their villages, but many others were either not permitted to return or had nothing to return to because their homes had been demolished by the fighting or, later, by the Israelis. The Arabs claimed that little or nothing was being done to help these unfortunate people because Israel wanted to create conditions which would make it necessary for them to continue on to Jordanian-held territory. The Israelis, in turn, contended that they were trying to revive the economy of the west bank so that more people could find employment.

At this writing it was impossible to determine exactly how much help Israel was giving to the newly displaced Arabs still under her dominion. It was clear, however, that it would be in Israel's best long-range interests to allow as many as possible of these refugees to return to their homes, to provide building materials and other aid to those whose properties had been destroyed, and to make every effort to find housing and work for those unable to return to their own homes. Otherwise, these hapless, uprooted Arabs would become economic burdens on the community and would grow increasingly frustrated, resentful, and hostile to Israel. Neither Israel's public image nor her economy, political position, and security would benefit from such a development.

The second issue arose from Israel's conquest of areas already containing nearly 550,000 Palestine refugees. Immediately after the June War, Israeli leaders announced that they would take the initiative in rehabilitating and resettling the refugees under their control. Some officials even began to speak optimistically about resettling all of them in the west bank and Sinai areas. A high-level committee was set up to study the matter and to recommend the best course of action. Well before the committee had had an opportunity to delve deeply into the situation, a number of Israeli officials began to discern the magnitude of the task. By the middle of August, 1967, they estimated that it would take between one and two billion dollars over a ten-year period to rehabilitate the refugees and other needy Arabs and to raise their standard of living close to that of the Israelis.[77] Even then, the success of such an undertaking would depend upon (1) large-scale financial assistance from the United States and other countries, as well as considerable contributions from Israel herself; (2) the full cooperation of most of the refugees, other Arabs, and their leaders in Israel; and (3) the tacit agreement of the neighboring countries that they would not urge the refugees to oppose the Israeli plan or obstruct the flow of waters from the Yarmouk River and other branches of the Jordan River into the Israeli-controlled west-bank sector.

There appeared to be little hope that Israel would obtain the cooperation required from the refugees and the Arab governments, and there was no definite indication as to whether the United States and other nations would be willing to provide all the necessary financial aid. Then, too, there was no assurance that the west bank and the Sinai Peninsula had enough potential resources to permit the resettlement of all the refugees there. The conclusions reached by those UN, American, and other experts who had made detailed studies in the past were that these areas could absorb only a limited number of additional inhabitants and that many refugees would have to cross international borders—including those of Israel—in order to attain economic independence. Defense Minister Moshe Dayan was reported by the *New York Times,* September 11, 1967, to have stated the previous day that it was impossible, at this time, to resettle a large number of the Arab refugees in the areas now occupied by Israel. Consequently, if Israel did not allow resettlement on her own land, it would be difficult to see how any ambitious resettlement plan could be successfully implemented. Of course, major desalinization plants could ultimately be helpful, but they would be very costly and, even under favorable circumstances, would take a long time to construct. In the meantime, the refugee population would increase by nearly 3 per cent each year. This would raise the number of refugees from 540,000 to 800,000 or more within ten years. Tens of thousands of native Arab inhabitants, primarily in the extremely overcrowded Gaza Strip, would also be in great need of economic rehabilitation and resettlement, and their population would mount as rapidly as that of the refugees. There was also much doubt as to whether many Israelis would be willing to allocate large amounts of their money and other resources to be invested in the occupied territories on behalf of the Arabs when some of these areas might ultimately be returned to the Arab countries.

Actually, Israel could give the impression of making considerable progress in resolving the problem of the refugees in the areas which she conquered. For example, by December, 1967, over 250,000 natives of the west bank, the Sinai Peninsula, and the Golan Heights of Syria, plus about 150,000 Palestine refugees (including many who were not residing in UNRWA camps) had left Israeli-held territories, and more Palestine refugees and other Arabs were leaving daily. If Israel were to persist in her refusal to allow more than a handful of them to return and if she were to encourage further departures, then her total refugee population would decline because of these departures, and Israel could resettle large numbers of the refugees who had not departed in the homes and other properties abandoned by the Syrians, Egyptians, Jordanians, and those Palestine refugees who had not been living in camps. Obviously, any "improvement" in the living conditions of these refugees which might have been made by these means would not have been accomplished so much through constructive efforts and sacrifices made by Israel as through the creation of an even larger refugee problem for several neighboring Arab states and through the expropriation of the property of those newly uprooted Arabs who were not permitted to return to their former homes and lands.

However, if Israel were to rehabilitate, resettle, and otherwise improve the lot of large numbers of the Palestine refugees under her rule—without, at the same time, aggravating the refugee problem in the neighboring Arab states—she would reduce significantly the dimensions of the refugee question. But, even then, a serious Palestine refugee problem would remain, for there would still be well over 700,000 of them in the Arab states (at least 160,000 in Lebanon, 140,000 in Syria, 5,000 in Egypt, and 450,000 in truncated Jordan, as of December, 1967), and their numbers would be increasing by about 21,000 per year because of the high birth rate alone, not counting those who might continue to come from the Israeli-held zones. Jordan's poor and greatly overpopulated east bank could never absorb the large number of both old and new refugees now living there. Lebanon and Syria would have great difficulties in fully integrating the Palestine refugees under their jurisdiction for internal, as well as external, political reasons. With only a few thousand Palestine refugees in her territory—although the total could grow substantially if Israel were to expel many of those in the Gaza Strip—Egypt, at least for the time being, no longer had any direct involvement with large numbers of Palestine refugees.

Because of the new Palestine refugee situation, Israel found a need to develop a different attitude towards and a new relationship with UNRWA. In earlier years, Israel had advocated the termination of UNRWA's mandate in order to compel the Arab governments to become more "realistic" and to make serious efforts at resettling the refugees within the Arab world. Now that Israel saw herself responsible for about 40 per cent of the Palestine refugees, she realized that she needed UNRWA just as the Arab states did. If UNRWA should cease to exist, Israel would have to assume the heavy burden of providing 540,000 refugees with food, clothing, education, and other essentials—or else give up the west bank and Gaza areas or expel as many refugees as possible. Israel refused to relinquish any occupied areas, partly, at least, so that she could use them to force the Arabs to the peace table. While Israel might continue to encourage a steady, though small and relatively inconspicuous, exodus of refugees, she could not force large numbers of them to leave quickly without arousing strong protests and seriously impairing her political position throughout the world. Obviously, as long as Israel held all the newly-acquired territories, she had little choice but to keep the greater part of the refugees and look to UNRWA to help her maintain them at the smallest possible cost. It would be in her best interests, as well as those of the refugees, if she cooperated fully with UNRWA.

The third issue facing Israel developed because, by December, 1967, the June War and Israeli policies had helped to turn more than 250,000 Syrians, Egyptians (this figure does not include over 300,000 Egyptians who moved from the west bank of the Suez Canal to safer locations), and Jordanians into refugees for the first time, and this figure continued to increase as more Arabs left Israeli-controlled areas day after day. This new and major refugee problem spawned new difficulties and dangers. The large numbers of uprooted Jordanians and Egyptians further exacerbated the already desperate economic conditions in these two countries. Although not overpopulated, Syria would have considerable difficulty in relocating and integrating the 100,000 persons who fled from the Golan Heights. This new Arab exodus created in the Arab world another large group of restless, frustrated, and angry Arab refugees who would not permit their governments and their own fellow countrymen to forget their plight, who would persistently demand action by their leaders to regain their homes and lands, and who would press harder than ever for the destruction of Israel. Even in the UAR, the old refugees from Palestine and the newer ones from the Sinai Peninsula and the Suez Canal's west bank would not be as isolated as the Palestine refugees in the Gaza Strip had been in the past, and they would be in a position to spread their feelings of frustration and of hatred for Israel directly to the Egyptian masses. It should have been obvious for years that there could be no Arab-Israeli peace as long as a major Arab refugee problem persisted. After June, 1967, more and more Israeli officials finally began to acknowledge this fact publicly, and the Israeli government even proclaimed its intention to try to resettle those refugees under her jurisdiction in order to reduce the dimensions of the refugee dispute. Yet at the same time, Israel initiated policies and actions which, by inducing large numbers of Arabs to leave the occupied territories and by refusing to readmit all but a small number of those who had applied for readmittance, added greatly to the scope and complexity of the entire refugee issue.

Many Israelis were especially concerned that if Israel held all the conquered territories permanently and did not thin out the Arab population there, then the Arabs, because of their higher birth rate, would ultimately become the majority. Even if this particular threat did not exist, most Israelis who wanted their country to be a strictly Jewish state would be unhappy to see the continuation of a large Arab minority in their nation. But on the other hand, the larger and the more explosive the Arab refugee problem, the less chance would there be for peace and the more manpower and resources would Israel have to allocate for military purposes. Then, too, by encouraging Arabs to flee to the east bank and by refusing to allow most of them to return to their homes on the west bank, Israel greatly complicated the difficulties for the hard-pressed and moderate King Hussein and strengthened the position of the militants in Jordan and elsewhere in the Arab world.

As long as Israel retained the conquered lands, reducing the problem would involve the following: (1) allowing as many as possible of the newly displaced Arabs to return to their homes, as called for by Security Council and General Assembly resolutions; (2) not encouraging more Arabs to leave the occupied zones; (3) drawing up a rehabilitation and resettlement program that would provide for the repatriation of as many as possible of the refugees under her control to their former districts and/or villages in Israel and for the compensation of those to be resettled elsewhere in order not only to help the refugees reestablish themselves and to reduce their hatred of and hostility towards Israel, but also to make possible partial implementation of UN General Assembly resolutions; (4) giving as much priority to economic development plans for the occupied areas as for Israel proper; (5) treating all newly acquired Arabs equitably. (For example, Israel had evicted, frequently with very little notice, hundreds of Arabs in the occupied territories, particularly in the Old City of Jerusalem, living on properties once belonging to the

Palestine Jews, according to the *New York Times,* June 14, 1967; yet, at the same time, she did not try to return those properties once owned by the newly conquered Arabs.)

Israel's June victory and territorial acquisitions presented her with a unique opportunity for constructive and beneficial actions with regard to the refugee question which could enable her to build an essential bridge of understanding with the Arab world. If, however, she should misuse this exceptional opportunity, she could well make an already bad situation much worse.

The Arabs After the June War

Their defeat in the June War, Israel's acquisition of large Arab areas, and the development of a new Arab exodus greatly altered and complicated the entire refugee predicament for the Arabs. As in the early years, the Arabs, too weak militarily and politically to influence Israel's policies and actions, had little choice but to seek the political support and financial aid of the UN and some of the major powers. As in the past, the Arabs were able to obtain the passage of UN resolutions which reiterated earlier decisions relating to the rights of the Palestine refugees, called upon Israel to permit the return of the recently displaced Arabs, renewed the mandates of UNRWA and the Conciliation Commission for Palestine, and expanded UNRWA's responsibility. But once again the Arabs were unable to secure the implementation of the repatriation provisions of General Assembly resolutions, despite their warning that there could never be peace in the Middle East until a "just" solution for the refugee question had been attained.

Unless most of the recently uprooted Arabs could be repatriated soon—and there appeared to be very little likelihood of this happening— Syria, Egypt, and Jordan could be faced with considerable political and security—in addition to economic—complications, as they were after the 1948 war. Without work and hope for the future, the new refugees could become very restless and resentful. With tens of thousands of displaced persons living in skimpy tents and other improvised shelters and with hundreds of Arabs still crossing daily to her east bank, Jordan, in particular, was facing a potentially explosive situation.

The Arab governments should do everything in their power to rehabilitate economically as many refugees as possible and even to integrate politically those refugees who might voluntarily agree to permanent resettlement in an Arab country. The Arab states should seek UN and other outside economic and financial aid to initiate large-scale development schemes which would help their own nationals, in addition to the refugees. They should cooperate wholeheartedly with UNRWA and all other international agencies providing refugee assistance and should allow accurate censuses of the old and new refugees within their territories. Arab leaders should carefully avoid provocative statements and actions which could aggravate the refugee situation. If they appealed to the refugees to return in order to promote active hostility to Israel and if they abetted terroristic and other militantly anti-Israeli activities among the Arabs within the occupied zones, then: (1) Israel's fear of and opposition to any significant refugee repatriation would grow; (2) Israel would be encouraged to take repressive measures against the Arabs under her jurisdiction and to induce more of these Arabs to leave; (3) Israel would be able to convince many UN members that such actions were justified; and (4) the Arabs would be unable to persuade the UN and the major Western powers to apply the firm and determined pressures which would be required to compel Israel to liberalize her policies towards the refugees and the Arabs in the occupied areas. Consequently, all Arab attempts to use the refugees for political purposes would be self-defeating and would gravely weaken the effectiveness of any Arab complaints that Israel was utilizing the unfortunate refugees as political pawns and bargaining weapons.

The Arab governments should adopt a positive, rather than a negative, approach to the refugee problem. They should try to help even those refugees who have remained under Israeli control. For instance, they should not prevent Arabs working in Kuwait and other parts of the Arab world from sending money to their families in the occupied sectors, and they should not obstruct constructive efforts by Israel to rehabilitate and resettle the refugees living within her jurisdiction. However, they would have reason to object if these refugees were to be resettled against their will, at the expense of other displaced Arabs, or primarily for political purposes—such as by deliberately thinning out the population in the Gaza Strip in order to make it less of a liability were Israel to annex it. Nevertheless, in the final analysis it would be to the best interests of the refugees in particular and of all the Arabs in general if the Arab leaders would seek in every possible way to alleviate the over-all refugee situation.

CONCLUSION

Extensive misunderstanding caused the UN and most of its members to oversimplify the refugee predicament, to seek vainly for some simple economic panacea, and to make the same costly mistakes over and over again. Notwithstanding the sound analyses and repeated warnings of a small number of experts on the Middle East, few UN and government officials seemed to have realized the following: (1) how much the attitudes of the Arabs and Israelis had been conditioned by mutual fear, hate, and distrust and how difficult it would be to bring the contending parties together in order to compose their fundamental differences until the intensity of these feelings had first been significantly diminished; (2) how deeply embittered and disappointed the Arabs had become over the failure of the international community—which they blamed for the unhappy plight of the refugees—to implement the repatriation and compensation provisions of UN resolutions and to rectify what they considered to be the grave injustice inflicted upon them; (3) how strongly opposed to repatriation most Israelis had become because they feared that a return of the refugees would bring a threat to Israel's security and "Jewishness" and because they wished to use the vacated Arab properties to facilitate the rapid absorption of large numbers of Jewish immigrants; (4) how difficult, time-consuming, and expensive it would actually be to reintegrate all of the refugees into the life of the area by resettlement and repatriation; (5) how effective had been the clamor and the pressures of the refugees on the political leaders in the Arab world; and (6) how closely interrelated and entangled the major Arab-Israeli disputes had become, making it impossible to deal successfully with the refugee question in complete isolation from the other basic issues.

Actually, while no miracles can be expected, certain constructive actions could and should be taken. The first and most urgent step is to care for pressing needs and to avoid repetition of the old Palestine War refugee problem. As the immediate needs of the newly displaced Arabs are being met, every effort must be made to resolve this new refugee situation before it becomes too deeply rooted. The UN and the large powers would have to apply firm pressures to enforce the UN resolutions of June, July, and December, 1967, and the Arabs and Israelis would have to show more understanding and flexibility. UNRWA must be given the support to promote that improvement in the psychological and political climate that is essential to the attainment of any permanent Arab-Israeli agreement. It must be provided with sufficient funds on a long-term basis to enable it (1) to extend relief, educational, and other essential services more efficiently and effectively to all the new and old refugees who require such assistance; (2) to carry out major economic development projects; and (3) to expand and accelerate the existing refugee training program. Before June, 1967, contributions to UNRWA were decreasing despite the fact that the numbers and needs of the Palestine refugees were increasing. This compelled UNRWA to meet its growing deficits from accumulated reserves, which, by the end of 1965, had fallen well below the $15,000,000 regarded as necessary to keep supplies in the pipelines and to cover temporary financial shortages when contributing states were late in meeting their pledges. After the June War, UNRWA found it imperative to provide emergency relief aid to large numbers of newly displaced Arabs, as well as to the Palestine refugees. This forced the agency deeper into debt. The United States, Sweden, and numerous other countries made special contributions to help UNRWA meet its more immediate fiscal requirements. Nevertheless, it remained uncertain whether these UN members would be willing to continue providing UNRWA with the additional financial support needed if it were to continue giving relief aid on an expanded basis for the indefinite future. In fact, as of December, 1967, pledges made by the various governments fell far short of the minimum amount requested by UNRWA for 1968. If the UN failed to provide the required funds, a number of Arab states would certainly face even more serious internal economic, political, and security problems, and there would be increased instability and strife in the area. Therefore, in the long run it would be far less costly in lives as well as money to appropriate the additional money required by UNRWA than to allow the already dangerous conditions in the Middle East to deteriorate still further.

Obviously, too, the more newly displaced Arabs the UN could persuade Israel to repatriate, the less money the world organization would have to raise for this fiscal year and for years to come. Because of a high birth rate, the number of refugees will increase rapidly, necessitating steadily rising relief, educational, and other expenditures. Consequently, for financial as well as humanitarian and political reasons, the UN must seek vigorously to bring about the return at least of most recently uprooted Arabs before the existing refugee situation becomes too solidified.

The major powers should offer large-scale financial assistance to those governments prepared to initiate major development schemes, apply the required pressures on the parties to take measures which could reduce the refugee problem, and open their own gates to interested refugees. They should also seek a deeper and more complete understanding of all aspects of the refugee and other Arab-Israeli issues and be more objective in their approach to all Arab-Israeli disputes.

In the years before the June War, most neutral experts concluded that a peaceful and lasting solution of the Palestine Arab refugee question could ultimately be found only if its terms were fairly consistent with the fundamental provisions stipulated in the pertinent General Assembly resolutions. Actually, practically every proposal made by non-Arab and non-Israeli sources was based on the conviction that, in general, the principles of repatriation, resettlement, and compensation as originally set down by the General Assembly in its Resolution 194(III) provided the most equitable basis for settling the refugee issue. Even recommendations made by such friends of Israel as Sweden, New Zealand, and the *New York Times* and by such Israelis as Dr. Martin Buber, members of Ihud, and sponsors of *The New Outlook* also called for a combination of repatriation (of at least a "token" or a "limited" number of the refugees), resettlement, and compensation.[78] Since the essence of the refugee problem remained the same after the June War as before it, any peaceful solution would still have to be based on the same combination of repatriation, resettlement, and compensation, and it would have to be implemented gradually and by stages because of the economic, psychological, and political difficulties which would confront Israel, the Arab states, and the refugees. The exact percentage of those who would be repatriated or resettled would depend largely upon the particular circumstances existing when a final refugee agreement is drawn up. Until such an agreement is reached and the reintegration process is completed, UNRWA would, of course, have to continue providing relief and other essential services.

There is little hope that a final solution of the refugee issue could be arrived at until the emotional climate in the Middle East has substantially improved and the Arabs and the Israelis have decided to seek a political solution to all their major differences. Moreover, any future solution of the refugee problem would entail considerable time, patience, money, perseverance, and sacrifice on the part of the UN and all the states directly and indirectly involved. Nevertheless, in the long run, a far higher price will probably have to be paid if this deadlock is not broken. Until it is, peace and stability in the Middle East will remain endangered.

CHAPTER VII

Armistice Complications and the Sinai War

Shortly after the four Arab-Israeli General Armistice Agreements came into effect in 1949, Arab and Israeli officials started to wrangle over the meaning of various provisions, and numerous incidents erupted along the demarcation lines. Differences also developed over Arab efforts to boycott and blockade Israel and over the use of Jordan River waters. Cumulative disagreements and conflicts exacerbated Arab-Israeli emotions and relations, leading to raids, retaliatory assaults, and finally a full-fledged war.

Differences soon arose between the Arabs and Israelis over the interpretation of the armistice agreements. The Arabs stressed those sections which stated that: (1) they were "dictated exclusively by military considerations"; (2) they would "remain in force until a peaceful settlement between the Parties [was] achieved"; (3) they were not intended "to weaken or nullify, in any way, any territorial, custodial or other rights, claims or interests which may be asserted by either Party in the area of Palestine"; and (4) the demarcation lines established by the agreements were "not to be construed in any sense as ... political or territorial" boundaries and were "delineated without prejudice to the rights, claims and positions of either Party ... as regards the ultimate settlement of the Palestine question." The Arabs also contended that under international law, armistice conventions ended only the military phase of a war. Therefore, a technical state of war continued to exist between the Arabs and the Israelis, and both sides retained all the rights under the international law of war except those involving the use of military force. On the basis of these armistice agreement provisions and their own contentions, the Arabs sought to justify their refusal to deal with Israel directly and to allow Israeli ships to use the Suez Canal and the Gulf of Aqaba, their application of an economic boycott, and their view that the demarcation lines and the demilitarized zones were temporary, provisional, and subject to change in any final peace settlement.

Initially, Israel had conceded that the armistice agreements dealt "only" with "military matters." She later claimed that the UN Charter forbade one UN member from exercising "belligerent rights" of any kind and from being in a state of war with another member. On this basis, Israel challenged the legality of the Arab boycott and blockade. She also held that, despite the fact that the armistice agreements were to provide only a temporary transition from war to peace, the Arabs acted as if they would never agree to make peace. As time passed, Israel also took the position that the demarcation lines were permanent, legal borders and all of the demilitarized zones were part of her sovereign territory.[1]

UN officials and members tended to support, at least in part, Israel's view that the UN Charter did limit the freedom of UN member states to apply belligerent rights. But they also held that, as stated by Acting Mediator Ralph Bunche, the armistice agreements were "not the final peace settlement." They merely signaled "the end of the military phase of the Palestine situation" and did not "prejudice" the final terms of any political settlement. The UN, rejecting Israel's claim that the demilitarized zones legally belonged to her, insisted that the ultimate sovereignty over these areas was to be established by future peace treaties.[2]

BORDER INCIDENTS AND RETALIATORY RAIDS

The frequent incidents in the earlier years were usually minor ones caused by private individuals and groups. But over the years they grew in intensity and scope—especially as the governments and their military forces became increasingly involved in them.

Most of the early incidents originated from innocent motives. Many Arab refugees, seeing no reason why they should not be able to return to their villages, sought to cross into Israeli territory. Israel, however, not wanting the refugees to return, took forceful measures against them as infiltrators. This strong reaction discouraged most refugees from trying to return home. Nevertheless, some of them, anxious to restore contacts with relatives, to reclaim movable properties, and to harvest their crops, were willing to take the risk.

For centuries Bedouins had moved about in disregard for, and frequently in ignorance of, international boundaries in their constant search for grass and water for their animals. A number of tribes had traditionally wandered about almost at will within an area encompassing the Egyptian Sinai, the Palestine Negev, and parts of Transjordan. Although Israel sought to prevent these tribes from entering her territory, the Bedouins, especially in periods of drought, felt it essential to move their flocks into Israel despite the dangers involved.

Many incidents also resulted from accidental border crossings by both Arabs and Israelis because the demarcation lines were often marked inadequately or not at all. This was a particularly grave problem along the frontiers between Israel and Jordan and between Israel and the Gaza Strip because the new demarcation lines in these areas did not follow the old, well-known Palestine borders. Both Arabs and Israelis were guilty of stealing (at times as a result of dire need) and smuggling, and these activities often led to violence. Even "errant livestock" occasionally precipitated incidents when they wandered across the frontiers. Under normal circumstances such events would have been considered harmless mistakes or ordinary transgressions which required only limited police action. Since the situation between Israel and her Arab neighbors was not normal, however, these minor border crossings often had serious political repercussions.

Certain policies and actions of the Arab and Israeli authorities also produced frontier strife. For instance, Israel established a number of "fortified" settlements right along the borders instead of a little distance away, and Israeli patrols frequently drove their military vehicles provocatively close to the demarcation lines despite UN Truce Supervision Organization (UNTSO) warnings against such close contacts between the opposing sides. The Arabs, in turn, encouraged incidents by sometimes employing inadequately trained and poorly disciplined border police and troops and by sending their patrols too close to the frontiers. But it was the government-inspired raids and counterraids that produced the most serious border crises.

UN officials recommended various measures which would help prevent border strife. They suggested that the demarcation lines, especially in the more sensitive areas, be clearly marked to prevent accidental crossings and that mixed border patrols be used to discourage incidents. They recommended, too, the setting up of local commanders groups which, by means of frequent meetings and phone communications, could more effectively discourage border clashes, return stolen properties, and quickly resolve most disputes on the spot.

Both the Arabs and Israelis accepted these proposals in principle and some of them were partly put into effect. Nevertheless, certain basic differences in points of view prevented them from being fully implemented. Because Israel sought to bypass the UN as much as possible and to encourage those direct contacts with the Arabs which ultimately might lead to a *de facto* recognition of Israel and her existing boundaries, she wanted only Arabs and Israelis to man the joint patrols, to place markers and barbed wire fences on the demarcation lines, and to carry out other UN proposals. The Arabs, on the other hand, opposed dealing directly with Israel in any way, insisted upon UN involvement in the implementation of the UN recommendations, and refused to go along with any move that might imply recognition of either Israel or the existing borders. So they opposed placing fences right on the demarcation lines and accepting joint patrols unless UN personnel participated in these activities. Despite these differences, some borders were finally marked, and some governments put up barbed wire fences on their own side of the demarcation lines. Mixed patrols were used only rarely and temporarily along a few sensitive frontiers. A local commanders organization established for a time by Jordan and Israel through UN auspices proved useful. However, Israel later refused to consent to a formal renewal of the existing local commanders agreement with Jordan because it required the signature of a UN representative and because Israel preferred to seek direct and high-level—rather than indirect and low-level—contacts with Jordanian officials. The local commanders organization was kept alive for a while longer by means of verbal agreements—but even these finally broke down. UN efforts to create a similar organization along the Egyptian-Israeli lines failed as a result of differences arising over the role to be played by the UN and over the type and level of the contacts to be established.[3]

UN officials also urged both sides to use only their best soldiers and police as border guards because poorly trained and undisciplined guards not only proved ineffective in preventing infiltrations, but often helped to precipitate border clashes by nervously shooting across the lines at the slightest real or imaginary provocation. All governments made some serious efforts to comply with this UN recommendation. Particularly in the Gaza area, UN officials pressed Israel and Egypt to withdraw their patrols, observation posts, and "defensive positions" back from the demarcation lines to a distance sufficient to reduce unnecessary physical contacts between their forces. Israel, protesting that this would involve the surrender of some sovereign control over her own territory, proved much more reluctant than Egypt to accept and carry out this UN proposal. In fact, Egypt not only accepted the UN suggestion "without reservation," but on a few occasions she unilaterally withdrew her troops some distance back from the demarcation lines and called for the setting up of neutral, no-man's land zones in the more sensitive areas.[4]

UN and Western officials requested Israel and the Arab states to allow complete freedom of movement to UN observers and the establishment of fixed UN observer posts where needed. All parties had, at one time or another, been guilty of interfering with observers' movements. On the whole, however, UN reports indicated that Israel was considerably more hesitant than were the Arab states about permitting the observers to move around freely and about accepting fixed observer posts on the usual ground that such measures derogated from her sovereign "rights." She was also much less willing than the Arabs to increase the authority of the Mixed Armistice Commissions (MAC's) and UNTSO. As indicated in an earlier chapter, during the Palestine War period Israel had begun to develop a suspicious and hostile attitude towards UN officials, agencies, and resolutions. Since then the Israelis frequently sought to weaken, while the Arabs sought to strengthen, UN involvement in the Middle East. Thus, instead of taking her complaints to the various MAC's or to the Security Council, Israel often tried to deal with them unilaterally. By 1951 she had stopped attending regular meetings of the Israeli-Syrian MAC, and after her 1956 Sinai invasion Israel withdrew all further recognition of the Egyptian-Israeli Armistice Agreement and MAC. Israel repeatedly ignored the warnings of UN and Western officials that such attitudes and actions would increase border tensions and conflicts and hurt the chances for peace.[5]

At times the Arab and Israeli governments took certain steps on their own initiative to prevent incidents. For example, Jordan passed special laws, used more border guards, gave "strict orders" to local authorities and military commanders, issued strong warnings by means of the press and radio, and removed Bedouins from the more sensitive frontier sections in an endeavor to suppress illegal crossings of the lines. In 1954 alone, nearly one thousand infiltrators were sentenced to jail terms, and suspended sentences were given to many others accused of lesser frontier violations. On a number of occasions, army trackers cooperated with UN observers and even with Israeli authorities in an attempt to identify and apprehend alleged infiltrators from Jordan. Egypt also passed laws providing stricter penalties for illegal crossings and generally urged her police and military officials to enforce these laws. In 1955, Lebanon moved 9,000 Arab refugees from the border area to prevent infiltrations. Israel, in turn, increased the number and improved the caliber of her own border police, pressed them to suppress crossings of the lines, and exchanged information on infiltrators with Arab officials when possible. These various Arab and Israeli measures helped somewhat, but they were not implemented as fully and consistently as they should have been, thereby permitting some avoidable incidents. In any case, the tense conditions in the area made some incidents inevitable no matter how sincerely and energetically the responsible governments and UN agencies tried to prevent them.

While most of the earliest border violations were brought about by unofficial and nonviolent infiltrations by individuals and small groups, in time force began to be used increasingly by both sides. As the number of casualties mounted, more and more Arabs and Israelis felt compelled to strike back in revenge. Raids by one side precipitated counterraids by the other. The resulting chain reaction soon caused family groups, local communities, and ultimately even national authorities to become directly involved in retaliatory activities.

Israel was the first state to develop a deliberate and official policy of retaliation.[6] From 1951 on, the larger reprisal raids were made by military personnel using advanced weapons and military tactics. Thus, it was obvious that the Israeli government had ordered these attacks, even though for a few years Israeli officials generally, though not invariably, denied any responsibility for them. By early 1955, however, Israeli authorities began to accept full responsibility for the retaliatory assaults made from Israeli territory. Prime Minister David Ben-Gurion was the major instigator of these acts of reprisal. Holding little faith in the UN and in its ability to protect Israel and believing that the Arabs "best understood sharp words and tough actions," Ben-Gurion contended that only by the use of superior force and by inflicting "two blows for one" would the Arabs be compelled to stop their hostile activities against Israel and to begin seriously considering making peace with her. Ben-Gurion's views were especially popular among the ultranationalistic elements of the population.[7]

Only a small number of Israeli moderates (such as those associated with Ihud) strongly opposed Ben-Gurion's militant policy. They warned that the retaliatory attacks would only further embitter the Arabs, drive them to increasing their own acts of violence, and gravely lessen Arab willingness and ability to make peace. Other Israelis, such as Foreign Minister Moshe Sharett, were not opposed to all retaliation, but they were conscious of the need to give full consideration to the timing, frequency, and extent of any raids and their potential effects on world opinion. For example, these Israelis were greatly distressed when Ben-Gurion, largely on his own initiative, ordered a major raid against Syrian territory in December, 1955, while Sharett was in the West seeking arms for Israel. This raid not only alienated many people in the West, but it also undermined Sharett's efforts to purchase weapons to match those being acquired by Egypt from the Soviet bloc. While Sharett remained as foreign minister he served as a brake on Ben-Gurion. But after Sharett left the government in the middle of 1956, he was succeeded by Golda Meir, who was as strong an advocate of a "tough" policy against the Arabs as was Ben-Gurion himself.[8]

Certain aspects of Israel's retaliatory policy especially angered the Arabs and proved particularly harmful to her position in the UN. In practice, Israel frequently went beyond the principle of "an eye for an eye" and sought to inflict many more casualties on the Arabs than she had originally suffered. For example, in October, 1953, in reprisal for the murder of an Israeli woman and two children, Israeli military forces attacked the Jordanian village of Qibya, killing forty-two men, women, and children and injuring fifteen other persons. At Nahalin (Jordan) in 1954, and in the Lake Tiberias and Gaza sectors in 1955, and in the Gaza and other areas in 1956, Israel took many more lives than she had lost. For the period from January 1, 1955, through September 30, 1956, UNTSO reported the following verified casualties: 496 Arabs killed and 419 injured compared to 121 Israelis killed and 332 injured.[9]

There were times when Israel responded to an act of violence within her territory with a retaliatory attack even when no definite proof existed that any neighboring Arab country was actually responsible for this act. In March, 1954, for instance, a bus was ambushed in Scorpion Pass in eastern Israel with the resulting loss of eleven lives. The Israeli-Jordanian MAC, after investigating the incident with the full cooperation of the Jordanian government, finally concluded that it could not determine who had committed the crime or where the criminals had come from. Nonetheless, Israel made a major reprisal assault on the Jordanian town of Nahalin. By late 1955, Israel had, with increasing frequency, refused to submit alleged incidents to the MAC's for investigation before retaliating. In 1956 the UNTSO Chief of Staff complained:

> At present the situation is that one of the Parties to the General Armistice Agreement makes its own investigations, which are not subject to check or confirmation by any disinterested observers, publishes the results of such investigations, draws its own conclusions from them and undertakes actions by its military forces on that basis. This is, of course, a negation of vital elements of the Armistice Agreement.[10]

At times, Israel applied her policy of retaliation not only as a response to prior Arab attacks, but also for other reasons. Since Israelis considered the armistice agreements to be "indivisible," they contended that they were justified in using armed raids as reprisals for any injuries suffered by Israel as a result of allegedly illegal boycotts and blockades. The Israelis hoped in this way to compel the Arabs to stop these particular activities. Then, too, after having successfully used her superior military power in 1948–49 to force the Arabs to negotiate armistice agreements with her, many Israelis, including such influential persons as Ben-Gurion and Golda Meir, became convinced that the Arabs could also be driven to the peace table by the repeated show and use of Israel's military might. Thus, on some occasions, Israel welcomed or even provoked incidents which would give her an excuse to retaliate with sufficient force to make the Arabs realize the necessity of making peace. For example, while secret negotiations were taking place between Jordanian and Israeli officials in September, 1950, Israel, according to an Israeli scholar and writer, "encouraged acts of provocation" to enable her to assault the town of Nakaraim on September 7 "in the hope of forcing the [Jordanian] Government to come to terms." [11] One of the most important reasons Israel invaded the Sinai in October, 1956, was to coerce Egypt into suing for peace.

Israel was not always satisfied with merely maintaining the armistice agreements indefinitely even though her frontiers might be kept reasonably quiet at the same time. On April 22, 1956, while Israel was awaiting a visit from UN Secretary-General Dag Hammarskjold, who was seeking ways to reduce tensions in the area, the *New York Times* correspondent in Israel reported:

> Many Israelis fear a temporary relaxation will benefit Egypt more than Israel since Premier . . . Nasser will use the time to train his army in new Soviet arms. For that reason there was widespread hope just before Hammarskjold arrived that Egypt would provide sufficient provocation for a major reprisal action by Israel. Just what good that would be done in terms of a long-range settlement is obscure, but the point to remember is that Israel doubts the Arabs will ever deal with this nation unless compelled to by defeat or fear of defeat. . . . The Israeli Government is not content with mere tranquillity. It is afraid that the calm produced will strengthen the Eisenhower administration's ability to resist internal pressures for sending arms to Israel. It also fears an illusion of peace will make arms hard to get from Western Powers.

Israel sometimes instigated or magnified border incidents in order, as another *New York Times* reporter stated, to make herself "so much of a nuisance" that the big powers would have to "worry about the Middle East situation" and about Israel's arms and border problems.[12] Israeli officials were under considerable political pressures, especially in election years, to take a stronger than usual stand against the Arabs, and this circumstance tended to encourage more and larger reprisal raids. Israel's policies were also influenced by the fact that the more threatened Israel appeared to be, the more freely would Jewish communities outside Israel provide her with the necessary financial and political support. Increased tensions with the Arabs also helped to strengthen national unity in Israel at a time when Israel was trying to forge hundreds of thousands of Jews with diverse backgrounds, including many from Arab countries, into one, unified people.[13]

In the earlier years, Arab retaliatory activities were generally carried out by individuals and groups on their own initiative. There were times when Arab civilians and local military personnel retaliated by firing or by making raids across the demarcation lines. Nevertheless, up to 1955, the Arab governments, partly because of their military inferiority vis-à-vis Israel, did not try to reply in kind even to the more serious Israeli assaults.

In the summer of 1955, however, Arab, and especially Egyptian, policy changed radically as a result of large-scale Israeli attacks on the Gaza Strip. The first one, costing the lives of thirty-eight Arabs and injuring thirty-one others, was made on February 28, 1955, shortly after Ben-Gurion returned to the government as defense minister. Although Israel sought to justify this strong action on the alleged ground that Egypt had been employing "aggressive" activities against her territory, the UNTSO Chief of Staff denied Israel's allegation.

This February 28 assault, which revealed that Israel had acquired some advanced weapons not possessed by Egyptian forces, was to have grave consequences for the Middle East. The Egyptian public and most of the officers who had experienced humiliating defeat in the Palestine War started pressing President Nasser to strengthen Egypt quickly so that she could strike back at Israel in case of further raids. Consequently, Nasser began both to seek advanced weapons and to arm and train Palestine Arabs for use in future reprisal assaults on Israel. In late August, 1955, after further Israeli attacks, Egyptian-trained Arab commandos, called the *fedayeen,* began to make raids so deeply into Israel that every Israeli town and village felt threatened. The Israeli people, now more emotionally aroused against the Arabs than ever before, insisted on even more forceful action by their government. Thus, instead of discouraging incidents and bringing peace nearer, as Israel in particular had hoped, the policy of retaliation had actually precipitated a dangerous chain reaction of raids and counterraids, dangerously heightened Arab-Israeli tensions, and brought the contending parties to the brink of war.

UN officials and Security Council members repeatedly warned the Arabs and Israelis that retaliatory actions not only posed a serious threat to peace, but they also violated the armistice agreements, existing Security Council resolutions, and the UN Charter itself. They maintained that because the cease-fire provisions of earlier resolutions were independent of the armistice agreements, these provisions must be observed "unconditionally." In short, one party could not legally justify its armed reprisals on the ground that the other party had already broken some part or another of the armistice agreement. Even the reservation for "self-defense" did "not permit acts of retaliation." UN and Western officials cautioned Israel in particular that as a result of the emotional and political conditions in the area, some incidents were inevitable no matter how hard the governments involved tried to prevent them. They urged all sides to avoid impetuous reactions and to keep the situation and particularly popular emotions under as much control as possible. While deploring infiltrations and acts of violence by private individuals and groups, UN and Western authorities vigorously condemned officially inspired raids, which were considered to be far more unjustifiable and far more dangerous to the cause of peace. Because Israel used military retaliations more frequently, over a much longer period of time, and on a considerably larger scale than the Arabs, Israel was reprimanded more often and more strongly than the Arab states were. Even Israel's warmest supporters on the Security Council voted for a number of resolutions which censured her for some of her major reprisals. They warned that such tactics would do more to hurt than to help her security in the long run and would "not produce peace negotiations." [14]

Lebanon-Israel

Relatively few incidents took place along the demarcation lines between Lebanon and Israel. Because these lines coincided with the old Palestine border, few accidental crossings took place. Possessing only a small military force, Lebanon was anxious to avoid giving Israel any cause for making large-scale attacks. Besides, hostility against Israel, at least among some of the Christians, was not as great in Lebanon as it was in other Arab states. The Lebanese government moved the Arab refugees away from the border areas and made other serious efforts to discourage incidents. Israel, considering Lebanon to be the least hostile and dangerous of all the neighboring Arab states and wishing to exploit all signs of Arab disunity, placed Lebanon in a special category among the Arab countries. Israeli officials stated that "Lebanon as a nation" was "innocent of evil designs on Israel." [15] Israeli and Lebanese frontier officials frequently cooperated through the MAC and sometimes directly to prevent or control troublesome situations. Both parties usually sought to play down the occasional incidents; consequently, no major crisis developed between the two countries.

Syria-Israel

From the beginning, practically all border differences between Israel and Syria were centered around the problems arising in the demilitarized zone and Lake Tiberias areas. The demilitarized zone, an area of less than 100 square miles stretching from above Lake Huleh to south of

Lake Tiberias, was composed of three separate sectors. The northern sector, once largely uninhabited and used by Arabs and Israelis for grazing and farming purposes, remained relatively free of trouble for many years. The central sector straddled the Jordan River between Lakes Huleh and Tiberias. The southern one was situated along the southeastern shores of Lake Tiberias. Because these two latter areas were more heavily populated, contained a large number of Arab and Israeli-owned properties, and had considerable economic and strategic value, they became the scene of most of the clashes. Israel tended to control the greater part of the demilitarized zone, especially those portions located west of the Jordan River.

Many of the major difficulties in this zone had their roots in a basic conflict between the view of Israel, on the one hand, and Syria and, to a large extent, the UN, on the other, as to the legal status of the zone. Israel claimed that the armistice agreement had given her sovereign authority over the whole zone, while Syria had been given no rights there of any kind. Only the MAC Chairman had been allowed a very limited authority in the zone, and its extent was to be determined by Israel alone. Neither the MAC nor the Security Council had any legal right to interpret the terms of the armistice agreement, to exercise any power in the zone, or to circumscribe Israel's position or dominion there. Israel contended that she could curb the movements of UN observers in the zone and did not have to obtain anyone's consent before starting drainage and other projects there. After 1951, she refused to attend regular meetings of the MAC, insisting that it had no jurisdiction over any issue involving the zone, but she continued to deal with some zone problems through the MAC on an informal basis.

Both UN and Syrian officials refuted practically all of the Israeli contentions. Relying heavily upon the authoritative interpretation of the armistice agreement by Ralph Bunche, who had helped to write it in 1949, UN officials held that: (1) the armistice agreement had left the question of sovereignty over the zone to be resolved by the final peace treaty—thus "neither Party could validly claim to have a free hand in the demilitarized zone over civilian activity"; (2) the civilian administration was to "take shape on a local basis under the supervision of the Chairman of the MAC," who was made responsible for the "restoration of normal civilian life in the area without prejudice to the ultimate settlement"; (3) both sides were to consult with the Chairman before carrying out any significant activities in the zone; (4) all zone police had to be recruited locally, and no outside police or military personnel and equipment and no more than strictly defensive works would be legally permitted; (5) no change could be made in the military *status quo* in the zone which would give one party a clear military advantage over the other; (6) the MAC was responsible for interpreting the armistice agreement provisions dealing with the area; (7) MAC observers and chairmen had to be allowed complete freedom of movement there; and (8) the two parties were obligated under the armistice agreement and various Security Council resolutions to attend all MAC meetings. UNTSO repeatedly complained that Israel was starting major projects in the zone without first consulting with the MAC Chairman; "Israeli police . . . exercised control over the larger part of the . . . Zone"; Israeli military personnel and "armored vehicles" had illegally entered the zone; Israeli fortifications beyond legal limits had been set up in the zone; Israel seriously restricted the movements of UN observers and the MAC Chairman there; and Israel's failure to attend MAC meetings and her efforts to limit the powers of the UN had "greatly weakened" UNTSO's authority.[16]

Some of these same complaints—especially those involving restrictions on the movements of UN observers, illegal fortifications, and the introduction of "National Guard and other military personnel" to support the zone Arabs—were sometimes made by UNTSO against Syria as well. UNTSO disagreed with Syria's contention that she too must be consulted on all activities going on in the zone. Otherwise, Syria's views on the zone were very close to those held by the UN.[17]

The Security Council repeatedly and fully supported all the views of the responsible UN officials, reaffirmed the validity of the armistice agreement, and sought to strengthen the authority of the MAC. Individual members, particularly the United States and Britain, gave verbal as well as diplomatic support to the UN agencies and officials involved. On at least one occasion, in October 1953, the United States went so far as to suspend all economic aid to Israel until she abided by the MAC Chairman's request that Israel stop work on a canal project in the demilitarized zone until he could authorize its continuance.[18]

According to UNTSO, incidents resulted from the "progressive extension of Israeli cultivation" and/or control "towards the East" in the demilitarized zone. For instance, starting in March, 1951, Israeli forces moved into a number of Arab villages, destroyed many houses and compelled hundreds of Arabs to flee to other parts of the zone or to Syria, where many set up rock dwellings along the rugged mountain slopes overlooking their former homes and lands. At first, Israel disregarded UNTSO requests to allow the Arabs to return to their villages and to compensate them for the properties destroyed. After the Security Council, on May 18, 1951, passed a resolution (S/2157) which firmly backed these requests, Israel finally permitted some of the displaced Arabs to return. However, she paid no compensation, set stringent restrictions on the movement of the Arabs living in the zone, and prohibited the traditional contacts between these Arabs and their relatives and friends in Syria and the Syrian-controlled part of the zone. Since some of these Arabs sought to continue these contacts despite the presence of Israeli police in the area, clashes became inevitable. Israeli farmers, at times supported by Israeli police and armored vehicles, moved on to Arab-owned lands in the zone and began to till the soil despite repeated protests from the MAC Chairman that such actions were not only illegal but would provoke strong Arab reactions. As the Chairman feared, the displaced Arabs living along the Syrian mountain slopes frequently vented their anger and feelings of frustration by shooting at the Israelis they saw working on their lands. Thus, many more incidents were spawned.[19]

Starting in 1951, serious difficulties arose in the demilitarized zone over Arab objections to Israel's efforts to drain Lake Huleh and the surrounding swamp areas to provide more arable land and to combat malaria. Israel sought to buy some Arab-owned lands for her project, but the Arab owners refused to sell. When Israel tried to continue her project anyway, some Palestine Arabs, with Syrian support, attempted to prevent the occupation of their lands. This led to exchanges of fire which became progressively more serious. The MAC Chairman ordered both a cease-fire and a cessation of further work by Israelis on Arab-owned lands. Denying Israel's claim of sovereignty over the zone and holding that Israel should have consulted with the MAC Chairman before starting her project in the first place, the UNTSO Chief of Staff supported the cease-fire order. At the same time he rejected Syria's contentions that her consent was required for the project and that it would alter the military *status quo* contrary to the armistice agreement. He concluded that the project would be legal if it did not interfere with the restoration of normal life in the zone and if it did not affect the rights of the Arab landowners. The Security Council passed two resolutions (S/2130 and S/2152/Rev. 1) supporting the cease-fire and cease-work orders and the views of the Chief of Staff. Israel was compelled to suspend further work until, despite Syrian objections, the Chief of Staff authorized its resumption on lands which were not Arab-owned and thus not the subject of dispute.

Major Israeli-Syrian differences also arose over Lake Tiberias. Syria's border reaches about thirty-three feet from the northeastern edge of the lake, near where most of the best fishing is found. Under the Anglo-French agreements of February 3, 1922, June 23, 1923, and February 2, 1926, the inhabitants of Syria were given "the same fishing and navigation rights on Lakes Huleh and Tiberias . . . as the inhabitants of Palestine" and also the right to "enjoy grazing, watering and cultivation rights" and to "cross the frontier freely" to enjoy these rights.[20] Whereas Syria and UNTSO maintained that these agreements were still binding, Israel contended that because she had never accepted them and, in any case, because they would be binding only if normal relations existed between Syria and herself, the agreements were no longer valid. Wishing to take all possible steps to foster direct contacts with the Syrians and their government, to bypass UN agencies, and to reassert her claims to sovereignty over the entire lake, Israel expressed a willingness to negotiate a new treaty with Syria which would restore the water rights contained in the earlier Anglo-French agreements and/or to give individual Syrians fishing permits but only on personal applications to Israeli authorities. Opposing any direct dealings with Israel, Syria rejected these proposals. Syrian officials insisted that if any permits were to become necessary, they must be issued only by the MAC Chairman. Since both sides were determined to uphold their "rights," incidents became inevitable, for the Arabs continued their efforts to use Lake Tiberias and Israel sought to prevent this by the use of force.[21]

Israel set up armed settlements like the "fortified" kibbutz of Beit Katzir along the shore area and used patrol boats to block Arab use of the lake and protect Israeli fishermen and fishing vessels. In earlier years, UN officials complained that Israel was illegally employing "armoured landing craft armed with machine guns and cannons as police boats." Not only were these craft used to protect Israeli fishermen, but their equipment was sometimes used to facilitate raids on neighboring Syrian villages, allegedly to retaliate against Arab interference with Israeli fishing boats and to discourage further Arab use of the lake. UN officials pointed out that every time one of these landing craft came close to shore, even when it was on the most innocent mission, the Arabs, fearing that this time it was on its way to another raid, would become so "alarmed" and nervous that they were "encouraged . . . to start shooting." Even "according to Israeli complaints, firing by Syrian positions was directed not at Israeli fishing craft but at Israeli patrol boats." Yet Israel frequently ignored UN warnings that continued patrolling too close to the shore when not absolutely essential would merely provoke Arab fire and precipitate unnecessary incidents. In fact, following such an incident on December 10, 1955, "between Israeli craft other than fishing boats and a Syrian position," Israel, during the night of December 10–11, made a major assault on Syrian territory north of the lake resulting in fifty-six Syrians killed, seven wounded, and thirty-two missing. UNTSO condemned this attack as completely "unjustified," especially since "no Israeli fishing boat" had "been fired at since the beginning of the fishing season" and no Israeli casualties had resulted from the alleged firing from Syrian positions. Because the Israeli military operation was on a scale requiring preparation long before the December 10 firing took place, UN officials implied that Israel had used, if not actually provoked, the firing incident as an excuse for her planned attack. On January 19, 1956, the Security Council passed a strongly worded resolution (S/3530/Rev. 3) condemning Israel for her "flagrant violation" and threatening her with more severe measures if she failed to "comply with its obligations." [22]

To reduce friction in the Lake Tiberias area, the UNTSO Chief of Staff, backed by the Security Council, urged both sides to take certain actions. Syria was asked to use every effort to prohibit her villagers and soldiers from firing at Israeli vessels and from interfering in any way with Israeli fishing on the lake and to authorize individual Arabs to apply for fishing permits from Israel. Israel, in turn, was pressed to employ only ordinary police boats, to keep them at least 250 meters from the shore, to permit normal and reasonable Arab use of the lake, and to allow a UN ship to patrol the lake. Both states were requested to permit the setting up of fixed observer posts in the more sensitive areas and the complete freedom of movement of UN observers in their territories in order to discourage future incidents, as well as to enable UN officials to be in a better position than in the past to determine which side was responsible for initiating illegal actions. Syria agreed to accept fixed UN observer posts, and the first was set up in September, 1956. She also expressed a willingness to allow greater freedom of movement for UN observers and to issue orders not to fire on or interfere with Israeli fishing activities, although these were not always abided by. Israel refused to sanction a UN patrol boat, and until the summer of 1957, she objected to the setting up of any UN observer posts on the grounds that these were "uncalled for," derogated Israel's sovereign "rights" over her own territory, and "would only encourage Syrian designs on the lake." Although Israel agreed to keep her patrol boats away from the eastern shore except when necessary to approach "for security purposes," UN officials reported that these boats continued to move close to shore even when security was not involved. Israel also continued to restrict the movements of UN observers and to object to the use of lake waters by the Syrians.[23]

Because the Israelis persisted in sending their patrol boats provocatively close to shore and in extending their areas of cultivation to more Arab-owned lands, because the Arabs did not stop trying to make use of Lake Tiberias waters, because UN observer facilities remained inadequate, and because Syrian-Israeli hatred did not diminish, incidents continued to take place.

Jordan-Israel

There were special factors which contributed to the strife between Israel and Jordan. The demarcation lines were 350 miles long, often irregular, and inadequately marked in many areas. In places like Jerusalem, the armistice lines frequently left thousands of bitter Jordanians and Israelis separated mainly by a barbed wire fence. Some lines cut through Arab villages, separating thousands of Arab homes in Jordan from their farm lands in Israel. Jordan also had been forced to absorb thousands of needy and aroused Bedouins expelled by Israel after the Palestine War. One-third of Jordan's population was made up of refugees, large numbers of whom lived in crowded camps very near the demarcation lines. The overwhelming preponderance found themselves with little to do but brood about their plight and dream of their return to their homes and their "homeland." As time passed without any significant progress made by either improving their economic conditions or making it possible to regain their properties, the refugees became increasingly bitter and frustrated. Another third of Jordan's population was made up of Arabs from Palestine areas annexed by Jordan. Their hatred of Israel and their desire for an Arab Palestine were as intense as those of the refugees.

For the first several years of the General Armistice Agreements the incidents were minor. By early 1953, however, the border situation, particularly in the Jerusalem area, became increasingly serious. Armed raids were launched by both sides, and Israel began to mount large-scale "retaliatory" attacks on Jordanian villages. The borders remained relatively free of major clashes from the latter part of 1954 until late 1955, but by 1956 tension had built up once again because Jordanian territory was being used as bases for raids on Israel by the *fedayeen*. Israel responded with major retaliatory assaults.[24] In the meantime, the Western governments had become so preoccupied with the worsening crisis over the Suez Canal that they were unable to deal effectively with the deteriorating situation along the Israeli-Jordanian lines.

Before the Sinai War, difficulties also arose between Jordan and Israel over the Mount Scopus area, located on the northern outskirts of Jerusalem. On July 7, 1948, the two governments agreed to divide this area into three sectors: a Jewish one which included the Hadassah Hospital and Hebrew University and which was completely isolated from the rest of Israel; the Arab village of Issawiya; and a third sector which included the Arabs' Augusta Victoria Hospital. The agreement provided that the entire area be demilitarized and only limited numbers of Arab and Jewish policemen under UN command were to be allowed in the respective sectors. The UN was to be responsible for the security and demilitarization of the area, to fly its flag on the main buildings, and to inspect all convoys carrying supplies to the civilians allowed in the Israeli sector to maintain the buildings there.[25]

Few difficulties arose over Mount Scopus in the early years. Realizing that incidents were more likely to occur if the Arabs and Israelis came into too close physical contact, UN officials prevailed upon the Arab villagers to evacuate those houses, to stop picking olives from those trees, and to refrain from cultivating those lands located within 50 meters of the fence surrounding the buildings in the Israeli sector. In 1952, however, Israeli police, ignoring UNTSO protests, began to patrol beyond the fence. By September, 1953, Israel had begun to send her patrols right up to the "outskirts" of Issawiya. By 1954, she had set up roadblocks across the only road between the Arab village and Jerusalem —thus forcing the villagers to use "rocky and dangerous slopes and hills" instead. Israel now also claimed sovereignty over the whole area between the fence and the village. Through such actions, Israel defeated UNTSO efforts to keep the contending parties separated by a strip of no-man's land, embittered still further the villagers, and triggered numerous incidents.[26]

Israel repeatedly complained to the UN that Jordan was not living up to those provisions of the armistice agreement which called for the "resumption of the normal functioning of the cultural and humanitarian institutions on Mount Scopus" and for "free access to the [Jewish] Holy Places and the cultural institutions" located in Jordan. Israel sought to activate the special committee provided for by the agreement in an effort to obtain Jordan's compliance with these armistice provisions. Despite the urgings of UN officials and the Security Council (in Resolution S/1907), Jordan refused to create this committee on the grounds that security considerations and Israeli failure to abide by various UN resolutions and other parts of the armistice agreement made Jordan's compliance impossible.

Egypt-Israel

Certain conditions which existed along the Egyptian-Israeli demarcation lines provided a breeding ground for incidents. While the armistice line from the Gulf of Aqaba to the Gaza Strip, except in the al-Auja sector, followed the old Palestine border, it was inadequately marked and passed through rough, barren territory with poor means of communication and few inhabitants other than Bedouins. Bedouin tribes frequently crossed the lines, either deliberately or accidently, in their incessant search for water and grass. Israel forcibly sought to keep the Bedouins out of her territory, not only because they might pose a threat to her security but also because she hoped to develop the Negev for her own benefit.

The strategic importance of al-Auja, located at a major road junction, and the conflicting views regarding its legal status furnished another potential source of trouble. The Egyptian-Israeli Armistice Agreement had provided that an area encompassing the village of al-Auja and its vicinity would be "demilitarized." The armed forces of both parties were to be completely excluded from the demilitarized zone. The MAC Chairman was to have considerable jurisdiction over the zone, and MAC headquarters were to be located there. No Egyptian military personnel were to be stationed "closer to al-Auja than al-Qouseima and Abou Aueigila."

Significant difficulties over the al-Auja Demilitarized Zone first developed in September, 1953, when Israel, after driving the indigenous Bedouins from the area, set up a kibbutz there. By this time, Israel had begun to claim sovereignty over the whole zone despite the objections of both UN and Egyptian officials. At first, the MAC denied Egyptian contentions that the kibbutz was illegal. But in September, 1954, the MAC reversed its position, for by then it had found clear "evidence tending to indicate the settlement was organized as a unit of the Israeli armed forces," and this was contrary to the terms of the armistice agreement.[27]

By September, 1955, Israel had illegally taken complete military control of the zone, built fortifications, and laid mine fields. In response to these Israeli actions, Egypt moved her own military forces into the area south of al-Auja, also in violation of the armistice provisions. Both sides started to restrict the movements of UN observers, and Israel refused to allow the MAC to hold any more meetings in the zone despite UN protests. Although by October both sides had agreed to a UN request to withdraw their troops from the prohibited sectors, on the night of November 1–2, Israeli forces made a sudden, major attack upon Egyptian troops and positions in Egyptian territory, killing fifty Egyptians and wounding forty others. Not only did this act increase hatred and tension between the Egyptians and Israelis, but it led to the permanent establishment of the Israeli army in al-Auja and to the further weakening of the position and authority of UN officials and agencies responsible for supervising and enforcing the armistice agreement. After that, Israel refused all UN requests to remove her troops and fortifications from the zone and to allow the MAC to meet in the zone and to supervise activities there.

The Gaza Strip was another source of friction. Even though it was only 50 kilometers long and approximately 4 kilometers wide, the Gaza Strip was crowded with over 50,000 native inhabitants and more than 200,000 Arab refugees. Since most of the natives were no longer able to earn a living, nor were they eligible for UNRWA relief, since they were not refugees, they ended up in a worse predicament than the displaced Palestinians. The packing of such a large number of needy and discontented persons into a small area with artifically created borders made incidents inevitable. The situation was aggravated when Israel established armed settlements and Egypt set up military outposts close to the demarcation lines and armed patrols were sent up to and along these lines. The resulting close contacts between the military personnel of both sides could not but provoke border clashes.

In the earlier years most incidents were relatively minor. The more serious ones involved illegal overflights, minelaying, shooting across the lines, and an occasional armed raid or "reprisal" attack. In June, 1950, as on the other frontiers, Israel started using large numbers of soldiers to make retaliatory assaults. Nevertheless, until February, 1955, the Gaza Strip did not experience as many major and dangerous border clashes as took place on the demarcation lines between Israel, on the one hand, and Jordan and Syria, on the other. In fact, by the latter part of 1954 the Egyptian-Israeli lines had become relatively quiet. However, on February 28, 1955, Israel made an unusually large military raid on the Gaza Strip, killing thirty-eight Arabs and injuring thirty-one. Israel sought to justify her action by claiming it to be a reprisal for earlier Egyptian aggressions. However, the UNTSO Chief of Staff reported to the Security Council that there had actually been "comparative tranquillity along the armistice demarcation lines during the greater part of the period November 1954 to February 1955." On March 29, 1955, the Security Council unanimously passed Resolution S/3378 which supported the UNTSO report and condemned Israel for her assault.[28]

Actually Israel's attack was prompted by a number of considerations which had nothing to do with the border situation. The return of Ben-Gurion as defense minister on February 17 brought back into power a man who believed, as the New York Times reported on March 2, 1955, that "Israeli restraint during the last seven months had been misinterpreted by the Egyptians as a sign of weakness" and that it was necessary "to teach Egypt a lesson and warn it not to push its hostile policy towards Israel too far." Ben-Gurion and his supporters also believed that the Arabs would never agree to make peace until they were forced to do so and that Egypt was the key to peace with the Arab world. In addition, these Israelis were alarmed about the possible military and political consequences resulting from the conclusion of an Anglo-Egyptian agreement in October, 1954, calling for the evacuation of all British military forces from the Suez Canal Zone within twenty months and from the signing of a military pact between Iraq and Turkey on February 24, 1955, with Western blessing. Israel feared that these developments would enable Egypt to strengthen greatly her military position vis-à-vis Israel by taking over British military bases in the canal area and would encourage the West to increase arms shipments to Iraq and other Arab countries. Some Israeli officials were so concerned about the rapid improvement in Egyptian relations with the major Western powers that they launched an attempt to undermine this trend. Israeli agents were instructed to attack American properties and citizens in Egypt and to make it appear as if this were the work of Egyptians—in the hope of causing friction between the United States and Egypt.[29] However, Egypt caught two Jewish ringleaders, tried, and executed them before their plans reached fruition. Even though Israel at the time denied the validity of Egyptian charges against the two Jewish saboteurs, later, as a result of a high-level political dispute within Israel known as the "Lavon Affair," these charges were confirmed. In any case, Israelis claimed that their assault on the Gaza Strip was partly meant to be a "retaliation" for the allegedly "illegal" and "inhuman" executions and for the Egyptian seizure of the Israeli ship *Bat Galim* while it tried to go through the Suez Canal in September, 1954. According to some reports, the Gaza raid brought about a major increase in the influence of those members of the Israeli government who believed in a "get tough" policy and who feared that "the quieter Israel is . . . the easier" it would be "for the Americans and the British to sell Israel down the river." [30]

The February 28 assault had serious and lasting consequences. Prior to February, 1955, anti-Israeli feeling in Egypt had been less virulent than in some other Arab states, and Israeli officials had even tended to express less hostility towards the Nasser regime than some other Arab governments. Since nearly all of the Palestine Arabs under Egyptian control had been confined to the Gaza Strip, which in turn remained considerably isolated from Egypt, they were unable to exert any influence on Egyptian policy towards Israel. Thus, the top Egyptian officials were able to concentrate their energies primarily on internal economic, social, and political reforms and to consider the Palestine question of only secondary importance. Moreover, before 1955, Egypt had not made any determined efforts to buy large amounts of arms from the outside world, and as one military authority observed, "the reorganization of the Egyptian army had only been toyed with so far." [31]

The February 28 attack radically changed the situation. Egyptian leaders interpreted this action and the return of Ben-Gurion to the government as presaging the beginning of a more aggressive Israeli policy designed to force Egypt into suing for peace in the same humiliating way Israel had compelled Egypt to seek an armistice in 1949. The sharp increase in the strength of the activist parties in the Israeli Knesset as a result of the July, 1955, election and the awareness that Israel had obtained advanced military weapons not yet possessed by Egypt added to their fears. To a proud and sensitive leader and people already smarting from earlier defeats, yielding to such blatant pressures without a struggle was unthinkable. Moreover, Iraq's joining the Baghdad Pact and Western efforts to build up Iraq to compete with Egypt for leadership within the Arab world heightened still further the anger and sensitivity of the Egyptians. As a result, Nasser found it necessary, as he himself put it, "to give defense priority over development" and to concentrate his attentions on his relations with Israel. Thus, instead of discouraging incidents and encouraging peace talks, Israel's February 28 assaults aroused increased hatred and fear among the Egyptians, weakened the position of the Arab moderates, forced Nasser to seek arms, and made the chances for peace more remote than ever." [32]

In the summer of 1955, Egypt was unable to obtain arms from the West on terms she could meet. She then turned to the Soviet bloc with more success. Whereas the resulting arms deal greatly strengthened Nasser's prestige in Egypt and throughout the Arab world, it seriously weakened his position in the West and aroused the deep concern of Israel. In the West, Nasser came under increasing attack by the press, television, and other news media, as well as by government officials and politicians. Secretary of State Dulles, who had already charged all neutralists with being immoral and practically tools of the Communists, became more and more hostile towards Nasser as he sought to adopt a neutral foreign policy and as his ties with Russia multiplied—notwithstanding the fact that the Nasser regime took strong measures against the Communists within Egypt. By late 1955, Nasser was accused of being pro-Communist, anti-West, and dangerous to both Israel and the West.

Israel, worried about the flow of large amounts of modern weapons into Egypt, embarked on her own search for more arms. To promote her appeal to the West, Israel belittled her own military strength, exaggerated the actual power of Egypt, and warned that she too would not hesitate to buy arms from the Communists if necessary. Actually, it would have taken years before Egypt could have trained and educated all the military technicians needed to use effectively the large amounts of advanced military equipment purchased. According to her own intelligence estimates, Israel at that time could have put 250,000 trained soldiers into the field within 48 hours, while all of the Arab states combined could have come up with only 205,000 men. Israel could have deployed nearly all of her troops against the Arabs while the Arab countries, for internal and other security reasons, could have used "probably less than half" of theirs against Israel.[33] So Israel continued to hold a significant military superiority over Egypt, as well as the other Arab states, and the threat to Israel's security was not an immediate one. The United States, anxious not to arouse Arab antagonism, agreed to sell Israel only a limited amount of small arms. At the same time, however, American officials quietly encouraged other countries, especially Canada and France, to sell Israel the latest war planes and other heavy equipment. By 1956, France had become Israel's primary source of supply for the most advanced weapons. Ironically, just as the February 28 attack had weakened the position of the moderates in Egypt, so Egypt's arms deal strengthened the influence of the extremists in Israel and helped to bring about the replacement of Moshe Sharett by Ben-Gurion as prime minister on November 2, 1955.[34]

Border incidents multiplied as a result of these developments. Egyptian officers and many Palestinians pressed Nasser to reply to Israeli assaults with even bigger military "retaliations." Nasser resisted these pressures, partly because he knew the Egyptian army was still no match for Israel's and that it would be very difficult to defend the narrow, vulnerable Gaza Strip, and partly because he did not want to give Israel an excuse for increasing the scope of her raids while Egypt's military position remained relatively weak. To placate his own aroused officers and people, Nasser initiated a commando training program for some of the refugees. Finally, after a strong Israeli attack on an Egyptian military position in the Gaza Strip in late August, 1955, small groups of these trained and armed *fedayeen* were sent to make raids in Israel. Since every Israeli village was now endangered and since many Israelis were being killed and injured, the Israeli public became increasingly aroused and the Israeli government stepped up the tempo of its own attacks on the Arabs. Thus, one act of violence led to another.

By the spring of 1956, Arab-Israeli—and especially Egyptian-Israeli —relations had become so explosive that the Security Council had to intervene. On April 4, the Security Council passed Resolution S/3575 which asked UN Secretary-General Dag Hammarskjold to go to the Middle East to do what he could to reduce tensions along the demarcation lines. On the eve of his departure, another serious border clash took place. Israel shelled the crowded town of Gaza, while Egypt fired on a nearby kibbutz. Egypt suffered approximately 160 casualties, mostly civilians; Israel had ten dead and wounded. Egypt was so incensed over her heavy losses that she initiated a new wave of *fedayeen* raids on Israel. Nevertheless, by late April, Hammarskjold was able to bring about a cease-fire and an agreement to accept at least some of his proposals—such as those leading to a greater separation of the forces of the two parties and to more freedom of movement on the part of UN observers—which were aimed at preventing further incidents. The resulting calm along the demarcation lines proved only temporary. The situation deteriorated again for a few weeks in July and then improved for several months. Finally, in late October, 1956, a major crisis developed when Israel invaded the Sinai.

ARAB BOYCOTT AND BLOCKADE OF ISRAEL

Even before Israel came into existence, the Arabs had tried to block the establishment of a Jewish state by launching an economic boycott. In December, 1945, the Arab League Council decided that all Arabs should refuse to buy goods produced by Zionist firms in Palestine. A special office was set up to prevent such goods from being smuggled into Arab territory.

After Israel became a state, the Arab League organized an extensive economic, financial, and personal boycott. By cutting off all types of Arab contacts and by discouraging foreign companies from dealing with Israel in any way, it was hoped that Israel's economic development would be seriously hampered. Foreign concerns were warned that if they set up branch factories or offices in Israel, sold patents and copyrights to her, or did anything which would bolster the "enemy" economically and militarily, they would then be placed on a blacklist and prohibited from carrying on any business activities within the Arab world. There were stringent regulations governing the movement of tourists and others who were usually forbidden to travel to or from Israel. While some Arab governments did not enforce the boycott regulations as strictly as did others, all of them were compelled by popular pressures to express strong support for the boycott.

The Arabs justified their boycott activities on the grounds that a state of war continued to exist, the Arabs had the "right" to take "defensive" action against an enemy which threatened their security, and Israel was refusing to abide by many UN resolutions. The boycott remained important to the Arabs, not only because it provided them with one of the few opportunities for doing something practical to hurt Israel, but also because it provided them with one of their rare bargaining weapons.

Israel attacked the Arab boycott as illegal and contrary to the armistice agreements and the UN Charter. She urged other governments to oppose the boycott by every means. Especially in the earlier years when Israel was seriously handicapped by a rapidly growing population and limited material resources, her economy was adversely affected by the boycott for she was completely cut off from what otherwise would have been her nearest and most natural markets and sources of supply. Thanks to massive outside economic and financial aid from the Jews of the world and from the United States and, later, from West Germany, as well as to the dedicated efforts of her own people, Israel's economy not only survived despite the boycott, but it was able to make considerable progress. Nevertheless, the Arab boycott continued to have some harmful consequences which the Israelis wished to eliminate. At times, Israel resorted to the use of military force in the hope of compelling the Arabs to sue for peace and to end their boycott, but this policy failed to achieve either goal. Israel was more successful, however, in eliciting protests from various Western governments against the Arab boycott. After repeated attempts, Israel's friends in the United States were finally able, in the summer of 1965, to convince Congress to pass a law encouraging American companies to refuse to comply with Arab boycott regulations. In 1965, too, Israel began a counterboycott against foreign concerns which had succumbed to Arab pressures—an effort Israel considered effective. Despite Western and Israeli protests and despite the fact that the Arabs also suffered economic losses from their policy, the Arab governments refused to let up on their boycott.[35]

Friction over the Suez Canal

Serious difficulties arose over Egypt's decision to prevent Israeli ships from using either the Suez Canal or the Gulf of Aqaba. On May 15, 1948, the day the Palestine War formally began, Egypt, establishing an economic blockade of Israel, started visiting and searching all ships passing through the canal suspected of transporting goods to Israel. On February 6, 1950, an official decree listed those items which would be considered contraband of war and thus subject to seizure when found on neutral ships going through the Suez Canal. Israeli vessels were subject to confiscation if they entered Egypt's territorial waters.

Egypt justified her actions on the basis of various contentions. The armistice agreement ended only the military phase of the war, so under the traditional laws of war, Egypt retained the legal authority to exercise the right of visit and search. Even Israel usually seized any Arab ships which entered her territorial waters. This indicated that Israel had also accepted the fact that a state of war still existed with all the corresponding belligerent rights short of actual military action. In any case, the UN Charter gave to all members the right of self-defense, and the

Suez Canal Convention of 1888 authorized Egypt to take whatever measures deemed necessary to protect her security. After all, Israeli ships could sabotage the canal and drop off spies and saboteurs inside Egypt if they were allowed to enter the canal. In both world wars Britain had interfered with enemy shipping in and around the canal for security reasons. Egypt was actually interfering with only a minute amount of goods and shipping passing through the canal, and shipping generally was not suffering any significant inconvenience or delay. Thus, as long as a state of war existed and Israel posed a threat to Egypt's security, Egypt had the "right" to prevent any use of the canal which might strengthen the military power of her enemy. After Israel brought the Suez dispute to the Security Council, Egypt also held that because the problem involved the interpretation of various international agreements and rules of international law, it was basically a legal issue which only the World Court, not the Security Council, could resolve. Egyptian delegates stated that if Israel agreed to abide by all prior UN resolutions, then Egypt would remove her restrictions on the use of the Suez Canal.[36]

As early as the summer of 1949 Israel had attacked Egypt's canal policy before the MAC. In November, 1950, and again in July, 1951, Israel argued, before the Security Council, that Egypt's "hostile acts" were: (1) contrary to the UN Charter which prohibits members from exercising belligerent rights against other members; (2) contrary to the armistice agreement; and (3) contrary to the 1888 Suez Canal Convention, which required Egypt to keep the canal open to all ships and goods in both peace and war. All nations should be concerned about Egypt's "illegal" policy because Egypt could use the restrictions being applied against Israeli vessels and goods as a precedent for interference with the shipping of other nations.[37]

The Western states with major maritime interests generally supported Israel's views and protested Egypt's restrictive canal actions. On September 1, 1951, by a vote of eight in favor and three abstainers (China, India, and the Soviet Union), the Security Council passed Resolution S/2298/Rev. 1, submitted by Britain, France, and the United States. This resolution denied that a state of belligerence still existed and found Egypt's interferences with shipping in the canal to be contrary to the armistice agreement, unnecessary for self-defense, and harmful to the interests of all countries. Egypt was called upon to terminate all interferences beyond those essential to the safety of boats in the canal. (At this time Russia had not yet reversed her policy of friendship with Israel.) Even though Egypt warned that she would not abide by the resolution, she did enforce her canal policy less strictly than before.

In the latter part of 1953, the Suez dispute again flared up. Israel became aroused when Egypt added "foodstuffs and all other commodities . . . likely to strengthen the war potential of the Zionists in Palestine" to the list of contraband and when Egypt detained two ships carrying cargoes to Israel. Israel, bringing the matter before the Security Council, asked it to pass a strong resolution with provisions for sanctions, if necessary, to compel Egypt to remove all "illegal" canal restrictions. Denying again that the Security Council had the authority to pass upon legal issues, Egypt claimed that since September 1, 1951, no ship or cargo had been confiscated even if it were going to Israel, and only fifty-five suspected vessels out of 32,047 using the canal had been inspected. She further announced that only foodstuffs going to the Israeli military forces would be subject to seizure, that blacklist regulations on foreign ships would be further relaxed, and that she would lift her blockade if Israel agreed to abide by all UN resolutions pertaining to Arab-Israeli questions.[38]

The major Western powers favored stronger UN action in principle. However, at that time Britain was trying to negotiate a treaty with Egypt favorable to Britain's future status in the Suez Canal area. By late 1953, the Soviet Union had apparently decided that she would have more to gain by giving up her friendly relations with Israel and cultivating the Arabs instead. On January 22, 1954, the Soviet Union for the first time vetoed a resolution (relating to a Syrian-Israeli water dispute) because the Arabs objected to it. Since the Western powers were not anxious to do anything which might further complicate Britain's negotiations with Egypt and help Russia strengthen her position within the Arab world, they left it to New Zealand to introduce a draft resolution (S/3188/ Corr.1) milder than that which either they or Israel actually wanted. Consequently, although the resolution expressed "grave concern" that Egypt had refused to live up to the 1951 resolution and called upon her to start abiding by it, no provision was made for enforcement. The United States also tried to placate the Arabs by reiterating her interest in seeing that all UN resolutions were carried out. Eight states voted for the New Zealand resolution, but the Soviet Union vetoed it. This veto helped Russia win more friends among the Arabs, but she lost some ground when, at the same time, she publicly called for "direct" negotiations between Egypt and Israel. The Arabs strongly objected to the idea of direct negotiations on any issue. Israel complained that while pro-Arab resolutions could pass the Security Council, none recognizing Israel's rights appeared "capable of adoption" because of the Russian veto policy.[39]

The Suez situation remained dormant for about six months before it exploded again. Israel tried for the first time to send one of her own merchant vessels, the *Bat Galim,* through the canal in late September, 1954. Egypt seized the ship and its cargo. Some reports claimed that Israel had deliberately provoked the incident in order to hamper negotiations between Egypt and Britain over the removal of British troops from the Suez Canal Zone and to force the Security Council to reconsider the whole issue of Israeli shipping in the canal. As a result of UN and Western pressures, on January 1, 1955, Egypt released the Israeli crew and expressed a readiness to release the boat and cargo but only through the MAC. In August, 1955, Israel complained about the two-day detention of a Dutch ship carrying goods to Israel. In June, 1956, Israel protested again when Egypt prevented the Greek vessel, *Pannegia,* from going through the canal with a cargo of cement from Haifa destined for Elath. Up to that point, Egypt had been allowing neutral boats to carry cargoes from Haifa for Elath through the canal. This action indicated a significant tightening up of Egyptian restrictions against Israel.[40]

After Nasser nationalized the Suez Canal Company in July, 1956, Israel found more effective support for her opposition to Egyptian restrictions on her ships and goods. As a result of this new and broader Suez crisis, the major Western governments, disturbed over Egypt's whole canal policy, began to develop a strong hostility towards Nasser. The Israelis were pleased wtih this new Western stance, especially since they had begun to consider Nasser the main threat to their future security. For the first time Israel was able to obtain powerful Western backing for her position that all available means should be employed to compel Nasser to end all canal restrictions.

Friction over the Gulf of Aqaba

Difficulties between Egypt and Israel arose, too, when Egypt extended her visit and search measures to the Gulf of Aqaba in the summer of 1950. The gulf, over 100 miles long and three to seventeen miles wide, borders Egypt, Israel, Jordan, and Saudi Arabia. The mouth of the gulf, about nine miles wide, contains the islands of Tiran and Sanafar which, though technically belonging to Saudi Arabia, had been occupied by Egypt with Saudi Arabia's tacit consent. The only navigable channel runs through the Strait of Tiran, within several hundred yards of Egypt's seacoast. Egypt had installed shore batteries at Sharm al-Sheikh to command the entrance to the gulf.

Egypt defended her right to restrict Israeli shipping in the gulf with the following arguments: Israel's control over the Elath area was illegal because she occupied it after the Egyptian-Israeli Armistice Agreement had been signed and in complete disregard of various UN Security

Council cease-fire resolutions. Thus, until the legality of Israel's owner-ship of Elath was authoritatively determined, "the fundamental issue as to whether the waters of [the Gulf of] Aqaba are or are not an inter-national waterway [could not] be discussed." For centuries the gulf had been an exclusive possession of the Arabs and the natural passageway for Muslims going to the holy cities of Mecca and Medina, and the Arabs wished to protect this passageway. All countries bordering the gulf, including Israel, considered their territorial waters to extend at least six miles from their shores. Since the gulf was generally less than twelve miles wide, practically all of it was under the territorial jurisdic-tion of the bordering states. Consequently, the gulf could not be classi-fied as an international body of water. The Strait of Tiran, lying wholly within the territorial jurisdiction of Egypt, could not be considered an international strait since it did not actually connect two portions of the high seas. In any case, a state of war continued to exist, and both inter-national law and the UN Charter gave nations the right of self-defense. Egypt was, therefore, legally justified in restricting the use of the gulf by enemy ships and by neutral vessels carrying contraband goods to Israel. In an exchange of letters with Britain in July, 1951, Britain had officially accepted Egypt's right to visit and search in the gulf. Also, the issues in-volved were legal in nature and should be dealt with only by the World Court, not the Security Council.[41]

For the first few years during which the port of Elath remained un-developed, few neutral vessels sought to use the gulf to reach Elath, and incidents were rare. Between 1951 and early 1955, according to Egyp-tian authorities, "only three" out of 267 vessels which entered the gulf were actually visited and searched, and no ship or cargo was seized.[42]

By 1955, Israel revealed an increased interest in the port of Elath as the main gateway for her trade and other contacts with the countries of Asia and East Africa. Because transportation facilities by land between Elath and the main cities of Israel were still inadequate, Israel had to depend on neutral ships to bring the cement and other commodities needed to build the port and new housing there. So when on July 3 Egyptian shore batteries, as a result of a misunderstanding, shelled a British ship carrying Muslim pilgrims, Israel took a serious view of the event even though she was not directly involved, for she feared that it presaged increased Egyptian restrictions on neutral vessels carrying goods to Elath. Israeli officials used this occasion to warn that she would use force if Egypt sought to hamper the transport of essential Israeli goods through the gulf. On September 11, 1955, Egypt announced that all ships seeking to enter the Strait of Tiran must obtain Egyptian per-mits beforehand. Nevertheless, in order to avoid a possible military showdown with Israel, Egypt made no serious effort until the 1956 Sinai War to prevent neutral ships from carrying cargoes to Elath.

Israel sought the backing of the UN and the Western governments on the Gulf of Aqaba question. As early as January, 1954, when she asked the Security Council to act upon Egyptian restrictions in the Suez Canal, she also urged the Council to force Egypt to stop interfering with shipping through the gulf. Israel contended that Egypt's hostile actions were contrary to the armistice agreement, the UN Charter, and the Security Council resolution of September 1, 1951. Moreover, since the gulf was "international waters" and under no state's jurisdiction, Egypt was "legally" bound to allow the right of innocent passage through the Strait of Tiran to all ships and goods. If Egypt refused to abide by her legal obligations and if the Security Council failed to act, then Israel held she would be justified in using all means necessary to defend her "rights" and interests. One of Israel's main objectives in attacking Egypt in October, 1956, was to assure herself of uninhibited use of the gulf.[43] According to Moshe Dayan, he and Ben-Gurion had sought Cabinet backing for military action to seize the Strait of Tiran and to open the Gulf of Aqaba to Israeli shipping in the fall of 1955. Most of the Cabinet advised against acting at the time, but they agreed to act when conditions were more favorable.[44]

SINAI WAR AND ITS AFTERMATH

So incensed was United States Secretary of State John Foster Dulles over Colonel Nasser's purchase of arms from the Soviet bloc, his recognition of Communist China, and his increasingly neutralist policies, that he concluded it was time to teach him a lesson. Accordingly, on July 19, 1956, Dulles suddenly withdrew the United States government's offer to help finance the High Dam for the Nile River at Aswan—in a deliberately undiplomatic manner.[45] Angered by what he considered an insult to Egypt's pride, President Nasser struck back with a drastic and dramatic action of his own. On July 26, he nationalized the Suez Canal Company and offered to compensate company shareholders for their bonds "at their value estimated at the closing rate on the Paris Bourse prior to the date on which this Law entered into effect." Future canal revenues would be used to help finance the dam project.[46]

The major Western powers, vigorously condemning Nasser's action, claimed that it violated the 1888 Constantinople Convention and posed a threat to freedom of navigation. They held that Egypt lacked enough technical and administrative personnel to manage the canal safely and efficiently. In addition, they accused Nasser of seeking to obtain complete control of the waterway to promote his political ambitions and to use it for "political blackmail." In August, 1956, the United States took the initiative to convene an international conference in London to deal with the situation. Despite the opposition of the Soviet Union, India, and other countries, eighteen of the conference participants recommended the setting up of an international authority to administer the Suez Canal.

Egypt, holding that such an international body would be even more restrictive of her sovereignty than was the old Suez Canal Company and that it would be equivalent to the establishment of a "collective colonialism" in Egypt, rejected the eighteen-nation proposal. Denying that her action was illegal, she contended that since the Suez Canal Company was merely a privately-owned company set up under Egyptian law, she had the legal right under international law to nationalize it as long as foreign stockholders were paid a just compensation. Egypt was willing to use arbitration, if necessary, to ascertain what a fair price would be. The existence of the old Suez company was not essential to assuring freedom of navigation through the canal as required by the 1888 convention. As proof of this, Egypt noted that while the convention was to last indefinitely, the Suez Canal Company concession was to expire in 1968. She expressed a readiness to abide by the 1888 treaty and to reaffirm this by formal agreement with the UN.[47]

Enraged by what they considered Nasser's intransigence, Britain and France pressed for military action to restore their "rights." Their attitude was greatly influenced by considerations which did not involve the principle of freedom of navigation. This became obvious as Egypt was able to run the canal effectively, despite the abrupt departure of nearly all of the Western canal pilots in response to the encouragement of their home governments, and as she refrained from interfering with the shipping of any country except Israel and offered to submit the legal aspects of the dispute to the World Court. To British ultra-nationalists, whose pride had already been badly hurt by the rapid decline of Britain's position in the world, the Suez Canal became a symbol of Britain's past glory. To them Nasser was an upstart who was challenging Britain's honor, as well as her vital interests, and who should be dealt with forcibly.

Similarly, French reaction reflected the bitter frustrations generated by repeated blows to French pride and prestige. Having suffered humiliating defeats during World War II and in Indo-China, French nationalists were reluctant to give up their last major possession in North Africa —Algeria. France blamed Egypt's material and moral support for the persistence of the Algerian rebellion. French public opinion gave very strong support to the use of armed power in order to save French pride, assure the rights of French stockholders in the Canal Company, and guarantee use of the canal for transporting oil and other commodities required by the French economy. After conferring, Britain and France started to build up their military forces on Cyprus.

Although the United States also mentioned the need for firm action, she had not intended to go as far as military intervention. In order to head off any drastic actions by Britain and France, the United States induced them, on September 12, to accept a new proposal—the creation of a Canal Users' Association. But Egypt refused to accept this new association.

Early in October the Suez controversy was finally brought before the Security Council. After both private and public discussions, Egypt, Britain, France, and the United States agreed upon a formula containing the following six principles: (1) there should be free and open transit through the canal without discrimination; (2) the sovereignty of Egypt should be respected; (3) the operation of the canal should be insulated from the politics of any state; (4) the manner of fixing tolls and charges should be decided by agreement between Egypt and the canal users; (5) a fair proportion of the canal revenues should be allotted to development; and (6) all differences between Egypt and the Suez Canal Company should be settled by arbitration. Britain and France then introduced a joint draft resolution containing the above principles and calling upon Egypt to accept the eighteen-nation plan for an international authority to administer the canal. On October 13 that part of the resolution containing the six principles passed unanimously. Because of Egyptian opposition to the second part, the Soviet Union vetoed it. Britain and France were unhappy because no international machinery was provided to enforce the principles. They were also dissatisfied with the idea of a Users' Association which claimed the authority to collect all canal tolls because not all ships were cooperating with it and because Egypt refused to recognize its existence. In addition, they became increasingly disillusioned with American policy. The outcome was that Britain and France secretly agreed to disregard the UN and the United States and took matters into their own hands.

The growth of the Suez crisis between Egypt and the Western powers at a time when Arab-Israeli relations had become ever more serious presented Israel with a favorable and rare opportunity which her leaders felt should be exploited. So the Israeli government decided October 25 to initiate a "preventive" war.[48] Most of the cabinet members favored a strike at Jordan to enable Israel to acquire some strategically important territory. Prime Minister Ben-Gurion, however, feared that an attack on Jordan would bring British forces into the contest and would antagonize the United States because of her friendly attitude towards Jordan. In any case, he preferred to deal first with the most powerful and dangerous

Arab opponent. An attack on Egypt was made even more appealing when Israel was assured that Britain and France were going to invade the Suez Canal [49] and when Israel realized how much Egypt had weakened her military strength in the Sinai and Gaza areas in a desperate effort to bolster her defenses around the vital cities of Cairo and Alexandria. Before the Suez crisis broke out, Egypt had stationed the bulk of her army, about 60,000 men, and her heavy military weapons along her borders with Israel. However, when Britain and France began to marshal their forces on Cyprus, Nasser moved most of his best troops and equipment to positions west of the canal. This gave Israel, for the first time in many years, an opportunity to invade Egypt without having to face more than a part—and by far the weakest part—of Egypt's military power.[50] Moshe Dayan frankly admitted: "If it were not for the Anglo-French operation, it is doubtful whether Israel would have launched her campaign; and if she had, its character, both military and political, would have been different." "The decisions on the campaign and its planning are based on the assumption that British and French forces are about to take action against Egypt." [51]

There were other major factors encouraging Israel to invade Egypt. Increasingly concerned about the violent *fedayeen* raids, Israel hoped to destroy *fedayeen* bases in Egypt and to discourage further attacks. Israel was also worried about the large amounts of Czech arms arriving in Egypt and about the military alliance which Egypt had formed with Jordan and Syria on October 24, 1956, with an Egyptian officer as commander-in-chief, because these developments, in time, could bring about a major shift in the balance of power in favor of the Arabs. Israel felt it would be to her advantage to act before Egypt could build up her military strength and before the Arab alliance could become effective. In order to justify her allegedly "preventive" war, Israel made it appear that she faced a "direct and immediate danger" which demanded quick action on her part. In actual fact, as Hanson Baldwin, military specialist for the *New York Times,* concluded after inspecting Egyptian military installations on the eve of the Israeli invasion, with the bulk of the Egyptian army on the western side of the canal, "there was no factual military indication of any imminent Egyptian attack." [52]

Israel was further encouraged by an international situation favorable to her. The Soviet Union was preoccupied with the revolt in Hungary and a threatened uprising in Poland. Since the West had become strongly anti-Nasser, the Israelis presumed that most Western countries would not seriously try to oppose—and some would even welcome—an Israeli attack which might cause the downfall of the hated Nasser regime. Moreover, since the United States was in the thick of a presidential election campaign, it was widely believed that President Dwight D. Eisenhower, a candidate for reelection, would not dare to risk antagonizing Jewish voters by opposing Israel's invasion.

Then too, the Suez Canal crisis had brought about a temporary convergence of British, French, and Israeli interests, and Israel tried to extract the greatest possible benefits from this unique situation. Franco-Israeli relations had not been especially friendly in the earlier years. In 1955 and 1956, however, both countries developed a common enemy in Egypt, and this pulled them into a virtual unofficial alliance. France became the strongest political supporter of Israel in the UN and her primary supplier of the latest fighter planes, tanks, and other military equipment. While relations between Israel and Great Britain never became close, their common opposition to Nasser brought them briefly together after Britain and France decided in secret talks held in the middle of October, to take military action against Egypt. Their plan was that Israel would invade the Sinai. As soon as Israeli troops neared the Suez Canal, Britain and France would order Egypt and Israel to withdraw their forces from the canal zone in order to permit Anglo-French military units to intervene and occupy the canal area on the pretext of protecting it from the ravages of war. Because of the warm ties which had developed between Israel and France, French officials handled most of the direct contacts with Israel, although the British Foreign Secretary did meet secretly with the Israeli and French Prime Ministers between October 22 and 24 to work out the final details of the military plans. Besides providing considerable military equipment, France also agreed to use her own fighter planes and naval vessels to help protect Israeli cities and seacoast areas from possible Egyptian air and sea attacks during the conflict. (Some reports even indicated that French planes and ships took an active part in the fighting in the Sinai, Gaza, and coastal areas.) Under these providential circumstances, Israeli leaders felt the moment was opportune to attack Egypt because Israel would be faced with "a minimum of resistance and with a minimum of unfavorable international repercussions." [53]

Israel was determined to achieve a number of objectives besides destroying *fedayeen* bases and Egyptian military power. She hoped to force an end of the Arab boycott, an opening of both the Suez Canal and the Gulf of Aqaba to her shipping, and the negotiation of a peace settlement with Egypt on Israel's terms. Once the leading Arab country had been compelled to sue for peace, the Israelis believed that other Arab states would quickly follow Egypt's example. Israel also expected to seize some valuable territory which could be kept permanently or used as a bargaining weapon. Although the Gaza Strip contained several hundred thousand bitter refugees and native Palestinians who could become a burden, Israeli leaders desired this area because of its great strategic importance to Israel. In fact, immediately after occupying the Gaza Strip early in November, Israeli officials made it clear that they intended to retain it indefinitely. For example, on November 10, Foreign Minister Golda Meir stated that the strip was an integral part of Israel and would remain so. On November 14, Ben-Gurion referred to it as "Israeli territory occupied by an invader." [54] Israeli actions supported these statements: a civil administration and a postal system were installed and steps were taken to improve various public services. Even as late as February, 1957, Israel started an elaborate development program there. Ben-Gurion also hoped to acquire part, if not all, of the Sinai Peninsula, and on November 7, 1956, he implied that the Sinai was "Israel's ancient right" and not properly part of Egypt. He and others wished to acquire control of at least the sector along the Gulf of Aqaba so that Israel would be better able to protect her ships in the gulf.[55]

To maximize the element of surprise, Israel pretended for days that she was mobilizing her forces to invade Jordan. When she finally launched her attack in the Sinai, she made it look like only a large-scale reprisal action. Consequently, for many hours after the initial assault Egypt was unaware of its true nature and extent, and her main attention remained fixed on the Anglo-French threat from Cyprus. By October 30 Nasser finally realized the seriousness of the Israeli attack, and he ordered his air force and 10,000 men to reinforce Egyptian troops in the Sinai and Gaza sectors. Only hours later, however, Britain and France issued a twelve-hour ultimatum ordering both parties to withdraw ten miles from the canal and to allow British and French soldiers to interpose themselves between the contending armies, allegedly for the purpose of protecting the canal. Faced with two major threats at the same time, Nasser decided to concentrate his limited power against what he considered the more dangerous one. Therefore, after the ultimatum had ended at 1930 hours on October 31 and after Anglo-French planes had begun to bomb Egyptian airfields and other military targets, Nasser decided to block the canal, to destroy the bridges over it, and to concentrate all his forces in an effort to protect his main strategic centers. At 0730 hours on November 1, he gave the order that all uncommitted Egyptian units in the Sinai Peninsula and the Gaza Strip were to withdraw westward over the Suez Canal and back into Egypt proper as quickly as possible. Even those units then engaged with the enemy were ordered to try to cross the canal while the bridges remained intact, preferably during the night of November 1–2.[56] (Moshe Dayan had written, "From the operational point of view we had to distinguish between the period up to the start of the Anglo-French action and the period after it. It may be assumed that with the launching of their attack, the Egyptian Air Force will cease its activity against us. Egyptian Army units in Sinai will almost certainly be ordered to withdraw into Egypt, and those remaining in their positions will find their morale lowered." Egypt issued a "general withdrawal order" to her forces east of the Suez Canal on November 1.[57])

Up to this point, the Israeli forces—reasonably well-equipped and benefiting greatly from the element of surprise, daring strategy, and superiority in training and mobility, as well as from the fact that Egypt had transferred most of her army west of the canal—had moved forward during the first two days, had overrun some Egyptian border positions, and had thrust deeply into the Sinai Peninsula in the more deserted areas. Nevertheless, the Israelis met some setbacks and some unexpectedly strong resistance at key points, such as at Abu Ageila and Mitla Pass, and Egyptian planes were causing numerous casualties. However, after November 1, Nasser's order to his troops to evacuate the area east of the canal and the Anglo-French air attacks (which destroyed many Egyptian planes and forced Nasser to withdraw the remnants of his air force to neighboring Arab countries to save it from total destruction) put a new light on the Israeli operations in the Sinai and suddenly simplified Israel's military problem. Now, with retreating Egyptian troops fighting largely rear guard actions and lacking any air support, Israeli forces were able to make swift progress in conquering the Sinai and Gaza areas.

As soon as news about the Sinai invasion reached the outside world, the United States took the initiative in calling for a meeting of the UN Security Council and in introducing a strong resolution because she considered Israel's action to be a flagrant violation of the UN Charter. This resolution (S/3710) called upon Israel to withdraw her forces behind the armistice lines "immediately" and upon all UN members to refrain from giving her any assistance so long as she "had not complied with the resolution." Only Britain and France opposed any action against Israel and only France seriously sought to justify Israel's invasion. Because these two powers had vetoed the American resolution and their planes had already started, on October 31, to attack Egypt, an Emergency Special Session of the General Assembly was called.

As soon as the General Assembly convened on November 1, the United States, believing that the Anglo-French action gravely threatened the future of the UN and world law, once again took the initiative in introducing a resolution (A/3256) which urged an "immediate cease-fire" and called for the "prompt withdrawal" of Israeli forces. This resolution passed by an overwhelming vote with only Britain, France, Israel, Australia, and New Zealand voting against it. Since of the four belligerents only Egypt had agreed to abide by the terms of the resolution, nineteen Afro-Asian states jointly introduced an even stronger cease-fire proposal (A/3275). This passed by a large majority on November 4. Israel agreed to accept a cease-fire, but only on conditions which would have given her most of her objectives. This was unacceptable to the General Assembly. In the meantime, Britain and France hurriedly began to land troops in the Suez Canal area in the hope of being able to seize all of it before having to accept a cease-fire. But pressures from the United States, the UN, and, in the case of Britain, from some Commonwealth members and British public opinion, plus threats from the Soviet Union finally compelled the two Western governments to accept a cease-fire on November 6, even though their forces had occupied only part of the canal. It took similar pressures and threats, as well as another UN resolution (A/3309), before Israel reluctantly agreed to a cease-fire on November 8.

On November 4, the General Assembly passed a Canadian resolution (A/3276) which provided for "the setting up, with the consent of the nations concerned, of an emergency international UN force to secure and supervise the cessation of hostilities in accordance with the terms" of prior resolutions. Under the leadership of the UN Secretary-General, a UN Emergency Force (UNEF) was hurriedly brought into existence. Several Scandinavian, Latin American, and Asiatic states provided UNEF with troops, who were rushed to the canal zone to take over as British and French units withdrew and also to man the lines between Egyptian and Israeli forces.

Israel tried to set major conditions to any withdrawal. However, since nearly all UN members felt that Israel should not be allowed to benefit in any way from her illegal aggression, they voted for a series of resolutions (A/3385/Rev. 1 on November 24, A/3501/Rev. 1 on January 16, and A/3517 on February 2) which demanded an immediate and unconditional Israeli withdrawal. Because American officials felt that an Israeli evacuation of the occupied areas was essential if the United States were to retain any influence in the Arab world and to foil Soviet designs there, they decided to help make it easier for Israel to yield to UN demands. They declared that: (1) they would insist that UNEF be stationed in the Gaza Strip and at Sharm al-Sheikh; (2) they considered the Gulf of Aqaba to be an "international waterway"; and (3) they were prepared to exercise American right of freedom of navigation through the Strait of Tiran and to join with other nations to secure general recognition of this right. Israel was not fully satisfied with these rather indeterminate American assurances. But, in view of increasing American pressures, Soviet threats, and calls for sanctions within the UN, Israel reluctantly agreed to withdraw on the basis of her understanding of the American declaration. Israel completed her troop withdrawal by March 8. Despite UN protests, she claimed that the Egyptian-Israel Armistice Agreement was no longer binding upon her and she refused to evacuate the al-Auja demilitarized zone.

Egypt agreed to allow UNEF troops to be stationed in the Gaza Strip, along the Sinai demarcation lines, and in key spots along the Gulf of Aqaba coast. The UN Secretary-General indicated that this was done only with Egypt's permission and that UNEF would have to leave whenever Egypt so requested. It had been originally hoped that UNEF troops could be stationed on both sides of the demarcation lines to enable them to do a more effective job of preventing incidents. Israel, however, refused to allow UNEF to operate on her soil on the alleged ground that it would infringe upon her sovereignty.

Israel soon found that she had won few of her objectives and even these were gained at considerable cost. While the Gulf of Aqaba was opened to Israeli shipping—at least for as long as UNEF units were allowed to remain in the area—Israeli shipping was still denied the use of the Suez Canal. The Israeli army destroyed considerable Egyptian military equipment, but Egypt quickly made up for these losses by seizing British military supplies stored in the canal zone and by purchasing more arms from the Soviet bloc. In short, Israel gained at most only a relatively brief military respite. The stationing of UNEF units along the demarcation lines kept the borders relatively free of ground incidents. Nevertheless, Israel's refusal to work through the armistice machinery seriously weakened the effectiveness of the Egyptian-Israel MAC. Far from declining, Nasser's position both in Egypt and in the Arab world was greatly strengthened by his resistance to the Israeli and Anglo-French invasions. Ironically, instead of bringing peace nearer, the Sinai War, by increasing Arab hatred and fear, by giving the Arabs still another reason for wanting revenge, and by further humiliating them, made the Arabs even more adamant in their refusal to come to terms with Israel. Besides, by exaggerating the extent of Israel's military victory and of Egypt's defeat in the Sinai, the Israelis became, as the *New York Times* reported on November 12, 1956, more overconfident and cocky and, therefore, "more difficult to handle" and less willing to make concessions.

The Suez affair strengthened the position of the Soviet Union in the Arab world and weakened that of Britain and France. Not only were the Arabs embittered by the Anglo-French assault on Egypt, but they were furious because these two states had deliberately aided and abetted Israel in her invasion. Even though the strong American stand against the attacking countries did restore some American prestige and influence in the Arab world, other actions, such as the freezing of Egyptian assets in the United States and the cessation of the CARE and surplus agricultural disposal programs just when Egypt needed them the most, tended to detract from the final gains achieved.

The Sinai War had unfortunate repercussions for the Arabs in Israel and the Jews in Egypt. Although the former revealed no real sign of disloyalty, Israeli Jews showed great distrust of them. For example, the Israeli government compelled many Arabs to move away from the more sensitive borders. At Kafr Kassem, Israeli border police callously killed nearly fifty innocent Arab villagers as they returned home from work in the fields without knowing that a curfew had been established. Even though the Israeli government expressed regrets for the attack on the villagers of Kafr Kassem and ultimately tried and punished those guilty of the killings, such actions hardly inspired the loyalty of Arab residents in Israel. For some years, the Jews in Egypt had been less troubled than those in some other Arab states. During the Sinai War, however, the Egyptian government felt obliged to detain some of its own Jewish citizens. Many other Jews, particularly those who were British and French nationals or stateless, were expelled from the country. Despite the fact that Egypt soon tempered her actions against her own Jewish citizens after the Israeli threat had disappeared, many felt so insecure that they left the country. Thus, the Sinai War undermined still further the position of Jews in the Arab world and Arabs in Israel, and this development, in turn, added considerably to Arab-Israeli distrust and hatred.[58]

BORDER PROBLEMS, 1957–1965

For several years after the Sinai War, the Arab-Israeli armistice lines remained relatively quiet. UNEF troops prevented any significant complications from arising along the Egyptian-Israeli lines. While more serious and more frequent incidents took place along the borders between Jordan and Israel and especially between Syria and Israel, even these were usually minor. In later years, however, border conflicts increased in number and intensity.

Egypt-Israel

With more than 5,000 UNEF soldiers stationed in the Gaza Strip, along the demarcation lines in the Sinai Peninsula, and in the Sharm al-Sheikh area overlooking the Strait of Tiran, few border incidents occurred. Though Israel refused to cooperate with the MAC, she submitted some of her complaints about alleged infiltrations to the commander of UNEF, who then sought to deal with the situation. The MAC continued to function with only Egyptian and UN officials participating in its activities. UNEF and the MAC were unable to prevent frequent illegal overflights by the aircraft and violations of territorial waters by the fishing vessels of both countries.

Occasional difficulties arose over Egyptian restrictions on Israeli vessels and goods seeking to go through the Suez Canal. While the UN was helping Egypt to remove the ships sunk in the canal during the Sinai War, Israel began to threaten that she would resort to force, if necessary, to insure her of unhindered use of the waterway once it was opened to traffic. The United States prevailed upon the Israelis not to create a new crisis over this issue, but she was unsuccessful in her efforts to persuade Egypt to terminate her blockade actions against Israel. Egyptian officials once again expressed a willingness to accept a World Court test of their canal policy and to end their blockade if Israel agreed to abide by the UN resolutions involving the Arab refugees and other Arab-Israeli problems.[59]

From the summer of 1957 until March, 1959, Egypt allowed forty-one foreign vessels, mostly chartered by Israeli companies, to go through the canal with Israeli goods. But in March, 1959, Egypt began to tighten her restrictions, partly in an effort to check the growth of Israel's trade with countries in the Far East and East Africa and partly because of the intense anti-Israeli feelings among the Arab masses. Egyptian leaders were placed under particularly great pressures to take strong action against Israeli goods going through the canal whenever Israel gave publicity to the affair. For example, in 1959 when the Danish ship *Inge Toft* was widely reported as approaching the canal with Israeli goods, Egyptian officials, who had allowed many such boats to pass quietly through the canal in the past, temporarily detained the *Inge Toft* despite Israeli protests. In this case, the United States, anxious to avoid giving Russia further opportunity to play up to the Arabs by vetoing another resolution opposed by them, used her influence on Israel to keep the matter off the Security Council agenda. More difficulties arose in 1960 and 1961 when Egypt confiscated Israeli-owned cargoes from a Greek vessel and a British freighter. After 1961, Egypt appeared to relax her restrictions on Israeli goods carried through the canal on neutral ships. Nevertheless, in August, 1966, Egypt seized trucks and excavating equipment on a Dutch vessel because it was believed that the cargo was owned by an Israeli bank. In short, while Egypt generally allowed Israeli goods to pass through the canal, she occasionally enforced her restrictive policy—apparently to prove to Arab nationalists that she was enforcing the blockade.[60]

Egyptian restraints on Israeli shipping not only embittered the Israelis but also caused increased anti-Egyptian feelings and actions in certain quarters in the United States. For instance, some seamen's unions picketed Egyptian vessels in American harbors, and a number of attempts were made in Congress to restrict American aid to Egypt because of her Suez Canal policy.

Jordan-Israel

For some years after the Sinai War, both Jordan and Israel tried to prevent border complications. *Fedayeen* raids from Jordanian territory ceased completely, while Israel refrained from escalating the minor incidents which occasionally occurred. The most serious difficulties arose in the Mount Scopus and no-man's land areas in the Jerusalem sector.

Conflicts over Mount Scopus emanated largely from two major factors. Despite UN protests, Israel insisted on keeping the only road between the Arab village of Issawiya and Jerusalem closed and on sending her police patrols right up to the outskirts of the village itself. A major disagreement also developed between Israel, on the one hand, and Jordan and the UN, on the other, as to the extent of UN authority over Mount Scopus and over the convoys used to supply the Israeli sector. For example, tension brought about by Israeli patrolling culminated in the May 26, 1958, killing of Colonel George A. Flint, chairman of the MAC, by shots from Jordanian territory. When Israeli patrolling became less provocative and when Israel agreed to open the road during the daytime, tension declined and fewer incidents took place. Differences also arose in 1957 and 1958 when Jordan charged that Israel was illegally sending oil and equipment by convoy to add to her military power on Mount Scopus. For many years, Israel, claiming sovereignty over her own sector, had restricted the movements of MAC and UNTSO officials even when they were formally instructed by the UN to investigate Jordanian accusations of illegal activities. In November, 1957, Israel finally agreed to permit a personal representative of the UN Secretary-General to check on Jordanian contentions that fortifications were being built there. However, some limitations were placed upon his movements as well. In the summer of 1958, UN officials removed a barrel from a convoy because it contained prohibited material. Jordan, in turn, persisted in her refusal to allow Israel to make use of the university and hospital buildings on Mount Scopus, as well as to have access to Jewish holy places in the Jordanian section of Jerusalem.[61] (Shortly after the June, 1967, war had ended, Israeli officials revealed that they had, in fact, been illegally smuggling military equipment to Mount Scopus. On June 21, 1967, the *New York Times* reported that Israel was displaying "an interesting exhibit of modern arms—machine guns, mortars, grenades, mines and other equipment smuggled into the enclave over the years." Even three jeeps and recoilless guns had also been smuggled in piece by piece.)

Certain bits of territory in the Jerusalem area had been made into neutral, demilitarized zones and no-man's lands during the Palestine War. Some of these were retained by the Jordanian-Israeli Armistice Agreement to keep the contending parties from having too close contact with each other in the more critical sections. On June 23, 1949, Jordanian and Israeli representatives signed an agreement which drew a line, sometimes referred to as the "civilian line," through the neutral zone around Government House, which once had belonged to the Palestine mandatory government and which had been made into the central headquarters of UNTSO. Since the Jordanian government had refused to ratify this agreement, Jordan considered that it had never come into legal force. Israel, on the other hand, contended that it had become binding on signature.

Despite the fact that both sides had disregarded the demilitarization provisions, these no-man's lands did not become a serious source of trouble until the summer of 1957. In July, 1957, Israel sent workers and police into that part of the area around Government House claimed by Israel under the June 23, 1949, agreement to plant trees as part of a "beautification project." Fearing that Israel was preparing the way for annexing this territory, Jordan moved some of her own soldiers into the demilitarized zone. Jordan also formally complained to the UN that Israel was illegally working on Arab-owned property. When Israel refused the appeal of the UNTSO Chief of Staff to suspend her project until the differences could be straightened out, the dispute was taken before the Security Council. On January 22, 1958, the Security Council unanimously passed Resolution S/3940, which asked Israel to suspend her tree planting activities until UNTSO had had an opportunity to survey the land records to determine whether Arab-owned lands were involved and until some provisions had been made to enable UNTSO to regulate civilian activities in the area. Mostly in response to strong American pressures, Israel reluctantly abided by this resolution.[62]

Syria-Israel

Even after the Sinai War, the demilitarized zone and Lake Tiberias continued to be the main trouble spots between Syria and Israel. In the earlier years, UN officials were able to keep to a minimum the number of conflicts within the demilitarized zone by convincing the Arabs and Israelis to maintain no-man's areas between the opposing parties. But in the latter part of 1957, incidents began to develop, according to UNTSO reports, from "the progressive extension of Israeli cultivation towards the East" and into the buffer area and "from Arab opposition to what they considered as encroachment on their land." As physical contacts between Arabs and Israelis increased and as Israeli farmers, often backed by armed Israeli police, began to work on Arab-owned and disputed lands, shooting incidents became inevitable. In January, 1960, the situation became increasingly tense as Israel began to dig a drainage ditch through the edge of the Arab village of Tawafiq in the southern part of the demilitarized zone. In an attempt to prevent serious clashes, the UNTSO Chief of Staff, after studying the conflicting land claims, established what he considered the proper limits of cultivation for both the Arabs and the Israelis. He also proposed the reestablishment of a buffer zone between these areas, a suggestion which the Arabs accepted and the Israelis rejected. When the Arabs sought to cultivate some property assigned to the Arab sector, an exchange of fire took place. Finally, on the night of January 31–February 1, Israel sent an armed force against Tawafiq. Because of the gravity of this assault, the Israeli-Syrian MAC, with only the Syrian and UN representatives present, met formally for the first time in years to condemn Israel for her action.[63]

Another grave crisis developed when, on December 4, 1962, Israeli tractors moved on to disputed lands in the southern sector. Syrian soldiers not only fired at the tractors but they also began to shell three neighboring Israeli settlements. This and subsequent incidents led Prime Minister Ben-Gurion to threaten to unleash a major assault against Syria if she persisted in shooting at Israeli settlements. Syria warned that she would fight back if attacked. By acting quickly, UN and Western officials were able to restore temporary peace.

Numerous incidents continued to take place, however, because Israeli tractors, often supported by armed police, insisted on moving into disputed areas and because the Syrians frequently reacted by firing at the tractors. On August 19, 1963, two Israeli farmers were killed while working with a tractor near Almagor, a few miles north of Lake Tiberias. Israel charged that Syrian soldiers had committed the crime. By this time, the more moderate Levi Eshkol had replaced Ben-Gurion as prime minister. Instead of immediately ordering a retaliatory raid, Eshkol submitted the matter to the Security Council. While many Israelis contended that the use of force would be more effective against the Arabs than any Security Council action, other Israelis, aware of the harm done to Israel's international position by past reprisals, believed that Israel would have more to gain by turning to the UN first. UNTSO's report on this incident did not try to assign any specific responsibility. However, it did report finding "tracks leading from the direction of the Jordan River to the ambush position . . . and the tracks returning in the direction of the Jordan River." [64]

Partly because they had hoped to weaken the influence of the advocates of force in Israel and because they had feared that if the Security Council did not give the Israelis some satisfaction in this case, Israel might still order a military reprisal against Syria and might refuse to resort to the UN again in the event of future incidents, the United States and Britain took the lead in condemning those responsible for the crime and in holding Syria at fault. On August 29, eight states voted for the Anglo-American resolution (S/5407) which implied that Syria was guilty, but the Soviet Union, once again supporting the Arabs, vetoed it. Despite the veto, Israeli officials, encouraged by the Western governments, decided to consider the large vote for the resolution as representing a "moral and political victory" for Israel, and this precluded the need for any retaliatory assault. Nevertheless, incidents continued to occur.[65]

Difficulties also persisted over Lake Tiberias. Israel insisted upon denying the use of the lake to the Syrian and demilitarized zone Arabs until they had obtained special permits from her. Israel also occasionally alleged that the Syrians had been harassing Israeli fishing and patrol boats. On March 8 and 15, 1962, heavy fire was exchanged between Israeli patrol boats and Syrian military positions near the northeastern shore of the lake. UN officials were unable to determine which side had started the shooting. Nevertheless, Israel, blaming Syria, launched a large-scale "retaliatory" assault against Syrian military posts and villages in the area on the night of March 16–17. In the fighting that ensued, both sides suffered casualties. While criticizing Syria for illegally maintaining and using such heavy military weapons in that particular sector, the UNTSO Chief of Staff accused Israel of continuing to send her patrol boats provocatively close to the shore even when it was not necessary to do so for security reasons. He claimed that Israel's action was unjustified and contrary to the armistice agreement. On April 9, the Security Council overwhelmingly passed Resolution S/5111 which strongly condemned Israel. Even Israel's best friends on the Security Council voted for the resolution and warned that her policy was doing more to aggravate than to alleviate the situation. In fact, the Chief of Staff reported that Israel's attack had left such an unfortunate "aftermath of tension" that it had actually fostered subsequent incidents. As will be discussed later, the situation in the Lake Tiberias area deteriorated again in 1966.[66]

JORDAN RIVER CONTROVERSY

By the early 1960's the rapidly growing Arab-Israeli competition for the limited water supplies in the Jordan River system had added yet another source of friction. Three major streams—the Hasbani, the Banyas, and the Dan—converge north of Lake Huleh to form the headwaters of the Jordan River. The Hasbani originates in Lebanon, the Banyas in Syria, and the Dan along the Syrian-Israeli border. Starting near Jisr Banat Yacoub, located below Lake Huleh in the Syrian-Israeli Demilitarized Zone, the Jordan River drops nearly 900 feet before it empties into Lake Tiberias. South of the lake the river descends through the Jordan Valley until it reaches the Dead Sea some 1,300 feet below sea level. The Yarmouk River, main tributary of the lower Jordan, flows westward along the Jordanian-Syrian frontier for a considerable distance before touching Israeli territory and joining the Jordan River four miles below Lake Tiberias. While all of the riparian states are in need of water, the Jordan River is especially vital to Jordan and Israel.

In the late 1930's and early 1940's, the Zionists, anxious to settle as many Jews as possible in Palestine, had water studies made by Walter C. Lowdermilk, James B. Hayes, and a private Zionist company. Lowdermilk and Hayes optimistically concluded that if the area's waters were properly utilized, Palestine could absorb up to four million more Jewish refugees. On the basis of these studies and conclusions, the Zionists advocated a unified, regional development program for the Jordan and Litani Rivers, even though the latter was wholly within Lebanese territory.

By the early part of 1950, Israel, using the Lowdermilk and Hayes proposals as a basis, devised an All-Israel Seven-Year Plan. This provided for the diversion of Jordan River water at Jisr Banat Yacoub to a proposed power plant at Tabagha. Most of this water was to be channeled westward to the Battauf Reservoir and then southward to the Negev. On September 3, 1953, Israel started digging a diversion canal at Jisr Banat Yacoub. When Israel sought to work on Arab-owned land in the area despite Arab opposition, shooting incidents occurred. The UNTSO Chief of Staff, backed by the UN and the United States, forced Israel to halt all work on Arab-owned properties. Since difficulties continued to arise with both Syria and the UN over canal digging operations within the demilitarized zone, in 1956 Israel decided to divert the water from Lake Tiberias, instead of from the river itself in the disputed demilitarized zone.

UNRWA commissioned an American engineering firm, Charles T. Main, Inc., to study the water problem in 1952–53. The Main Plan which resulted recommended a regional and unified development program for the entire Jordan River system. In October, 1953, President Dwight D. Eisenhower sent Eric Johnston, then head of the Motion Picture Association, to the Middle East to urge the Arab and Israeli governments to accept this new proposal. Unfortunately, Johnston's first trip took place at a time when Arab-Israeli tensions were on the rise as a result of a number of bloody border clashes. After several more journeys to the Middle East in 1954 and 1955, he did obtain major Arab and Israeli concessions which greatly narrowed some of the differences between them; serious political and psychological obstacles, however, continued to hamper progress. Arab-Israeli hatred and fear remained intense. Arab officials were concerned that an acceptance of the Johnston Plan (a modified version of the Main Plan) might be interpreted as an implied recognition of Israel—a development which would be most unpopular among the Arab masses. Moreover, the Arabs insisted that the UN must be fully involved in the implementation of any agreed water program. Israel, distrustful of the UN, opposed having it involved in any supervisory activities. The further deterioration of Arab-Israeli relations in 1956, leading to the Sinai invasion, destroyed all further hope of obtaining Arab-Israeli acceptance of any regional water proposal. After 1956, both sides felt free to develop their own unilateral projects.[67]

In 1958, Jordan, with American financial help, started work on a forty-two-mile East Ghor Canal to irrigate more than 30,000 acres of land along the eastern banks of the lower Jordan by means of a gravity diversion of Yarmouk waters. This canal was completed in 1963. Jordan also initiated work on a larger Yarmouk project to increase the land to be irrigated on both sides of the lower Jordan and to supply Jordan and Syria with electric power.

By 1960, the Arabs showed mounting anxiety over the substantial progress being made by Israel in carrying out her plans to divert Jordan waters to the Negev. The Arabs were especially concerned that the Israeli project would: (1) deprive Jordan of badly needed water; (2) endanger Arab security by allowing Israel to absorb large numbers of Jewish immigrants, thus enabling her to increase her potential military power through a much larger population; and (3) lessen the chances of Israel ever permitting the repatriation of the Arab refugees since Jewish immigrants would have occupied all the available land. Pressed by Syria, the Arab League started to discuss the matter and to consider various proposals (including one calling for impeding the flow of those Jordan River headwaters located in the neighboring Arab states) which might thwart Israel's diversion plans. In 1960, the Arab League Council claimed that Israel's undertaking was "an act of aggression against the Arabs, which justifies Arab collective defense." [68] Israel, in turn, warned that she would regard any effort to cut off the flow of Jordan waters as a "threat to peace" and would use any means necessary to prevent such a development. Because no Arab state except Syria was then prepared to take any practical steps to deal with the water dispute, an Arab-Israeli confrontation over it was postponed.[69]

By late 1963, as Israel's project rapidly neared completion, rising Syrian pressures and popular concern over the situation forced the Arab governments to act. The Arab Chiefs of Staff, convening in December, 1963, supported Syria's call for the use of military power, if necessary, to compel Israel to halt her water diversion efforts. President Nasser and other Arab leaders, however, realized that the Arab armies were still relatively weak and greatly preoccupied with fighting in Yemen and in the Kurdish areas of Iraq, that serious inter-Arab frictions continued to exist, and that the Western powers would probably intervene on Israel's behalf if she were attacked. President Nasser therefore requested an urgent meeting of all the Arab heads of state to check the grave trend towards a war on Israel which had developed within the Arab world and to seek and agree upon some nonmilitary course of action which might placate the angry Arab masses. At a conference in Cairo in the middle of January, 1964, the Arab leaders decided on a plan to divert the flow of those headwaters and tributaries (the Hasbani, Banyas, and Yarmouk Rivers) located in the neighboring Arab countries. If completed, this scheme would substantially decrease the amount and greatly increase the salinity of the waters left in the Jordan River for Israel's use. The leaders also decided (1) to reduce inter-Arab frictions and increase inter-Arab cooperation; (2) to create a unified military command which would coordinate the power and strategy of all Arab armies to protect the Arab states carrying out the project from an Israeli attack; (3) to request that all Arab governments help finance the Arab water diversion scheme, as well as a proposed military build-up in Lebanon, Syria, and Jordan; and (4) to ask Ahmad Shukairi, the Palestine representative to the Arab League, to continue his efforts to set up a "Palestine entity" which would enable the Palestinians to play a more effective role in dealing with Israel.

While the summit conference decisions eliminated any immediate danger of war, they did not diminish the basic Arab-Israeli differences over the Jordan River. In fact, Israel found herself faced with a grave potential threat to her vital water supplies. Israeli officials intensified their warnings that they would resort to military force to prevent the successful completion of the Arab plans to divert the Jordan's head-waters. By the summer of 1964, the first stage of Israel's project had been completed, and water, although more saline than desired, began to flow to the Negev area.

At a second summit conference held in September, 1964, the Arab leaders agreed to press ahead on their diversion plans, which now clearly envisaged the damming of the Banyas and Hasbani Rivers in order to divert their flow through an eighty-mile canal to a proposed Makheiba Dam on the Yarmouk River in Jordan. These waters, when added to those already in the Yarmouk, were to help Jordan develop even more electric power and irrigated land. After some delay, Lebanon, Syria, and Jordan commenced work on their respective diversion schemes.

While the Arab and Israeli water undertakings did not bring about a major military confrontation, the increasingly bitter water dispute helped to intensify Arab-Israeli tensions and to encourage attacks by each side on the diversion projects of its opponent. Actually, the next serious border clash took place in November, 1964, near the point where the Israeli, Syrian, and Lebanese frontiers converge and in an area containing major springs that feed the Dan River in Israel. It started on November 3 with an exchange of fire between Syrian and Israeli forces when Israeli workers sought to reconstruct a "track" and to build a drainage ditch on territory claimed by Syria as well as Israel. In spite of UNTSO's attempts to prevent further Israeli activities until a survey could be completed to ascertain the exact location of the border in this sector, on November 13, Israel sent a military patrol into the disputed area. Syrian soldiers reacted to this move by firing upon the patrol. Soon the two sides were using heavy weapons against both military and non-military targets. Finally, Israel ordered her air force to bomb and strafe Syrian roads, villages, and military positions in order, according to Israel, to show Syria that she would not be permitted to shell Israeli border settlements "with impunity." [70]

After investigating the situation, the UNTSO Chief of Staff reported that there was doubt as to whether the controversial track penetrated into Syria in some places. He therefore recommended that a survey be made by an impartial team of experts. He asked Syria to stop firing warning shots and to take her complaints to the MAC instead. He also urged Israel to suspend all activities in the disputed sector until a survey had been completed and to attend MAC meetings. The United States took the lead in criticizing the parties for resorting to force and in supporting the Chief of Staff's conclusions and suggestions. Britain joined the United States in submitting a draft resolution (S/6113) which "deplored" the renewal of military activities, requested a survey of the disputed area, and asked the two governments to cooperate with the MAC in every way. The Soviet Union continued to back the Arab point of view. The resolution received eight votes on December 21, but it was vetoed by the Soviet Union on the ground that it placed "victim and aggressor" on the same footing.[71]

Frequent incidents—usually involving shots fired by Syrians at Israeli tractors while working on land claimed by the Arabs to be theirs and occasional exchanges of fire across the demarcation lines—continued to occur. In March and May, 1965, Israel took advantage of incidents along the northern segment of the frontier to direct artillery and tank fire against buildings, bulldozers, and other equipment used by Syria in constructing access roads which came within 100 yards of Israeli territory in some places and which led to the site of a proposed canal designed to divert water to the Yarmouk River in Jordan, thus bypassing Israeli territory. Israel's heavy guns caused such severe damage that Syria's diversion efforts were greatly impeded. On July 14, 1966, Israeli planes strafed tractors and earth-moving machinery used in constructing a water diversion canal eight miles inside of Syria.[72]

REVIVAL OF ARAB COMMANDO AND ISRAELI RETALIATORY RAIDS

From the end of the Sinai War until the beginning of 1965, the most serious clashes took place between Israel and Syria; Israel used armed reprisals only against Syria. In early 1965, however, the situation along the Israeli-Jordanian demarcation lines suddenly became critical as a result of the activities of a new, militant organization known as *al-Fatah*. Composed of a small number of Palestinians familiar with Israeli territory, this group was created in December, 1964, with Syrian help. One of its primary goals was to keep alive the emotional attachments of the younger refugees to Palestine as the national homeland. *Al-Fatah* began a series of raids aimed especially at dynamiting water pipelines, pumps, and wells in order to disrupt Israeli water projects. Although *al-Fatah* had its home base in Syria, it found it easier and safer to cross the longer Israeli border with Jordan than the shorter and more strongly defended Syrian-Israeli frontier. Most Arab governments did not support this new organization for they felt it was too extremist and was trying to drag the Arab world into an untimely war with Israel.[73]

After infiltrators had blown up a grain silo and a house on the night of February 27–28, Prime Minister Levi Eshkol, pressed hard by those who accused him of being too vacillating and soft in his Arab policy, cautioned Jordan that she would be held responsible for any further raids from her territory. Since the commando attacks persisted, Israel again decided to deal with her border problems by resorting to her military power rather than to the UN. On May 27, 1965, Israeli army units carried out a series of assaults against what Israel claimed to be the bases of operations used by the "saboteurs" in the Jordanian villages of Sjuneh, Jenin, and Qalqilya. Five Arab civilians were killed, four civilians and three soldiers wounded. Despite the severity of this armed reprisal, border incidents and *al-Fatah* raids continued to take place. On May 31, an exchange of fire in Jerusalem caused the deaths of two Israeli civilians and injuries to four others. According to Israel, in early June and again in early July, "marauders" from Jordan attacked two Israeli settlements, a railroad, and a forester's observation tower. Finally, after a water well was blown up in Eyal on September 2, Israeli military units crossed into Jordan and destroyed eleven irrigation pumps near Qalqilya. The Israelis left pamphlets which warned the villagers to stop giving shelter to Arab raiders; yet, the commando operations continued. In April, 1966, infiltrators destroyed a water pipeline, set explosives in an Israeli frontier village, and placed a land mine on an Israeli road. On the night of April 29–30, Israeli soldiers attacked and blew up fourteen houses in two Jordanian villages on the alleged ground that these villages had been used by Arab "terrorists" to stage assaults on Israeli civilian targets. Israeli officials charged that of forty-three commando raids made since the end of 1965, thirty-three had been "from Jordan." Israel insisted that she had made every effort to avoid casualties among the Jordanian civilians, but Jordan claimed that three civilians had been killed, and six civilians and soldiers injured. This latest retaliatory attack also failed to bring border incidents to a halt.[74]

Israel contended that *al-Fatah* was using bases in Lebanon as well. According to Israel, "marauders" from Lebanon had committed a "bomb outrage" on October 27, 1965. In response, on October 28, Israeli military units crossed the frontier, blew up the home of a Lebanese village chief, and destroyed three water reservoirs in another Lebanese community. One Arab woman died as a result of the raid, labeled by the Israelis as a "warning action." Even though the United States had for a long time quietly urged all parties to avoid rash actions, she took advantage of this assault on Lebanon to express her opposition to Israel's policy of retaliation openly and vigorously. In November, the State Department Press Officer warned Israel that the United States could "not condone" armed reprisals and that these would only make the task of UNTSO "more difficult." The Israelis, however, were aware of the contradiction between Washington's request for restraint on their part and America's failure to exercise any appreciable restraint in her own actions in Vietnam, where the United States did not hesitate to employ the weapon of retaliation. As a result, American ability to influence Israel's policies towards the Arabs was greatly weakened. In any case, too, despite the October 28 action, "saboteurs," according to Israel, continued to enter Israel from Lebanon.[75]

Israeli officials conceded that the real "source and principle initiative for the *al-Fatah* operations came from Syria." Yet, until July, 1966, Israel responded to *al-Fatah* raids with armed reprisals only on Jordan and Lebanon. This was due, in part, to Israel's contention that each country was directly "responsible for the activities" from her "soil"— but also due to the fact that because of the difficult and unfavorable nature of the topography of the Syrian border area, Israel found it much easier and far less costly to mount land attacks against Lebanon and Jordan than against Syria.[76]

As early as January, 1966, Israel had contended that Arab infiltrators were beginning to enter Israeli territory directly from Syria. Israel charged that on January 28 members of *al-Fatah,* in their "first" attack from Syria, damaged a water pipeline in northern Israel before escaping to Lebanon. Israel held that two Israeli farmers had been killed and another was injured when the tractors they were driving were blown up by mine explosions on April 18 and May 16. Tension rose rapidly after the May 16 incident; Israeli officials warned Syria that "this state of affairs cannot continue." [77]

Despite Israel's warning, border infiltrations persisted. After accusing Syria of responsibility for four acts of minelaying and sabotage within a single twenty-four-hour period and of causing the deaths of two Israelis and injuries to two others, Israel, on July 14, ordered her air force to bomb and strafe engineering vehicles and other equipment being used eight miles inside Syria on the project to divert the Banyas River. This attack precipitated a battle between Syrian and Israeli planes. Realizing the gravity of the situation, both parties brought the problem to the UN Security Council. After discussing the issue, the Security Council rejected, by a vote of six in favor with nine abstentions, a draft resolution (S/7437) submitted by Mali and Jordan, which called upon the Council to "condemn Israel's wanton attack." While deploring Israel's military reprisal, some Council members decided not to vote for the resolution because it failed to condemn activities on the part of *al-Fatah* and Syria as well. The Security Council ended its debate without taking any steps to deal either with the Syrian and Israeli complaints or with the underlying conditions which had helped to produce border conflicts.[78]

By the middle of August, 1966, the border between Jordan and Israel had quieted down once again. Some reports indicated that both Lebanon and Jordan had been earnestly trying to prevent *al-Fatah* from using their territories as bases of operations. As a result, Arab commandos found it increasingly necessary to initiate their raids from Syria. This development exacerbated relations between Israel and Syria.[79]

The Israel-Syria situation became critical when, on August 15, both countries fought a major battle with planes, artillery, and patrol boats in the Lake Tiberias area. Israel contended that the trouble started because Syrian shore positions opened fire when an Israeli police boat tried to aid another patrol vessel which had accidentally run aground along the northeastern shore of Lake Tiberias. Syria held that an Israeli "gunboat" had been the first to open fire on a Syrian outpost. Israel claimed to have shot down two Syrian MIG's and to have silenced Syrian coastal batteries. Syria maintained that her planes had destroyed or damaged more than ten "gunboats" and "their base on the southern shore" of the lake in a "punitive operation to retaliate against Israeli aggression." Syrian officials also stated that because the Security Council had failed to pass a resolution condemning Israel for her July 14 air assault, they had decided to adopt a "new strategy toward Israel." In effect, Syria would no longer resort to the UN in case of any future Israeli "aggression." Instead, as she had done on August 15, she would "not confine herself to defensive action but would attack defined targets and bases of aggression within" Israel. Some reports indicated that this new, more belligerent Syrian policy was initiated partly in an attempt to win greater popular support within Syria, where the existing government was facing strong internal opposition, and throughout the Arab world. Syrian officials had for years complained that other Arab governments had been failing to take a strong enough stand against the enemy. Prime Minister Eshkol, pressed by many Israelis to adopt an even tougher position against the Arabs, warned Syria that any further Syrian assault would be met by "effective countermeasures." The army weekly *Bamahane* quoted Israeli Chief of Staff Major General Itzhak Rabin as declaring that bloodless warning raids, such as those against Jordan and Lebanon, would not be enough to pacify the frontier with Syria. Equating the situation with that which had existed in 1955 and 1956 with Egypt, he implied that strong military action might be needed against Syria, as was then needed against Egypt. UN officials were finally able to obtain a promise from both sides to maintain a cease-fire. In addition, Syria appeared to have taken a somewhat more moderate line in a note sent to the Security Council on August 24.[80]

Several days after a land mine had, on October 7, killed four Israeli policemen and wounded two others while they were on patrol duty, Israel requested an urgent meeting of the UN Security Council. She complained that armed groups operating from Syria had been committing acts of aggression against Israeli citizens and property and that high Syrian officials had been making open threats against Israel's territorial integrity and political independence. Syria denied responsibility for the activities of the Palestinian commando groups and maintained that she would not act as a police force to help Israel's security by trying to halt the infiltration operations of al-Fatah.[81]

During the Security Council debates, the major Western countries pressed Syria to recognize her "responsibilities" to prevent raids from being mounted from her soil. The Soviet Union, Bulgaria, and the UAR expressed concern over Israeli "threats of aggression" against Syria. Other Security Council members appealed to both sides to exercise restraint. The United States and Britain introduced a draft resolution (S/7568) which noted that al-Fatah had been responsible for a series of raids into Israel, reminded Syria of the need to fulfill her obligations by taking all essential steps to prevent the use of her territory as a base of operations for acts constituting a violation of the General Armistice Agreement, and called upon Syria and Israel to cooperate fully with UNTSO and the MAC. After a week of unsuccessful attempts at reaching a consensus among all Council members, on November 3, six delegations introduced a proposal (S/7575) which asked the Security Council to "deplore" the recent incidents, invited Syria to strengthen her measures to prevent actions violating the armistice agreement, requested Israel to cooperate with the MAC, and urged both parties to refrain from acts that might increase tension. This six-power draft received ten favorable votes on November 4, but Russia vetoed it on the grounds that it was too "one-sided" and that it wrongly implied that Syria was to blame for the al-Fatah incursions. The United States and Britain did not press for a vote on their resolution for it would obviously have been vetoed by the Soviet Union. Israel once again expressed her great disappointment at the fact that Russia constantly prevented any proposal objected to by the Arabs from being passed by the Security Council. Nevertheless, Israeli officials contended that the large vote for the six-power draft represented a rebuke to Syria and a political and moral victory for Israel.[82]

The situation along the Syrian-Israeli demarcation lines became less troubled for a couple of months after the Security Council discussions. A number of observers, including a few Israelis, attributed the improvement not only to the Security Council debates, but also to two other major developments. In early November, 1966, Syria and Egypt signed a defense pact which enabled Nasser, who opposed any military showdown with Israel at least until the Arab world was adequately prepared for war, to exercise a greater measure of restraint on Syria. The Soviet

Union, anxious to avoid a major upheaval in the Middle East, urged Syrian leaders to restrict the scale of Arab guerrilla operations and to tone down calls for a war of liberation against Israel.[83]

Tension between Syria and Israel had hardly subsided somewhat before a grave crisis developed unexpectedly between Israel and Jordan. Early on Sunday, November 13, two powerful Israeli armored columns assaulted the Jordanian towns of as-Samu, Jimba, and Khirbet Karkay, located west of the Dead Sea and south of Jerusalem and Hebron. As a result of this large-scale military operation—the biggest since the Sinai War—Israeli forces killed three civilians and fifteen soldiers, wounded seventeen civilians and thirty-seven military personnel, destroyed 140 houses, a clinic and a school, and damaged many other buildings. In the process, the Israeli forces suffered one dead and ten wounded. Israel insisted that this action was a reprisal provoked by a series of thirteen terrorist attacks, involving murder and sabotage, launched from Jordanian territory over the prior six months. Israel expressed anger particularly over those raids which had resulted in the derailment of a train and injury to one Israeli on October 27, the dynamiting of two houses and the wounding of four civilians in the Romema quarter of Jerusalem on October 8, and the explosion of a land mine under a military vehicle on November 12 in the Hebron-Dead Sea area, which killed three soldiers and injured six others. Israeli officials stated that their retaliatory assault was meant to be a "warning and a deterrent" to the inhabitants of those villages which harbored and aided the "saboteurs" who planted mines in Israel and an indication of Israel's determination not to allow attacks against her citizens to proceed unchecked. They also claimed that "so long as the Security Council has not adopted effective measures to stop the aggressor, it is the duty and right of an attacked state to defend itself." [84]

Israel's major assault provoked sharp reactions in both the Arab world and in the UN. Israel's military action intensified Arab hatred and bitterness and strengthened the position of the more militant Arabs at the expense of the Arab moderates. Inside Jordan, the angry and frustrated Palestinians initiated numerous demonstrations and riots, demanded the arming of the border villagers, and pressed for strong reprisals. Leaders of the Palestine Liberation Organization, as well as officials in Syria and Egypt, accused King Hussein of being a traitor. Syria even began to offer aid to those Jordanians who sought the overthrow of the Hussein regime. For several weeks, the Jordanian monarchy was seriously threatened, but the army was finally able to restore internal order and security. Nonetheless, the as-Samu affair weakened

Hussein's position both within Jordan and within the Arab world and made it more difficult for the monarch to continue his relatively moderate policy towards Israel and to avoid a violent Jordanian military response to any future Israeli reprisal action. The Israeli attack further widened the grave split which already existed between Jordan, backed by Saudi Arabia, on the one hand, and Syria and Egypt, on the other.[85]

King Hussein accused the Russians and the Arab Communists of whipping up the efforts being made to overthrow his regime. Yet, some reports indicated that the Soviet government had actually been exerting a moderating influence on Syria. While Soviet leaders had no special desire to see Hussein remain in power, they nonetheless feared that his overthrow would lead to serious upheavals in the Middle East and to the military intervention of the United States in the area. On December 4 the Communist Party newspaper, *Pravda,* appealed for the maintenance of peace in the Middle East and condemned any provocations which might undermine peace there.[86]

The Arab League Defense Council met in early December to discuss the tense situation which had developed. The Council unanimously agreed that Iraq and Saudi Arabia should send troops into Jordan to help strengthen her defenses against Israel. Fearing that military contingents from other Arab states might be used to intervene in Jordan's internal affairs and that Israel might use the movement of these forces as an excuse for invading Jordan, King Hussein refused to allow Iraqi and Saudi military units to enter his country. (Shortly after the Defense Council had announced its decision, Israeli officials warned that they would not "tolerate" the stationing in Jordan of troops from other Arab countries.) Hussein claimed that his agreement to accept outside military assistance was dependent upon the following two conditions: Jordan must be faced with an immediate military threat from Israel, and Egypt must ask for the withdrawal of UNEF soldiers from her territory and must replace them with Egyptian military divisions being used in Yemen. Most Arab governments contended that Jordan had originally accepted the Defense Council's decision without conditions, and some Arab officials accused Hussein of sabotaging Arab defense plans. In short, the Defense Council's meetings and endeavors led not to greater Arab unity and strength but to greater friction and disagreement than before.[87]

Shortly after the Israeli reprisal action, Jordan asked the Security Council to deal with the matter. Jordan urged the Council to brand Israel an aggressor and to impose economic sanctions against her. While deploring the continuation of Arab commando raids on Israel, nearly all Security Council members, led by the United States, strongly criticized

Israel. As in the past, they contended that large-scale government-planned and organized military retaliations were far more serious violations of the UN Charter and the armistice agreements than incidents primarily caused by nonofficial groups and individuals. They also held that armed reprisals did not actually help either Israel's security or reputation. Most delegations found it difficult to understand why Israel attacked a country like Jordan that had been trying to keep the borders peaceful and had been following a relatively moderate policy towards Israel. They urged the Security Council to take firm action to prevent future military reprisals by Israel. After intensive discussions among the delegates, Mali and Nigeria submitted Resolution S/7598 which stated that the Security Council "censures Israel" and "emphasizes to Israel that actions of military reprisal cannot be tolerated and if they are repeated, the Security Council will have to consider further and more effective steps as envisaged in the Charter to ensure against the repetition of such acts." On November 25, the resolution was passed by a vote of fourteen in favor with only New Zealand abstaining. It was reported that the United States and other Western countries had decided to support a straight and forceful censure of Israel without referring directly to Arab commando activities largely because they wished to do everything possible to bolster the delicate and threatened internal position of King Hussein.[88]

Israel's assault was widely condemned outside the UN. Many Western officials and observers noted that Israel had attacked Jordan, not Syria, apparently because of the following reasons: (1) the rugged, uphill terrain along the Syrian border would make any land assault on Syria difficult and costly; (2) the recent Syrian-UAR defense pact might require Egypt to intervene on Syria's behalf in the event of an assault by Israel; (3) the Soviet Union might decide to provide assistance to Syria; (4) the militant group of Baathists (Arab socialists) in control of the Syrian government might decide to hit back with considerable force regardless of the risks involved; and (5) Jordan, because of her moderate leadership, relative military isolation, and susceptibility to American influence, was not likely to strike back and to precipitate a major military crisis. These officials were shocked by Israel's drastic action. They considered it to be a gross and dangerous "mistake" which helped to undermine the position of Hussein's regime, to embarrass the United States, and to enhance the influence of Russia and the more extremist groups in the Arab world. Responding quickly to prevent the overthrow of the Jordanian monarchy and to protect its own prestige in the area, the U.S. government not only supported the strong Security Council resolution censuring Israel, but also sent additional naval vessels to the eastern Mediterranean and airlifted several million dollars worth of defensive weapons and equipment to Jordan in order to bolster Hussein's internal position; to make it clear to Hussein's opponents within the Arab world that the United States continued to stand behind him; to preclude the need for Jordan to turn to the Soviet Union for arms (as Syria and Egypt were urging); and to demonstrate clearly to Israel how greatly displeased the American government was with her assault on as-Samu. American officials also began to consider the possibility of pressing the UN to send an international force, similar to UNEF, to man the sensitive Israeli-Syrian and Israeli-Jordanian borders. But when Israel indicated her opposition and when it was realized that such a move would merely add to the UN's financial difficulties, the United States dropped the idea and offered, instead, to help Israel to improve her border defenses.[89]

Israeli leaders refused to concede that their assault on Jordan had been a mistake, claiming, rather, that it had brought a decline in terrorist raids and had enabled King Hussein to find and eliminate his internal enemies. Nevertheless, as a result of the unexpectedly serious and dangerous repercussions within Jordan, the Middle East, and the UN, many Israelis—including some officials—expressed misgivings about the target, questioned the size and strength of the attack, and wondered whether armed reprisals really were the best long-range answer to Israel's chronic border problems and whether they were not hurting the cause of lasting peace. They complained that the as-Samu affair had tended to undermine an Arab regime which had provided a major stabilizing influence in the Middle East and to hurt Israel's prestige in the UN and in the world. A number of Israelis, as well as non-Israelis, even charged that Premier Eshkol had ordered the assault primarily to strengthen his own political position, "to hide the weaknesses of his domestic economic policies," and "to take Israeli minds off problems at hand." [90] Some reports indicated that shortly after the raid even members of Eshkol's own Mapai Party had started to question his leadership openly. In any case, despite Israel's "warning" action against Jordan and her efforts to seal her frontiers against al-Fatah forays, by the middle of January, 1967, border incidents and infiltrations by Arab commandos began to occur again with increasing frequency.[91]

By the end of 1966 and early 1967 the Syrian-Israeli frontier once again became the scene of a series of incidents. Some of these, involving exchanges of fire across the demarcation lines, were precipitated when Arab and Israeli farmers began to work on disputed lands in the demilitarized zone. (This troublesome situation developed annually at the beginning of the planting season.) Other incidents resulted from the revival of land-mining activities in Israel by Arab guerrillas. Border tensions reached the critical stage by the middle of January. After a mine blast killed one Israeli and injured two others at a soccer match, Premier Eshkol gave notice on January 17 that Israel would not continue to put up with "Syrian attacks." On January 18–19, in cables sent to Presidents Lyndon Johnson and Charles de Gaulle, he warned that the situation was "grave" and that there was a "legitimate limit even to self-restraint." He also asked the two Western leaders to do what they could to make Syria halt her "aggressive" actions. In support of Israel's move, a delegation of American Jewish leaders met with Under Secretary of State Nicholas Katzenbach and pressed the government to issue a "stern warning" to Syria.[92]

In order to head off any further deterioration of conditions, UN Secretary-General U Thant urgently appealed to Israel and Syria to hold an emergency meeting of the MAC. The two parties accepted U Thant's appeal. On January 25 the Syrian-Israeli MAC held its first meeting since February 16, 1960, on the Syrian side of the Banat Yacoub bridge. In a joint statement issued as a communiqué by UNTSO, Israel and Syria reaffirmed their commitment to refrain from all kinds of hostile or aggressive actions, as provided for in the UN Charter and the General Armistice Agreement. The MAC also began to discuss an agenda item which called for efforts to bring about a "practical arrangement on problems of cultivation on the Armistice Demarcation Line in order to secure a peaceful atmosphere . . . for farmers and civilians in the area." At this and two other sessions, held on January 29 and February 2, the Israelis and the Syrians failed to find any common ground. Differences arose over Israel's claim to sovereignty over the demilitarized zone and over what matters were to be discussed first. Israel, contending that the problem of cultivation was the only item on the agenda, submitted a proposal for dealing with this matter. Syria insisted that Israel must remove her armed forces and fortifications from the demilitarized zone, that the zone Arabs must be allowed to return to their lands, and that the status of the zone must be determined before other issues could be considered. When it became evident that a deadlock had been reached, the fourth MAC meeting, originally scheduled for February 9, was postponed indefinitely. In the meantime, border strife had temporarily declined in intensity and scope, and President Johnson had taken advantage of the opportunity to remind the parties that the United States would "resolutely oppose the use of force or the threat of force by one state against another in the area." [93] Nevertheless, by the middle of February, 1967, both Syria and Israel complained about new exchanges of fire and mine-laying, and tensions began to mount once again.[94]

Before the outbreak of war in June, 1967, there were periods of relative quiet along the demarcation lines, and on these occasions popular emotions did abate somewhat, but sooner or later another major clash would again arouse Arab-Israeli hostility. Every time blood was spilled and lives were lost as a result of border incidents, raids, and armed reprisals, Arab-Israeli hatred and fear mounted, and this development, in turn, deepened and widened the rift between the two groups. Consequently, relative peace and tranquility along the frontiers never managed to prevail long enough to allow Arab and Israeli emotions to subside sufficiently to enable the moderate leaders on both sides to feel free to consider those compromises so essential to the solution of any one of the major Arab-Israeli problems; like some other unresolved international problems, they festered and eventually led to war.

As already shown, Israeli policies and actions contributed to conflicts and tensions along the demarcation lines. For example, Israel's failure, especially in the early years, to abide by UN resolutions relating to the Arab refugees made a solution of the refugee problem impossible. Consequently, the disgruntled and frustrated refugees spread their bitterness throughout the Arab world and launched forays against their enemy.

Israel ignored repeated warnings from UN officials and insisted upon (1) taking illegal control of the al-Auja DMZ, most of the Syrian DMZ, and parts of the no-man's lands between Jordan and Israel; (2) occasionally sending her patrol boats close to the northeastern shore of Lake Tiberias; and (3) launching large-scale "reprisal" attacks, at times even when the frontiers had been relatively quiet, and for initiating a "preventive war" in October, 1956, despite the fact that such actions usually caused an increase in border tensions and conflicts and in Arab animosity.

Instead of cooperating fully with the UN agencies and officials who were earnestly trying to discourage incidents and maintain tranquility in the area, Israel frequently placed obstacles in their path, such as restricting UN observer movements, refusing to allow UNEF units on her side of the lines, and refusing, with rare exceptions, to attend the Syrian-Israeli MAC after 1951. UN officials were convinced that the clashes resulting from Israel's drainage, tree-planting and other projects could have been avoided if Israel had shown "more patience and restraint and less determination to undertake unilateral decisions." [95] On the occasions when Israel did give prior notification of her work plans to the proper MAC, incidents were usually avoided. Israel's impatience with the investigating procedures of the various MAC's had also led her to make several unwise and unnecessary retaliatory attacks.

As for the Arabs, many of their policies and actions before the June War also helped to cause incidents and contributed to the aggravation of Arab-Israeli relations. At times, the Arabs restricted the movement of UN observers, failed to cooperate adequately with UNTSO and the MAC's, and limited the number of UN observer posts placed on their soil. Syria, on occasion, fired too quickly on Israeli tractors in the demilitarized zone and on Israeli patrol boats on Lake Tiberias, instead of submitting her complaints to the MAC. Jordan refused to allow the "resumption of the normal functioning of the cultural and humanitarian institutions on Mount Scopus" and the free access "to the [Jewish] Holy Places" in her territory as required by her armistice agreement with Israel. Egypt's interferences with Israeli use of the Gulf of Aqaba and the Suez Canal created additional and serious sources of friction. Egypt, as well as Israel and the UN, failed to seek a ruling from the World Court on the legality of her restrictions on Israeli shipping.

In 1955 and 1956 and again starting in 1965, some Arab governments facilitated or promoted *fedayeen* raids on Israel despite the fact that they would greatly disturb Israel and provoke armed reprisals. As indicated in Chapter VI, the Arabs were partly responsible for the failure to resolve the refugee problem, which played a major role in preventing more tranquil and normal relations from developing between Israel and themselves. Moreover, a number of Arab leaders frequently made violent statements threatening the very existence of the state of Israel, thus giving the Israelis considerable reason for being concerned about their security and about Arab intentions. Too often these leaders sought to enhance their personal popularity by appealing to the strong passions of their own people, rather than to promote calm and to relax tensions in the area by urging moderation and patience.

Moreover, other countries and the UN shared in the responsibility for the persistence of the dangerous conditions in the Middle East. In all the years between the Palestine War and the June, 1967, conflict, neither the major powers nor the UN made a consistent or determined effort to come to grips with the fundamental differences in the viewpoints of the Arabs and the Israelis and the emotions which sharpened and hardened them and made them so resistant to a solution. During the periods of relative calm when Arab and Israeli leaders were in the most favorable positions to make concessions to clear the path for a final settlement of their differences, the big powers and the UN usually felt it unnecessary to intervene. However, every time a major crisis arose, they would suddenly make some attempt to deal with the underlying causes, but in the meantime Arab-Israeli bitterness and hostility would have become so intense that no outside efforts at conciliation could possibly succeed.

Over the years, the UN passed many resolutions dealing with border and other armistice problems, but it rarely tried to implement them. It must be stressed, however, that the UN is not a superstate and is only an instrument for international cooperation without any independent capacity to act on its own in order to enforce its decisions. Therefore, it cannot be held responsible for its failure in dealing with Arab-Israeli disputes. The fault lies, instead, with its members—and especially with the most powerful ones—who alone have the means to make the UN function effectively.

In reviewing the events which followed in the wake of the Arab-Israeli Armistice Agreements, it was unfortunate that, during the years following the Palestine War in 1948, neither the Arabs and the Israelis, on the one hand, nor the UN and its powerful members, on the other, gave adequate consideration to the inevitable consequences of the many incidents and conflicts on the Arab-Israel borders. If another Arab-Israeli confrontation were to be averted, it was imperative for all parties directly and indirectly involved to make more determined efforts to maintain calm on the extremely sensitive demarcation lines. This would have required not only a more effective UN presence as a buffer between the hostile sides, but also greater Arab and Israeli patience with and understanding of each other's feelings and problems and the frustratingly slow process unavoidably involved in all UN actions aimed at achieving peace and justice. In addition, this would have demanded more enlightened and courageous leadership in both the Middle East and the world organization. Because these did not materialize, violence along the Arab-Israeli borders persisted, mutual hatred and fear mounted, and tensions remained high. Such developments, in turn, proved once again to be more conducive to war than to peace.

CHAPTER VIII

The June War

During the years following the Palestine War of 1948, the Arabs and the Israelis maintained unyielding and hostile attitudes towards each other, and the UN and the major powers failed to deal objectively, realistically, and resolutely with those Arab-Israeli feelings and differences which remained the principal obstacles to a peaceful Arab-Israeli settlement. In fact, many of the policies and actions of the major powers were so misguided that they served to aggravate, rather than ameliorate, the over-all situation in the Middle East. By the spring of 1967, as a result of impatient and belligerent actions and threats and grave miscalculations, the Arabs and Israelis found themselves once again drifting towards another momentous crisis.

DEVELOPMENTS LEADING TO WAR

During the first three months of 1967, though some incidents occurred along the Jordanian-Israeli lines, and *al-Fatah* used Jordanian and Lebanese territories as bases of operations for several raids, the Syrian-Israeli frontier remained the most serious trouble spot. On the one hand, Israel persisted in sending tractors to plough "disputed" lands in the demilitarized zone—even though it was obvious that the Syrians would fire on them. Syria, on the other hand, continued to support Palestine refugee commando activities in order to undermine Israel's sense of security, to discourage foreign investments and Jewish immigrants, and to encourage emigration from Israel—even though it was clear that Israel would, sooner or later, react forcibly.

On April 7, one of the most serious military clashes between Israel and the Arabs took place on the Syria-Israel border as a result of a cultivation dispute. Israel claimed that Syria had triggered the affair by shooting at an "unarmed" tractor working on "Israeli lands."[1] Syria, in turn, contended that Israel had deliberately sent an "armed" tractor to work on "disputed" land and had opened fire on a Syrian position in order to give Israel an excuse to make a major attack. Syria also charged that Israel was determined to seize the entire demilitarized zone and even to encroach on Arab-owned land.[2] Although the fighting began with only light weapons, both sides soon employed artillery, mortars, and tanks. Israel took this opportunity to apply a "calculated response" to what she considered "intolerable" interference with Israeli cultivation efforts.[3] In order to neutralize the topographical advantage enjoyed by Syrian military positions in the mountains overlooking Israeli-controlled territory, Israel ordered her planes to bomb and strafe both Syrian military targets and border villages. This large-scale reprisal action was meant not only to silence Syrian guns and tanks, but also, according to Israeli Chief of Staff General Itzhak Rabin, to convince Syria that "there's a limit to encroachment, that the Syrians will not determine the type of weapons to be used in these encounters and that while this time the action was in connection with a border dispute the same lesson can be applied in other areas,"[4] presumably as a reply to commando forays. After many hours of conflict, the United Nations Truce Supervision Organization (UNTSO) was finally able to arrange a cease-fire.

The April 7 clash and Israel's major "reprisal" action had a number of important and far-reaching consequences. While there were some Israeli casualties and property damage, Syria suffered much greater losses in lives and property primarily because of the Israeli air assaults on Syrian villages. Israel claimed that her pilots had shot down six Syrian MIG's and had chased others to the outskirts of Damascus. Syria contended that four Israeli planes had been destroyed and that Israel had used napalm bombs against innocent Arab villagers. Israel acknowledged that despite her armed reprisal, "attacks" on Israeli tractors did not stop and that "a rash of stepped-up sabotage, shelling and mining incidents" developed along her borders with Syria, Lebanon, and Jordan.[5]

This Israeli air strike led the Arab governments quickly to pledge their support to Syria, but it also caused increased bickering among some of the Arab states. Cairo newspapers complained that the Jordanian air force had not tried to help the Syrian planes even when they were being shot down in Jordanian air space. Jordanian newspapers and radio announcers, in turn, charged that, as had happened when as-Samu was raided, Israel's air assault had brought not a single reaction from Syria's ally, the UAR, and that Egypt preferred fighting fellow Arabs in Yemen to helping fellow Arabs against Israel. The April 7 air attack multiplied the pressures on Egyptian leaders to take a more direct and active role in supporting their Syrian ally the next time she was attacked.[6]

The Israelis, who held Syria primarily responsible for the *al-Fatah* terrorist raids, responded favorably to their government's action. They felt relieved that neither Russia nor the UAR had tried seriously to intervene and that, unlike the as-Samu affair, other governments and peoples had reacted apathetically to Israel's military action. Thus encouraged, the Israelis tended to believe that they could continue using large-scale military retaliations with relative impunity. In addition, the extensive freedom of movement allowed to Israeli pilots over Syrian territory on April 7 appeared to indicate that "unlimited pursuit" had become "firmly established in Israeli Air Force strategy"—and this opened the way for possibly even bigger and more far-reaching reprisal air strikes against Syria[7]

Because in the early part of May Arab commandos were showing increasing daring and proficiency, even main roads used by civilians were being mined, and Syrian officials were making "threatening" statements, Israel complained to the UN and started to issue strong and blunt warnings to Syria. Prime Minister Levi Eshkol stated on May 7 that Israel had ". . . no other choice but to adopt suitable counter-measures against the foci of sabotage and their abettors"; on May 14 he made it clear that Israel would "choose when, where, and how to reply to the attacker." [8] Other Israeli officials also added sharp warnings. Then, on May 13, the *New York Times* revealed that Israeli leaders had "decided that the use of force against Syria" might be "the only way to curtail increasing terrorism. . . . Any such Israeli reaction . . . probably would be of considerable strength but of short duration and limited in area. . . . The comments being heard [in Israel] in recent weeks, and especially since last weekend [have been] stronger than those usually heard in responsible quarters." Reports within the Arab world even claimed that a senior Israeli military officer had stated that Israel "would carry out military operations against Syria in order to occupy Damascus and overthrow the Syrian Government."[9] Israeli leaders were soon to discover that they had seriously miscalculated the consequences of their exceptionally tough warnings.[10]

Syria formally drew the attention of the UN to the Israeli "threats" and to the *New York Times* report; yet Syrian leaders continued to make bellicose statements and speeches of their own. They also sought the support of other Arab states, and on May 14, they indicated that they would invoke their defense agreement with Egypt in the event of another Israeli attack. Most Arab governments expressed their readiness to aid Syria.[11]

These events placed President Nasser in a quandary. For several years, he had been cautioning the more militant Arabs that the Arab states were still too militarily weak and divided to be able to challenge Israel successfully in a war and that in any case, the United States would probably support Israel if she were invaded. He had signed the defense pact with Syria perhaps in the hope that it would place him in a better position to restrain the pugnacious Syrian leaders, and for several months he was able to exert some restraint. Consequently, in May, 1967, Nasser, with his best troops tied up in Yemen and with the Arab world more bitterly divided than ever, preferred to wait until the Arabs were far better prepared for a military showdown.[12]

Nevertheless, he was also confronted with a number of major developments within the UAR and the Arab world and between Israel and Syria which, he believed, required that he make some concrete gesture of military support for his ally. Egyptian economic conditions had been deteriorating, especially since the United States had cut Egypt off from purchasing American surplus food under Public Law 480, which had enabled the UAR to buy about $150,000,000 of badly needed wheat each year on easy payment terms. Many Egyptians had been growing increasingly restless because of these economic conditions and the endless war in Yemen. Nasser himself was frustrated over the lack of progress in Yemen. Other Arabs, particularly King Feisal of Saudi Arabia, were aggressively challenging his leadership within the Arab world, where his position had weakened considerably. Nasser was also greatly irritated by repeated taunts from Jordanians, Saudis, Syrians, and other Arabs—as well as an occasional Israeli—that he preferred to "hide" behind the skirts of the UN Emergency Force and that when Israel launched large-scale reprisal assaults against Jordan and Syria, he spoke bravely but acted meekly. Many non-Arabs, too, accused him of posturing and contended that his bombastic talk was not to be taken seriously. Not only did Israeli leaders begin to make strong threats against Syria, but on May 13, Nasser received diplomatic reports, particularly from Syria and Russia, which claimed that Israel was building up her forces for a military attack on Syria on May 17 in order, among other aims, to unseat the Syrian government. Nasser was apparently led to believe, moreover, that the Soviet Union would support Arab action countering an Israeli threat to Syria. He also realized that Syria would not hesitate to call on Egypt for military assistance if Israel initiated any assault. Thus, to deter an attack on Syria, to save his declining prestige and influence in the Arab world, to quell the charges that he was lacking courage to face Israel, and to prove his dependability to his fellow Arabs, Nasser felt that he was left with no choice but to take a "calculated risk" and to prove that he was ready to employ his military power to help protect his ally. On May 15, he put his armed forces on alert and, on May 16, on an emergency footing; he began to move large numbers of troops to the Sinai area.[13]

It was obvious that as long as UNEF troops were stationed along the entire demarcation lines between Israel and Egypt, Nasser could not actually move his army in support of Syria if Israel did attack—in which event his motives might still be impugned by Israel as well as by most Arabs and he might still be accused of posturing. So he took a step he probably would not have taken if the pressures on him had not multiplied.[14] On May 16, Egypt insisted that some UNEF units leave their positions along certain parts of the demarcation lines so that Egyptian soldiers could take over. UN Secretary-General U Thant maintained that UNEF had to be withdrawn completely or be allowed to patrol the entire length of the borders as in the past. Consequently, on May 18, Egypt formally requested that UNEF be fully withdrawn. Some unconfirmed reports indicated that Nasser had anticipated and, possibly, even hoped that the UN would try to delay UNEF's actual removal for he was not anxious to risk a military confrontation with Israel.[15] Even though he believed that Egypt's request was unwise and untimely, U Thant decided to order UNEF's quick departure for several reasons: (1) because Egypt was a sovereign state and had originally permitted UNEF to operate on her territory only with the understanding that it would leave whenever she asked for its withdrawal, he had no alternative but to comply after discussing the matter with representatives of the countries providing contingents to UNEF; (2) Egyptian soldiers were already occupying some UNEF posts, and he wished to insure the safety of UNEF personnel; and (3) two major contributors to UNEF, India and Yugoslavia, both warm friends of the UAR, had indicated that they would order their own units to leave, regardless of any decision that U Thant might make, because they felt that Egypt had the legal right to demand UNEF's removal at any time.[16] Recognizing the dangers that would follow without an adequate buffer between Israel and Egypt, the Secretary-General strongly urged Israel to permit UNEF to take up positions on her side of the lines because he felt that UNEF's presence would be just as effective on her territory as it had been on Egyptian soil. Israel replied that this would be "completely unacceptable,"[17] and on May 19, UNEF ceased to exist. The Egyptian and Israeli military forces found themselves face-to-face, and the Palestinian commandos felt free to operate from the Gaza Strip for the first time since the 1956 Sinai War. With these developments, tensions in the area mounted and the Arabs and Israelis found themselves on the brink of another violent confrontation.

The fact that UNEF forces had been withdrawn from Sharm al-Sheikh overlooking the mouth of the Gulf of Aqaba, as well as from the Egyptian-Israeli demarcation lines, deepened the crisis and presented Nasser with yet another dilemma. Compelled to dispatch Egyptian troops to the area, he was subjected to great pressures from all parts of the Arab world to reinstate the restrictions on Israel's use of the gulf which had existed before the Sinai War. Some of his most bitter Arab rivals began to ask him pointedly what he intended to do once the first Israeli vessel sought to pass through the Strait of Tiran. Aware that Israel might react to such a step with military force, yet not wishing to appear afraid to stand up to Israel and anxious to bolster his position as the primary leader in the Arab world, Nasser announced, on May 22, that the Gulf of Aqaba was henceforth closed to all Israeli ships and to all other vessels carrying strategic materials to Israel.[18]

By these various moves Nasser demonstrated his readiness to run the risk of war. But, as most reports indicated, he really wished to avoid it because he felt that the United States would intervene on behalf of Israel, that the Arabs were not as well prepared for a military showdown as they should have been, and that the Arabs should wait until they were more united and militarily stronger so that victory for them could be definitely assured. James Reston, in two Cairo dispatches to the *New York Times* on June 4 and 5, stated that Egypt did "not want war, . . . [was] certainly not ready for war," and had been making little preparation within Egypt proper for war. At the same time, UAR leaders hoped that they had "raised the cost of war high enough so neither the Americans nor the Israelis [would] pay the price." Nasser's military build-up in the Sinai and his request for the removal of UNEF were, as many Western and even some Israeli officials conceded, more political than military maneuvers. He was anxious to discourage Israel from attacking Syria and, at the same time, to enhance his position and reputation within the Arab world. Even "Israeli sources," according to a *New York Times* report published on May 19, believed that "Syria had bluffed the UAR into becoming more involved in the Syria-Israel dispute than Cairo had intended." [19]

Once UNEF had withdrawn from the demarcation lines and Egyptian troops had taken over there and at Sharm al-Sheikh, Nasser assured foreign diplomats and U Thant that all he had intended to do was to deter Israel from striking Syria and to restore those conditions along the Israeli-UAR borders and at the mouth of the Gulf of Aqaba which had existed before Israel had invaded the Sinai. He contended that the UN General Assembly itself had insisted in 1956 and 1957 that Israel should not profit in any way from her aggression. Since the General Assembly had been unable to prevent Israel from continuing to enjoy some benefits from her illegal action, he held that the UAR was taking the initiative to deprive Israel of them. As soon as he had achieved his most immediate political objectives, Nasser was content to sit back and go no further. He stressed that he would not be the first to initiate a military attack. He apparently felt confident that his forces were reasonably prepared for a test of strength if it should come and that he had Soviet support in case of a showdown, especially if the United States were to intervene on Israel's behalf. (High Syrian and Egyptian officials had gone to Moscow in late May to consult and returned home believing they had received assurances of Soviet support for the Arabs, according to the *New York Times,* May 30, 1967.) He also appeared to be gambling that the UN and the United States would somehow apply enough pressures on Israel so that she would not resort to war merely to reopen the Gulf of Aqaba to her shipping. Nasser was able to make a sudden and dramatic comeback as the undisputed leader in the Arab world and appeared to be winning a major political victory at Israel's expense, but he was to discover in a matter of days that he had seriously miscalculated and that his gamble would be extremely costly.[20]

Until May 17, Israel considered all the military activities in the neighboring Arab states to be nothing more than political maneuvering within the Arab world, and she took them in her stride. But after Egypt had demanded that UNEF be withdrawn and she had begun to build up her forces in the Sinai and Gaza Strip areas, and after other neighboring Arab states had put their armies on the alert, Israeli officials became apprehensive and ordered a partial, later a complete, mobilization. Israel became even more aroused by Egypt's reinstatement of restrictions on Israeli shipping in the Gulf of Aqaba. This disturbing development did the most to create war fever among her people. Actually, restrictions, at least as publicly announced, probably would not have had the dire economic consequences most Israelis envisaged. Rarely had Israel used her own merchant vessels in the gulf, so the prohibition on her ships would not have had any significant economic effect. The only important strategic item being shipped through the gulf in large quantities was oil. Most other articles were basically nonstrategic and could presumably have been transported by neutral ships. Moreover, Israel received less than ten per cent of her imports through the gulf.[21] Nevertheless, the principle of freedom of navigation for their vessels and goods had become an extremely sensitive issue and a matter of national honor for the Israelis, and they did not want Egypt to control a waterway which they considered vital to their interests. Over the years, the Israeli government had repeatedly proclaimed that the closing of the Strait of Tiran would be regarded as an "act of war" and that it would use whatever force was necessary to counter any such move. Thus, in late May, Prime Minister Levi Eshkol, like Nasser, found himself in a quandary. On the one hand, there was a strong popular outcry against the new "blockade," and powerful politicians like Moshe Dayan began to demand quick military action to "reopen" the gulf. Opponents within Eshkol's Mapai party, as well as outside it, had been questioning his competence as a leader and accused him of being too lenient in his policies towards the Arabs. On the other hand, the United States and other Western countries were urging him to exercise restraint; according to various reports, he personally wished to avoid war if at all possible. Again, like Nasser, Eshkol finally bowed to popular and political pressures and assumed a tough and relatively inflexible stand.[22]

Until the end of May, Arab gestures of unity tended in some cases to be only symbolic, and considerable disunity and antagonism persisted within the Arab world. For example, Cairo and Amman radios continued their bitter war of words, while relations between Egypt and Jordan remained strained. This situation provided a kind of reassurance for Israel. On May 30, however, King Hussein, influenced by his own Arab nationalist feelings and the desire to maintain his precarious position by placating the aroused Palestinians (both refugees and others) who made up two thirds of Jordan's population, traveled to Cairo and signed a five-year mutual defense pact with President Nasser. Although this military agreement would require considerable time before it could be effectively implemented, it quickly deepened Israel's fears for her security.[23]

During the third week of May, when the situation in the Middle East started to deteriorate, Secretary-General U Thant appealed to all parties to act with moderation, urged Israel to reactivate fully the Israel-Egyptian MAC because it was needed more than ever since UNEF had been withdrawn, and warned the Security Council that the situation had grown more "menacing" than at any time since 1956. He blamed *al-Fatah* raids and Israeli reprisal attacks, threatening statements made by Israeli and Arab leaders and the removal of UNEF for the rapid deterioration of the situation. While he was on his way to Cairo on May 22 to confer with President Nasser, Egypt announced that she was restricting Israeli shipping through the Strait of Tiran, and this gave U Thant another major problem to discuss. He urged Nasser to lift the "blockade" temporarily because Israel was threatening to go to war. The Egyptian leader expressed a willingness to cooperate with the UN to prevent an armed conflict but held that he could not reopen the gulf to Israel. On his return to New York, U Thant reported to the UN Security Council that the situation was extremely grave and warned that "a peaceful outcome" would "depend upon a breathing spell" which would "allow tensions to subside." He strongly urged "all the parties concerned to exercise special restraint, to forego belligerence and to avoid all other actions which could increase tension, to allow the (Security) Council to deal with the underlying causes of the . . . crisis and to seek solutions." He also stated that the Egyptian leaders had "assured" him that "the UAR would not initiate offensive action against Israel." He recommended that the MAC machinery be revitalized and used to help relieve the explosive conditions between Israel, on the one hand, and Syria and Egypt, on the other.[24]

In the meantime, at the urgent request of Canada and Denmark, the Security Council met on May 24 to consider the grave situation. Israel and the Arab states were allowed to present their views to the Security Council. Israel, denying that she had massed troops on the Syrian border, noted that a report from U Thant had verified this. She strongly criticized U Thant's hasty removal of UNEF. She also charged that the Arabs were planning to make war against her. In evidence of this, she referred the Council to the many bellicose statements being made by Arab leaders and the massing of Arab military forces near her borders. She accused the Arab states, especially Syria, of aiding and abetting terroristic attacks on Israel and held that she could not be expected to submit to such actions without some response. She demanded that the Arabs withdraw their troops and stop threatening her survival. She also complained that the blockade of the Gulf of Aqaba (1) was a "gross violation" of the UN Charter and international law, including the terms of the 1958 Geneva Convention on the Territorial Sea; (2) was a "blow at the sovereign rights of other nations" and an "act of aggression" and of "war" against her; and (3) threatened to strangle her economy and to endanger her security. She warned that, as a measure of "self-defense" under Article 51 of the UN Charter, she would use her own military power to reopen the gulf if the UN and/or the world powers were unable to do this themselves "without delay." She held that when she was persuaded to withdraw her troops from Sharm al-Sheikh after the Sinai War, she had been "promised" that Egypt would never be allowed to close the gulf to her shipping, and she insisted that the promise be fulfilled.[25]

The Arabs quoted strong statements made by Israeli leaders and pointed to Israel's military build-up as "proof" clearly indicating that Israel had been planning to make a major attack on Syria. They accused Israel of preparing to start an aggressive war against the Arabs over the Gulf of Aqaba dispute. They insisted that they had mobilized their own forces as a purely defensive measure. They repeated the arguments presented in 1954, namely, that Egypt had the legal "right" to restrict Israel's use of the gulf because (1) the Arabs were still in a state of war with Israel, and this allowed them to take proper security measures as provided for by the rules of war; (2) Israel's occupation of Elath was illegal for it came about after the Egyptian-Israeli General Armistice Agreement and in complete disregard of various Security Council truce, cease-fire, and troop withdrawal resolutions; (3) the 1956 "aggression" did not change the legal status of the gulf and of Egypt's right to impose restrictions on enemy shipping; (4) the gulf was primarily an internal, not an international, body of water since in many places it was less than twelve miles wide, and all the coastal states considered their territorial jurisdictions to extend at least six miles from shore; and (5) Egypt was not denying any state "innocent passage" nor actually "blockading" the Strait of Tiran since normal shipping was not being prohibited. However, she had the "right" to prohibit Israeli vessels and strategic commodities destined for her enemy from passing through her territorial waters because, with the existence of a "state of war," such passage could not be considered "innocent." Egypt contended that in July, 1953, the Israeli-Egyptian MAC had backed her position on this point. At that time, the MAC had resolved that the ships of one party were not to be permitted to pass through the territorial waters of the other, thus "setting a legal precedent that no innocent passage could be attributed to combatant parties." The Arabs pointed out that the United States had established restrictions on shipping to Cuba and China. They further maintained that since the UAR had not signed the 1958 Geneva Convention, she was not bound by it. In any case, the convention would apply "in time of peace only."

The Arab delegates also insisted that Israel be made to live up to those UN resolutions which dealt with the refugee and other Arab-Israeli issues. They complained that the same states demanding immediate solution to the problem of navigation in the Gulf of Aqaba did "not display the same sense of urgency and concern for the fate of one and a quarter million human beings whose right to repatriation . . . has been solemnly proclaimed and reaffirmed in no less than eighteen resolutions of the General Assembly. . . ." They asked: "If the Arab states today were to declare that the non-compliance of these resolutions was a *casus belli,* would they not be on far more solid ground than Israel, which claims a right which it does not possess under international law and on which the UN has taken no position?" They not only denied responsibility for *al-Fatah* raids, but they blamed both Israel, who had failed to abide by the repatriation and compensation provisions of UN resolutions, and the UN and the major powers, who had failed to implement these resolutions, for the frustration, hostility, and terroristic activities of the Palestine refugees. It was argued that, because for nineteen years the refugees had not been allowed by Israel to attain by peaceful means those rights established by repeated UN decisions, they had no choice but to resort to force. Israel, not the Arab states, was therefore basically responsible for the existence and actions of such groups as *al-*

Fatah. The Arabs also contended that the Israelis should be the last to complain about the tactics used by *al-Fatah* since it was they who had "first" used the weapon of terrorism in the Middle East during the mandate period and who had acclaimed those Jews who had participated in bloody guerrilla warfare against the British as brave patriots. If Israel could look back and consider the bombings and snipings of the Sternists and Irguns before 1948 as heroic and legitimate actions, the Arabs wondered why they could not also consider as equally heroic and legitimate similar activities by Palestine commandos who were "merely" seeking, with the only means left to them by Israel and the UN, to undo "grave injustices" and to gain those "rights" promised to them by the world organization. The Arabs asked why the Western states were giving priority to the navigation issue over other pressing matters and were ready to use force on Israel's behalf but not on behalf of the natives of Southwest Africa, Rhodesia, and the Arab refugees. The Arabs urged the Security Council to strengthen the UN armistice machinery in the area, to compel Israel to withdraw from her "illegal" occupation of demilitarized zones and no man's lands, and to order her to abide by all obligations under the armistice agreements. The UAR submitted a draft resolution (S/7919) which requested the Security Council to carry out these suggestions. In addition, they maintained that they too had the right under Article 51 to take individual and collective defensive measures and warned that the entire Arab world would fight if Israel attacked any Arab country. Nevertheless, they "assured" the Council that they did "not contemplate any offensive action." [26]

In the UN Security Council, the Soviet Union and Bulgaria consistently and vigorously backed the Arabs, while India and Mali also provided occasional support, particularly for the Arab position on the Gulf of Aqaba dispute. The Communist states insisted that Israel had moved her troops to the Syrian border and that the Knesset defense and foreign policy committees had authorized the initiation of "military operations against Syria." They warned that, "should anyone try to unleash aggression in the Near East, he should be met not only with the united strength of the Arab countries but also with strong opposition from the Soviet Union and all peace-loving states." While in public Russian diplomats used militant language, in private they urged restraint on both sides for they feared that an Arab-Israeli war might bring about a military confrontation between the big powers—and this they wanted to avoid at almost all costs. They also held that the fighting in Vietnam had helped to precipitate the crisis in the Middle East and that any agreement to end the war in Vietnam would facilitate efforts to alleviate the situation in the Middle East.[27]

American officials found themselves under tremendous pressures from aroused and very active pro-Israeli groups, individuals, and politicians to carry out their promise to open the Strait of Tiran by force, if necessary, and to intervene militarily if Israel were attacked by the Arabs. In response, the U. S. government increased and alerted its military forces in the eastern Mediterranean. In a major address on May 23, President Johnson denied Egypt's right to interfere with the shipping of any nation in the Gulf of Aqaba and assured Israel and her supporters that the United States was "firmly committed to the support of the political independence and territorial integrity of all the nations" in the Middle East and would "strongly" oppose "aggression by anyone in the area, in any form, overt or clandestine." According to a *New York Times* report on May 24, 1967, the government "quietly reassured the Israelis that it will meet its commitment to oppose an Arab invasion of Israel." At the same time, American officials were seriously concerned that a major Arab-Israeli conflict might escalate into a world war. So they urged restraint upon Israel—who had made it clear that she would act militarily if the gulf were not opened quickly to her shipping—until they had a chance to deal with the problem through diplomatic channels.[28]

The United States first pressed for action through the UN. In the Security Council she took the lead in sharply criticizing U Thant for withdrawing UNEF so hastily and in denying the legality of Egypt's "blockade" of the Strait of Tiran. On May 31, she introduced an "interim" draft resolution (S/7916) which called upon the parties concerned, as a first step, to comply with the UN Secretary-General's appeal to "exercise special restraint, to forego belligerence and to avoid all other actions which could increase tension" in order to provide an essential "breathing spell." The resolution also encouraged the immediate pursuit of diplomacy in the interests of pacifying the situation and seeking reasonable, peaceful, and just solutions to all major Arab-Israeli problems. The United States interpreted the resolution to mean that Egypt would have to reopen the Gulf of Aqaba to Israel, at least for the time being.[29]

The Arabs expressed a willingness to accept a resolution calling for a cooling-off period as long as it did not require the lifting of the restrictions on Israeli shipping in the gulf. Because the American proposal contained such a requirement, the Arabs opposed it and accused the United States of acting on behalf of Israel. They further complained that when Israeli leaders threatened an attack on Syria, the United States remained "mute." But now that Israel was being threatened, the United States was ready to use armed force to protect her.[30] The American draft was supported by most of the Security Council members, but the Soviet

Union, to show her solidarity with the Arabs, rejected it. Although American officials soon discovered that their resolution could not pass because of this opposition, they refused to modify it.[31]

Once the United States realized that she could not obtain the approval of the Security Council for any resolution acceptable either to the West or to Israel, she resorted to diplomatic efforts outside the UN, urging both the Arab and Israeli leaders to do everything possible to avoid war. But because by this time all Arabs considered the United States to be acting as a partisan of the Israelis and because her relations with such key states as Syria and the UAR had been deteriorating—from the cessation of further sales of surplus wheat in the case of Egypt—the American government found that it was less able than ever to exert influence on the Arab countries.[32]

In contrast, American relations with Israel were good, and the United States was in an excellent position to apply pressures on her. However, pro-Israeli sentiment was so strong in Washington and throughout the country that Israel was encouraged to refuse to make any concessions and to use force. In fact, the *New York Times* reported on May 29, 1967, that President Johnson

> has been described as extremely sympathetic to the Israelis' eagerness to defend their southern sea route and as ready to support them in this objective. But in the crucial question of tactics, the President is also described as convinced that a hasty Israeli use of force would confuse the rights and wrongs of the controversy. He is said to be concerned that Israel might jeopardize much of the sympathy and support that she has painstakingly built up in the United States, Western Europe and Scandinavia.

Nonetheless, American officials pressed Israel at least not to make an immediate test of the blockade and to give them a little time in which to seek a peaceful solution acceptable to her. The Israelis were assured that, if this effort failed, the United States would act unilaterally to open the gulf. Some Israelis, like Foreign Minister Abba Eban, also urged the Israeli cabinet to delay any military action to allow more time to win over more support in the UN and the world at large and to lessen the chance that Israel would be blamed for starting a war. Eban reminded members of the cabinet that Israel had hurt herself badly in 1956 when she suddenly attacked Egypt without first trying to convince world public opinion of the "justness" of her action. As a result of these urgings and arguments, Israel agreed to give the United States a little more time.[33]

The United States tried to obtain agreement among the major Western maritime nations for creating an international naval task force to test the "blockade," but only the Netherlands was willing to go along with such a drastic step. Most governments were reluctant to take a strong stand for it would not only jeopardize their economic, financial, and political interests in the Arab world, but it could precipitate a clash with the Arabs which might lead to an involvement with Russia as well. The United States, shifting to a milder course of action, joined Britain in drawing up an international declaration to be submitted to all maritime powers for their signature. The declaration stated: (1) the Strait of Tiran and the Gulf of Aqaba were "international waterways" in which ships of all nations had a right of free passage; and (2) the signatories were prepared to "assert" this right on behalf of ships flying their own flags and to join with others to secure general recognition of this right. While the declaration did not commit any of the signatories to use force in support of Israel's right to use these waterways, the United States hoped that it would provide a basis for some states to do just that, if it became necessary. She also hoped it would lead to negotiations with Nasser about removing his proclaimed "blockade." However, not only most Western governments, but even some United States senators were not in favor of using the declaration as a basis for any military action. Britain also began to waver on the issue of the use of force, especially because of her fear that Russia might react violently.[34]

Realizing that Egypt would not voluntarily rescind her "blockade" measures and that there was little support in the West for the use of force against her, some American and British officials proposed offering Nasser a face-saving compromise solution. In return for accepting, in principle, Egypt's territorial sovereignty over the Strait of Tiran and for allowing restrictions to continue on Israeli vessels, he might be willing to let neutral craft pass through carrying goods of all kinds to Israel. These officials felt that Nasser had "left the door open" for discussing "such a compromise." They argued that since Israel had rarely sent her own merchant ships through the gulf even when it had been open, the acceptance of such a restriction on her own boats would inflict no practical hardship.[35] In fact, just before war actually broke out, Nasser agreed to send one of his top aides, Vice-President Zakariya Mohieddin, to consult with President Johnson on the gulf issue.[36] The United States was especially hoping to keep the crisis under control long enough for it to cool off to the point where a political solution could be found.

Even though the United States and Britain were actively seeking some compromise for the navigation dispute by early June, and some Western diplomats continued to believe that there was still a chance Nasser might be willing to make limited concessions, Israel repeatedly proclaimed that she would not accept any compromise, that "nothing less than complete noninterference" with Israeli shipping would be "acceptable" to her, and that she was "determined" to make her "stand on the Gulf of Aqaba." [37] Israel rejected all proposals by the UN Secretary-General, Britain, and others that the UN armistice machinery be strengthened in the area and that an "adequate UN presence" be stationed on both sides of the Egyptian-Israeli demarcation lines.[38] In short, Israel once again revealed both her great distrust of the UN—even when it was seriously trying to interpose itself between the hostile parties in a desperate attempt to preserve peace—and her strong conviction that in the final analysis she must depend completely upon her own will and strength to insure her security and to promote her interests.

As the Arab armies concentrated near Israel's borders, as many Arabs intensified their clamor for war, and as the UAR announced her "blockade" of the Gulf of Aqaba, Israel's apprehension mounted, and she hastened mobilization. Israel's military activities and increasing demands within Israel for a "preventive war" in turn caused the Arabs to accelerate their own military preparations. This cycle became more and more difficult to control as events generated their own irresistible momentum and outran the intentions of those who had set them in motion.

Initially, the responsible leaders on both sides had neither wanted nor planned for war. Grave miscalculations, however, were made by all the principal parties directly and indirectly concerned. The militant Palestinians and Syrians underestimated Israel's sensitivity and forceful opposition to border incidents and commando raids. President Nasser seriously misjudged the severity of the reactions in Israel and in the West to his provocative actions in the Sinai and Gulf of Aqaba areas, as well as the ability of the UN and the United States to hold Israel in check. Moreover, Egypt and the other Arab states greatly overestimated their own military power vis-à-vis Israel and the extent of the aid they would actually receive from the Soviet Union.

The Israelis, in turn, failed to realize that (1) as long as the Arab refugee problem remained unresolved, Arab hostility and terroristic activities would persist; (2) as long as they cultivated "disputed lands," border conflicts would keep Arab-Israeli emotions and tensions high; and (3) they could not continue to threaten and mount large-scale reprisal attacks without eventually eliciting violent responses from the Arabs. Both the Arabs and the Israelis committed themselves to such inflexible positions that they found it increasingly difficult to back down without losing "face."

The Soviet Union helped to incite the Arabs and to encourage them to take bold and dangerous positions, then deluded herself into believing that she could exert enough restraint to keep developments from reaching the point of actual war. American officials—by giving strong support to Israel on a number of major issues, particularly that involving the Gulf of Aqaba, and by assuring her that American power would be used to guarantee her security and survival—undoubtedly encouraged Israel to be more uncompromising and militant than anticipated. The United States also misjudged the bitterness of the Egyptian reaction to her refusal, a few months earlier, to continue selling the surplus wheat which Egypt needed desperately. While this action was not taken in the deliberately undiplomatic manner in which Dulles had turned down Egypt's request for aid to build the Aswan Dam, nevertheless it seriously aggravated American-Egyptian relations and impelled Nasser to take a stronger anti-West and anti-Israeli stand. In addition, the United States failed to recognize how much her own military actions in Vietnam had promoted militancy in the Middle East and reduced the likelihood that Russia would cooperate with American efforts, inside or outside the UN, to head off the Arab-Israeli crisis.

WAR

While Arab bellicose statements and military moves helped to bring the Middle East to the brink of an armed conflict and while the Arab leaders took an active part in a dangerous war of nerves, Israel actually initiated warfare on the morning of June 5. Ever since the start of the crisis, some Israelis, like retired General Moshe Dayan, had pressed for military action. This pressure became even more compelling after the UAR closed the Strait of Tiran to Israeli shipping. At first the Israeli cabinet was closely divided on what response should be made. Prime Minister Levi Eshkol and Foreign Minister Abba Eban urged restraint and recommended that the United States be given a reasonable opportunity to find an acceptable solution through diplomatic and political means. They warned that any precipitate military move by Israel might bring about Soviet intervention and might, as had happened during the Sinai War, alienate most governments and peoples, especially in the West. Even Ben-Gurion advocated a cautious policy. After it had become clear that the United States could not obtain sufficient backing for a resolute stand on the gulf dispute, most Israelis again insisted, as on critical occasions in the past, that their government disregard the UN and the wishes of other states and act unilaterally. Especially after King Hussein suddenly signed a military pact with Nasser on May 30, thereby confronting Israel with the military unification of two of her most powerful neighbors, internal pressures forced Eshkol to bring all parties except the Communist into a coalition government, to appoint activist Moshe Dayan as defense minister, and to take measures necessary to break both the gulf "blockade" and the tightening Arab "vise" around Israel. On June 3, the new cabinet voted overwhelmingly in favor of a "preventive war" and left it to Eshkol and Dayan to determine when to strike. The day they selected was June 5.[39]

For many years, Israel's military strategy had been based upon making full use of the element of surprise, striking the Arabs before they had become too unified and powerful, taking the offensive from the beginning in order to win a quick victory, and concentrating as much power as possible on the strongest foe first. In early June, although Arab mobilization was well advanced and Algeria, Iraq and other Arab states had promised to send troops to aid Israel's Arab neighbors, the Arab leaders still had not had adequate time in which to concentrate their military forces along the Israeli borders and to coordinate their military plans. Israeli military advisers had expressed confidence that Israel could readily defeat the Arabs, but they urged that Israel attack before the Arabs had the opportunity to become better prepared militarily and while they were not expecting such a move. They warned that the longer Israel delayed action, the stronger and more united her enemies would become and the more casualties the Israeli armed forces would suffer in the ultimate conflict. At this time, too, the Arabs were not yet expecting Israel to attack, and the crisis gave her a unique opportunity for a surprise assault—she was able to explain her mobilization as merely a move to counter Arab mobilization.

The UN Security Council was actively debating the Middle East crisis. The United States and Britain were continuing their search for a solution to the Gulf of Aqaba question, and President Johnson had agreed to discuss the Middle East situation with a high level Egyptian official around June 7. On top of all this, Israeli officials, including Moshe Dayan, were making public statements which appeared to give the impression that Israel was willing to give Anglo-American diplomacy more time before taking action. By early June, Israeli propaganda and diplomacy, aided greatly by the intemperate and warlike language being used by Arab leaders, had won over to Israel's side a large part of world public opinion, particularly in the West. Although President Johnson urged restraint on Israel, he did not make it absolutely clear, as President Eisenhower had done in October, 1956, that the United States would oppose Israel if she made the first military move. Besides, it appeared as if he were requesting that Israel merely delay belligerent action and not demanding that no such action be taken regardless of the time element. In any case, pro-Israeli and anti-Egyptian sentiment was so strong in the United States generally and in the highest levels of government and most Americans were so convinced that Israel would be justified in taking any "necessary" military measures that Israel saw little need to worry about any hostile American reaction to her striking the first blow. Moreover, if Israel had miscalculated her own power and that of the Arabs, she still felt reasonably confident that the United States would come to her aid if her security and survival were seriously endangered. Firm American support and the presence of the powerful U.S. Sixth Fleet in the eastern Mediterranean also reduced the likelihood that the Soviet Union would intervene militarily on the side of the Arabs. Besides, Israel was aware that she would have great difficulty in maintaining full mobilization indefinitely. But with a large percentage of her manpower in uniform, she was suffering economic losses from lowered production, and even her tourist trade was gravely affected. All these factors led Israeli leaders to the conclusion that conditions were favorable for an all-out military attack on the Arabs.[40]

By attacking and defeating the Arab states, Israel sought (1) to eliminate all further commando raids and border conflicts; (2) to destroy as much of the Arab armed forces and their equipment as possible in order to remove any potential Arab military threat for some years to come; and (3) to make sure that her ships would never again be denied the right to use the Gulf of Aqaba. She also hoped to open the Suez Canal, to compel the Arabs to enter direct peace negotiations with her, and to cause the overthrow of the more militant Arab governments, especially that of Syria.

At least initially, Israeli leaders probably differed on whether Israel should seek additional lands as well. In any case, on the day the war began, both Prime Minister Eshkol and Defense Minister Dayan asserted on the Israeli radio that Israel's war aims did not include territorial aggrandizement. Dayan said, "Soldiers of Israel, we have no aim of territorial conquest. Our sole aim is to bring to naught the attempt of the Arab armies to conquer our country and to destroy the encircling blockade and aggression." [41] Israel soon reversed her position on this particular point.

Although Israel claimed that the Arabs had actually started the war by directing artillery fire on Israeli border villages and by sending Egyptian tanks and planes "toward" the border, it was clear that Israel —following tactics similar to those successfully employed in the Negev and Galilee sectors in October and December, 1948, and in the Sinai War in 1956—again used alleged provocations as an excuse to initiate the all-out military attack which caught the Arabs completely by surprise.[42] Just before 8 A.M. local time, Israel suddenly launched devastating air strikes on military airfields in the UAR, and later on those in Syria, Jordan, and Iraq, in order to break the back of Arab air power right from the start. Because the Arabs had not been prepared for this action and because Israeli aircraft had flown very low and through gaps in the Arab radar system, Israeli pilots destroyed most of their enemies' planes on the ground within the first several hours of the war. This spectacular military blow paved the way to victory.

Employing daring, mobility, and speed and taking full advantage of their almost unchallenged control in the air, Israeli armor and mechanized infantry took the offensive against Egypt and, a few hours later, against Jordan as well. On the southern front, several Israeli columns— fighting day and night, constantly and relentlessly pressing ahead to keep the Egyptian forces off balance and to encircle them when possible, and depending greatly upon their air power to bomb and strafe Egyptian tanks, artillery, and supply units—were able, within three days, to conquer the Gaza Strip, Sharm al-Sheikh, and nearly the entire Sinai Peninsula to the east bank of the Suez Canal. At the same time, other Israeli units using relatively similar tactics defeated Jordan's army and occupied the Old City of Jerusalem and all Jordanian territory on the west bank of the Jordan River. Without air cover and without trees and other vegetation to provide protection, the Egyptian and Jordanian tanks, artillery, trucks, and infantry, forced to move and fight mostly over desert areas, were easy targets even at night for the alert and well-trained Israeli pilots. The Israeli air force by relentlessly attacking exposed Arab soldiers and by cutting off their supplies, shattered Arab morale and left them helpless. Israel delayed her invasion of Syria until she had defeated Egypt and Jordan and UN-sponsored cease-fires had come into effect on these two fronts. Once the Israeli forces launched their offensive in the north on June 9, they were able to concentrate almost their whole air force and the greater part of their ground units against a much weaker opponent. Even though the fighting was bloody and bitter and the rough uphill terrain slowed the Israeli mechanized forces to some extent, the Syrian forces gave way under the brutal pounding from the air. Hostilities had generally ceased by the evening of June 11 when both sides agreed to and abided by the fourth cease-fire resolution passed by the Security Council. Since Lebanon did not directly enter the conflict, no combat took place between her and Israel.[43]

There were many factors which contributed to Israel's swift and conclusive victory. As in earlier wars, the Israelis started out with excellent military intelligence, supply, and communication services; well-trained and disciplined soldiers had great fighting spirit and the skill to make full use of modern military equipment and techniques; highly competent military leaders who had effectively coordinated air and ground units into a single, mobile striking force had devised a daring, offensive strategy and a unified command; and benefitted from short lines of communications. The element of surprise enabled her to destroy the greater part of Arab air power on the ground, leaving her in almost complete command of the skies. Because of the terrain, air superiority was an especially decisive factor. The Arabs had not had a chance to unify their varied military forces and commands and to organize all their armed manpower for effective deployment against Israel. Then too, as Hanson Baldwin, military analyst for the *New York Times,* wrote on June 8, 1967:

> Since the vaunted superiority in numbers of the Arab armies was never brought to bear on the fighting fronts, Israel probably had an over-all numerical superiority in the troops actually involved and a clear-cut superiority in firepower and mobility in the actual battles. . . . Many of the more than 2,000 tanks and self-propelled guns used by the principal Arab armies do not appear to have been engaged at all. . . . President Nasser appears to have retained . . . [most of his] troops to maintain his precarious foothold in Yemen, to perform internal security duties in Egypt, and to provide a reserve for the defense of the Suez Canal and of Egypt proper.[44]

The expectation that the U.S. would probably come to their rescue in case of an unexpected military setback which would threaten their survival probably encouraged the Israeli leaders to take a more daring, all-out offensive gamble. This gamble paid off, at least militarily.[45]

The third military confrontation of the Arabs with the Israelis revealed that though Arab armed forces had improved, they suffered from many of the earlier deficiencies. They still lacked able political and military leaders and well-trained, dedicated, offensive-oriented officers. Their soldiers were not adequately trained to use the sophisticated weapons supplied by the USSR. While both the officers and the enlisted men were able to fight reasonably well from fixed, dug-in defensive positions, they were far less adept at carrying out an offensive military campaign requiring mobility, maneuvering, and coordination of all branches. The average Arab soldier still could not match his Israeli counterpart in discipline or fighting spirit. Arab intelligence, communications, radar, and supply services remained weak. As in the 1948 conflict, Arab disunity, overconfidence, and failure to mobilize and concentrate all effective military power against Israel helped pave the way to another humiliating defeat.[46]

When war broke out on June 5, most of the world's governments were extremely anxious to bring the conflict to a halt as quickly as possible, not only because they wished to prevent bloodshed, but especially because they greatly feared that American and Soviet commitments to come to the aid of the disputants might draw them into the military struggle. Both the Soviet Union and the United States were so fearful of finding themselves, through some miscalculation, at war, that they quickly made use of the "hot-line" link between Moscow and Washington to assure each other that they would make every effort to end the fighting in the Middle East and to avoid precipitate actions which might cause an escalation of the Arab-Israeli confrontation.

When the UN Security Council hurriedly convened, Israel took the offensive politically and diplomatically, as she had already done militarily. Israel was greatly aided by her careful and astute diplomatic and propaganda efforts, American sympathy and support, and the short-sighted and bellicose public speeches and show of military force by the Arabs during the preceding weeks. Consequently, even though she had been the one to initiate offensive operations and even though the Arabs, despite their provocative statements and military moves, had not actually intended to start a war, Israel was able to convince most people, especially in the West, and most UN delegates that the Arabs, by "illegally" closing the Gulf of Aqaba and by calling for Israel's extermination, were really the aggressors and that they had pushed her into exercising the "right" of self-defense as provided for under Article 51 of the UN Charter. Israel also contended that (1) the Arabs were sending tanks and planes "toward" her borders when she decided to "defend" herself; (2) since the UN could not reopen the Strait of Tiran and provide her with protection against Arab threats, she was justified in taking all necessary action to protect her own vital interests and to repel "aggression"; (3) her armistice agreements with all the Arab countries except Lebanon had not worked to keep the peace and therefore were no longer valid; and (4) she would reject any cease-fire proposal which required her to withdraw her troops from the conquered areas until the Arabs agreed to negotiate a peace settlement.[47]

The Arabs denied that they had started the war and sought to defend their own views and actions. They claimed that (1) since their planes were caught by surprise on the ground, it was obvious which side was the aggressor; (2) Article 51 applied only "if an armed attack occurs" against a state, so even if the movement of Arab troops close to Israel's borders, the closing of the Strait of Tiran, and the natural love of the Arabs for bombastic and overly-dramatic language were considered ill-advised and/or illegal, the fact remained that these actions could not be classified as "an armed attack" in the meaning of this article; (3) the Arabs had the "legal right" to restrict enemy shipping from using the gulf and, in any case, the navigation dispute, since it involved a disagreement over a rule of international law, should have been brought before the World Court and not made the basis for starting a war; (4) Egypt had requested the removal of UNEF and the Arabs had mobilized their forces and sent them to their Israeli frontiers because Israel had threatened Syria, and the Arabs, therefore, under the terms of Article 51, had the "right of individual and collective self-defense," which right would have been exercised, as required by the article, only if and when Syria had actually been subjected to an Israeli military assault; (5) if Israel feared an invasion by the UAR, she could easily have prevented it by accepting U Thant's suggestion that UNEF units be moved to her side of the demarcation lines and by agreeing to the proposals made by the Arabs and others that the Egyptian-Israeli MAC be strengthened and made more effective; (6) if Israel were justified in going to war merely because the UN had been unable to accomplish all the things desired by Israel, then the Arabs would also have been justified in resorting to force because the UN had failed to implement many of its own decisions favorable to the Arabs or even to provide the Arabs with security from Israeli assaults; and (7) Israel had constantly ignored and belittled the UN. They held that Israel's military attack should be strongly condemned especially because it came at a time when the Security Council was still trying to deal with the situation and was asking the Arabs and the Israelis to show restraint, when, in response to UN and American urgings, Egypt had "clearly" and formally declared her "intention not to initiate any offensive action," when the UAR was seeking ways to strengthen the Egyptian-Israeli MAC so it could keep peace along the borders, and when President Nasser was about to send a high Egyptian official to discuss the Gulf of Aqaba and other problems with President Johnson. They warned that the UN would be setting a dangerous precedent if it allowed any aggression to go unpunished. While the Arabs at first opposed a cease-fire, they soon reversed themselves when it became evident that the Arab forces were being overwhelmed by the Israelis. When they were finally prepared to accept a cease-fire, they insisted that it also call—as similar cease-fire resolutions had usually stipulated in the past—for the withdrawal of all military forces to the positions held before the conflict had broken out.[48]

At a series of urgent Security Council meetings, all Council members favored a cease-fire resolution but disagreed as to whether or not it should be unconditional. At the beginning, the Soviet Union, once again vigorously backing the Arabs, accused Israel of being the aggressor and pressed the Security Council to order an Israeli withdrawal from occupied areas, as well as a cease-fire. The United States, on the other hand, supported Israel's demand that any request for a cease-fire must be unconditional. As soon as the Russians realized that the decisive Israeli air victory had made the Arab military position virtually hopeless and that a continuation of the conflict would merely mean greater losses of territory, manpower, and equipment for the Arabs, they finally decided to vote for draft resolution S/7935, submitted by the President of the Security Council after consultations with Council members. This resolution, which called upon the "governments concerned," as a "first step," to take "forthwith" all measures for an "immediate cease-fire," was unanimously approved by the Security Council on June 6.[49]

Initially, the Arabs refused to accept the resolution (S/Res 233) because it passed "in silence" the question of which side was the aggressor and it failed to call for an Israeli withdrawal from conquered areas. They urged that sanctions be applied against Israel because of her "treacherous" and "premeditated attack." They also vehemently accused the United States and Britain of having given Israel intelligence information and even direct military support in the air strike on the Arab states. Many Arab governments broke diplomatic relations with, and several also stopped oil shipments to, the United States and Britain. In addition, they expressed great disappointment in the Soviet vote for the resolution. After the Arab military situation had become increasingly desperate and the Security Council had passed Resolution 234, which demanded a cessation of all military activities at 2000 GMT on June 7, first Jordan, on June 7, and then Egypt, on June 8, agreed to a cease-fire. Israel had consented to it on June 7, but only on the condition that all Arab belligerents also accepted and abided by it. Hostilities between Israel, on the one hand, and Jordan and the UAR, on the other, had generally stopped by June 8–9, but both Jordan and the UAR complained to the UN that Israel had continued her advance and occupied territory not held before the cease-fires had gone into effect.[50]

Although Syria had reluctantly agreed to a cease-fire on June 9, fighting between Israel and Syria intensified on June 10 and 11. Israel claimed that the Syrians were continuing to shell Israeli border villages and that this forced her to take "defensive actions" to silence the Syrian artillery and tanks involved in the shooting. Syria, in turn, insisted that she was not at fault and that the Israelis were persisting in their invasion so that they could annex Syrian territory and occupy Damascus. Actually, a number of reports held that Israel, after having defeated the UAR and Jordan and after having shifted her planes and best forces to the northeast frontier, deliberately launched a large-scale assault on Syria, despite the cease-fire, in order (1) to seize the strategically important Syrian heights (which overlooked and dominated the Israeli-controlled plains north and east of Lake Tiberias), the headwaters of the Banyas River, and the springs which feed the Dan River; (2) to deal a crushing blow to that Arab country considered mainly responsible for *al-Fatah* raids and which had been the primary proponent in the Arab world of a war to "exterminate" Israel; and (3) to humiliate the militant Syrian leaders so badly that they would be overthrown. The fact that large Israeli land and air forces were striking deeply into Syria and well beyond the Syrian guns and tanks allegedly breaking the cease-fire clearly indicated that the objective of Israel's military activities embraced far more than merely the silencing of Syrian fire on her villages. The Arabs repeatedly protested to the Security Council and pressed that body to order Israel to halt her "invasion" of Syria. They also accused the United States of deliberately delaying Council action to allow Israel enough time to gain her objectives.[51]

In an attempt to bolster her prestige and position in the Arab world, where many Arabs had begun to accuse her of "running out" on them when they needed her most and of working with the United States against their interests, the Soviet Union (1) broke diplomatic relations with Israel on June 10; (2) introduced a draft resolution (S/7951/Rev. 1) which, among other things, "vigorously condemned" Israel's "aggressive" activities and violations of Security Council resolutions and demanded that Israel halt her military operations, withdraw her forces behind the 1949 armistice lines, and respect the status of the demilitarized zones; (3) held a meeting of Communist bloc leaders in Moscow who issued a statement promising to aid the Arabs if "aggression" did not stop and to make every effort to bring about the withdrawal of Israeli troops from the occupied areas; (4) warned that she would rearm the Arabs if Israel did not withdraw from occupied Arab areas; and (5) threatened to demand the application of sanctions if Israel failed to abide by UN decisions.[52] The increasing vehemence of the Russian threats caused the United States and other Security Council members to press Israel to halt her advances before the Russians felt it necessary to intervene. Because of these pressures and the passage, on June 9 and June 10, of resolutions 235 and 236—which ordered a cessation of hostilities "forthwith and a prompt return of forces to the original cease-fire positions"—and because she had already achieved most of her immediate military objectives in Syria, Israel agreed to stop all hostilities at 6:30 P.M. GMT, on June 11.[53]

AFTERMATH

Once the cease-fires had gone into effect on all fronts, Russia again concentrated her efforts in the Security Council on bringing about a condemnation of Israel and a withdrawal of her forces to behind the armistice lines. After slightly modifying her resolution (S/7951/Rev.3), she insisted that the Council vote on it. On June 14 the resolution was defeated. Only four states (Russia, Bulgaria, Mali, and India) voted in favor of the paragraph which "condemned" Israeli "aggression." Ethiopia and Nigeria joined these four countries in voting for a second operative paragraph demanding an immediate and unconditional Israeli withdrawal.[54]

The United States led the opposition within the Council to the Soviet proposal and was largely responsible for its defeat. In the interim, she had introduced a draft resolution (S/7952/Rev.3) that made an Israeli withdrawal dependent upon the "establishment of viable arrangements" which would be brought about by means of discussions "among the parties, using such third party or UN assistance as they may wish" and which would also involve "the renunciation of force . . . , the maintenance of vital international [navigation] rights, and the establishment of a stable and durable peace." Realizing that this resolution would be vetoed by Russia, the United States did not ask that it be put to a vote. As for the charge that their planes had participated in the fighting, the United States and Britain not only vigorously denied it, but they offered to have this matter investigated by the UN.[55]

The Arabs accused the United States of being anti-Arab and pro-Israel, of deliberately misleading the Arabs into thinking that Israel would hold off an attack until all diplomatic efforts had been exhausted —thus helping Israel to catch the Arab forces off guard, of working and voting in the Security Council to defeat any resolution opposed by Israel, and of disregarding her "obligations" under the UN Charter to condemn aggression and to insist, as she had "correctly" done in 1956 and 1957, that an aggressor should not be allowed to enjoy the "fruits" of his "illegal" actions. They wondered why the United States did not want the UN to determine who had actually initiated offensive operations on June 5 and why Israel had attacked while "the Council was seized of the problem and while talks and negotiations and efforts were being undertaken . . . to find a peaceful solution." They went on to ask why the President and other American officials had, before and even after the outbreak of war, repeatedly committed the United States, both inside and outside the UN, to safeguarding the political independence and territorial integrity of "all" countries in the Middle East and to being "impartial" in dealing with the issues and states in the area, and yet, making no effort to fulfill their pledges now that the Arabs, and not the Israelis, would benefit. They questioned whether the United States would have been so reluctant to carry out her commitment had Israel been the vanquished party and the Arabs the victors. They warned that they would not negotiate with the aggressor, would not accept this injustice, and would see to it that the injustice was "undone." [56]

Although, in time, many Arabs began to concede that British and American planes had probably not helped Israel during the war, nearly all Arabs nevertheless continued to believe that the United States had at least indirectly encouraged Israel to attack, delayed Security Council action until Israel had made substantial territorial gains—especially at the expense of Syria, and helped to defeat all efforts to obtain an Israeli withdrawal. In American newspapers they read reports which directly and/or indirectly quoted high government officials, including Secretary of State Dean Rusk, as stating that they were "quite happy" and "pleased" to see Israel win the war and that her victory was also "quite a victory for the West." They witnessed the tremendous outpouring of strong pro-Israeli and anti-Arab sentiments, not only from American Jews but from the overwhelming preponderance of the American people. Even the inexplicable attack by Israeli air and naval units on the clearly-marked American communications ship *Liberty* on June 8 while it was in international waters off the Sinai coast did not cause any weakening of these deeply-rooted pro-Israeli feelings, despite the fact that thirty-four American sailors were killed and seventy-five were injured. For these reasons, the Arabs, including large numbers of those who had been favorably disposed towards the West, became increasingly unfriendly to the United States, and American prestige and influence in the Arab world plunged to its lowest levels. Then too, most Arabs felt that since they could not expect any assistance from the United States despite their desperate economic and military situation, they had no choice but to look to the Russians for aid.[57]

With Israel the situation was reversed. She denounced the Soviet Union for being pro-Arab and anti-Israel and accused the Russians of aiding and abetting the Arabs in their endeavors to destroy Israel. Had it not been for Soviet weapons and political support, the Arabs could not, Israel claimed, have threatened to make war on her and the Arabs would have been more willing to come to the peace table. She charged the Russians with distorting the facts of the Middle East situation, backing the anti-Israel militants in the Arab world, mistreating the Jews in the Soviet Union, and disregarding their UN Charter obligations. The Israelis, too, wondered whether the Soviet Union would have been so anxious for cease-fire and withdrawal resolutions had the Arabs been victorious. They insisted that Russia would have them move "backward to belligerency" rather than "forward to peace," and that they could not be expected to withdraw their forces until the Arabs were ready to insure Israel's peace and security—and this could be done "only" through a peace settlement achieved by direct negotiations.[58] In the meantime, Russian-Israeli relations deteriorated rapidly, while the Soviet government found itself facing some opposition to its pro-Arab and anti-Israeli position from Rumania and a number of Communist leaders and their followers in some of the Western countries.[59]

Having failed to obtain Security Council approval for her resolution (S/7951/Rev.3), the Soviet Union intensified her efforts on behalf of the Arabs both inside and outside the UN in order to offset the growing Arab discontent which stemmed from what the Arabs considered inadequate Russian military and political backing during the war crisis and also to exploit to the maximum the bitter anti-American and anti-British feelings which had developed in the wake of the Arab defeat. Because the Arabs were so enraged with the West and because they quickly discovered that only the Russians were willing and able to provide the considerable political, military, and economic aid which they desperately needed, the Soviet Union did not find it difficult to restore and even to extend her influence in the Arab world.[60]

As soon as hostilities had ended, Russia began to rush military and economic aid to the Arabs. She flew new MIG's and airlifted other badly needed military equipment to the UAR and other Arab states, but not only to help her recoup some of her lost prestige. Other reasons were: (1) to restore some of the military balance of power between the Arab countries and Israel so as to discourage Israel from trying to seize more Arab territories; (2) to strengthen the political bargaining position of the Arabs in case efforts were made to force upon them a political settlement with Israel; (3) to bolster the existing governments in Egypt and Syria to prevent their overthrow by political factions perhaps less friendly towards Russia; and (4) to make the Arabs more dependent upon her and thus to increase her power in the area. Russia even offered to rearm such pro-Western countries as Jordan so as to undermine further the position of the United States and to strengthen her own in those parts of the Middle East where she had made little headway. Within a relatively short period, the Soviet government replaced approximately half of the MIG's and nearly half of the tanks lost by Egypt during the war. Some of the new replacements included the latest planes and tanks which had not been sold to the UAR before.[61]

After rather serious clashes had taken place between Egyptian and Israeli forces at numerous points along the Suez Canal, Egypt expressed fear that Israel was trying to seize not only Port Fuad and the small marsh area round it along the northeastern shore of the canal (the only section of Egyptian territory east of the waterway which had remained in Egypt's hands at the time of the cease-fire) but parts of the west bank as well. Russia lost no time in dispatching some naval vessels to Alexandria and to Port Said, across the canal from Port Fuad, as a warning to Israel not to advance any further. In June and July, high Soviet officials, including President Nickolai Podgorny, visited Cairo and other Arab capitals to assess the situation first-hand and to assure the Arab leaders that Russia would supply them with military and economic assistance. At the same time, the Russians, anxious to avoid a further deterioration of conditions in the Middle East, urged the Arabs to be cautious and moderate and stressed the need for a political, rather than a military, solution to their differences with Israel. In the second week of July, Communist bloc leaders meeting in Budapest agreed to press for an Israeli withdrawal from occupied Arab areas and to pledge long-range economic aid to strengthen the Arab countries which had suffered the most. The Russians apparently decided that because of the immense economic and political investments already made in the Arab world and of the unique opportunities which existed for further Soviet penetration, they should continue to provide costly and urgently needed help to the Arabs.[62]

The Soviet Union took the initiative in requesting an emergency session of the UN General Assembly in the hope of winning enough support there to pass a resolution similar to the one she had unsuccessfully submitted to the Security Council. Despite the opposition of the United States and Israel, the overwhelming majority of the members of the UN approved the Soviet request, and the Fifth Emergency Special Session convened on June 17.

To provide further evidence of Russia's determination to help the Arabs, Aleksei N. Kosygin, chairman of the Council of Ministers, came to the UN to press for General Assembly action against Israel. He submitted a draft resolution (A/L.519) which (1) "vigorously" condemned Israel's "aggressive activities"; (2) called for an immediate and unconditional withdrawal of Israeli forces to behind the armistice demarcation lines; (3) demanded that Israel "make good in full" all damages inflicted; and (4) appealed to the Security Council to take "immediate and effective measures in order to eliminate all consequences of the aggression." The Arabs fully endorsed this proposal, but the United States and Israel led the opposition to it. Because most delegates felt that it was too one-sided, the resolution failed to pass. Russia was undoubtedly aware from the beginning that her proposal would not muster the required two-thirds vote, but she must have felt that it would demonstrate her staunch support of the Arabs' cause. In the meantime, she exerted every effort to obtain passage of a draft resolution (A/L.522/ Rev.3) introduced by Yugoslavia on behalf of seventeen Afro-Asian states and herself. This draft called on Israel to withdraw to positions she had held prior to June 5 and requested the Secretary-General to ensure compliance and to designate a personal representative to assist him in securing such compliance. It also asked the Security Council to consider all aspects of the Arab-Israeli problem and to seek peaceful solutions for them.

The American delegates took the lead in backing many of Israel's views and in working to defeat those resolutions strongly opposed by her. In particular, they firmly supported Israel's refusal to withdraw from the conquered sectors unconditionally and her insistence upon a negotiated settlement which would give her most of the goals which she was seeking. They even toned down their former pledges to protect the territorial integrity of all states in the area in the hope that Israel could gain more defensible borders.[63] In addition, the United States submitted a draft resolution (A/L.520) which considered that the main objective was a "stable and durable peace" to be achieved through "negotiated arrangements with appropriate third party assistance based on": (1) the "mutual recognition" of the "political independence and territorial integrity of all countries" in the Middle East, encompassing recognized boundaries and including disengagement and withdrawal; (2) freedom of innocent maritime passage for all ships; (3) a "just and equitable solution" of the Arab refugee problem; (4) the registration and limitation of arms shipments to the area; and (5) the recognition of the right of all sovereign nations to exist in peace and security.

Since no other nation openly supported this resolution, the United States never pressed for a vote on it. American officials, instead, concentrated their efforts on defeating the Yugoslav proposal, which for a while appeared to be fairly sure to pass—especially because Israel's harsh peace terms, her encouragement of the Arabs living on the west bank of the Jordan River to leave their homes, and her annexation of the Old City of Jerusalem had caused much of world opinion to move away from her. In an attempt to draw support away from the Yugoslav draft, the United States encouraged some Latin American delegations to present a competing proposal.[64] The Latin American draft (A/L.523/Rev.1) (1) requested Israel's withdrawal; (2) asked the parties concerned to end the state of belligerency; (3) reaffirmed that there should be no recognition of the occupation or acquisition of territories through force; and (4) requested the Security Council to continue working with the parties to insure withdrawal, the end of the state of belligerency, freedom of transit in international waterways, full solution of the refugee problem, and the establishment of demilitarized zones. Since the overwhelming preponderance of UN members actually favored the principle of an Israeli withdrawal, had the Latin American draft not been submitted, chances were that the Yugoslav proposal would have been adopted. Now, however, all the states which sought a withdrawal were split between those for a conditional and those for an unconditional withdrawal—with Western and Latin American delegates mostly backing the conditional, and the Afro-Asian and Communist delegates mostly supporting the unconditional type of withdrawal.

Israel unequivocally rejected the Yugoslav proposal. She contended that it was "one-sided" and that it ignored the "facts" that the Arabs were the ones who had been threatening Israel's existence and who were responsible for the war. She charged that its objective was to restore to the Arabs what they had lost through their own "illegal" actions and that it would merely revive those conditions which had led to the war in the first place. The Yugoslav draft was "a prescription for renewed hostilities" and not for peace. There could be, she insisted, no Israeli withdrawal from conquered areas until there was an Arab "withdrawal from belligerency, from hostile actions, from war preparations, from the obdurate refusal to recognize the sovereign equality of states." The Israelis held that they had made a serious mistake in giving up Egyptian territory after the Sinai War on the basis of certain promises and understandings which never materialized. By relinquishing these strategic areas they had merely endangered their security and made it possible for the UAR to "plan for" her "annihilation." They felt "justified," therefore, in demanding that the Arabs agree to make peace before any decision would be made about an Israeli evacuation of the occupied territories.[65]

They also maintained that by "starting" the war, the Arabs had automatically made the armistice agreements "null and void." Consequently, Israel no longer recognized either the armistice machinery—such as UNTSO and the MAC's—or the old demarcation lines, demilitarized zones, and no-man's lands between herself and Syria, Jordan, and the UAR. She also asserted that the cease-fire lines and present situation could "only be exchanged for a negotiated peace settlement" which would establish "mutual recognition" and "agreed frontiers and security arrangements." As long as the Arabs alleged that a state of war continued to exist, then Israel would be in a "reciprocal state of war" with them. The Israelis repeatedly expressed their dissatisfaction with the UN, its agencies, and its efforts in the Middle East. They charged that "when Israel was in dire peril . . . , the UN decided not to intervene, . . . [but] to get out of the way" [66] and that the world organization had been unable to provide Israel with her "elementary right to security, uninterrupted development, maritime freedom and peaceful existence."

Since Israel could not, therefore, "depend" upon the UN or the major powers to insure her peace and security, she would not yield her territorial acquisitions on the mere promises of others, and she would retain control over them until she could convince the Arabs to negotiate a peace settlement. Although Israel concentrated her attack on the Yugoslav draft, she was also far from pleased with the Latin American proposal, principally because it called for an Israeli withdrawal without demanding that the Arabs negotiate directly with her and it assigned to the UN a greater role than Israel wanted the world organization to assume in any Arab-Israeli settlement.[67]

While the Arabs were not completely satisfied with the Yugoslav resolution, they backed it with vigor, for they realized that they would be unable to obtain General Assembly approval for any proposal which contained stronger terms. The Arab delegates to the UN contended that (1) Israel's continued occupation of Arab lands was "illegal," "unacceptable," and "intolerable"; (2) an unconditional withdrawal, as provided by the Yugoslav draft, was an absolute prerequisite to the examination and resolution of any other Arab-Israeli issue; (3) Israel's "sneak" attack on June 5 was not "an isolated example but part of a deliberate Israeli expansionist policy"; (4) Israel had "flouted" UN resolutions relating to the Arab refugees and Jerusalem, "mistreated" Arabs in the occupied areas, "looted" Arab properties and "driven" thousands of Arabs from their homes; and (5) by rejecting all recommendations aimed at strengthening the UN's presence in the Middle East and the UN's role in dealing with Arab-Israeli disputes, by "disregarding" the UN Charter and UN resolutions, and by proclaiming, as Foreign Minister Abba Eban had, that Israel would refuse to comply with a General Assembly withdrawal resolution even if it were to pass by a vote of 121 to one, Israel was showing her "utter contempt" for the UN and was proving that she was concerned not with attaining fair solutions to the existing problems but with "dictating" her own peace terms. "To permit Israel to retain gains as a bargaining weapon," they maintained, was "to permit the aggressor to use the fruits of his aggression to gain the ends for which he went to war." Not only would this be "immoral" and "illegal," but it would set a "dangerous precedent" which would "encourage" Israel to try to expand again at the first opportunity. It would, in addition, embolden other states to use force and to "strike the first blow," especially since one major lesson learned from the June War was that "victory goes to the one who strikes first," and it would "undermine" the "very foundations" of the UN and international law.[68]

Arab delegates complained that the Latin American draft was

"slanted on the side of Israel" and ignored the UN Charter, UN resolutions, and the Arab-Israeli armistice agreements. Despite Israel's contentions that these agreements were no longer in effect, the Arabs insisted that (1) no state had the legal right under international law to terminate a treaty unilaterally; (2) since the UN had helped to draw up these agreements and had endorsed and helped implement them by passing resolutions and setting up UNTSO and the four MAC's, Israel could not dissolve them without the sanction of the world organization; (3) in 1956–57 and since the June War UN officials and/or organs had denied Israel's right to declare the agreements null and void; (4) the Arabs considered both Israel and themselves still bound by the armistice treaties and urged the UN to strengthen and enforce them; and (5) any disagreements arising under these and other international conventions, such as those involving rights of navigation, should be resolved by the World Court, the only body qualified and empowered to decide legal issues. With deep bitterness, the Arabs again accused the United States of aiding and abetting Israeli aggression and Israel's efforts to impose her own views and demands even when they "conflicted" with the UN Charter, UN resolutions, and international conventions. Finally, the Arabs warned that they would never accept an Israeli "diktat" (dictation) and that another war would be inevitable if Israel did not completely withdraw her forces from all conquered Arab territories.[69]

Most major Western powers did not back Israel quite as wholeheartedly as did the United States. Britain and Canada, for example, supported the view that an Israeli withdrawal must be accompanied by Arab acceptance of her right to live and of an end to belligerency. At the same time, however, they proposed that the UN dispatch a high level mediator to the area to seek some common ground between the opposing sides and to enlarge and strengthen the UN truce supervision operations in the area. In short, they recommended that the UN play an even more active and important role in trying both to prevent clashes along the cease-fire "lines" and to seek, by quiet diplomacy, some bases for limited Arab-Israeli concessions and agreements—a step which Israel, at least, strongly opposed. Britain held that, according to the UN Charter, "war should not lead to territorial aggrandizement," warning Israel that if she annexed the Old City of Jerusalem, she would "not only isolate" herself from "world opinion" but would make it more difficult to achieve final peace with the Arabs.[70]

In an official statement issued after a cabinet meeting on June 21, President Charles de Gaulle, disregarding considerable internal political dissension, strongly censured Israel, once France's unofficial ally, for having been the one to start offensive operations despite his warning not to do so and his promise to come to her rescue if her survival became endangered. He urged that while the Arabs should accept Israel's right to exist, a complete Israeli withdrawal from all occupied territories must take place before any progress could be made in resolving the other Arab-Israeli disputes. In the UN, France advised the Israelis that the "war settled nothing and has made everything more difficult." She also announced that she would not recognize Israel's latest territorial acquisitions. Holding that the Vietnam conflict played an important role in creating those conditions in the Middle East which ultimately produced war, France contended that any improvement in the Vietnam situation would help alleviate the Arab-Israeli situation. She also pressed for action and agreement on the part of the big powers on the Middle East crisis. France not only approved the Yugoslav proposal, but she urged other nations to vote for it.[71]

On July 4, the General Assembly voted on a number of draft resolutions. Only two less controversial proposals passed. One [A/RES/2253 (ES-V)] called upon Israel to rescind her annexation of the Old City of Jerusalem. The other [A/RES/2252(ES-V)] dealt with various humanitarian and refugee problems. The Yugoslav draft received fifty-three votes in its favor, forty-six against, and twenty abstentions—less than the required two-thirds majority. Most Asian, some African, and three European states (France, Greece, and Spain) joined the Arab and Communist blocs in voting for it, while nearly all the Latin American and Western European nations, plus eight African countries, joined Israel and the United States in voting against the resolution. The Latin American proposal received fifty-seven favorable votes (most of which came from North and South America and Western Europe, while some came from Africa) and forty-two negative votes (most from Asia, the Arab world, and the Communist bloc, plus some from Africa). Twenty members, including France and Israel, abstained. Israel was delighted that neither proposal calling for her withdrawal passed the Assembly. The Arabs, on the other hand, were disappointed with the Soviet Union's failure to obtain passage of a resolution demanding an unconditional Israeli withdrawal. However, their bitterest feelings were directed at the United States, for they held her primarily responsible for the defeat of the Yugoslav draft.[72]

Russia, embarrassed at having summoned an emergency session of the General Assembly without being able to produce a successful withdrawal resolution for the Arabs, desperately sought to arrange a compromise proposal with the cooperation of the United States. The two countries worked out a draft which, in essence, called for an Israeli withdrawal to the positions held before June 5 and asked all UN members to acknowledge the right of Israel to exist in peace and security as an independent nation free from any state of belligerency. However, the Arabs, led by Algeria and Syria, emphatically rejected the Soviet draft because they considered its language even less satisfactory than that used in the Latin American proposal. As soon as they realized that this move had merely offended the Arabs, the Soviet Union quietly put aside the new proposal and joined the United States, despite Arab opposition, in voting for a resolution which adjourned the General Assembly "temporarily" and requested the Security Council to resume, "as a matter of urgency . . . its consideration of the tense situation in the Middle East." Through this resolution for adjournment, the General Assembly conceded its inability, largely as a result of the serious split between Russia and the United States over the Middle East situation, to deal effectively either with the more immediate issues in dispute or with the basic obstacles which continued to block the path to an Arab-Israeli peace.[73]

While the General Assembly was still debating the Middle East crisis in the early part of July, clashes began to take place along the various cease-fire lines, especially the one between Israel and the UAR. After the war had ended, Israel and Syria had agreed to allow UN observers to be stationed along their cease-fire lines. Israel had accepted them only as cease-fire observers and not as representatives of UNTSO and the MAC's, whose existence and authority she no longer recognized. (In keeping with this position, Israel returned Government House, the old UNTSO headquarters located on the outskirts of Jerusalem, to the UN with the understanding that the "sole function and concern of General Bull and his staff is with those cease-fire resolutions of the Security Council and no longer with the General Armistice Agreements and the now obsolete arrangements of the past." This Israeli view of the armistice treaties and machinery was not endorsed by the UN Secretary-General.[74]) Israel insisted that the observers confine themselves to observing and reporting. In addition, she restricted their movements in the occupied territories. For their part, the Arabs insisted that UNTSO, the MAC's, and the armistice systems were still in effect. Despite these opposing opinions, the observers carried out their assignments and helped reduce friction along the lines where they were posted.[75]

Unfortunately, similar arrangements were not made for observers either along the cease-fire lines between Jordan and Israel or along the Suez Canal, which was blocked by a number of ships apparently sunk by the UAR during the June War. Starting on July 1, the canal became the scene of serious fighting involving, on occasion, the use of planes, tanks, and artillery. Both sides suffered many casualties. Finally, on July 8 both the UAR and Israel asked for an urgent meeting of the

Security Council. In the charges and countercharges Israel blamed Egypt, while Egypt accused Israel of starting the fighting in an effort to seize not only Port Fuad and the area around it on the east bank of the canal but also Port Said and other territories on the west bank. In fact, the UAR was apparently so concerned about Israel's intentions in the northern sector of the waterway that she invited Soviet naval vessels to visit Port Said to discourage any Israeli move.[76]

The Security Council met on July 8 and 9 to consider the complaints of the opposing parties. The nonpermanent members devised an agreement (S/8047) requesting UNTSO Chief of Staff General Odd Bull to "work out with the governments of the UAR and Israel as speedily as possible necessary arrangements to station UN military observers in the Suez Canal sector under the chief of staff." The proposal was accepted without dissent and without a formal vote on July 9.

The UAR and, especially, Israel were not completely in favor of accepting UN observers. Egypt's primary concern was that the stationing of observers on each side of the Suez Canal might tend to legitimatize it as a permanent frontier. The reference to the "Suez Canal sector" and not to a "line" in the Security Council agreement helped to make it somewhat more palatable. However, when she accepted the Council's proposal on July 10, she did so with the understanding that it was a "purely provisional measure" and that the observers would be allowed to stay only until Israeli forces withdrew from the area.[77]

In Israel, the opposition to the Security Council's move was much greater. For years the Israelis had been trying to get the UN out of the Middle East, partly because of their "disappointing experience" with UN observers in the past and partly because they feared that third-party interposition would remove pressures on the Arabs to consider peace talks. The Israeli cabinet was deeply split on the issue and some members, like Moshe Dayan, were reported by the *New York Times,* July 12, 1967, as urging not only the rejection of this Security Council proposal but also the removal of all UN observers along the other cease-fire lines. Many Israelis expressed a preference for having Arab and Israeli local commanders contact each other directly and work out necessary arrangements to keep the peace along their lines. Israel finally and reluctantly yielded, not only because she was embarrassed by the fact that Egypt had already agreed to cooperate with the UN but because of the powerful pressures which Western governments had brought to bear and because of the possibility that the new arrangement might help to formalize the canal as a new boundary.[78] Even then, differences between the contending parties delayed the implementation of the agreement. Israel wanted the observers on each side to communicate directly, while Egypt insisted that all contacts must go through the chief of staff's office in Jerusalem. At least for several months Egypt's position on this point prevailed. Israel also maintained that the cease-fire line ran through the middle of the Suez Canal and that either her boats had the right to use the waterway or neither party should have the right. Egypt held that at the time of the cease-fire, no Israeli vessel had yet been in the canal. Therefore, the cease-fire line was on the east bank, and Israel did not have the right to go beyond it for any reason. Even though their differences on this point were not reconciled, the UN observers took up their posts at 1600 GMT on July 17.[79]

The controversy over the use of the Suez Canal caused several serious skirmishes as Egypt forcibly sought to prevent Israeli ships from sailing on the waterway, and Israel, in turn, tried to stop the UAR from using it unilaterally. Many casualties, especially among Egyptian civilians in the major west-bank cities, resulted from these clashes, and UN observers had great difficulty, at times, in arranging lasting cease-fires. Israel had started to use the canal to facilitate the transport of supplies to her troops along its banks and, more important, to set precedents for the establishment of freedom of navigation through it. The UAR was determined to keep Israeli boats out of the waterway because she did not want such precedents set. To prevent further bloodshed, the chief of staff finally suggested that there be a cessation of navigation on the canal by both sides for a period of one month. This proposal, accepted by Egypt and Israel, went into effect on July 27. Late in August, both states agreed to extend the shipping prohibition indefinitely. Egyptian vessels were allowed to navigate the waterway only to deliver provisions to those ships stranded in the canal when it was blocked. This extension of the agreement notwithstanding, serious clashes continued to occur because of alleged attempts by one side or the other to use the waterway.[80]

From the beginning, Egypt had indicated that she would not open the canal as long as Israeli troops occupied the east bank. President Nasser undoubtedly felt that the Suez Canal was his most effective bargaining weapon to force an Israeli withdrawal. He hoped that the commerce of Western countries would be so adversely affected by the closure that all the necessary pressures would be applied to compel Israel to leave Egyptian territory. However, the United States, who had the most influence over Israel, was only slightly affected, for only a very small part of her trade went through the canal. Most of the other Western countries were not as seriously handicapped as Nasser had anticipated. Actually, ever since 1956, the companies which produced oil—the main commodity traditionally routed through the canal—had begun to transport their oil in huge tankers too large for the canal, and they had to go around Africa. Moreover, major discoveries of oil had been made in North Africa, and Europe began to draw much of its oil needs from there. Of the Western nations, Britain was hurt the most, but even she made no major effort to compel Israel to withdraw. In the meantime, countries in South Asia, the Middle East, and East Africa sustained considerable losses because of the higher shipping costs and the decline in the tourist trade.[81]

Actually, the nation that suffered the greatest financial loss from the blockade of the Suez Canal was Egypt herself. The approximately $200,000,000 which had been earned from transit fees represented a major portion of Egypt's foreign currency earnings. The wealthy oil-producing Arab states, Kuwait, Saudi Arabia, and Libya, however, provided the UAR with about $75,000,000 immediately after the war. About $266,000,000 more was pledged on September 1, 1967, in the summit conference held by the Arab states in Khartoum, Sudan. These contributions, plus considerable belt-tightening in Egypt, helped Nasser to keep the canal closed despite large financial losses. In any case, Israel's announcement that once the waterway was reopened she would demand the right to use it seriously complicated matters for Nasser. If he opened the canal and did not continue to keep Israeli ships out of it, he would be met with a great outcry from the whole Arab world, and his rivals would find themselves with an ideal situation to exploit. On the other hand, if he tried to prevent Israeli ships from entering a re-opened canal, Israel might employ her superior military power and her control of the east bank to use force to get her shipping through, to close down the waterway from her side, or to try to seize the entire canal. As long as the other Arab governments supplied him with adequate funds, he could avoid the dangerous dilemma that would arise from trying to unblock the waterway under these precarious conditions. Meanwhile, there was always the possibility that a sufficient number of Western nations would eventually find the prolonged blocking of the canal so costly that they would start pressing for Israel's evacuation of Egyptian territory. In the interim, the deadlock over the Suez Canal persisted without an end in sight.[82]

During the last several months of 1967, many incidents and some large-scale clashes occurred along the Egyptian-Israeli and Jordanian-Israeli cease-fire lines, Arab guerrilla activities were stepped up, and Israel revived her policy of retaliation. On at least one occasion, the situation became so perilous that the UN Security Council had to intervene.

The most serious and damaging conflicts took place between Israel and the UAR. During some exchanges of fire across the Suez Canal, the Israelis shelled Egyptian towns, particularly Ismailia and Suez. Because civilians began to suffer heavy casualties, the UAR evacuated approximately 350,000 inhabitants from the principal cities along the west side of the waterway. On October 21, Egyptian vessels, using radar-guided missiles supplied by Russia, blew up the destroyer *Elath* with heavy losses in the same area near Port Said where Israeli ships had sunk two UAR torpedo boats on July 12. Israel contended that the *Elath* had been on "routine patrol" and had remained more than thirteen miles from shore. Egypt, claiming a twelve-mile territorial sea, charged that the Israeli warship had been only ten miles away and heading for Port Said in a "provocative" manner. (The UNTSO Chief of Staff reported the destroyer to be "11 nautical miles" from the port.) Egyptian national pride and self-confidence were given a lift by the destruction of the largest vessel in the Israeli navy. However, the Israelis were so infuriated that on October 24 their forces, using an exchange of fire across the canal as an excuse, directed such heavy artillery barrages on the city of Suez that Egypt's two main oil refineries, which supplied 80 per cent of her gasoline and cooking and heating fuel, were either demolished or badly damaged; other industrial plants were also hit. This severe attack, obviously meant to be a reprisal action, was a serious blow to Egypt's already shaky economy. Tensions mounted so rapidly that the Security Council felt it necessary to intervene. On October 25, a resolution condemning all violations and reaffirming the need for strict observance of the cease-fire was passed unanimously. U Thant asked for and received permission to increase the size of the UN observer force and to set up nine more observation posts on both banks of the Suez Canal. Nevertheless, the sinking of the Israeli warship and the grievous blow dealt to Egypt's productive capacity further heightened Egyptian and Israeli animosity and weakened the chances for moderation and conciliation on the part of the two antagonists.[83]

Numerous exchanges of fire also took place between Israeli and Jordanian troops. Starting in early November, Israel began to accuse Jordanian army units of providing covering fire to enable Arab terrorists to escape from pursuing Israeli soldiers. Two serious incidents and reprisal actions occurred in the third week of November, 1967. On November 20, during an exchange of fire across the Jordan River, Israeli artillery shelled the Karama refugee camp two miles east of the river and caused many casualties among its inhabitants. Israel alleged that the camp was being used as a staging area by Arab commandos. On November 21, after further firing by both sides, Israeli planes crossed into Jordanian airspace and strafed some tanks taking part in the conflict. The fighting caused considerable damage, numerous casualties, and increased tensions. Again on January 8, 1968, after an unusually heavy artillery battle broke out across the Jordan River, Israeli jets attacked Jordanian positions. Despite the Israeli strikes, occasional exchanges of fire across the Jordan River persisted.[84]

Arab terrorist activities were also stepped up in the latter months of 1967. While there were a few mining incidents in the Sinai and in the Gaza Strip and an occasional attempt at sabotage in the Golan Heights sector, the great preponderance of the commando attacks was mounted either from Jordan or from the occupied west-bank area itself. Arab guerrillas used explosives against small factories and other buildings and planted mines on roads and railway tracks. Numerous clashes developed between Israeli border patrols and Arab raiders, and both sides suffered casualties. Israel was able to seize and arrest many Arab infiltrators, and houses suspected of harboring them were leveled. A number of towns and villages were placed under martial law with strict curfews enforced in an attempt to bring Arab guerrilla assaults to a halt. Although Israel accused Syria, Algeria, and Egypt of training and arming Arab "saboteurs," she also charged Jordan with helping to protect and to provide bases of operations for *al-Fatah* and other extremist groups. Israeli officials warned that they would not hesitate to stage reprisal raids "with ground forces outside our borders" if Jordan and Syria did not stop promoting forays against Israel. Syria denied responsibility for the existence and operations of the Palestinian activist organizations. King Hussein and other Jordanian officials publicly opposed terrorist actions on the ground that they would merely give Israel an excuse to take harsh measures against the Arabs in the occupied territories and to make reprisal attacks on nearby Arab countries. Jordanian authorities made some efforts to discourage and even to arrest infiltrators; but many Jordanian citizens and soldiers sympathized with the Arab militants and there were large numbers of bitter and unemployed refugees from the Palestine and June Wars who were ready and anxious to join the ranks of the various commando organizations.[85]

Thus, as of the early part of 1968, "border" incidents, Arab guerrilla raids, and Israeli armed reprisals persisted. Moreover, because of American-Soviet disunity and the limited size and restricted authority of UN observer forces in the Middle East, the UN was unable to act very effectively to prevent bloody clashes and to lower tensions in the area. Consequently, the situation along the cease-fire lines remained unstable and fraught with great danger.

ANALYSES

Instead of settling the Arab-Israeli dispute, Israel's overwhelming victory and the humiliating defeat of the Arabs, the considerable loss of life, the extensive destruction and the vast territorial changes which resulted from the June War, and the bloody skirmishes which followed in its wake served only to deepen the fear, distrust, and hostility of the Arabs and Israelis and to compound the complexities of the Arab-Israeli dilemma. Actually, all of those who were directly or indirectly involved with the Arab-Israeli problem—Israel, the Arab states, the major powers, and the UN—shared responsibility, in one degree or another, for the June conflict and its aftermath.

Israeli Position and Responsibility

Israel's policies and actions, as well as those of the Arabs, were responsible for setting off the chain of events which eventually led to war in June, 1967. The festering refugee situation was primarily responsible for Arab guerrilla raids as well as for much of the anti-Israel feelings in the Arab world. Consequently, the most logical and effective way to have brought commando activities to an end was not to have mounted armed reprisals, which merely inspired more, not less, terrorist operations, but to have made determined efforts to deal with the real root cause: the unresolved refugee problem. Moreover, Israel's large-scale retaliatory assaults on as-Samu in November, 1966, and on Syria on April 7, 1967, and the serious threats of yet another and possibly bigger attack on Syria made openly by Israeli leaders in the second week of May, 1967, had been major factors in inducing President Nasser to build up his forces in the Sinai, to request the withdrawal of UNEF, and to order the closing of the Strait of Tiran to Israeli shipping.

Ironically, President Nasser and King Hussein had been bitter enemies and rivals for years—and this Arab disunity had added greatly to Israel's security. It was Israel's assaults on Jordan and Syria and her open threats against Syria which suddenly brought these former Arab antagonists to sign a military pact on May 30. Therefore, if this move by Nasser and Hussein did pose a potential threat to Israel, she had a great deal to do with bringing it about. At any rate, the new Egyptian-Jordanian "defense" agreement could not have represented any immediate danger for it was still only on paper. It would have taken the two countries many months, at the minimum, to have turned their alliance into an effective military instrument against Israel. The very competent and highly respected Israeli military intelligence was well aware that (1) Israel continued to hold a substantial military lead over the

Arabs; (2) the Arab forces were far from sufficiently trained and organized for successful offensive operations against her; and (3) in June the UAR was not seriously preparing or planning to invade Israel, a fact which Western correspondents in Cairo readily observed and reported to their newspapers. Not only had American, as well as Israeli, intelligence been predicting before June 5 that Israel could win a war against the Arabs without great difficulty,[86] but both the American and French governments had assured Israel that they would come to her aid if it became absolutely necessary. In short, while Israel was fully justified in her concern for the hostile statements and actions of the Arabs and the long-range implications in their efforts to achieve greater military unity, Israel's security and existence were not as greatly or immediately menaced as it was made to appear.

Furthermore, if the Israeli leaders had really believed that an invasion was imminent and Israel's survival was at stake, they could easily have precluded any Arab attack by accepting U Thant's urgent suggestion that UNEF be allowed to take up positions in their territory. This could have been arranged very quickly by a transfer of men and equipment over an extremely short distance. She could also have accepted proposals made by U Thant and others that the observer staff of the Egyptian-Israeli MAC be enlarged and made more effective. With a strong UN presence along Israel's borders and the United States Sixth Fleet in the Mediterranean, the UAR could not have seriously considered invading Israel. By firmly and unhesitatingly rejecting U Thant's proposals, Israel indicated that she was less interested in thwarting an Egyptian attack than she was in making sure that a UN presence did not frustrate her own ability to strike at the UAR at the time of her own choosing. Israel's strategy has been to attack the Arabs and destroy as much of their military manpower and material as possible before they had an opportunity to unify their separate armed forces and to develop superior power. From the short-range military point of view this might be considered sound strategy. But, if the Arabs persisted in their efforts to build and, when necessary, rebuild their military unity and power, Israel's strategy would require, first, that Israel always be the one to deliver the first blow and, second, that Israel start a "preventive war" whenever deemed essential—and that could be every few years or so. As it would not be reasonable to expect the Arabs, with much greater manpower and other potential resources, to desist from trying to attain military power at least equal to, if not greater than, that of Israel, Israel's strategy would obviously doom the Middle East to an endless series of wars and preclude any hope for a real Arab-Israeli peace. Also, having learned the costly and humiliating lesson of the June War that the side which hits first has the better chance to win, it would be logical to assume that the Arabs might sooner or later adopt Israel's successful strategy of striking the first blow, and that could very well mean that all-out surprise attacks would become the order of the day in the Middle East.

The Israelis were understandably aroused and concerned when the UAR suddenly reinstated her former restrictions on Israeli use of the Strait of Tiran. Nevertheless, no matter how ill-advised and "illegal" this action might have been, it did not justify starting a war. Articles 2 and 33 of the UN Charter clearly require all members to settle their disputes, no matter how serious or threatening, by "peaceful means" alone. The sole exception is that provided in Article 51, which permits a government to resort to force only if "an armed attack occurs," and the closing of the Gulf of Aqaba could not be classified as "an armed attack" under the Charter. The Israelis feared that this UAR blockade would hurt their economy, would pose a threat to them, and would not be dealt with firmly enough by the UN, and their feelings of frustration were natural. However, over one million Palestine Arab refugees had been living under distressing conditions and in frustration for nineteen years, and the UN had never seriously tried to compel Israel to abide by those resolutions which provided for their repatriation and/or compensation. Besides, Israel had committed her share of "illegal" actions, as have other countries, and millions of peoples have felt helpless and frustrated. If every UN member could—unilaterally, arbitrarily, and with impunity—resort to force at any time it felt threatened or suffered from some "illegal" or "hostile" policy of another member, then the UN Charter would be rendered meaningless and international relations would be thrown into chaos. Then, no nation, not even Israel, would benefit from the anarchy that would ensue. If the UN and world law are to have any chance to survive and to be strengthened so that they could better serve the cause of peace and justice between nations, no country, whether Arab or Israeli, should be allowed to start a "preventive" or an "aggressive" war. No matter how unsatisfactory and frustrating it might be for the Arabs and the Israelis, they must completely fulfill their obligations under the Charter by using only peaceful means for resolving their differences.

As conceded by UN, American, and other Western officials and experts, "A legal controversy exists as to the extent of the right of innocent passage through these [Gulf of Aqaba] waters." [87] The more confident the Israelis were about their legal rights, the more willing they should have been to bring the matter before the World Court. The Security Council itself could and should have asked the Court to hand down an advisory opinion. Especially in the light of obligations as set down in the UN Charter, the legal issues should have been resolved before any responsible action could have been decided upon—and only the World Court had the authority and the competence to decide the legal question involved. Once the court had handed down a decision, the Security Council, finally assured of the legally correct course of action and already authorized by Article 94 of the Charter to enforce court "judgments," could then have taken whatever measures required to implement it.

Through her victory, Israel gained some but not all of her major objectives. She was able to destroy a large amount of Arab, especially Egyptian, military equipment and considerable numbers of military personnel. In doing this, Israel was able to alter the balance of power in the area heavily in her favor, at least for the time being. The Gulf of Aqaba was opened, and her forces were in a position to keep Egypt from using the Suez Canal as long as she could not also use it. She had seized vast sections of Arab territories, including some strategically valuable areas. The crisis had released a tremendous upsurge of emotional, economic, and political support from world Jewry and it enabled her to strengthen her ties with the United States. In addition, her swift and decisive defeat of the Arabs not only weakened Arab morale and self-confidence, but it also heightened Israeli morale and prestige. Her major territorial conquests and her powerful military machine placed her in a strong bargaining position in case the Arabs were prepared to negotiate a final peace settlement.

But Israel did not put an end to all "border" incidents and guerrilla raids, as she had hoped to do. While the positions of the hated leaders in Egypt and Syria were greatly shaken, Presidents Gamal Abdel Nasser and Noureddin al-Atassi continued in power. Even extremist Ahmad Shukairi remained as head of the Palestine Liberation Organization, until December, 1967, and *al-Fatah* continued its commando operations. The Suez Canal was closed to Israel as well as to all other states. Within a few months Russia had replaced the greater part of all the military equipment losses of the UAR, Syria, and Iraq. By further antagonizing and humiliating the Arabs, by conquering and holding the "sacred" national soil of three Arab states, by annexing areas containing shrines revered by Muslims, by weakening the position of many Arab moderates, by helping to create yet another major Arab refugee problem, by magnifying their own feelings of superiority, and by demanding far tougher peace terms than they had demanded before June 5, 1967, the Israelis were soon to discover that their tremendous military victory did not bring them any closer to their most cherished goal of all—a final peace settlement on their own terms.

Israel paid a considerable price for her gains. Some 679 Israelis were killed and 2,563 wounded in the armed forces alone,[88] not counting the civilian casualties, especially in Jerusalem. In the months following the war, the Russians broke diplomatic relations with her, assumed a violently anti-Israeli and strongly pro-Arab stand, refused to permit any more Soviet Jews to migrate to Israel, and looked with greater suspicion on the loyalty of their own Jewish nationals. Israel's formerly very close ties with France were seriously weakened, and France ceased to sell her military equipment. Hostility to her increased in non-Arab Muslim countries, including Turkey and Iran, who had maintained diplomatic and/or economic relations with her in the past.

By seizing vast Arab territories, Israel also became responsible for approximately 540,000 Palestine Arab refugees and another 500,000 Jordanians, Egyptians, and Syrians. Large numbers of the refugees and other Arabs, especially those in the Gaza Strip, were either unemployed or underemployed. The standard of living in the occupied areas was lower than that in Israel proper, and this created economic complications. After the initial shock of defeat had worn off, the Arabs in the west-bank and Gaza Strip areas began to show their bitterness and discontent by strikes, demonstrations, refusal to cooperate with Israeli authorities, and various acts of terrorism. The Palestine Liberation Organization, *al-Fatah,* and other groups established after the June War launched a campaign of sabotage and guerrilla attacks from bases both in the occupied sectors and from the neighboring Arab countries with, according to some reports, the active aid of Syria and Algeria and later Iraq and the UAR as well. Conflicts arose between Arabs and Israelis within the occupied areas not only because two incompatible nationalisms were involved, but because there was a clash between two different cultures and religions. By employing severe punitive measures, such as the blowing up of houses believed to have been used by commandos, and by arresting suspected trouble makers, Israel was able to restore relative order and normal life in the conquered territories. Strong opposition to Israeli rule persisted, however, and the harsh measures introduced to keep the Arabs submissive merely deepened Arab hatred of the Israelis. There was even danger that this hatred and hostility of the newly subjugated Arabs might spread to the approximately 300,000 Israeli Arabs who had generally accepted their status as Israeli citizens and who had never before created any significant security problem. In brief, Israel would probably find it increasingly difficult and costly to hold on to the occupied sectors.

The Israelis also found themselves on the horns of a dilemma. While most of them wanted to retain permanently much, if not all, of the lands wrested from the Arabs, at the same time they wished to keep Israel a strictly Jewish state. But the annexation of these territories would add well over a million Arabs to the 300,000 already in Israel proper. Some demographic experts warned that the much higher Arab birth rate could put them in the majority in ten to twenty years if Israel retained all the conquered areas and their inhabitants. Israeli Jews could then maintain political control of their state either by disenfranchising the Arabs and treating them practically as a colonial people or by trying to expel as many of them as possible from their homes. In either case, Israel would not only further provoke the Arabs everywhere and make it even less likely that they would ever accept her, but she would lose a considerable amount of the political support and the greater part of the sympathy which she had so painstakingly built up over the years in many parts of the world, especially in the West. Israel could, moreover, find herself facing a problem similar to that which had confronted Britain in the post-World War II period in Palestine—except that this time the Israelis would be playing the role once assumed by the British, and the Arabs, like the Palestine Jews, would seek through terrorism and civil disobedience to drive out their hated rulers. In short, if the Israelis annexed all the captured lands and they were to grant the Arab community equality of opportunity and status, as would be required under a democratic government,[89] they could in time lose control of their state. On the other hand, if they sought to maintain Jewish domination, they could do so only by denying the Arabs political rights and treating them as a subject people—in which case, real democracy would cease to exist in Israel, and nineteenth-century imperialism would again rear its head to the embarrassment not only of the Israelis themselves but also of their friends and supporters.

The bitterness engendered by the June War spread strong anti-Israeli feelings even to those Arab countries which had not been too greatly concerned with the "Palestine" question in the past. The Jews still living in the Arab world found themselves increasingly distrusted and disliked by their Arab neighbors and many of them decided to leave.

By renouncing the armistice agreements and by claiming that only a cease-fire existed between her and the Arabs, Israel left the legal situation more confused than it was before June 5. Actually, armistice treaties normally provide a much firmer legal basis than cease-fires for prohibiting a resumption of hostilities. Security Council cease-fire resolutions are imposed from the outside, while only armistice agreements provide direct legal commitments between the antagonists themselves. In 1948 and 1949, for these very reasons, the UN pressed for armistice conventions to replace truces and cease-fires. By rejecting the continued existence of UNTSO and the MAC's and by insisting that the authority and functions of the UN cease-fire observers be strictly limited, Israel made it far more difficult for the UN and its agencies to discourage "border" incidents and clashes and to maintain relative tranquility in the area. Moreover, it is hard to understand the antipathy of many Israelis to UN agencies and officials in the Middle East, especially since practically all military personnel assigned by the UN to UNTSO and the four MAC's have usually come from relatively pro-Israeli Western countries and none from pro-Arab areas.[90] In fact, if the objectivity of these UN officials were subject to question, it would be the Arabs who would have more reasons to distrust them because of their background. In any case, the UN has denied Israel's right to terminate the armistice agreements and the UN resolutions and machinery connected with them and has contended that they are still legally in force. It is certainly logical to assume that the more anxious Israel is to avoid unnecessary strife with her hostile neighbors, the more willing she should be to welcome as much of a UN presence as would be required to provide an effective buffer between her and the Arabs. Obviously, as long as blood is shed along the cease-fire lines, passions will not subside sufficiently to permit the moderate leaders on both sides to work out their differences rationally and peacefully.

Arab Position and Responsibility

Arab—especially Syrian and Palestinian—bellicose language and actions helped to bring the Middle East to the brink of war in May, 1967. By resorting to force to halt Israeli cultivation of "disputed lands," by countenancing and aiding *al-Fatah* commando attacks, and by calling for war against Israel, the Syrians increased Israeli anger and concern, encouraged Israeli retaliation, and heightened Arab-Israeli tensions. The taut situation was further strained when Egypt decided to call for the withdrawal of UNEF, to build up her forces in the Sinai, and to close the Gulf of Aqaba to Israel. Blustering and irresponsible Arab oratory inflamed still further the tense state of Arab-Israeli affairs. While threatening a neighboring country was not, of course, as serious an offense as actually invading her, Article 2 of the UN Charter forbids not only the use of force, but also the "threat . . . of force against the territorial integrity or political independence of any states." Therefore, while it was Israel that first initiated offensive operations on June 5, the Arabs contributed greatly to the grave deterioration of those conditions which ultimately led to war.

The June War had many painful consequences for the Arabs. The UAR, Jordan, and Syria sustained heavy losses in military manpower and equipment, causing the balance of power to swing even more heavily in Israel's favor. While large-scale military aid from Russia narrowed the imbalance, the armed forces of Jordan, the UAR, and Syria had been so severely mauled and their morale and self-confidence so seriously shaken that it would take them some time to recover.

The war also had grave economic effects, particularly for Jordan and Egypt. The west-bank area, including the Old City of Jerusalem, had been the most fertile and productive part of Jordan; tourists visiting the holy shrines there were her biggest source of foreign exchange. The more than 200,000 west-bank residents who fled to the east bank multiplied economic difficulties. Most experts agreed that the east bank alone could not survive without continuous and considerable foreign economic assistance. As for Egypt, she found herself in desperate straits because the closing of the Suez Canal, the loss of her productive oil wells in the Sinai, and the sharp decline in the tourist trade were depriving her of foreign exchange at the rate of several hundred million dollars a year. Her economic position was further handicapped by the need to relocate tens of thousands of Egyptian refugees from the Sinai and Suez Canal areas, by the vast destruction of her oil refineries in Port Suez, and by the interruption of normal economic and financial relations with some of the major Western nations. Although the wealthier Arab governments and the Soviet Union provided aid to Egypt and these same governments and some Western countries and private groups donated funds to Jordan, both of these Arab nations found it necessary to cut down drastically on administrative expenses and economic projects and to put austerity programs into effect.

As for political repercussions, their unexpected and mortifying rout left the Arabs stunned, uncertain, and frustrated. But much to the surprise of those who had expected the debacle to topple President Nasser, the Arabs rallied to his support and urged him to remain as their leader. Not only did Russia's timely economic, political, and military backing bolster Nasser's position, but actually there was no other outstanding leader in the Arab world to whom the confused and desperate Arabs could turn. Though King Hussein's army was soundly beaten, he found new popularity among his people (most of whom were bitterly anti-Israel and anti-American), because he dared to fight on the side of Egypt and because he seemed to be veering a little from his staunchly pro-Western position. Despite the major roles they had played in provoking the war and setting up the Arabs for their humiliating defeat, the extremist Syrian and Palestinian leaders continued in power. In the months to come, however, there could develop a period of political and social ferment and even of violent upheaval in some of the Arab countries, as had taken place after the Palestine War in 1948.

Many Arabs raised blunt and angry questions about the causes for the military defeat. Some of the more perceptive Arabs attributed it to their inferior political and military leadership and institutions, their relatively backward society, their lack of adequate education, technological know-how, and discipline, their serious disunity and selfish rivalries, their feeble propaganda which had failed to present the Arab position properly, and their blustering, overly-dramatic oratory, which allowed the Israelis to make it appear as if the Arabs were the true aggressors and the Israelis were merely "innocent victims," thus causing the Arabs to lose and the Israelis to gain decisive diplomatic and political support during and after the war.[91] More and more Arabs demanded that quick and determined action be taken to overcome these deficiencies so that the Arabs would never again have to suffer crushing defeat. Arab discontent and impatience could increase to the point where they would threaten the positions of the existing leaders and cause considerable instability in some Arab countries. Such a development would not make it easier for Arab officials to consider a settlement with Israel.

This third Arab-Israeli conflict also brought about major changes in inter-Arab relations. For a short time, the Arabs were compelled to put aside their differences and close ranks against the common foe and against the bitter consequences of defeat. But soon the facade of unity gave way again to traditional disarray, even though the Arab leaders held a number of small conferences and finally a full-scale summit meeting. Algeria, Syria, and the extremist groups among the Palestinians pressed for more aggressive policies and actions against Israel, including guerrilla warfare, and for maintaining the economic boycott of the United States and Britain. On the other hand, Egypt, Jordan, and other Arab countries urged a more moderate course towards both Israel and the West. They stressed the political as well as economic advantages to be gained by improving Arab relations with Great Britain and the United States. Only the United States, they contended, could compel Israel to give up her conquered territories. However, because of the weakened position of some of the governments, the violently anti-Israel emotions of the Arab masses, and the readiness of the Arab extremists to attack any Arab official who gave the slightest indication of coming to terms with Israel, most moderate Arab leaders continued to feel that they could not deal more realistically with the Arab-Israeli issues facing them. For the time, these circumstances prevented them from making positive contributions toward resolving the Arab-Israeli dilemma, but it was hoped that the more responsible leaders would make every effort to avoid policies and actions which would only exacerbate the already dangerous state of affairs and that they would exert every effort to quiet popular feelings and to improve the political climate in the Middle East. In the final analysis, the precipitation of another crisis and a fourth military confrontation would not be to the benefit of any state in the area and would, like the other Arab-Israeli wars, only multiply and complicate the problems.

Positions and Responsibility of the Major Powers and the UN

In the months preceding the outbreak of war in June, 1967, Russia and the U.S., by directly or indirectly supplying military equipment and providing strong support to the Arabs and Israelis, helped to heighten tensions and to encourage intransigent attitudes in the Middle East. Once the crisis had developed, American and Soviet partisanship, disagreement, and conflicting interests rendered the Security Council powerless to stop the drift towards war. In fact, because the United States and the Soviet Union failed to use their great influence on the disputants on behalf of peace, they shared greatly in responsibility for the war.

After the conflict had broken out, the United States and the Soviet Union did cooperate sufficiently to bring about cease-fires between the combatants. However, their readiness to cooperate largely ended at this point. By aggravating Soviet-American relations, intensifying American and Russian partisanship and support of their respective friends in the Middle East, the war actually helped to diminish the ability and willingness of the superpowers to exert a moderating influence and to act constructively in dealing with Arab-Israeli problems.

While the UN succeeded in bringing military hostilities to an end, the world organization soon found that its position in the Middle East had been seriously weakened as a result of the war. Largely because of Israeli opposition, UNTSO and the MAC's were no longer able to function effectively, thus leaving cease-fire observers with very limited authority as the only meaningful UN presence between only some of the parties: namely, between Israel, on the one hand, and Syria and the UAR, on the other, but not between Israel and Jordan. Before June, 1967, the Arabs and Israelis were able to submit their complaints to the respective MAC's (or to UNEF in the case of Israel when incidents occurred on the Egyptian front), and some of them were handled quickly and resolved in the Middle East by the responsible UN organs. In the months following the June War, however, complaints no longer could be disposed of in the area, and they had to be referred to the Security Council. Consequently, without UNTSO, the MAC's, and UNEF, with only a relatively small number of cease-fire observers possessing inadequate power, and with considerable disagreement persisting between Russia and the United States, the UN's ability to prevent clashes and to come to serious grips with the basic issues was gravely weakened.

Conclusion

The June War not only did not settle any of the basic issues in dispute, but it added to them. As often happens in the aftermath of war, the death, misery, and destruction it caused deepened and accentuated Arab-Israeli hatred and hostility. Without an adequate UN presence to inhibit militancy, there were more frequent and bloody frontier clashes, commando forays, and reprisal attacks in the months following the war than had taken place for many years before it. It soon became clear that, notwithstanding occasional periods of relative calm along the cease-fire lines, the underlying situation remained explosive.

It is essential, therefore, that everything possible should be done to discourage violent actions and reactions on the part of the Arabs and Israelis. One important and useful step which should be taken in this connection would be to press for an increase in the size and authority of the UN cease-fire observers and for their deployment for the first time between Israel and Jordan. While such observers have not succeeded in maintaining complete tranquility where they have been stationed, nevertheless, they have been extremely helpful in keeping down the number of incidents, in bringing fighting to a halt when it did take place, and in providing some stabilizing influence in the areas where they have been able to operate. It is especially important that these observers be kept in the area for as long as necessary for their premature withdrawal could have dangerous consequences.

Every effort should also be made to persuade Arab and Israeli leaders to avoid rash actions, to exercise as much patience and restraint as possible, and always to submit their complaints to the proper UN agencies. The adverse conditions which still prevail in the area will continue to make some incidents inevitable regardless of the measures taken to prevent them. Every government, therefore, should try to minimize the incidents that do occur and to put them in their proper perspective in order to keep popular emotions from being unduly aroused. As many UN members and officials have repeatedly stressed, there is a vast difference between attacks launched by private persons and groups and those engineered by governments themselves. Deplorable as the former type of action might be, officially inspired military assaults are much less excusable. They constitute far more serious violations of the armistice and cease-fire agreements, as well as the UN Charter, and they have proved to be considerably more destructive and dangerous to the cause of peace.

There is considerable doubt as to whether UN-imposed Security Council cease-fires and a small number of cease-fire observers with limited powers would be able to maintain relative quiet in the area for an indefinite period. Therefore, more effective peacekeeping machinery must be devised if there is to be any hope of avoiding further hostilities between Israel and the Arab states. This would involve either the revival and expansion of UNTSO and the MAC's (according to UN officials, the original armistice agreements remained in effect since Israel had no legal right to terminate, unilaterally, valid conventions and those UN resolutions recognizing and helping to implement the provisions of these conventions) or the setting up of new agencies to take their place. In any event, new demilitarized buffer zones should be established, and UN forces, similar to UNEF, should be stationed on both sides of the frontier in the more sensitive areas. If new agencies are set up, they should be empowered to deal with as many of the local incidents and problems as possible. In addition, determined efforts should be made to see to it that all parties cooperate fully with UN officials in the area. To make these proposals workable, Israel's opposition to the expansion of UN activities and responsibilities in dealing with Arab-Israeli disputes would have to be overcome and the Arabs and Israelis made to realize that a strong UN presence could play a vital role in preventing unnecessary bloodshed and strife and in creating the calm atmosphere in the Middle East which is so essential to providing a basis for an Arab-Israeli peace.

CHAPTER IX

Arab-Israeli Peace

As soon as the Palestine War had ended, numerous attempts were made to bring about an Arab-Israeli peace settlement. However, for many years few officials realized how difficult and complex the Arab-Israeli dispute actually was and how deeply rooted Arab-Israeli distrust and antipathy had become. Too frequently, therefore, the UN and Western governments oversimplified the whole problem and sought to deal only with its more superficial aspects. In the meantime, much valuable time was lost while the situation generally deteriorated.

PEACE EFFORTS, 1949–1956

UN Conciliation Commission

Set up under the General Assembly's Resolution 194(III) of December 11, 1948, the UN Conciliation Commission was to prepare a plan for the internationalization of Jerusalem and to "facilitate the repatriation, resettlement and economic and social rehabilitation of the refugees and the payment of compensation" to them. The resolution also called upon the Arab and Israeli governments to "seek agreement by negotiations conducted either with the Conciliation Commission or directly, with a view to a final settlement of all questions outstanding between them." [1] Israel, while unhappy about some provisions, could not vote because she was not yet a UN member. The Arab members voted against the resolution, although within a few months they were to become the strongest advocates of many parts of it.

Since separate talks with Arab and Israeli leaders in the Middle East proved fruitless, the commission persuaded the governments of Egypt, Jordan, Lebanon, Syria, and Israel to meet in Lausanne, Switzerland, in April, 1949. On May 12 it succeeded in having the Arab states and Israel sign two identical but separate protocols stating that the signers were willing to use the map attached showing the 1947 partition resolution boundaries as the "starting point and framework for the discussion of territorial questions." The Arab signature revealed that the Arabs had significantly shifted their position from outright opposition to the partition resolution to partial support of it, because continued opposition to it would be self-defeating and because UN enforcement of its provisions would compel Israel to give up at least part of her territory. However, Israel made clear soon after she was admitted into the UN that she would not abide by the territorial and many other provisions of the November 29, 1947, and December 11, 1948, resolutions. The Arabs continued to show great reluctance to accept Israel's very existence.[2]

Discouraged by the Conciliation Commission's lack of success, despite its own close diplomatic support of commission efforts, the American government took steps of its own towards promoting reconciliation. On May 29, President Truman sent Israel a note blaming her more than the Arab states for the impasse, protesting her failure to make concessions at the Lausanne conference on the refugee and boundary issues, and threatening to reconsider his government's attitude towards her. By late summer, 1949, American officials had become reasonably convinced that the Arab leaders would be willing to negotiate a peace treaty with Israel if she would agree to repatriate a substantial number of refugees and give up sufficient territory in the south to restore land contact between the Arab areas of North Africa and Asia. Israel refused to consent to any territorial concessions, but, bowing to American pressures, she reluctantly agreed to repatriate 100,000 refugees—only, however, if this were part of a final peace settlement and Israel could resettle them as suited her economic and security needs. Later, she offered to take all the refugees and native inhabitants in the Gaza Strip if she were allowed to annex this area. Not only were the proposals unacceptable to the United States, the UN, and the Arabs, but strong opposition within the country forced the government to withdraw them.[3]

In 1950, the commission suggested the setting up of mixed committees to study and discuss various issues in dispute in an effort to combine in a single procedure Arab wishes for commission involvement with Israeli desires for direct negotiations. However, the Arabs held that they would accept this procedure if Israel first accepted UN resolutions dealing with the refugee and other problems, while Israel insisted on direct negotiations and no mediatory role for the commission.

Meanwhile, in late 1949 and 1950, King Abdullah of Jordan had secret talks with Israeli representatives. Because of the strong anti-Israeli feelings among Arabs generally, Abdullah sought meaningful concessions from Israel. However, while the Israeli foreign ministry suggested some generosity, Ben-Gurion and his military advisors opposed this. In fact, they "encouraged acts of provocation on the Jordan frontier in the hope of forcing the [Jordanian] government to come to terms." [4] Although Abdullah and the Israelis began to achieve some agreement on the bases for negotiations, premature publicity, from Israeli sources, according to some reports, created such a furor among Arab nationalists that Abdullah was forced to break off further contacts with the Israelis.[5]

There was also evidence of circumspect communications early in 1950 between Israel and Egypt. Not only had anti-Israeli feelings been less intense in Egypt than in some other Arab areas, but the ruling Wafd Party had not been in power during the Palestine War, and it enjoyed strong popular and political support within the country. Hoping to become a leader of the Arab world, Egypt was anxious to obtain from Israel a corridor in the southern Negev connecting Egypt with the other Arab countries, as well as the repatriation of some of the refugees, in the possible exchange for the Gaza Strip and the lifting of the blockades of the Suez Canal and the Gulf of Aqaba. However, the closer Israel felt she was to an agreement with Jordan, the less willing she was to meet Egypt's terms. This stand destroyed any chance for peace with the most important Arab country. Since Egypt feared that territorial grants to Jordan would advance Abdullah's ambitions for a Greater Syria and undermine Egyptian influence in the Arab world, Egyptian officials launched an open attack on Abdullah's dealings with Israel.[6]

As one Israeli author put it, "The golden opportunity for arriving at a final settlement in the Middle East had been lost for a long, long time to come." [7] This was most unfortunate because certain favorable conditions were soon to disappear: the Cold War had not entered the picture; Western prestige was reasonably high; and demarcation line tensions were not yet acute. Even Israeli officials admitted, as reported by the *New York Times,* December 29, 1950, that despite strong public statements, some Arab leaders really wanted peace. Their main problem was "to discover a formula to allow them to begin negotiations with Israel." The only opening for success would have been some dramatic and face-saving concessions by Israel on the refugee and territorial issues, which might have involved some sacrifice but would not have been an exorbitant price for achieving peace and reasonably normal relations with the Arab world. By recognizing Israel and terminating the state of war, the Arabs would also be making some sacrifice and Arab leaders would be taking serious risks. Israel's refusal to compromise, the growth of inter-Arab rivalries, the violent death of Abdullah, and the development of the Huleh swamp dispute in 1951 brought to a close this period of hope for peace.[8]

On May 25, 1950, the United States joined Britain and France in the Tripartite Statement of Policy, binding the three nations to oppose "the use of force . . . between any states" in the area and to supply only those arms to Israel and the Arab countries which would be needed for "legitimate self-defense." This probably discouraged major military aggression for the time being but failed to bring an Arab-Israeli peace agreement.

At a Paris Conference in September, 1951, the Conciliation Commission presented its own peace plan. This not only differed considerably from the provisions of existing General Assembly resolutions dealing with the refugees, but it also provided for territorial adjustments, creation of a Jordan River water authority, making Haifa a free port, and arrangements for the economic development of the entire area. The Arabs insisted that any territorial agreement had to be based upon the provisions contained in the UN partition resolution. They once again contended that they would be willing to negotiate a peace settlement with Israel either through the Conciliation Commission or through mixed commissions consisting of representatives of both parties—but only on the basis of existing UN resolutions. They also objected to any shift from strict enforcement of the UN resolutions and charged that Israel's open immigration policies would have to be altered for they posed a threat to Arab security.[9]

Israel claimed that the exodus of Jews from Iraq and other Arab countries had resulted in an exchange of populations which freed Israel from accepting the return of Arab refugees and that "major considerations of security and of political and economic stability made the return of any refugees impossible." Agreeing in principle to the payment of compensation, she felt that her ability to pay was affected by the Arab threat to her security and the Arab boycott and blockade. Israel maintained that the May, 1948, Arab invasion made the original partition resolution "obsolete." Believing she had a better chance of pressing for direct negotiations if the commission did not exist, Israel asked the General Assembly to replace the commission with a UN Good Offices Committee to assist the parties to get together to resolve their own differences.[10]

The Paris Conference was doomed to failure from the beginning. During this period Arab-Israeli relations were exacerbated by disputes over Israeli use of the Suez Canal and drainage of the Lake Huleh area, British-Arab relations were becoming strained, and anti-Western feeling was on the rise. Consequently, many Arabs now objected to further cooperation with the Western-dominated commission. In fact, by forcing a public airing of Arab-Israeli differences, the Paris Conference actually helped to aggravate the situation.

On January 25, 1952, the General Assembly passed Resolution 512(VI), urging the commission to "continue its efforts to secure the implementation" of earlier resolutions "on Palestine." The commission, despite its new mandate, refrained from embarking on another attempt to deal with the over-all problem on the grounds that the attitudes of the parties had "not changed" and the disputants had not requested it to play an active role.[11]

During 1952 and into 1953 there were reports of Egyptian peace feelers through the Foreign Minister of Pakistan, of Ralph Bunche acting as an Egyptian-Israeli intermediary, and of Western diplomats in the Middle East being "more hopeful" regarding the prospects for an Israeli-Arab peace than they had "been at any time since" the Palestine War. Egyptian newspapers and government officials dared publicly to advocate negotiations with Israel. The Israeli and Lebanese chiefs of staff met on the frontier to deal with border problems. The formal head of Egypt's new military regime, General Muhammad Neguib, assuming power in July, 1952, was considered a moderate on the Palestine issue, and his young officers were expected to concentrate on internal reforms. But the disputants remained unready to make essential mutual concessions, and in 1953 Arab-Israeli tensions rose as the relative quiet along Arab-Israeli demarcation lines came to an end.[12]

The Arabs asked the General Assembly's Seventh Session to implement existing UN resolutions by pressuring Israel to abide by their provisions. To the dismay of the Arabs, however, eight states (Canada, Cuba, Denmark, Ecuador, the Netherlands, Norway, Panama, and Uruguay) submitted to the *Ad Hoc* Political Committee draft resolution A/AC.61/L.23, which urged the governments concerned to enter, at an early date, into "direct negotiations." Although to obtain wider support the sponsors later revised their proposal to include a request that the contending sides bear "in mind both the resolutions and the principal objectives of the UN on the Palestine question," including the religious interests of third parties, they also made clear that their main intention was to emphasize the use of direct negotiations by the disputants without any prior conditions—even those contained in UN resolutions.

The Arabs bitterly accused the eight sponsors of deliberately repudiating existing resolutions and asking the UN to "wash its hands of the Palestine dispute." They complained that the UN was "standing by" and enforcing its decisions on Korea, but not those on Palestine. The Arabs, never really content with the composition of the Conciliation Commission (France, Turkey, and the United States), charged it with being predominantly pro-Israel and insisted that more "truly" neutral countries be added to its membership. They warned that, if passed, the eight-power proposal would merely drive the opposing sides further apart than ever before.[13]

Most Asian and African, as well as some Latin American, states also opposed the eight-power draft on the ground that it disregarded existing resolutions. Roman Catholic members especially objected because it did not provide for the internationalization of Jerusalem. In an attempt to support the Arab position, four Muslim governments submitted joint draft resolution A/AC.61/L.25, which reaffirmed past resolutions, requested the Conciliation Commission to continue its efforts to implement them, and recommended an increase in the commission's size.

Israel vigorously backed the eight-power proposal. Her delegate also indicated the type of peace terms which his government sought: (1) binding mutual guarantees against aggression; (2) elimination of the demilitarized zones; (3) minor border rectifications; (4) the resettlement of the refugees outside of Israel; (5) talks on refugee compensation; (6) an end of the Arab boycott and blockade, as well as of the state of war; and (7) regional cooperation in such fields as health, communications, and economic development for the benefit of all states in the area.[14]

While the eight-nation proposal passed the *Ad Hoc* Political Committee, it ran into difficulties in the Plenary Meetings of the General Assembly. The Philippines offered an amendment requiring that Arab-Israeli negotiations be based upon UN resolutions, especially those providing for the internationalization of Jerusalem. Since this was defeated, the resolution lost the votes of a number of Roman Catholic countries. More votes were lost when Prime Minister Ben-Gurion made two poorly-timed statements. In these he said that there could be ". . . no cession of territory, but there could be minor adjustments of pieces of land to straighten out the frontiers"; Israel would "not under any circumstances" allow any refugee repatriation; and Jerusalem "cannot be an issue for negotiations." [15] These completely uncompromising remarks, as the Haitian delegate put it, "raised doubts" in the minds of some delegates "as to Israel's respect for prior General Assembly resolutions," and they further alienated the Roman Catholic delegations. The Soviet Union, holding that the Conciliation Commission was a tool of American imperialism in the Middle East, opposed the resolution because it would continue the life of the commission. As a result of these developments, the resolution failed to obtain the two-thirds vote required for final passage despite the strong support it received from Israel, the United States, and many European and Latin American countries.[16]

Having unexpectedly come close to a major defeat at the Seventh

Session of the General Assembly and fearing to take any step which might cause the UN to replace existing resolutions with less favorable ones, the Arabs decided against requesting the General Assembly to debate the over-all Palestine question—at least for the next few years. While the Arabs remained very unhappy that the UN was not seriously trying to enforce its decisions, it was generally believed that keeping past resolutions legally alive, even if they were not enforced, was far better than not having these resolutions at all, for they strengthened the Arab bargaining position and made it more difficult for the UN to wash its hands of the problem.

The Middle 1950's

Shortly after President Dwight D. Eisenhower took office in January, 1953, both he and his secretary of state, John Foster Dulles, proclaimed that, unlike the strongly pro-Israeli Truman administration, they intended to deal with Arab and Israeli differences more objectively. They felt that undue governmental partisanship had undermined the position of the United States in the strategically important Arab world and had even weakened her ability to influence the Arab attitude towards Israel. In an important speech on June 1, 1953, shortly after returning from a trip to the Middle East, Dulles set down his views on the Arab-Israeli dispute. He reaffirmed support for the 1950 Tripartite Declaration and his government's intention to be "impartial" and to seek to "allay the deep resentment" of the Arabs against the United States for helping to create Israel. He held that the parties concerned had "the primary responsibility of bringing peace to the area." Nevertheless, the American government would "not hesitate by every appropriate means to use its influence to promote step-by-step reduction of tension in the area and the conclusion of ultimate peace." He held that "some of the refugees could be settled in the area presently controlled by Israel," although "most . . . could more readily be integrated into the lives of the neighboring Arab countries." He reported that while "the Israelis feared that ultimately the Arabs might try to push them into the sea," the Arabs were "more fearful of Zionism than Communism" and concerned that the United States would become the "backer of expansionist Zionism." He advised Israel that she must "become part of the Near East community and cease to look upon [herself], or be looked upon by others, as aliens to this community" if she wished to be ultimately accepted in peace and friendship by the Arab world. The Arabs were pleased with Dulles' visit to their capitals—the first made by any United States Secretary of State—and with some aspects of Dulles' statement. Nevertheless, they were unhappy with his failure to deal with the boundary and Jerusalem issues and with his suggestion that "most" of the refugees should be resettled instead of repatriated. The Israelis resented some of Dulles' remarks and objected to his proposal that "some" of the refugees should be repatriated. In any case, Dulles' recommendations did not change the situation.[17]

On April 9 and May 1, 1954, Henry A. Byroade, assistant secretary of state for Near Eastern, South Asian, and African affairs, warned that the "emotions" of the Arabs and Israelis were still so intense that any immediate or dramatic solution of the problem was "impossible" and that progress on even limited issues in dispute would be "at best exceedingly difficult." Yet, the situation was so fraught with danger that the United States had to do what she could, no matter how unpopular the action might be, "to assist both parties to arrive at any arrangement which both sides would accept as satisfactory." He criticized the Arabs for their "negative" stand towards Israel and asked them to reconcile themselves to the fact of Israel's existence. He also urged Israel to "drop the attitude of the conqueror," to accept her status as a Middle Eastern state, and to assure the Arabs that unlimited Jewish immigration would not threaten their security. Whereas the Arabs had become used to such outspoken and critical remarks aimed at them by American officials, this was a new and unpleasant experience for the Israelis and their American friends. Not only did a number of pro-Israeli groups in the United States object openly to Byroade's comments, but even the Israeli government formally protested some of them.[18]

The statements by Dulles and Byroade revealed that the American government had abandoned all hope that any major progress could be made in the near future to resolve basic Arab-Israeli disputes and that it had decided to leave the primary job for making peace to the Arabs and Israelis themselves, with the United States doing what she could from the sidelines to encourage the parties to move towards a step-by-step solution of their differences. Consequently, in 1953 and 1954, the United States, while ready to offer advice and criticism, did not try to formulate and push any general peace plan of her own—and neither did any other major power.

In 1954, some Arab and Israeli officials sought to handle their differences through third parties and even through clandestine contacts outside the Middle East. According to Israeli newspaper reports (*Maariv* and *Yediot Akhronat* in their August 4, 1961, editions[19]), Israeli and Egyptian representatives met for quiet talks in Paris. The Egyptians expressed "a willingness to reach a secret agreement with Israel on the normalization of relations without a formal peace agreement." The "main proposal" discussed was one "to maintain a tranquil border and to create direct contacts in a European capital as a base for clearing controversial matters or conflicts." Egypt "was to agree to the passage of Israeli cargo through the Suez Canal; though not under the Israeli flag." The Egyptians explained that, because of the intense feelings of the Arab masses against Israel, "Egypt's status among the Arab countries," and the still uncertain internal position of the new military regime, "their government could not reach an open normalization of relations" with Israel. "The top Israeli foreign office people, headed by M. Sharett . . . , appreciated" the Egyptian government's position and recognized the value of normalizing relations with Egypt even if this had to be done behind the scenes. They regarded such a step as a "chance to break the ring of Arab hostility against Israel." These hopeful moves came to naught, however, when "another executive arm" of the Israeli government initiated an action against Egypt—espionage and sabotage activities associated with the "Lavon Affair." Jarred by this hostile Israeli move, the Egyptians "abruptly" terminated all further contacts with the Israelis. Thus, Israel once again was largely responsible for the failure of reasonably hopeful, if limited, negotiations.

By late 1954 the tranquility of the Arab-Israeli demarcation lines, the evacuation of British troops from the Suez Canal area, and the quiet talks between Egyptian and Israeli representatives led British and American officials to initiate an intensive review of the whole situation.[20] However, the large-scale Israeli attack on the Gaza Strip of February 28, 1955, followed by further raids and counterraids, destroyed what opportunities might have existed for peace. The shift of the Soviet Union to an increasingly pro-Arab position, Russia's efforts to expand her own influence within the Arab world at the expense of the West, and the belief that outside intervention was needed to break the existing deadlock led first the United States and then Britain to assume the initiative in offering peace proposals.

In August, 1955, John Foster Dulles suggested certain peace terms requiring compromises on the refugee and territorial issues, and his action was actively supported by both Britain and the UN. While the Arabs complained that the Dulles proposals were contrary to UN resolutions and were too vague on such subjects as border adjustments, the Israelis objected to any significant boundary changes and refugee repatriation. Dulles also tried to induce the leaders of both political parties in the United States to keep the Arab-Israeli question out of the forthcoming election campaign because he considered the Russian threat to American interests in the Middle East far too serious to allow political partisanship at this critical stage. The Arabs naturally welcomed such a move; Israel was not pleased with it, and Israeli sympathizers in the

United States vigorously expressed their disapproval. Dulles' initiative, therefore, failed to achieve any concrete results either in the Middle East or in the U.S.[21]

In a speech on November 9, 1955, British Prime Minister Anthony Eden, after warning the Arabs and Israelis about the growing Soviet threat to the Middle East, offered his own services and those of his government in settling the Arab-Israeli dispute. Although he did not use the word *mediation,* his offer was interpreted as implying that he had this in mind. He asked Israel and the Arab states to "make some compromise" between the UN partition resolution boundaries and the present armistice lines. He stated that "if there could be an accepted arrangement between them about their boundaries, we—Her Majesty's Government and, I believe, the United States Government and perhaps other powers too—would be prepared to give a formal guarantee to both sides." While the American government backed Eden's proposal in general, it did not specifically accept his territorial recommendations, and some State Department experts doubted that mediation would be either accepted or successful. Israel, vehemently rejecting Eden's suggestions, made it clear that she would refuse to make any territorial concessions. She accused Britain of trying to help Jordan acquire the Negev so that Britain could obtain a military base there to replace the one given up in the Suez Canal zone. In spite of British efforts to reassure Israel that she would not be asked to give up any substantial amount of territory, Israeli officials remained cold to the Eden plan. On the other hand, the Arabs—and especially the Egyptians—reacted much more favorably. Egypt agreed to accept Eden's offer to mediate, but insisted she would not hold direct talks with Israel. Some reports indicated that Egypt's positive response was partly influenced by a British promise not to try to press other Arab states to enter the Baghdad Pact.[22]

American and British officials continued to retain high hopes that a peaceful solution could still be worked out and to cooperate closely towards that end. They were particularly encouraged by reports that Arab leaders in Egypt, Iraq, and Lebanon were privately expressing a willingness to negotiate with Israel without demanding the full implementation of UN resolutions. Western diplomats in the Middle East felt confident that Egypt would be willing to accept peace if she obtained a land bridge with Jordan, if Israel accepted some repatriation and compensation of the refugees, and if a new status were devised for Jerusalem.[23] Israel, however, persisted in her refusal to agree to any significant alterations in the *status quo* or to outside mediation, and this caused, as the *New York Times* noted on November 17, 1955, another potentially favorable "opportunity" to be "missed."

Early in 1956, Britain asked France and the United States to join her in discussing ways to compel the opposing parties to come to terms with each other and to "put teeth" into the 1950 Tripartite Agreement. This initiative resulted only in a joint communiqué in February, 1956, in which Prime Minister Anthony Eden and President Dwight Eisenhower (1) held that an Arab-Israeli peace was urgently needed; (2) stated that their governments were willing to contribute to a peace settlement by providing financial help and by "guaranteeing agreed frontiers"; and (3) expressed a hope for a solution of the refugee question.[24] When violence erupted along the Arab-Israeli borders in the spring of 1956, the UN Secretary-General was sent on a mission to the Middle East. His efforts to calm the situation proved only temporarily successful. Golda Meir's replacement of Moshe Sharett as foreign minister stiffened Israeli government opposition to outside mediation and removed the most effective moderating influence in the cabinet. In October, 1956, Eden renewed his offer of help in reaching a peace agreement. But this was completely unacceptable because right then Britain and France were massing troops in Cyprus for use against Egypt, and Israel was preparing to invade the Sinai.

Israel's demand in late 1956 and early 1957 for direct peace negotiations before withdrawing her troops from the Sinai in accord with General Assembly resolutions and UN pressures was not supported by the United States and other UN members. Although Israel had hoped that her victory over Egypt would force the Arabs to the peace table, the Sinai invasion made the Arabs even less willing than before to deal with Israel. The Anglo-French assault on Egypt weakened Western prestige and influence and strengthened the Soviet's position within the Arab world, thus diminishing the ability of the West to apply pressures on the Arabs and increasing the power of the Russians to work against any improvement in Arab-Israeli relations.[25] At a July 16, 1957, press conference, Secretary of State Dulles indicated that for the time being the United States would assume a less active role. Only the British, despite their attack on Egypt, continued to present relatively detailed recommendations for a peace treaty.[26]

RECONCILIATION EFFORTS, 1957–1967

Even after the Sinai War, UN and Western officials continued to believe that the Arab refugee dispute remained the key barrier to peace and they sought ways to resolve the refugee situation. Nevertheless, both the UN Secretary General and Dr. Joseph E. Johnson, who had been requested to study the refugee issue, reported in the late 1950's and early 1960's that neither the refugee nor the peace problem could be effectively dealt with until the basic psychological and political obstructions had been overcome. Despite these warnings, the UN made no serious efforts to come to grips with the fundamental difficulties and merely kept requesting the UN Conciliation Commission to continue and even to step up its efforts despite the unfavorable conditions which prevented any real progress from being made.[27] Draft resolutions asking the Arab and Israeli governments to enter into direct negotiations—encouraged by pro-Israeli delegations primarily from Africa, Latin America, and northern Europe—failed. Most UN members realized that the Arabs, far from abiding by the proposed resolutions, would be angered by their passage.

From 1959 and on, the United States not only strongly supported the peace efforts of the UN Secretary-General, Dr. Johnson, and the Conciliation Commission, but she made some efforts of her own. Late in 1959, American officials quietly sought to bring about peace talks between Israel and Egypt, but without success. In the 1960 presidential election campaign, both John F. Kennedy and Richard M. Nixon, the Democratic and Republican candidates, sought to attract Jewish votes by taking a pro-Israeli stand. Pressed by a number of American Zionist and pro-Zionist organizations, Kennedy promised that, if elected, he would actively work for peace talks between the Arabs and the Israelis. Soon after Kennedy took office, these same groups protested that he had not yet taken the action which he had promised during the election campaign. By this time, however, President Kennedy had been more fully briefed on the complexities of the Arab-Israeli question, the stakes of the United States in the area, and the strong Arab objections to direct negotiations with Israel. Undoubtedly, the President was further inhibited when Prime Minister Ben-Gurion, as reported in the *New York Times* on April 1, 1961, openly expressed his vigorous opposition to any mediation efforts by outside nations, including the United States, because he apparently feared that a mediator would try to pressure Israel into accepting some refugee repatriation and into making significant territorial concessions.[28]

Despite these developments, President Kennedy, seeking to improve Arab-American relations, sent letters to the heads of the states of Jordan, the UAR, Lebanon, Iraq, and Saudi Arabia in May, 1961. The President reiterated American support for those UN resolutions dealing with the refugee question, and he held that his government would use its "influence toward a just and peaceful solution" of the over-all Arab-Israeli problem. The letters, however, made no specific reference to the important boundary and Jerusalem issues and did not dispel the distrust of America's Middle East policy among the Arabs, who were far more interested in American actions than in American rhetoric. In his written reply, President Nasser challenged Kennedy to create the atmosphere of confidence needed for the solution of Middle Eastern disputes by proving that United States policy in the Middle East was in fact inspired solely by her own interests and not by the interests of "world Zionism." Since Kennedy was unable to satisfy the Arabs on this matter, the Arabs continued to harbor serious misgivings about American motives. Nevertheless, in 1962 and 1963, the American government persisted in using quiet diplomacy—but without success.[29]

In 1962–63, a dangerous arms race started, especially between Israel and Egypt, involving heavy tanks, supersonic planes, and advanced rockets and missiles. Each side began accusing the other of seeking to acquire or build atomic weapons and warned that it would initiate a "preventive war" if its opponent appeared to be attaining a significant lead in this field. Israel, anxious to maintain her military superiority, called for a halt to the arms race and for a stabilization in the military *status quo*. If these could not be brought about, she insisted that she should be enabled to purchase enough weapons to offset Arab military acquisitions. Israel and her American supporters pressed the United States either to agree to a defense pact with Israel or to guarantee her security against any future Arab assault. The American government, not wishing to weaken still further its position within the Arab world, rejected Israel's request for an alliance. However, American and British officials announced they would not stand by and allow any state to be invaded and destroyed by any other state in the Middle East. The Arabs, on the other hand, objected to any freezing of the military *status quo* in such a way as to force them into a permanent position of military inferiority vis-à-vis Israel. They contended that, because the Arab world was divided into many political entities and was much larger in size and population than Israel, Arab arms needs were considerably greater than those of Israel. Consequently, even equality in weapons between Israel and themselves would in fact mean inequality in actual power and security for the Arabs. The Arabs, therefore, sought to acquire enough military equipment to turn the balance of power in their own favor.[30]

Both the Communist and Western states contributed to the Arab-Israeli arms race. The Soviet bloc was the chief supplier of weapons to some Arab countries in the Middle East, especially to the UAR, Syria, and Iraq. France, Canada, the United States, and, for a time, even West Germany were the principal sources of arms for Israel. While Russia's action was obviously based upon her desire to strengthen her position and influence within the Arab world, the Western governments stated that they were merely trying to maintain the existing balance of power.

By 1966, the United States and Britain started to provide advanced military equipment to Saudi Arabia and Jordan, primarily to build up the prestige of their conservative and pro-Western regimes against the more "radical" governments of Syria and Egypt. These moves caused Israel to become further concerned about her security and Syria and Egypt to feel the need for even more arms to counterbalance those of their Arab opponents as well as those of Israel. So the United States found herself arming both Arabs and Israelis while, at the same time, she was still actively trying to halt the growing Middle Eastern arms race.[31]

By 1963–64 differences over the Jordan River water became increasingly ominous. Palestine Arab commando incursions starting in early 1965 from bases in Jordan, Lebanon, and Syria led to reprisal attacks. Pressures inflamed by the large-scale Israeli assault on as-Samu in Jordan during November, 1966, led even moderate King Hussein, faced with internal and external threats, to proclaim that Jordan would hit back in the event of another Israeli raid. Despite nearly unanimous UN condemnation of Israel for the as-Samu assault, Israel's government and most of her people continued to express their belief in the policy of armed reprisals. Consequently, Arab-Israeli tensions and animosity continued to grow.

With inter-Arab rivalries becoming more acute and the internal positions of several Arab governments weakening, summit conferences were held to lessen inter-Arab differences, but the attempts at unity were only temporarily successful. In April–May, 1965, Tunisia's President Habib Bourguiba broke with Egypt's President Nasser, partly because of Bourguiba's proposal to make peace with Israel on the basis of UN resolutions. Saudi Arabian-Egyptian relations deteriorated once again over Egyptian support of the republican government in Yemen. Bitter feelings persisted between Syria and several Arab states, including her erstwhile partner, Egypt. Opposition to Saudi Arabian King Feisal's effort to organize and lead a bloc of conservative countries brought about closer ties between Syria and the UAR, widened the split between Feisal and Nasser, and strained relations between Egypt and Jordan as King Hussein became more deeply associated with Feisal's new move. Syria and Egypt began to form a progressive bloc to counter Feisal's efforts. Extremist elements, especially in Syria and among the Palestine Arabs, advocated the overthrow of Hussein on the ground that he was soft towards Israel and a pawn of the West. By late 1966, several Arab governments felt insecure, with reports indicating that even the Nasser regime was losing popular support largely because of the costly war in Yemen and of internal economic difficulties.

These rivalries and insecurities impelled Arab leaders to assume strong stands against Israel. Since even the moderates did not dare openly consider anything less than the elimination of Israel, Bourguiba's April, 1965, offer of peace on the basis of UN resolutions was attacked even by officials who privately concurred with Bourguiba's reasoning. With the Arab League's organization of the Palestine Liberation Organization in 1964 under the leadership of extremist Ahmad Shukairi and the Syrian government's support of the activities of *al-Fatah,* the Palestine Arabs' uncompromising views undermined the influence of Arab moderates and encouraged Arab officials to express militant anti-Israel sentiments.

In the middle 1960's, rivalries between leading personalities and political parties for control of the government intensified in Israel as well, and this trend tended to weaken the influence of the Israeli moderates. When Levi Eshkol replaced the militant Ben-Gurion as prime minister in 1963, it was hoped that he would adopt a more moderate and flexible policy towards the Arabs, and for a few months he did. But his attitude changed due to the rapid increase in Arab military power, the growth of border incidents and raids, the persistence of the strongly nationalist and anti-Arab feelings among his own people, and his internal political difficulties—such as the rise of a personal and political enmity between Ben-Gurion and himself, the continued political strength of the activist parties, and the existence of a delicate balance of power in the Knesset. Eshkol soon felt compelled to revert to the use of armed reprisals and to take a tough, uncompromising stand against the Arabs.

By the middle 1960's, most UN members, including the United States, considering that the political and emotional climates in the Middle East made further peace efforts not only futile but possibly even harmful, set aside such activity. Instead, they concentrated on trying to prevent a deteriorating situation from becoming worse, especially by working to quiet the troubled demarcation lines. Both UN and American officials urged the Arab and Israeli governments to take all possible measures to avoid raids and border clashes. The United States offered Israel equipment which would aid her to check infiltrations across her frontiers. Moreover, the American government sought to head off any large-scale military attack by either side by warning repeatedly that it would take all necessary action to counter such a move. By December, 1966, even the Soviet Union, after helping to arm the Palestine Arab commandos and Syria (as well as a number of the other Arab states) and after endeavoring for years to promote instability in the Middle East, finally started to use her influence in Syria to forestall any drastic moves which might seriously threaten peace in the area. Some reports also indicated that the UAR had applied her own moderating pressures on the militant Syrian leaders because she opposed any premature military confrontation with Israel. Nevertheless, *al-Fatah* raids and Arab-Israeli border incidents and tensions persisted.[32]

UN RECONCILIATION EFFORTS AFTER THE JUNE WAR

In May, 1967, Syrian-Israeli differences over cultivation of land in the demilitarized zone, Palestinian commando raids on Israel, Israel's large-scale reprisal attack on Syria and her threat to launch yet another assault, and Egypt's removal of UNEF and her reinstatement of the blockade of the Gulf of Aqaba brought the Middle East to the brink of war. The world waited anxiously for UN action, but the deep American-Soviet split over the Middle East rendered the Security Council powerless. American efforts to press for steps aimed at a peace settlement proved unrealistic.

Fighting was brought to a halt only after Israel had overrun Jordan's west bank, Syria's Golan Heights, Egypt's Sinai Peninsula, and the Gaza Strip. At the General Assembly's Fifth Emergency Special Session a number of UN members, including the United States, initially believing that Israel's overwhelming military victory would compel the Arabs to be more "realistic," backed Israel's demand that her withdrawal be conditioned upon Arab readiness to accept Israel's right to existence and freedom of navigation. However, other than passing resolutions calling upon Israel to rescind her measures annexing the Old City of Jerusalem, to allow the newly uprooted Arabs to return to their homes, and to treat the inhabitants in the occupied areas humanely, neither the Security Council nor the General Assembly could agree on any action which might bring the antagonists closer to a peace settlement.

Both a draft resolution (A/L.522/Rev.3) submitted by Yugoslavia which called for the unconditional withdrawal of Israeli forces from all territories occupied since June 4 and a draft (A/L.523/Rev.1) offered by Latin American members—which requested an Israeli withdrawal, reaffirmed that there should be no recognition of the acquisition of territory through force, and asked for an end to the state of belligerence, freedom of transit in international waterways, and a full solution of the refugee problem—were defeated in the General Assembly. Moreover, a compromise American-Soviet proposal, which called for an Israeli withdrawal and asked all UN members to acknowledge the right of Israel to exist in peace and security and free from a state of belligerence, was never formally submitted because of strong opposition by the more militant Arab governments.

Nevertheless, in the UN there was overwhelming agreement on the need for strengthening the UN presence, aiding the refugees, and preventing an arms race. There was also widespread support for the principle of an Israeli withdrawal since the UN charter prohibited territorial acquisition by means of force. But most Western nations and Israel disagreed with most Communist and all Muslim and Arab countries over whether such a withdrawal should be unconditional, as well as over what the UN role should be in bringing about a peace settlement. Because the member states, particularly the United States and the Soviet Union, could not reach agreement, the UN again was unable to act effectively.

Meanwhile, Israel's demands mounted and her peace terms stiffened. Initially, Israel held that she sought only to destroy the Arab military threat and reopen the Gulf of Aqaba—not to gain territory. Shortly after her victory her territorial goals appeared to extend only to Jerusalem's Old City and possibly to the Gaza Strip, strategic areas in Jordan's west bank, and Syria's Golan Heights. Then she began to insist on her right to use the Suez Canal as well as the Gulf of Aqaba. More militant political groups like the Herut party and large numbers of ordinary Israelis urged that Israel hold all or nearly all of the conquered lands. By the summer's end Prime Minister Eshkol and other top officials were referring to a "Greater Israel" and asserting that Israel needed "natural" borders, and there were no frontiers "more natural" than the Suez Canal and the Jordan River.[33] Though the Arabs sought through third parties to ascertain what points Israel was willing to bargain, the Israelis insisted they would not reveal their terms until the Arabs started to negotiate.

Moreover, while Israel at one time might have been satisfied with an Arab declaration ending the state of belligerence, she quickly reached a point where she would accept nothing less than a complete and final peace treaty which would not only terminate the state of war but also formally acknowledge Israel's existence and right to live in peace and security and would provide for demilitarized zones in Arab territories along the more exposed parts of her eventual borders. Israel also announced repeatedly that she would never depend upon the "unreliable" promises and assurances of the UN and/or the big powers for her security and that peace must be achieved only through direct negotiations between Israel and her Arab neighbors. As far as Israel was concerned, the old General Armistice Agreements and machinery had ceased to exist because, she alleged, the Arabs had started the war; the cease-fire arrangements could "only be superseded" by final peace treaties; and the Suez Canal would remain closed until her right to use it was conceded. Some Israeli officials believed that if life were made sufficiently uncomfortable and precarious for the Arab states they would have to adopt a "more realistic" attitude and have to accept peace with Israel largely on her own terms.[34]

Within Israel there was some disagreement as to how much of the new territories they should yield and whether areas like Jordan's west bank should be annexed directly or made into an autonomous Arab state controlled by Israel. The latter suggestion was supported by those Israelis who feared that outright annexation of this area with hundreds of thousands of Arabs would greatly alter the country's Jewish character. They pointed out that Israel could claim that, by setting up such a separate Arab political unit, she was fulfilling for the first time the terms of the 1947 UN partition resolution. In this way, Israel could more readily justify her refusal to return the west bank and Gaza Strip. When it appeared that the Israeli government might be trying to seek out those west-bank Arabs who would be willing to participate in a scheme for establishing such a Palestine Arab entity, Arab nationalists in the occupied sectors and in the neighboring Arab countries issued warnings that any Arab who agreed to cooperate with Israel in such a scheme would be considered a traitor and would be dealt with accordingly.[35]

In the meantime, Israel opposed any effort at mediation by either the UN or any government. When Britain and other states recommended that the UN authorize its Secretary-General to dispatch a prominent figure to the Middle East to serve in several capacities, including that of a mediator, Israel urged the UN to confine itself to pressing both sides to enter into direct negotiations. She also bitterly assailed Yugoslavia's President Josip Broz Tito when he actively sought to promote a peace plan which he had drawn up in August. This plan called, first, for a complete Israeli withdrawal from all occupied areas. Once this was accomplished, then Israeli ships would be allowed to use the Gulf of Aqaba; her cargoes and her ships sailing under flags of other countries would be permitted to use the Suez Canal; the Palestine Arab refugees would be fully indemnified; the Arab states would declare the end of the state of belligerence; and the big powers would be asked to guarantee Israel's borders. Israel accused Tito of being pro-Arab, angrily rejected his intervention, and firmly stated that his proposal was "wholly unacceptable from beginning to end." [36]

After the June War, nearly all Arabs opposed recognizing and negotiating directly with Israel and insisted upon the return of all their lost territories. However, the Arabs disagreed strongly on what policies to follow in order to deal with the consequences of their military defeat.

Taking the initiative immediately after the June War, King Hussein pressed for an early summit meeting of the Arab leaders, urged upon the Arabs new more realistic attitudes, and asked permission from

Nasser and other Arab leaders to seek a compromise political settlement. Israeli reports claimed he had indirectly tried to contact Israeli officials to ascertain what their price would be for the return of the west bank and Jerusalem's Old City. These accounts maintained that Hussein had expressed willingness (1) to terminate the state of belligerency; (2) to acknowledge Israel's armistice borders and her possession of Elath on the Gulf of Aqaba; (3) not to press for the enforcement of UN resolutions calling for refugee repatriation if the United States furnished financial help to resettle the refugees in her own territory; (4) to provide Israel with a corridor to the Wailing Wall; and (5) to demilitarize the west-bank sector. Israel, however, was reported to have rebuffed his efforts and insisted upon direct negotiations and far more extensive concessions by Jordan and fewer concessions by Israel. While Hussein could not convince all the Arab leaders of the urgent need for an early summit conclave, he managed to confer with Nasser and President Houari Boumedienne, of Algeria, in Cairo during the second week of July. However, he was not invited to attend conferences held by Nasser with Boumedienne, President Nureddin al-Attasi, of Syria, President Abdel Rahman Arif, of Iraq, and Ismail al-Azhari, chairman of the Sudanese Supreme Council of State, during the middle of July in Cairo. All Arab foreign ministers convened in Kuwait on June 17–18 to prepare a unified Arab policy and strategy for the Fifth Emergency Special Session of the UN General Assembly, but they were unable to find any common basis for an agreement as Hussein had hoped they would. In the latter part of June and early July, he visited Washington, London, Paris, and other Western capitals in a vain attempt to obtain military equipment and especially political support which would enable him to regain his lost territories.[37]

King Hussein's efforts to bring about an early summit meeting and a unified Arab policy failed largely because the Arab leaders were seriously split. Presidents al-Attasi and Boumedienne, and Ahmad Shukairi of the Palestine Liberation Organization insisted that the Arabs should not compromise with Israel or give up the struggle against her. They urged the Arabs to initiate guerrilla warfare in order to keep Israel off balance and to force her to give up the conquered areas. They pressed for the strengthening of the existing oil embargo and economic boycott against the United States, Britain, and other countries considered to have been pro-Israel. In contrast, the more moderate leaders, led by Hussein and Nasser, contended that the Arabs were and would remain for some time too militarily weak to challenge Israel, and, therefore, they should try to salvage as much as possible from their disaster by diplomatic and political means. They felt that they had to view the situation more realistically and agree to make concessions in return for an Israeli with-drawal from their lands. Such concessions could include ending the state of war by means of a UN Security Council resolution, allowing Israeli ships to use the Gulf of Aqaba, and allowing Israeli goods to go through the Suez Canal on vessels not flying the Israeli flag. Tunisia's President Habib Bourguiba even proposed that the Arabs stop talking about de-stroying Israel and consider negotiating a definitive peace settlement with her on the best terms they could get. But the other Arab leaders did not dare to go this far, for their own internal political positions were too weak and the Arab masses had still refused to consider their military defeat as anything more than a temporary setback and their anti-Israeli passions had not abated. The moderates also became increasingly aware that a continuation of the oil embargo and economic boycott would be self-defeating since these measures actually affected the economy of the Arabs more adversely than that of the Western nations against which they were applied. In addition, they finally recognized the fact that it would be to their ultimate advantage to restore normal relations with the United States and Britain because only these Western powers could provide the pressures required to compel Israel to yield her conquered territories.[38]

After Ismail al-Azhari of the Sudan had joined Hussein in calling for a summit meeting and Nasser had been won over to the idea, two foreign ministers' conferences were held in the first and fourth weeks of August to prepare the way for the gathering of the Arab leaders in Khartoum at the end of August. The more militant presidents of Algeria and Syria refused to attend for they realized that the moderates would dominate the affair and they apparently did not want to be associated with any moves aimed at seeking a compromise settlement with Israel. Both of these states sent their foreign ministers to Khartoum, but only the Algerian delegate actually participated formally in the meetings. The Syrian representative boycotted them and returned to Damascus before the summit conference had come to an end. The King of Libya and the President of Tunisia, unable to attend because of ill health, sent high ranking officials. The King of Morocco, opposed to any top-level Arab convention, dispatched his Premier. Ahmad Shukairi appeared on behalf of the Palestinians, but to show his disapproval of the trend of affairs he refused to attend the final session.[39]

President Nasser and King Hussein urged the summit to agree to seek a political solution which would help eliminate the harmful conse-quences of their defeat. Both men made it clear that their economic and financial conditions were desperate and they were not in a position mili-tarily or otherwise to renew the war. The success of the conference was greatly facilitated when President Nasser and King Feisal of Saudi Arabia accepted a compromise proposal made by Sudan's Premier Ismail al-Azhari to settle the Yemen dispute. (Under this plan, which later was rejected by the Republican leaders of Yemen, Saudi Arabia would cease supplying aid to the royalists; Egypt would withdraw her troops from Yemen; and Iraq, Morocco, and the Sudan would form a committee of three to supervise the implementation of the agreement.) The resolutions adopted on September 1 reflected the views of the Arab moderates. While the summit found it necessary, largely as matter of form, to reiterate certain phrases and positions so popular with the Arab masses—such as there could be "no peace with Israel" and "no recognition of Israel" and the Arab states would work for the "maintenance of the rights of the people of Palestine in their nation"—it also called for "unified efforts at international and diplomatic levels to eliminate the consequences of [Israeli] aggression and to assure the withdrawal of the aggressor forces . . . from Arab lands." No references were made to military action or to the need to destroy Israel. It was also reported that both Hussein and Nasser had expressed a readiness to make some substantial concessions to Israel, and Nasser had indicated a willingness to accept the plan offered by President Tito. The conference also agreed to set up a fund of 135,000,000 pounds sterling (at that time worth approximately $378,000,000) to be distributed among the states which had suffered the greatest economic losses from the war, not only to help them overcome their desperate economic plight but also to strengthen their political bargaining position and to make it possible for Egypt to keep the Suez Canal closed. The UAR was to receive about $266,000,000 and Jordan over $100,000,000 yearly for as long as "the consequences of aggression" remained. Payments were to be made on a quarterly basis by the oil-rich states of Kuwait, Saudi Arabia, and Libya, and this provision gave these three Arab nations some potential influence over the future policies and behavior of Nasser in particular. To establish such a fund, the summit decided to lift the oil embargo. There was also a tacit understanding that an effort would be made, primarily through King Hussein, to improve Arab relations gradually with the United States and to win American support for an Israeli withdrawal from occupied Arab areas. The summit conference, according to the view of most neutral observers, displayed a considerable amount of realism and moderation and had probably gone as far as it could go, considering the intense passions of the masses, the weakened position of many of the Arab leaders (Nasser himself had to remove a potential threat to unseat him just before leaving for Khartoum), and the violent opposition to any show of moderation by the more militant Syrian,

Algerian, and Palestinian leaders. In fact, these extremists began a vigorous campaign against the decisions of the summit meeting and made it clear that they would not abide by them.[40]

Despite the unchanged and unyielding attitude of the Arab militants, the Khartoum conference cleared the way for the Arab moderates to seek a political solution and to offer, in exchange for their conquered lands, important concessions short of actually recognizing Israel and negotiating formal peace treaties with her. Because many Arab governments had broken diplomatic relations with the United States and because, in any case, the American position was still considered pro-Israel, the more moderate Arab leaders decided to work through the UN General Assembly, which convened on September 19 for its Twenty-second Session.

While there were some advantages to be derived from waiting for the intense emotions of the Arab masses to subside somewhat and for their military strength and bargaining power to improve before pressing for action, the Arabs were at the same time becoming concerned that the longer Israel remained in possession of their territories, the more firmly she would consolidate her position there and the harder it would be to extricate them from her control. For these reasons, they were anxious for the UN to make some decisive move which would compel Israel to remove her forces from the occupied areas. At the same time, however, they realized that they could not obtain a two-thirds majority in the General Assembly for a resolution calling for an unconditional withdrawal and that they would have to be prepared to make some meaningful concessions in return. Both before and after the opening session of the General Assembly, most Arab governments revealed that they were far more willing than they had been during the Fifth Emergency Special Session to accept a compromise settlement. In fact, they even expressed interest in the possible revival of the Latin American and the United States-Soviet proposals which had been offered to them during the General Assembly meetings in July and which they had turned down. Moreover, moderate Arab delegates such as those from Lebanon went so far as to declare before the General Assembly that while they could not recognize Israel and negotiate a formal peace treaty with her, they would be willing to accept a "peaceful settlement of the present crisis" achieved through the UN, and an Israeli withdrawal could be followed "by the establishment of peaceful conditions guaranteeing the renunciation of the use of force and the security of all states in the region." They held that the UN had a "real opportunity" to achieve peace in the Middle East and warned that if "this opportunity" were "missed," it might "never come again." [41]

By October, according to various reports from the *New York Times,* the Associated Press, the United Press International, and private observers,[42] some Arab leaders, including President Nasser, were privately showing an even more "realistic" and flexible approach than they were able to express publicly because of the intense anti-Israeli passions of the Arab masses. They were especially anxious to deal with the highly sensitive issues by means of quiet diplomacy, rather than more open procedures, and to find the most favorable face-saving formula possible which would enable them to justify to their own people the making of unpopular concessions. By the middle of October, the Arabs began to express a preference for action through the Security Council so that they could tacitly go along with any compromise resolution which might be passed without having, since no Arab state was a member of that body, to take a direct and public stand. In this way too they could place the responsibility on the Security Council for any distasteful conditions which they might have to abide by in return for an Israeli withdrawal. The Associated Press reported on October 16 that some "diplomats familiar with the Egyptians' thinking" believed that the UAR "would accept" a five-point plan then being discussed by UN delegates. This plan provided that: (1) Israel would withdraw her forces in "stages coordinated with steps to settle other problems"; (2) coexistence would be established "guaranteeing the renunciation of the use of force and the security of all states" in the Middle East; (3) the Palestine Arab refugees "would be settled permanently, preferably in the places of their own choice, and Israel would pay a substantial share of the cost"; (4) there would be freedom of navigation through the Suez Canal and the Strait of Tiran for "all states without restriction"; and (5) "sensitive zones between Israel and the Arab countries would be demilitarized, with the definition of permanent frontiers left for later." After meeting with President Nasser, Sir Dingle Foot, British Labor Party M.P., stated, according to the *New York Times* of October 15, that the Egyptian leader was prepared to negotiate a political settlement with Israel through the UN or some other third party. While Nasser expressed a wish to use the 1949 armistice agreements as the basis for the discussions, he "did not necessarily mean that boundaries and other peace considerations must return to their 1949 status." The *New York Times* correspondent in Egypt concluded, in a report published on October 22, that "on the question of direct negotiations, Cairo is likely to be adamant for a long time [because of the strong unpopularity of such a move within the Arab world]. But on points of dispute aside from formal recognition, one can find in this city today much room for accommodation." In the first part of November, 1967, some accounts stated that

Nasser was so anxious to find a political solution that he was willing to make more concessions than ever before. He was said to have agreed to accept the five principles proposed in June by President Johnson as the basis for peace in the Middle East—the right of all nations to exist, justice for the Arab refugees, freedom of navigation for all states through international waterways, limits on the arms race, and recognition of the political independence and territorial integrity of all countries. Nasser set two conditions: Israeli troop withdrawal from occupied Arab areas and a just solution for the Arab refugee problem. He was also said to have elicited a promise from Algerian, but not Syrian, leaders that they would not try to denounce and embarrass him if he succeeded in reaching a political settlement with Israel. In addition, Egypt was reported as having indicated a desire to restore diplomatic relations with the United States.[43]

Moreover, apparently with at least the initial encouragement of the UAR and some other Arab states, King Hussein took the initiative for the Arabs in the first part of November, by visiting Bonn, Paris, and Washington in an effort to win further support for the Arab cause in the West and to press for action by the UN Security Council, which had become deadlocked over the Arab-Israeli dispute. He held that the Arabs had agreed upon a "new and positive approach" and were willing to give a "great deal" to bring about a solution to the Middle East crisis. While the Arabs were still not yet prepared to recognize Israel and negotiate directly with her, he stated that they were now ready to recognize "Israel's right to exist in peace and security," to end the state of belligerence, and to allow her shipping to use the Suez Canal and the Strait of Tiran "if the right conditions were reached in a general settlement." In particular, Israel would have to give up her conquered territories, including the Old City of Jerusalem, whose absorption by Israel was "totally unacceptable." He urged Israel to "offer some terms" for the Arabs to "consider" and to "match" the concessions submitted by the Arabs. He also warned that Israel's failure to propose an acceptable solution to the refugee issue would be a "death blow to any hope she may have for acceptance of her other proposals;" that unless a satisfactory solution were arrived at "soon" the Arab militants would dissipate the "existing mood of moderation" in the Arab world and the "struggle" between the Arabs and the Israelis would go on until either the Arabs were "subjugated" by Israel or Israel were destroyed by the Arabs; and that "if the Jew and Arab are to live in peace, the alien quality of Israel must be diminished" and the Israelis must become "more Eastern and less European." Although Hussein claimed he was speaking on behalf of all Arabs, the Syrians made it clear that he was not representing them. At that time, some Egyptian officials held that Hussein's views were generally similar to those of their own.[44]

In the fall of 1967, the UN, encouraged by the more moderate attitude of some Arab leaders and pressed by the UN Secretary-General, engaged in intensive behind-the-scenes diplomatic talks on the assumption that the disputants could be more conciliatory in private than in public. When it became clear that disputes could not be resolved in New York City, most UN delegates placed their hopes in sending a UN representative to the Middle East to find some way of resolving the Arab-Israeli problem. However, neither the Arabs nor the Israelis and their respective supporters could agree on the functions, powers, and goals of a UN representative. A draft resolution (S/8227) submitted by India, Mali, and Nigeria provided that: (1) Israel should withdraw from positions seized since June 4; (2) all nations in the Middle East should terminate the state of belligerency and settle all disputes by peaceful means; (3) every state in the area must respect the sovereignty, territorial integrity, and political independence of the others and has the right to be secure within its borders; (4) there should be a "just settlement" of the Palestine Arab refugee problem; (5) there should be guaranteed freedom of navigation in accordance with "international law through international waterways"; and (6) a special UN mediator should be dispatched to the Middle East to coordinate efforts to achieve the purpose of the resolution. While the Arabs and their friends, including Russia, backed this proposal, Israel and the United States strongly opposed it. In fact, the United States warned that she would refuse to cooperate in carrying it out if it were adopted. Hoping to block this three-power draft and sharing Israel's views that the UN should not try to impose its own solution on the parties, that any withdrawal must be linked to a final peace treaty, that direct negotiations were essential for achieving lasting peace, and that Israel should be allowed to keep some of the conquered areas to give her more "defensible borders," the United States also submitted a draft resolution (S/8229) of her own. This stated: (1) "armed forces" should withdraw "from occupied territories," without specifying whose forces were involved and whether all territories should be given up; (2) "territorial inviolability" should be guaranteed through measures, including the establishment of demilitarized zones and of "secure and recognized" boundaries; and (3) the UN should send a representative to the Middle East "to establish and maintain contacts with the states concerned with a view to assist them in the working out of solutions." The Arabs and the Soviet Union firmly rejected the American draft, claiming that it was pro-Israel and that it ignored the UN Charter and UN resolutions. Efforts made by several Latin

American countries to present a compromise proposal based upon the draft the Latin Americans had submitted to the emergency session of the General Assembly in June proved unsuccessful for, while it was accepted by the Arabs, it was turned down by Israel.[45]

Britain assumed the initiative in trying to break the existing deadlock in the Security Council because she feared that if the UN failed to act in time, conditions in the Middle East would soon deteriorate and an opportunity for peace would be lost forever. Thus, on November 16, she introduced a draft resolution (S/8247) which sought to provide a compromise formula reasonably acceptable to all sides. After "emphasizing the inadmissibility of the acquisition of territory by war and the need to work for a just and lasting peace in which every state in the area can live in security," the draft affirmed that the establishment of such a peace should include the application of the following two principles: withdrawal of Israeli armed forces from territories occupied in the recent conflict and termination of all claims or states of belligerence; and respect and acknowledgment of the sovereignty, territorial integrity, and political independence of every state in the area and their right to live in peace within secure and recognized boundaries free from threats or acts of force. It further affirmed the "necessity": (1) "for guaranteeing freedom of navigation through international waterways in the area"; (2) "for achieving a just settlement of the refugee problem"; and (3) "for guaranteeing the territorial inviolability and political independence of every state in the area, through measures including the establishment of demilitarized zones." It also requested the UN Secretary-General to designate a special representative to proceed to the Middle East to "establish and maintain contacts with the states concerned in order to promote agreement and to assist efforts to achieve a peaceful and accepted settlement in accordance with the provisions and principles in this resolution."

While the resolution passed unanimously on November 22, Syria, as well as the Palestinian leaders, denounced it because it "ignored" earlier UN resolutions and the "roots of the problem." The Arab states and Israel also disagreed in their interpretations of it. Israel held that "only" after permanent peace with secure and recognized boundaries had been established could the other principles of the resolution be "given effect." The Arabs, in turn, contended that Israel must withdraw from all the occupied territories as a first step. In any case, by their votes and statements, the overwhelming preponderance of the UN members revealed widespread agreement on the following basic points: (1) the UN Charter required Israel to give up the Arab areas seized in the June War; (2) there should be no state of belligerence; (3) all countries should have the right to exist in peace and security and to enjoy innocent passage through international waterways; (4) the UN must play an active and essential role in dealing with the entire problem; and (5) only a "just" peace could be dependable and lasting.[46]

On November 23, U Thant appointed Gunnar Jarring, the Swedish ambassador in Moscow, as special representative. Ambassador Jarring had held diplomatic posts in several countries in the Middle East, had been a Swedish delegate to the UN from 1948 to 1964, and had been sent on a peace mission by the UN Security Council in 1957 to deal with the Kashmir dispute. Despite his considerable talents and experience, the UN Special Representative faced a formidable task as he began a series of visits to Middle East capitals on December 12. In fact, so long as deep Arab-Israeli distrust, hostility, and conflicting national interests persisted, so long as internal political instabilities and rivalries continued to exist within Israel and the Arab world, and so long as the two superpowers remained seriously divided, neither the UN nor any of its agents would be able to bridge the wide psychological and political gaps which continued to separate the Arabs and Israelis and to bring about a peace settlement despite U Thant's clear warning that "if . . . no progress is made towards resolving the root causes of conflict, within a few years at the most there will be ineluctably a new eruption of war." [47]

ANALYSES

The Arab States

Over the years preceding the June War, the official Arab position before the UN was generally as follows: The Palestine Arabs had been grievously wronged by the Zionists and the UN, and it was their responsibility to rectify this injustice. The UN should at least have implemented those resolutions providing for the repatriation and/or compensation of the refugees, the internationalization of Jerusalem, and the establishment of a Jewish entity containing approximately one-third less territory than the pre-June, 1967, State of Israel. By reiterating or recalling these same provisions in later resolutions, the General Assembly had reaffirmed their continued existence and validity. Actually, the real dispute was the one between the UN and Israel, who had adamantly refused to abide by UN decisions, and the real problem was not to seek new solutions, but to carry out existing ones. It would be harmful to the interests of the world community for the UN to submit to the *fait accompli* and to allow Israel to disregard its resolutions.

The Arabs also insisted that they would not consent to direct talks with Israel. However, on numerous occasions, at least in the earlier years, Arab delegates stated before the General Assembly that their governments would be willing to negotiate a peace settlement if (1) the UN would act as an intermediary; (2) the Arabs were recognized as a "single party"; (3) UN resolutions would be used as the basis for the discussions; (4) the major powers would provide assurances that "territorial encroachment by Israel upon the Arabs" would "never be allowed"; (5) Israel would "desist from aggravating the dangerous disequilibrium between population and the absorptive capacity of the land, by putting an end to its policy of [unlimited] immigration"; (6) the the Arabs were aided in acquiring sufficient arms for defense purposes; and (7) "no obstacle" would be "put in the way of their developing the closest national ties among themselves." On several occasions, some Arabs even indicated that they would agree to negotiate directly with Israel if she would first accept the principles laid down by UN resolutions. Only then would the Arabs consider making peace with Israel and ending their boycotts, blockades, and other similar measures which provided them with their only effective bargaining weapons against Israel. Even some high Arab officials expressed a readiness to consider peace with Israel on these terms.[48]

However, by the middle 1960's, as a result of heightened tensions with Israel and growing instabilities and dissension within the Arab world, Arab leaders found it increasingly advantageous politically to take, at least publicly, a more obdurate and bellicose stand towards Israel, and a few of them, particularly the Syrian and Palestinian ones, even began to advocate a war to destroy Israel. Especially during the latter period, Arab views on the subject of war or peace with Israel differed considerably from person to person, state to state, and time to time, depending upon the various and often changing circumstances which happened to prevail.

The Arabs complained that continued, large-scale immigration and extensive aid from world Jewry and Western governments added substantially to Arab insecurity by enabling Israel to become considerably more powerful. Moreover, Israel's successful efforts to develop closer ties with Western countries and especially with the large, influential Jewish groups living there greatly concerned the Arabs. From the beginning, many Arabs considered Israel not only to have expansionist ambitions of her own, but also to be a wedge deliberately set up by imperialistically minded Western governments to enable them to maintain their dominance over the Middle East. Having suffered under Western colonial rule for many years, most Arabs became highly suspicious of Western motives and policies and hypersensitive about any move which could restore Western control over their area. The Arabs frequently contended that they would not fear and distrust Israel if she existed completely on her own. But they believed that an Israel actively supported by powerful governments and wealthy and influential world Jewry deeply worried them. Consequently, the Arabs were very reluctant to accept and negotiate with Israel as long as she could call upon the backing of such formidable allies. Israel, in turn, not only refused to give up her ties with her Western and Jewish friends, but she sought to strengthen them, thus adding to Arab apprehension and unwillingness to deal with her.

Most Arabs believed that, because of their greater manpower and their resources, time was on their side. There was, therefore, no need to hurry the settlement of the Arab-Israeli problem, whether by negotiations or by war. Any negotiations should wait until the Arabs had achieved military superiority and a more favorable bargaining position over Israel. If the matter had to be resolved by war, then it should be delayed until the Arabs were far better prepared to fight Israel. In fact, by the early 1960's, many Arabs became convinced that since Israel refused to comply with UN resolutions even in part, then war with Israel was virtually inevitable, for they were denied the opportunity to right by peaceful means any of the wrongs done to the Palestine Arabs. Some Arab leaders, however, were very concerned that either Israel or the Arab extremists would force them into a war before they were prepared to win it. All Arabs recognized the need for increasing the power and influence of the Arab world, and many of them urged that these be accomplished through quicker economic, social, and political modernization, greater unity and military strength, and enlisting additional friends and supporters throughout the world. Some Arab officials and intellectuals warned against the resort to force because they believed that war frequently created more difficulties and problems than it resolved. They especially feared that a major military confrontation between the Arabs and Israelis might not be confined to the Middle East and that it might precipitate a disastrous atomic war; and that, in any case, the United States and possibly other Western countries might intervene against the Arabs and on the side of Israel. A number of Arabs, including relatively important officials, believed that if the Arabs remained sufficiently calm and patient, once the Arab world had become united and powerful, Arab differences with Israel would ultimately be resolved without war, to the general satisfaction of the Arabs.[49]

The Arabs were justified in their criticism both of Israel for refusing to cooperate with UN agencies in the Middle East and to abide by many UN resolutions and of the world organization itself for failing to implement its own decisions. However, the Arab position on this would have been much stronger had the Arabs themselves cooperated more fully with all UN bodies and complied with all parts of all resolutions dealing with various Arab-Israeli disputes. Not only did the Arabs disregard the UN partition resolution by resorting to force in 1948 and, at times, hinder the constructive efforts of UNTSO and the MAC's, but the demand for UNEF's withdrawal by the UAR in May, 1967, contributed greatly to the precipitation of the June War. While the Arabs generally revealed a considerably greater willingness than the Israelis to respect and cooperate with the UN organs and personnel, they frequently benefited more from the UN than did the Israelis. Thus, it was much easier for them to accept UN decisions and presence in the Middle East. The real test of Arab sincerity towards the world organization would come when the Arabs had achieved military superiority and when they began to consider the UN to be more of a handicap than a help in their relations with Israel.

While some Arab officials indicated a willingness to consider a peaceful settlement with Israel on the basis of UN resolutions, the more extremist leaders—occasionally even the more moderate ones when faced with difficult internal conditions—made bellicose statements. These not only were contrary to the principles of the UN Charter but actually served the cause of Israel and discredited that of the Arabs. By widely publicizing the more warlike Arab speeches and by convincing many people in various parts of the world that the Arabs were unjustifiably unreasonable and belligerent and were intent on aggression, the Israelis were able to obtain considerable military and economic aid from the Western nations, as well as commitments to come to her assistance in case of an Arab attack, and to justify their refusal to make concessions. In addition, the more the Arabs called for a "war of liberation," the more reluctant were the UN and the United States to enforce those resolutions which favored the Arabs and which could be used to strengthen the Arab military position against Israel.

Though it is easy to understand the reluctance of most Arab officials to take a public stand in favor of moderation as long as the Arab masses remained violently anti-Israel and Arab activists were ready to undermine their position, these circumstances did not justify those ill-advised actions in the middle 1960's which inflamed popular passions further and aggravated an already explosive situation. Many speeches, especially by the Syrians and Palestinians, were unduly intemperate. Official aid and encouragement given to Palestine Arab commando groups, particularly by Syria, and inadequate Arab efforts to prevent border incidents aroused Israeli fear and hostility, heightened Arab-Israeli tensions, and caused unnecessary bloodshed. Palestinian and Syrian extremists seemed bent on promoting a military confrontation, despite the lack of preparedness. The June fiasco made all Arabs realize, in retrospect, the soundness of the position of the moderates who had warned that Arab threats or use of force would encourage Israel to initiate military acts and enable her to win tremendous moral and material support throughout the world and to justify her armed attack as legitimate self-defense.

In short, rigidity and blind emotionalism, lack of foresight and realism, inept and divided leadership, too much reliance on force and too little on the UN, and a penchant for exaggerated oratory obstructed the path to peace and led the Arabs to another military disaster.

Humiliated, stunned, weak, and uncertain after their June defeat, the Arabs nevertheless revealed agreement on some major points while disagreeing on others. Blaming Israel for starting the war and the United States for supporting her—politically and economically if not militarily—they insisted they would never be reconciled to the loss of their lands. A UN failure to compel Israel to withdraw, they insisted, would set a dangerous precedent, undermining world law and opening the way to another Middle East war. As long as Israel retained control over Islamic holy places, it would be impossible not only for the Arabs but for all Muslims to forgive and forget, and some non-Arab Muslim countries might, under the banner of a holy war, provide the Arabs with military assistance in order to wrest control of their revered shrines from alien hands and make them freely accessible to Muslims from all over the world. The Arabs adamantly refused to negotiate directly because this could imply recognition of Israel and would enable Israel to disregard the armistice agreements and those UN resolutions she did not like, to legitimatize her illegal conquests, and to extract the maximum concessions through her superior power. The Arabs also held they could not be expected to settle their differences while foreign troops remained on their soil.

Syrian, Palestinian, and other Arab militants, despite the fact that their shortsighted, uncompromising, and aggressive policies had helped to bring on the disastrous June War, continued to insist that the Arabs should organize guerrilla operations and turn the Israeli-occupied areas into bases for underground resistance to deny Israel the fruits of her victory, to keep anti-Israeli feeling alive, and to soften her up for an eventual Arab attack. Believing that their government still depended for survival on inciting the passions of the masses, Syrian officials in particular saw advantages in perpetuating Arab-Israeli strife. Moreover, the extremist leaders could not now agree to moderate their stand without admitting that their former aggressive policies had in fact been wrong. Misguidedly, these Arab militants believed that only by force could the Arabs redress their grievances, despite the fact that, since

Israel would be able to maintain her military lead for some years, she would be able to inflict far more damage on the Arabs than they on her. Not only would such an approach stiffen her refusal to withdraw, but it might actually encourage her to seize more territory and to justify such action on the ground that she needed still more "defensible borders." She might even be encouraged to persist in her policy of "preventive war" and again attempt to smash Arab military power before it seriously threatened her, while placing primary blame for such drastic action on the Arabs. Furthermore, extremist Arab threats of "extermination" merely helped Israel to continue to receive much support, as well as sympathy, from her friends abroad. In the light of these threats the United States in particular would maintain her effort to keep Israel alone better armed than the combination of her Arab neighbors.

The Arab extremists also overlooked the fact that the ultimate fate of Israel would never be determined by the Arab world alone, no matter how powerful it might become. The events of 1967 demonstrated that the United States would continue to play a crucial role, in or out of the UN, thanks not only to United States government policy but to the emotional commitment to Israel of so many individual Americans. Therefore, even if the Arabs eventually achieved military superiority over Israel, they still could not hope to defeat an Israel backed by the incontestable power of the United States.

Furthermore, the Arabs could not be confident of receiving direct military help from the Russians. In June, 1967, the Soviet Union made every effort to steer clear of the actual fighting in order to avoid any confrontation with the United States regardless of the fact that the Arabs were being soundly defeated. Even if Russia would be willing to intervene militarily on the side of the Arabs, this could provoke a general war.

In today's world, wars can no longer be used to any nation's long-term best interests. If every government resorted to armed force whenever it deemed it desirable, then there would be no hope that man would ever be able to develop a more effective world organization and world law. Common sense would therefore dictate that no government, regardless of how frustrated it might feel, should use or be allowed to use war as a means to bring about change, no matter how "just" this might appear to be.

For many months after the June War the moderate leaders in Jordan and Egypt, disagreeing with the Arab militants, sought a political solution. Swallowing a great deal of pride, they expressed a willingness to recognize Israel's right to peace and to the use of the Gulf of Aqaba if she would withdraw from territories occupied in the June War and would cooperate in attaining a just solution of the Arab refugee problem. Though insisting upon an Israeli withdrawal, a few Arabs privately conceded the possibility of a phased withdrawal coinciding with the fulfillment of Arab obligations with the understanding that direct talks might eventually be possible after Arab emotions had a chance to abate and Israel demonstrated her good faith. Nevertheless, the anti-Israeli passions of the Arab masses, the obdurate and militant stand maintained by the Syrian and Palestinian leaders, and the precarious position of some of the Arab regimes made it virtually impossible, at least for the time being, for Israel's more moderate Arab neighbors to make all the drastic concessions which Israel demanded. Moreover, because Israel had refused to retreat from her tough views and because Egypt's military power and self-confidence had grown considerably, there were indications by the latter part of 1967 that the Egyptian leaders had become increasingly pessimistic about the chances for an acceptable political solution of their differences with Israel, and their own position had hardened in some ways. For example, whereas earlier the UAR had indicated she might consider allowing Israeli ships to pass through the Suez Canal under certain conditions, President Nasser, in a speech on November 23, held that he would not lift the restrictions on direct Israeli use of the canal under any circumstances. There was also a growing conviction that another war was inevitable and that the Arabs should do everything possible to prepare themselves for it. Nevertheless, Egyptian spokesmen insisted that while they ruled out a peace treaty, they still wanted to reach a peaceful solution of the Arab-Israeli problem. In fact, in late February, 1968, there were reports that Egypt had even expressed a readiness to negotiate indirectly through UN Representative Gunnar Jarring if Israel would agree to abide by UN Security Council Resolution 242 (1967) of November 22, 1967, which called, among other things, for an Israeli withdrawal from conquered areas. In early March, however, after serious anti-government riots of students and workers had broken out in the UAR and after Israel had removed the designation of "enemy territory" from the occupied sectors and had given some of them Jewish Biblical names, the UAR position hardened once again.[50] According to the *New York Times* of March 9, 1968, the authoritative Egyptian newspaper *Al Ahram* reported that the Egyptian government had formally informed Dr. Gunnar Jarring that it would now reject any proposal for negotiations with Israel, direct or indirect. *Al Ahram* stated that Egypt took this position because Israel's latest move regarding the occupied areas "proved" Israel's "aggressive and expansionist" plans and showed that she was not ready to accept the Security Council resolution and because time was on the side of the

Arabs and was needed to "correct the military imbalances." These developments did not make Dr. Jarring's assignment any easier.

It had become clear that by early March, 1968, the views of some of the moderate Arab leaders had become less flexible and conciliatory. Their continued fear of Israel and concern for their own political positions and even their lives are understandable. Nevertheless, at least the more responsible officials should have realized that, unless they seriously tried to temper their language, calm popular emotions, avoid all hostile activities, and give indications that they truly want to live in peace with Israel, then neither would Israel voluntarily accept the return of even the new refugees and give up the conquered lands, nor would the UN and the United States be willing to exert the pressures on Israel which would be required to compel her to do so. Moreover, as long as the Middle East remains in turmoil, Arab plans for economic and social progress and UN efforts to bring about peace will be seriously handicapped.

Israel

Before the June War, Israel's position was basically as follows: The Arab "invasion" in May, 1948, made all the UN resolutions on Palestine null and void, and they could not be brought back to life. The radically altered conditions after the Palestine War made a return to the original partition scheme unthinkable and required a new solution. In any case, the Arabs were not genuinely interested in peace; what they really sought was the destruction of Israel. There was only one road to peace, and that was "through direct . . . negotiations" between the Arabs and the Israelis "in order to achieve a mutual settlement without any prior conditions." Such a settlement should: (1) end the state of belligerency and require Arab recognition of Israel; (2) maintain the existing borders and territorial integrity of Israel; (3) provide mutual guarantees against aggression reinforced by commitments from the major powers; (4) resettle all Arab refugees outside of Israel; (5) end the Arab boycott and blockade and establish normal economic, transit, and other relations in the entire area; (6) assure Israel of adequate water from the Jordan River; and (7) continue the existing balance of power between the Arab world and herself. In return, Israel would consider: (1) giving Jordan a free port at Haifa; (2) reviving a limited reunion of families plan and paying some compensation to the Palestine Arab refugees; (3) cooperating with the Arabs in the economic development of the area for the benefit of all parties; and (4) making "minor agreed mutual adjustments at certain" points on the borders "where there are hindrances to the daily life of the population," as long as the Arabs would also give up an equivalent amount of land.[51]

Israeli actions and policies were based on several premises. The only deterrents to Arab aggression were Israel's superior military power and the application of this power against the Arabs. There was little or no hope for a peaceful settlement with the Arabs except one brought about by the use or threat of superior force. Major concessions to the Arabs would only weaken Israel and further enhance Arab ability and determination to attack her. Time would somehow lend "stability to existing facts" and perpetuate the *status quo* in Israel's favor. Moreover, to insure their country's security, Israeli leaders pursued three primary objectives: (1) to prevent the Arabs from gaining enough military unity and might to bring about a major shift in the existing balance of power; (2) to strengthen Israel by increasing her industrial and military production, by purchasing from abroad those advanced weapons which could not be produced domestically, by continuing to press for more immigrants (especially those possessing valuable skills), and by maintaining Israel's lead in the fields of education, science, and technology; and (3) to widen and deepen friendships throughout the world and to convince other peoples and governments of the justness of their cause.[52]

It was true, as Israel complained, that the Arabs forcibly opposed the UN resolution of 1947 partitioning Palestine and that only later, when the partition lines were more favorable to them than the prevailing situation, did they decide to insist upon its implementation. However, the Israelis also supported the resolution only when it served their interests and repudiated it when it became an obstacle. The General Assembly did not accept the Israeli contention that the Arab invasion had voided the partition resolution, since it reiterated this decision in its Resolution 273(III) of May 11, 1949, which admitted Israel into the UN, and subsequent ones such as Resolution 512(VI) of January 26, 1952.

Israel's insistence upon direct negotiations as the only path to peace was prompted by her desire to bypass UN resolutions, to extract the maximum bargaining value out of her superior military power, and to obtain an implied *de facto* recognition of her statehood. Despite the assertion of Israeli officials that the main obstacle to peace was the unwillingness of allegedly self-serving Arab leaders, they must have been aware that no Arab leader, regardless of his personal inclinations, could agree to direct parleys for three major reasons. Firstly, Israel had most to gain and the Arabs most to lose from any move that ignored UN resolutions and that compelled the Arabs to negotiate from a position of weakness. In fact, President Nasser was reported to have told Western diplomats in late 1955 that "he would be willing to negotiate with Israel, but could not do so as long as Egypt was militarily inferior." [53] Secondly, observing the continued opposition of the Arab masses to any dealings with Israel, the Israelis should have recalled how popular emotions had prevented their own government from holding direct talks with West German officials for many years. Thirdly, because of their insecure internal positions and bitter rivalries, Arab leaders felt it necessary to assume hard anti-Israel stances. Some Israeli officials frankly conceded that whenever political divisions within the Arab world increased, the Arab governments had to appear more militant, and that only when they were more secure and rivalries muted could Arab leaders consider coming to terms with Israel.[54] Whenever the Arab countries seemed to be moving towards greater unity and any one Arab leader appeared to be growing more powerful, Israel expressed deep concern and sought to do what she could to impede this trend. Naturally, strong Arab leaders and a more unified and confident Arab world might have posed a greater military threat to Israel. Yet any Arab leader needed precisely these circumstances before he could consider concluding an unpopular peace with Israel.[55]

Israel's calls for direct talks, therefore, bore, as one Israeli put it, "... no relation at all to reality" and were made primarily to enable Israel to gain "propaganda value" out of the inevitable rejections.[56] But whatever short-term propaganda advantages Israel gained, the calls for direct talks only further antagonized the Arabs. Moreover, Israel's insistence that negotiations must be carried on without prior conditions was itself a major condition which proved to be a major obstacle to peace. Had Israel been willing to accept some conditions and abide at least in part by certain key UN resolutions in the earlier years, when the Arab leaders were in the best position to come to terms with her and when most of them would probably have been satisfied with some face-saving formula, an Arab-Israeli peace settlement might then have been achieved.

Israeli leaders made it clear that under no circumstances would they accept any change in the status of their section of Jerusalem, any refugee repatriation (other than admitting a small number of refugees under a limited reunion-of-families scheme), or any modification of the existing frontier, other than minor, mutual border rectifications. Actually, whenever an Israeli official revealed the slightest flexibility on these subjects, ultra-nationalist spokesmen immediately attacked him, and he usually retreated with the explanation that his remarks did not really involve any yielding on these issues. Consequently Arab officials asked "What's the use of negotiation?" [57] According to the *New York Times,* July 29, 1957, one Israeli official admitted, "Of course, we would sit down with the Arabs at any time, but what would the Arabs really gain from this?" Consequently, it was unrealistic for the Israelis to ask that the Arabs, already suffering from hurt pride, voluntarily waive all rights under UN resolutions and surrender to Israel's terms without being able to obtain any of their own objectives in return.

Some Israelis began to criticize their government's rigid position and belief that somehow if it denied concessions long enough the Arabs and the UN would give up requesting them. They held that Israel needed "new leadership" which dared "to envisage new horizons," had greater "imagination" and flexibility, and was prepared to do some "rethinking in the field of Arab-Israeli relations." They warned that Israel had to choose "one of two alternatives: the *status quo* of no peace, the constant danger of war—and an enormous security burden, increased conflicts and difficulties—or the possibility of peace at the price" of some important concessions to the Arabs.[58] The Israeli government paid no heed to this perceptive advice.[59] By refusing to help resolve the Arab refugee problem and making it impossible for the Arabs to attain by peaceful means even part of the rights established by UN resolutions, the Israelis further embittered the Arabs and convinced them that they had no alternative but to maintain boycotts and resort to force in order to obtain justice.

Israel's frequent hostility towards the UN was reflected not only in her defiance of even those UN resolutions supported by her warmest friends, but also in her lack of cooperation with such UN agencies in the Middle East as UNEF, UNTSO, and the MAC's. Closer cooperation with these agencies and permitting the stationing of UNEF forces on her side of the border, particularly in late May, 1967, not only would have precluded what Israel considered a necessary defensive war, but could even have encouraged prospects for peace.

The disparaging attitude of many Israelis towards the Arabs created one of the most formidable obstacles to peace. Even such leaders as Ben-Gurion laid claim to a moral, intellectual superiority over the allegedly backward Arabs. The insistence that Israel must remain a Western nation and not become "Levantine" indicated that many Israelis opposed any meaningful integration of Israel into the life and ways of the Middle East and this despite the facts that 65 per cent of her Jewish population was Oriental in origin and that her location made her forever an integral part of the area.[60]

Perceptive Israelis criticized both the manner and tone used by Israeli officials when speaking of the Arabs and the "distorted picture," depicting the Arabs in the "gloomiest colors," which was being presented by the Israeli schools and press. In addition, they stressed that, while the Arab-Israeli question was a "political one, . . . its roots" were "psychological," and it would "never be resolved without a psychological transformation on our part, which may ultimately bring about a similar transformation on the other side"; and that Israel's lack of understanding of the Arabs and the "psychological gulf" which had grown between Arab and Jew contributed "to the deepening of Arab hatred for Israel, and of Israeli hatred for the Arabs." They charged Israeli officials with being "very shortsighted" in believing that Israel's "power and deterrence and the prevailing discord and disunity among her neighbors" would insure her security forever because Arab disunity and military inferiority could and probably would sooner or later be overcome. They warned that until the Israelis became more understanding of and sensitive to Arab feelings and aspirations, brought about a "far-reaching change of values in [their own] thinking and feeling . . . towards the Arab peoples," and began to accept themselves as an integral part of the area in which they lived, there could be little hope that Israel would ever find real friends among her neighbors or lasting peace and security.[61]

Israel's relations with her own Arabs also had important repercussions on the issue of an Arab-Israeli peace. Although the Israeli government did work to improve their economic, educational, and health standards and finally lifted military rule in the Arab areas late in 1966, even Israeli Jews admitted that the Israeli Arabs continued to be treated as second-class citizens, that they were looked down upon as inferiors, and that the government had not yet produced a fully effective and farsighted minority policy. The Arabs still suffered from inequalities in the fields of education, politics, internal travel, and employment opportunities (especially for white-collar positions). Some rooming houses refused to admit Arabs. Thousands of Arabs who had been forcibly removed from their villages by Israeli authorities were not allowed to return to their former homes. Very often, Israel gave first consideration —such as in providing roads, water, electricity, and schools—to her Jewish inhabitants, and the Arabs were often the victims of "the last-in-first-to-go employment rule." Although the Israeli Arabs had not posed a threat to Israel's security, even during the Sinai War period, most Israeli Jews, including officials, continued to distrust the Arabs, especially the Muslims.[62]

Before the June War, increasing numbers of Jews—particularly those associated with the Communist and Mapam Parties, Ihud, *The New Outlook* magazine, and the Sephardi (Oriental) Jewish community—deplored their government's attitude and policies towards Israeli Arabs and pressed for a radical change in them. They cautioned that Israel's restrictions created more "needless ill will, both among her own Arabs and in the outside world," than she gained in any meaningful security. Israel could not "treat" the Arabs as inferiors, aliens, and even enemies and at the same time "demand that they treat us as friends." "A feeling of inequality and discrimination" would "prevent Israeli Arabs from integrating into the life of the new state and make them easy prey of hostile propaganda against Israel." Because the position of the Israeli Arabs played an important role in the relations between Israel and her Arab neighbors, the practice of discrimination would merely "deepen distrust and enmity," "poison Arab-Jewish relations," and "serve as an obstacle in the way of real peace." The manner in which Israel dealt with the Israeli Arabs would provide a "test of the democratic character of the Jewish State." Besides, "it must not be forgotten that the Jews formed a national minority in many lands" and they "always fought for equal rights." If Israel "succeeded in fully absorbing the Arab minority—not only economically, but morally and psychologically as well"—this would enable the Israeli Arabs to become a constructive "bridge between Israel and its neighbors," instead of a potential fifth column, and would produce the "first" essential step on the road to peace with the Arab world.[63] Unfortunately, these discerning admonitions were generally ignored by the Israeli leaders.

Israel's immigration policy also sharpened Arab-Israeli differences. During the mandate period the Arabs actively opposed the migration of substantial numbers of Jews to Palestine. After Israel became a state, the Arabs were deeply concerned that continued large-scale immigration would lessen the chances for the repatriation of the Palestine Arab refugees, help to create a more powerful and dangerous opponent, and encourage, if not indeed compel, an overpopulated Israel to expand her borders. For these reasons, Arab officials usually insisted that one essential condition for peace was Israel's agreement to terminate her policy of unlimited immigration. Israel repeatedly rejected this condition, primarily because she felt that a larger population was vital to her future. Nonetheless, increased security for her meant greater insecurity for the Arabs.

After the June War Israel believed that (1) the Arabs would come to terms with her only if compelled to do so by the threat or use of superior military power; (2) a comprehensive and favorable peace settlement must be achieved by direct negotiations and without regard to UN resolutions; (3) if the UN and other third parties would refrain from interfering, the Arabs would finally realize that they had no choice but to negotiate with Israel to extricate themselves from their desperate economic, military, and political situation; (4) Israel must depend only upon herself and her own strength to insure her security and that she alone was entitled to determine her vital interests and how they should be secured; (5) large-scale immigration of Jews and continued access to modern arms from the West were essential to her security; and (6) every effort had to be made to maintain the balance of power in her favor indefinitely.

Just as she had claimed that the Palestine War made the 1947 partition resolution null and void, Israel began to contend that the June hostilities had automatically terminated her armistice agreements with the Arabs. She refused to evacuate any part of the newly conquered areas until the Arabs negotiated a comprehensive and final treaty which would formally recognize her existence and maritime rights and provide her with more defensible borders and with guaranteed safeguards for her security, including restrictions on Arab arms and demilitarized zones on the Arab side of the ultimate boundaries. The cease-fire situation could be altered only by specific, public, and contractual commitments. Israel also insisted she would reject the establishment of any intermediate position between cease-fires and a final peace settlement. She warned that she would respect the cease-fire lines and agreements only on a reciprocal basis, strongly implying that she would reply to Arab terroristic and "border" attacks with armed reprisals. Other than proclaiming that her annexation of the Old City of Jerusalem was an irrevocable act, that she would never go back to the armistice demarcation lines, and that she would insist upon obtaining more "defensible borders," Israel was vague about what specific territorial demands she would present to the Arabs in any peace conference. Israel was equally enigmatic about what she would actually contribute towards resolving the refugee problem. In December, 1967, she proclaimed her readiness to "negotiate a five-year plan for the rehabilitation of the refugees and their final integration into the economic life of the region." However, not only was she aware that the Arabs would reject any direct negotiations with her, but she refused to divulge any details of her proposed plan. Concerning Jerusalem, she expressed a willingness to give an extraterritorial and "universal status" for the holy places, but they would remain under her sovereignty. In the meantime, the strong support extended by the United States, the indecisiveness of the UN, and the impotence of the Arabs made the confident Israelis feel that they were not subject to anyone's authority, that they could act arbitrarily and unilaterally, and that they could largely dictate their own peace terms.

Not only did Israel begin to establish several Jewish settlements in the occupied sectors, but Israeli leaders began (1) to refer to a "Greater Israel"; (2) to claim that Jordan and Egypt had no legal claim to the west bank and the Gaza Strip areas and that Syria could not be permitted to regain control of the Golan Heights because of the danger to Israeli villages; (3) to press for large-scale Jewish immigration, especially from the West, so that "Israel's bargaining position over the disposition of the occupied lands would be improved with a larger Jewish population needing land for new settlement" and that the existing population balance of Jews ("64 per cent") to Arabs ("34 per cent") would remain favorable to the Jews despite the much higher Arab birth rate; and (4) to contend that "when we have four or five million Jews in Israel, nothing will be able to injure our state or cast doubt on its existence." [64] It appeared from these developments and statements that Israel's territorial and other ambitions and demands had greatly expanded and that the only peace settlement which would be acceptable to her would be one based largely on her own terms.

After acknowledging that Israel's victory over Egypt in the Sinai War in 1956 had provided Israel temporarily with more security, David Ben-Gurion also noted, "Basically, however, the [Arab-Israeli] problem has not been solved; it is doubtful whether war can solve historical problems at all, although sometimes it is unavoidable to stave off some great and growing immediate danger." [65] This profound statement could also be applied to the June War, which, while providing Israel with another breathing spell, did not bring lasting peace any nearer. In fact, had Israel won a less complete victory in June, 1967, then, on the one hand, Israel would not have become so ambitious and her peace terms would not have been so exacting and, on the other hand, the psychological obstacles to peace in the Arab world would not have been so great. According to the *New York Times* of December 13, 1967, even Defense Minister Moshe Dayan "warned that Arab leaders were less prepared now than before the June War to agree that Israel existed as their neighbor," and he and other Israeli officials were pessimistic about the chances for a peaceful settlement of Arab-Israeli differences.

Impartial observers such as U Thant, friends of Israel, and even some Israelis concluded that any "realistic appraisal of Arab politics" and of popular Arab emotions clearly indicated that the Arab governments could not yet consent to deal directly with their foe and agree to an unfavorable peace settlement and that any Arab official who did would find himself in serious political and personal peril.[66] In any case the UN Charter provides not only for direct negotiations, but also for mediation, conciliation, and other useful methods for the pacific settlement of disputes. It could even be to Israel's ultimate disadvantage to compel moderate leaders to enter face-to-face negotiations before the Arab masses were reasonably prepared for them because such action could actually cause their downfall and replacement by more militant leaders.

Early in 1968, Israel modified her position slightly and expressed a readiness to begin negotiations with the Arabs in the presence of UN

Representative Jarring. However, she also insisted that the parties then move quickly to face-to-face talks. Reports began to circulate in February that the UAR would be willing to negotiate through Jarring on the basis of the November 22, 1967, UN Security Council resolution. At this point, Israel initiated two untimely actions—removing the designation of "enemy territory" from occupied areas and expelling an Arab leader from the former Jordanian section of Jerusalem—which helped both to bring about a hardening of the Arab position on the issue of negotiations and to lessen, at least for the time being, any chance that existed for the success of the Jarring mission.[67]

Intense anti-Arab feelings among his people and his bitter personal and political friction and rivalry with popular Defense Minister Moshe Dayan made it very difficult for Prime Minister Levi Eshkol to assume a more accommodating stand—even if he wanted to. Moreover, Israeli officials were so deeply divided on future policies that, according to the *New York Times* of December 6, 1967, "Even cabinet ministers believe that the Government will fall if it is forced to decide what is negotiable and what is not . . . The cabinet is a crisis Government, expanded on the eve of war to include nearly every faction represented in Parliament. It is designed for war and as such has not coped with the more subtle problems of peace. It has not, for example, been able to agree on a common policy on the occupied west bank of the Jordan River." In fact, if a peace conference were actually held, it could cause a major government crisis in Israel because of the disagreements which existed over what peace terms Israel should be ready to offer.[68]

Nevertheless, Israel's generally uncompromising stand appeared not to take into adequate account the modification in the position of all the Arab countries involved except Syria. After some Arab officials openly expressed the desirability of resolving their differences with Israel through peaceful means and the need to accept her existence as a fact of life, the *New York Times* reported on November 12, 1967:

> "It may not sound like much to an American," said one U. S. diplomat with years of experience in the Middle East, "but they are actually swallowing quite a bit of their pride to say these things in public. It has taken a great deal of courage for King Hussein. He's sounding reasonable to us and that makes him sound unreasonable to many Arabs. Some nut might well take a shot at him when he gets home."

The same edition also noted that "since then [early September, 1967] moderation has been on trial in the Arab world." In other words, if

Israel failed to match in time the flexibility and concessions of responsible Arab leaders, they would become discouraged and perhaps even be
replaced by militants. Then all hopes for peace and stability in the
Middle East would vanish. As of early March, 1968, there was some
doubt as to how long the moderates could maintain their accommodating
position in the face of the vituperative opposition of the Arab extremists
and the obdurate attitude of Israel. It was to Israel's best interest to
strengthen the position of the moderate Arab leaders.

The Israelis would benefit from a study of their own history. They
would discover that the Zionists were able to prevail largely because
pre-1948 Zionist policy was flexible and Arab policy rigid. They would
also see that the Arabs would be more likely to make greater concessions
right after defeat than later when they had rebuilt their military power
and gained self-confidence.

In both words and deeds, Israel gave the impression that she was
often confusing a paper peace treaty with genuine peace. For instance,
according to the *New York Times* of June 30, 1967, Gideon Hauser,
Israeli delegate to the UN, told reporters, "A piece of paper signed by
the Arab countries and us would be enough to satisfy us." Since under
international law an armistice agreement has as much binding legal force
as a peace treaty and since Israel has contended she would not accept a
return to the old General Armistice Agreements because the Arabs have
allegedly not abided by them, how would Arab signatures on a document labeled a peace treaty make any significant difference? A formal
peace treaty by itself could not *ipso facto* eliminate the deeply-rooted
animosities and conflicting national interests. Besides, even though
formal peace treaties might not be feasible for the time being, this need
not preclude the possibility of developing peaceful and stable relations
between the opposing parties, such as developed between the United
States and Japan well before the terms of the final peace treaties had
been settled.

Over and over again, history has revealed that a harsh imposed
peace, especially against a foe that has greater potential resources and
manpower than does the victor, does not endure and that the more
repugnant it was the more likely it would sow the seeds of another war.
Because they learned these costly lessons from history, after World War
II the Western governments offered fair and generous peace settlements
to Germany, Japan, and Italy. This farsighted policy, which sought to
heal and not deepen the physical and psychological wounds of war,
brought, even more quickly than could have been foreseen at the time,
moderate and friendly leaders into power in the defeated states and
provided a permanent peace between those who were, only a few years

earlier, the most bitter enemies. So what is needed in the Middle East is not merely another piece of paper, but a just peace that will have a chance to endure. If the Arabs were compelled to give in to Israeli demands at a time of military weakness, once they succeed in shifting the balance of power (and eventually they should be able to do so because of their greater potential resources) they would be under irresistable pressure to fight for their rights. Of course, Israel could continue to launch a "preventive war" every time the Arabs began to grow too strong, but this could require her to go to war every few years. This would become increasingly intolerable, not only to the Arabs, but to the UN and the world community as well.

The frequent conflicts which have taken place along the Arab-Israeli cease-fire lines have clearly indicated that the more "natural" and "defensible" borders provided by some of the conquered Arab lands have not proven less conducive to incidents than the old armistice lines. Moreover, even if Israel kept all the conquered territories, she would still remain, geographically, a small and vulnerable country in a sea of hostile Arabs, on both sides of her borders, with no assured protection against supersonic airplanes and guided missiles. Even the development of atomic weapons by Israel could be balanced by Arab production of them or their acquisition from China or Russia. Because most of her population is concentrated, Israel would generally be more vulnerable than the Arabs in any localized atomic conflict. Moreover, a nuclear war would be almost certain to spread, and even the beginning of a nuclear arms race would radically increase tensions in the Middle East and between the big powers.

It could be that Israel, at least for the months following the June War, deliberately set conditions so unacceptable that the Arabs could not possibly agree to them in order that she could both justify her retention of the occupied areas and place full responsibility on the Arabs for the failure to achieve any peace treaty. For example, a correspondent who has generally been friendly toward Israel, Joseph Alsop, wrote in a syndicated column published in the (Philadelphia) *Evening Bulletin* on November 14, 1967,

> Among Israel's friends in America, even on the highest level of the U. S. Government, and among almost all other Western policy-makers, the hard realities of the situation are not at all clearly understood. The central reality is the high probability that Israel actually does not want the kind of Middle Eastern peace King Hussein has been talking about simply because it would involve an approximate return to Israel's former borders. . . .

But behind this Israeli insistence on no repetition of 1957 is the calculation that the Arab leaders will probably never be able to bring themselves to offer the kind of signed and sealed agreement the Israelis are demanding.

The reasons for making this assumption are all too simple. The great majority of Israelis from Prime Minister Levi Eshkol and Defense Minister Moshe Dayan to the humblest private in the army, are determined never to give back the more important conquered territories, especially the Gaza Strip and above all the West Bank of the Jordan.

During an intensive inquiry in Israel, in fact, I recently encountered only one leader, Foreign Minister Abba Eban, and only a single private person who doubted the wisdom of hanging onto all these territories and, therefore, having to hold down by main force an internal Arab minority of more than one million.

Since the overwhelming majority of Israelis wish to retain the territorial conquests, but wish to avoid blame for doing so, having the Arabs refuse to negotiate is intensely convenient to Israel.

Israel could effectively refute the accuracy of this "assumption" by Mr. Alsop and others only by showing greater readiness for conciliation and compromise and by clearly indicating, for instance, in wholeheartedly accepting UN mediation, that her primary concern was, in fact, to attain a just and lasting peace and not to expand her borders at the expense of her neighbors in defiance of the UN Charter. But, if Israel were more seriously concerned with retaining most of the conquered Arab lands and with achieving a "Greater Israel" than with working for a final settlement with the Arabs, then she would have to reconcile herself to remaining an armed fortress, for genuine peace and security would continue to elude her and she would, sooner or later, have to forfeit most of the sympathy and support which she had won for herself, especially in the West.

By continuing to belittle and often to flout the authority of the UN, Israelis have clearly indicated that they still do not sufficiently recognize the vital role played by the world organization in the very creation of their nation and in promoting peace and stability in the area. Israeli attitudes and actions have done much to undermine the authority of UN agencies and their ability to deal effectively with the area's problems. Of course, as long as Israel maintains military superiority she might feel that she could dispense with the UN and that its presence might even hinder the attainment of her own objectives. However, once the Arabs can shift the balance of power in their favor, a strong and respected UN might prove the decisive factor for Israel's survival. Israel should, therefore, welcome that UN assistance which U Thant and other experts believe to be indispensable to any successful move for a solution to the Arab-Israeli problem. In fact, UN mediation could offer important advantages. For example, it could temper Israel's peace terms and make it easier for Israeli officials to justify to their own people the offering of major concessions to the Arabs. Moreover, the Arab masses would be more likely to submit to UN than Israeli demands. Both the UN and the major powers would feel more obligated to enforce a peace settlement through UN auspices than through direct negotiations, and all parties to the settlement would be more likely to abide by its provisions.

If Israel sincerely wanted peace and genuine security, she would also have to try to understand Arab feelings, to redress justifiable Arab grievances, and especially to alter her own attitude towards the Arabs, by starting to consider herself as a natural part of the Middle East. In this connection the Sephardi or Oriental Jews in Israel could play a most useful role. Although these Jews from Africa and Asia already outnumber the Ashkenazi Jews from the West, their economic and political immaturity and lack of education have prevented them from gaining influence. In fact, their situation has created serious economic, social, and political problems for Israel. Because the Sephardi Jews do not share the superiority complex and Western cultural ties of the Ashkenazi Jews nor the aversion of the "Levantine" way of life, and because they share with the Arabs the feeling of being looked down upon by the Western Jews, there is less of a psychological gulf between them and the Arabs. Some Sephardi community leaders contend that the Oriental Jews could contribute quite "a lot . . . towards breaking the regrettable impasse" between Israel and her Arab neighbors and convincing all Israelis of the need to integrate Israel into the Middle East culturally and psychologically.[69] Consequently, if the Oriental Jews attain a higher status in their country, with the Israeli Arabs they could someday help bridge the gap between Israel and the Arab world. Until Israel moves in these directions there can be little chance for lasting peace and stability in the Middle East.

The United States

In the years following the Palestine War, the United States initiated efforts to resolve the Arab-Israeli question, but she failed to make headway because (1) there was inadequate understanding of the unique and complex nature of the problem; (2) American officials were frequently subjected to powerful, partisan pressures; and (3) the American government usually waited for a crisis to occur, when conditions were least favorable, before pressing for a compromise solution. Consequently, the United States oversimplified the entire problem, wasted much invaluable time, and allowed several "golden opportunities" for a settlement, especially in the earlier years, to slip by forever while fruitlessly seeking some simple and painless formula for peace.

In the months following the June War, the United States continued to play a major role in the search for peace in the Middle East, but again it was often not a constructive one. While she was proclaiming objectivity and a desire for a "peace of reconciliation" acceptable to all parties and not imposed by anyone, she proceeded to make other statements and perform deeds which did not attest to her impartiality and which could not possibly contribute to the kind of peace that she professed to favor. Powerful pro-Israeli pressure groups, strong pro-Israeli sentiments among large segments of the American population, and internal political considerations generally prevailed over the considered advice of many experts and even over America's best long-term interests in determining American policies relating to the Arab-Israeli problem. As a result, many of these policies were so misguided and biased that they were ineffective and, at times, detrimental.

When Israel appeared to be threatened, American officials kept repeating that the United States was firmly committed to protect the territorial integrity of "all" nations in the Middle East. But when the territorial integrity of the Arab nations was endangered by the Israelis, the United States made no attempt to carry out this commitment and, thereby, gave cause to the Arabs to accuse her of applying a double standard. In fact, American officials frankly welcomed Israel's triumph, hailing it as a victory for the West. The United States introduced resolutions in the UN which generally favored the Israelis and opposed those which were objectionable to them. The United States also supported their refusal to withdraw from occupied areas, except as part of a final peace settlement, as well as their wishes to retain some of the conquered territories and to acquire more "defensible borders"—notwithstanding the fact that this would constitute a serious breach of UN principles—to end the state of belligerence, and to guarantee the rights of sovereign nations to exist in peace and security with recognized boundaries and to enjoy innocent passage through international waterways. While maintaining that the status of Jerusalem must not be decided "unilaterally," the United States did not support the UN resolutions which required the Israelis to rescind their annexation of the Old City, and she completely ignored earlier UN decisions calling for the internationalization of the Holy City. Moreover, shortly after the June hostilities, American officials provided economic aid and, later, even agreed to sell war planes to Israel in order to help her overcome economic and military losses caused by the war and to strengthen her bargaining position.

At the same time, despite the serious economic and military situation faced by pro-Western Jordan, for at least seven months the United States pointedly refused to give new economic assistance or to make military equipment available to King Hussein in the hope that he would then, in sheer desperation, decide to break ranks and agree to negotiate with Israel. In addition, the United States generally rebuffed the initial feelers put out by the UAR to restore diplomatic relations. The American government initiated efforts to restrict the sale of arms to nations in the Middle East at a time when Israel still held a substantial military lead over the whole Arab world in order to perpetuate Israel's military superiority over the Arabs and insure Israel's security even though this would mean continued insecurity for the Arabs. For example, according to the *New York Times* of June 11, 1967, whenever American officials referred to the necessity to "preserve a balance of power" between Israel and the Arabs, they "have always meant enough arms for Israel from all available sources to enable her to defend herself against all Arab challengers without the need for direct United States intervention in any war"; in short, the balance must be kept heavily in Israel's favor for this would be the only way to insure that American involvement would never be required. While these American policies pleased Israel and encouraged her to maintain her uncompromising stand, they embittered the Arabs and forced them to turn more and more to the Soviet Union for material help and political support.[70]

For a while after the June conflict, some American officials had apparently hoped that if Israel's forces remained in the conquered areas and the United States refused to aid any of the Arabs, within a short time, as the Arab masses became aware of the true dimensions of their military disaster and as the economic and political situation became increasingly desperate in Egypt and Jordan, pressures would build up for a settlement with Israel in order to bring about an Israeli withdrawal from vital Arab territories and a reopening of the Suez Canal. Undoubtedly, there was also the hope that the more extremist Arab leaders would be held responsible for the Arab calamity and would be overthrown and replaced by more moderate, pro-Western, and "realistic" Arabs. In anticipation of such developments, these officials concluded that time would work in favor of peace. But, as weeks and months passed, it became increasingly evident that these expectations would not materialize. In fact, between the Soviet economic, military, and political assistance on the one hand and the pro-Israeli policies of the United

States and the increasingly rigid stand assumed by Israel on the other, even the most militant Arab regimes were able to survive, the position of the pro-Western Arab moderates was weakened, and the path was cleared for the Soviet Union to extend her influence within the Arab world at the expense of the West. Then, too, despite the serious economic and political hardships involved, the Arabs refused to undergo what they considered further humiliation by submitting to a "dictated" peace with the hated enemy. Consequently, as the summer months went by, the United States grew more and more concerned about the extensive inroads Russia was making in the Arab world and about the hardening attitude of Israel and her expanding territorial ambitions. While leaving the initiative largely to the Arab governments, American officials, by the latter part of 1967, indicated a desire to restore normal relations with most Arab states, as well as a willingness to resume economic aid and the sale of military equipment to some of the more pro-Western Arab countries.

Even though the United States continued to back many Israeli views, at the same time, during the summer and fall of 1967, a few American officials began openly to criticize a number of Israeli policies and actions. For instance, these officials publicly as well as privately chided Israel for: (1) annexing the Old City of Jerusalem in defiance of UN resolutions and world public opinion; (2) setting up Jewish settlements in occupied Arab territories and giving other indications that she intended to retain large parts of these areas; (3) limiting the number of newly uprooted Arabs allowed to return to the west-bank sector; (4) resisting the idea of sending a UN mediator to the Middle East; and (5) insisting obdurately that she would accept nothing less than direct and open peace talks and would reject any quiet mediatory efforts by any third party—despite the fact that it was impossible even for the moderate Arab leaders to negotiate directly with Israel because popular emotions were still violently opposed to it. These officials also felt that not only did recent attitudes and actions of the Israelis conflict with their former position and with American views, but they also would not serve the cause of peace. They became greatly disturbed because time was no longer "working . . . on the side of a peaceful settlement," and they urged the UN Security Council to relieve the situation, not by passing meaningless resolutions but by providing a quiet forum for serious behind-the-scenes talks, for they were the only kind of negotiations in which the Arab leaders could dare to participate. At least some American officials began to realize that an Arab-Israeli peace could not be achieved by some dramatic conference which would settle all Arab-

Israeli differences in one stroke and that progress would have to be achieved, if at all, slowly and piecemeal through quiet diplomacy and third-party mediation and through pressures.[71]

Although the United States was the only nation that could apply effective pressures on Israel, powerful pro-Israeli lobbyists and internal political conditions (especially the fact that 1968 was a presidential election year) prevented their application. The American government actually agreed to supply Israel with economic aid and military equipment apparently without seriously trying to use them as levers to persuade her to moderate her policies towards the Arabs. Consequently, as long as Americans remained strongly pro-Israeli, influential groups sponsoring the Israeli cause remained very active, politicians in the Democratic and Republican parties felt the need to outbid each other for the important "Jewish vote," and official American rebukes remained only verbal in nature, Israel did not feel the need to alter her tough attitude and demands or to abide by UN resolutions; American ability to exert a moderating influence on the Arabs was impaired. Moreover, despite the better understanding on the part of some of her officials of the actual requirements of the complex Arab-Israeli situation, the United States appeared to be without a definite and constructive Middle East policy and to be either unable or unwilling to furnish the determined, farsighted, objective, and effective leadership which was so badly needed and which only she was in a position to provide.

The Soviet Union

Over the years, by exploiting American blunders, by giving substantial economic and military aid to key Arab states, by using her Security Council veto to support the Arabs, and by firmly opposing the Israeli-British-French invasion of Egypt in 1956, the Soviet Union was able to increase her influence in the Arab world despite the facts that nearly all Arab governments followed anti-Communist policies within their own domains and that no Arab leader wished to substitute Soviet domination for Western influence in his country. While the Russians did not want war, they fostered strife in the hope of undermining the Western position and facilitating their own penetration.

The Soviet Union had badly miscalculated the situation just before the June War. In fact, her strong support of the Arab cause, her direct or indirect encouragement to the militants, and her misleading intelligence reports concerning an alleged Israeli military build-up along the Syrian frontier were major factors which helped to lead to the June War and to set up the Arabs for their disastrous defeat; for a very brief period this even caused some Arab resentment to build up against the Russians.

Nevertheless, in the months following the June War, the Soviet Union, eschewing any pretense of neutrality, led the Communist, Muslim, and a number of Afro-Asian states in championing the Arab cause. For many years, Russia had wanted to play a major role in the strategically important Middle East. The disastrous Arab defeat, the pro-Israeli stand taken by most of the Western countries, the Arabs' desperate economic, military, and political situation, and the refusal of the United States to help most of them in any way gave the Soviet Union a unique opportunity to undermine the position of the West in the Arab world, to make the Arabs feel that she was their only powerful friend and supporter, and to attain that deep penetration into the area which she had always desired. Russia, therefore, pressed the UN to condemn Israel and to compel her to withdraw from occupied areas unconditionally. She provided the Arabs with large-scale economic aid and military equipment and sent her military and political officials and some naval vessels to the Arab states. In addition, taking advantage of the situation, she rapidly and greatly increased the size of her fleet in the Mediterranean Sea and strengthened her position in Yemen. There were occasions when the Soviet Union, trying to salvage something for the Arabs and herself at the UN, worked with the United States to draw up compromise proposals. But, as soon as the Arabs objected, the Russians hastily withdrew sponsorship of them. The Soviet Union had so clearly identified her own position and interests with those of the Arabs that an Arab surrender to Israeli demands would have seriously damaged the Soviet image and influence in the Middle East, as well as elsewhere, because it would have been interpreted as a sign of Russian weakness and unreliability.

Even though the Russians were content to allow Arab-Israeli friction to persist as a means for further weakening the Western position in the Middle East, at the same time they did not want to see another Arab-Israeli war occur; nor did they want an escalation which might bring about a military confrontation between the United States and themselves. Consequently, at least until early 1968, the Soviet leaders provided the Arabs with only enough arms to enable them to deter further Israeli efforts at expansion and to strengthen their bargaining position but not enough for them to consider an early renewal of hostilities. In fact, in the fall of 1967 Russia began to criticize the Arab extremists in Syria and Algeria, to warn the Arabs that they must be less militant and more realistic, and to throw increasing support behind the more moderate Arab governments. Even the traditionally pro-Western King of Jordan was offered Soviet economic and military aid. In short, while Russia did concede that the Arabs should ultimately accept Israel's right to exist, she placed her primary emphasis on vigorously supporting those Arab contentions with which she concurred. In the process of providing the Arabs with economic, military, and political help, she tended to encourage them, just as the United States tended to encourage Israel, to be more unyielding than they might otherwise have been.[72]

The Russians were able to exploit and aggravate anti-American and anti-Israeli emotions in the Arab world and thus extend their own influence. Whether the Soviet Union's propaganda and political gains would be permanent, however, would depend upon what the United States would do to restore her own position among the Arabs and how far Israel would go in initiating the reconciliation process.

Not wanting a general war but unwilling to witness the return of American influence, the Russians appear to welcome the continuation of enough strife and instability in the Middle East to destroy the chances of an Arab-Israeli reconciliation. Nevertheless, if they can be made to understand fully that this is a perilous policy and that as long as conflicts and tensions persist between Arabs and Israelis there will always be a danger of a world conflagration, then they might someday realize their need to thaw the Cold War, to become more objective in dealing with Arab-Israeli issues, to restore diplomatic relations with Israel, to support Arab and Israeli moderates, and to cooperate with other major powers in the UN in order to work for and then guarantee a just and mutually acceptable settlement.

France and Britain

At first, France followed what she considered to be a balanced position between the antagonists. While holding that every nation had "the right to live and see its security guaranteed," France continued to urge an Israeli evacuation of the occupied areas as an "obvious preliminary" to peacemaking and refused to recognize the acquisition of new territory by the use of force. France believed that while agreement among the big powers, the restoration of diplomatic relations between Russia and Israel and between the United States and Egypt, and UN assistance and involvement were all essential to the attainment of any Middle East settlement, there was no quick and easy way to break the deadlock. She warned that it would do more harm than good to push ahead too rapidly and too prematurely. However, by the latter part of 1967, France, seeing an unusually favorable opportunity to expand her influence in the Middle East, initiated major efforts to promote closer ties with the Arabs. In November and December, French oil companies concluded an agreement with Iraq which gave them the right to prospect for new oil fields. France offered economic assistance to Syria and indicated that she would resume the sale of arms to those Arab countries which had not been directly involved in the June conflict. Moreover, on November 27, President de Gaulle once again strongly criticized Israel for disregarding the advice he had given to her in late May and for being the first to start a military offensive. In addition, he stated that the Jews were "at all times an elite people, sure of themselves and domineering." These French actions and de Gaulle's statements brought about a major improvement in Arab-French relations. At the same time, however, they also caused a serious deterioration in Franco-Israeli relations and led to strong attacks on de Gaulle, who was accused of being anti-Semitic by Israel's friends in the United States and elsewhere in the West, as well as in France.[73]

Of the Western powers, Britain made the most serious attempt to maintain a balanced position between the Arabs and Israelis and to work constructively for peace in the Middle East. Britain agreed with the United States that the Arabs should recognize Israel's right to exist and to enjoy security and maritime rights, but, unlike the United States, she insisted that Israel must withdraw completely from all Arab lands occupied since June 4, including the Old City of Jerusalem, for territorial aggrandizement by conquest violated the UN Charter. Britain gave even greater emphasis than either France or the United States to the role of the UN in dealing with the crisis. In fact, she took the lead in urging that UN agencies in the Middle East be expanded and made more effective, in pressing for greater UN intervention, and in winning unanimous Security Council approval on November 22, 1967, for her compromise resolution, which provided for the dispatch of a UN representative to the Middle East to work towards a final Arab-Israeli settlement. Britain's success in obtaining widespread support for her proposal demonstrated how much more effective a government could be in promoting helpful measures on behalf of peace if it earnestly tried to maintain an impartial position between the contending sides. As she was anxious to reopen the Suez Canal and to restore full economic and diplomatic relations with all Arab nations, as well as to play a more active role in bringing about an Arab-Israeli settlement, Britain took the initiative in reestablishing contacts and normal diplomatic relations with the UAR.[74]

These views and actions of Britain and France prompted Israel to accuse them of being pro-Arab. Nonetheless, they enabled the West to restore some of its lost prestige and to exert a moderating influence in the Arab world and also allowed the Arabs to feel a little less dependent upon the Communist nations for understanding and support.

CONCLUSION

As of early 1968, mutual Arab-Israeli hate, fear, and distrust were as acute as ever. The intermittent shedding of blood caused by clashes along the cease-fire lines, raids by guerrillas, and armed reprisals by Israel, the existence of more than 1,500,000 bitter and restless Arab refugees dispossessed and dispersed by the Palestine and June Wars, and the continuing Israeli occupation of vast Arab territories containing one million discontented Arab inhabitants prevented any abatement in these hostile emotions. Still firmly convinced that by denying the Palestine Arabs their elementary "right" to national self-determination and by establishing an "alien" and "dangerous" state in their midst, the Zionists and the West committed a grave injustice against the Arab world, the Arab masses remained vehemently anti-Israel and unwilling to accept either their defeat or Israel's existence as final. Arab extremists, particularly among the Palestinians and Syrians, persisted in vociferously opposing any compromise settlement with Israel and in advocating an unrelenting struggle against her. Because of popular passions, internal instabilities, and pressures from the extremists, even the moderate Arabs did not dare go too far in yielding to Israeli demands. Most Israelis, on the other hand, continued to believe in the efficacy of force, the effectiveness of armed reprisals, and the concept of "preventive war" and to ignore the urgent need for developing more conciliatory policies and a deeper understanding of the Arabs and the bases for their grievances and especially for making every endeavor to narrow the harmful psychological gulf between the Israeli Jews and the Arabs, including those under Israeli control. Sharp personal and political rivalries among top leaders in Israel served to harden still further Israel's stand vis-à-vis the Arabs. Therefore, despite occasional periods of tranquility and UN efforts, the underlying situation remained potentially explosive.

As matters stand, three alternatives present themselves to the Arabs, the Israelis, the UN, and the powers concerned.

The *first* is to let events continue to run their course largely unimpeded. This will perpetuate and heighten hostilities and will lead inevitably to another violent military confrontation which could precipitate a world war.

The *second* is to press for direct negotiations and formal peace treaties in the immediate future. This would not only prove to be a futile effort in the face of two opposing parties who remain psychologically and politically unready for a meaningful compromise peace settlement, but a premature forcing of an acrimonious airing of Arab-Israeli antagonisms and differences would accentuate hatred and hostility and once again divert the world's attention and efforts from the issues which are at the heart of the whole problem. The almost inevitable failure of any such conference would produce severe recriminations between the antagonists and a dangerous disillusionment among those whose hopes for peace had been unduly raised. It would also heighten the conviction among both Arabs and Israelis that the only alternative left was war. Even if, somehow, one side were compelled to accept undesirable peace terms, this would not only result in a meaningless paper peace, but could precipitate the overthrow of moderate Arab regimes by extremist elements.

The *third* alternative is for all interested nations to make concerted efforts, especially through the UN and quiet diplomacy, to reduce the scope and intensity of Arab-Israeli differences through a step-by-step approach, with elapsing time used intelligently and constructively. Whenever possible, every effort must be made to arrive at partial solutions for the different Arab-Israeli disputes—and this can be accomplished without formal peace treaties—and to exploit every possible area of compatibility so as to narrow the scope of the over-all problem, to promote better understanding, and to develop a reasonably acceptable *modus vivendi*. Each advance would help reduce Arab-Israeli animosities and improve the general climate in the area, thus facilitating the next advance. Trying to force the pace of peace would not only be futile, but it could destroy whatever headway which might have been achieved and jeopardize further progress. This evolutionary process would be exasperatingly slow and would require great patience, perseverance, and the sincere and determined cooperation of the disputants as well as of the UN and the major powers. While there could be no guarantee of its success, it is the only realistic and potentially fruitful procedure which offers the slightest hope of slowly, if not imperceptibly, moving the opposing sides from a state of belligerence to a state of peace.

Perhaps the *first* prerequisite to this third alternative is that all parties concerned permit themselves to become better informed in an area now clouded with ignorance and confusion, intended and unintended. This would not be an easy task, for most people do not welcome knowledge and evidence which challenge their prejudices and expose their shortcomings and ulterior motives. The extreme nationalists, who have considerable influence in the areas of education and communications in practically all the countries of the world, would resist the dissemination of the objective truths because the revelation of those truths might prove embarrassing to their own states. Nevertheless, every effort should be made to provide government officials and their peoples, especially in the Middle East and the West, with more accurate, objective, and complete information about all facets of the Arab-Israeli question. Only then would these officials be able to face squarely and deal effectively and farsightedly with the deep-lying passions and grievances which have been responsible for Arab-Israeli differences and animosity.

The most important fact that must be clearly understood is that the Arab-Israeli problem is a complex and emotional one which cannot be dealt with simply and on a purely rational basis. The deep-seated feelings of the masses will not be easily or quickly dispelled no matter what measures the UN or the big powers or the Arab and Israeli leaders might take. Even well-intentioned proposals for ambitious water desalinization and other economic development projects, earnest appeals to reason, and a glowing depiction of all the material advantages the Arabs and Israelis could derive from peace and cooperation will not only prove to be futile, but they could further embitter the hypersensitive Arabs in particular. For many years the Arabs have resented all references to how backward they were, especially in comparison with the Israelis. Moreover, neither they nor the Israelis would surrender national pride and interests for any potential economic rewards, no matter how tempting they might be. No proud people of any other nation would either. In any event, as UN Secretary-General U Thant noted, there can be "no solution" in the Middle East "if the human factor is ignored. The problem will become susceptible of solution only if the interests of human beings are kept in mind." [75]

The *second* prerequisite lies within the framework of the United Nations. The UN must do more than pass resolutions and deal fitfully with the problem's superficial aspects. It must maintain sustained and active involvement for as long as necessary, reducing tensions, strengthening the UN presence in the area, intensifying its peace-making efforts during periods of relative calm when conditions and emotions are more conducive to mutual accommodation, removing root causes of differences, and determinedly, impartially, and urgently enforcing its charter's principles and its own resolutions—especially those relating to a just solution of the Arab refugee issue, prohibition of the use of force and acquisition of territory by military conquest, and the rights of all states to live in peace and to enjoy innocent maritime passage through international waterways. The UN must augment and strengthen its observer and peace-keeping machinery and expand its constructive non-political programs in scope and depth—for the Middle East in general as well as for the Arab refugees. This should include not only the operations of UNRWA, but the UN Technical Assistance Program, the World Health Organization (WHO), Food and Agricultural Organization (FAO), and the UN Educational, Scientific, and Cultural Organization (UNESCO) in close cooperation with the governments in the area and various other agencies, both public and private.

Everything possible should also be done to strengthen the UN as a whole, for the more powerful and respected it becomes, the less likelihood that either side would resort to force and the more likely that both parties would finally decide they had no alternative to resolving their disputes by peaceful means. In fact, there can never be dependable peace and security in the Middle East or anywhere else in the world until the destructive forces of fanatical nationalism and international anarchy have been overcome and the UN has acquired the will and the power to enforce its decisions.

The *third* prerequisite is the shift in United States government policy which might strengthen the UN along the lines discussed. No other country has been in a position to play as important a role as the United States in enforcing UN decisions and in bringing peace to the Middle East. To achieve such a peace, however, the United States must abandon her partisanship and many of her self-defeating policies, tear down the "paper curtain" which has seriously obstructed the free flow of objective information, and acquire a more complete and accurate understanding of all basic aspects of, and points of view on, the Arab-Israeli problem. Only by assuming a more enlightened, consistent, and objective position will the American government and people be able to regain the confidence and trust of all peoples in the Middle East, to exert effective and constructive influence on them, and to assist them in arranging a just and lasting peace. To provide a reliable basis for a permanent solution, she must press the contending parties to abide by the principles and decisions of the UN and to employ only peaceful means for resolving their differences. In order not to set a dangerous precedent which could have grave consequences for the future of the UN and the world, the possession and/or the use of force must not be allowed to become the determining factor in settling disputes between states.

In this connection, the United States could set a better example for other nations by making more determined efforts to find a peaceful solution to her conflict in Vietnam. American policies and military actions relating to Vietnam have tended to encourage other countries, including those in the Middle East, to resort to armed might, instead of to more pacific procedures, to attain national objectives. The use of military power to compel her enemies in Vietnam to negotiate a peaceful settlement fully satisfactory to her presents a difficulty in convincing the nations in the Middle East, particularly Israel, that it is not in their best interests to use war or other means of coercion as instruments of foreign policy. An end to the Vietnam War, too, would eliminate one of the most formidable obstacles to cooperation between Russia and the United States on the issue of Arab-Israeli peace.

The United States could also greatly advance the cause of peace in the Middle East by seeking, on the one hand, to ease her own tensions with the Arabs and to bolster the positions of the moderate Arab regimes and, on the other hand, by firmly impressing on Israel the absolute need for her to stop thinking of her future only in terms of force, to show greater flexibility, and to make generous concessions if she is ever to attain real peace and security. In addition, the United States, in conjunction with other major powers, could formally commit herself to guaranteeing the security of Israel and the Arab states—and this time on a completely equal basis—if and when a final peace settlement were reached. Such a guarantee might encourage both sides to make substantial concessions without the fear that they would be endangering their security. For such efforts to succeed, American officials must courageously educate the American public about the Arab-Israeli problem, stand up to any and all partisan internal political pressures, intelligently and effectively apply the pressures available to them, work through the UN as much as possible, and seek the cooperation of Russia and other major powers.

The *fourth* prerequisite to the step-by-step alternative is for the Soviet Union also to become better informed and more objective in her approach to the Arab-Israeli question. The Russians must also cooperate with the United States and the UN in thawing the Cold War in the Middle East and elsewhere, in enforcing UN decisions, and in applying firm and unrelenting pressures in order to reduce tensions in the Middle East and to make both antagonists seek peaceful solutions to their differences. They could also extend large-scale economic assistance and political and military guarantees to both sides to facilitate, first, the attainment and, then, the implementation of any fair and mutually acceptable peace settlement which might ultimately be worked out.

The *fifth* prerequisite is based upon certain favorable changes taking place within the Arab states and Israel which could facilitate the evolutionary process towards peace. In the Arab world, the achievement of greater economic, social, and political maturity and greater Arab unity would enhance Arab pride and self-confidence and diminish extreme Arab nationalism and hypersensitivity. These developments could, in some ways, make it easier for Arab leaders to soften their adamant and hostile posture against Israel and to deal more realistically and farsightedly with her. In conjunction with equally constructive Israeli efforts, Arab officials could then work gradually and quietly to relax their boycott, to prevent border incidents, and to seek compromise agreements in

limited fields in the hope that these measures would produce a conciliatory atmosphere and a base for further useful endeavors. Assuming the
initiative, even in the face of vociferous opposition, moderate leaders
must undertake the difficult but essential task of educating and condition-
ing their peoples to accepting Israel as an irrevocable, if painful, fact of
life and to accept any just and reasonable compromise settlement. Whatever the past wrongs done to them, the Arabs must realize that only
through peaceful means can justice be enduringly served and their
legitimate goals be rationally attained.

As for Israel, if steps could be taken to bring about an abatement in
the extreme Israeli nationalism, a reduction of the harmful effects of her
bitter internal personal and political rivalries on her relations with the
Arabs, and a deeper understanding of the Arab position, then Israeli
leaders could also be encouraged to adopt more flexible and constructive
policies. In particular, the Israelis must begin to realize that: (1) they
will not always be able to depend upon their superior military strength;
(2) Israel's long-term prospects for survival will depend not on power
alone, but on a change in her attitude of superiority and on a lasting
reconciliation with the Arabs; (3) the use of force not only violates the
UN Charter but usually complicates problems rather than solves them;
(4) radically different qualities and policies are needed for winning
peace than for winning war; and (5) the more generous the peace terms
and the more easily the Arabs could live with them, the less the Arabs
would feel the need to resort to force.

The *sixth* prerequisite is for both the Arabs and the Israelis to realize
that some mutual concessions must be made and risks taken in order to
open the way for some early progress towards resolving the most pressing issues in dispute if the situation is not to deteriorate, if both parties
are to avoid even more serious sacrifices and risks in the future, and if
real peace is ever to be attained.

Israel, therefore, must agree to withdraw from occupied lands in
accordance with UN principles and resolutions. As long as Israel retained
complete control of these areas, the Arabs would not and probably
could not make peace with her. Moreover, even friends of Israel have
warned that if Israel held on to these lands she would be reviving
nineteenth-century imperialism and undermining her own democratic
institutions. To facilitate a withdrawal, a revived and expanded UNEF
could, as was done after the Sinai War, take control over areas as they
are evacuated and maintain its presence between the contending sides.
The withdrawal itself could take place in stages to be matched by reciprocal Arab actions. Ultimately, demilitarized zones and UNEF units
could be established on both the Arab and Israeli sides of the eventual

borders. If there is to be any hope of maintaining such zones and UNEF's presence in the area for any considerable length of time, all parties involved should be dealt with on an equal basis. If such zones and UN troops were placed on only one side, there would build up, sooner or later, greater national resentment towards their continued existence than if they were established on the other side of the border as well. Besides, with UNEF on both sides, the situation could still be kept stable should one party later request its withdrawal, for UNEF would continue to function in the territory of the other nation. As long as UNEF is stationed in the area, neither the Arabs nor the Israelis could seriously contemplate attacking across the frontiers. If it becomes necessary to give added encouragement and even incentive to Israel to give up the conquered sectors, the UN and/or the big powers could guarantee that her safety would not be imperiled by her withdrawal. Israel's future safety and survival would be far better safeguarded by returning the captured lands and receiving, in return, not only a chance at peace, but UN forces and probably also formal assurances from some major powers to come to her rescue if and when she were threatened. The final boundaries could, of course, allow for some territorial changes as long as they were arranged by mutual consent.

Along with withdrawal from the occupied areas, Israel must co-operate with UN efforts for a just solution of the Palestine Arab refugee problem. This would have to be solved by a combination of repatriation, resettlement, and compensation—more or less in keeping with UN resolutions on the subject. Israel would naturally have to permit the repatriation of some refugees and contribute substantially to the compensation of the others. The Arab states would have to cooperate with the resettlement of the greater part of the refugees who would almost surely prefer to live under Arab jurisdiction. The UN and its member states could assist by providing funds for resettlement and by facilitating the migration of some refugees to countries outside of the Middle East. The elimination of the refugee problem would remove one of the most formidable obstacles to the normalization of Arab-Israeli relations and it would help bring stability to the area.

The Arabs, in turn, must terminate the state of belligerency with Israel, as well as give up any thought of trying to exterminate her. This could be accomplished by UN action and Arab acquiescence until the Arab leaders are in a position to make more formal arrangements with Israel. UN forces could be stationed along Arab-Israeli lines and the UN and the great powers could provide a guarantee for Israel's independence and territorial integrity until these arrangements could be concluded. In addition, the Arabs would have to accept the right of Israel to use the

Gulf of Aqaba and the Suez Canal. If necessary, UNEF units could be returned to the Strait of Tiran section. Complications over the Suez Canal would be minimized if Israel were to delay sending vessels under her own flag through it until emotions in the Arab world subsided and if she subsequently used it with a minimum of fanfare. Pressures by the UN and the big powers could make it easier for the Egyptian government to justify the lifting of restrictions on Israeli shipping.

Both the Arab and Israeli governments would also have to make every effort to discourage border clashes and guerrilla and reprisal activities. Since some incidents will be inevitable, they should be minimized as much as possible and they should not be made the cause for counteractions. All parties should cooperate fully with those UN agencies responsible for handling such matters. In fact, both Arabs and Israelis should welcome any increase in the size and the authority of any UN presence in the area—if they were truly interested in preventing strife.

Of course, there could be no assurance that either the Arabs and Israelis or the UN and the big powers would be willing to take the steps outlined above. In fact, to date there has been little or no indication that they were actually prepared to do so. Moreover, this evolutionary process would be frustratingly slow and uncertain of success. Nevertheless, if, before it is too late, all the parties concerned should seriously try to make the necessary efforts and concessions and take the risks involved, then there would be a chance that the emotional and political barriers to peace could be gradually dissipated and the general atmosphere in the Middle East could someday be sufficiently improved to enable the Arab and Israeli leaders to face and compose their differences intelligently and realistically.

There are those who are convinced that the Arabs and the Israelis can never attain real peace and friendship. Naturally, the present outlook is not promising, but a careful study of history reveals that there might be some cause for hope. For many centuries Arabs and Jews lived together in relative peace and harmony. It was the rise of extreme forms of Arab and Jewish nationalisms, mostly in the twentieth century, which precipitated the serious breach between the two Semitic peoples. Thus, their hostility is of fairly recent origin and not based upon some ancient animus. History has demonstrated that as various peoples in Western Europe became politically mature, the intensity of their nationalist feelings and their hostility towards their former foes greatly diminished. If such bitter, traditional rivals and adversaries as the British and French were finally able to temper their extreme nationalist emotions, to overcome their mutual animosity, and to develop relatively close and friendly ties, is it so completely inconceivable that the Arabs and the Israelis, despite their violent antagonism of today, might also undergo the same metamorphosis sometime in the future? If the pressing economic, political, and security needs in the modern world have compelled large, powerful countries and former enemies, such as France and Germany, to form a Common Market and to contemplate the possiblity of a political federation, is it not even more essential that the much smaller, weaker, and poorer states in the Middle East should someday seek to combine in a similar manner and for similar reasons?

The concept of some kind of an Arab-Israeli unity is not new. A few Israeli Arabs and Jews and at least one Israeli group (Semitic Action, founded in 1958) openly urged the Arabs and the Israelis to work towards a federal union.[76] At least until the June War, there were a few individuals, including government officials, in the Arab world who were convinced that war was not the wisest means for settling the Arab-Israeli question and who suggested that the best solution would be the forming of a regional federation which would include both Arabs and Jews.[77] Obviously, only a handful of Arabs and Israelis have so far accepted this view, and there is little chance that any Arab-Israeli integration could be achieved in the foreseeable future. However, if the adverse conditions and sentiments in the Middle East could someday be improved, what now appears to be only a hopeless dream could ultimately become a more realistic objective. Since recent history has revealed that radical transformations can take place among even the bitterest of enemies, a similar conversion in the Middle East at some later date is certainly not beyond the realm of possibility.

As a matter of fact, the ideal, long-term solution for the Arab-Israeli dilemma would be the establishment of a federal union of the Arab states and Israel, because peace treaties between sovereign states frequently leave many actual and potential problems and dangers. For example, since a peace settlement would not eliminate the unreliable balance of power system, it would leave each side constantly worried about its security. The Arabs would always be fearful of the effects of any large-scale immigration into Israel on her military power and of continued economic and political support for Israel from world Jewry and the West. The Israelis, in turn, would remain forever concerned about the superior manpower and resources of the Arab world and about every move which might bring about closer Arab unity and increase Arab military capabilities. Competition for arms and allies would never cease. Major obstacles to the uninhibited movement of persons and goods across national boundaries, to the full exploitation of the region's water and other resources, and to the general economic development of the area as a whole would continue to exist. The position of the Arabs in

Israel and the Jews in the Arab countries would remain precarious. The threat of incidents and even of war would persist. All parties would constantly be tempted to disregard those particular peace terms which hampered the attainment of their national ambitions. Only a federation could eliminate most, if not all, of the complications and hazards which would certainly follow in the wake of just another peace settlement; only a federation could insure lasting peace and security for both the Arabs and the Israelis.

In any event, so long as ignorance and misunderstanding persist, so long as passions are inflamed and two extreme nationalisms continue to be relentlessly pitted against each other, and so long as no determined and constructive efforts are made—especially through the UN and quiet diplomacy—to reduce gradually the scope and intensity of Arab-Israeli animosity, then not only a federation but peace itself in the Middle East will remain only a forlorn hope and dream.

CHAPTER X

After the June 1967 War, 1968–1976

While the imperatives and the imponderables in the Arab-Israeli dilemma have remained virtually intact since the first edition was completed in early March 1968, many important developments involving the Palestinians, as well as the Arabs and Israelis, have taken place; whereas many of these have added significantly to the complexities of the Arab-Israeli problem, some have provided new opportunities for dealing with it. Moreover, not only the United States and the USSR, but also many other nations have found their vital interests increasingly affected and endangered by the Arab-Israeli conflict and the failure to resolve it.

THE PALESTINIAN ISSUE FROM THE JUNE 1967 WAR TO THE OCTOBER 1973 WAR

Among the most decisive and far-reaching consequences of the June 1967 war were the spreading and intensifying of Palestinian nationalism; the establishment of new, militant, and ideologically oriented commando organizations; the rise of new, activist leadership within the Palestine Liberation Organization (PLO); and the emergence of the Palestine resistance movement as a major force in Arab politics and in the Arab-Israeli conflict. Over the years, common suffering and frustrations served to unite the Palestinians, while the rapid spread of mass education became an effective instrument for spreading and deepening nationalist consciousness among an ever-increasing number of them.

In fact, for many years after the 1948 Palestine War, the Arab-Israeli problem was considered by the UN, all the major powers, and even by Arab governments as one involving Israel and the neighboring Arab states. The Palestinians were looked upon merely as refugees and their plight as a humanitarian one. Moreover, prior to the 1967 hostilities most Palestinians were politically inert, and the enforcement of UN

356

resolutions which provided for their right to repatriation or resettlement with compensation would probably have reasonably satisfied them. Relatively few Palestinians—and only Syria among the Arab states—seriously supported such small activist Palestinian nationalist groups as al-Fatah.

After the 1967 war, the UN, the big powers, and Israel continued to consider the Arab-Israeli dispute to be between Israel and the Arab states; and, for some years, virtually all peace plans (such as Security Council Resolution 242) referred to the Palestinians only as refugees. Even such key Arab countries as Egypt, Jordan, and Lebanon, while beginning to pay some lip service to the Palestinian nationalist cause, were prepared to accept a final peace settlement based on Resolution 242. However, a number of Arab states—including progressive Iraq and Algeria, as well as conservative Saudi Arabia and Kuwait—joined Syria in opposing any solution, including Resolution 242, which did not take into adequate account Palestinian national rights. Thus, a serious disagreement developed among the Arabs themselves on the Palestine issue.

Until the 1967 war, most Palestinian nationalists had looked to President Nasser and the military power of the Arab world as the primary instruments for achieving the liberation of Palestine on their behalf. However, after the disastrous 1967 war, because the Palestinians had lost faith in Arab military power, because some Arab governments were seeking a settlement which disregarded Palestinian national aspirations, and because Israel was rapidly establishing Jewish settlements in many parts of the occupied territories, resistance leaders concluded that there was urgent need for the Palestinians to take the military initiative against Israel in order to keep alive anti-Israeli feelings among the Arab masses and force Arab governments to back the Palestinian cause, to disrupt Israel's economy and soften her for an eventual Arab military attack aimed at liberating all of Palestine, and to frustrate both Israel's efforts to consolidate her position in the conquered areas and also all efforts to press for a final peace settlement which provided for the continuation of the State of Israel and the return of the West Bank to Jordanian control. While these leaders continued to depend heavily on various Arab countries for essential military, economic, and political support and for bases for training and launching operations against Israel, they sought a greater degree of freedom to pursue their own goals as they deemed best.

After the resignation of the controversial Ahmad Shukairi on December 24, 1967, as chairman of the PLO, leadership of this important organization—which had been recognized by most Arab governments as the spokesman for the Palestinians—fell to younger and more activist and popular Palestinians such as Yasir Arafat. While the PLO soon became the umbrella organization for the various fedayeen groups which joined it, each group retained its own organization, leadership, and freedom of action. Serious differences developed among them over ideology and the methods to be used to achieve their generally agreed upon goal, namely, the dismantling of the "Zionist State of Israel" and its replacement with a secular, democratic state of Palestine in which all Palestine Arabs and Jews were to "live in peace and equality." Al-Fatah, which became the most important element in the PLO, and its leader, Arafat, who became the chairman of the PLO and the most popular and influential of all Palestinian leaders, eschewed political ideology and sought to avoid taking sides in the Arab cold war in order to win over and retain the backing of as many Palestinians and Arab governments as possible for the long, hard struggle against Israel. Most of the other resistance organizations—such as Saiqa, formed from the Syrian faction of the Baath Party and trained, equipped, and backed by Syria; the Popular Front for the Liberation of Palestine (PFLP) under Dr. George Habbash; the Popular Democratic Front for the Liberation of Palestine (PDFLP) under Naif Hawatamah; the Popular Front for the Liberation of Palestine, General Command, under Ahmad Jabril; and the pro-Iraqi Arab Liberation Front—were generally more militant and ideologically motivated. Some of them, such as the PFLP and the PDFLP, contended that Palestinian goals could be achieved only after revolutionary changes had been brought about within the Arab world.

Shortly after the 1967 war, the Palestinian commando organizations formed resistance groups within the occupied territories and launched a campaign of sabotage and guerrilla attacks on Israel both from within the West Bank and Gaza Strip areas and from neighboring Arab countries, especially Jordan. These highly publicized exploits in the face of the military impotence of the Arab states restored some of the damaged pride of the deeply humiliated Arabs and enhanced the prestige and self-confidence of the fedayeen. Nevertheless, official and popular Arab support for the resistance movement remained limited until the Israelis made a large-scale assault on the Karama refugee camp and commando base on March 21, 1968. The Palestinians, together with Jordanian troops, put up such a stiff fight and inflicted such unusually heavy casualties on the Israeli forces that the resistance movement was suddenly given a great boost; virtually overnight, there developed a substantial increase in the backing of Arab governments and the Arab and Palestinian masses. The movement now entered the mainstream of inter-Arab politics and became a major factor to be reckoned with in any attempt to resolve the Arab-Israeli question. Moreover, fedayeen activities against

Israel were intensified and received greater support from Arabs within the occupied territories.

The stepped-up guerrilla attacks provoked a great surge of anti-Arab and anti-Palestinian feeling in Israel and strengthened the position of the more militant and uncompromising Israeli factions. Israel branded the commandos as irresponsible terrorists whose avowed goal was the destruction of Israel and intensified her efforts to justify her refusal to agree to the ultimate establishment of a Palestinian state and to negotiate with the PLO and other "terrorist" organizations. Israel initiated reprisal, punitive, and "preventive" attacks on alleged fedayeen bases in neighboring Arab states. Israel also took tough and increasingly effective measures in the occupied areas—such as blowing up houses suspected of being used by commandos, detaining hundreds of suspected Palestinians, expelling potentially troublesome Palestinian leaders, moving some Palestinians from critical areas, strengthening border defenses, and restricting political activities—in order to destroy resistance movement cells, to discourage local Palestinian cooperation with guerrilla units, to prevent the formation of any serious, organized anti-Israeli political movements, and to limit fedayeen infiltrations.

Finding their attempts to mount successful guerrilla attacks on Israel increasingly frustrated, some of the more radical commando factions, such as the PFLP, began a campaign of plane hijackings, kidnappings, bombings, and shooting Israelis and their supporters in Europe and elsewhere in order to make the world more acutely aware of the plight and aspirations of the Palestinians and to hurt Israel's economy by discouraging tourism. Some of the more moderate Arabs and Palestinians strongly criticized plane hijackings and other terrorist activities aimed at civilians outside Israel and contended that they served to discredit the Arab and Palestinian causes. In fact, most states in the world condemned these terroristic operations and, by the middle 1970s, they were greatly reduced through international and regional efforts. Even the most militant Arab governments such as Iraq and Libya also started to discourage plane hijackings by refusing to allow such planes to land in their territories.

While Egypt and Syria were able to maintain effective control over commando groups within their territories, the power, influence, and ambitions of the fedayeen organizations in Jordan and Lebanon grew to such an extent that they became virtually a state within a state and they mounted raids against Israel almost at will. These developments led to bloody military confrontations between commando forces and the Jordanian army in September 1970 and again in July 1971 and ended with the complete expulsion of the PLO and various commando factions from Jordan. This left Lebanon as the primary base for the resistance movement's military, political, and propaganda operations. The new situation was to result in vastly accelerated Israeli reprisal, punitive, and preventive military assaults by air, land, and sea on those refugee camps and Lebanese villages which, according to Israel, contained terrorist bases; in virtual Israeli control over some border areas in southern Lebanon; and in increased Palestinian military and political involvement in the long-standing sectarian, economic, social, and ideological disputes within Lebanon, including the long, bloody civil war which began in April 1975.

Since by the early 1970s the resistance movement's position in parts of the Arab world and its ability to injure Israel by military action had been significantly weakened, some moderate Palestinian leaders decided to place more stress on political and public relations activities and less on the use of force and even to consider—despite the bitter opposition of the more militant Palestinians—adapting themselves, cautiously and quietly, to the growing trend in the Arab world toward a compromise political settlement with Israel.[1] By exploiting Israel's inflexible stand and by intensifying their political and propaganda efforts, the more moderate Arab and Palestinian leaders were able to generate more sympathy and political support for the Palestinian cause not only within the UN, the Third World, and the Communist bloc, but also within Western Europe and even, to a more limited extent, the United States.

Third World nations were the first to back the Palestinian cause. As early as September 1969, an Islamic summit conference supported the national rights of the Palestinians and admitted a PLO representative to its meetings. Starting in September 1970, conferences of nonaligned countries advocated respect for the inalienable rights of the Palestinians, and in 1973 these conferences began to recognize the PLO as the legitimate representative of the Palestinian people. Although prior to 1970 the USSR considered the PLO and various fedayeen groups as "adventurers" in the Middle East conflict, after Arafat began a series of visits to Moscow in 1970, Russia began to develop closer relations with the Palestinian resistance movement and to provide it with military and political assistance. Most Palestinian leaders welcomed this assistance even though Soviet officials also urged them to accept a compromise peace settlement which would require them to recognize the existence of a State of Israel within the pre-1967 boundaries. The more radical Palestinians preferred the Communist Chinese position which more fully supported their political goals.

As the number of Western Europeans recognizing the national rights of the Palestinians mounted, U.S. State Department spokesmen and

President Nixon began, in 1970 and 1971, to concede publicly that there could be no lasting peace in the Middle East without "addressing" the "legitimate . . . interests" of the Palestinian people.[2]

While the great preponderance of Israelis continued to back their government's refusal to recognize the Palestinians as a separate national community and to negotiate with them, an increasing number of Israelis began to hold, as Israeli historian Yohoshua Aireli stressed, "No Israeli-Arab peace can be based . . . on the refusal to recognize the right of the Palestinians to shape their own destiny." [3]

Especially significant progress on behalf of the Palestinians was made at the United Nations. In December 1969, the UN General Assembly not only reiterated the provisions of earlier resolutions dealing with the Arab refugees from the 1948 and 1967 wars, but also passed Resolution 2535B (XXIV) which mentioned, for the first time, the "inalienable rights of the people of Palestine." General Assembly resolutions passed in the fall of 1970 and in subsequent years recognized that the "people of Palestine are entitled to equal rights and self-determination" in accordance with the UN Charter and that "respect for the rights of the Palestinians is an indispensable element in the establishment of a just and lasting peace." Thus, by the outbreak of war in October 1973, the great majority of the countries of the world had begun to support the national "rights" of the Palestinians, as long as this was not inconsistent with the existence and security of the State of Israel within the pre-1967 borders. By this time also, many states had accepted the PLO as the legitimate representative of the Palestinian people.

Peace Efforts: 1968–October 1973

In early 1968, UN Special Representative Gunnar Jarring began discussions with Israeli, Egyptian, and Jordanian officials in an attempt to carry out his mandate to help "achieve a peaceful and accepted settlement in accordance with the provisions and principles" of Security Council Resolution 242. Jarring did not meet with with Syrian and Lebanese representatives because Syria had rejected Resolution 242, and Lebanon, while accepting the resolution, preferred not to be included in the negotiations since she had not participated in the 1967 war.

Jarring soon discovered it was impossible to make any headway because of the many differences that could not be reconciled. Israel still wanted to bypass the UN and to negotiate directly with the Arabs using her formidable bargaining position—based on her superior military power and her control over Egyptian, Syrian, and Jordanian territories—to compel the Arabs to make peace largely on her own terms. She claimed that Resolution 242 provided only a basis for direct Arab-Israeli negotiations and not a detailed blueprint for a final peace settlement and that it allowed her to retain some occupied areas for security purposes. Questioning the sincerity of Arab readiness for peace, Israel refused to withdraw from any conquered lands until the Arabs had agreed to formal, contractual peace treaties with her. Egypt and Jordan, in turn, contended that Resolution 242 set down specific guidelines for a peace settlement and required Jarring to implement them without any changes; both the UN Charter and Resolution 242, by stressing the inadmissibility of acquiring territories by force, required Israel to withdraw from all areas, including East Jerusalem, seized in 1967; and the Arabs would negotiate only through Jarring and would accept a formal agreement implementing Resolution 242 with the UN Security Council and not with Israel. There were signs, however, of some increasing realism and flexibility in the positions of Egypt and Jordan. For example, on July 3, 1968, the Egyptian Foreign Minister publicly stated that "we accept the realities and one of these is Israel." [4] By early 1969, Egypt and Jordan were willing to accept a phased Israeli withdrawal simultaneously with Arab implementation of other parts of Resolution 242; and Jordan was prepared to make some border modifications.[5]

Secretary of State Dean Rusk held private talks with the Egyptian and Israeli foreign ministers in November 1968 in an attempt to revive the Jarring mission. Rusk proposed the return of the Sinai to Egypt in return for a signed peace agreement which would end the state of belligerency and provide, among other things, for the permanent stationing of UN peacekeeping forces at Sharm al-Sheikh. However, he found the basic differences between the Egyptian and Israeli positions too great to bridge. Since the Johnson Administration was soon to come to an end, Rusk refrained from pressing his diplomatic efforts.

After assuming office in January 1969, President Nixon and Henry Kissinger, his chief foreign policy adviser, sought, consistent with their balance of power theories, to deal with the Middle East in the context of the worldwide rivalry between the United States and the USSR. Since their primary concerns were to prevent the escalation of Soviet influence in and possible superpower military confrontation over the Middle East, they considered it essential to improve American relations with the Arab world and to seek ways to defuse the Arab-Israeli conflict. At the same time, however, Nixon continued the Johnson Administration's policy of keeping Israel militarily stronger than the Arabs because he believed it would help bolster America's position in the Middle East vis-à-vis that of Russia and deter the Arabs from starting a war. As he was not prepared to take the initiative to promote a settlement and he wanted to limit Russian involvement in any negotiating process, Nixon preferred to work through the Jarring Mission.

In March 1969 Jarring submitted specific questions to the contending parties to ascertain if there had been any changes in their points of view since he had last contacted them. Since the replies indicated little change and Jarring was unable to make any headway, France, anxious to restore her influence in the Middle East, and Secretary General U Thant, aware that the UN was unable to act effectively without the cooperation and support of the major nations, then urged the big powers to become more directly and actively involved.

In April 1969, the Big Four (the United States, Russia, Britain, and France) began a series of meetings—which continued intermittently into 1971—in an attempt to bolster Jarring's hand by seeking agreement among the major powers on a general formula for a peace settlement and on ways to ensure Israel's security in the hope that Israel would then be encouraged to be more flexible on the territorial issue. At times, the United States and the USSR also held bilateral meetings, especially in an endeavor to promote an agreement between Egypt and Israel. Egypt and Jordan welcomed big power intervention in the hope that it would compel Israel to accept the principle of complete territorial withdrawal. Israel, however, firmly opposed any outside intervention, even by her closest friend and supporter, the United States.

Since both Jarring and the Big Four had failed to break the deadlock and since a dangerous war of attrition had been initiated by Egypt in order to inflict heavy manpower and economic losses on Israel and to convince Israel and the major powers that Egypt would not peacefully accept an indefinite Israeli occupation of the Sinai, the United States decided to take the initiative to deal with the deteriorating situation. In a speech on December 9, 1969, Secretary of State William Rogers, after asserting that American policy would be a "balanced one," outlined what the United States considered to be essential elements in any peace settlement. After reiterating those principles of Resolution 242 which dealt with the territorial integrity, independence, and security of all states in the Middle East and with freedom of navigation and the refugee problem, Rogers acknowledged the need for a "negotiated settlement" and stated that "any changes in the pre-existing lines should not reflect the weight of conquest and should be confined to insubstantial alterations required for mutual security" and that "we do not support expansionism." He rejected "unilateral actions by any party to decide the final status" of Jerusalem and indicated that, while it should be a "unified city" with free access for all faiths and nationalities, both Jordan and Israel should have roles "in the civic, economic, and religious life of the city." Rogers also called for a complete Israeli withdrawal from the Sinai in return for Egypt's acceptance of a final peace agreement. Moderate Arab leaders saw much of value in the Rogers Plan. Israel, however, so strongly objected to it that, although it remained for years official American policy, the United States refrained from openly and actively pressing it. On December 18 the United States submitted a proposal at a meeting of the Big Four which provided for an Israeli withdrawal from the entire West Bank, except for marginal territorial changes, and a just settlement of the Arab refugee problem in return for a Jordanian acceptance of a "state of peace." Israel quickly and firmly rejected this proposal as well.[6]

By January 1970, the war of attrition had turned so badly against Egypt that President Nasser sought and obtained Soviet pilots and missile crews to help defend Egypt from Israeli air attacks. Increasingly alarmed by the rapid expansion of the Soviet military position in Egypt, the United States built up Israeli armed power still further and proposed a plan which provided for a cease-fire, military standstill zones on both sides of the Suez Canal, and the revival of the moribund Jarring Mission. In August both sides accepted this plan and a cease-fire went into effect. However, Israel refused to participate in any further talks through Jarring until Egypt had halted the illegal movement of Russian-supplied ground-to-air missiles into the canal zone area and had restored the military conditions there to their original situation. Egypt, in turn charging Israel with violations of the standstill agreement, refused to comply with Israel's demand. In response to UN and American urgings and especially to American promises to provide her with more Phantom planes and other military equipment and with urgently needed loans, Israel finally decided in late December to resume the talks.

While the more militant Arabs remained as opposed as ever to any peace with Israel, by the end of 1970 several important developments enabled some key Arab governments to soften their positions still further. The crushing defeat of the Palestinian commandos at the hands of the Jordanian army in September 1970 made it possible for King Hussein to be more flexible. Israeli sources even claimed, despite Jordanian denials, that Hussein had met secretly with Israeli officials in November 1970 and in subsequent years in unsuccessful attempts to promote a peace settlement.[7] Anwar Sadat, who became president of Egypt following the death of Nasser on September 28, 1970, was more inclined and better able than Nasser to give priority, when dealing with the Arab-Israeli problem, to Egyptian interests as against those of the Arab world. A much more moderate and pragmatic leader, Hafez Assad, had assumed power in Syria in November 1970. Moreover, increasing numbers of Arabs in Egypt and other countries had become more psychologically prepared to accept the reality of Israel's existence and the imperatives for a political settlement with her.

However, Israel's official position had not softened. Distrustful of Arab intentions and convinced that time was on their side and they could maintain military superiority indefinitely, that Israel had more to gain than lose from prolonging the *status quo,* and that any attempt to seek a detailed Israeli peace program would cause the downfall of the delicately balanced government coalition which was deeply divided on territorial and other issues, Israeli officials refused, despite the urgings of some American officials and some Israelis, to take any serious peace initiative and decided to sit tight politically and to wait for the Arabs to become "realistic" to the point where they would make the first move. In fact, since for historical and/or security reasons some political leaders and considerable numbers of Israelis wanted to retain permanently all—or nearly all—of the occupied areas, they preferred maintaining the *status quo* indefinitely to seeking a peace settlement, for it would require Israel to relinquish a substantial part of these areas.[8] In the meantime, Israel continued to establish a rapidly growing number of new Jewish settlements in those areas which she intended to retain permanently as a minimum even in the event of a peace settlement. Settlements had already been set up or were planned to be set up throughout the Golan Heights and Gaza Strip areas, along the west bank of the Jordan River, around East Jerusalem and between Jerusalem and Hebron, along the Gulf of Aqaba to Sharm al-Sheikh, and in the northeastern part of the Sinai just below the Gaza Strip—with one settlement there ultimately intended to become the city of Yamit with a population of over 200,000. From the beginning Israel's settlement policy was to cause a deep division within Israel. Extreme nationalists and some religious groups backed it, and some of them even sought to establish unofficial settlements on their own. Not only did the Arabs, the UN, and even the United States criticize this policy, but Israeli doves strongly opposed it and warned that, by creating *fait accomplis* which their government might not be able to undo in the future, even if it wanted to, and by strengthening Arab belief that Israel was more interested in holding on to Arab territories than in achieving peace, it would produce serious obstacles to peace. These doves also contended that lasting peace and security for Israel would depend far more on attaining friendly relations with the Arabs and Palestinians than on mere military power and territorial expansion, and that it was up to Israel, the victor with undiminished pride, to take the initiative to begin the process of gradual reconciliation. Moreover, they have warned that continued control over the occupied areas and ultimate annexation of all or most of them with one million Arab inhabitants would sooner or later undermine Israel's position as both a Jewish and democratic state. The doves in Israel, however, were far too few in number to have any significant influence on Israeli policy.

In February 1971, with big power approval, Jarring tried a new tactic. In an *aide-memoire* to Israel, he asked her to commit herself to withdraw from all parts of the Sinai and to abide by UN resolutions dealing with the refugee problem with the understanding that satisfactory arrangements would be made for freedom of navigation for Israeli shipping and for Israeli security along the final Egyptian-Israeli borders and at Sharm al-Sheikh. In an identical *aide-memoire* to Egypt, he asked Egypt, in return for regaining the Sinai, to commit herself to making a peace "agreement with Israel," ending all states of belligerence and acts of hostility from her territory, and respecting Israel's independence and right to live in peace within secure and recognized borders. Egypt agreed to "enter into a peace agreement with Israel," specifically and formally referring to "Israel" for the first time, and to accept the other conditions. Egypt's favorable response earned for her considerable praise throughout the world, and some American officials and even a number of Israelis felt that Egypt had now agreed to make all of the basic concessions demanded by Resolution 242 for peace.[9]

Israel not only refused to make the requested commitments on the refugee and territorial issues even though the withdrawal commitment applied only to the Sinai, but she ignored American advice and insisted on stating bluntly in her reply that she would "not withdraw to the pre-June 5, 1967 lines." Israel's unyielding stand was criticized both at home and in many parts of the world, including Western Europe and the United States where Israel was being held increasingly responsible for the impasse in the peace efforts.[10]

Since Israel's negative reply had brought the Jarring Mission to a halt, American officials decided to take the initiative by trying a new step-by-step approach. Following a conditional offer by Sadat in April 1971 to reopen the Suez Canal, the United States began to press for an interim settlement in the canal area between Israel and Egypt in the hope that this would ultimately create a better climate for more general peace talks under Jarring. While Egypt insisted that an interim agreement must clearly state that it was only the first stage in an Israeli withdrawal from all occupied territories, Israel refused to make such a commitment. American officials continued for many months to press for an interim step and even proposed that Egypt and Israel hold "proximity talks" in New York City with American representatives acting as an intermediary. But differences between the Egyptians and Israelis remained too great to be overcome. For some months in 1971 the United States held up the sale of more planes to Israel in an attempt to pressure her into softening her stance. But this tactic did not work. With presidential and congressional elections approaching, and apparently unwilling to risk antagonizing pro-Israeli factions in congress (which, as a result of the greatly expanded Soviet military role in Egypt since early 1970, now included many conservative, anti-Communist members as well as the usual liberal ones) and among the American public, President Nixon agreed in January 1972 to sell Israel more Phantom and Skyhawk planes.

By the latter part of 1971, President Sadat was beginning to lose faith in the sincerity of American efforts at mediation and to warn that 1971 would be the "year of decision," implying that he would resort to war if necessary to regain his lost lands. Since he repeated similar warnings in 1972 and yet he did not act, many Americans, Israelis, and even Arabs concluded that he was only bluffing and that his threats should not be taken too seriously.

In the fall of 1971, the Organization of African Unity (OAU) sent four African heads of state to Egypt and Israel in an endeavor to break the deadlock. Egypt agreed to make peace with Israel and to abide by all parts of Resolution 242 as requested by the OAU delegation. Israel, however, refused to state formally and unequivocally, as was also requested, that she did not seek the annexation of Arab territory. Israel's refusal so embittered many African leaders, including those who had been her good friends, that her political position in Africa began to deteriorate rapidly, while that of the Arabs was significantly strengthened.

In early 1972, the new UN Secretary General, Kurt Waldheim, held numerous discussions with Arab and Israeli diplomats in New York and he traveled to the Middle East in the hope that he could bolster the Jarring mission by means of his own personal diplomacy. However, he too failed to break the stalemate. Similar attempts by him in subsequent years also proved to be fruitless.

In a speech in Damascus on March 8, 1972, President Assad stated publicly for the first time that Syria would accept Resolution 242 provided that Israel withdrew from all Arab lands occupied in 1967 and that the "rights" of the Palestinians were recognized as part of a final peace settlement.[11] As the *Christian Science Monitor* concluded on March 9, this statement "apparently" brought "Syria at least formally into line with the policy of Egypt." In July 1972, encouraged by King Faisal of Saudi Arabia, Sadat—who was already disappointed with Russia's failure to provide Egypt with the most advanced weapons and the strong political support he felt he needed, and now convinced that only the United States was able to help the Arabs regain their lost lands —suddenly expelled thousands of Russian military personnel in the hope that this drastic, risk-fraught move would convince the United States of his sincere desire for peace and for closer ties with the West and encourage the United States to start applying more effective pressures on Israel. While some American officials felt that the United States should take advantage of the unique opportunity provided by Sadat's action and Assad's more moderate stand to enhance America's position in the Arab world at Russia's expense, the Nixon Administration continued to provide Israel with substantial economic and military aid and to back Israel in the UN, where it used one of its rare vetoes on September 10 to kill a Security Council resolution censuring Israel for large-scale land and air attacks on Lebanon and Syria following a Palestinian commando attack on the Israeli Olympic team in Munich.

Disappointed in America's failure to respond favorably to Sadat's and Assad's moves, the Arabs turned to the UN General Assembly once again for support. In December 1972, the Arabs were able to win even wider backing than ever before for the passage of another strong resolution providing for a complete Israeli withdrawal and the rights of the Palestinians. Israel found herself increasingly isolated, with only the United States and a few smaller countries still generally, but not fully, supporting her position. Israel repeatedly accused the UN General Assembly of being biased against her and dominated by an Arab-Communist bloc. As long as she remained confident of substantial American military and economic backing and of the use of the American veto in the Security Council when needed, Israel felt that she could safely disregard General Assembly resolutions and Arab threats to resort to force if their occupied lands were not returned by peaceful means. For example, Jon Kimche, an Anglo-Zionist writer, noted that large-scale American aid "had strengthened Israel's armed forces to a point where they were the masters of the Middle East. . . . Why then . . . should Israel" make "concessions to Egypt or anyone else? . . . 'Why change,' became the slogan for 1972 and . . . 1973. Israel had everything she could want—except peace. . . . The Government therefore believed that the best thing they could do . . . was to go on making sympathetic noises for a peace settlement [and] to be generally accommodating without any commitments. . . . Crucial, however, in this Israeli calculation was the assumption of continuing American support, diplomatic, military and financial. The majority of the Cabinet believed that they could rely on this for some years to come in view of the . . . agreements concluded with the Nixon administration." [12]

Until early 1973, the moderate Arabs continued to hope that once the 1972 elections were held and American military involvement in Vietnam was terminated, the Nixon Administration would feel better able and thus more willing to initiate more effective means for implementing Resolution 242. But these hopes were soon dashed. Not only did Nixon refuse to give the assurances Sadat sought through the dispatch of a special envoy to Washington in February 1973, but during a visit by Prime Minister Meir in late February and early March, Nixon assured her of continued American support and agreed to sell forty-eight more Phantoms and Skyhawks. According to the *New York Times,* March 12, 1973, on her return to Israel Prime Minister Meir stated that there was "no basis" for a change in her Middle East policy; and there was no change.

Increasingly disillusioned by the United States, Sadat intensified his threats to resort to war if it became necessary and King Faisal began warning that he would deny friendly relations and oil to any Western nation that worked against Arab interests. Sadat decided to try one more political move. He called for Security Council discussion of the Middle East situation in the hope that it would lead to the passage in that influential body of a resolution which would include provisions on territorial withdrawals and Palestinian rights similar to those already contained in UN General Assembly resolutions. Such a resolution was jointly introduced by eight members of the Security Council, and, despite strong American and Israeli opposition, thirteen of the fifteen members (including Britain, France, Austria, and Australia) voted for it on July 26, 1973. China abstained because she felt that the resolution was too weak. The United States vetoed the resolution on the grounds that it was unbalanced and that it would have "undermined" Resolution 242, which was "the one and only agreed basis" on which a settlement in the Middle East could be constructed. This vote revealed that not only Israel but even the United States had become virtually isolated in the UN. Moreover, according to the *New York Times,* September 21, 1973, even Israeli officials were reporting that Israel's "image" had suffered throughout the world, "particularly in Western Europe" where there were signs of increased "impatience" and where she was being viewed "as truculent, unbending, unwilling to compromise." [13]

The Arabs were further aroused, this time against Russia as well as the United States, when, in a lengthy communiqué issued at the conclusion of talks between Nixon and Brezhnev in the latter part of June 1973, there was hardly any mention of the Middle East and no reference of any kind to Resolution 242. Fully convinced now that all paths to a peaceful return of occupied Arab lands had been blocked by Israeli intransigence and American and Soviet unwillingness to act, the leaders of Egypt, Syria, and Saudi Arabia concluded that they were left with no alternative to war.

THE OCTOBER 1973 WAR AND ITS AFTERMATH

Egypt and Syria, with the backing of Saudi Arabia, decided to initiate a limited war in the hope of breaking the political stalemate and getting a political process started by jarring the major powers and Israel into realizing that the Arabs would no longer accept the indefinite prolongation of Israeli occupation of Arab territories seized in 1967. They also hoped to unite the Arab world and regain some of the occupied areas in order to strengthen their bargaining position and to restore Arab pride and dignity.

Using the element of surprise, the greatly improved Egyptian and Syrian armies made significant advances in the early stages of the war. But once the superior Israeli military forces had been fully mobilized, they drove the Syrian army beyond the 1967 lines and crossed to the west bank of the Suez Canal where they threatened to cut off the Egyptian Second and Third Armies deployed on the east bank. By applying powerful pressures, the United States and the USSR were able to terminate the war before Israel could win a smashing victory and inflict on the Arabs another humiliating defeat in the belief that a military stalemate would provide a better psychological and political basis for peace negotiations after the war. The war, however, did not end before the superpowers had rushed vast amounts of military supplies to their respective clients and had come close to a military confrontation on October 25–26, 1973, when the Russians, responding to urgent appeals for help from Egypt, threatened to intervene to save the Egyptian Third Army from Israeli forces—which, despite two UN Security Council cease-fire orders, continued advancing in an attempt to destroy it— and when the United States called a worldwide alert as a warning to the Soviet Union. Angered by the massive American arms aid sent to Israel during the conflict, the Arabs applied an oil embargo against the United States and cut down on oil shipments to Western Europe. Because the Security Council quickly dispatched a UN emergency force to supervise the Egyptian-Israeli cease-fire and the United States applied determined pressures on Israel, major combat was ended and the dangerous tension between the superpowers was relieved.

UN Security Council Resolution 338, passed on October 22, called not only for a cease-fire but also for immediate negotiations between the parties in order to implement Security Council Resolution 242. In early November Secretary of State Henry Kissinger flew to the Middle East to establish a more stable cease-fire between Egypt and Israel and to pave the way for the negotiations called for in Resolution 338 through a conference to be convened in Geneva in December. As a result of his meetings with Arab leaders, Kissinger was able to develop relatively friendly relations with Kings Hussein and Faisal and President Assad and warm personal ties with President Sadat. Henceforth, Egypt was to become the keystone of American policy toward the Arab world and Kissinger was going to depend heavily on personal diplomacy in trying to deal with the Arab-Israeli problem and to improve America's position in the Middle East.

The October War, the Arab oil embargo, and the rapid rise in oil prices—which generated a sense of urgency and greater realism, at least for a time—had many important, far-reaching effects on the major parties directly and indirectly involved in it.

Because the Israelis had suffered heavy losses and had to retreat in the early phase of combat, the war produced a profound emotional and psychological shock to their feelings of complacency and security; more uncertainty about their future and less faith in their leaders; more questioning about such deeply accepted assumptions that the Arabs lacked the technical and innate abilities to pose a serious military threat and that, as long as Israel remained strong and held on to the strategic occupied areas, Israel could indefinitely maintain the *status quo;* greater respect for the Arabs and their capabilities; and the realization that Israel had suffered a major political and diplomatic defeat leaving her more dependent on the United States and more isolated in the world than ever before. Israeli doves warned that the October War had demonstrated that Israel could never have lasting peace and security until she was prepared to make those territorial and other concessions needed to provide a basis for reconciliation with the Arabs, including the Palestinians. They urged their government to assume a more flexible position and to take the initiative for peace. The Israeli hawks, however, continued to insist that the Arabs did not really want peace and understood only force. They claimed that the occupied areas helped save Israel from greater losses and dangers during the war. They rejected any significant concessions on the territorial and Palestinian issues and any outside intervention and mediation. They preferred retaining the *status quo* to any settlement requiring major concessions.

Despite the radical changes brought about by the war and the urgings of American officials and some Israelis even in her own government, Prime Minister Golda Meir reluctantly held fast to her earlier unyielding strategy,[14] which was, according to Terence Smith of the *New York Times,* July 13, 1975: "to hold on to every inch of occupied territory until the Arab states were ready to negotiate—on Israel's terms. Israel's aim was to demonstrate to the Arabs that they had no feasible military option; therefore, no real choice but to conclude a peace agreement. . . . The aim was to stand fast until the Arabs came around. . . . Parallel to this strategy, Israel had to beat back various [UN and U.S.] diplomatic initiatives that she felt would give the Arabs an escape hatch."

Mrs. Meir continued to state unequivocally that Israel would hold on to substantial parts of the occupied territories and would never recognize or negotiate with any Palestinian group, especially the PLO, or allow any Palestinian state to be set up between Israel and Jordan. She sought to fight off American pressures for more flexible policies and more urgent action and to delay negotiating on the overall Arab-Israeli problem. She did not trust the Arabs or big power and UN guarantees and she even had "deep doubts about the value of an American guarantee." [15] The December 31 elections resulted in significant losses for the ruling Labor Alignment and an eight-seat gain in the Knesset for the hawkish Likud, indicating increased popular support for the hardliners and, thereby, making it more difficult for the Israeli government to soften its stand.

When native-born Yitzhak Rabin became prime minister following Golda Meir's resignation in April 1974, there was hope that the new leader would adopt more flexible policies. However, even as late as July 13, 1975, Terence Smith, concluded: "Mr. Rabin's strategy today differs from his predecessor's only in nuances." He had not softened to any significant degree Israel's stands on the territorial and Palestinian issues and he was still trying to "buy" time, while avoiding a "break with the United States," in the hope that "in a few years . . . new energy sources may be developed and Arab economic and political power may decline. Then Israel would be in a better bargaining position."

The October War intensified Palestinian nationalism, not only among the Palestinians in the occupied areas but also among the Israeli Arabs, thus adding to the internal tensions and difficulties for Israel. Moreover, by the end of October 1973, twenty-six out of thirty-three African states had broken diplomatic relations with Israel and many Latin American nations were moving toward a neutral position. On November 5, 1973, even pro-Israel Holland and Denmark voted with all the other members of the Common Market for a resolution calling not only for Israel's right to exist in peace and security, but also for an Israeli withdrawal from all areas seized in 1967 and the recognition of the "legitimate rights" of the Palestinians. Japan took a similar position. This mounting Israeli isolation was due not only to the oil weapon but also to increasing impatience with Israeli inflexibility and a sharpened awareness that the Middle East was not the only area that would seriously suffer from a failure to resolve the conflict.

The 1973 war, like the one in 1967, further intensified and spread nationalist feelings among Jews throughout the world and caused a further increase in their emotional, financial, and political backing of Israel. Israel also benefited from the skill, financial resources, and/or dedication of many thousands of new immigrants from the West and Russia. More recently, however, the number of immigrants has sharply declined while the number of Jews leaving Israel has grown significantly.

As for the Arabs, the October War broke the "curtain of fear," restored Arab pride and self-confidence, and strengthened their bargaining position. The Arabs gained still greater political support at the UN and throughout the world. The UN General Assembly continued to pass by very large majorities resolutions calling on Israel to withdraw from all occupied lands, to cease illegal activities in the occupied area, to carry out earlier decisions relating to Jerusalem and the 1948 and 1967 Arab refugees, and to recognize the legitimate national rights of the Palestinians. On the other hand, the war had also demonstrated that Israel remained considerably more powerful than the Arabs and that the United States would do everything possible, including risk a conflict with Russia, to insure Israel's survival and security. Moreover, after years of wasting invaluable resources on wars and preparing for wars, Egypt, Syria, and Jordan were anxious to concentrate their efforts on badly needed economic development. Consequently, most Arabs and all major Arab governments except those of Iraq and Libya were better prepared psychologically and politically than ever before to accept the reality of Israel's existence and to negotiate a final peace settlement. In fact, an Arab summit meeting in November 1973—with only Iraq and Libya not represented—unanimously gave Egypt and Syria the green light to negotiate such a settlement.

The war and Egypt's respectable military performance revived and strengthened the credibility, prestige, and influence of President Sadat in the Arab world, and this enabled him to take the lead in pressing for peace negotiations. Since Sadat had been convinced that Kissinger and the Nixon Administration had finally adopted a new, more balanced attitude and were seriously trying to promote a fair peace, and since he had little faith in the USSR, Sadat—despite the obvious risks involved and the warnings of some Egyptians and other Arabs who were not yet as fully convinced as he was about America's reliability—decided to place almost complete faith in American willingness and determination to move

Israel to make all the concessions required for peace. Top American officials and even some Israelis became increasingly convinced of Sadat's sincere desire for peace and felt that this provided a favorable opportunity to promote a peace settlement. Sadat's views were warmly backed by King Faisal of Saudi Arabia, who had begun to play a leading role in the Arab world.

President Assad of Syria, whose position had also been enhanced by the war, formally accepted Security Council Resolution 242 when he accepted Security Council Resolution 338 calling for a cease-fire, thus indicating a willingness to accept the existence of Israel. Syria pressed not only for the return of all lands occupied in 1967, but also for Palestinian participation in any negotiating process. While Syria's relations with the United States were to improve, the Syrians remained distrustful of American efforts; and there were more militant Syrians who continued to oppose any compromise settlement with Israel.

The 1973 war intensified and spread Palestinian nationalism, substantially affected the resistance movement, and brought it increased outside support. After considering Israel's continued military superiority and her determination to maintain her existence, America's virtually complete commitment to Israel's security, and the obvious readiness of all the front-line Arab states, including Syria, to make peace with Israel, some of the more moderate Palestinian leaders began to conclude that their goal of a secular, democratic state of Palestine achieved by means of force was unrealistic. They feared that unless they scaled down their demands to more realistic levels the United States might succeed in bringing about a final settlement which would not provide in any way for Palestinian national aspirations and which would restore the West Bank to Jordan, thus preventing the Palestinians from ever attaining their own state even in part of Palestine. Moreover, not only Egypt, but also Syria and the USSR encouraged the Palestinians to reduce their demands and to participate in any forthcoming negotiations. Therefore, as *Le Monde* reported on November 6, 1973, "in the light" of a "detailed analysis of the regional and international situation," al-Fatah leaders "reached the conclusion that it is imperative, in the supreme interest of the Palestinian people, to accept a compromise" which would provide for the existence of a state of Israel. On February 19, 1974, the two largest and most moderate commando groups, al-Fatah and Saiqa, plus the PDFLP, approved a document calling for the establishment of a Palestinian state in any parts of the occupied areas evacuated by Israel. This trend was further strengthened by Egyptian and Syrian acceptance of disengagement agreements with Israel in January and May. In fact, on June 8, 1974, the PLO National Council voted overwhelmingly to authorize Arafat to attend a reconvened Geneva Conference provided that the national rights of the Palestinians were recognized as a major issue before the conference. However, as the *New York Times* reported on June 9, while moderate leaders "conceded privately" that the goal for a secular, democratic state was "no longer realistic," they could "not say so publicly" because of internal political considerations.[16]

Naturally, not all members of the more moderate commando groups went along with their leaders. Moreover, the more militant but also much smaller and less influential PFLP and Arab Liberation Front were so vehemently opposed to this trend toward compromise that they left the PLO Executive Committee in September 1974, forming what became known as the Rejection Front, and worked to undermine it. Some of those backing the new trend did so with the expectation that the Palestinians would have to accept a limited goal permanently. Others did so with at least the hope that it would be only a stage toward ultimately achieving their full original goal of a single, democratic state, either by evolutionary or revolutionary means.

Although Russia's position with Syria and the Palestinians remained firm after the war, her relations with Egypt deteriorated as Egypt moved rapidly closer to the United States. The USSR was unhappy with the leading role played by Kissinger in promoting a settlement. Nevertheless, Russian leaders, having been badly shaken by the closeness of the superpower confrontation during the war and still anxious to keep *détente* alive, realized that there was great need to resolve, or at least to stabilize, the Arab-Israeli dispute and that only the United States had sufficiently good relations with the opposing sides to mediate effectively. In any case, Kissinger's efforts were still aimed primarily at dealing with only peripheral matters and he publicly conceded that there could be no final overall settlement without Soviet involvement. Russia insisted that negotiations on the overall problem be held at Geneva, where she was a co-sponsor with the United States, and she continued to give substantial political and diplomatic support to the Arab and Palestinian causes. Although the USSR drastically cut down on her supply of advanced military equipment to Egypt as Egyptian-Soviet relations deteriorated after the war, Moscow helped to rebuild Syria's armed power to the point where it was significantly greater than before the war. Increasingly, Russia was to look to Syria and no longer to Egypt as the keystone of her own policy in the Middle East. Soviet-Israeli relations remained as bad as ever despite some quiet, direct, and indirect contacts made between Israel and Soviet diplomats in New York and elsewhere.

Until the October conflict, the United States believed that as long as she kept Israel militarily more powerful than the Arabs, the Arabs would not dare start a war and the United States could safely and indefinitely remain on the sidelines while occasionally prodding the parties until some day they would finally decide to negotiate their differences. The war destroyed American complacency and made the United States more aware of the fallacy of some of her major assumptions and of how vital an Arab-Israeli peace was to her best interests. The Nixon Administration concluded that the war had provided a unique but fleeting opportunity to promote a peace settlement and that the United States should exploit it. It was felt that the United States had to play a much more active, direct, and balanced role than before and to be prepared to apply greater pressures on the parties, especially Israel. Although the Geneva Conference called for by Resolution 338 met briefly on December 21–22, 1973, American officials believed that it would be unrealistic to seek an overall settlement in one initial effort. They therefore decided, with the approval of Israel, Egypt, and Saudi Arabia, to attempt a step-by-step approach and to proceed at a pace which the political realities in the area and in the United States would allow in the hope of gradually cutting down the size and scope of the Arab-Israeli problem and creating ultimately a more favorable atmosphere for a complete settlement.

Employing time-consuming shuttle diplomacy, as well as both pressures and economic and political incentives, Kissinger was able, notwithstanding the opposition of Arab and Israeli hawks, to arrange disengagements between Egypt and Israel on January 17, 1974, and Syria and Israel on May 29. These provided for Israeli forces to withdraw to positions some 15 to 20 miles east of the Suez Canal and to evacuate all new territories seized in Syria in October 1973 and a sliver of land captured on the Golan Heights in 1967, including the town of al Quneitra. Buffer zones manned by UN peacekeeping forces were established to keep the opposing parties apart. Both agreements stated that they were not to be regarded as a final peace settlement but only a first step toward one based on Resolutions 242 and 338. Syria and Egypt obtained the return of some of their lost lands and American promises of economic aid. Israel, in turn, was able to demobilize part of her army, to gain more time, and to receive renewed assurances of continued American economic, political, and military support. The United States obtained an end of the oil embargo, the renewal of diplomatic relations with Egypt and Syria, and greatly improved relations with much of the Arab world, especially Egypt.

Kissinger then sought to maintain the momentum and to bypass the controversial Palestinian issue by pressing for an Israeli-Jordanian disengagement accord for the West Bank. American, Israeli, and Jordanian officials contended that only Jordan should negotiate with Israel over the West Bank and that Palestinian interests would be protected through Jordan. On her part, Jordan indicated that once she regained the West Bank she would allow the Palestinians there to decide their own future. Since Israel was unwilling to consider more than token concessions, Kissinger's efforts to work out such an accord failed. After King Hussein joined other Arab leaders at a summit meeting in Rabat in late October 1974, in proclaiming the PLO to be the sole legitimate representative of the Palestinian people and the only Arab organization to negotiate for the West Bank, some Israeli as well as American officials expressed deep regret that Israel had not been more forthcoming with Hussein while there was still a chance to negotiate a West Bank settlement without any PLO involvement.

The positions of the PLO and Arafat were significantly enhanced politically and diplomatically when, despite bitter Israeli and American opposition, the UN General Assembly on October 14, 1974, invited the PLO to participate in the approaching deliberations on the Palestine question, on November 14 heard a statement by Arafat, and on November 23 gave UN observer status to the PLO. In 1975 several UN agencies also extended observer status to the PLO. These major gains strengthened the position and influence of the more moderate Palestinian leaders; encouraged them to place more emphasis on political and public relations and less on military activities; and gave them greater incentive to assume a more flexible stand. Nevertheless, they felt that they had to be cautious in their public statements and to leave the door open for retreat to a tougher stand if they were unable to achieve sufficient progress toward even their limited goals by political means. The PLO and Arafat became increasingly popular among Palestinians everywhere, including those in the occupied areas. The Rejection Front and other militant Palestinians, however, maintained their own hardline policies, sought to undermine the trend toward peace, and continued to press their terrorist activities.

While Prime Minister Rabin refused to soften his own views on the Palestinian and PLO issues, a number of leading Israelis—including officials such as Foreign Minister Yigal Allon and Information Minister Aharon Yariv, former Foreign Minister Abba Eban, Elie Eliacher, the Sephardi leader, and many others—warned him of the need to assume a more positive and flexible position.[17] An editorial in the liberal Israeli magazine *New Outlook,* July–August 1975, stated: "Peace without [the Palestinians] is impossible and peace with them may now be possible for the first time since before 1948. Growing sections within the PLO . . . openly advocate a peaceful solution to the conflict based on partition according to the 1967 borders. Pursuit of this path would be in Israel's best interest—these elements would be encouraged by an Israeli recognition of the Palestinians and a willingness to negotiate with them."

During 1974 there were a number of serious fedayeen raids on Israel, some of which had been deliberately initiated by the more militant commando groups in an attempt to frustrate efforts for peace. Israel, in turn, launched large-scale attacks on Lebanese territory, inflicting heavy casualties. These assaults raised tensions and emotions in the area and compounded the obstacles to peace.

During 1974 a new Palestinian resistance movement, known as the Palestinian National Front, came to the surface on the West Bank, and it was held responsible for many acts of sabotage and guerrilla actions. Israel arrested hundreds of suspects in an attempt to break up this organization and to halt its terroristic activities. For over a week following Arafat's appearance before the UN General Assembly, large numbers of Arabs held demonstrations in various parts of the West Bank, including East Jerusalem. These developments reflected growing nationalism, frustration, and opposition to continued Israeli rule. The Israeli government made inadequate efforts to deal constructively with the root causes of this rising unrest. Israel had improved the economic lot of the people and allowed a significant measure of local self-government with the help of the relatively conservative and traditional leaders who were generally prepared to cooperate with Israeli officials. But the Palestinians were given no political rights or voice beyond the local level and nothing was done to work toward providing them with what they wanted most of all —to be free of alien rule and to have their own national state. Not until late November 1975 did Israel seriously try to introduce limited home rule on the West Bank, and, as the *Jerusalem Post* noted on January 2, 1976, this move had come far too late and it failed to neutralize the PLO, for the PLO had by that time "established itself too firmly as the voice of the Palestinians to be defied either in Jordan or the West Bank." Moreover, many Israeli actions and policies—such as the expulsion of alleged troublemakers, the expropriation of Arab lands, administrative detentions, and the establishment of more and more new Jewish settlements—not only were being repeatedly condemned as illegal by the UN, the Human Rights Commission, the International Red Cross, and other international bodies, but were causing rising bitterness and hate for Israel and growing support for the PLO and various commando organizations both inside and outside of the occupied areas. In short, Israeli policies were creating both an explosive situation within the occupied territories and also still more serious obstacles to peace with the Arab world.

In March 1975, Kissinger made a major effort to achieve a second Egyptian-Israeli disengagement agreement. Israel insisted that she could not make another substantial withdrawal unless Egypt made a formal pledge of non-belligerency, while Egypt held that she could not be expected to virtually end the state of war except as part of a final peace settlement. Despite unusually stiff American pressures, Israel refused to soften her stand and Kissinger's mission failed. Sadat, nevertheless, continued to trust Kissinger and to seek further American mediation. To demonstrate his sincere desire for peace, he reopened the Suez Canal on June 5 and rebuilt the canal cities. Meanwhile, President Gerald Ford and Kissinger blamed Israel for the failure; and, in order to show their displeasure and to apply pressures on her, they ordered a reassessment of American policies in the Middle East and halted action, for the time being, on any new military assistance to Israel. These developments led to a chill in American-Israeli relations and to intensified efforts by Israel to mobilize her American supporters. On May 23, 1975, seventy-five senators sent a joint letter to Ford demanding continued strong economic, political, and military aid to israel. This letter weakened the Administration's leverage over Israel and encouraged Rabin to stand his ground with the expectation that he could ultimately get, as had repeatedly happened in the past, largely what he wanted without having to make distasteful concessions.[18]

Although by the spring of 1975 an increasing number of American officials urged the government to abandon step-by-step diplomacy and try for an overall peace settlement, the Ford Administration, considering such a move politically unfeasible, pressed once again for a second Egyptian-Israeli accord. Employing a combination of pressures and tempting incentives, Kissinger was able to arrange by September 1, 1975, a second Sinai agreement (Sinai II) which provided for: an Israeli withdrawal from the Abu Rudeis oil fields and from the length of the Mitla and Gidi passes; a new buffer zone controlled by a UN peacekeeping force; American monitoring of the new pact by aerial reconnaissance and the manning by some two hundred American technicians of three surveillance stations; the transit of the Suez Canal by non-military Israeli cargoes; and a mutual commitment to resolve the Arab-Israeli conflict only by peaceful means. No specific reference was made to the Golan and Palestinian issues.

Egypt was able to regain some land, to ensure greater protection for the Suez Canal, and to obtain American promises to provide economic aid and to make a serious effort to bring about another accord for the Golan Heights. While this second interim agreement and Sadat's trip to the United States in late October helped to promote even warmer Egyptian-American relations than ever, they brought about a major deterioration in Egypt's relations with Syria, Jordan, the PLO, and Russia and a decline in Sadat's influence in the

Arab world. Egypt was criticized for virtually removing herself from active confrontation with Israel, thereby depriving the other Arabs of the leverage needed to promote further Israeli withdrawals and the rights of the Palestinians. Sadat claimed that the United States had secretly promised him that she would not only work for another Syrian-Israeli agreement, but also prevent any Israeli attack on Syria and insure Palestinian participation in any Middle East settlement; and Egypt would go to Syria's aid in the event Syria was attacked by Israel.[19] Because many Arabs believed that the United States was now deliberately helping Israel stall for time to enable her to preserve the *status quo*,[20] faith in the United States and in the sincerity of her role as an objective mediator declined within the Arab world.

Israel accepted the new agreement because she did not want to antagonize the Ford Administration again; the United States offered such major, tempting economic, military, and political concessions (including billions of dollars in economic aid and the most advanced planes and weapons, as well as commitments to coordinate with Israel American political policies pertaining to the Arab-Israeli problem and not to recognize or negotiate with the PLO until it accepted Resolution 242 and recognized Israel's right to exist) that Israel felt that she could not afford to resist; and the agreement would neutralize Egypt, thus greatly weakening the Arab military threat, and would give her more time to strengthen her bargaining position to the point where the Arabs would finally be compelled to negotiate on "Israeli terms."[21]

Prime Minister Rabin frankly conceded that the agreement "gave Israel greater freedom of action in the political sphere," left Syria "in an inferior political and military position," and enabled Israel to "emerge from the agreement stronger militarily as well as politically."[22] Consequently, he felt better able to resist American pressure for greater concessions. In fact, he continued to take such a tough stand on the Palestinian and other major issues that, according to the *New York Times,* December 14, 1975, he was "now being criticized by the more moderate mainstream of the ruling Labor Party. These are the people who hoped Mr. Rabin would replace Mrs. Meir's negative absolutism with a flexible, conciliatory policy that might finally achieve a negotiated breakthrough with the Arabs. Instead, the moderates charged, Mr. Rabin has proven even more rigid and obdurate than his predecessor. Where Mrs. Meir said no, Mr. Rabin says never. If she chose to ignore the Palestinians, he goes a step further and pledges never to negotiate with them." The moderates also felt that his continued unyielding stand had caused a further deterioration in Israel's position in the international community and even in the United States, where increasing numbers of Americans, including warm friends of Israel in Congress such as Senators Charles Percy and Adlai Stevenson, were becoming impatient with Israel's negative attitude.[23]

On December 10, 1975, a group of prominent Israelis, who also were unhappy with their government's hardline position, formed the Israel Council for Peace between Israel and the Palestinians. The Council called on Israel to change her policy and accept a Palestinian state alongside Israel on the basis of mutual recognition. Contacts were made abroad between Council members and the PLO as the more moderate PLO leaders moved to consider coexistence with Israel and a dialogue with Israeli doves. But the doves then were relatively few in numbers and had little political influence; and PLO hardliners strongly opposed meetings with any Israelis who were Zionists.

By the latter part of 1975, the American government began to reveal a slight shift on the Palestinian issue. On November 12, 1975, Deputy Assistant Secretary of State Harold Saunders submitted to a congressional subcommittee a paper which conceded that "in many ways, the Palestinian dimension . . . is the heart of the conflict"; there will be no peace until "Palestinian interests" are "expressed in the final settlement"; some Palestinians were prepared to consider "coexistence between two separate Palestinian and Israeli states"; and the United States would maintain an open mind on the subject.[24] Moreover, the United States did not seriously try to stop invitations to the PLO to attend Security Council meetings in December 1975 and January 1976, and she urged Israel to drop her boycott and attend these meetings. American officials also indicated a willingness to consider PLO participation at a reconvened Geneva Conference if the PLO would first recognize Israel and terminate all terrorist activities.

Kissinger sought to promote another Syrian-Israeli interim accord in order to keep up the momentum and to alleviate a growing split in the Arab world which had heightened inter-Arab tensions and threatened to undermine the influence of Sadat and other Arab moderates. Since Israel refused to discuss anything more than "cosmetic" territorial changes on the Golan Heights and indicated that, even in a final settlement, she intended to retain most of the area, Syria concluded that she had little to gain through further American mediation.

In the fall of 1975 the UN General Assembly passed by overwhelming majorities resolutions which, among other things, called upon Israel to withdraw from "all territories" occupied in 1967; reaffirmed the national rights of the Palestinians and established a committee to recommend means for fulfilling these rights; resolved that the PLO should be invited to all UN forums dealing with the Middle East; asked the Security Council to implement all relevant resolutions on the Middle East; and called upon all states to refrain from providing Israel with economic and military aid as long as she remained in the occupied areas. The one resolution which passed by only a narrow margin and which generated very bitter responses from Israel, the

United States, and some Western European countries, classified Zionism as a "form of racism." In early December, the PLO, at the initiative of Egypt, participated for the first time in Security Council discussions when that body took up Lebanon's complaint against recent large-scale Israeli air raids.

During Security Council debates on the Middle East situation in January 1976, several nonaligned members, in cooperation with the Arabs, submitted a resolution which affirmed the "inalienable national right of self-determination" of the Palestinian people, including "the right to establish an independent state in Palestine," and called for the withdrawal of Israeli forces from "all the Arab territories occupied in 1967." To obtain broad support, the resolution also affirmed the "sovereignty, territorial integrity and political independence of all states in the area and their right to live in peace and security within secure and recognized boundaries." The key Arab states and some moderate Palestinians went along with this resolution even though, with this latter provision, it affirmed the existence of Israel. The United States found herself the only Security Council member who opposed any reference to Palestinian "rights." Fearful that Israel would refuse to go along with any further efforts to reach a peace settlement if the basic framework for negotiations set by Resolution 242 were seriously altered, the United States vetoed the resolution on January 26. Even the *New York Times* conceded on January 27 that the PLO representative had "struck a relatively moderate line" during the Security Council debates. After the American veto, however, many moderates were embittered and concluded that there was little hope of achieving anything meaningful through the United States and the Security Council. Some Arabs, therefore, began to call for the reconvening of the Geneva conference.

In January, 1976, Israel pressed the United States to try for a Jordanian-Israeli agreement, even though at the time there seemed to be extremely little chance for success. Negotiating a separate peace treaty with Israel would pose serious risks for King Hussein and would jeopardize the closer military and political relations which he had been developing with Syria. Moreover, the Rabin government had committed itself not to give up any part of the West Bank without first placing this matter before the voters; and there was vigorous opposition to any withdrawal from any part of the West Bank from some members of the government coalition and from powerful hawkish elements in the Knesset and the country.

In late January 1976, Rabin came to the United States to insure continued large-scale and long-term American economic, military, and political support of Israel. While he received most of the assurances he wanted—including an American agreement not to recognize the PLO and accept a Palestinian state[25]—he found significant differences between American and Israeli positions on key issues. As reported by the *New York Times* on January

29, "despite repeated pleas from President Ford and . . . Kissinger to adopt a flexible negotiating attitude, . . . Rabin offered no new initiative" and he "indicated no urgency about continuing negotiations." Washington urged him "to accept the American policy to offer to sit down with the PLO if it would acknowledge Israel's existence," but "Rabin showed no flexibility on this issue." There were serious differences on the territorial issue as well. Whereas Israel had repeatedly made it clear that she intended to retain major parts of the occupied areas, Israeli officials were "privately convinced that the [1969] Rogers Plan represents more-or-less official American policy"[26] and this plan called for only "insubstantial" territorial changes. Moreover, while the United States was anxious to avoid letting the peace efforts come to a grinding halt, *Newsweek* reported in its February 9 issue that a high Israeli official had stated: "The watchword here [Jerusalem] is motion without movement." President Ford admitted being angry because the Israelis kept "stalling" and "dragging their feet" and were so confident that their influence in Congress and among the American public was so strong that they could always put enough "domestic pressure" on him to avoid making "any concessions."[27]

On March 30, 1976, Israeli Arabs held a general strike in many towns to protest their government's expropriation of Arab-owned land, which was aimed in large part to promote Jewish settlements in the predominantly Arab Galilee in northern Israel. The strikes led to riots, causing six deaths, many injuries, and hundreds of arrests. According to the *New York Times* of March 31, the riots "reflected the growing political awareness among the Israeli Arabs and the cumulative discontent of a group that feels it has suffered political, economic, and social discrimination since 1948." Moreover, increasing numbers of Israeli Arabs were being influenced by the rising tide of Palestinian nationalism. Since in the past the Israeli Arabs had been relatively loyal and quiescent, these riots represented an ominous new element confronting Israel and caused many Israelis, including members of the cabinet, to call for an urgent review and reevaluation of Israel's policy toward her Arab minority and for effective remedial actions to facilitate the full economic, social, political, and psychological integration of these Arabs into Israeli life and politics.

Tensions also began to mount on the West Bank as the April 12 municipal elections there approached. Unrest and strife had developed as a result of Palestinian fear that Israel might extend her control over the Muslim holy places in Jerusalem, opposition to continued searches of homes and arrests without trials of suspected "troublemakers," heightened frustration as a result of nine years of Israeli rule, and growing militancy and support for the PLO among the younger Palestinians.

On March 22 the UN Security Council convened at the request of the Arabs to discuss Israel's policies in the West Bank, including East Jerusalem. In a statement before the Security Council on March 24, the American delegate, William Scranton, held that "the occupation of territories in the 1967 war has always been regarded by the world community to be an abnormal state of affairs"; certain Israeli practices—such as the deportation of Palestinians and the setting up of Israeli settlements on the West Bank— were "illegal"; the United States "does not recognize unilateral actions altering the status of Jerusalem"; and the presence of Israeli settlements in the occupied areas was an "obstacle" to peace.[28] Although these remarks represented well-known official American views of long standing, Israel nevertheless strongly and formally complained about them. The Arabs, in turn, welcomed them and hoped that they might presage a further shift in American policy. However, on March 25 the United States vetoed a resolution which received the favorable votes of all other members of the Security Council, including Britain, France, Italy, Sweden, and Japan. The resolution not only recognized the right of all states in the area, including Israel, to live in peace and security within secure and recognized borders, but also deplored Israel's actions changing the status of Jerusalem and called upon her to rescind these and to stop expropriating Arab lands and establishing settlements in occupied territories. While the veto headed off a crisis between Israel and the United States, Rabin nevertheless contended that the critical American statements before the Security Council were "damaging" to Israel and that Israel would not give up East Jerusalem and would continue her settlements policy despite American opposition.[29]

The April local elections in the occupied territories resulted in an overwhelming victory for nationalist and leftist candidates, most of whom were pro-PLO. The results not only presented a new challenge to the Israeli government, but gave great weight to the PLO claim that it had widespread support in the occupied areas. While many Israelis were shocked and perturbed by the election outcome, some of them urged their government to reassess its occupation policies and to negotiate the future of the West Bank more realistically and constructively with the new leadership. Many Israelis deplored the government's failure to make any serious effort over the years to develop broad, moderate Palestinian political organizations and leadership for the West Banik as a whole which could have provided Israel with a more pliant alternative to the PLO for negotiating the future of that area. Some dovish elements argued that it was now more imperative than ever for Israel to accept an independent Palestinian state on the West Bank with proper security arrangements in order to avoid an ultimate explosion there. Even the New York Times warned in an editorial on April 14: "The direction signs point ultimately to an end, not a tightening, of the military occupation, in the long-run interests of Israel as much as the Arabs west of the Jordan."

Although major disturbances on the West Bank ceased immediately after the elections, they flared up again a week later as a result of a two-day march through the area by 20,000 Jewish nationalists and activists of the Gush Emunim movement, who sought to dramatize their claim that Israel had the right to establish settlements everywhere on the West Bank and to retain all of it permanently. Arab riots, demonstrations, and strikes broke out again in many towns and villages, including East Jerusalem, as a protest against the march; and these led to bloody clashes between Israeli security forces and young Arabs. Some Israelis criticized their government for allowing the provocative march to take place and called for a reevaluation of the entire settlements policy. However, Prime Minister Rabin toured the settlements and, according to the *New York Times* of April 21, he told their inhabitants: "These settlements are here to stay for a long time. . . . We don't establish new villages only to pull them down later."

By the spring of 1976, President Ford had become increasingly preoccupied with the forthcoming presidential elections in which he faced tough challenges from Ronald Reagan in the Republican primaries and from Jimmy Carter in the final elections. Both of his opponents had taken a strongly pro-Israeli line in order to win over powerful pro-Israeli voters and financial supporters. Ford, therefore, not only made no attempt to take any new peace initiatives, but began to woo these same voters and financial supporters. For example, he vetoed a Security Council resolution on June 29, 1976, which reaffirmed the "inalienable rights of the Palestinians' and the creation of a Palestinian "entity" in the West Bank and Gaza Strip; and, in the late stages of the campaign, agreed to supply Israel with the modern weapons she was seeking.[30] He, as presidents before and after him, justified the large-scale arms aid to Israel on the grounds that it would make her feel more secure and, thus, more "willing to accept some risks in the search for peace." But he was also to admit that even though the United States had helped the Israelis become "stronger militarily than all their Arab neighbors combined, yet peace was no closer than it had ever been."[31] After his defeat in the elections, Ford was to take a tougher stand with Israel. On November 11, 1976, the United States joined in a UN Security Council consensus statement which expressed concern about Israeli policies in the occupied territories and called upon her to ensure the safety, welfare, and security of the inhabitants as required by the Fourth Geneva Convention of 1949 and to facilitate the return of the refugees from the 1967 war.[32]

As for Kissinger, his peace efforts had largely run down after Sinai II. He saw no hope of achieving further steps whether on the Syrian or Jordanian fronts. While he knew that at some point the Palestinian issue had to be confronted, he geared much of his diplomacy to circumvent and delay dealing with it. He was reluctant to try for an overall settlement not only because he would have to involve the Palestinians, as well as the Russians, in the peace process, but also because he was convinced that it would fail—and Kissinger hated to fail.[33] According to a leading Israeli newspaper, *Davar* (November 12, 1976), Kissinger accepted Israel's views on the PLO; he, "like Israel, did not believe in the possibility of peace"; and he sought to defend the *status quo,* which favored Israel, while any overall settlement would require many more concessions than Israel was prepared to make. According to another leading Israeli newspaper, *Haaretz* (November 5, 1976), "Israel's reasons for preferring interim settlements are based on the assumption, that has become firmly established among us in recent years, that America is not particularly interested—any more than Israel is—in the establishment of full peace between us and the Arab countries."[34]

THE LEBANESE CIVIL WAR, 1975–1976

American peace efforts in 1976 were also sidetracked by the intensification of the Lebanese civil war and increased Syrian and Israeli involvement in it. The failure of the Kissinger step-by-step approach to involve the Palestinians and to bring about an overall peace settlement left the Palestinian issue unresolved. This heightened the hostility between right-wing Lebanese Maronites (most of whom were supporters of either the Phalangist Party or ex-president Camille Chamoun), who wanted to rid Lebanon of the Palestinians and their mostly Muslim Lebanese supporters. The Palestinians, however, felt that Lebanon constituted their last effective base of operations which must be retained at all costs and that the Maronite-controlled army and the Phalangist militia were out to destroy them and their movement in Lebanon. These factors—together with other important internal social, economic, ideological, and psychological forces—helped to ignite the civil war in April 1975 which pitted rightist Christians against Lebanese Muslims and Druze supported by the Palestinians.[35]

For years many Maronites had sympathized with the Israelis, who were considered to be, like themselves, a product of the West and a threatened minority in a Muslim-dominated Middle East. For years, too, Israeli leaders had sought to cultivate closer ties with the Maronites.[36] Thus, during the civil war these right-wing Christians sought and received from Israel extensive military aid—such as arms, training, and, at times, even direct artillery and other military support in South Lebanon. The Maronites hoped that Israel would help them not only drive out the Palestinians but also retain their long-standing domination over Lebanon. The Israelis helped in order to exploit anti-Palestinian feelings and to emasculate the Palestinian resistance movement and remove it as an active element in any future Arab-Israeli peace negotiations; to further divide and distract the Arab world so as to lessen any Arab political and military threat; and to delay any American efforts to reconvene the Geneva Conference and gain more time to strengthen her own bargaining position vis-à-vis the Arabs before agreeing to enter any serious peace talks.[37]

When fighting in Lebanon intensified following the failure of reconciliation efforts by Syria in April 1976, and when it appeared that one side (Muslim-Palestinian) might defeat the right-wing forces, Syria intervened militarily. She feared that any attempted domination by one faction would only perpetuate instability and strife and could bring about the partition of Lebanon on sectarian lines—and such developments might have adverse repercussions in a religiously divided Syria, increase chances for an Israeli intervention, and weaken her own influence in a neighboring country which had uniquely deep historical ties with Syria and which provided a strategic buffer vis-à-vis Israel. Syrian intervention had American support because the United States hoped Syria could help the pro-Western Christians and end the brutal civil war. Even Israel acquiesced in the intervention to save her Christian allies, inflict severe damage on the Palestinian commando groups, and split Syria's military forces and divert some of them from the Golan Heights.[38]

Through American mediation, Syria and Israel reached a tacit understanding in which Israel accepted Syrian military presence in parts of Lebanon as long as Syria accepted Israel's security interests in south Lebanon; did not send her forces south of a "red line," which ran from below Sidon eastward to the Syrian border; and did not bring into Lebanon surface-to-air missiles.[39]

In October, Saudi Arabia intervened and helped to bring about an end to the civil war and to create an Arab peacekeeping force—consisting mainly of Syrian troops with token units from several other Arab states—to restore some element of law and order to Lebanon.

The Lebanese civil war (1) weakened the military and political bargaining positions of the Arabs and Palestinians, thus increasing the willingness of some of them to take a more flexible negotiating position vis-à-vis Israel; (2) brought a temporary halt to United States peace efforts at a time when the more moderate Labor Alignment was still in power in Israel; (3) caused the Arab-Israeli and Lebanese problems to become much more interrelated than ever before and caused Lebanon, which had previously sought to remain as neutral as possible in the Arab-Israeli conflict, to become ever more involved in it; (4) made it increasingly more obvious that a solution to the Lebanese problem could not be wholly achieved without a corresponding solution to the Palestinian issue, thus making Lebanon's stake in an overall Middle East peace settlement greater than ever; (5) exacerbated relations between the contending parties in Lebanon and left Lebanon more fragile, unstable, and subject to the danger of renewed civil strife and armed conflict than ever; (6) resulted in Syria and Israel being more deeply involved militarily and politically in Lebanon, thereby heightening the danger that the situation in Lebanon could trigger another Arab-Israeli war; and (7) added major complications in the way of resolving the Arab-Israeli conflict.

Having suffered severe military setbacks and casualties in Lebanon, moderate PLO leaders felt the urgent need to be more flexible and to go along with any reasonable peace process if they were to have any realistic opportunity to attain even part of their objective.[40]

During the civil war, the United States had indirect contacts with the PLO to elicit its help in providing security protection for hundreds of American and other Western nationals as they were evacuated by ship during heavy fighting in Beirut in June and July 1976. In addition, the PLO began to provide regular security protection for the United States embassy and American diplomats in Beirut.[41]

While there was a great decrease in incidents along the Israeli-Lebanese border itself during the civil war, many occurred on other fronts. There was an unsuccessful attempt by several guerrillas in May to infiltrate from Jordan; there were two plane hijackings in June and September 1976; and there were some bombings and rocket attacks from within Israel which caused casualties. In the occupied territories there were many demonstrations, strikes, and clashes with Israeli police and troops in protests over continued Israeli rule and settlements activities; over differences concerning the respective rights of Muslims and Jews to pray in the mosque built above the Tombs of the Patriarchs in Hebron; and over attempts by some Israeli religious extremists to ignore the law which forbade them to enter and pray on the Muslim Holy Place, the Temple Mount, in East Jerusalem.

Israel used tough police and military measures to quell demonstrations, causing deaths and injuries among the demonstrators; continued to build new settlements in the occupied areas; and employed the use of severe curfews. These actions aggravated the tensions and unrest thus precipitating more demonstrations, strikes, and clashes with increasingly harsh responses from the Israelis—in short, creating a series of vicious cycles. The UN General Assembly and Human Rights Commission criticized these Israeli policies and actions; and, with United States support, the UN Security Council on November 11, 1976, unanimously deplored Israel's settlements activities and once again declared invalid Israel's absorption of East Jerusalem.[42]

In the fall of 1976, a number of Arab and other states—including Egypt, which had concluded that the step-by-step process had finally reached a dead end—began to press for reconvening the Geneva conference to revive efforts to promote a comprehensive Middle East peace settlement. The Soviet Union supported this move, partly to help restore her waning influence in the area. She proposed the following guidelines for the conference: (1) a total Israeli withdrawal to the pre-1967 lines; (2) a Palestinian state; (3) acknowledgment of the right of all states in the area, including Israel, to live in peace and security; (4) PLO participation in the conference; and (5) Big Power guarantees of a settlement. On December 9, 1976, the UN General Assembly passed by an overwhelming majority a resolution calling for the reconvening of the Geneva Conference by March 1, 1977. The 122 votes cast in favor included nearly all of the Western powers. Only the United States and Israel voted against it, while 8 members abstained. In an earlier resolution, the General Assembly also called for, among other things, a Palestinian state, Israeli withdrawal to the 1967 lines, and PLO participation in any conference.[43]

CHAPTER XI

The Carter Administration, Israel, the Arabs, and Palestinians, 1977–1980

JANUARY–MAY 1977

When the Carter Administration took over in January 1977, it gave high priority to dealing with the Middle East situation. Greatly influenced by a 1975 report *(Towards Peace in the Middle East)* by a Brookings Middle East Study Group (which was composed of a number of leading American Jews, American experts on the Middle East—including the author—and noted American scholars, several of whom became top-level advisors of President Jimmy Carter), administration leaders concluded that the step-by-step approach had exhausted its potential, leaving key elements of the Arab-Israeli problem unresolved. Unless these elements were soon addressed, rising tensions in the area would generate more violence and thereby undermine not only vital United States influence and interests in the area but also, ultimately, Israeli security; enable the Soviet Union to exploit the situation to her advantage; and trigger another Arab-Israeli war which could bring about a superpower confrontation. Thus, they felt, it was in America's best national interests that the administration take the initiative to seek a comprehensive settlement through a reconvened Geneva Conference and to act as quickly as possible since a president enjoyed more leverage in dealing with critical issues in his first year in office than in subsequent ones. It was agreed that the United States must serve as a fair and objective mediator (even if this led to strains with Israel and created domestic political risks) and seek as much agreement as possible between the parties to the conflict on the basic principles of a final settlement before going to Geneva. Moreover, it was clear that Israel and the Arabs could not reach such an agreement on their own without strong encouragement and inducements from the United States.[1]

Since the Soviet Union had vital interests in the Middle East; had the capacity either to obstruct or help promote a settlement through her influence over key parties to the conflict; had already sent signals indicating her desire to cooperate with the United States in bringing about a peace settlement through a Geneva conference; and, in any case, would be co-chairman of any reconvened conference, it was considered essential to involve the Soviet Union at some stage in the negotiating process and in the arrangements and guarantees which any successful settlement would require. However, until the Geneva conference the Soviet Union would not be actively involved in the peace process, but merely kept informed about developments during United States negotiations with the parties directly involved in the conflict.[2]

In line with the Brookings report, the administration also agreed that a fair and enduring settlement should be based upon an agreed trade-off between Israel's requirements of peace and security and Arab requirements of return of territories occupied in 1967 and of the right of national self-determination for the Palestinians. This would require: (1) an Israeli withdrawal to the 1967 lines with only minor border adjustments; (2) a peace treaty which would not only end the state of war but also provide for full normalization—diplomatically, economically, and culturally; (3) various security arrangements and guarantees; (4) a solution of the Palestinian national rights problem by establishing either an independent state if it accepted all the obligations and commitments of the peace settlement or—the solution actually preferred by Administration leaders—a voluntary federation between Jordan and a Palestinian entity; (5) the participation in the negotiations of credible Palestinians—including the PLO if it was prepared to accept Resolution 242 and Israel's right to exist; and (6) some reasonable solution to the Jerusalem problem which would provide for at least unimpeded access to the holy places and free circulation throughout the city for all.[3]

In the initial phase, United States diplomacy in early 1977 involved high level consultations to ascertain the views of Arab and Israeli leaders and then to try to narrow the differences between them in order to get as much prior agreement as possible on a comprehensive framework of principles that would serve as a guide to ensuing negotiations at a Geneva conference to be reconvened in September 1977. President Carter not only played an active role in diplomatic talks and committed his prestige and influence to the peace process, but he also began deliberately to reveal through public comments the broad outlines of what the United States considered fair principles for an overall settlement in an attempt to educate the American public and Congress and gain their support. He especially stressed the need for an Israeli withdrawal to pre-1967 lines with only minor border changes, full peace and normalization, and a Palestinian ''homeland.''[4]

The administration found all Arab leaders, including Syrian President Hafez Assad, receptive to active American mediation and to working out principles for an overall settlement before going to Geneva.[5] The Arabs opposed negotiating directly and individually with Israel because she had the stronger bargaining power which she would use to avoid the Palestinian issue and the withdrawal provisions of Resolution 242 as interpreted by the rest of the world, including the United States. They preferred negotiating at a conference where the support of the superpowers and UN resolutions for virtually complete withdrawal and for Palestinian rights would help counterbalance their own weak bargaining position. The Arabs were generally united on the principles of any final settlement and the need for PLO representation at Geneva. They opposed immediate normalization of relations with Israel following a peace treaty because that was not required by or even mentioned in Resolution 242 and because, in any case, existing hatred and mistrust would require normalization to come about only gradually over a period of time. Nevertheless, according to President Carter and Secretary of State Cyrus Vance, no Arab leader "rejected the idea of ultimate normalization out of hand"; and Arab leaders were prepared to sign peace treaties with Israel as part of an overall settlement.[6]

While the Arabs were united on principles for a final settlement, they were divided on procedural matters, reflecting largely mutual suspicion and distrust. Egypt, as well as Israel, preferred that separate Arab delegations attend Geneva and that the committees to be set up there be organized on a geographical basis (Egypt-Israel, Jordan-Israel, etc.) to deal with each territorial issue separately. Jordan and Syria, however, wanted a single pan-Arab delegation to go to Geneva and the committees there to be set up on functional lines (territories, security arrangements, refugees, etc.) because they felt that they needed a combined Arab delegation to strengthen their weak bargaining position vis-à-vis Israel and they could thereby be better able to prevent another separate Egyptian deal as in Sinai II in 1975 at the expense of Syria and the Palestinians.[7]

While Carter got along well with all Arab leaders on both personal and substantive levels, he, like President Ford before him, found Prime Minister Rabin, who visited the United States in March 1977, "cold," "rigid," and difficult to deal with.[8] As Rabin himself admitted in his memoirs, Israel did not want a reconvened Geneva conference and he tried to "lay the matter of Geneva to rest" because at such a conference Israel would be faced by a united Arab delegation with Palestinian participation of some kind and by the presence of both superpowers and their pressures on her to make far greater territorial and political concessions than she was prepared to make even in return for peace treaties with the Arabs.[9] Israel preferred direct negotiations with each Arab state separately because only in this way could she hope to circumvent the extensive withdrawal requirement of Resolution 242, ignore the Palestinian issue, and make maximum use of her superior bargaining position either to obtain peace agreements largely on her own terms or to maintain an acceptable status quo. Israel had especially hoped to be able to make a separate peace with Egypt and by that means to split the Arabs and strengthen still further Israel's bargaining power in dealing with the remainder of the territorial and Palestinian issues.[10] After Rabin's visit, administration officials were convinced that he had shown a "lack of interest in pursuing negotiations for peace" and he was "stonewalling" and "playing for time."[11]

Israel's official positions at this time were basically (1) direct negotiations were the only realistic way to peace; (2) Israel must retain substantial portions of the occupied territories on all fronts for "security" reasons because Israel trusted neither the Arabs nor the world community in so far as her security was concerned; (3) the question of Jerusalem was "not negotiable"; (4) Israel would never accept a Palestinian state as it could threaten Israel's security; (5) Israel would never negotiate with the PLO—a "terrorist organization"—even if the PLO altered its charter and agreed to accept 242 and Israel's right to exist; and (6) Israel insisted on full and immediate normalization of relations following any peace agreement on the grounds that this was the only way the Arabs could prove that they really wanted peace.[13] The Labor government, but not the Likud opposition, was willing to give up heavily populated areas in the West Bank in return for a full peace primarily because most Labor party leaders believed that the permanent retention of these areas with about 800,000 Palestinians would change the Jewish character of Israel; either undermine Israel's democracy if the inhabitants of the annexed areas were not given full rights, or turn Israel into a colonial power if such rights were denied; and threaten Israel's security from within because of the existence of a large, hostile population in her midst.

On June 29, 1977, leaders of the European Economic Community (EEC) issued a declaration which supported Carter's views. It held that a peace settlement should be based on Resolution 242 and on recognition of the "legitimate right of the Palestinian people to its national identity" in the form of a "homeland." It held that representatives of the Palestinian people must be included among those taking part in peace negotiations.[13]

MAY 1977 ISRAELI ELECTIONS TO THE SADAT INITIATIVE

The victory of Menachem Begin and the Likud in the May 1977 elections in Israel had profound effects on the situation in the Middle East and United States peacemaking efforts. The "Covenant" of the Herut party (the dominant element in Likud) claimed Jewish sovereignty over the whole of Palestine, including Transjordan (present-day East Jordan); its "insignia" showed a map of the two banks of the Jordan River united by a gun and an inscription "only this way"; its "slogan" was "the two banks of the Jordan—this one is ours and that one too"—and these have "never been officially discarded."[14] The Herut party claimed all of these areas on historical, religious, ideological grounds, although it toned down its demand for the area east of the Jordan River. However, the Labor party claimed only parts of the occupied territories and primarily on security grounds. Immediately after the election Begin contended that the West Bank (which he called Judea and Samaria) and the Gaza Strip (later to be referred to by Israel as the Gaza District) were integral parts of Israel's sovereignty which had been "liberated" during the 1967 war and which would never be given up for any reason; and indicated that under no circumstances would he accept a Palestinian state and negotiate with the PLO at Geneva or elsewhere even if the PLO changed its charter and recognized Israel. Begin was to interpret Resolution 242 in such a way that Israel did not have to make withdrawals on all fronts[15] as Labor itself had been conceding was necessary to some degree. Consequently, Israel's position under Begin was to harden still further and he was even less prepared than Labor to go to Geneva and to make the concessions essential to the success of American peace efforts.

Begin quickly initiated policies and actions that would reinforce Israel's claim to the occupied territories and would establish "facts on the ground" which would make it increasingly more difficult for any future Labor government to give up any part of these areas even in return for a peace treaty. Thus, he accelerated the pace of building new settlements and, unlike the Labor government—which, except for the Jerusalem area, had generally concentrated most settlements in lightly populated strategic areas which it intended ultimately to annex—he deliberately established settlements in all parts of the West Bank and other occupied areas and especially close to major Arab population centers; his government announced on April 14, 1977, that Israel would extend government services to the inhabitants of the West Bank and Gaza; and he began to assert Israeli authority over these inhabitants in an even more forceful way than was the case in the past. Begin also began to mount large-scale air, land, and sea "retaliatory" and "preemptive" strikes against the Palestinians who were making rocket and artillery attacks on northern Israel and to intervene more openly and actively on behalf of the Israeli-backed right-wing Christians fighting Palestinian forces in south Lebanon. The Israel Cabinet even voted to support the Christians in all parts of Lebanon in time of need.[16] These developments led to increased guerrilla attacks on and bombings in Israel; to more demonstrations, strikes and clashes with Israeli police and troops; and to a deeper conviction on the part of the Arabs and Palestinians that Israel preferred maintaining the *status quo* to making essential concessions for peace. Begin ignored repeated warnings by American officials that if he "maintained these positions, there was no prospect of further progress" toward peace since the Arabs and Palestinians would be discouraged by them from cooperation.[17]

While visiting Washington in late July 1977, Begin protested Carter's continued reference to a Palestinian "homeland" and to the need for Israel to return to the 1967 lines with only minor border changes and asked Carter to stop publicly presenting these views. Carter agreed to this and he did comply; but he also asked Begin, in return, to stop authorizing new settlements. Begin not only refused to commit himself, but on his return to Israel his government recognized as permanent several new settlements.[18] Begin's hardline policies and personal image antagonized not only administration officials but also some members of Congress and even members of the American Jewish community—although most Jewish leaders confined their opposition to the more blatant policies and actions of Begin to private criticism so as not to appear as undermining Israel's position and security.[19]

Secretary of State Cyrus Vance made a trip to the Middle East in August to make one more serious effort to reach some agreement on common principles and also to seek agreement on the procedures involved in convening the Geneva conference. Vance reported that Arab leaders were still prepared to go to Geneva and sign peace treaties with Israel as part of a comprehensive settlement and "showed a readiness to compromise." While he was unable to narrow substantive differences between Arabs and Israelis, he did make some progress with both on procedural matters. But he reported that he was "extremely discouraged" after talks with Begin, because he refused to moderate his views and actions.[20]

Within days after Vance's visit to Israel, the government announced that Israeli social services in the fields of education, health, and welfare were to be extended to the Arab populations of the West Bank and Gaza—a move widely interpreted as a step toward annexation—and that more new settlements would be established. Administration officials again complained that these actions made it increasingly more difficult for them to "persuade the Arabs to go forward with the peace process" and the "settlements policy seemed to us to be one of deliberate provocation" so as to undermine efforts to go to Geneva.[21] Carter even bluntly told Foreign Minister Dayan that the Israelis were "more stubborn than the Arabs, and you put obstacles on the path to peace."[22]

Carter was so provoked that he considered a possible "public showdown" with Israel—especially over the settlements dispute because even some members of Congress were prepared to support him on that issue. He complained that "we are financing their conquest and they simply defy us in an intransigent fashion and generally make a mockery of our advice and preferences."[23] But for domestic political reasons, Carter was reluctant to apply pressures on Israel and he assured Foreign Minister Dayan that he would not impose any peace settlement on her.[24] This reluctance, according to one key administration official, increased Israeli confidence that Carter would not stand fast and would accommodate if pressed by domestic supporters. This also convinced even moderate Arabs and Palestinians that since the United States would not apply essential pressures, there appeared to be little real hope that the United States-sponsored peace process would actually succeed.[25]

In September, American officials concluded that Begin's views and actions forestalled any chance of achieving agreement between the Arabs and Israelis on general principles as a framework for a peace settlement before going to Geneva. Therefore, they concentrated on dealing with procedural differences—such as how the Palestinians would be represented at Geneva—in the hope that if this could be resolved, progress could be made on substantive issues after a conference had been reconvened.

The PLO wanted an invitation to the Geneva conference, and the Palestinian National Council (PNC) session in March 1977 had authorized PLO attendance. On August 9, a PLO spokesman said the PLO would participate in negotiations on the basis of Resolution 242 if it were modified to add a reference to Palestinian national rights.[26]

While American officials were anxious for a dialogue with the PLO, they felt bound by the 1975 Sinai II commitment to Israel not to negotiate with the PLO until it had accepted Resolution 242 and recognized Israel's right to exist. Although this commitment had not actually excluded "occasional informal contacts,"[27] in practice the United States avoided them and had been depending upon indirect contacts through third parties, such as the Saudis and Egyptians. In August and September major efforts were made through an American contact and the Saudis to get the PLO to accept Resolution 242 with (1) the suggested reservation that it did not consider the resolution to make "adequate reference to the question of the Palestinians" and their right to a homeland; and (2) the statement that "it is recognized that the language of Resolution 242 related to the right of all states in the Middle East to live in peace." The United States felt that if the PLO accepted 242 with these suggestions, it would imply recognition of Israel's right to exist and would in effect cancel the wording in the PLO Charter relating to the extinction of Israel.[28] The United States would then be able to talk with the PLO. However, the United States also made it clear that only the parties invited to the original Geneva conference in 1973 could decide who would be invited to participate at a reconvened conference—thus giving Israel a veto over PLO participation—and that the United States would not commit herself to go beyond merely holding talks with the PLO. Begin had also stated flatly that it would be fruitless to prepare a role for the PLO at the conference by trying to get the PLO to recognize Israel since Israel would not accept or deal with the PLO under any circumstances.[29]

During the summer of 1977, the PLO debated the issue of accepting Resolution 242 with the language recommended by the United States as a means of initiating discussions with her. While Arafat and a few other moderate PLO leaders wanted to accept the United States proposal because they believed it might open the way for an important step forward for the PLO, most members of the PLO Executive Committee decided in a late August meeting that the potential risks were greater than the potential benefits. The majority felt that accepting Resolution 242 risked disrupting the fragile consensus within the PLO without guaranteeing that the PLO would even be invited to Geneva, much less being guaranteed help in achieving a national homeland. In fact, since Begin made it clear that he would never accept a Palestinian state or deal with the PLO at Geneva or anywhere else even if it agreed to the conditions called for by the United States and since the United States had not been willing to pressure Israel even on the much lesser matter of settlements, then there was little or no chance that the United States would go so far as to persuade Israel to withdraw from the West Bank. Most PLO leaders refused, therefore, to give up their main bargaining chip unless they received reasonable assurances of getting something of substance in return. In their view, recognition could be used only once as a bargaining chip and should be used only in the context of a fair solution to the Palestinian problem. As one American expert on the Middle East put it:

> The problem ultimately came down to a question of trust: if the Palestinians were to make the commitments required by the Americans, would the Americans then deliver something worthwhile in return? The Palestinians argued . . . that for them to take the drastic step that recognizing Resolution 242 constituted for them it would not be sufficient to be rewarded only by the opening of vaguely defined "talks" with Washington.[30]

OCTOBER 1, 1977, JOINT US–USSR STATEMENT

Since in September the United States was preparing what she hoped would be the last steps before reconvening the Geneva conference, she concluded that it was time to bring the Soviet Union, the co-chairman, more into the picture on the assumption that any agreement with her would improve the chances for its success. A joint statement was negotiated and then made public on October 1, 1977.

The statement declared that the United States and the USSR were convinced of the need to achieve a comprehensive settlement of the Arab-Israeli conflict which would be based on: an Israeli withdrawal "from territories occupied" in 1967; the resolution of the Palestinian question, including insuring the "legitimate rights" of the Palestinian people; the termination of the state of war; and the establishment of normal peaceful relations on the basis of mutual recognition of the principles of sovereignty, territorial integrity, and political independence. To insure security between Israel and her neighbors, demilitarized zones, UN troops and observers, and international guarantees would be used. Representatives of the Palestinian people must participate in the work of the conference.[31] This statement was generally consistent with the views the United States had openly been presenting and reflected important Soviet concessions. While the United States did accept the term "legitimate *rights*" (instead of *"interests"*) for the Palestinians for the first time, the USSR had reluctantly agreed to: (1) leave out any references to the PLO, to a Palestinian state, and to a withdrawal from "all" or "the" occupied areas; (2) include a reference to normal peaceful relations— something not mentioned in 242; and (3) use the much more limited term "legitimate rights" and not "legitimate *national* rights." No mention was made of Resolutions 242 or 338 only because the United States insisted on referring only to these particular resolutions while Russia wanted to refer to these and all other pertinent UN resolutions—particularly those calling for a Palestinian state. They compromised by not mentioning any UN resolution.[32]

Since Israel had from the beginning accepted the Soviet Union as cochairman of the Geneva conference, since administration officials had kept Foreign Minister Dayan informed about the negotiations with the Soviet Union prior to October 1, and since they considered that the statement contained nothing startlingly new and was largely a procedural matter required to reconvene the conference, they were not prepared for the furor which developed after its publication.

Israel immediately denounced the statement. She objected especially to the use of the term "legitimate *rights*," claiming that these were code words for an independent Palestinian state; to the failure to refer to Resolutions 242 and 338; and to the wording on withdrawal (even though the same wording was used in 242). She insisted that she would not go to Geneva on the basis of the statement. Dayan even threatened to appeal to American Jews and Congress against Carter over the statement. American Jewish leaders, members of Congress, the media, and others also condemned the statement and accused Carter of reinjecting Soviet influence into the Middle East. Vance contended that Israel was so opposed to the entire United States peace initiative that she decided to use the statement as a means "to kill it"—a tactic, he held, that Israel had "used many times" in the past.[33]

Carter was so shaken by the great furor aroused and by the considerable political damage this could cause him domestically that he decided to make a hasty retreat by disassociating himself from the statement as quickly as possible. In an address before the UN General Assembly on October 4, he referred to the statement as only a procedural initiative and disavowed any intention of imposing a settlement on anyone.[34] Moreover, on the night of

October 4–5, he negotiated a "working paper" with Dayan which: (1) reaffirmed Resolutions 242 and 338 as the "agreed basis" for reconvening Geneva; (2) stated that "acceptance of the Joint U.S.-USSR Statement . . . by the parties is not a prerequisite for the reconvening of . . . the conference"; and (3) established procedures which would allow only Palestinians who were not PLO representatives to be present at Geneva and they would be part of the Jordanian delegation.[35]

The Arabs and even Arafat and some other PLO leaders had "welcomed" the statement (especially since it referred to "legitimate rights" and held that representatives of the Palestinian people must participate in the work of the conference), even though there was no mention in it of the PLO and a Palestinian state. Arafat and others considered it to be a significant step forward and "a fundamental basis for a realistic settlement in the Middle East."[36] But while Carter's retreat calmed the Israelis, it angered the Arabs and Palestinians, who saw it as yet another United States capitulation in the face of Israeli and domestic political pressures. One top administration official warned that this hasty retreat would: (1) encourage the Israelis to feel that they could always get their way by applying threats and pressures; (2) convince the Arabs and Palestinians that no constructive results could come out of Geneva; and (3) make it more difficult for the PLO to accept 242.[37]

The Soviet Union also reacted bitterly and attacked the working paper and Carter's virtual repudiation of the joint statement after the USSR had made important concessions. In fact, she withdrew these concessions and began to insist once again on total Israeli withdrawal, a Palestinian state, PLO involvement at Geneva, and no reference to normalization. Nevertheless, the Soviet Union made no serious attempt to block the continuation of American efforts to go to Geneva. After all, the USSR would still be there as co-chairman.

In October and November, the United States again endeavored to resolve the procedural obstacles to Geneva. Even though the confidence of the Arabs and Palestinians in the United States had been seriously shaken, they were still willing to go there because they had no better alternative. Jordan, Saudi Arabia, and the United States were actively trying to overcome procedural differences between Assad and Sadat and were making progress in getting an agreement on a single Arab delegation, including Palestinians, to attend the plenary meeting, with national delegations making up the subcommittees and the Jordanians and Palestinians sitting together on the subcommittee dealing with the Palestinian issue. There were still United States-Israeli differences over the settlements and PLO representation. But on the whole Secretary Vance concluded that "substantial progress" had been made, sent a letter on November 12 to an Arab Foreign Ministers conference in Tunis expressing confidence that the remaining procedural obstacles could be overcome, and felt that "in fact, we appeared on the verge of reconvening the conference when Anwar Sadat . . . undertook his historic trip to Jerusalem."[38]

But Israel's official position on key issues had not changed. According to Foreign Minister Dayan, Israel had been prepared to go to Geneva since October 10, 1977, on the basis of Resolution 338 with Israel, Egypt, Jordan, and Syria as participants. There would be separate subcommittees on a geographical basis to negotiate separate treaties. Israel was prepared to make significant withdrawals from the Sinai and a partial withdrawal from the Golan Heights, but no withdrawal from "Judea, Samaria, and the Gaza District." She would not accept United States contentions that Resolution 242 required withdrawals on all fronts and that a settlement should provide for a Palestinian entity. Israel also insisted on full and immediate normalization.[39] Nevertheless, Israel really preferred the continuation of the *status quo* to making major territorial and political concessions as required by 242 and the United States. To justify her refusal to make these concessions, she claimed that she did not believe that the Arabs really wanted peace and that, therefore, any concessions she made would only be used to further threaten Israeli security.[40]

Fighting between Palestinians and Israeli-backed Christians in south Lebanon escalated in early November. Israeli settlements came under Palestinian fire on November 6 and 8, killing three Israelis. On November 9, Israel launched a large-scale airstrike, killing more than 100 people and leveling two farm villages in the Tyre area.[41] These developments raised tensions and did not help the peace process.

THE SADAT INITIATIVE

For some time Sadat had been interested in achieving an agreement with Israel, as long as he could obtain something for the other Arab parties as well. Actually, Sadat, as well as many other Egyptians, had felt that Egypt had sacrificed enough for the other Arabs and Palestinians and that the time had come to do what was to Egypt's interests regardless how the Arabs reacted. In any case, he believed that Egypt was so important to the Arab world that the other Arabs would have to follow Egyptian leadership whether they were consulted or liked it or not. Therefore, even while he was going along with United States efforts to reconvene Geneva and with active efforts by the Arab foreign ministers to unify Arab plans and strategy for Geneva as he himself had urged and while Secretary of State Vance and Egyptian Foreign Minister Ismail Fahmy were telling him that progress was being made to going to Geneva and the deadlock could soon be broken, Sadat nevertheless initiated secret talks between high level Egyptian and Israeli officials in Morocco, starting in September. By bypassing the United States and the other Arabs, Sadat hoped to attain an informal agreement directly with Israel on matters of substance before Geneva reconvened with the expectation that once such an agreement had been achieved Jordan and Syria would have to go along and the Geneva conference would have a better chance to succeed. Israel welcomed the talks because she saw them as a golden opportunity to make a separate deal with Egypt which could split the Arabs and disrupt the path to Geneva.[42]

Sadat had been shaken by the manner in which the United States had hastily retreated when the October 1 joint United States-USSR statement had come under attack from Israel and her American supporters. Moreover, Sadat received a personal letter from Carter urging him to break the deadlock by some dramatic move. Sadat interpreted this to be an admission of Carter's domestic weakness and his lack of will to push through a comprehensive settlement. Besides, Sadat, who had a flair for the dramatic and an exaggerated "sense of his role in history," had grown impatient with the slow pace of the negotiations and the haggling over procedural matters. As Sadat himself contended, it was time to break out of the cycle of formal procedures and come to grips with what he considered to be the root cause of the problem—namely, "the psychological barrier" created by "a wall of suspicion, fear, hate, and misunderstanding." Therefore, there was need to try a completely new approach which would bypass all formalities and procedural technicalities by pulling down the barrier of mistrust.[43]

Despite the vigorous opposition of his foreign minister (who strongly opposed the move and resigned over it) and without seriously considering the enormity of the problem and weighing the potential harmful consequences to the peace process, to Arab unity, to Egypt's relations with the other Arabs, to Arab—and even Egyptian—bargaining position vis-à-vis Israel; without having any idea whether Begin would respond with comparable good will; and without having any real plan as to what would follow his trip, on November 9 Sadat announced suddenly and unexpectedly in the Egyptian Parliament that he was ready to go to Jerusalem to address the Knesset on the question of peace. Begin quickly invited him to come to Israel and the invitation was accepted.

Sadat told the Kneset that he had come to eliminate the "psychological barriers" between Arabs and Israelis, to prove that the Arabs "accept living with you in permanent peace based on justice," and to overlook the past and shape a new life to save Arabs and Israelis from more wars. He insisted that he was for a comprehensive settlement based upon (1) Israeli withdrawal from all territories occupied in 1967; (2) Palestinian self-determination, including an independent state; (3) right of all states in the area to live in peace within secure borders; (4) an end to the state of belligerency; and (5) a commitment to administer relations in accordance with those principles of the UN Charter pertaining to the nonuse of force.[44]

Begin's response was not conciliatory. He accused the Arabs of being the aggressors and blamed them for the failure to achieve peace. He reiterated or implied his long-standing peace terms: "full, real" peace with completely normal relations; treaties negotiated with each Arab state separately; no withdrawals on all fronts; and retention of Samaria and Judea as parts of "Eretz Israel."

Sadat was disappointed in the content and tone of Begin's reply; and he quickly realized that his trip to Jerusalem had not produced the basic shifts in Israel's attitudes and position as he had expected. Nevertheless, he persisted in pressing his initiative, to which his prestige was now committed. He called for a conference to be held in Cairo and invited Israel, Syria, Jordan, the PLO, the United States, the USSR, and the UN to send representatives. He claimed that this would be a step toward a Geneva conference.

Secretary of State Vance went to the Middle East in mid-December and made an unsuccessful effort to get the agreement of Sadat and Begin to reconvene the Geneva conference. Despite a personal plea from Carter, Begin refused to make a clear statement on accepting the principle of withdrawal on all fronts to encourage the other Arabs to at least attend the Cairo conference. Consequently, only representatives from Israel, Egypt, the United States, and the UN attended it. Since Begin was not interested in making the Cairo meeting a stepping stone to Geneva, no progress was made. As his Defense Minister Ezer Weizman stated, Begin, while seeing some risks involved in going along with the Sadat initiative and particularly with accepting subsequent United States pressures to make concessions which he did not want to make, he also saw a golden opportunity "to use every ruse to sabotage the peace efforts" leading to Geneva and to promote Israel's long-standing goal of separating Egypt from the other Arab states as a means of weakening Arab bargaining power and making it easier for Israel to hold on to the remainder of the occupied territories and to ignore the Palestinian problem.[45]

The Sadat initiative forced Begin to spell out more specifically Israel's peace plans—especially on the Sinai and Palestinian issues—to balance Sadat's proposals and to show that Israel also would make some concessions for peace. He formally indicated that he was prepared conditionally to make a phased withdrawal from all or nearly all the Sinai. On the Palestinian issue, he presented, in late December, an autonomy plan for the West Bank and Gaza. Under this plan, Israel would abolish the military administration and provide limited "administrative autonomy for the residents." Israel would retain responsibility for security and public order. While insisting on her right to claim sovereignty to Judea, Samaria, and the Gaza District, for the sake of a peace agreement she was prepared to leave the question of sovereignty in these areas "open" for the time being.[46]

According to Weizman, because of the strong criticism of this plan within his own Herut party—critics claimed that autonomy would lead to a Palestinian state—Begin soon began to water down his proposals and to make it clear that "he was giving up the Sinai to protect himself against" having to make "any eventual concessions in the West Bank"; while the United States and Egypt saw autonomy as a step toward national self-determination, Begin saw it as an end goal; he also saw it as a chance to gain time to establish facts on the ground (such as settlements) to deprive his plan of any content and make it impossible for any future Israeli government to give up these areas even in return for peace with the Arabs; and he counted on his watered down autonomy plan to discourage the Arabs and Palestinians from going along with it.[47] In fact, Begin accelerated the settlements program and initiated major attacks on Lebanon in March, 1978, which not only angered the United States and Egypt, but further diminished the chances that other Arabs would back Sadat's initiative. An angry Carter wrote:

> Whenever we seemed to be having some success with the Arabs, Begin would proclaim the establishment of new settlements or make provocative statements. This behavior was not only very irritating, but it seriously endangered the prospects for peace and Sadat's status both in Egypt and with the Arab world. The repeated Israeli invasions or bombings of Lebanon also precipitated crises.[48]

Even Weizman candidly concluded: "Israel seemed to be finding every possible tactic to impede the peace process." He also stated that despite Sadat's visit to Jerusalem, many Israelis and government ministers continued to distrust Sadat and the Arabs; many ministers were "afraid of peace" and "most" of them were not really interested in a peace settlement for they preferred the situation before Sadat's initiative when there were no serious pressures for changes in the *status quo* and for making concessions which they did not want to make.[49]

Begin's uncompromising position so angered Sadat that he gave up on further talks with Israel. Even Labor party leaders, as well as many Israeli doves, criticized Begin's policies and actions, especially on the Palestinian and settlements issues. In the spring of 1978, at the initiative of some Israeli military reservists and students, the Peace Now movement was formed as a means of pressing Begin to be more forthcoming to help salvage Sadat's initiative. A letter from 350 reserve officers, backed by the leftist Mapam party and some Labor party leaders, was sent to Begin. It held that Israel was squandering an invaluable opportunity for peace by refusing to recognize the changes which had taken place in Arab society since the 1967 war; to make territorial concessions in exchange for peace; to recognize the significance of the Palestinian movement and the changes which had taken place in it; and to end the settlement policy. The letter expressed fear that continued rule over occupied areas would ultimately undermine Israeli democracy.[50]

Saudi and Jordanian leaders exercised public restraint while they awaited the results of Sadat's visit to Jerusalem. They were torn between their private hope that the initiative would succeed and their fear that it would not. They especially warned Sadat that his action must not lead to a separate peace for this would split the Arab world and greatly weaken its position vis-à-vis Israel. They felt that prompt actions by the United States and positive responses from Israel were essential to enable them to support Sadat. When Israel's responses were not positive and the initiative was floundering, the Saudis and Jordanians—and other moderate Arabs—began to criticize Sadat. Sadat responded by bitterly attacking all of those who opposed him, thus further antagonizing even the most moderate Arabs who had been wishing him well.

Iraq, Libya, and South Yemen, who were true rejectionists in the sense that they were opposed to any peace treaty with Israel on any terms, vehemently attacked Sadat and his initiative.

Both Syria and the PLO, however, while strongly condemning Sadat and expressing great distrust of his motives, tried "to keep their options open."[51] Syria was angry not only because Sadat had failed to consult his allies beforehand even though they had vital interests at stake, but also because she felt that his initiative had undermined Arab unity (which Syria believed was essential to providing the Arabs with a sufficiently credible military threat to encourage Israel to make the concessions required for an overall peace settlement) and had strengthened Israel's bargaining position to the point where she would be even more rigid than ever on the Palestinian and Golan issues. Syria joined the Arab Front for Steadfastness and Confrontation not because she opposed a peace process but because she was convinced that the initiative would do more to cripple than advance the chances for a fair comprehensive settlement, which was the only realistic way she felt she could regain the Golan Heights.

Thus, in the statements following meetings of this Front in Tripoli in early December and in Algiers in early February 1978, Syria backed wording which, among other things, (1) criticized the initiative because it could "destroy all possibility of establishing a just and honorable peace that would safeguard the national rights of the Arab nations" and of the Palestinians and that would "ensure the liberation of its occupied territories"; and (2) stated that the "Arab nations will continue action on behalf of a just peace."[52] In fact, Iraq walked out of the Tripoli meeting on the grounds that Syria was insisting on a "capitulatory course" by refusing to close the door on a peace settlement.[53] In an interview with *Newsweek* (January 16, 1978), Assad said that Sadat had:

> weakened the Arab stand. . . . Sadat is now on the way to a separate deal. Don't confuse [a] separate agreement with an overall settlement and real peace in the area. . . . He has given up both the war and the peace options. . . . We [Assad and Hussein] have opted for the road to peace, not war. [Sadat's route will] not lead to peace. Peace cannot be achieved without Arab unity. [The Steadfastness Front is not] rejectionist. [It held that] Sadat had destroyed peace efforts. We didn't say we were against peace.[54]

ISRAELI INVASION OF LEBANON, MARCH 1978

Peace efforts were further complicated by the developments which took place between Israel and the Palestinians in March 1978.

Because the PLO had suffered serious losses and divisions during the Lebanese civil war; because both Carter and Sadat had attacked the PLO's refusal to go along with Sadat's initiative and claimed that the PLO had now forfeited any right to participate in the peace process; and because they feared that Egypt and the United States were working for a separate peace, PLO leaders felt the need for some spectacular guerrilla operation to convince the United States and Israel that the PLO and Palestinian rights could not be ignored with impunity in any peacemaking process and to try to reunite PLO ranks split by the civil war. Thus, on March 11, on the eve of a planned visit by Begin to Washington, al-Fatah commandos landed on a beach in Israel and seized a bus with the intention of using the passengers as hostages for release of Palestinian prisoners in Israel. Israeli troops stormed the bus and in the fighting 36 Israelis and 8 commandos were killed, 76 Israelis were wounded and 2 commandos captured.[55]

On March 14, Israel responded with a large-scale air, land and sea invasion of south Lebanon in which Israel seized all of south Lebanon up to the Litani River. Because the invasion caused heavy casualties (over 1,000 civilian Palestinian and Lebanese dead) and 100,000 to 200,000 Palestinians and Lebanese to flee their homes, Israel was widely condemned by many countries. The United States was angered not only by what Carter called the "terrible overreaction by the Israelis," but also because Israel had used American weapons, including cluster bombs, in the operation "contrary to our agreement when they were sold"; because the invasion hurt Sadat, the United States, and the peace process; and because when Begin met Carter on March 20 in Washington Begin continued to pursue a hard line.[56] Consequently, United States-Israeli relations were to reach a very low point.

On March 19, the UN Security Council passed a United States-sponsored resolution which called on Israel to withdraw from all occupied Lebanese territory and established a UN Interim Force in Lebanon (UNIFIL) to facilitate her withdrawal and to take up positions in south Lebanon to try to prevent further incidents and conflicts. After strong American pressure, Israel completed her withdrawal on June 13, but she refused to allow UNIFIL—and later even regular Lebanese army units—to enter a strip about five miles wide along the entire Lebanese-Israeli border, leaving it under the control of a right-wing Christian-led militia which had been trained, armed, and financed by Israel to serve as her surrogate force. For all intents and purposes, Israel continued to control that entire strip.

CAMP DAVID

In a final desperate effort to salvage the situation, Carter invited Begin and Sadat to come to Camp David in early September to make an all-out effort to break the deadlock in negotiations which had developed.

Sadat came to Camp David in a weakened position because by splitting the Arab world, he lost all the bargaining power a united Arab world would have provided him; by having gone to Jerusalem, he had yielded his major card—non-recognition of Israel; and by having so greatly committed his prestige and future to the success of his initiative, he now was under great pressure to come out of Camp David with some kind of agreement, even if it required major concessions on his part.

Because he had committed his own prestige and political future—just before a presidential election year— to the success of Camp David, President Carter also had much at stake and felt he could not afford to have it fail. He was, consequently, in a "weak position vis-à-vis Begin."[57]

Begin, on the other hand, was in a strong bargaining stance vis-à-vis both Carter and Sadat. He knew he had to pay some price for an agreement with Egypt, involving the return of the Sinai. But because the Sinai had never been part of Eretz Israel and was largely desert, it was easier to give up than any other occupied area; and, in any case, by yielding it he would be in a stronger position to hold on to the rest of the disputed territories, to perpetuate the split in the Arab world, and to ignore the Palestinian issue. Thus, he had something to gain if Camp David succeeded on his terms. Since he and many of his ministers were quite content with the *status quo* and unhappy about making any substantial concessions—even in the Sinai—a failure at Camp David, while spelling serious political consequences for both

Sadat and Carter, could be considered the best of all possible results by those Israelis who did not want to relinquish any land, even in the Sinai and even for peace. This put him in a position in which he could virtually demand an agreement largely on his own terms or threaten to agree to no terms. After all, he had been repeatedly assured by Carter that the United States would not apply pressures on him to accept any agreement he opposed—and this encouraged him to believe that he could always in the end get his way with the United States.[58] Consequently, Begin had very little to lose and much to gain whether the negotiations succeeded largely on his terms or failed altogether.

Carter's greatest hope was to achieve a framework for an Egyptian-Israeli treaty which could be closely linked to a framework for a comprehensive settlement that could, in turn, help resolve the critical Palestinian issue. At the outset, he felt that this close linkage was the "single most important issue" so as not to end up with merely a separate peace. He was also concerned about getting an Israeli commitment to a long-term settlements freeze because he was convinced that as long as Israel continued to establish "facts on the ground" there would be little incentive for the Arabs and Palestinians to cooperate in a peace process when they—and even the United States—were convinced that Begin's settlements policy provided firm proof that he was not seriously willing ever to exchange territory for peace.[59]

However, as Carter complained, Begin had come to the conference without altering his basic positions. He showed "inflexibility on all the issues"; "seemed completely unconcerned with the Palestinian problem"; insisted on Israel's right to veto all "decisions made by the local citizens [under Palestinian autonomy] on any subject"; and debated every point tenaciously.[60] According to Dayan, Begin opposed any mention of the wording in Resolution 242 which referred to "the inadmissibility of the acquisition of territory by war"—even though the Camp David Accords were to call for implementing Resolution 242 "in all its parts"—because he did not intend to give up any territory outside of the Sinai.[61]

After 13 days of heated debate, threatened walkouts, and major rescue operations by Carter and concessions by Sadat, the parties at Camp David agreed on two accords. The first, "A Framework for the Conclusion of a Peace Treaty between Egypt and Israel," provided that Egypt and Israel would make a good faith effort to conclude a peace treaty within three months on the basis of: (1) a phased withdrawal of Israeli forces from the Sinai over a three-year period; (2) demilitarized zones, a peacekeeping force, and other security arrangements; and (3) the establishment of full normal diplomatic, economic, and cultural relations nine months after the treaty was signed.

The second accord, "A Framework for Peace in the Middle East," provided for a comprehensive settlement based on the negotiation of peace treaties which would carry out Resolution 242 "in all its parts"; resolve the "Palestinian problem in all its aspects"; provide for various security arrangements and the establishment of normal diplomatic, economic, and other "good neighborly relations"; and provide "full autonomy" for the inhabitants of the West Bank and Gaza Strip by allowing them to elect a self-governing authority whose powers and functions would be determined by negotiations between Israel, Egypt, Jordan and representatives of the inhabitants. This authority would replace the existing military government for a transitional period of five years. Within three years after the beginning of the transitional period, there would be negotiations between Egypt, Israel, Jordan, and representatives of the inhabitants to define the final status of the West Bank and Gaza with the final results having to 'recognize the legitimate rights of the Palestinian people and their just requirements" and the right of the Palestinians to "participate in the determination of their own future" by having the agreement on the final status submitted to a vote by "elected representatives" of these inhabitants.

The framework for peace did not contain any reference to Jerusalem because the parties could not agree on the wording of such a reference. Egypt and Israel submitted separate letters to Carter indicating their positions on this issue. Carter sent letters reiterating the long-standing United States position that the future of Jerusalem must be decided by negotiations and not by any unilateral decision by Israel. At Israel's insistence, the Golan Heights was not specifically mentioned, but Egypt and the United States interpreted the reference to implementing Resolution 242 in the framework as applying the principle of territorial withdrawal to the Golan Heights as well as to other occupied areas. Begin did not agree with this view since he refused to concede that Resolution 242 required withdrawals on all fronts. In fact, the two accords contained many ambiguous phrases and wording which, while they made it possible to reach an agreement at Camp David, also allowed for conflicting interpretations later; and there was no clear and close linkage between the accord dealing with an Egyptian-Israeli treaty and the one calling for a comprehensive settlement "largely because Carter in the end acquiesced to Begin's vague formulas"—and, as one high administration official complained, these "came back to haunt us in the subsequent phases of the negotiations."[62]

Begin appeared to have made important concessions at Camp David. He agreed to withdraw from the Sinai and dismantle settlements there. He agreed to the wording "legitimate rights" of the Palestinians and to the need for resolving the Palestinian problem "in all its aspects" and to providing "full autonomy" for the Palestinians and their right to "participate in the determination of their own future." Thus, he was, for the first time, formally accepting the existence of a Palestinian issue and the right of at least the

Palestinians in the occupied areas to become involved in the negotiating process. In addition, he agreed to carry out Resolution 242 "in all its parts." Carter also had believed that he had received a separate commitment from Begin to accept a five-year settlements freeze.

Despite strong opposition within his own party, Begin was to carry out his commitments to withdraw from the Sinai and to dismantle the settlements there. However, on virtually all other major controversial issues, Begin was to interpret them in ways which were radically different from the interpretations of both Carter and Sadat. Begin was attacked by the hawks in Israel who accused him of giving up too much in the Sinai (even the Labor party opposed a complete withdrawal from that area and there was widespread opposition to dismantling the settlements) and on the Palestinian issue (with strong objections to accepting the terms "the legitimate rights" of the Palestinians and "full autonomy" with Palestinian involvement in deciding the future of the West Bank and Gaza). So Begin felt the need to convince the hawks in his own party that he had really given up nothing new. Thus, within hours after Camp David he was making public statements in which he denied he was obliged to withdraw on other fronts; to provide anything more than limited administrative autonomy for the inhabitants of the West Bank and Gaza; to ever give up Israel's "claim to right of sovereignty" over these areas—and especially Jerusalem; to allow the inhabitants any say in determining their own future; and to stop new settlements beyond three months.[63]

An irate Carter claimed that Begin was making

> negative statements to Jewish audiences. . . . Begin's statements were certain to alienate the moderate Arab and Palestinian leaders and to impede any further progress on the Palestinian and West Bank issues. . . . [Carter warned Begin that] his remarks were making it impossible for them [Arab and Palestinian leaders] to join in any further discussions. . . . I had a feeling that he really didn't want any early talks involving the Palestinians and other Arabs. . . . [Carter asked Begin to cooperate, yet] he announced plans to expand the West Bank settlements and revealed that he was thinking of moving his office to East Jerusalem. . . . Begin wanted to keep two things: the peace with Egypt and the West Bank . . . [and he used] the settlements and East Jerusalem issues to prevent the involvement of the Jordanians and the Palestinians.[64]

Carter again spoke of a possible "showdown" with Israel; and some administration officials and members of Congress urged him to threaten to use a cut in economic aid as a means to get a change in some of Begin's policies and actions, but Carter did not go through with any showdown.[65]

Sadat signed the Camp David accords despite their serious flaws and the opposition of his own top advisors because failure to come to some agreement would be a clear admission that his initiative had failed and that he had gambled and lost a great deal not only for Egypt but for the entire Arab and Palestinian causes, and because Carter urged him to do so. He still trusted Carter and took him at his word when he promised to stand firm on United States interpretations of the accords. Sadat saw the "Framework for the Conclusion of a Peace Treaty between Egypt and Israel," in which Israel agreed to withdraw completely to the pre-1967 lines, as a model for similar treaties with Jordan and Syria. But according to Weisman, Begin saw it as "the precise opposite. As far as he was concerned, the withdrawal from the Sinai would be the end of the story."[66]

Initially some moderate Arabs, such as King Hussein, were willing to give the Camp David accords a chance by waiting to see how they would be interpreted and implemented. Hussein sent a list of questions about the many vague terms used in the accords and sought American interpretations of them. The American reply to Hussein on the Palestinian, settlements, withdrawal, and even East Jerusalem issues appeared to be somewhat reassuring. However, after the Arabs and Palestinians heard Begin's interpretations of the Camp David accords and Israel's commitment on settlements and after seeing no effective responses to these by the United States, even moderate Arabs began to attack the accords and to be convinced that they would lead only to a separate peace and nothing more. Therefore, Jordan and Saudi Arabia, stated that the accords were an "unacceptable formula for a definitive peace."[67]

President Assad was not surprised by the accords and their failure to mention the Golan Heights since he did not trust Israel, Egypt, or the United States and felt that the accords were meant to isolate Syria and the Palestinians. Since he was convinced that Israel would never willingly give up the Golan Heights and accept Palestinian rights and that the United States would not press Israel to do so, he believed that the only hope of achieving these goals was for the Arabs to be united and strong in order to be able to pose a strategic threat to Israel as a lever for bargaining purposes—and now the Camp David accords would leave the Arabs more divided and weaker than ever.

The PLO and the Palestinians in general reacted bitterly. Since the PLO was completely ignored and since Begin made it clear that any autonomy allowed would be a very limited one and Israel would never relinquish the West Bank and Gaza, neither the PLO nor the inhabitants of the occupied areas were prepared to cooperate with the Camp David process. They complained that by authorizing even a five-year transition period, the accords bestowed "legitimacy" upon continued occupation while from the beginning the world community had insisted that the occupation was illegal; that a five-year transition period would give Israel enough time to establish so many settlements as to alter the face of the territory when the question of the future of the territory came up; and that Israel was given a virtual veto on most key subjects, so that she could merely object and thus retain the *status quo* indefinitely.[68]

On November 5, 1978, an Arab summit meeting in Baghdad issued a statement which (1) condemned Egypt and the Camp David accords; (2) warned Egypt that if she signed a separate peace treaty she would be subjected to an economic and political boycott; (3) transferred Arab League headquarters from Cairo to Tunis; and (4) set down its own peace formula: a full Israeli withdrawal; the right of the Palestinians to their own state; and the right of every state in the area to live in peace and security, as stated in Resolution 242. Even Iraq, a leader in the past of the real rejectionist movement, now voted for this peace plan which indicated a willingness to accept Israel's existence and make peace with her.[69]

THE EGYPTIAN-ISRAELI PEACE TREATY

Egyptian and Israeli representatives started negotiations in Washington in October, 1978, to work out a detailed peace treaty as provided for in the Camp David accords. However, major differences quickly arose so that negotiations were to drag on beyond the three-month deadline set at Camp David.

The United States was actively involved in trying to overcome the differences and was successful in narrowing them. Matters were further complicated in early 1979 by the fall of the Shah and the rise of Islamic fundamentalism, which concerned not only Egypt and the United States but also Israel, who had benefited from good relations with the Shah, especially in the way of an assured supply of oil; the outbreak of serious fighting between China and Vietnam; and the entry of United States-USSR SALT negotiations into a critical stage. By March 1979 the major issues still unresolved involved whether Israel could get preferential access to Sinai oil; whether Palestinian autonomy would start quickly with some self-government for Gaza with Egyptian involvement before being extended to the West Bank at a later date; and whether there would be an exchange of ambassadors upon signing of the peace treaty or later.

In early March, Carter met with Begin in Washington. Although Begin asked the United States for greatly increased economic and military aid, he rebuffed all of Carter's pleas for a settlements freeze and other acts of accommodation. Carter and Vance were convinced that Begin's provocative policies and actions were deliberately aimed at discouraging other Arabs and

Palestinians from joining any peace talks and making it more difficult for the United States and Egypt to reassure them that the Camp David accords provided a meaningful process that could ultimately lead to the fulfillment of Palestinian rights and a fair settlement between Israel and her other Arab neighbors.[70]

Even Foreign Minister Dayan and Defense Minister Weizman continued to disagree with Begin's intransigence and dilatory policies, very restrictive definition of Palestinian autonomy, and settlements policy. Weizman contended that the Israelis "were afraid of peace" because it would require greater concessions on all fronts than they were prepared to make, thereby making perpetuating the *status quo* more desirable than any peace based on undesirable terms.[71]

Carter then decided that he had to travel to the Middle East and initiate shuttle diplomacy to salvage the situation. He assured the Egyptians that he was committed to a comprehensive peace which would resolve the Palestinian issue and that an Egyptian-Israeli treaty would be only the "first step" toward that goal. Despite strong opposition to some parts of the treaty in his own cabinet, Sadat felt that the success or failure of his initiative was at stake and that he had little choice but to trust Carter's assurances and accept the treaty despite the flaws it contained.

Begin also had serious opposition in his own party and government—some strongly objected to giving up all of the Sinai and all of the settlements there and two cabinet members voted against the treaty. But Begin saw a golden opportunity to remove Egypt from the confrontation states and, thereby, making it easier for Israel to retain the remainder of the occupied areas. To soften the opposition, Begin stated unequivocally that Israel would never give up the Gaza District, Samaria, and Judea, including East Jerusalem, and never accept a Palestinian state.[72] These assurances might have lessened opposition to the treaty in Israel, but they only increased opposition within the Arab world both to the treaty and to the entire Camp David peace process which, in their estimation, had only ended up by further dividing the Arabs and making a truly comprehensive peace settlement more difficult than ever to achieve.

After wringing concessions from both sides—and especially from Sadat—Carter was finally able to complete negotiations on an Egyptian-Israeli treaty, which was signed in Washington on March 26, 1979. While the treaty's preamble stated that there was "urgent necessity" to settle all aspects of the Arab-Israeli conflict and that the treaty was only the first step toward a comprehensive peace, the treaty itself contained nothing which specifically linked its implementation to actual progress on the Palestinian issue. Therefore, to all intents and purposes Egypt had agreed to a separate peace with only the unrealistic hope on the part of Sadat, that somehow United States assurances and pressures and Israeli goodwill would somehow enable further movement to be made on other fronts.

The treaty mainly provided for a phased Israeli withdrawal from all of the Sinai within a three-year period and a dismantling of Israeli settlements there in return for Egypt's (1) ending the state of war and all political, economic, and other hostile actions from her territory; (2) establishing full normal and friendly diplomatic, economic, and cultural relations upon the completion of an interim Israeli withdrawal within nine months; (3) accepting security arrangements which provided for limited forces zones (which especially limited Egyptian sovereignty there), international peace-keeping forces, and early warning systems; and (4) guaranteeing the right of Israel to use the Suez Canal and the Strait of Tiran.

Israel also obtained from the United States a memorandum of agreement on March 26 which provided for (1) American support in case of any violation of the treaty by Egypt; (2) greatly increased United States economic and military aid; (3) an American pledge to guarantee Israeli access to oil for 15 years; (4) a United States commitment to veto any Security Council resolution which might adversely affect the treaty; and (5) reiteration of all prior commitments to Israel—especially those made by Kissinger in 1975.[73]

Egypt and Israel began to implement the treaty without any serious hitches, and provisions for Israeli withdrawals and mutual normalization procedures were carried out as stated in the treaty.

According to Defense Minister Weizman, who helped negotiate the treaty, "Begin and his supporters" were so "alarmed by the Egyptian-Israeli peace treaty" that they eroded it "by provocative settlements programs and unnecessary land confiscations, trumpeting verbal challenges to the world as they withdrew into their mental ghetto." Although Begin had played a decisive role in negotiating the agreement,

> no sooner had the treaty been signed then Begin gave up promoting the peace process. Instead of forging ahead into a new era, he withdrew into his pipe dreams. At the same time, he began to treat this peace we had struggled for as something banal, almost despicable. I was increasingly dissatisfied with Begin's retreat from decisions he himself had authorized.[74]

Begin reiterated his views on the withdrawal, settlements, Palestine state, and PLO issues. He called the PLO a "syndicate of murderers" who will "never be any partner to negotiations with Israel" even if it changed its stance and accepted Resolution 242 and Israel's right to exist.[75] Moreover, although Carter repeated his warning that Israel's settlements were undermining American efforts to involve moderate Arabs and Palestinians in the peace process; and in 1979–1980 the UN, the Parliamentary Council of the Coun-

cil of Europe, and the leaders of the EEC passed resolutions which criticized
the settlements as being illegal and obstacles to peace, Begin publicly announced that Israel would "pay no attention" to any world criticism involving settlements.[76] In fact, he even accelerated his settlements program. More
settlements were established close to such major Arab cities as Nablus and
Bethlehem and he authorized some Israelis to live and set up a school in the
heart of Hebron, a move which was soon to precipitate many incidents.
Moreover, in May, 1979, Sharon called for an intensive settlements program
for the next 20 years; and in September, 1979, the government for the first
time allowed and even encouraged private Israeli citizens and businesses to
buy and build on Arab lands in the occupied territories.

The Labor party and some American Jews also criticized placing settlements in highly populated Arab areas; and Defense Minister Weizman and
former chief of staff Haim Bar-Lev contended that such settlements were not
necessary for security reasons and undermined autonomy talks and other peace
negotiations.[77] But, as David Shipler of the *New York Times* reported (May
31, 1979), such negotiations were "precisely what the Government of Prime
Minister Begin [did] not want."

Arab world reactions to the treaty—especially in the light of Begin's
statements and actions—were quick and sharp. In a summit meeting in
Baghdad on March 31, Arab leaders adopted a resolution calling for political, diplomatic, and economic sanctions against Egypt. Egypt was now left
more isolated than ever before in the Arab world.

This common feeling about Egypt's desertion of Arab unity encouraged
former enemies in the Arab world, such as Iraq and Syria, to close ranks to
try to establish an Eastern Front against Israel. But this unity was not to last
and began to disintegrate after the outbreak of the Iran-Iraq war in 1980,
with Syria backing Iran while Jordan and other Arab states backed Iraq.

The growing divisions between the Arabs undermined Syria's hope that
a strong and united Arab world—or even an Eastern Front—could strengthen
her position to the point where she might be able to recover the Golan Heights.
Statements by Sharon in April 1979 and Begin in May 1979 that Israel would
never give up the Golan Heights even in a peace settlement with Syria[78] and
the inability of the United States to change even those Israeli policies to which
Carter had vigorously and repeatedly objected, led Syria to conclude that
there was not much point in cooperating with any American-sponsored step-
by-step peace process which, in any case, would do more to obstruct than
to promote a comprehensive settlement and an Israeli withdrawal from the
Golan Heights. In the meantime, tensions between Israel and Syria mounted
in 1979 and led to some clashes between Syrian and Israeli planes on June
27 and September 24, 1979, in which Syria lost a total of eight aircraft. On
October 7, Syria shot down an unmanned Israeli drone flying within Syrian
airspace.

The PLO was angry with Sadat because he had made a separate peace which would reduce still further Palestinian chances of gaining their right to national self-determination. Consequently, relations between the PLO and Egypt were to deteriorate still further. The PLO was also angry with Carter, who continued to criticize the PLO and who accepted the resignation of Andrew Young as United States ambassador to the United Nations because in August 1979 he had met with a representative of the PLO in his capacity as acting president of the UN Security Council. Yet, PLO leaders still sought some dialogue with the United States. By this time, according to one American expert, the PLO had

> dropped hints that their future policies might be more moderate than those of the past. By the year's end, the PLO had received unprecedented recognition in Europe, as well as in virtually all of the Third World. Even within the United States, significant currents of opinion were calling for some kind of dialogue between the United States and the PLO. The mainstream of the PLO welcomed these developments and anticipated that at some point contacts with the American government would take place.[79]

Although the PLO had been repeatedly rebuffed by both Israel and the United States, it continued to make substantial headway in Western Europe and at the UN. Arafat and other PLO leaders met with top officials in Austria, Spain, Italy, Belgium, Portugal, and Greece. In November 1979, Italy accorded the PLO political recognition and in March 1980, Austria extended full diplomatic recognition. In September 1979, the Irish Foreign Minister, speaking formally for the European Economic Community (EEC) at the UN General Assembly, strongly criticized Israeli policies, supported Palestinian national rights, and for the first time mentioned the need for the PLO to have a role in the peace process. In April 1980, the Parliamentary Assembly of the Council of Europe condemned Israeli settlements policy and called on Israel to recognize Palestinian right of self-determination.[80]

The UN General Assembly passed resolutions condemning the Camp David accords and the Egyptian-Israeli peace treaty and continued to pass annual resolutions providing for the complete Israeli withdrawal from all territories occupied in 1967, including East Jerusalem; the right of the Palestinians to their own state; the PLO to act as the only legitimate representative of the Palestinian people and to participate in peace negotiations; economic sanctions against Israel if she refused to withdraw; and the right of the Arab refugees from the 1948 and 1967 wars to repatriation or compensation. Numerous General Assembly, as well as some Security Council, resolutions criticized Israeli settlements and other Israeli policies and actions in the occupied areas.

On July 11, 1980, even the World Jewish Congress said that the solution of the Arab-Israeli conflict should include "due recognition of the legitimate rights of the Palestinian people."[81]

AUTONOMY TALKS

After the Egyptian-Israeli peace treaty came into force, the United States restricted her efforts largely to preventing excessively negative reactions to it; carrying out her role in the withdrawal and security provisions of the treaty; and trying to promote quiet negotiations on the future of the West Bank and Gaza. The United States became increasingly preoccupied with her security interests in the Middle East as a whole as a result of the turmoil in Iran and the Russian invasion of Afghanistan. Moreover, Carter no longer wanted to play an active and direct role in dealing with the politically sensitive Arab-Israeli conflict because he feared that it might result in "political suicide" in the light of the approaching 1980 presidential election year.[82] Therefore, he appointed Robert Strauss, an influential American Jew, as Middle East negotiator to promote Egyptian-Israeli talks on Palestinian autonomy.

While some progress was made on water rights and several other technical matters, no agreement was achieved on such critical issues as the ultimate status of the West Bank and Gaza; Israel's settlements policy; security arrangements; who would be permitted to vote for a self-governing authority and how much actual authority it would have; and what chance, if any, the inhabitants would have in determining their own future. Secretary Vance held that "Israel's retreat from full autonomy" as stated in the Camp David accords and her "unwillingness to declare a moratorium on the creation of new settlements" had "struck an almost mortal blow to the hopes for success" in the autonomy talks.[83] Even Defense Minister Weizman complained that "rather than viewing autonomy" as the beginning of self rule" as the United States and Egypt interpreted the Camp David accords to provide, "Begin saw it as the way to prevent Israeli withdrawal" and as an end in itself; he had so watered down the autonomy concept by the "restrictions and qualifications" he had "imposed" that he had "reduced the autonomy plan to a caricature of genuine self rule"; and he "backed away from implementing the autonomy agreements because his desire for annexation under the old Herut dream ultimately overcame the vision in him that would strive for peace."[84] Dayan told Carter that there was no chance for any progress in the talks as long as Begin remained in power because Begin "was firmly committed to retaining maximum control over the West Bank in spite of the Camp David commitments" and he opposed any further peace negotiations since they could only lead to American pressures to make additional disagreeable political and territorial concessions.[85] Dayan (on October 21, 1979) and Weizman (on May 25, 1980) ultimately resigned because they strongly disagreed with Begin's intransigence and dilatory actions and his refusal to implement meaningful Palestinian autonomy and to change his settlements policy.[86]

Although many Israelis, American Jews, and congressmen also opposed Begin's hardline policies and actions, the United States confined herself to mere verbal protests and criticisms and failed to take any effective actions— even economic ones—to elicit more forthcoming Israeli policies.[87] Consequently, American credibility was undermined to the point that Jordan and the moderate Palestinians in the occupied territories concluded that there was no useful purpose served in cooperating with the American-sponsored autonomy talks.

THE OCCUPIED TERRITORIES

Tensions in the occupied territories increased as a result of the Egyptian-Israeli treaty, the annexation of East Jerusalem,[88] attempts by religious extremists to force their way onto the Temple Mount, and conflicts between religious Jews and Arabs in Hebron and between settlers and Arab inhabitants in and around other populated centers. They were further exacerbated after Yitzhak Shamir replaced Dayan on March 10, 1980, as Foreign Minister and especially after Ariel Sharon became Defense Minister on August 4, 1981, and assumed responsibility for the occupied territories, because the government then began to take an even tougher line there in dealing with demonstrations, strikes, and rock throwers and in seeking to discourage any signs of support for the PLO and any displays of nationalist sentiments through cultural and other activities. There was a great increase in the use of curfews, collective punishments, arrests and detentions, demolition of houses of suspected terrorists, expulsion of Palestinian mayors and other leaders, travel restrictions, closing of schools and universities, forced land expropriations, and the use of live ammunition in combating demonstrators and rock throwers which resulted in numerous Palestinian casualties. Settlers were armed and "allowed" and sometimes even encouraged to take the law into their own hands with impunity.[89] The government also put off local elections which were due to take place in 1980 because of fear that PLO-backed candidates would win again as they had in 1976.

Israeli doves and some Labor party leaders criticized the harsh policies and a number of military reservists began to publicize accounts of orders to beat, humiliate, and intimidate the inhabitants.[90] Even Moshe Dayan said: "It seems to me that the military government sometimes treats the local residents like a tyrant treats natives" and "regards the residents as enemies that have to be subjugated, not as a people that we must live with."[91]

Harsh Israeli policies and actions led to more Palestinian demonstrations and strikes, as well as stone throwing, bomb and grenade attacks, and sniper firing. These caused many Israeli casualties and led to even tougher Israeli crackdowns, which provoked still more violent reactions by the inhabitants and thereby created more vicious cycles. Not only was there an increase in settler attacks on Palestinians and their properties, but there were also the beginnings of organized Jewish "terrorists" activities—including some bombings, grenade attacks, and attempts to blow up Islamic and Christian religious institutions.[92]

These attacks and counterattacks led to a serious deterioration in the occupied areas; to intensified Palestinian opposition to continued Israeli occupation and support for the PLO and Palestinian right to self-determination; to increased divisions within Israel between those who opposed and those who backed the government's actions; and to a weakening of Israel's position within the world community, including Western Europe.

Israel helped establish Village Leagues based primarily in the less nationalistically-oriented rural areas in an effort to weaken and replace PLO influence in the West Bank and to win over some leaders and generate popular support for Israel's policies and ultimate objectives there. Village League leaders were given funds which were to be used to provide economic development for those towns willing to cooperate. But the Leagues gained little popular support. Moreover, even League leaders expressed opposition to Israeli annexation of the area and rejected autonomy as an end in itself.[93]

JERUSALEM

Shortly after the 1967 war, the Israeli government proclaimed all of Jerusalem a single, united city under Israeli administration and had for all intents and purposes annexed it. Although nearly all countries, including the United States, refused to accept the legality of this action, Israel insisted that Jerusalem would forever be united under her rule. Moreover, she extended its borders until it ultimately encompassed a significant part of the West Bank.

On July 30, 1980, one day after the UN General Assembly had passed by a vote of 112 to 7 against and 20 abstentions a resolution calling for a Palestinian state and for an Israeli withdrawal from all territories occupied in 1967, including East Jerusalem, the Knesset passed a bill which more formally made "complete and united Jerusalem" the *de jure* capital of Israel to again make it clear that Israel would never give up any part of Jerusalem even as part of a peace settlement.

This action led not only to strikes and demonstrations in the occupied areas and throughout the Muslim world, but also to strong criticisms and protests from the United States, Western Europe, and the UN. The State Department publicly criticized Israel's action and held that the United States would not accept any "unilateral national legislation dealing with Jerusalem"; and, although the 1980 election campaign was in full swing, Carter reiterated the long-standing United States policy that the future of Jerusalem "can only be decided through negotiations."[94] (From the beginning the United States had considered East Jerusalem to have the status of occupied territory under Resolution 242.)[95] On June 13 Western European leaders meeting in Venice had already warned Israel against any change in the status of Jerusalem and held that they would never recognize any such change; and the Vatican stated that it regarded the move "very seriously."[96] On August 20, the UN Security Council, by a vote of 14 with the United States abstaining, called for the removal of all embassies then located in Jerusalem. Virtually all states involved, including the Netherlands and many Latin American states, complied with the resolution.[97] On December 15, the UN General Assembly also censured Israel for her action.

Israel ignored these protests. Thousands of Israelis, together with units from the pro-Israeli Lebanese militia in south Lebanon, marched in Jerusalem in support of the Knesset's action. On December 3, an Israeli government committee approved a plan which would increase the population of Jerusalem by one-third.[98]

Various Jewish religious zealots advocated expelling Arab inhabitants from the Muslim quarter of East Jerusalem, taking control over the Temple Mount, and destroying the Aqsa and Dome of the Rock mosques in order to rebuild the Jewish Temple. For example, some zealots tried, in September 1980, to build a tunnel under the Temple Mount; in July 1982, to forcibly evacuate some Arab inhabitants from the Muslim quarter; in March 1983, to seize control of the Temple Mount; and in January 1984, to destroy the mosques there with explosives. In April 1982, an Israeli soldier, apparently a supporter of Rabbi Meir Kahane, a religious and political fanatic, shot his way into the Dome of the Rock and sprayed it with gunfire, killing two and wounding nine. Some of these extremist actions led to angry Arab protests and riots throughout the occupied territories and they were condemned by many Israelis and the Israeli government.

Studies by Merion Benvenisti, a former deputy mayor of Jerusalem, and Israeli Professor Alex Weingard showed that while there were no physical barriers in Jerusalem, the Arab and Jewish inhabitants there remained sharply divided economically and socially with "little communication between them outside the market place." According to Benvenisti, they remained consciously separated and lived within "two separate systems with little integration" and with widespread discrimination against the Arabs. "Take away Israeli coercive powers, and the city splits on the ethnic fault line." Thus, according to Weingard, Jerusalem was not truly a "united" city.[99]

UNITED STATES 1980 ELECTIONS

In 1980 the Carter administration became increasingly preoccupied with the presidential election campaign. Political advisors warned against doing or saying anything which might antagonize influential pro-Israeli groups. Carter's opponents in both the primary and final elections had begun to take a strongly pro-Israeli stand. On March 1, 1980, the United States voted for a Security Council resolution that strongly condemned Israel's settlements policy. Israel and pro-Israeli groups protested so forcefully that Carter felt it necessary to publicly repudiate the vote and to claim that it came about as a result of a breakdown in communications. On April 30, the United States vetoed a Security Council resolution affirming the right of the Palestinians to their own state. While the United States did not veto Security Council resolutions on June 30 and August 20 criticizing Israel's moves on Jerusalem, she did abstain. In presidential debates with Ronald Reagan on October 28, Carter strongly criticized the PLO as a "terrorist organization." In fact, both candidates tried to outbid each other for support of the pro-Israeli voters.[100]

During the campaign Ronald Reagan made some pro-Israeli statements which greatly conflicted with several traditional official American positions. He held that, while Israeli settlements were obstacles to peace, they were not illegal; he promised not to talk with the PLO even if it accepted Resolution 242 and Israel's right to exist; and he claimed that all of Jerusalem should remain under Israeli sovereignty.[101]

WESTERN EUROPE'S ATTEMPTED PEACE INITIATIVE

Western Europe had been deeply concerned about the great potential dangers which would arise from the lack of serious progress in bringing about an overall peace settlement. In early 1980, because autonomy talks had been suspended, the Camp David agreements seemed to be at a dead end, and Carter was so preoccupied with the election campaign that peace negotiations had been placed on a back burner and because European leaders felt that the impasse could be broken only by bringing the Palestinians into the peace process, EEC members decided that they should take the initiative by introducing a Security Council resolution which would combine the basic principles in Resolution 242 and provisions for the right of the Palestinians to self-determination and for PLO participation in peace negotiations. They believed that such a resolution could encourage moderate PLO leaders to openly accept Resolution 242 as part of a broader resolution.[102]

However, because the United States warned that she would veto such a resolution, the EEC decided to drop the idea of a resolution and, instead, to issue a declaration, which it did on June 13, 1980, in a summit meeting in Venice. This declaration went further than ever before in support of Palestinian aspirations and the PLO. It called for (1) "the right to existence and to security of all states in the region, including Israel"; (2) Palestinian "right to self-determination"; (3) "PLO association with the negotiations"; (4) nonacceptance of any unilateral changes in the status of Jerusalem; (5) a halt in "illegal settlements, as well as modifications in population and property in the occupied Arab territories"; and (6) and an "end to the territorial occupation which it [Israel] has maintained since . . . 1967." [103]

While Israel quickly denounced the Venice Declaration, many Arabs welcomed it. Even moderate PLO leaders held that it contained positive aspects; but they criticized its failure to specifically provide for a Palestinian state and to recognize the PLO as the only legitimate representative of the Palestinian people. They and other Arabs were especially disappointed because Western European leaders had watered down the language of the original version of the declaration as a result of United States pressures and had confined themselves to a mere declaration which contained no provisions for implementation. [104]

The United States was unhappy with the declaration and sought to discourage any further European peace initiative. She successfully opposed European efforts at a NATO meeting to draft a similar statement and at the UN to present a Security Council resolution which, like the one presented in January 1976, combined the principles of Resolution 242 with the right of the Palestinians to self-determination.

Nevertheless, many Western European governments were anxious to improve their ties with the Arabs and even with the Palestinians. Nearly all allowed the PLO to open information offices; several gave diplomatic status to the PLO; Arafat and other PLO officials were repeatedly received by top officials in most Western European countries; and EEC spokesmen at the UN repeatedly expressed support for Palestinian national rights, including a "homeland." In later years this was upgraded by using the word "state" and requiring PLO involvement in any peace process. Some European leaders openly began to criticize the Camp David accords and the Egyptian-Israeli peace treaty on the grounds that they left the Palestinian question unresolved and failed to facilitate a comprehensive peace settlement. [105]

The Reagan Administration, Israel, the Arabs, and Palestinians, January 1981–March 1985

The election of Ronald Reagan was welcomed in Israel, but caused dismay in the Arab world. The Arabs had hoped that a reelected Carter would feel sufficiently free of domestic political pressures to finally apply effective pressures on Israel so she would be more flexible, especially on the Palestinian issue.[1] The Arabs were particularly worried about the strongly pro-Israeli appointments (especially Alexander Haig as Secretary of State) Reagan made after the elections, and about the lack of knowledge about the Middle East on the part of virtually all top appointees.

Reagan and two of his top advisors—Haig and Richard V. Allen, National Security Council adviser—judged the Arab-Israeli conflict not on its own merits but in terms of East-West confrontation. They believed that Israel was America's most important and dependable ally against the Soviet Union in the Middle East. Soon after taking office, Reagan continued to express hostility to the PLO, accusing it of being composed of a "bunch of thugs"; changed the long-standing United States position on Israeli settlements by claiming they were not illegal; became primarily preoccupied with the alleged Soviet threat to the Gulf region and not the Arab-Israeli conflict, which was considered to be of only peripheral importance; and sought to promote a "strategic consensus" in the Middle East against the Soviet Union and her surrogates (which he assumed Syria and the PLO to be) with the cooperation of Israel, Egypt, Jordan, and Saudi Arabia.[2]

In April, Haig went to the Middle East to try to convince the conservative Arab leaders of the Soviet threat and of the need to join a strategic consensus. Saudi and Jordanian leaders told Haig that Israel and the unresolved Arab-Israeli conflict and Palestinian problem, not the Soviet Union, remained their primary concern and source of danger; were the main reasons for the turmoil and instability in the area; and provided the Soviets with "troubled waters in which to fish." They held that they could not fully and openly cooperate with the United States politically and militarily until there was an acceptable comprehensive Arab-Israeli settlement based on UN resolutions. They warned that continued failure to bring about such a settlement would weaken their position, would undermine America's position to the benefit of the USSR, and sooner or later would provide the greatest threat to uninterrupted Western access to Middle Eastern oil.[3]

According to the *New York Times* (April 18, 1981) the Reagan Administration assured Israel that it would not openly criticize her military attacks on Lebanon. Thereby, it gave Israel's army and air force "a new flexibility" which Israel was busy using by making "air strikes and ground assaults against Palestinian guerrilla bases" and in support of Israeli-backed rightwing Christian militia forces fighting Palestinians in south and central Lebanon.

On April 28, Israeli planes shot down two Syrian helicopters in the Zahle area where Phalangist forces had come into conflict with Syrian troops while the Phalangists were trying to extend and strengthen their positions there. This caused the Syrians to move in SAM-6 anti-aircraft missiles to defend their own positions in the Bekaa Valley. Israel demanded the immediate removal of these missiles and threatened to attack them if they were not removed.[4]

Reagan dispatched an able and experienced diplomat, Philip Habib, to the Middle East to prevent an Israeli-Syrian conflict. The United States also sought the help of the Saudis to obtain Syrian cooperation.

While the Syrian missile crisis remained unresolved, on June 6 Israeli planes flew over Jordanian and Saudi airspace and bombed an Iraqi nuclear plant near Baghdad. Begin claimed that it was an act of self-defense on the alleged grounds that the plant would be used to build atomic weapons—a charge which was denied by the International Atomic Energy Agency (which had recently inspected the plant), the French (who were helping to build the plant), and a Congressional research service in Washington.[5] Nearly all states, including the United States, condemned the attack. The United States even temporarily suspended delivery of four F-16 planes because of it. The leader of the Labor party also criticized the bombing and accused Begin of "acting out of electoral considerations which ignore the national interest."[6]

The attack and violation of Jordanian and Saudi airspace, followed by continued reconnaissance flights over Saudi Arabia, humiliated the Arabs and embarrassed Sadat. Even pro-Western Arab leaders were angry with the United States because American planes had been used in the bombing and because in a news conference on June 16, Reagan, after condemning the attack, went on to hold that he recognized "the Israeli preoccupation over" Iraqi hostility and he "could not see Israel as a threat to neighboring countries," while "Israel had been under threat from the beginning."[7] Israel's action made it more difficult than ever for Reagan to convince even the most conservative Arabs that Russia and not Israel was their primary threat.

Although the polls in Israel had been showing the Labor alignment ahead of the Likud, the Likud nevertheless won the election on June 30, 1981. Begin felt that his reelection had given him a clear mandate to carry out an authentic, ideologically-based, hard-line Likud policy. While in the past the Likud government had some less militant leaders in such key positions as Foreign Minister (Dayan) and Defense Minister (Weizman) who had played a somewhat moderating role in forming Israel's policies toward the Arab states and in the occupied areas, the new administration was to be dominated by hard-core Herut ideologists and by such leading hawks as Ariel Sharon as Defense Minister and Yitzhak Shamir as Foreign Minister—both of whom had opposed the Camp David accords and the Egyptian-Israeli peace treaty and advocated using military force to attain political as well as military goals.[8]

After the election, Israel accelerated her settlements activities, continued her tough line in the occupied areas, and launched a series of "preemptive" air strikes against Palestinian targets in Lebanon. Since the PLO retaliated against these attacks with shell and rocket fire on northern Israeli towns, the conflict became even more intense. After one Israeli large-scale air strike in July against the Palestinians in Beirut had caused heavy casualties (150 dead), Western European countries, the UN Security Council, and the United States condemned this costly attack and deplored the escalating violence. The United States ordered a delay in the delivery of six F-16s and directed Philip Habib to seek a cease-fire between the Israelis and Palestinians.

Working through UN and Saudi intermediaries, the United States negotiated indirectly with the PLO as well as directly with Israel. Agreement was reached and a cease-fire came into effect on July 24. Israel accepted the cease-fire because she feared the consequence of further deterioration in United States-Israeli relations. Israel's heavy attacks causing many civilian casualties were being criticized not only by some Israelis and administration officials, but also by congressmen and the American media. Later on, however, since the PLO unexpectedly abided by the cease-fire, some Israel officials began to have second thoughts about accepting it. They began to fear that this might convince the United States that the PLO was a responsible negotiating party which could be depended upon to keep any agreements it made and that this might encourage the United States to consider closer contacts with the PLO.[9]

Some Palestinian leaders saw major advantages in the cease-fire. They held that by negotiating, even if indirectly, with the PLO, the United States and Israel had at least implicitly recognized the PLO as a legitimate party to the dispute. Moreover, by abiding by the cease-fire they could prove that they could be responsible negotiators.

While during the cease-fire no incidents were initiated from Lebanon, two unsuccessful guerilla operations were attempted from Jordanian territory on August 11, 1981 and January 30, 1982. Moreover, some extremist Palestinians attacked Israeli diplomatic missions in Athens (August 11, 1981), Paris (March 3, 1982), and Vienna (May 15, 1982), and a synagogue in Vienna (August 2, 1981); and bombed a Jewish district in Antwerp (October 20, 1981) and a Jewish restaurant in West Berlin (January 15, 1982) causing a large number of casualties. There were also some grenade and bomb attacks against Israelis within the occupied territories, causing still more casualties.

In a news conference on August 8, 1981, Saudi Crown Prince Fahd presented a new eight-point peace plan which called for an Israeli withdrawal from all territories occupied in 1967, including East Jerusalem; recognition of the right of the Palestinians to their own state; the establishment of a UN mandate over the occupied areas for a short period after an Israeli withdrawal; and the removal of settlements from occupied areas. The plan also recognized "the right of all states in the region to live in peace"—which Saudi Prince Saud on November 5 and President Reagan on November 10 interpreted as implying recognition of Israel.[10]

Israel quickly rejected the plan. Western Europe generally supported it. Although the United States held it was at least a starting point for negotiations, she strongly objected to parts of it.

While only Libya rejected the plan outright, there was considerable hesitation to support it on the part of several Arab states, especially since Saudi Arabia had been unable to obtain meaningful support from the United States for the plan and some Arab leaders preferred to delay discussion of it until after April 1982, when Israel's intentions to withdraw fully from the Sinai had been tested.[11] Thus, the plan failed to be adopted at an Arab summit in Fez in late November.

Arafat held that the plan was a "good beginning" and a "good basis for a comprehensive and lasting peace in the area." However, some other PLO leaders objected to the plan because it failed to refer to the PLO and its role in any peace process.[12]

There was increasing unrest in Egypt during the summer of 1981. There were clashes between Copts and Muslim fundamentalists and economic conditions had not improved despite peace with Israel. There was also rising opposition, especially among the fundamentalists, to widespread corruption, Sadat's life style, his close ties with a strongly pro-Israeli United States, and his failure to resolve favorably the Palestinian and Jerusalem problems. On October 6, one small group of Muslim fanatics assassinated Sadat. His successor, former Vice President Husni Mubarak, sought to improve Egypt's relations with other Arabs and took strong stands on behalf of the PLO and the Palestinian issue. However, he was reluctant to do anything which might antagonize Israel who was still in the process of withdrawing from the remainder of the Sinai and of facing strong internal opposition to the complete dismantling of Israeli settlements in the Sinai. Even after Israel's withdrawal had been completed in April 1982, he repeatedly stated that Egypt would abide by the Egyptian-Israeli treaty. But he also warned that Egypt's normalization of relations would be affected by Israeli actions. While wanting to retain good ties with the United States, Mubarak did not want Egypt to be as dependent and trusting of her as Sadat had been.

US–Israeli Memorandum of Understanding, November 30, 1981

While the Reagan Administration's primary concern in the Middle East, as elsewhere, remained the "Soviet threat," there were serious divisions within the administration about how best to deal with it in the Middle East. Haig believed that Israel provided our primary strategic asset in the area and pressed for closer military ties with her. Secretary of Defense Caspar Weinberger and the Pentagon, however, believed that the large, economically and geopolitically important Arab world was also vital to America's strategic interests. Therefore, according to the *New York Times* (February 15, 1982) Weinberger, who believed that the United States had neglected her ties with friendly Arabs because of "being hostage to Israeli policy," urged that greater pressures be applied against Israel to make concessions on Arab-Israeli problems and that more advanced weapons be sold to moderate Arabs. Thus, after a year in office, the Reagan Administration remained divided and had not yet formulated a clear, consistent policy toward the Middle East.

In the autumn of 1981, the administration made two important moves. By means of determined efforts it was able to obtain the consent of Congress for the sale of AWACS to Saudia Arabia despite powerful opposition on the parts of Israel and her American supporters. This was consistent with the views of Weinberger and the Pentagon. However, Haig pressed for and succeeded in getting Reagan's approval to negotiate with Israel a Memorandum of Understanding on Strategic Cooperation, despite Pentagon opposition. This agreement provided for the strengthening of United States-Israeli strategic cooperation against threats to the Middle East "caused by the Soviet Union or Soviet-controlled forces from outside of the region" and for the establishment of a coordinating council and working groups to deal with research, military cooperation, maintenance facilities, and other matters. The agreement helped relax tensions which had developed between the United States and Israel.[13]

Israelis, however, were divided over the agreement, which passed the Knesset on December 2, 1918 by a vote of only 57 to 53 with 2 abstentions. Many Israelis felt that the agreement was too one-sided because it tied Israel to American strategic aims vis-à-vis the Soviet Union without committing the United States to help Israel against the Arabs. They believed that Israel should concentrate on her own defense against the Arabs. While Israel objected strongly to Weinberger's views, she was convinced that as in the past, she had "taken on the United States time and again and [had] seemingly won." [14] When Reagan wrote Begin to assure him that the United States was committed to maintaining Israel's qualitative technical edge over the Arabs, it was clear that Begin need not fear great pressures for concessions. Moreover, Israeli leaders were so convinced that Israel was strong enough to resist making concessions, that in early May, 1982, the Knesset even went so far as to approve a policy statement approving Begin's plan to extend Israeli sovereignty over the West Bank following the interim period called for in the Camp David accords. [15]

The Memorandum of Agreement angered the Arabs, who charged that it marked a major qualitative change in the United States alignment with Israel and that it provided a commitment to continued support of Israeli "aggression and expansionism." [16]

ANNEXING THE GOLAN HEIGHTS

While international attention was concentrating on the December crisis in Poland, on December 14, 1981 the Israeli Knesset passed a bill which extended Israeli laws, jurisdiction, and administration to the Golan Heights. There was strong opposition in Israel to this move—especially among those who felt that since Israel already had complete control over the area, this action would only create unnecessary provocations and even problems with the United States. Labor forced a vote of confidence on the annexation and this was defeated by a relatively narrow vote of 57 to 47. [17]

The United States responded on December 18 by suspending the recently signed Memorandum of Understanding and United States-Israeli relations were to deteriorate again. The EEC condemned the annexation on December 15 and on December 17 the UN Security Council passed by a unanimous vote a resolution which called upon Israel to rescind her decision. Several African countries which had been considering restoring diplomatic relations with Israel now changed their minds. [18]

The Arabs, especially the Syrians, reacted angrily. The annexation, followed in early 1982 by statements by the Israeli foreign and defense ministers that "Israel will make no more [territorial] compromises" and "this means the Golan Heights as well," [19] further strengthened Syrian conviction that Israel would never willingly give up any part of the Golan even in return for peace and favorable security arrangements.

While the Druze inhabitants living on the Golan had been relatively quiet over the years, they now began to demonstrate against the annexation and Israeli efforts to force Israeli citizenship on them. Demonstrations and riots went on for months and these led to many arrests, curfews, and the use of gunfire against demonstrators. These developments caused increased tensions and opposition to Israeli occupation.

THE INVASION OF LEBANON

According to a leading Israeli correspondent and writer, Amnon Kapeliuk, Sharon had admitted "preparing for the invasion of Lebanon since his nomination as minister of defense last August (1981). . . . Even a partial budget for the war had been projected" and Chief of Staff Rafael Eitan enthusiastically supported the idea. Then, Begin, Sharon, and Eitan waited for a pretext—"any pretext"—to launch the invasion. They came close to doing this in February and April, 1982. Since the cease-fire on the Lebanese border was holding and the PLO stressed its intention to abide by it, Begin then announced that any attempt anywhere in the world against Israel—and not only from Lebanon, the original intention of the cease-fire agreement—would be considered as a violation of the cease-fire.[20]

For Sharon's plan to succeed, Israel needed the cooperation of the Phalangists and the acquiescence of the United States. In January 1982, Sharon informed the Phalangists of his plan, which included the seizure of Beirut. Since Phalangist leaders had for years been urging the Israelis to intervene militarily in Lebanon in order to drive out the Palestinians and the Syrians, they readily supported the plan.

The Chief of Israeli Intelligence in February and Sharon in May discussed the plan with Haig and other American officials. Sharon presented it not as a mere local measure "but as a Grand Design with repercussions favorable to Western interests in the global balance."[21] Haig saw the invasion as an opportunity to benefit the United States by driving out of Lebanon the Syrians and the PLO, whom he considered Soviet allies; facilitating a broad solution to the Lebanese problem favorable to the United States; and speeding up autonomy talks. Thus, according to Zeev Schiff, a leading Israeli writer on military affairs, Haig did not oppose the plan and Israeli leaders were "convinced . . . that the final green light had come from Washington."[22]

Sharon's "Grand Design" had major political and military objectives. He wished to destroy PLO military and political positions in Lebanon not only to protect Israeli border settlements but also to erase all symbols of Palestinian nationalism there in order to demoralize the inhabitants of the West Bank and Gaza by convincing them that they no longer had a viable spokesman and that they therefore had no alternative to accepting permanent Israeli rule. According to Schiff and others, after winning in Lebanon, Sharon planned on turning "Israel's military might against Jordan to impose a new political order there as well" which would make East Jordan the Palestinian state to which the Palestinians in Lebanon and the West Bank could be transferred.[23]

Sharon also intended on driving Syrian military forces and political influence from Lebanon and to install a Phalangist-dominated, pro-Israeli, and anti-Syrian and anti-PLO government there which would make peace and become allied with Israel. Begin and Sharon also hoped that the invasion would provide some political and psychological compensation for the unpopular withdrawal from the Sinai and reunite the hawkish community which had been split over Camp David and the Egyptian-Israeli peace treaty.[24]

Two important factors made the invasion possible. Since the Egyptian-Israeli peace treaty had split the Arab world and removed the danger of any military response from Egypt, Israel was able to leave her southern flank only lightly defended while she conducted an all-out optional war to the north. Moreover, American failure to act more forcibly than she did when Israel attacked the Iraqi reactor and annexed East Jerusalem and the Golan Heights and the conviction that United States officials had actually given them a "green light" encouraged Israeli leaders to believe that there would not be any meaningful United States opposition to the invasion.[25]

In the early months of 1982, Israel built up a large military force near the Lebanese border and waited for some incident which could be used as a "pretext" for the invasion. For months, the United States media was full of reports about an impending invasion and Israeli generals and diplomats frankly stated that it was only a "matter of time" before Israel took action.[26]

Since PLO leaders knew that they would be no match for the powerful Israeli military forces and since they felt that they had achieved something important from the cease-fire, they concluded that they should act with restraint and avoid providing Israel with an excuse for an attack. Thus, the PLO kept the Israeli-Lebanese border quiet since the July 1981 cease-fire.[27]

On April 21, Israeli jets attacked PLO positions in Lebanon, killing 23 and wounding many others. Israel claimed that this was a retaliation for the death of an Israeli soldier in south Lebanon. The PLO deliberately did not respond. On May 9, Israeli planes attacked again killing 16 and wounding 54. This time the PLO fired on northern Israel, but carefully avoided causing any casualties. Arafat issued a statement saying the PLO would continue to abide by the cease-fire.[28]

On June 4, anti-PLO Palestinians (who belonged to the dissident Abu Nidal group which had been outlawed by the PLO and had not been operating from Lebanon) seriously wounded the Israeli ambassador to Britain. The PLO denounced the attack and denied responsibility for it.[29] Nevertheless, the Israeli cabinet ordered a major airstrike on Beirut, which killed at least 45 and wounded 150, mostly civilians, and which finally provoked the PLO into shelling northern Israel, killing one person and injuring five others. Israel used this incident as an excuse to launch a full-scale attack.[30]

Begin and Sharon had led the Israeli cabinet, the Knesset, and even the United States to believe that the invasion would be a limited operation involving the seizure of a security strip some 40 kilometers wide in order to prevent further shelling of northern Israel. The cabinet members gave their approval on that basis.[31] But Sharon did not stop there because he had more sweeping plans which required going to Beirut and bringing Syrian forces into the war.

Although the Syrians sought to avoid being drawn into the conflict, on the fourth day of the invasion Israeli forces initiated clashes with them, thereby precipitating heavy fighting. After receiving a warning from the Soviet Union that further attacks on the Syrians would have global implications, Reagan pressured Israel to agree to a cease-fire which came into effect on June 11.[32] However, the cease-fire did not last long and there was considerable intermittent fighting, with Syria suffering heavy military losses.

The Maronites at first welcomed the invasion and cooperated militarily with it. But after Israel had cut off West Beirut on June 14 and surrounded PLO forces there, the Phalangists were unwilling to take on the very costly task of attacking and defeating them, as requested by Israel; and this refusal angered the Israelis. Moreover, after Israel by means of her military pressure and resources had helped Bashir Gemayal, military leader of the Phalangist militia, to be elected as president of Lebanon on August 23, he realized that he had to develop greater independence from the Israelis if he was to be able to rule a united Lebanon, the majority of whose population was not Christian and bitterly opposed to close ties with Israel. Thus, he proved to be less willing to cooperate with Israel, especially in agreeing to negotiate as soon as possible a peace treaty with her. This caused the Israelis to become increasingly disenchanted with him.[33]

On June 5, UN Security Council Resolution 508 ordered an immediate and simultaneous cease-fire. On June 6, the Security Council unanimously passed Resolution 509 demanding observance of the earlier cease-fires and a full withdrawal of all Israeli forces ''forthwith and unconditionally'' to the internationally recognized border. After Israeli forces continued to bomb Beirut and inflicted heavy civilian casualties and vast destruction, the Security Council, with American support, passed further resolutions criticizing Israeli attacks, cease-fire violations, and blockade of Beirut. On August 18, the UN General Assembly closed a four-day emergency session by approving three resolutions which criticized Israel's invasion, demanded an end to it, and called for sanctions against Israel if she failed to comply. These Assembly resolutions passed by large majorities with only Israel and the United States voting against them.

The United States reacted to the invasion with a number of carefully nuanced statements which deplored the new "outbursts of violence," but stopped short of actually condemning Israel. The Reagan Administration generally shared Israel's goals of driving out Palestinian and Syrian forces from Lebanon and establishing a pro-Israeli and pro-Western Christian-led government which would make peace with her. While several Administration officials, such as Defense Secretary Caspar Weinberger, wanted a tough stand against the invasion, on June 19 Haig tried to justify it by claiming that it was merely "a culmination of a long period of unacceptable instability in southern Lebanon."[34] On the whole, the government's attitude remained equivocal. The United States voted for a number of Security Council resolutions which criticized Israel's invasion and the heavy civilian casualties which resulted from it and, on the basis of an administration report which indicated that Israel might have violated a United States arms agreement by using cluster bombs, she halted the shipment of cluster bombs while she reviewed the matter. Yet, she vetoed a number of other Security Council resolutions which condemned Israel for failing to withdraw from Lebanon, called for an Israeli pullback from the Beirut area, and called for cutting off economic aid to Israel until she withdrew. The media and even some members of Congress strongly criticized those Israeli military actions which were causing large civilian casualties. Begin faced great hostility when he met with the Senate Foreign Relations Committee on June 22 and even Reagan strongly critized Israel after she began to heavily bomb and shell Beirut. Public opinion polls showed that increasing numbers of Americans now opposed the invasion. Yet, by early 1983 Congress not only opposed reducing aid to Israel as some urged, but actually increased the amount of aid over past years. The administration acquiesced in this move.[35]

Western European governments were much more strongly aroused over the invasion. The EEC denounced it as a "flagrant violation of international law" and as another obstacle to peace in the area and insisted on an immediate Israeli withdrawal. The United States rejected Western European calls for formal condemnation of Israel at a NATO summit in Bonn. Although on July 27 France joined Egypt in introducing in the Security Council a joint draft resolution calling for a diplomatic settlement of the Lebanese crisis and mutual recognition by Israel and the PLO, it was not pressed to a vote because of American opposition. Therefore, European leaders concluded that they were powerless to act until the United States was prepared to cooperate.[36]

In an attempt to prevent the Israelis from invading West Beirut and to stop the bloody fighting, the United States took the lead in negotiating an agreement which provided for the safe evacuation of PLO forces from West Beirut. Once again the United States and Israel became involved in indirect negotiations with the PLO. The agreement provided for an international force composed of troops from the United States, France, and Italy to enter West Beirut and supervise the safe withdrawal of PLO as well as some trapped Syrian military forces by sea and land. The PLO agreed to withdraw only after receiving a formal written guarantee from the United States which stated that the "governments of Lebanon and the U.S. would provide appropriate guarantees of . . . the safety" of "law abiding Palestinian noncombatants left behind in Beirut, including he families of those who have departed."[37]

In late August the multinational force took up positions, and PLO and Syrian forces were evacuated without incident by September 1. American troops left by September 10 and those from France and Italy left shortly there-after.

On September 14, president-elect Bashir Gemayel was killed in a bomb explosion. In response, on September 15–16, Israeli forces invaded and took control of West Beirut. Since this action caused heavy civilian casualties, it was widely condemned, even by the United States, as well as by a Security Council resolution which was passed by unanimous vote on September 17.

On September 16, Israel allowed Phalangist militia units to enter the Sabra and Shatilla refugee camps in West Beirut and in four days they slaughtered many hundreds of their civilian inhabitants. This brought about an even more intense and widespread condemnation of Israel not only by the UN Security Council on September 19, the EEC, and many Americans, but also by large numbers of Israelis who strongly criticized their government for allowing the massacre to take place. In fact, on September 25, more than 350,000 Israelis demonstrated in Tel Aviv to protest their government's conduct during and following the massacre and demanded an independent inquiry to ascertain responsibility for it.

A high-level Israeli commission of inquiry reported on February 8, 1983, that the Phalangists had "direct responsibility" for the massacre, but that since Israel was the "occupier" of the territory involved, she was responsible under international law for the safety of the people there. It also held that Defense Minister Sharon and three generals had "indirect responsibility" and they should, therefore, either resign or be dismissed. The commission criticized Begin and Shamir for their roles and felt that they had a "certain degree of blame," but it did not recommend any action against them.[38] Sharon resigned, but he was kept on as minister without portfolio with reduced power and influence.

The Arabs and especially the Palestinians were furious because the United States had failed to live up to her formal guarantee of the safety of the Palestinian civilians left behind in Beirut. Demonstrations were held by Israeli

Arabs and by Arabs in the occupied areas. Egypt recalled her ambassador as an expression of condemnation.

The United States joined by France, Italy, and Britain, hurriedly sent new peacekeeping forces to Lebanon. The first units began arriving on September 24.

Several Israeli dovish groups strongly and publicly opposed the war from the beginning and thousands of their members demonstrated and submitted letters and petitions against it. On June 26, 20,000 demonstrated in Tel Aviv under the banner of The Committee Against the War in Lebanon and on July 3, 100,000 demonstrated under the banner of Peace Now. Other anti-war groups (such as There is a Limit, Soldiers Against Silence, and Parents Against Silence) sprang up during the war. Before the invasion, a number of Israeli leaders questioned whether Israel's security really required a major invasion and some Labor party leaders opposed getting into a war. After the invasion began, however, the Labor party and the great preponderance of the people backed it. But support for the war declined after Israeli forces kept driving beyond the 40 kilometer mark to Beirut, casualties began to mount on all sides, and it had become clear that Israel would not be able to achieve her objectives and had become even more isolated than ever within the world community. According to Zeev Schiff, the apparent "green light" given by the United States to the initial invasion and the "moderate and indifferent U.S. reaction" to Israel's military advances beyond 40 kilometers "weakened the hand of those elements in Israel—both in the parliamentary opposition and in the general public—who opposed extending the war further into Lebanon and thus helped insure that the offensive would not be limited to the defense perimeter of the Galilee townships and villages."[39] Open opposition to the invasion increased greatly after the Sabra and Shatilla massacres. The Labor party now backed and participated in large-scale demonstrations against the government's conduct of the war. Many leading Israelis (including a former president, foreign minister, and chief of staff and even the Israeli ambassador who had been injured in London), as well as major newspapers (*Davar, Haaretz, Maariv, Jerusalem Post, Yediot Aharonot*), also began to criticize the war.[40]

THE RESULTS OF THE WAR

While the war had destroyed the PLO military and political structures in south Lebanon and the Beirut area and had compelled PLO leaders and thousands of commandos to leave Lebanon, it failed to resolve any important aspect of the Arab-Israeli conflict and even to achieve major goals Sharon had in going to war. In fact, the war was to have many adverse consequences for Israel, as well as for Lebanon, the United States, the Palestinians in Lebanon, and the cause of peace in the Middle East.

During the war itself Israel suffered a large number of casualties (nearly 500 dead and several thousand wounded). Even after the war had ended, Israel continued to suffer additional hundreds of casualties during her occupation, especially in south Lebanon. Israel's economy had been seriously damaged by the large financial burdens of the war and the occupation. The war had dampened Israeli spirit and self confidence, weakened the national consensus, and caused serious polarization and divisions, especially between Oriental (Sephardic) and Western (Ashkenazi) Jews, which led to some violent confrontations between hawkish and dovish elements of the population, particularly during anti-war demonstrations, and to growing concern among many liberal Israelis about the future of their country. For the first time the nature of the state and the mission of her army and military policy were being seriously questioned and even military morale seemed to be at an "all-time low." Many Israelis were also concerned that the invasion had badly tarnished Israel's image in the eyes of the world and had further isolated Israel within the international community.[41]

On the other hand, the war also strengthened the peace movement in Israel and made more Israelis aware of the limits of military power and of the inability of Israel to resolve the Palestinian problem and to rearrange the Middle East to Israel's liking by the use of force alone. Many felt that future governments would have to be more cautious in their use of force and in going to war without a national consensus.

The war caused large casualties among the Palestinians, both military and civilian; destroyed their main military, political, and administrative bases in Lebanon; and helped ultimately to create a split in the PLO. It also caused emotional hardship for large numbers of Palestinians, because when they left Beirut many commandos had to leave their families behind without protection and means for their support.

At the end of the war the PLO remained a viable organization in which Arafat, despite his diminished powers, remained as the only leader with broad support, especially in the occupied territories and the diaspora. Because many Palestinians believed that they had fought well during the conflict, their pride and morale remained high. Moreover, the picture of the suffering and homeless Palestinians was greatly sharpened as a result of the war and this brought increased sympathy and support for the Palestinian cause throughout the world. The military defeat of the Palestinians did not, as Sharon had expected, cow the Palestinians in the occupied areas and cause them to be more cooperative with Israel's goal of retaining permanent control over them. In fact, Israel's invasion brought increased tension and opposition to Israeli rule in these areas and increased support for the PLO not only in the West Bank and Gaza, but also among the Israeli Arabs.[42]

Some Palestinian commandos had begun to slip back into the Beirut area, especially from northern and northeastern Lebanon. Moreover, the PLO continued to operate against Israel from Lebanon and Jordan, although on a much diminished scale. Three rockets were fired from Lebanon in 1983 and 1984, and two rockets from Jordan in August 1983, without causing any casualties. Several unsuccessful attempts were made to land commandos by small boats. The PLO began to put most stress on encouraging attacks on Israelis by the inhabitants of occupied areas.

The invasion not only caused huge casualties and physical destruction in Lebanon, but also helped to destroy the fragile balance which had existed in Lebanon since the end of the 1975–76 civil war and to further deepen the rift within that country. Therefore, when Israel, after arming both Druze and Phalangists, suddenly withdrew from the Shuf Mountains of Lebanon, this move reignited a violent civil war as both Druze and Phalangists sought to seize control over the evacuated areas.

In significant ways Israel's position in Lebanon was to end up worse than before. The killing, wounding, and uprooting of many thousands of Lebanese, as well as Palestinian, civilians as a result of the invasion produced another generation of hatred. Ties with Phalangist political leaders were to be weakened and distrust between them and Israel was to grow. Although Israeli forces had at first been welcomed by many Shiites in south Lebanon, continued Israeli rule, which was often oppressive, led to almost daily attacks by an increasingly hostile Shiite population against the occupying forces.

While the Syrians had suffered heavy casualties and military equipment losses during the war and their position in Lebanon was temporarily weakened, the Soviet Union, by providing the most advanced planes, missiles and other weapons, quickly rebuilt Syria's military power to the point where she was much more powerful—and, therefore, a greater military threat to Israel—than before the invasion. The USSR also sent thousands of her own military personnel and technicians and publicly committed herself to come to the aid of Syria if Syria proper was attacked. Syria also soon restored her strong political influence in Lebanon, while that of Israel and the United States declined.

The Soviet Union had suffered temporary setbacks because she failed to come to the aid of Syria and the PLO during the war and because of Syria's military defeat. However, after Syria had been rearmed and Soviet military personnel was brought into Syria in great numbers and after both Israel and the United States failed to attain their objectives in Lebanon, the Soviet Union's position in the Middle East ended up stronger than before the invasion.[43]

While, at first, American influence in Lebanon had increased, United States officials soon discovered that they had been sucked into a dangerous role there without fully understanding the complicated internal situation which existed and the implications of the misguided policies which were ultimately followed there. She was to end up suffering the loss of many Marines, the loss of influence in Lebanon, and a severe blow to her prestige and credibility throughout the Middle East, especially after she withdrew the Marines from Lebanon. Moreover, she found that both she and the Soviet Union had increased their commitments to their respective clients, resulting in a greater potential for a superpower confrontation in the future.[44]

The Israeli invasion also hurt Egyptian-Israeli relations. Although Egypt stated she would abide by her treaty with Israel, she recalled her ambassador and broke off autonomy talks until Israel completely withdrew from Lebanon. Cultural, commercial, and diplomatic contacts dropped off sharply and a situation labelled a "cold peace" developed. There was increased belief in Egypt that Sadat's policies had been based on false assumptions and had helped isolate Egypt in the Arab world and made possible the invasion of Lebanon. There was also increased disillusionment among many Egyptians over America's role and policies in Lebanon and the Middle East and disappointment in her inability to prevent the invasion and to obtain an early Israeli withdrawal from Lebanon.

THE REAGAN PEACE PLAN

The 1982 Israeli invasion compelled the Reagan Administration to reassess its Middle East policy. In late summer, the United States sought to exploit whatever advantages she thought had been derived from the invasion: the military defeat of Syria resulting in the diminished influence of both Syria and a discredited Soviet Union in Lebanon and elsewhere; the destruction of the PLO military and administrative infrastructure in Lebanon; and the election of a strongly pro-Western and pro-Israeli president, Bashir Gemayel. Naively anticipating an early withdrawal of both Israeli and Syrian, as well as PLO, forces from Lebanon, administration officials concluded that this would be a propitious time to initiate a new Middle East peace process which would bypass Syria and the Soviet Union and involve only Israel, Jordan, and those Palestinians who were willing to accept something less than an independent state.

Thus, on September 1, 1982, Reagan announced a peace plan which provided that: (1) the Arab-Israeli conflict should be resolved through negotiations which would bring about an exchange of territory for peace, as called for by Resolution 242; (2) the Palestinians in the West Bank and Gaza would have "full autonomy" over their own affairs during a transitional period, at the end of which a self-governing Palestinian entity would become associated with Jordan; (3) the United States would not support the use of additional land for new settlements; (4) the United States would not support either an independent Palestinian state or permanent Israeli rule over the West Bank and Gaza; and (5) while Jerusalem would remain undivided, its final status would be determined through negotiations in the context of an overall Middle East settlement.

In a note ("Talking Points") sent to Begin on September 8, Reagan also held that (1) the United States opposed the dismantling of existing Israeli settlements in the occupied areas; and (2) withdrawal would be made only in return for real peace, and the extent of the withdrawal would be influenced by the extent and nature of the peace and the security arrangements provided for—thus opening the way for Israel to retain far more land than the limited, if any, territorial changes which had been envisaged by the framers of Resolution 242.

While no reference was made in the plan to Syria and the Golan Heights, State Department officials held that the plan's reference to Resolution 242 would cover the Golan problem as well. Nevertheless, by concentrating on the involvement of Jordan, while ignoring Syria and the PLO, the plan clearly revived the step-by-step process and stressed direct negotiations and a piecemeal approach as against a comprehensive settlement by means of a Geneva-type conference.[45]

Arab leaders quickly responded to the Reagan initiative by announcing on September 8 their own eight-point peace plan formulated at an Arab summit conference held in Fez. This called for (1) a complete Israeli withdrawal from all territories, including East Jerusalem, occupied in 1967; (2) the dismantling of Israeli settlements in occupied territories; (3) a guarantee of the right of worship for all religions in Jerusalem; (4) a Palestinian state under the leadership of the PLO; (5) compensation to Palestinian refugees not repatriated; and (6) UN Security Council guarantees for the peace and security of all states in the region.[46]

Soviet leaders called the Reagan Plan a "farce" and an attempt by the United States to arrogate for herself alone the right to determine the future of the Middle East. They reaffirmed their support for the PLO and warned it to stay clear of the Reagan initiative for fear that if the PLO cooperated, Russia could once again be locked out of any Middle East peace settlement. Having suffered humiliation because of the defeat of Syrian arms and her inability to help the Palestinians in Lebanon, Moscow did not want to suffer another political defeat at the hands of the United States. Thus, Soviet leaders warned that they would not be pushed around and, to enhance Soviet credibility as a superpower, they strengthened their ties with the PLO and

Syria. To help discourage Arab and Palestinian support for the Reagan plan, the USSR praised the Fez plan and called for an international conference to resolve the Arab-Israeli conflict. Moreover, Leonid Brezhnev proposed on September 15, 1982, his own peace plan which called for (1) a total Israeli withdrawal; (2) establishment of a Palestinian state; (3) a return of East Jerusalem to Arab rule and free access to all holy places for all religious groups; (4) assurances of the security for all states in the area, including Israel; (5) the end to a state of war; and (6) a guarantee of any final settlement by the Security Council. The most significant difference between this and the Fez plan was the specific reference in the Russian proposal to "Israel," while the Arab plan provided only tacit or implied reference to her.[47]

The United States considered the Fez plan to be a positive step forward since it accepted, if only by implication, Israel's right to exist. Nevertheless, she was not happy with its proposals for a Palestinian state under PLO leadership, the dismantling of Israeli settlements, and a complete Israeli withdrawal.

Begin immediately and firmly rejected both the Reagan and Fez plans. He reiterated Israel's opposition to any further territorial withdrawals and to any Palestinian entity. Since, he claimed, the Reagan plan deviated from Camp David and would create a "serious danger" for Israel, he refused to negotiate with any party on the basis of this proposal. Israel's rejection was coupled with the announcement of the establishment of some new settlements and of a plan to settle 1.4 million Israelis in the occupied areas in the next thirty years. Israeli officials called these moves Israel's "answer" to Reagan. The State Department objected to these actions and charged again that they "raised the question about Israel's willingness to . . . exchange land for peace," thereby making it more difficult to get even moderate Arabs and Palestinians to enter any peace talks as long as settlements continued to be established.[48] Even members of Congress and some leading American Jews criticized Israel's settlements policy and opposition to the Reagan plan, which was backed by such major American Jewish groups as B'nai B'rith and the American-Israeli Public Affairs Committee.

Israel not only ignored these protests, but responded by launching a major television, radio, and newspaper campaign to boost the settlement drive and to encourage private developers to build low-priced villas and apartments and by establishing more new settlements near major Arab cities. Many Israelis complained that the large sums being spent annually on settlements were largely responsible for the growing government deficits. Some Israelis even held that unconditional American economic aid and United States vetoes of Security Council resolutions whenever they labelled the settlements as illegal worked to strengthen the pro-settlement movement in Israel and to weaken the position of Israeli opponents of this movement.[49] Even the Labor party, which saw merit in the Reagan plan, charged that Begin was trying to scuttle it by his accelerated settlements program in the hope that this would discourage Hussein from cooperating with it. Begin feared that if Jordan cooperated, then not only would the United States apply tougher pressures on Israel to make concessions, but it also would precipitate an awkward debate in Israel over the merits and risks of territorial compromise in return for peace.[50] But despite the support for the Reagan plan by the Labor party and many American Jews, on September 8, by a vote of 50 to 36 the Knesset rejected the plan.

King Hussein expressed a willingness to go along with the plan if the United States would pressure Israel to stop her settlements program and to withdraw from Lebanon. He felt that he needed some proof of American and Israeli good faith before he could take the risk of cooperating. However, since the United States failed to obtain either a settlements freeze or an Israeli withdrawal from Lebanon, Hussein concluded that the United States would not seriously try to compel Israel to withdraw from occupied territories as called for not only by Resolution 242 but also by the Reagan plan itself. Hussein was also angered by Congressional opposition to the sale of advanced weapons to Jordan and especially by the fact that some members of Congress were insisting that there should be no sale until Hussein formally cooperated with the Reagan plan while not, at the same time, setting similar conditions on the sale of arms to Israel—even though Israel had already rejected the plan outright, while Hussein was clearly seeking ways to cooperate with it. Despite his pessimism, however, he continued to express interest in Reagan's initiative. He held discussions with PLO and other Arab leaders in an attempt to work out a common approach to negotiations under it. In the meantime, he was hoping to receive more encouraging signals from the United States.

Arafat did not reject the Reagan plan outright as the more militant PLO leaders urged him to do. While he felt that it had serious flaws—especially since it rejected a Palestinian state and failed to recognize the PLO—he also saw some "positive elements" in it and he sought to explore both the potential of the plan and the intention of the American government. He indicated that he and others would be encouraged to accept the plan if it were expanded to include a reference to the national rights of the Palestinians and/or if the United States gave meaningful assurances that these rights would be seriously addressed in the peace process. In meetings of the PLO Central Committee (November 26, 1982) and the PLO Executive Committee (January 27, 1983), the Reagan plan was criticized, but not explicitly rejected. Arafat continued talks with Hussein and hoped that this would prove to the Americans that he was serious about wanting to seek a political solution.[51] But the United States gave none of the assurances requested.

Moderate PLO leaders found some encouraging developments within Israel. Before the Lebanese War, virtually all of them had felt that the gulf between Israelis and Palestinians was too wide to bridge. But the many demonstrations—and especially the massive ones following the massacres at Sabra and Shatilla—which took place in Israel against the war in Lebanon had a profound effect on some of these leaders. According to Eric Rouleau, a respected French expert and writer on the Middle East, some PLO leaders told him that they now believed there was a chance that the gulf could be bridged after all. Farouk Khaddoumi, the PLO's "foreign minister," told him that he hoped that the Israeli opposition movement could bring about an Israeli withdrawal from occupied territories and the "coexistence between our peoples" based on a two-state solution.[52] Arafat encouraged more contacts between the PLO and Israeli doves; and he spoke with a number of them in December 1982 and January and February 1983.

In the middle of February 1983, the PLO National Council (PNC) met in Algiers and passed resolutions which, among other things, allowed Arafat to continue talks with Hussein as long as they were based on the right of the Palestinians to have an independent state before discussing a confederation with Jordan; considered the "Fez summit resolution as the minimum for Arab political action"; expressed support for the Brezhnev plan, which had called for peace between the Arab states and Israel, referring specifically to Israel by name; and criticized the Reagan plan, but did not directly reject it.[53]

In March 1983, Arafat informed American officials through intermediaries that an agreement with Hussein was still possible if the United States would recognize the right of the Palestinians to self-determination, because this would enable him to win enough support within the PLO for the Reagan plan. But the United States did not respond to this move.[54]

Nevertheless, Arafat, realizing that the PLO's military defeat and withdrawal from much of Lebanon had seriously weakened any military option, continued to seek a political solution. Thus, he held further discussions with Hussein and in April they came to a tentative agreement on a joint negotiating formula which combined elements of the Reagan and Fez plans; accepted the principle of a future confederation; and provided for setting up of a negotiating team which would be composed of Jordanian officials and non-PLO Palestinians chosen by Arafat.[55]

Arafat sought the support of other PLO leaders in Kuwait before finalizing the agreement with Hussein. Most of these leaders opposed it because they did not trust either Hussein or the United States; saw no chance that either the United States or Israel would change their opposition to any Palestinian state; and did not want to risk splitting the PLO until they were given enough American assurances that they would get something meaningful in return. There were also fears that Arafat might accept something less than an independent state.[56] Thus, the agreement collapsed and Hussein contended that it was now up to the PLO on its own to deal for the Palestinians.

Syria opposed the Reagan plan, which made no direct mention of either Syria or the Golan Heights, thereby, as *Time* stated in the April 25, 1983 issue, "leaving the Syrians with no incentive to cooperate." In Syrian eyes, the Reagan plan had revived the step-by-step process which would strengthen Israel's bargaining position while weakening that of the Arabs and would leave the Golan issue to a later stage when Syria would face Israel alone and her bargaining position would be weaker than ever. Syria felt that as long as the Arabs were weak and divided, direct, bilateral peace negotiations could only lead to an imposed peace on Israeli terms. That is why Syria insisted on achieving an overall peace settlement by means of an international conference in which all the parties, including the superpowers and the PLO, would be present and which would be based on UN resolutions. President Assad complained in February 1983 that the United States was concerned only about Israeli security and not that of the Arabs and Palestinians even though, because of their military inferiority, their security was more threatened than that of Israel.[57] Syria expressed deep concern about Israel's annexation of the Golan Heights and of the American tendency to ignore the Golan issue.

Nevertheless, she was anxious to avoid a confrontation with the United States and continued to indicate her interest in a comprehensive settlement, in which Syria would recognize and make peace with Israel if she withdrew from all territories occupied in 1967, including the Golan Heights, and recognized Palestinian right to self-determination.[58] In April 1983, Syria even expressed a willingness to modify her position on the Reagan plan if the United States would support an Israeli withdrawal from the Golan Heights, as well as the West Bank and Gaza.[59]

THE ISRAELI-LEBANESE WITHDRAWAL ACCORD

After the massacres in the Shatilla and Sabra refugee camps in the middle of September, a new peacekeeping force (composed of military elements from the United States, France, Italy, and Britain) was quickly organized and sent to Beirut to promote greater security and stability and to protect any threatened Palestinian and Lebanese civilians there. The United States also hoped that the force would strengthen the pro-Western Gemayel government, especially by helping to rebuild its army and expand and consolidate its authority; to facilitate the withdrawal of Syrian and Israeli armies from Lebanon; and to check Syrian influence there.

At first, the American Marines were welcomed by the Palestinians and all Lebanese factions. The Palestinians and Muslims hoped that the Marines could help protect them from the Israelis and the Phalangists. Gemayel and the Phalangists hoped that the Marines would help bolster their own positions. For a time, the peacekeeping force played a neutral and useful role in providing some security and stability and in facilitating an Israeli withdrawal from Beirut.

By early 1983, serious tensions were to develop between American and Israeli military units in Lebanon and even between the American and Israeli governments. A number of well-publicized incidents took place between American Marines and Israeli soldiers as a result of differences concerning the territorial limits for Israeli patrols. The United States also complained that the Israelis were using excessive firepower during patrols and that Israeli military presence in Lebanon was illegal and should be ended as soon as possible. The Israelis, in turn, accused the Marines of providing a shield for guerrilla attacks on them and insisted that they would not leave Lebanon until Syria withdrew and Lebanon came to formal terms with them.[60] United States-Israeli relations became so bad that in March 1983 the United States suspended delivery of some F-16 planes and the State Department commended an article[61] written jointly by former presidents Gerald Ford and Jimmy Carter for the February 1983 edition of *Reader's Digest* in which Ford and Carter contended, among other things, that: (1) Arab leaders had indicated their readiness "to live in peace with Israel," but continued Israeli occupation of Arab lands was "the major obstacle to any moderate Arab initiatives for a peaceful resolution of differences"; (2) the Palestinians needed a "home in which their legitimate rights might be exercised"; and (3) "there is little doubt that the PLO is the political entity recognized in the Arab world as speaking for the Palestinians."

In late 1982, the United States turned her efforts away from the Reagan plan and concentrated on dealing with the Lebanese problem first. Thus, she pressed negotiations for a withdrawal agreement between Israel and Lebanon. At the time, it appeared to Shultz that the positions and influence of Syria and Russia, as well as of the Palestinians and Lebanese Muslims and Druze, had been so weakened by the war that they could be safely ignored and that they would have to go along with whatever Lebanese-Israeli accord which was agreed upon. Syria had indicated that she would withdraw from Lebanon if Israel did, but Shultz gave no heed to Syria's condition that Israel must first withdraw unconditionally as the June 1982 Security Council resolution demanded.[62] Shultz also paid no heed to the advice of nearly all of his diplomats in the Middle East not to ignore the views and interests of the Syrians and of the opposition elements in Lebanon, and not to underestimate the harmful consequences of a separate and one-sided agreement. Shultz, however, expected the Saudis to help win Syrian and Lebanese opposition support and even believed an early Syrian and Israeli withdrawal could be attained and then the United States could concentrate on a Middle East peace process once again. Shultz was so determined to achieve his first diplomatic victory as Secretary of State that he was willing to risk his prestige by getting involved personally in shuttle diplomacy.[63]

The Israeli government was eager to obtain a treaty with Lebanon which would provide security arrangements and ultimate normalization of relations so it could counter the rising criticism within Israel against the war by being able to claim that Israel had made substantial security and political gains from the invasion. Thus, both Israel and the United States applied strong pressures on Gemayel to accept a withdrawal agreement which contained security and political provisions favored by Israel, despite the strong opposition to it from Syria and other Arab states, as well as from Lebanese Muslim leaders who warned that it would destroy the fragile internal Lebanese consensus which existed. The agreement was finally signed on May 17, 1983, after protracted negotiations and Shultz's personal intervention.

The treaty provided for (1) an end to the state of war; (2) various security arrangements for Israel in south Lebanon, including the establishment of a security zone where only limited Lebanese armed forces and military equipment would be allowed and where the pro-Israeli militia under Major Saad Haddad would be integrated into the Lebanese army; (3) limits on Lebanese air defense missiles outside the security zone; (4) a joint Liaison Committee to supervise arrangements by land, sea, and air; (5) liaison offices, with full diplomatic privileges and immunities, to be established in each other's capital; and (6) further negotiations to take place after Israel's troop withdrawal to promote a normalization of relations. In addition to the treaty, the United States and Israel signed another private agreement which provided for: (1) no Israeli withdrawal until Syria and the PLO had also fully withdrawn; (2) Israel's right of retaliation against any attacks from Lebanon; and (3) American help to ensure that Lebanon abided by the treaty.[64]

Since some Israelis claimed that the treaty was equivalent to a peace treaty and a *de facto* recognition of Israel and since the separate United States-Israeli agreement went far beyond the treaty itself by allowing Israel to add major conditions to her withdrawal and to launch retaliating and other kinds of attacks on Lebanon even after a complete withdrawal, the treaty became even more unpalatable to its opponents in Lebanon and throughout the Arab world. Even Labor party leaders criticized it. They contended that the security arrangements it contained were less satisfactory than those in actual existence in the past. Yitzhak Rabin also held that the United States had "erred" when she "focused on an agreement between Lebanon and Israel that did not embrace the Syrians."[65] On May 16, the Knesset approved the treaty by a vote of 58 to 8 with 46 abstentions, mostly from Labor.

In Lebanon, not only Muslim and Druze but also many Christians (including Greek Orthodox, Greek Catholics, Armenians, and non-Phalangist

Maronites in northern Lebanon) strongly opposed the treaty, especially because it gave so much to Israel, restricted Lebanese sovereignty over her
own territory, and virtually compelled Lebanon to repudiate her Arab affili-
ation and commitments. Opposition was to be so intense within Lebanon that
the treaty became one of the greatest obstacles to that reconciliation among
the various Lebanese factions which President Gemayel and the United States
were pressing for.

While Syria, as well as other Arab states, would not have objected to a
very limited Israeli-Lebanese security arrangement, Syria denounced the
withdrawal accord and separate United States-Israeli agreement not only because she had not been consulted and her political and security interests had
been ignored, but also because they (1) infringed upon Lebanon's sovereignty and independence; (2) detached Lebanon from the Arab world, making her a virtual client of Israel and weakening the Arab front vis-à-vis Israel; (3) allowed an Israeli presence and right to intervene militarily in Lebanon,
thereby posing a threat to Syria; (4) enabled Israel to achieve major benefits
from her "illegal" invasion; and (5) equated Syria's entry into Lebanon (which
had taken place at Lebanon's invitation to save the Christians in 1976 and
which had been welcomed by the United States and sanctioned by an Arab
League mandate) with Israel's unrequested and illegal invasion. Syria warned
that she would not support reconciliation efforts in Lebanon until the new
treaty had been abrogated and would not pull out her forces until Israel had
withdrawn hers unconditionally.[66]

Although the Lebanese Parliament gave its consent to the withdrawal treaty,
Gemayel put off formally ratifying it. Even though the treaty had not formally been finalized—and, in fact, was ultimately abrogated—nevertheless,
an Israeli liaison office was established in Beirut and began to function, and
economic and tourist relations were developed.[67]

THE UNITED STATES AND LEBANON

When Amin Gemayel became president, he had the good will of even
many non-Christians in Lebanon. In December 1982 the United States took
over primary responsibility for training and equipping the Lebanese army and
the combination of American trainees, Marines, and the Sixth Fleet offshore, and frequent American declarations of firm support for his government led Gemayel to believe he could now do without the backing of Israel
and Syria and he could still restore Maronite power in Lebanon without having to make major concessions to the Muslims and Druze. Thus, he sent in
his American trained and equipped army into West Beirut and cracked down
heavily on the Muslims and Palestinians there, while he allowed the Phal-

angist militia and political and other institutions to continue to operate unhindered in East Beirut and elsewhere. After Israeli forces withdrew from the Shuf Mountains the Phalangists tried to move in, precipitating serious clashes with the Druze there and reigniting a full-fledged civil war. Although in the past Lebanese Muslims and Druze often had serious differences with Syria, right-wing Christian efforts to restore their dominance in Lebanon forced them to turn increasingly to Syria for arms and political support. After the Phalangist-controlled army openly came out in support of the Phalangist forces who were fighting a losing battle with the Druze in the Shuf Mountains, major Druze and Muslim elements in the army broke away and this further intensified the conflict.[68]

The United States, who had originally reentered Lebanon to play a neutral and stabilizing role, ended up becoming increasingly involved militarily on one side—the Gemayel government and its Phalagist-controlled army. As a result, the United States was no longer playing that neutral role which had been initially welcomed and supported by all major factions and, consequently, American Marines increasingly became objects of attack by anti-government factions; and this, in turn, led to American naval bombardments and, later, also air attacks on anti-government and even Syrian positions. This changed American role and military actions and her strong opposition to terminating or even revising the Israeli-Lebanese withdrawal treaty, as demanded by most Lebanese factions and Syria, exacerbated internal divisions in Lebanon and prevented any progress in efforts at reconciliation; strengthened Syrian hostility to the United States and the Gemayel government; embarrassed and antagonized moderate Arabs who were angered when the United States started firing at fellow Arabs, both Lebanese and Syrians; ended any hope that the United States could continue to play a useful stabilizing and mediating role in Lebanon; worried our Western European allies; and forced Syria to move closer to Russia, thereby increasing Soviet influence.[69]

Moreover, for many months the United States had become so involved in trying to deal with the Lebanese problem that she largely ignored the Arab-Israel conflict and efforts to resolve it. She failed to press the Reagan plan on the ground that it was necessary to resolve the Lebanese conflict before turning to dealing with the broader problem of a Middle East peace settlement.[70]

ISRAELI INVOLVEMENT IN SOUTH LEBANON

Since Sharon's grand design had failed, Israel started trying to find some way to withdraw from Lebanon with at least her minimum objective intact—namely, providing security for northern Israel, especially by forming ties with the local population and the Israeli-dominated Haddad-led militia in south Lebanon. Israel even sought to get some Shiites to join the Haddad forces and the pro-Israel village leagues (similar to those in the West Bank) being established in south Lebanon. However, Israel's disregard for the religious sensitivities (such as by pushing through a large Shiite religious procession, using dogs—considered by Muslims to be "dirty animals"—against the people, and arresting religious leaders) and her harsh occupation policies (such as shooting at demonstrators, declaring curfews, blowing up houses of sus- pected trouble markers, and establishing road blockades and following other policies which seriously hurt the local economy) antagonized the Shiites and their religious leaders and strengthened the Islamic fundamentalist move- ment among the people. Initially, the Shiites had welcomed the Israelis for freeing them from Palestinian control and presence which had caused them to bear the brunt of Israel's retaliatory and preemptive attacks. But contin- ued harsh and prolonged Israeli rule caused the Shiites, with the encourage- ment of their religious leaders, to turn against the Israelis, and they, not the Palestinians, began to make daily attacks on the Israelis, causing both far more casualties than the Israelis had suffered in northern Israel at the hands of the Palestinians prior to the invasion and also a serious security threat to the Israeli forces in south Lebanon. As the *New York Times* reported on July 22, 1984, south Lebanon became "a nightmare for occupied and occupiers alike."[71]

Increasing numbers of Israelis began to criticize both the war and the occupation, especially as the cost in both lives and money continued to mount daily. Even many of those who had supported the war originally had grown disillusioned with its failure to achieve the original ambitious military and political objectives and with the heavy and unending cost of the conflict. Labor party leaders advocated an early withdrawal by stages after building up the pro-Israeli militia and an intelligence infrastructure in south Lebanon and relying on quick reaction forces from northern Israel.[72]

UN AND OTHER PEACE EFFORTS, 1983–84

A special UN General Assembly Conference on Palestine was held be- tween August 29 and September 7, 1983, in Geneva on the basis of a De- cember 1981 General Assembly resolution which called for such a confer- ence in order to heighten awareness of the Palestine problem and to find ways of enabling the Palestinians to achieve their national rights. The conference was attended by delegations from 117 UN members (including 8 non-Com- munist European countries), observers from 20 other members (including all other Western European states), and 100 non-governmental organizations, including the PLO. The United States and Israel did not attend in any capacity.

The conference passed the "Geneva Declaration of Palestine" which: (1) called for the convening by the UN of an international conference on the Middle East based on the UN Charter and all pertinent UN resolutions in which all parties, including the PLO, as well as the United States, the Soviet Union, and other concerned countries, would participate on an equal footing with the aim of achieving a comprehensive, just, and lasting solution to the Arab-Israeli problem; (2) urged a concerted international effort to resolve the Palestine question based on the right of the Palestinians to establish their own state and on the right of all states in the Middle East to exist within secure and internationally recognized borders; (3) reiterated the preamble of Resolution 242 providing for the inadmissibility of the acquisition of territory by force and stressed the need for an Israeli withdrawal from all occupied territories, including East Jerusalem; (4) held that Israeli settlements and other occupation policies and practices were contrary to international law and UN resolutions; (5) declared null and void Israeli actions involving Jerusalem; (6) called on member states to refrain from providing any aid to Israel which would help her continue her occupation and disregard of UN resolutions and Charter; and (7) asked the Security Council to use appropriate means to ensure Israeli compliance with UN resolutions.

In a statement at the conference, Arafat reiterated PLO support for the Fez summit resolutions, the Soviet peace proposals, and the French-Egyptian draft Security Council resolution which had never been pressed to a vote because of American opposition. He also supported the convening of an international conference as called for by the conference declaration.[73]

On December 13, 1983, the UN General Assembly, by a vote of 124 (including all Arab members) to 4 (Australia, Canada, Israel, and the United States), with 15 abstentions, approved the Geneva Declaration's call for a conference and requested the UN Secretary General, in consultation with the Security Council, to undertake preparatory measures for such a conference. In December, the General Assembly also passed a number of other resolutions, in most cases by large majority votes and with only Israel and the United States and occasionally Canada voting against, which reiterated its prior stands on territorial withdrawal, settlements, East Jerusalem, Golan Heights, Israeli practices in the occupied territories, and the right of the 1948 refugees to repatriation or compensation.[74]

Israel's delegate to the UN claimed that the "core of the Arab-Israeli conflict was the unwillingness of Arab governments to accept and coexist with a sovereign Jewish state, irrespective of its size and boundaries." He objected to the "distorted presentation of the Arab-Israeli conflict as the root of all Middle Eastern problems and as the sole danger in our region to world peace. The area was plagued by numerous conflicts and tensions." He called the PLO a "terrorist organization" which was being given preferential treatment by the UN.[75]

The Arab delegates, in turn, claimed that Israeli "aggression," "illegal occupation," and failure to abide by UN resolutions and the denial of the inalienable rights of the Palestinians were the primary reasons for the failure to bring peace to the Middle East. They further contended that what Israel "feared most was peace" and she was doing everything possible to "avoid" it.[76]

The United States held that peace "could only come about through direct, unconditional negotiations among the parties to the conflict" and that she would oppose any resolutions which would hinder such negotiations and which would dictate the terms of any final settlement.[77]

In June 1984, the UN Secretary General visited the Middle East to ascertain views concerning the convening of the international conference as called for by the General Assembly. He found Egypt, Syria, Jordan, Lebanon, and the PLO in favor of such a conference, while Israel and the United States opposed it. Although Britain, France, and Holland felt it would be inadvisable to convene a conference until Arab and Israeli positions had been brought closer together, all other countries consulted supported such a conference.[78]

In February 1984, President Mubarak spoke with President François Mitterand of France about the possibility of reviving their joint Security Council draft resolution. Because of continued American opposition to it, both leaders concluded that the time was not yet ripe for pressing the matter. But in March 1984, the EEC Foreign Ministers issued a declaration which stated that a settlement should include the right of all states in the Middle East, including Israel, to existence and security; the right of the Palestinian people to self-determination, with all this implies; non-recourse to force and non-acquisition of territory by force; PLO association with the negotiations; and mutual recognition of the existence and rights of the parties to the conflict. They also called for a stop in settlements and for the negotiations to take into account the Reagan and Fez plans.[79] But the Europeans again refrained from pressing any peace initiative because of continued American opposition to such a move. However, President François Mitterand of France indicated that France would like to play a major role in bringing about a peace settlement. He made a trip to the Middle East in November 1984 to ascertain the views of the key parties and to see what he could accomplish through personal diplomacy. But he was unable to make any progress on the matter.[80]

US–ISRAELI STRATEGIC AGREEMENT, NOVEMBER 1983

By the summer of 1983, the administration had grown increasingly frustrated because of a number of developments. The Reagan initiative was getting nowhere; the Palestine autonomy talks remained suspended; the Iraq-Iran war continued unabated; Soviet troops were still in Afghanistan; US-USSR relations had deteriorated after the downing of a Korean civilian plane; and administration officials remained as deeply preoccupied as ever with the alleged Soviet threat to the Middle East and the rest of the world. Moreover, the Israel-Lebanon withdrawal accord had proven to be a failure; and, as a result, Shultz, who initially had expressed some understanding of Palestinian and Arab positions, had a "major change of heart." He blamed Syria and Saudi Arabia for this failure and Jordan and Saudi Arabia for not cooperating with the Reagan plan. He had become so "disillusioned about Arab objectives" that by late 1983 he began pushing for closer United States-Israeli relations and a tougher joint American-Israeli posture in Lebanon which could force Syria out of Lebanon and weaken Soviet influence.[81]

Administration leaders became even more frustrated and annoyed as a result of the car bombing of Marine headquarters in Beirut on October 23, with heavy casualties; and of the decline in American influence in Lebanon while Syrian influence was growing there. With increased domestic demands for a Marine withdrawal and with an election year in the offing, the administration's position in Lebanon was proving to be an embarrassment and political liability; and officials began to seek ways of freeing themselves from this liability as quickly as possible. Whereas in late 1982 and early 1983 United States-Israeli relations were strained and the United States considered Israel a major obstacle to peace and was pressing her to withdraw from Lebanon, by late 1983 some American officials were now trying to justify Israel's invasion and urging her to stay on and use her military power to counter Syria, bolster the Gemayel government, and get the United States out of the bind she found herself in in Lebanon.[82] They began to consider Israel the central element in United States Middle East policy and strategy and to put major emphasis on the use of power and not just diplomacy.[83]

While Shultz was pressing for a strategic agreement and closer ties with Israel, American military and Middle Eastern experts opposed this. Weinberger, some top generals, and some State Department experts, concerned with the larger strategic realities in the Middle East and convinced that the United States already had close enough military ties with Israel, warned that a formal military accord with Israel would unnecessarily antagonize the Arabs, undermine American interests in the Arab world, and undercut any mediatory peacemaking role the United States could play.[84]

Influenced by the pressure of events in the Middle East, more congenial leadership in Israel (Shamir replaced Begin and Moshe Arens replaced Sharon), and domestic political considerations, Reagan decided that another attempt at strategic cooperation with Israel was called for. After some negotiations, on November 29 an agreement for "military and political cooperation" was concluded. This provided for the establishment of a "joint political-military group to examine ways to enhance United States-Israeli cooperation." The group was to give "priority attention to the threat to our mutual interests posed by increased Soviet involvement in the Middle East. Among the specific areas to be considered are combined planning, joint exercises and requirements for prepositioning U.S. equipment in Israel." Included in the agreement were United States pledges to increase military aid to Israel; to negotiate an accord on reciprocal duty-free trade; to provide military aid to help Israel develop the Lavi fighter plane; and to provide access to secret electronic technology.[85]

Israel gave no *quid pro quo* for the new arrangement. Although the United States urged her to show more flexibility on key Arab-Israeli issues, Israel did not change her opposition to a settlements freeze, the Reagan plan, and sales of advanced weapons to Jordan and Saudi Arabia.[86]

Nevertheless, by getting Israel to agree to focus United States-Israeli military planning on how to counter Russia in the region, this represented a serious modification of Israel's traditional military orientation and alarmed many Israelis, including military commanders, who felt that it diverted efforts from dealing with immediate Arab threats. Labor party leaders also feared that it would unnecessarily antagonize the USSR while the emigration of Soviet Jews was still possible. Israeli doves feared that it would encourage Israeli hawks to drag Israel into a war with Syria.[87]

Even the most pro-Western Arabs were embittered by the new arrangement. They were already aware of and resigned to long-standing close military ties between Israel and the United States. But by drawing even more forceful attention to these ties, these Arabs, including Egyptians, felt that the agreement embarrassed America's Arab friends, undermined American credibility, and made it much more difficult for moderate Arabs and Palestinians to cooperate with her peace efforts. Arab bitterness was further increased by the fact that the agreement was preceded by renewed delivery of cluster bombs to Israel and was followed by American air strikes and naval bombardments against Syrian positions in Lebanon.[88]

Even Reagan's closest friends in Western Europe opposed the idea of building up Israel to act as the West's point man against Syria and critized United States attacks on the Syrians and anti-government forces in Lebanon. They increasingly questioned American judgment, policies, and actions in the Middle East; but they made no serious effort to take any determined initiatives of their own in dealing with either the Lebanese or Arab-Israeli problem.[89]

THE 1984 UNITED STATES ELECTION CAMPAIGN

By late 1983 Reagan's political advisers were warning him of the need to remove the Marines from Lebanon and to avoid doing anything to antagonize the pro-Israeli lobbies and voters because of the forthcoming elections. Although for many months he had been claiming that Lebanon was vital to American security interests and the continued presence of the multinational force was essential to Lebanon's peace and stability, Reagan nevertheless decided to pull the Marines out. In March, 1984 they were transferred from land to naval vessels offshore, leaving the Gemayel government to fend for itself and further undermining United States credibility in the Arab world. Because of strong pressures from Israel and her supporters in Congress, he cancelled plans to sell advanced antiaircraft missiles to Jordan and Saudi Arabia. To allay Israeli fears about American pressures to make concessions, administration officials made it known that there would be no new peace initiative on any aspect of the Arab-Israeli problem in the near future. In fact, on May 18, 1984, Donald H. Rumsfeld, the latest special United States envoy to the Middle East, resigned and he was not replaced. Moreover, while insisting that the Reagan plan was "still alive," a White House official admitted, according to the *New York Times* (Feb. 3, 1984), that even if Hussein agreed to cooperate with the plan, the United States would not press Israel "too hard."[90]

During the Democratic party's primary campaign, most leading contenders also actively wooed pro-Israeli voters and financial contributors. After Mondale had been nominated, he and Reagan continued to compete for pro-Israeli support by making speeches which were largely sympathetic to Israeli and Jewish concerns.[91] The two candidates did disagree on one controversial matter. Mondale and the Democratic party platform, as well as many members of Congress from both parties, advocated moving the United States embassy from Tel Aviv to Jerusalem, while Reagan opposed it. A widely backed proposal to do this was submitted in Congress. Although the Reagan administration had already backed away from some important positions on the Arab-Israeli conflict which all prior administrations had supported—such as settlements were illegal and Resolution 242 allowed for only minor border changes—it did hold fast to the traditional American position which was that East Jerusalem was "occupied territory" and, while it should not be divided, its final legal status should be determined only through peace negotiations.[92]

Administration officials warned that any embassy move would undermine America's ability to press the peace process and would create serious dangers to Americans and American institutions throughout the Muslim world. Consequently, some congressional backers of the move began to express their concern and privately hoped that the proposal would not come to a vote. The congressional session ended without a vote, but its prime supporters insisted that they would bring it up again in the next session of Congress. While some Israelis questioned the advisability of any move at this stage, others felt that it would further hurt the United States position in the Arab world and thereby force the United States to become closer to and even more dependent on Israel than ever before.[93]

Most Arab leaders welcomed Reagan's election, partly because he had opposed moving the American embassy and especially because they believed that he would then be freer of domestic political constraints in dealing with the Arab-Israeli problem during this second and last term of office as president.[94] Israeli officials saw no danger to their interests in Reagan's reelection, especially since the new Congress would remain strongly pro-Israel.[95]

THE OCCUPIED TERRITORIES, 1983–84

In late 1983 and the early months of 1984 there were Palestinian bomb and grenade attacks on Israelis within Israel and the occupied territories, resulting in many casualties. For example, bombings of Israeli buses on December 7, 1983, and March 5, 1984, resulted in a total of 7 dead and 55 wounded; and grenades and gunfire on February 24 and April 1, 1984, caused 2 dead and 47 wounded. On April 12, 1984, four Palestinians from Gaza seized a bus and tried to use the passengers as hostages to free Palestinian prisoners in Israel. Israeli troops stormed the bus, leaving one passenger dead and 7 injured. Two guerrillas were killed on the bus and the other two were later beaten to death while under police interrogation.[96]

Although on April 13, 1983, General Moshe Levy replaced General Rafael Eitan as Chief of Staff, easing somewhat the treatment of the inhabitants in the occupied areas, Israel continued her tough policies. The Knesset also approved two new laws on January 3, 1984, which would extend Israeli legislation to the West Bank and Gaza Strip—thus adding one more step to possible annexation.[97]

One major new development in early 1984 was that the government finally decided to crack down on Jewish "terrorism." For some years, there had been a rise in Jewish attacks against the Arabs in the occupied territories, leading to a cycle of violence. After Likud came to power in 1977 and

Sharon became Minister of Agriculture and later Minister of Defense and General Eitan was made Chief of Staff, the settlers were encouraged to arm themselves and allowed to use force whenever they deemed it appropriate with little effort made by the government to control, investigate, and punish even those illegal settler actions which led to deaths and injuries, as well as to considerable property damage. The establishment of settlements close to major Palestinian cities created a situation ripe for violence. The government set up a commission headed by Deputy Attorney General Yehudit Karp to investigate growing settler attacks on the Arab inhabitants and their properties. The Karp Commission report, submitted to the Knesset in May, 1982 (although it was not made public until February 1984), documented hundreds of crimes and acts of harassment committed by the settlers, criticized the government for failing to press the investigation of these activities and to punish those found guilty, and charged that some Israeli politicians had interfered in some investigations involving Jewish suspects. Because the government largely ignored the report and there continued to be much political interference in law enforcement efforts, the chairperson resigned in protest.[98]

The extent and sophistication of the attacks indicated the existence of a well-organized underground "terrorist" organization, which was finally penetrated by agents of the government. In early 1984, for the first time the Israeli Cabinet issued a policy statement holding that settlers should not be permitted to take the law into their own hands. Following an unsuccessful attempt on April 27, 1984, to bomb five Arab-owned buses in East Jerusalem—which if not thwarted would have caused hundreds of casualties—the government began to arrest and hold for trial those accused of various illegal attacks. Members of the "terrorist" organizations and their supporters came mostly from Gush Emunim (an extremist nationalistic, religious group which had spearheaded the settlements movement), and included army officers and reservists. Arrested settlers admitted to the planting of bombs on Arab buses, machine gun and grenade attacks on Hebron College, planting car bombs which maimed two Palestinian mayors, and unsuccessful attempts to bomb a Hebron mosque and the Al Aqsa and the Dome of the Rock mosques.[99] What added to the seriousness of the situation was the fact that Jewish "terrorist" activities received considerable support from the public and even from some officials. A *Haaretz* poll in June, 1984, indicated that 32 percent held that the anti-Arab actions were "totally justified" or had "certain justification," although 60 percent held they were not justified.[100] There were demonstrations for, as well as against, the "terrorists"; and the Deputy Speaker of the Knesset joined one of the pro-terrorist demonstrations, while the co-chairman of the World Zionist Organization visited those arrested to indicate his support of them. The Minister of Science also expressed his support.[101]

According to the Philadelphia *Inquirer* (May 9, 1984) some Israeli officials held that the "primary motivations" of the Jewish "terrorists" "apparently were retaliation for terrorist attacks against Jews and an effort to
persuade Arabs to leave the West Bank," because while they wanted to annex that area, they did not want to end up with a large Arab population.
According to Nadav Safran, not only followers of Rabbi Meir Kahane but
also many followers of Likud wanted to push the Palestinians out of the West
Bank, even if they had to expel them by force.[102]

THE JULY 23, 1984, ISRAELI ELECTIONS

In interviews and statements before the Israeli elections, Prime Minister
Shamir presented his government's position on any peace negotiations. He
stated that "his government no longer accepted the old negotiating formula
of trading land for peace with the Arabs" and that "almost nobody wants to
give up any territory."[103] "We hold territorial compromise to be unrealistic
and unavailable. If it is realized that the Likud government is durable and
stable then all these international factors will have to come to terms with our
programme and enter those international negotiations leading to comprehensive peace."[104] Denouncing the Labor party's approach, he said: "Unfortunately, those among us who hint to the Jordanian monarch . . . that if and
when they hold the helm of power in Israel 'there would be something to
talk about' are working against the interests and the future of the State of
Israel."[105] He reiterated that he would not favor any territorial compromise
with Jordan and would demand a final settlement based on West Bank autonomy or some other mutually agreed arrangement "under the sovereignty
of Israel. . . . But one of the options may be that this [present] situation
continues. Nobody has discussed it so far, but it can be a solution."[106] He
opposed the convening of a new Middle East peace conference and claimed
that only by direct negotiations between Israel and its neighbors can the
problem be solved. But he rejected any kind of talks with the PLO, considered to be a terrorist organization out to destroy Israel. He insisted that
"Israel will not halt the building of settlements. . . . We will build without
pause. . . . We have to build. It is our mission on this land. We have to
have more cities, more centers of population."[107]

According to the *Jerusalem Post* (December 25, 1983) there was still the
"fear in official Jerusalem that a militarily defeated Arafat might opt for a
political solution," a move which "could pave the way for a revival" of the
Reagan plan and possible pressures on Israel.

Ariel Sharon, who had greatly strengthened his political position since
being forced to resign as Defense Minister in early 1983 and who, after Be-

gin resigned as leader of Likud, even mounted a strong if unsuccessful challenge to Shamir in April 1984 for leadership in the Likud, stated, while campaigning for the election, that a vote for Likud would "help guarantee that Israel will never have to give up any more territory for peace with the Arabs."[108] Moreover, in late August, 1984, Sharon was quoted by *Maariv* as saying that the "East Bank of the Jordan River [present day Jordan] was also Israel's, though not yet in its hands"—apparently reviving the traditional Herut party claim to both banks of the Jordan River.[109] The return to power of Sharon worried many Israelis, who feared that he might further divide the country and someday lead Israel into another war.[110]

Labor leaders and their party platform asked Jordan to join the peace process without preconditions on the basis of Resolutions 242 and 338. However, Israel would not return to the pre-1967 lines. Israel would be guided in determining her border needs by (1) security considerations; (2) preservation of the Jewish character of Israel; (3) the achievement of Zionist goals; and (4) the desire to maintain an enlightened democracy. Thus, they would be prepared to give up to Jordan densely populated parts of the West Bank and Gaza Strip, but would retain all strategic areas—those mostly defined in the old Allon Plan which left 30–40 percent of the West Bank under Israeli sovereignty—and the Jordan River would become Israel's "security border." They would not give up East Jerusalem and most of the Golan Heights, not accept an independent Palestinian state, and not deal with the PLO. The Palestinian problem would have to be resolved within a Jordanian-Palestinian framework. A Labor government would try to revive autonomy talks with Egypt; would not establish new settlements in densely populated areas, but would not uproot any presently existing settlements in any peace agreement; would seek security arrangements so Israel could withdraw from Lebanon as quickly as possible; and would transfer broad responsibilities and power on civilian matters to local authorities, protect individual rights and use full authority against Jewish terrorism in the occupied areas.[111]

The leaders of Mapam, an important left-wing partner with Labor in the Labor alignment, recognized, in the light of the "upheaval caused by the war in Lebanon, the Reagan plan, . . . growing signals from the Arab world expressing a readiness to reach an accommodation with Israel," and "the need to formulate a new, more advanced position on the Israeli-Palestinian and Israeli-Arab conflict which could help promote peace." They advocated "a resolution of the Israeli-Palestinian conflict . . . based upon the mutual right to self-determination." They would talk with any Palestinian element which recognized Israel and renounced terrorism.[112]

Several smaller hawkish parties (Tehiya, National Religious Party, and Kach) opposed giving up any territory and backed the settlements program. Rabbi Meir Kahane, leader of Kach, also openly advocated expelling all Arabs, not only from the occupied areas but even from Israel herself. Two small parties (The Progressive List for Peace and the Communist Democratic Front for Peace and Equality) advocated a complete withdrawal from all territories, including East Jerusalem, occupied in 1967, mutual recognition, and the acceptance of a Palestinian state and the PLO as representative of the Palestinian people. The dovish Citizens Rights and Peace Movement and Shinui insisted on Israel retaining all of Jerusalem but urged negotiating with any representative Palestinian element on the basis of mutual recognition.[113]

The July 23, 1984 Israeli elections revealed that Israeli society was deeply divided and without a consensus on critical issues, whether internal or external. With 120 seats in the Knesset, the voters failed to give either the Labor alignment (winning 44 seats) or Likud (with 41 seats) a clear mandate to rule and split their votes among so many parties that 15 of them won seats. Ten parties won 2 to 10 seats, while three [including Kach] won one seat each. To most Israelis, the winning of more than 25,000 votes and one seat in the Knesset by Rabbi Kahane was a disturbing element because he clearly disparaged democracy and praised Jewish terrorist activities and because his election revealed that his views were supported by much more than a handful of fanatics.[114] The election results appeared to signal a further drift to the right and the hardening of Israel's attitude toward the Palestinians.[115]

Shamir remained Prime Minister of a caretaker government for many weeks while Labor leader Shimon Peres sought to find enough supporters from the smaller parties to establish a coalition government under Labor leadership. Failing to achieve this, Peres and Shamir finally agree to a broad coalition government which would include both Labor and Likud with Peres as Prime Minister and Shamir as Foreign Minister for the first half of the five-year term of the Knesset and then they would exchange positions for the second half. Rabin became Defense Minister, while Sharon became Minister of Commerce and Industry.

Peres and Shamir concurred on some important aspects of the Arab-Israeli problem, but they also had serious disagreements over other major aspects. For example, Peres spoke of holding back on new settlements, while Shamir and Sharon advocated more of them. Peres called upon Hussein to meet directly and without conditions to start peace negotiations, but Shamir warned that any attempt by Labor to negotiate with Jordan would cause a split in the government coalition.[116] A weak coalition government which lacked a clear mandate and which contained leaders with greatly divergent points of view would clearly be unable to present more flexible positions on the Palestinian and territorial issues.

The United States administration had been hoping for a clearcut Labor election victory because Labor had been more receptive than Likud to the Reagan plan and appeared to be more flexible on the settlements, territorial, and Lebanese issues. But the administration preferred the Likud in some ways—particularly its views on the Soviet threat and the United States-Israeli strategic agreement. However, since the Israeli government was so weak and divided and since the United States had already been embarrassed by the failure of the US–sponsored Lebanese-Israeli withdrawal agreement, administration officials were reluctant to press any American-sponsored peace process.

The Arabs and Palestinians generally saw little to choose from between Likud and Labor, since Labor was not more flexible on the issues of Jerusalem, the role of the PLO, a Palestinian state, and return to the 1967 lines with only limited border changes. Yet they were more concerned about a Likud than a Labor victory because Likud would provide no hope of any territorial concessions; would be readier, especially with Sharon in a position of influence, to resort to force against them; and would be less prepared to stop settlement activities and to lighten its heavy-handed rule over the inhabitants of the occupied territories. But they feared that a coalition government would only perpetuate Israel's inflexibility and prevent any significant progress toward a comprehensive settlement which they could reasonably accept.

While dovish parties had won a significant number of seats in the Knesset, they still remained a small minority with little or no political influence on the government. The Israelis were so divided that even another election in the near future would probably not bring about any significant political improvements in Israel from the Arab, American, and Israeli doves' points of view.

ISRAEL AND LEBANON, 1984

In 1984, because she was suffering almost daily casualties, her battered economy was being hurt by the high costs of occupation, and popular demand for withdrawing was growing, Israel was anxious to negotiate a withdrawal agreement with Lebanon as long as it provided satisfactory security arrangements. She no longer demanded that Syrian and PLO forces, which were still present in eastern and northern Lebanon, must withdraw before she did. Israel had sought to obtain American involvement, especially in obtaining certain assurances from Syria, but American officials were reluctant to face another failure in the Middle East and therefore insisted she would intervene actively only when assured of a successful outcome.[117]

Israel agreed to accept an enlarged role by UNIFIL, despite her past distrust of and even hostility to the UN and its peacekeeping role in general. She wanted to divide south Lebanon into at least two zones. The first zone, falling between the Israeli-Lebanese border and the Zahrani River, would be controlled by the South Lebanon Army, which she armed and controlled, in coordination with Israeli troops. A second zone, between the Zahrani and Awali rivers, would be patrolled by an enlarged UNIFIL with possibly some token Lebanese army units. She wanted Syria to commit herself in some way not to move her forces into areas to be evacuated by Israeli units and not to allow Palestinian commandos to operate from her controlled territory against northern Israel. In addition, Israeli wanted to be able (1) to patrol Lebanese coastal waters with her navy; (2) to fly reconnaissance missions over Lebanon; (3) to move her ground forces in and out of south Lebanon as her security required; and (4) to use force against hostile elements who attacked from south Lebanon. Israel was now more concerned about future Shiite, rather than Palestinian, attacks across the border and about the danger of transforming Shiite areas in south Lebanon into a premanently hostile zone.[118]

Lebanon, backed by Syria, agreed to negotiate with Israel, but only on narrow security concerns and under UN auspices. She, as well as Syria, rejected Israeli conditions and insisted upon a complete and unconditional Israeli withdrawal without any infringements on her territorial sovereignty. Lebanon wanted UNIFIL to be expanded and to help her maintain security, but she also insisted that her own army should play the primary role in taking control over all of south Lebanon to the Israeli border.

On November 8, 1984, Lebanese and Israeli army officers met in the presence of UNIFIL officers to begin negotiations on the terms of an Israeli withdrawal. Since the talks dragged on without any substantial progress, in the middle of January 1985, Israel announced her own phased, three-stage withdrawal plan which would end up leaving a zone along the border that the South Lebanon Army would control with Israeli military backing.[119] This would, to all intents and purposes, largely restore a situation which had existed before the 1982 invasion of Lebanon—a situation that had not produced peace and stability in the area. Moreover, an Israeli withdrawal could trigger a conflict between Shiites and those Christians and militiamen who supported Israeli rule in south Lebanon, strengthen the Islamic fundamentalist movement in Lebanon, and be seen as a victory for Shiite-based national resistance.

THE PALESTINIANS

For years Arafat had been able to retain the support of even the more militant elements in al-Fatah, as well as in some other PLO factions, because his relatively moderate policies had brought about substantial progress in the areas of diplomacy and public relations and, thereby, had raised hopes that this progress could ultimately produce through peaceful means a Palestinian state in at least part of Palestine. However, by 1983, many Palestinians had concluded that his conciliatory efforts had reached a dead end with not even a mini Palestinian state in sight because of continued Israeli and American adamant opposition to it. Therefore, increasing numbers of Palestinians—including many of his followers in al-Fatah—were convinced that the political approach had failed and, therefore, the only option left was that of "armed struggle." They lost faith in Arafat's leadership and joined the ranks of the Palestinian rejectionists who had all along opposed any attempt at a settlement with Israel either because they refused to accept the continuance of the state of Israel under any circumstances or because they were convinced it would be useless to seek a compromise settlement since Israel was not and would not be prepared to accept one which provided for even a small Palestinian state.

Despite the objections of some commando groups, Arafat had agreed to withdraw his forces from Beirut and to accept United States guarantees that the Palestinian civilians left behind would be protected. The massacres which followed made many Palestinians furious not only at the United States but also at Arafat for having trusted the United States. Many opposed Arafat's acceptance of the Fez plan and his readiness to discuss with Hussein possible means for cooperating with the Reagan plan. He was accused of being prepared to accept something less than an independent Palestinian state; making too many vital decisions on his own; making too many concessions to the United States without getting anything in return; condoning corruption and high living at top levels of the PLO; and giving key military positions to incompetent officers closely associated with him.[120]

Thus, in May 1983 this growing opposition to Arafat and his policies led to a revolt on the part of some military officers and armed elements within al-Fatah units in Lebanon; and they soon began to receive support from some of the more militant commando groups and from Syria. The mutineers demanded that Arafat return to the original PLO goals of liberating all of Palestine through armed struggle; and share his powers, clean up corruption, and reorganize the PLO. With essential Syrian backing, the rebels were able to defeat forces loyal to Arafat in the Bekaa valley. After Arafat returned in September, 1983, to Tripoli, in northern Lebanon, his forces were defeated again and Arafat was compelled to leave Lebanon with his men by sea in December 1983.

Although the rebels failed to win support for their cause outside of the immediate areas in northern and northeastern Lebanon under Syrian control, Arafat's position was nevertheless weakened by the open rebellion and for many months it was uncertain if he could survive politically. But his military forces outside of Lebanon and especially the political and administrative apparatus of the PLO (now dominated more than ever by al-Fatah loyalists), as well as the great majority of the Palestinians in the occupied territories and the disaspora, remained loyal to him. Most Arab governments, especially the conservative ones, continued to back him. Even before the mutiny and following the 1982 PLO defeat in Lebanon, Arafat had already begun to build up his support in the occupied areas to make up for the loss of his base of operations in Lebanon. Although they criticized his mistakes and many disagreed with some of his policies and actions, most Palestinians continued to believe in the sincerity of his intentions and his loyalty to the Palestinian cause. Moreover, to them he remained a "father figure," the "symbol of Palestinian nationalism," and the only spokesman with an international stature who could speak effectively for the Palestinians.

Living under hated Israeli occupation for so many years and concerned about Israel's determined efforts to establish many settlements and to foster other "facts on the ground," the Palestinians in the occupied territories were growing increasingly desperate for some kind of early peace settlement which would free them from Israeli rule. Since many did not believe that armed struggle could succeed, they backed the relatively conciliatory policies of Arafat. Some were even prepared to become associated directly with Jordan in some fashion if this were the only way to enable them to escape from permanent Israeli control. Consequently, support for Arafat remained strong within the occupied areas and there even were rallies on his behalf.[121]

With his commando forces weakened and dispersed and with direct access to Israel closed to the PLO, Arafat felt it necessary to put greater emphasis on the call for more armed struggle from within the occupied areas and, at the same time, to show greater political flexibility on the Arab and international levels. The split in the PLO gave to the more pragmatic leaders greater freedom to openly choose and push the diplomatic option—but only at the risk of further widening and perpetuating this split. Apparently, Arafat was prepared to take this risk. After leaving Tripoli in late December 1983, he met with President Mubarak and tried to improve his relations with Egypt and to restore Egypt's role within the Arab and Islamic worlds in the hope that these could help strengthen his own political base, counter Syrian hostility to him, weaken Egyptian support for the Camp David accords, and ultimately enhance Arab and Palestinian bargaining positions vis-à-vis both Israel and the United States. Urged on by moderate West Bank leaders, he also revived discussions with Jordan to find some basis for a unified strategy in any peace process and for some kind of future ties between Jordan and a Palestinian entity. Not only were these moves bitterly condemned by anti-Arafat Palestinian groups and Arab governments, but even many Palestinian supporters of Arafat in the disaspora criticized his unilateral moves in these areas. While the United States expressed some satisfaction, Israel indicated her displeasure with Arafat's meetings and improved relations with Egypt and Jordan.[122]

Arafat and other moderate Palestinian leaders continued to support the Fez and Brezhnev plans, the Egyptian-French draft Security Council resolution, and the UN General Assembly's call for convening an international peace conference. These leaders continued to oppose recognizing Israel as a "precondition to negotiations," but some indicated that they could support "mutual recognition" in the framework of a peace process. Arafat told John B. Oakes, former senior editor of the *New York Times* (March 18, 1984), that he had "but one card to play—recognition—and I would be stupid to throw it away unless I get something substantial in return. Give me a package deal . . . I've sent many signals to open a dialogue [with Israel] but without response." Another top PLO leader claimed that PLO moderates would welcome an American peace initiative if they thought the United States could deliver—but because of the credibility problem, especially after the massacres at Sabra and Shatilla, "it is not worth taking the risk."[123] Even some Israelis began to contend that changes had taken place in the "thinking," "doctrine," and "attitude" of the PLO toward Israel and that the moderate PLO elements were ready for a political solution. They held that the split within the PLO proved the genuiness of this readiness.[124]

By March 1984, support for the anti-Arafat rebels began to wane even in the refugee camps near Damascus. Many unsuccessful efforts were made by some PLO leaders and by various Arab governments to bring about a reconciliation between Arafat and President Assad. Even the USSR tried as well. At first, the Soviet Union backed Arafat against the rebels and urged Syria to stop her attacks on his forces in Lebanon. The Soviets felt that Arafat's leadership and PLO unity were essential for it to remain an effective force. But when it became clear that reconciliation between Assad and Arafat would not readily take place and she had to make a choice of sorts, by late November 1983, the Soviet media began to give great stress to supporting the PLO with less specific mention of Arafat—and in December 1984 no Soviet diplomat attended an Arafat-led PNC meeting in Amman.

The United States hoped that the split would encourage the West Bankers to give up on the PLO and ask Hussein to negotiate a deal with Israel. But this did not happen for they stood by Arafat and the PLO, and both Arafat and the PLO survived the crisis created by the split.

Likud leaders welcomed the split in the hope it would weaken the PLO. But they were concerned that the split might also free Arafat to develop even closer relations with Egypt and Jordan and press more openly and strongly for a political solution, thereby precipitating stronger pressures by the United States to revive the Reagan plan and negotiations under it. According to a leading Israeli writer and journalist, Amnon Kapeliuk, the Likud government still feared negotiations "because it refuses to contemplate the idea of returning an inch of the territory occupied since the 1967 war." [125] After he became Foreign Minister in the new coalition government, Shamir continued to reveal his concern when, following Arafat's greatly improved ties with Mubarak and Hussein, he said: "I do not think that anyone in Israel views as positive an excessive intimacy between Hussein and Arafat" for this would bring closer to the West Bank "the voice of the PLO terrorist organization." [126]

The split within the PLO persisted with three separate factions coming into existence. On one side was by far the largest faction composed primarily of al-Fatah loyalists and some independents who, despite some disagreements with Arafat, backed his leadership and his strategy to try to promote the Palestinian cause by diplomatic and political means. On the other extreme was the newly formed pro-Syrian National Salvation Alliance, which was composed of al-Fatah rebels, the PFLP-General Command, the Libyanbacked Palestine Struggle Front, and the Syrian-dominated Saiqa and which insisted on Arafat's removal as PLO leader before taking part in any reconciliation efforts and in any further PNC meetings. In the middle was the newly-formed Democratic Alliance, which was composed of the Popular Front for the Liberation of Palestine (PFLP), the Democratic Front for the Liberation of Palestine (DFLP), the Palestine Liberation Front (PLF), and the Moscow-oriented Palestine Communist party. This latter group opposed giving Hussein a mandate to negotiate on behalf of the PLO, as well as Arafat's closer ties with Hussein and Mubarak and his tendency to act on his own. It preferred more stress on armed struggle and less on diplomacy, which it felt had no chance to succeed as a result of the negative positions on the Palestinian issue taken by Israel and the United States. Since it did not want a permanent split in the PLO, its leaders met with Arafat in June 1984 in an unsuccessful attempt to heal the rift.

After extensive efforts to end his feud with Assad had failed and since he was still convinced that it was necessary to ally the PLO with Jordan, Egypt, and other moderate Arab states and to put stress on what he considered to be the most realistic, if not the only, option available—that of diplomacy—to promote the Palestinian cause, Arafat finally decided to risk a permanent split in the PLO. Having failed to obtain the permission of Algeria or Yemen to hold a PNC conference in those countries, he finally accepted Jordan's invitation to meet in Amman. According to the *New York Times,* this decision showed his continued "readiness for moderation" and "signaled Arafat's intention to inject the PLO or its remnants . . . into any future peace talks with Israel alongside Jordan and Egypt" because he did not want to be "left out" of any future talks. [127] But it was made against the advice of some of his own supporters who held that a permanent split would weaken the PLO and its claim to be the sole legitimate representative of the Palestinian people, and could be exploited by various Arab governments which might try to play one faction off another. They also argued that while a split would be justified if it speeded up the attainment of a Palestinian state, there was no indication that Israel would agree to essential concessions no matter how forthcoming the PLO was or that the United States would press her to do so. Thus, a split would have been brought about "for nothing."[128]

Both the National Salvation Alliance and the Democratic Alliance refused to attend the Amman conference. Although the DFLP did send observers, it also demanded that the PNC session should not make any further concessions aimed at reaching a negotiated settlement on the Palestine problem. Israel refused to allow a large number of delegates from the occupied areas to attend despite the fact that they could have provided a moderating influence and helped Arafat obtain a clearer mandate for pushing the diplomatic option, indicating that Israeli leaders were more concerned about a moderate PLO than a rejectionist one.[129]

Before the conference convened on November 22, Moscow called in the leaders of the PFLP and the DFLP to discuss ways of averting a breakup of the PLO. These leaders promised not to participate in any rump gathering to form a rival to the PLO, although they did not attend the Amman meeting. Possibly not to antagonize Syria, the Soviet Union did not send her usual delegation as observers to the conference.

King Hussein addressed the PNC opening session and renewed his call for an international peace conference under UN auspices and based upon Resolution 242: an exchange of territory for peace. The conference, dominated by supporters of Arafat, objected to Hussein's stress on Resolution 242 alone. It also reelected Arafat as leader and established a new executive Committee of 14 members, which included two moderate former West Bank mayors (one of whom was assassinated in December, 1984); which left three seats vacant for the PFLP, DFLP, and Saiqa in an attempt not to break completely with these important dissident factions; and which would be dominated by Arafat loyalists. It also empowered Arafat and the Executive Committee to develop a joint strategy with Jordan for a negotiated Middle East peace settlement and to continue exchanges with Egypt; restated the PLO opposition to Camp David; and called for a UN-sponsored international peace conference. Heeding a warning of the DFLP, the conference did not produce any new peace initiative, but it also did not give up any old ones. Moreover, it tried to keep the doors open to Syria and the PLO factions backed by her.[130]

The Israeli government did not welcome the results of the Amman conference and the continuation of close PLO ties with Jordan and Egypt, with Likud members of the coalition government taking the toughest line. Foreign Minister Shamir warned Labor party leaders that if they sought to enter negotiations with Jordan on the return of even part of the West Bank to her, this would split the country's bipartisan government. Shamir's warning bolstered the position of those Palestinian militants who had been contending that there was no hope of success through the diplomatic-political option because of Israel's adamancy and, therefore, the only path left was that of armed struggle. These militants would also claim that the ability of a Shiite-backed national resistance movement to force Israeli forces to withdraw from south Lebanon shows that armed struggle might work after all. In any case, a hardline position by the Israeli government would further strengthen the position of Palestinian and Arab rejectionists.

SYRIA

By the spring of 1983, President Assad's relations with Arafat had begun to deteriorate. Distrust and bad feelings had existed between them for some time, especially since Syrian troops fought the Palestinians during the 1975–76 Lebanese civil war. When, in late 1982 and early 1983, Arafat, without first consulting Syria, began to negotiate both with Hussein over the possibility of jointly working through the Reagan plan and also with Lebanon on a possible PLO withdrawal from that country, Assad became concerned that more separate deals would be made which ignored Syria and weakened her bargaining position, thereby lessening her chances of regaining the Golan Heights. He was also concerned at the time that some extremist PLO groups might try to make attacks on Israeli troops in Lebanon which could drag Syria again into an unwanted war with Israel. In addition, Syria, already badly isolated in the Arab world, saw the PLO as a bargaining chip which she needed to control in order to protect her interests in Lebanon and in a larger Arab-Israeli settlement.[131] Thus, when in the spring of 1983 a serious split developed within al-Fatah, Syria backed the anti-Arafat elements, resulting in a worsening of relations between Arafat and Assad. Although on a number of occasions in the past Arafat and Assad have been able to make up after serious differences had developed, there has been no sign up to this writing that these differences can be overcome, at least for the foreseeable future.

In 1983 and 1984 Syria had become a major political and military actor in Lebanon. While some American and Israeli officials began to charge that Syria wanted to annex all or part of Lebanon, many experts, including some Israeli ones, disagreed with this view.[132] Even Richard Murphy, American Assistant Secretary of State for Near Eastern and South Asian Affairs and a former United States ambassador to Syria, told the Senate Foreign relations Committee on October 19, 1983: "I do not believe Syria has any intention of redrawing the political boundaries between it and Lebanon or any basic desire to absorb Lebanon. . . . Syria's interest in Lebanon is that it not be a threat to Syria'' and that it not be used by Israel as a "base or corridor which could threaten Syria.'' [133] Syria also wanted a friendly Lebanon who retained her Arab identity, who would not allow the military presence of Israel on her soil in any form, and who remained under traditional Syrian influence. [134]

On the whole, the situation between Israeli and Syrian forces had stabilized somewhat by 1984. Even though their lines were very close in eastern Lebanon and Israeli artillery was within easy range of Damascus and even though Israel occasionally attacked Palestinian positions within Syrian-controlled territory, both sides sought to avoid a direct military conflict. On June 14, 1984, Syrian and Israeli troops clashed directly near the Syrian-Lebanese border for the first time since 1982; but this incident was quickly contained. On June 28, 1984, Israel and Syria exchanged prisoners of war—six Israelis and 291 Syrians—plus the bodies of five Israelis via the Golan Heights and with the help of the International Red Cross and the UN peacekeeping forces on the Golan. This further helped relieve some of the tension in the area.

The Israeli public was anxious to get Israeli forces out of Lebanon and it was in no mood to start a war with Syria. [135] Some Israelis actually hoped that Syria and Israel could come to some kind of understanding on the division of Lebanon into spheres of influence and provide the basis for some kind of peaceful coexistence. A number of Israelis, including the former Chief of Staff, Mordechai Gur, was even prepared to accept continued Syrian military presence in Lebanon as long as the Syrians helped prevent Palestinian attacks against Israel from the areas they controlled in Lebanon. In fact, some felt that Syrian presence in Lebanon could prove to be "a lesser evil" and that Syria would feel it was to her advantage to prevent Palestinian attacks. [136] While negotiating a withdrawal agreement with Lebanon in November–December 1984, Israel sought some kind of understanding from the Syrians that they would not try to move into any areas to be evacuated by Israeli forces; but Syria was not yet willing to commit herself to protect Israel's border or to limit the movement of her forces.

Syria clearly did not want any military showdown with Israel—at least until she had been able to rectify the military imbalance which stood heavily in Israel's favor. Nevertheless, Syrian and Israeli forces remained in close proximity and major differences persisted between them over the unresolved Arab-Israeli conflict with little hope of any early movement toward their resolution.

By late 1983, United States-Syrian relations had deteriorated very badly. The United States was annoyed because Syria had strongly opposed the Reagan plan and the Israeli-Lebanese withdrawal agreement and had improved her military and political ties with Russia. Some American officials began to see Syria as an ally of Russia and, therefore, as much of an enemy to the United States as Russia was and to accuse her of promoting terrorist activities against the United States, including the car bombing of the Marine headquarters in Beirut. Secretary Shultz even began to accuse Syria of being the main obstacle to peace in Lebanon and in the Arab-Israeli conflict and to urge closer United States ties with Israel and tougher actions against Syria.

Syria was bitter not only because the United States had bombed and shelled Syrian positions and had accused her of being responsible for abetting acts of terrorism and of being a Soviet client, but also because Syria felt that the United States was trying to isolate her and to disregard Syrian interests in both the Lebanese and Arab-Israeli conflicts. Syria was also convinced that the United States was more concerned about promoting Israeli security and territorial ambitions and American anti-Soviet policies than about achieving a fair and comprehensive Middle East peace settlement. Since American officials kept linking Syria with the USSR, Syrian leaders concluded that even the United States-Israeli strategic agreement was partly aimed at them, as well as at the USSR.[137]

But despite worsened relations in much of 1983, by late 1983 and early 1984, both Syria and the United States sought ways to improve relations. Realistically concluding that only the United States could help her get back the Golan Heights, Syria began to give repeated signals of her desire to improve relations.[138] In December, 1983, Foreign Minister Khaddam stated that "at no time should the United States lose the mediating role" in Lebanon.[139] In early 1984, Syria released a captured American airman. President Assad sent a message to Reagan indicating a desire to hold talks and he later told American envoy Rumsfeld that the United States could "play an effective role in the Middle East if it would adopt a neutral attitude in the Arab-Israeli conflict."[140]

Some American officials, seeking a face-saving way to withdraw the Marines from Lebanon, began to feel that Syria now held the key to peace in Lebanon and in the Middle East and began to attach greater importance to Syria's role. They believed that Syria's policy had become more cautious and that she was beginning to make some headway, with Saudi help, to achieve a cease-fire and steps toward reconciliation in Lebanon and to bolster the Gemayel regime—goals the United States had been pushing.[141]

The serious illness of Assad in late 1983 concerned the United States for she feared that any successor to him would prove to be much more difficult to deal with. As *Newsweek* wrote on December 19, 1983: "Both Washington and Jerusalem consider Hafez Assad a man with whom they can strike a deal—if only after very hard bargaining. And like him or not, they would rather confront the Lebanese mess with him than without him.'' By the summer of 1984, following the abrogation of the Israeli-Lebanese withdrawal accord, Syria was able to bring about a more effective, although a still fragile, cease-fire and a unity government of sorts representing the leaders of all the major factions in Lebanon. On July 25, Assistant Secretary of State Richard Murphy told a congressional subcommittee that Syria was now playing a more ''cooperative'' and ''helpful'' role in restoring stability in Lebanon and that there was no solution in the area without taking into account the interests of Syria, as well as Israel.[142] However, while United States–Syrian relations improved somewhat, especially over the Lebanese situation, they remained strained over the overall Arab-Israeli conflict.

CHAPTER XIII

Analyses and Conclusions

THE ARABS

Many important changes in the views of the Arabs have taken place since the 1967 war. By the early 1970s, more and more Arab leaders had begun to recognize the reality of Israel's existence and her ability, especially with overwhelming United States support, to ensure that existence. Thus, they realized the need for a political solution to the Arab-Israeli problem. Egypt and Jordan formally accepted Resolution 242 which, while calling for an end to the state of belligerency and the right of every state in the area "to live in peace and security within secure and recognized boundaries free from threats or acts of force," did not actually require peace treaties, formal recognition of Israel, or direct negotiations; and they cooperated with Gunnar Jarring's efforts to implement the resolution. Lebanon was prepared to cooperate as well, but she held that since she had not entered the 1967 war and had no territorial differences with Israel there was no need for her to become formally involved in any negotiations. Some Arab countries, such as Syria, Iraq, Algeria, and Libya (after the overthrow of the monarchy in 1969), still refused to accept Israel's existence under any circumstances and, therefore, were "rejectionists" in the truest sense of the term. Other Arab states rejected Resolution 242 only because it did not provide for the political rights of the Palestinians.

By 1971, however, President Assad had indicated willingness to go along with Resolution 242 if it would provide for these Palestinian rights as well. Following the 1973 war, he formally accepted Resolution 242 when he accepted Security Council Resolution 338 which called for a cease-fire and for negotiations to implement Resolution 242. As explained earlier, in 1977 when the Carter Administration was holding discussions with Israel and the frontline Arab states in an attempt to seek a comprehensive settlement through a revived Geneva conference, all of these Arab states indicated that they were now prepared to go well beyond the requirements of Resolution 242 by expressing a willingness to negotiate directly with Israel by means of a reconvened Geneva conference which, if successful, would lead, among other things, to a formal peace treaty with and recognition of Israel. There were also indications that they would consider full normalization of relations with time.

Following the Sadat initiative and Camp David, even former rejectionists such as Iraq and Algeria accepted the November 1978 Baghdad Conference resolution which called for a peace settlement which would provide not only for an Israeli withdrawal to pre-1967 lines and a Palestinian state, but also for the right of every state in the area to live in peace and security as stated in Resolution 242, thus at least implying recognition of the existence of Israel. Libya continued to oppose any peace settlement with Israel and remained the only true rejectionist. Nearly all Arab states opposed Sadat's initiative, the Camp David accords, and the Egyptian-Israeli peace treaty not because they opposed any peace agreement with Israel, but because they felt that these developments would split the Arab world, weaken the Arab bargaining position vis-à-vis Israel, and make it easier for Israel to reject calls for further concessions, thereby doing more to obstruct than to promote the chances of ever achieving a fair and lasting overall peace settlement that would resolve the Palestinian and other territorial issues as well.

Thus, in another Arab summit in Tunis in November 1979 the Arab leaders reiterated their support for the Baghdad Conference resolution; in September 1982, they agreed to the Fez plan; and in the late summer and the fall of 1983 they backed UN resolutions calling for an international peace conference. All of these moves called for a peaceful settlement with Israel and clearly indicated that Arab views toward Israel had changed. It must be recalled that for years many Israelis and others had been insisting that Egypt's hostility toward Israel would never change and she would never voluntarily make peace with Israel. Yet, Egypt's views did change and she ended up making a full-fledged peace treaty with her former enemy.

Therefore, as Mordechai Bentov, a signatory of Israel's Declaration of Independence and a former cabinet minister, stated: "It is absurd to maintain that nothing has changed on the Arab side."[1] Yaacov Shimoni, a former Israeli diplomat and senior official in the Foreign Ministry, wrote in the *Jerusalem Post* (June 12, 1984): "The repeated assertion that there is nothing new on the Arab side, no change in PLO attitudes, is . . . politically and conceptually false and dangerous." Many other Israelis, such as former Defense Minister and presently Minister Without Portfolio, Ezer Weizman, former Foreign Minister Abba Eban, leaders and followers of the various Israeli peace movements, dovish political parties, and some members of the Knesset, specialists on the Middle East, and others, believe that the key Arab leaders are prepared for peace and urge, as Weizman did, that "the time has come for us to settle our conflict with the Arab world as a whole."[2]

As early as 1979, in an article in the World Zionist Organization publication *Israel Digest* (May 4, 1979) Nissim Rejwan wrote: "Today one can speak safely of a near-consensus among Arab governments everywhere that a peace settlement with Israel can be reached—and the State of Israel consequently accepted—given certain conditions." In an interview in 1979, Nahum Goldmann, former president of the World Jewish Congress, the World Zionist Organization, and the Conference of Presidents of Major American Jewish Organizations, said in an interview that "most of the Arab world, including Syria and Iraq, but with the exception of Libya, are in principle ready to accept the existence of Israel."[3]

In 1983 former presidents Carter and Ford in a joint article in *Reader's Digest* (February 1983) wrote that "the Arab leaders had indicated their readiness . . . to live in peace with Israel." Deputy Secretary of State Kenneth W Dam stated in an address on April 11, 1983: "Today Arab leaders are talking about *how*—not *whether*—to make peace with Israel." (Italics are used in the original address.[4]) Dr. Harold Saunders, who has dealt with the Arab-Israeli problem as a top official in the National Security Council and the State Department for as many years as any other American official wrote: "By 1981 it was accurate to state that the leaders of each of Israel's neighbors were prepared to make peace with Israel."[5]

While nearly all Arab states have, for some years, been prepared to make peace with Israel, they have insisted that it be based upon those principles which have been accepted by the overwhelming preponderance of the nations of the world, including those from Western Europe and elsewhere who are good friends of Israel, and which are stated in Resolution 242 and those other resolutions that deal with the Palestinian issue. These principles are (1) an Israeli withdrawal from territories, including East Jerusalem, occupied in 1967 with, at the most, minor and mutual border rectifications primarily involving Israel and the West Bank area; (2) the right of the Palestinians to national self-determination, including their own state, under the leadership of the PLO; (3) a fair resolution of the 1948 and 1967 Arab refugee problems based on UN resolutions; (4) an end to the state of war and all hostile activities; (5) security arrangements and guarantees; and (6) the right of all states in the area to live in peace and security. Front-line states have been prepared to negotiate and sign a peace treaty with Israel on these terms, and such a treaty would provide recognition of Israel and a process for normalization of relations. (Even the Israeli-Egyptian peace treaty did not provide for immediate, full normalization.)

In the past, most Arab states welcomed American peace initiatives and hoped to achieve their goals through them. More recently, however, even the most moderate Arab leaders have been reluctant to enter United States-sponsored negotiations because they were convinced that Israel, even under a Labor government, would never be prepared voluntarily to negotiate the kind of settlement they believe is in accordance with the "territory for peace" formula envisaged by Resolution 242, and that the United States cannot or will not apply the pressures needed to obtain essential Israeli concessions; because they believe that the United States has become so allied with Israel and so committed to give priority to her interests that the United States no longer can play the role of honest broker; and because they have lost confidence in American ability to deliver—especially after the United States failed to save the Shah, to stick it out in support of the Gemayel government, to deliver on promises to attain a settlements freeze and an early Israeli withdrawal from Lebanon, to promote real autonomy for the Palestinians, and even to carry out her own peace plans and to prevent Israel from taking actions and following policies which the United States has repeatedly criticized as both obstacles to peace and also harmful to American interests in the Middle East.[6]

Thus, even Arab moderates have preferred a negotiating process through a UN-sponsored international peace conference rather than through United States-sponsored direct talks not only because they no longer trust American impartiality but also because they know that the Arab bargaining position vis-à-vis Israeli is so weak, especially since Egypt ceased to be a serious part of the equation, that it can be strengthened only by means of an international conference in which the remainder of the confrontation states can work together and UN resolutions and the presence of major Western European states and the Soviet Union can be used to counter America's pro-Israeli posture and to bolster the weak Arab bargaining position. Arab leaders have been pressing the Western European states to play a more active and decisive role in the peace-making process by taking more of an initiative, but without much success. Moderate Arab governments have improved relations with the USSR and have insisted that she too should be involved in any peace negotiations.

Moderate Arab leaders also fear that unless their is some movement soon toward a peace settlement which they could accept, Israel will continue to establish so many facts on the ground that they could ultimately make the process virtually irreversible; Palestinian impatience and frustration will grow to the point that there will be a return to terrorism and armed struggle; and Islamic fundamentalist forces, which in recent years have been gaining support particularly among the youth and which have been especially aroused over the Jerusalem and Palestinian issues, will threaten their regimes and destabilize the area.[7]

The Arab world has been plagued by such serious divisions and bitter hostility that Arab ability to promote their cause has been greatly weakened. Nevertheless, a considerable degree of Arab unity, at least among the key Arab states, has always been and remains essential to promoting a just and durable peace in the Middle East. While the Arabs have been generally united on the goals of a comprehensive settlement, they have disagreed on how to achieve them.

However, the Arabs, even if they could again overcome their deep differences as they have occasionally done in the past in the face of an Israeli threat, will still not have much of a military option, at least for the foreseeable future, because Israel, solidly backed by American power and resources and a nuclear capability, can remain militarily stronger than the Arabs for the indefinite future, especially since her military policy has been dominated by the concept of a "preventive war," i.e., attacking the Arabs at the time of her own choosing and before the Arabs have been able to rectify the existing military imbalance in Israel's favor. Since the Soviet Union has been careful to avoid an open conflict with the United States, she cannot be depended upon to counter all-out United States support of Israel. Therefore, any return to an extremist stand would not only cost the loss of most of that valuable worldwide sympathy and political support which the Arabs have won largely as a result of their adopting more flexible and moderate policies and which provide them with one of their greatest sources of political strength, but could result in another major military defeat. Consequently, frustrating as it might be, it would be in the best interests of the Arabs to maintain as flexible and pragmatic a position as possible and continue seeking a solution through more effective political, diplomatic, and public relations activities while working to build their unity, strength, and bargaining power, and seeking to gain the support of those forces in Israel and the United States which are actively working for a fair and lasting peace.

Although Libya and the more militant elements in other Arab countries still refuse to make peace with Israel under any circumstances, none of them is now in a position to prevent a reasonably acceptable peace settlement. However, if essential steps toward peace are not taken within a reasonable period of time and if more and more Arabs lose all hope of ever being able to achieve such a settlement by peaceful means, then the more extremist forces within the Arab world would gain increased strength and influence and the more moderate leaders themselves would, sooner or later, either have to take a more militant stand or be replaced. It must be noted that it was moderate Sadat who, in desperation, decided to resort to war in 1973 because he found barriers to all political roads to peace—whether through the United States, the UN, the Big Four, or the Organization of African Unity.

EGYPT

Many Egyptians have become increasingly disillusioned with the Sadat initiative and the Camp David process. Even though these developments had led to Egypt's reacquisition of the Sinai, they had not led, as originally anticipated, to a comprehensive peace settlement which would have resolved the Jerusalem, Palestinian, and Golan issues and to substantially improved economic conditions for the Egyptian masses. Moreover, Egyptian sovereignty over the Sinai remained limited because of the military terms of the Egyptian-Israeli peace treaty and a small but important territorial dispute in the northeastern corner of the Sinai persisted. Many Egyptians felt that these developments had isolated Egypt in the Arab world and had given Israel a free hand to attack the Iraqi reactor, annex Jerusalem and the Golan Heights, and invade Lebanon while Egypt stood helplessly by. As elsewhere in the Middle East, supporters of the Islamic traditionalist movement have been growing both in numbers, especially among the young, and also in their demand for Egypt to reunite with the Arab world and work to restore Arab control over East Jerusalem and to promote Palestinian national rights. Mubarak insisted that Egypt would abide by the Camp David accords and the Egyptian-Israeli peace treaty, but he rejected Israeli interpretations of major parts of them. He accused Israel of disregarding both the spirit and the terms of these agreements and of being the chief obstacle to improved relations between Egypt and Israel and to the achievement of a comprehensive peace settlement.

Mubarak improved his relations with Arafat, continued to consider the Palestinian problem to be the core of the Arab-Israeli conflict, and urged the United States to open a dialogue with the PLO. Egypt also improved her relations with such Arab states as Jordan, Iraq, and Saudi Arabia; and with Arafat's help, Egypt was invited back into the Islamic Conference Organization. Mubarak exchanged visits with Hussein in November and December 1984 in an attempt to develop closer cooperation and to devise a joint Arab peace strategy to promote the Arab and Palestinian causes. Mubarak urged the moderate Arabs to unite in order to strengthen their bargaining position and to press the United States to launch a new Middle East peace initiative which would be based upon a merging of the Reagan and Fez plans so as to provide more forthrightly for the right of Palestinian national self-determination. While supporting the call for a UN-sponsored international peace conference, Mubarak felt that all other possible avenues should also explored.[8]

When he visited Washington in March 1985, Mubarak tried to persuade President Reagan to play a more active mediating role in the Middle East and, as a first step, to invite a Jordanian-Palestinian group to come to the United States for talks with American officials. The Reagan Administration was reluctant to go along with Mubarak's suggestion.

The Egyptians have grown increasingly unhappy with American failure to press Israel to achieve a settlements freeze, withdraw from Lebanon, and make progress on real Palestinian autonomy. They were also particularly upset as a result of the United States-Israeli strategic agreement and the public statements of high American officials who contended that Israel was America's primary if not also only valuable and dependable "strategic ally" in the Middle East. They felt that Egypt had won the right to be considered equally as a strategic ally and that any statements to the contrary put Egypt and other close Arab friends in an awkward position and place further obstacles in the path of peace. In a confidential document submitted to the United States in support of an Egyptian request for increased economic aid, Egypt portrayed herself as a "critical strategic asset" to the United States.[9]

While Egypt held some joint military exercises with the United States and continued to receive large-scale American economic and military aid and while United States-Egyptian relations remained generally good, Mubarak was less trustful of the United States and wanted to be less dependent on her than Sadat had been. Moreover, American credibility had been weakened in Egypt, as elsewhere in the Arab world. Thus, Egypt restored full diplomatic relations with the Soviet Union and refused to provide formal military bases on her soil. Egyptian impatience with both the United States and Israel was growing. Also growing was the fear that continued failure to make real progress toward achieving a fair and final resolution of the overall Arab-Israeli conflict would ultimately lead to increased strife and instability in the Middle East and could also ultimately lead to the unraveling of the Egyptian-Israeli peace treaty itself. Mubarak still hoped, however, that the moderate Arabs and Palestinians could unite with a common strategy and that President Reagan would feel free enough from domestic political constraints in his second term so that he would be willing and able to launch and seriously press a new and more favorable peace initiative.[10]

JORDAN

For many years, Jordan has been prepared to make peace with Israel. At times, Jordan even sought through secret talks to achieve a separate peace, but Israel was never willing to pay the territorial price required to enable King Hussein to risk such a move. After criticizing Sadat for making a separate treaty and after committing himself to recognize the PLO as the sole legitimate representative of the Palestinian people, Hussein found it more difficult to follow Sadat's path. He now felt that he needed at a minimum the agreement of Arafat and some key moderate Arab leaders before negotiating again with Israel.

In late 1982 and early 1983, Hussein, believing he had American assurances on a settlements freeze and an early Israeli withdrawal from Lebanon, was cautiously optimistic about the chances of peace. But he was soon to lose his optimism and his confidence in American ability and willingness to press the Israelis on these and other critical matters. Since he was convinced that the Likud government would never voluntarily make the required concessions and that only the United States could change Israel's inflexible position, he felt that he first needed concrete evidence that the United States would finally apply the appropriate pressures on Israel before he could reasonably be expected to take the serious risks involved in fully and unilaterally cooperating with the Reagan plan. But despite Hussein's pleas, the Reagan Administration failed to press the Israelis even to accept the plan itself. Confidence in the United States was further shaken because (1) the United States kept reassuring the Israelis that she would not use military and economic aid to compel Israel to make any concessions; (2) American Marines were suddenly withdrawn from Lebanon even after reassuring the Gemayel government of United States support and after insisting that Lebanon was so vital to United States security that they would not be forced out; (3) the United States negotiated a strategic accord with Israel which indicated that the United States would continue to give Israel all-out support and priority over the Arabs, even over the question of peace itself; (4) Congress failed to authorize the sale of advanced weapons to Jordan because of Israeli opposition; and (5) Congress also sought to move the American embassy from Tel Aviv to Jerusalem, a move considered by Hussein to be a "slap" at Jordan and "the last straw that breaks the camel's back."[11] Thus, Hussein felt badly let down by the United States.

In an interview with the *New York Times* (March 5, 1984), Hussein sharply criticized the United States. He charged that she had become so pro-Israel and so influenced by the pro-Israeli lobby that she was no longer acceptable as a mediator because, by becoming an ally of one of the protagonists, she could no longer be an impartial broker. Moreover, past reliance on the United States as the sole mediator had not produced any desired results. Therefore, while recognizing the important role the United States could play in any peace process, Hussein began to press for a broadly-based, UN-sponsored international peace conference in the hope of being able to counter American pro-Israeli influence with the countervailing influence of Western Europe, the Soviet Union, and the UN itself and to "provide an international umbrella to offset Israel's current dominance in the region."[12] But the United States and Israel opposed such a conference.

On the other hand, Hussein was also concerned that complete inaction in the peace process would strengthen the militant nationalist and Islamic fundamentalist forces in Jordan and elsewhere and, thereby, work to destabilize the area and his own regime. Thus, he remained torn between his belief that the Arabs and Palestinians, because of their disunity and relative weakness vis-à-vis Israel, could not regain the occupied territories without vital American help, and his equally strong belief that the United States was so committed to Israel that she would not press her to make meaningful concessions. Yet, hoping against hope that a reelected Reagan, now free of domestic political constraints, might still decide to initiate some positive moves and provide some encouraging signals, Hussein continued to express willingness to cooperate with even a peace process led by the United States, since this appeared to be the only possible option left to him. He met with Arafat and Mubarak to try to work out some joint strategy in the event peace negotiations might somehow be resumed in 1985. But he was not optimistic, for he did not believe American policy would actually change enough, at least in the near future.[13]

Hussein has frequently been accused of lacking courage because he has not been willing to cooperate fully with the Reagan plan until he received some assurances of getting something meaningful in return for the risks taken. Considering the fact that American officials, ever since the failure of the Israeli-Lebanese withdrawal agreement, have frankly refused to take the lead and assume the risks in any Middle East peace process or even in any negotiations dealing with an Israeli withdrawal from Lebanon unless they had some prior assurances and guarantees that their efforts would prove to be successful, one cannot readily fault Hussein for taking a similar position.[14]

In any case, there are two major risks in prematurely pushing Hussein to participate openly in any United States-sponsored peace process involving the West Bank and Gaza areas. In the first place, if he joined such a process even when it was virtually doomed to fail, as it would under present circumstances, the resulting failure could undermine his moderate, pro-Western regime and leave the situation in the Middle East more perilous and unstable than before. In the second place, if he is pushed into seeking a settlement only for the West Bank and Gaza areas, then Syria would feel that, since her own interests were being ignored and even undermined by another step-by-step process which would leave her with less chance than ever to regain the Golan Heights, she would have no choice but to do all she could to sabotage this step. In neither case would the cause of real, lasting peace in the area be well served.

Moreover, Jordan should support Palestinian efforts to achieve an independent state before negotiating on a voluntary basis some kind of economic and political union. If the stage of a Palestinian state is bypassed, many Palestinians would feel bitter and frustrated at the failure to achieve their primary nationalist goals, and the Palestinian problem may persist. Such a development would not help the cause of peace and stability in Jordan, as well as in the Middle East.

LEBANON

Before 1969–70, Lebanon lay only at the fringes of the Arab-Israeli conflict and she tried hard not to become directly involved in it. However, Lebanon's position was radically changed as a result of the failure to resolve the Palestinian problem; the establishment in Lebanon of the PLO's primary political and military bases of operations against Israel following the PLO's expulsion from Jordan, resulting in many Palestinian and Israeli attacks across the Lebanese border; active Palestinian, Syrian, and Israeli involvement in the 1975–76 civil war; Israeli invasions of Lebanon in 1978 and 1982; and Syrian and Israeli occupation of large parts of Lebanon. Thus, for years now, Lebanon has been enmeshed in the Arab-Israeli problem whether she wanted to be or not.

Even though the PLO's major military and political power was badly mauled and largely driven out of Lebanon by Israel in 1982, some thousands of Palestinian commandos remain inside Lebanon, primarily in Syrian-controlled areas of northern and northeastern Lebanon. There also have been reports that small numbers have already returned to the Beirut area. These commandos do not presently pose any major military or political problem for either Israel or Lebanon and probably will not as long as Syria can and will control them. Israel's main problem recently has been with the Shiites, not the Palestinians, in south Lebanon. Moreover, the Lebanese government's main problems have been with Israel over south Lebanon and with internal divisions involving its own squabbling sectarian groups, not with the Palestinians. But for the indefinite future there will still be hundreds of thousands of Palestinian refugees, whether living in camps or not, and some thousands of commandos still living in Lebanon. They could pose a serious long-term internal and external problem for Lebanon until the Palestinian problem has been resolved sufficiently to allow the refugees and commandos either to leave Lebanon for their homeland or somewhere else or to remain voluntarily on a peaceful basis and without further need to use Lebanon as a base of political or military operations against Israel. With a final solution of the Palestinian problem, Israel would no longer feel the need to retain control of south Lebanon whether through her own army or through an Israeli-controlled local militia and Syria would be encouraged to remove her own forces from Lebanon.

While these developments would help remove some major obstacles to Lebanon's attempts to restore unity and stability in her territory, many internal political, security, social, sectarian, psychological, and other major obstacles to peace and reconciliation will remain to be overcome. Peace in Lebanon—with or without the involvement of the Palestinians and the Arab-Israeli conflict—will remain a fragile one for quite some time to come.

SAUDI ARABIA

Although American officials have too often unrealistically overestimated the power that Saudi Arabia actually has to influence events in the Arab world, there is no doubt that in recent years she has been playing an increasingly important role in the Middle East because of her oil, financial resources, religious position, leadership in the Gulf and the Arab world, and potential ability to provide some useful assistance in resolving the Lebanese and Arab-Israeli problems. She has already been helpful on a number of occasions in dealing with internal Lebanese conflicts and for a number of years now she has tried to provide a moderating influence in dealing with the Arab-Israel conflict.

In recent years she has supported moderate Arab and Palestinian leaders in their efforts to reach a political solution with Israel and indicated that, as Crown Prince Fahd said in a 1980 interview in the *The Washington Post* (May 25, 1980), "If Israel would declare its sincere intention of withdrawing from the lands occupied in 1967, Saudi Arabia would do its utmost to bring the Arabs to cooperate and work for a full settlement." Saudi Arabia has especially insisted that Israel withdraw from all occupied lands in order to return East Jerusalem and its Muslim holy places to Arab control—as guardian of the two holiest cities in Islam, (Mecca and Medina), Saudi Arabia feels very strongly about the Jerusalem issue—and to provide for Palestinian right to self-determination and Syria's reacquisition of the Golan Heights.

She has sought to promote Arab unity, partly in the conviction that it would strengthen Arab bargaining power and help bring about a fair peace. She opposed Sadat's initiatives and United States efforts at step-by-step diplomacy because she believed these would divide the Arabs and weaken their position. She has sought to work by consensus rather than by forceful leadership as Sadat tried to do.

Thus, while improving her ties with Egypt, Saudi Arabia has not yet followed Hussein's lead to restore diplomatic relations with Egypt because she feels that Egypt was ostracized by an Arab summit and this decision can be altered only by another summit meeting. She also has not backed Jordanian and Egyptian efforts to isolate Syria. Recently she has unsuccessfully sought to resolve differences between Arafat and Assad.[15]

United States-Saudi relations have always been fairly close and they became even closer after the Soviet Union invaded Afghanistan, the Shah was overthrown, and the Islamic fundamentalist movement seemed to pose a threat to Saudi Arabia and the Gulf states. Relations have been based on mutual security needs and a relatively similar outlook on nearly all matters of mutual concern except for the Arab-Israeli problem and whether the Soviet Union or Israel and the unresolved Palestinian question pose the greater threat to

Saudi Arabia. The Saudis have been increasingly disappointed because of what they consider American failures in dealing with the Arab-Israel and Lebanese conflicts and in refusing to sell to Saudi Arabia and Jordan all the arms requested, and because of the United States-Israeli strategic accord and the congressional attempt to move the American embassy to Jerusalem. As long as the United States continues to give all-out support to Israel and refrains from taking effective action to resolve the overall Arab-Israeli question in accordance with principles accepted by most nations, Saudi Arabia feels she must avoid negotiating any formal alignment with and providing military bases to the United States.[16]

SYRIA

As mentioned earlier, President Assad, aware that Israel was too powerful to be defeated in a war, supported various American, Western European, UN, and Arab proposals for a comprehensive peace settlement because he felt that the best chance of regaining the Golan Heights was through diplomatic and political means.

Many former American officials and diplomats who had actively dealt with the Arab-Israeli problem in past years, as well as a number of experts on the Middle East, have considered Assad to be "pragmatic," "realistic," and "cautious" and to prefer a peaceful settlement as long as this option remained open and would enable him to regain the Golan Heights.

For example, following his discussions with Assad in 1977, Secretary of State Vance concluded that Syria was prepared to negotiate a peace settlement.[17] Talcott W. Seeley, former United States ambassador to Syria and a leading expert on that country, wrote in *The Christian Science Monitor* (April 9, 1983), "Assad is ready for peace" and this is an "important reason why Syria has kept the door open to the U.S.," who alone has the potential to bring about a just, comprehensive peace settlement. Dr. William Quandt, a former high-level National Security Council official, wrote in the *New York Times* (June 30, 1983) that Syria was still interested in peace if the United States "convincingly" said she still stood for the principles of withdrawal in return for peace and is prepared to promote a balanced peace settlement. Dr. Harold Saunders, a former high-level official in both the National Security Council and State Department, also wrote that "the leaders of each of Israel's neighbors," including Syria, have been "prepared to make peace with Israel."[18] Nadav Safran, Harvard specialist on the Middle East, wrote in an op-ed page article in the *New York Times* (December 16, 1981) that Syria would negotiate a peace settlement if given enough reason to believe that she could benefit from it and that "on the two occasions [prior to 1981] when the U.S. seemed to advance the peace process in earnest [the summer of 1974 and the summer of 1977], the Syrian government made its willingness to negotiate unmistakingly clear. Yet the Syrians gained little on either occasion from stating its willingness to negotiate.''[19]

According to the *Wall Street Journal* (September 15, 1983) and *Newsweek* (December 19, 1983), some Reagan Administration and State Department officials, and even some Israelis, believed that Assad was a man ''with whom they can strike a deal—if only after hard bargaining''; ''Assad can be brought around and would accept a new U.S. peace proposal which could help open the way for Israel's return of the Golan Heights[11]; and ''Syria is a reliable negotiating adversary, who, though difficult, will deliver if a deal is struck.'' The *New York Times* reported (October 8, 1984) that ''Israeli officials seem to have a good deal of trust that when the Syrians agree to something, whether orally or in writing, they do it.''[20]

Syrian officials have held that they were for a comprehensive peace settlement which would provide for a complete Israeli withdrawal from territories occupied in 1967, a Palestinian state, an end to the state of war, and the right of all states in the area to live in peace and security. As early as 1977, in discussions with Carter Administration officials, Syria indicated that she was prepared to consider a temporary demilitarization of the Golan Heights with a UN peacekeeping force maintaining a presence there and even ultimately diplomatic and other normal relations with Israel, although she felt that because of existing distrust and animosity, it would take time before full normalization could be attained.[21] Syrian officials supported the idea of a UN-sponsored international peace conference for this would enable the Arabs to counter American support of Israel and strengthen their own bargaining position.[22]

Although for years the Syrians had been willing to participate in negotiations leading to a comprehensive peace settlement, the Camp David accords, the Egyptian-Israeli peace treaty, Israeli annexation of the Golan Heights and East Jerusalem, the Reagan plan, the Israeli-Lebanese withdrawal agreement, the United States-Israeli strategic agreement, hardline statements by Begin and other Israeli officials on the Palestinian and territorial issues (with Begin and Sharon insisting that they would ''never'' give up the Golan even in return for peace,[23]) and repeated assurances by American officials that no pressures would be applied on Israel, convinced the Syrians that the United States and Israel were trying to isolate them and to ignore the Golan issue; Israel would never be prepared voluntarily to make the essential concessions for peace; and the United States had become so partisan and allied to Israel that she would not apply the pressures needed to extract these concessions. Syria opposed the Reagan plan and other piecemeal diplomatic efforts because she feared that if they succeeded they would eventually leave the Golan as the last issue to be dealt with and, consequently, would also leave her with an even more reduced bargaining power than ever while the Golan remained in Israel's hands. Since Israel was not prepared voluntarily to return the Golan Heights and Syria did not have the military power to regain it by force alone, Syria had concluded from the beginning that only Arab unity, strength, and cooperation would provide a credible strategic threat and bargaining power to persuade Israel to negotiate a withdrawal from all the occupied areas. That is why she so vehemently opposed Sadat's initiative and subsequent developments leading to a separate peace.[24]

Once Egypt was detached from Arab military and political might, Syria still hoped she could build respectable military and political strength by forming an eastern front around Syria, Jordan, Iraq, Lebanon, and the PLO. After this front failed to materialize and Syria found herself virtually isolated in the the area, she decided to try to build up her own military power to the point where she alone could bargain or threaten Israel from a more equal position. President Assad said at a news conference in Damascus in late December 1984: "There has to be a balance between Syria and Israel, or else the [comprehensive] peace we seek will not be realized."[25] Since he and the other Arabs had no effective leverage to use against Israel, Assad concluded that negotiations with her under current circumstances would be "fruitless."[26]

To improve her bargaining position, Syria needed additional military and political help from the Soviet Union and the more isolated she was the more she needed it for any strategy which involved either peace or war. Therefore, although the Syrians distrusted the Soviets and had much more in common culturally and ideologically with the West and would have preferred making a deal with the United States if only she would play a more impartial and effective role as peacemaker, they felt that they had no choice but to continue turning to the USSR for support and to avoid antagonizing the only major power willing and able to help them.[27]

But despite large-scale military aid by Moscow, Syria was still no military match for Israel, and Israel, with massive American assistance, could maintain her military lead for the indefinite future. Moreover, there was always the danger for Syria that if she succeeded in narrowing the power gap between herself and Israel, Israel would precipitate a "preventive war" at a time of her own, not Syria's, choosing and at a point when Israel was still sure of winning a war. So, Syria's military option remained unrealistic. Nevertheless, her political bargaining position had been strengthened, especially by the growing realization that without Syrian involvement in a peace process and without a fair solution to the Golan Heights issue, an overall, lasting solution to the Arab-Israeli problem was not possible.[28]

Syria has not always played her own hand very well. Too often, her officals have been strident and bombastic in their statements and they have done poorly in the area of public relations. Thus, they have not helped to promote a better understanding of their real position and case. Their rhetoric made it easier for the media and Israelis and others to claim they were really rejectionists, even when they were basically willing to accept and make peace with Israel if the peace terms were fair enough. Syria's recent backing of the militant PLO factions as a tactical means of getting at Arafat further complicates matters for her, because she could be charged with being a rejectionist through her support of Palestinian rejectionists and because strengthening these Palestinians could complicate her efforts in the future when the situation might be more favorable for achieving what she has indicated her preference really was—a just and lasting comprehensive peace settlement. Moreover, these Palestinian rejectionists might try to press their concept of armed struggle against Israel to the point where Syria could again be sucked into another costly and ill-timed conflict with Israel. For the long term at least, Syria really has much more in common with the goal (of a fair, comprehensive peace based on UN resolutions) and the means used to achieve this goal (UN-sponsored international conference) advocated by the moderate Palestinians supporting Arafat than with the goals and means proposed by the Palestinian rejectionists now in her camp. Thus, Syria must seek ways whereby she can restore close ties with Arafat and his moderate followers. In the final analysis, support from Palestinian moderates will do much more than support from the rejectionists to promote Syria's best interests.

When Assad was seriously ill with heart trouble in late 1983, there was great concern about future Syrian leadership and policy. Although Assad has regained his health, the risk of another serious illness remains. Any successor would be in a much weaker political position within Syria and he would, therefore, have much greater difficulty in making those unpopular decisions which would be required by any future peace negotiations, especially in the face of the rising power of militant religious fanatics within Syria. Moreover, a new leader might not be as able, pragmatic, and cautious as Assad has been. Nevertheless, any new leader would have to face problems and constraints (including Israeli military superiority and continued all-out United States backing and a cautious Soviet policy) similar to those Assad has been facing, and he too would have to be concerned about the harmful consequences of precipitating a war with Israel which would bring another humiliating Syrian defeat. Since there would be greater uncertainties in dealing with a new, untried, and weaker leader, it would clearly be preferable that a serious peace process takes place while Assad was still in power.

But no matter who is leader, failure to provide Syria with peaceful means for attaining legitimate goals supported by the world community, the overwhelming preponderance of which calls for an Israeli withdrawal from the

Golan Heights, could have serious consequences to the Middle East and to the world. Although Syria still prefers the peaceful path, sooner or later she might give up all hope in the effectiveness of this path and she might feel compelled, as in October 1973, to resort to force even when chances for military defeat remained great. Moreover, any new Syrian-Israeli conflict not only would prove to be far more destructive because of the more sophisticated weapons both antagonists would have in their arsenals, but also could bring about the active involvement of the two superpowers in support of their client states.

THE PALESTINIANS

Prior to the 1973 war, the PLO insisted on achieving the total liberation of Palestine through armed struggle and the establishment there of a single, secular, democratic state. However, after the war, for reasons discussed in Chapter X, the views of the more pragmatic Palestinian leaders began to change. In fact, starting in 1974, the annual Palestine National Council (PNC) resolutions stopped referring to the "liberation of Palestine" through "armed struggle" and the establishment of a "secular, democratic state"; and the moderate elements in the PNC started considering for the first time accepting (1) the establishment of a Palestinian state in those areas evacuated by Israel and (2) an invitation to attend a reconvened Geneva conference even though this could be considered an implied acceptance of both Security Council Resolution 242, which would have been the basis of any negotiations there, and also the existence of the State of Israel. In addition, the PLO, under Arafat's leadership and with the support of a large majority of the Palestinians, began to stress political, diplomatic, and public relations activities as opposed to armed struggle alone.

These major modifications in the goal and means to be used to achieve it caused a serious split within the PLO. The smaller, more extremist groups—such as the Popular Front for the Liberation of Palestine (PFLP), the Arab Liberation Front (ALF) and the Palestine Liberation Front (PLF)—withdrew from the PLO Executive Committee in 1974 in protest. As noted by former Foreign Minister Abba Eban in an interview in *New Outlook* (Tel Aviv, September 1975), such a split was inevitable. Eban stated:

> As with every movement of revolutionary violence, there are usually two schools of thought. There is one school which says: let us stick to our texts, to our dogmas . . . , even if this means we suffer on the diplomatic front. Others say: if you want to enter the diplomatic arena, half a loaf is better than no loaf at all. We can go around indefinitely

reaching no result if we stick to our text. So let us cut our losses and get what we can out of what remains.

The "dogmatic" Palestinians belonging to the first school of thought rejected this "half a loaf" solution, while those belonging to the second school—led by Arafat—finally, if reluctantly, concluded that half a loaf was better than none, thus being willing to settle for a small Palestine, while keeping alive the vision that someday they might be able to attain the whole loaf by peaceful means.

By giving up their more extreme aspiration and tactics, the moderate Palestinians were able to win wider political and public support throughout the world because most countries, while prepared to back Palestinian national rights, were not also prepared to accept the elimination of the State of Israel and the use of terrorist activities. Thus, the PLO received recognition from over 100 countries throughout the world (including in Western Europe), obtained overwhelming backing (even from Western European states) for favorable UN General Assembly resolutions, and also gained wide popular support and a better image in the media. This progress encouraged moderate leaders and their followers to continue on this path in the hope that it would ultimately pay off. However, this path did not lessen Israel's opposition to the PLO and a Palestinian state, even if only a mini one, and did not win meaningful support from the United States. Since Arafat's path of moderation did not pay off and there was no payoff yet in sight, by 1983 increasing numbers of moderate Palestinians who had supported it in the past began to lose faith in its feasibility and to join the rejectionists, leading to a split in al-Fatah and the PLO.

In fact, it is important to understand that, at least since 1974, the real rejectionists have been composed of two major elements. One element, for dogmatic reasons, would have rejected half a loaf even if it were offered to them. Other rejectionists, however, were not unequivocally opposed to accepting only half a loaf, but they became convinced that Israel never would voluntarily and peacefully give it up and that the United States would never apply the needed pressures on her to do so. Believing, therefore, that no peaceful means would ever actually be available for achieving even those limited goals which nearly the entire world considered as legitimate, they concluded that they were left with no choice but resort to armed struggle. In that case, they had nothing to lose by going for the whole loaf, and not just half a one. They accused Arafat of being naive and unrealistic and of merely wasting precious time trying to attain the unattainable through peaceful means.[29]

Over the years, as indicated earlier, Arafat and other moderate PLO leaders have indicated their willingness to negotiate a peace settlement with Israel as long as it provided for their right of national self-determination. Their sentiments have been expressed in statements and interviews; joint communiques with various heads of state; PNC resolutions; declared interest in attending a reconvened Geneva conference in 1977; support for various UN Security Council draft resolutions (including those vetoed by the United States, as in January 1976, or never put to a vote because of an American threat of veto, as in the case of the joint French-Egyptian draft resolution) and also General Assembly resolutions which called for convening an international peace conference; support for the United States-Soviet communique of October 1, 1977, and the Brezhnev plan, both specifically calling for Israel's right to exist in peace and security, as well as the Fez plan which at least implied this; discussions with Hussein and Mubarak to work out a "peace" strategy; talks with Israeli doves; many signals, if often ambiguous and cautious ones, to the United States; encouragement of active peace efforts by Western Europe; and a readiness to break with the Palestinian rejectionists even if this would split the PLO.

Some Palestinians have claimed that PNC resolutions since 1974 had already provided new interpretations of their Charter. While the Charter spoke of "liberating Palestine" "only" through "armed struggled," these resolutions stopped using these terms and called, instead, for establishing a Palestinian state in the areas to be evacuated by Israel; have placed stress on diplomatic and political means; and have clearly supported various peace proposals which provided for the existence and security of Israel. They have noted that the American constitution has been changed far more by new interpretations than by formal amendments; that the Herut party's charter, symbol, and songs claim both sides of the Jordan River and these have never been changed; and that the new interpretations by Arafat and others have even led to a split in the PLO, indicating their seriousness and genuineness.[30]

Many Israelis, including former high-level officials, military officers, and diplomats, as well as leading experts on the Arab world, members of the Knesset, and others, believe that the PLO has changed and urge their government to negotiate a peace settlement providing for Palestinian national rights with proper security arrangements for Israel. According to Yaacov Shimoni, a former diplomat and senior Foreign Ministry official, despite the rhetoric from some PLO leaders and the unchanged PLO Charter,

> changes . . . have occurred. [While it is regrettable that the Charter has not been changed] it should be borne in mind that movements or organizations seldom formally change their solemn, sacrosanct charters: if they no longer fit changed circumstances, they are often allowed to "fade away" or are re-interpreted rather than amended. (Examples

could be adduced from Israel's and the Zionist movement's own experience.) . . . Anyhow, for most movements political circumstances and necessities have usually been more important than the texts of their charters. . . . The repeated assertion that there is nothing new on the Arab side, no change in the PLO attitudes, is . . . politically and conceptually false and dangerous.[31]

The Israel Council for Israeli-Palestinian Peace stated in a resolution on June 23, 1983: "In the last few years, the PLO leadership has indicated many times to Israel and the U.S. its readiness for a political solution. The present situation [split in al-Fatah] proves these messages were genuine and sincere. Otherwise, the PLO extremists would not have rebelled as they have."[32] A leading Israeli specialist on the Arabs, Matti Steinberg, said in June, 1984, that because of the split "we shall be able to conclude that Arafat has embarked unreservedly on the political path. In the matter of position and ideology, he has already crossed the Rubicon." In the view of Professor Yehoshua Porath, another leading Israeli expert, "a majority coalition" backing Arafat is pressing "the political line, which seeks to achieve a [peace] settlement through an advanced agreement with Jordan with Egyptian backing."[33] Yehoshofat Harkabi, former head of Israeli military intelligence and a leading expert on the Arab world, contended that "as an ethnic group" the Palestinians "are entitled" to their own "nation state" and he condemned the "sour-faced refusal to ever negotiate with the PLO, forever and ever."[34] Former Foreign Minister Abba Eban wrote that an "Arab destiny in the West Bank was inevitable"; Israel should work to establish a Palestinian state which would not be hostile to Israel's security; and if the PLO agreed to participate in an international peace conference, "this will mean that it has modified its ideology."[35] Aharon Yariv, a former minister and head of military intelligence, warned that "there would be no peace without the recognition of the Palestinian rights to self determination."[36] Mordechai Bentov, a former cabinet minister, held that since "our fate, our security, our future . . . are all dependent upon a resolution of the Palestinian problem," Israel should "declare that it is ready" to accept "a Palestinian state."[37] Israeli Reserve General Mattityahu Peled, a leader in the Israeli peace movement who has had extensive contacts with Arafat and other top PLO officials, held that "it is clear from a series of resolutions taken by the PNC that such acceptance [of Israel] cannot be doubted."[38]

As indicated earlier, many officials, area specialists, and others in the West have become convinced that Arafat and other moderates were finally prepared to accept half a loaf no matter what the PLO Charter said and that the PLO must be brought into the peacemaking process.[39]

Moderate PLO leaders have preferred negotiating a comprehensive settlement through a UN-sponsored international peace conference which would be attended by all parties to the dispute, including the PLO, and the major powers in the hope that this would strengthen their weak bargaining power vis-à-vis Israel and this would also give greater weight to the UN resolutions which favored their cause. They have insisted that any peace settlement should provide (1) an independent Palestinian state, which could and would later voluntarily agree to federate with Jordan (although many West Bankers have become so concerned about the pace of Israeli *de facto* annexationist activities that, if necessary, they would be willing to have their area returned to Jordan in some form if this would be the only way of avoiding having to live indefinitely under Israel rule); (2) a solution of the 1948 and 1967 Arab refugee problems based on UN resolutions; and (3) the right of all states in the area, including the Palestinian one, to live in peace and security with effective security arrangements, including peacekeeping forces, demilitarized zones, and international security guarantees, for which they feel a weak and divided Palestinian state would have more need than a powerful Israel. At least at one time, they indicated that they would consider a UN administration of the West Bank and Gaza during a brief transition period while Israeli forces were withdrawing from them.[40]

Moderate Palestinian leaders have continued to oppose unilateral recognition of Israel as a precondition for negotiations, although, as mentioned earlier, some have indicated that they would consider this if assured that it could lead to Palestinian participation in the peace process and ultimately to their own state. Otherwise, they would insist on "mutual and simultaneous recognition" in the framework of a peace process.

Over the years, Arafat has been criticized by many, including some of his sympathizers in the West and in Israel, on the grounds that he gave so much stress to maintaining PLO unity that he was compelled to be too cautious and ambiguous and to base his policies on the lowest common denominator, leaving him with too little flexibility to enable him to fully convince others of the sincerity of his willingness to accept and make peace with Israel.[41] Moreover, American officials and others, including Israeli doves, have contended that it would be to the PLO's advantages to clearly accept Resolution 242 and Israel's right to exist because this would (1) enable the United States to enter talks with the PLO; (2) weaken Israel's argument that the PLO was out to destroy her; (3) strengthen the hands of dovish groups in Israel; and (4) further enhance the PLO's image here and abroad. The PLO was also warned that if it held on to its "bargaining chip" of recognition too long, it could ultimately become worthless if Israel continued her *de facto* annexation of the occupied areas.

If the bargaining chip was ever to have been played, the best time would have been in the summer of 1977 when the Carter Administration was seriously trying to involve the PLO in the peace process and when it was also willing to allow significant qualifications to the PLO's acceptance of Resolution 242. Arafat was prepared to play this "chip" at that time, but the majority of the PLO leaders opposed this because, as indicated earlier, they lacked faith in American credibility and willingness to produce something meaningful in return. After the Sadat initiative the Carter Administration took a tougher line on the PLO and on the issue of an independent state. The Reagan Administration has been even more hostile to both of these, while Israel has not lessened her own hostility.

While moderate Palestinians have understood the potential advantages of playing their card, they have stressed the constraints, risks, and other drawbacks to doing so before receiving assurances, at least from the United States, that they would get something tangible in return. They have also argued that recognition is not essential to negotiation, as was proved by United States negotiations with North Korea, China, and North Vietnam in the past. Recognition usually comes at the end, not at the beginning of a negotiating process. Since Israel has consistently insisted on negotiating only from a position of strength and on not giving up any of her own bargaining chips without getting something in return, it was unfair to press the PLO to do something Israel has refused to do. Israel, in any case, has repeatedly proclaimed that she would never deal with the PLO and never accept a Palestinian state even if the PLO unilaterally recognized her, so recognition would not bring about any change in Israel's inflexible position. Moderate Palestinians also claim that: winning greater backing in Israeli public opinion, while useful and desirable, would still not really bring about a significant change in Israel's adamant position; the United States has promised at most to talk with the PLO in return for recognition, but without committing herself to go beyond talk; the United States has repeatedly stated that she would not apply pressures on Israel to change her stand and she stated clearly, at least in the last several years, that she opposes the establishment of an independent state no matter what the PLO does; and unilateral recognition would further split the PLO.

Even Israeli Reserve General Mattityahu Peled, who has for years sought to promote an Israeli-Palestinian dialogue and peace agreement, concluded after carefully analyzing the pros and cons of a unilateral recognition, that "in terms of practical politics, such unilateral recognition would bring no immediate results because the government of Israel" would "still refuse to recognize the rights of the Palestinian people" and because the American government would still offer the PLO too little in return. "With no tangible results other than a shift in public opinion, then the merits of such a [PLO] move are dubious indeed" and could lead to harmful consequences to Palestinian moderates who would have taken a risk without achieving any gains in return. (Peled concluded that only if the United States made some dramatic move, such as by inviting the PLO to participate in the peace process under its own banner, would the PLO leaders be able ''to declare unilateral recognition'' and, at the same time, to ''withstand an ensuing storm'' within the PLO. [42])

Peled and others have stressed some important points which have been frequently overlooked or inadequately considered. If Arafat were to take some dramatic gamble—such as recognizing Israel unilaterally—and this failed to achieve any tangible results, it could prove to be dangerously counterproductive. For example, a failure could kill whatever little hope which still exists among many moderates that the path to a fair peaceful settlement was still open; could generate greater support for those who claim that the only realistic path remaining was that of armed struggle; and could encourage a great increase in guerrilla and terrorist activities in the Middle East and elsewhere. In short, since premature recognition could have more harmful than helpful consequences, it is not unreasonable for moderate Palestinians to insist upon some assurances that they would get something meaningful in return for taking the great risks involved. As a matter of fact, some Palestinian moderates have already paid with their lives for pursuing the path to peace. Therefore, one can understand when Palestinian moderates say that before they jump into a pool they want first to make sure that there is enough water there.

The present serious split within the PLO does in some ways provide Arafat and the moderates greater freedom to ignore the extremists and to pursue the diplomatic and political path more vigorously than in the past. However, there are important groups (such as the PFLP and the DFLP) which have not yet fully joined the extremist anti-Arafat movement but which have warned Arafat that they would irrevocably break with him if he initiated unacceptable diplomatic moves. Moreover, many of his own present followers might desert him if they think he is going too far and too fast without some guarantees, at least from the United States, that the Palestinians would benefit substantially by this. Any evaluation of the justification for Arafat's insistence on some assurances beforehand must take into consideration the fact that for many months the Reagan Administration has frankly indicated its reluctance, especially after the fiasco of the Israeli-Lebanese withdrawal accord, to stick its neck out by playing an active role in promoting another Israeli-Lebanese withdrawal agreement or even another Arab-Israeli peace process unless it was given some assurances from the parties directly involved that its efforts were certain of being successful. Therefore, since neither the United States nor Israel are prepared to provide enough incentives and assurances to enable Arafat to take further major risks, he will feel compelled to continue acting with greater caution than he would like. His recent moves to convene a PNC conference and to improve relations with Jordan and Egypt in the face of strong Syrian and Palestinian rejectionist opposition indicate he is willing to take big risks up to a point, but to safely go much beyond this he especially needs American incentives and willingness to assume her own share of risks for peace.

Some Palestinian moderates have also been constrained by their fear that if they negotiated from their present position of weakness they could be letting themselves "into a trap." Consequently, some have argued in favor of waiting until such time as the balance of forces in the region has changed in their favor. For example, one moderate leader said: "In my view there will not be a political solution in the near future. Not because we do not want one but because the Israelis do not want one. In view of the existing balance of forces in the region, I do not think that the U.S. wants to exert pressure on Israel."[43]

Clearly the overwhelming majority of the Palestinians first want their own state and then have it negotiate some kind of federal or confederal relationship with Jordan. There already are very close personal and family ties between large numbers of Palestinians in Jordan and those in the occupied areas and elsewhere; and a small, weak, and divided Palestinian state would need close association with Jordan, for economic, political, and military reasons. If this stage of an independent state were to be bypassed, however, it would not advance the cause of peace and stability in Jordan or in the Middle East as a whole, because it would leave many Palestinians (especially in the diaspora) bitter and frustrated and some might refuse to give up their struggle for their own state. Thus, an immediate Jordanian solution could end up leaving the Palestinian question still alive and unresolved. After all, for the Palestinians—like all nationalists including the Zionists—an independent state has been the primary objective and the whole purpose for their costly struggles over many decades.

While the Palestinian goal of a small state of their own is considered a legitimate one by nearly all of the nations of the world, there still is the question of the means to be used to achieve that goal. With Israel backed by the United States and retaining for the foreseeable future overwhelming military superiority, with deep splits in the Arab world persisting, and with the PLO militarily weak, divided, and dispersed, the armed struggle option is not a realistic one. Thus, under existing circumstances, a return to armed struggle alone not only would almost certainly fail again to attain its objective, but could also undermine the substantial diplomatic, political, and public relations gains made by the PLO and the Palestinian cause throughout the world. While these gains have not yet produced the desired state, the fact remains that without them the PLO bargaining power and its position in the world would be considerably weaker than it presently is. Therefore, turning away completely from the political path would actually do the Palestinians more harm than good. Thus, the moderate Palestinian leaders must remain realistic, pragmatic, and even patient and be prepared to seize any reasonable opportunity and take any reasonable risks to get their own state even if in only part of Palestine, because if they return to the past insistence on gaining all of Palestine through armed struggle alone, then the danger would be very great that they would end up, as in 1948, with nothing at all.

However, it must be realized that even the moderate Palestinians will remain unwilling to give up the armed struggle option altogether because it, together with non-recognition of Israel, remains one of the very few bargaining chips still available to them. In their eyes, the use of—or at least the threat to use—armed struggle would help ensure that neither Israel and the United States nor the rest of the world will once again place the Palestinian issue on the backburner and try to forget it. Americans and Israelis, as much as any other peoples, should recognize and recall one very important lesson from history: if you deny any people peaceful means for legitimate change, you then leave them with no alternative to the resort to force. After all, we Americans in 1776 and the Israelis prior to the 1948 war clearly understood and acted on the basis of this very lesson.

Moreover, the fact remains that for years there has been no realistic alternative to the PLO and Arafat if the Palestinians are to be brought into any peace process. As even the European Economic Community and some Israelis themselves have stressed, no fair and lasting comprehensive peace settlement can be achieved without associating the PLO in some meaningful way in the negotiating process. No matter what the rationale is for Israel's opposition to the PLO, the facts are that the PLO under Arafat's leadership has been widely recognized throughout the world, including Western Europe, as well as by the great preponderance of the Palestinians both in the occupied areas and the diaspora as the only legitimate representative of the Palestinian people; and that there is, in any case, no realistic alternative to it (at least as of this writing) except some small rejectionist groups. The Palestinians in the occupied areas were never able, because of Israeli opposition, to develop a competitive organization: and, in any case, they have for years clearly accepted the PLO as their only representative. Even if it were possible to develop another alternative, it would take many years before any new leaders could acquire sufficient influence, prestige, and confidence to enable them to make the very unpopular concessions required for peace with Israel.

Thus, the only viable alternative now is not between the PLO and some as yet unformed organizations, but between the more moderate and the more militant factions within the PLO. The wisest move, therefore, is not to ignore and bypass the PLO, but to exert every effort and provide every possible incentive to strengthen the position and influence of its more moderate

leaders and to help them rally increased support among the Palestinian masses
for a peaceful settlement. Only Arafat now still has the stature and backing
to move the PLO toward such a settlement, but even he has to move cautiously and avoid making too many unpopular commitments publicly until
he had received far greater assurance that he has so far that his moderate
efforts have a chance to produce reasonably favorable results. He will have
to deliver on a Palestinian state or, sooner or later, face further and even
more serious challenges to his leadership.

The survival of a reasonably unified PLO under Arafat's moderate leadership is vital to the cause of peace and stability in the Middle East and to
the chances, small as they might be today, for the Palestinians to attain their
state through peaceful means. Therefore, it is very important that a serious
and constructive peace process be undertaken very soon and while Arafat is
still leader of the PLO and while the great majority of the Palestinians continue to support him and his conciliatory path, because only under these favorable circumstances can a just and lasting comprehensive Middle East peace
settlement have a chance of being brought to fruition. But time is of the
essence. If with time there is no movement on the peace front, then more
and more moderate Palestinians will lose all hope in Arafat's peaceful path
and will join the rejectionists. While this trend would be welcomed by Israeli and Palestinian hawks, it cannot be welcomed by those who still hope
for a fair and durable peace settlement.

ISRAEL

After the 1967 war, Israel continued to profess a desire for a peace settlement, but only if it were based largely on her own conditions. Because
neither the Arabs nor the world community would consent to her conditions
and because Israel's coalition governments were deeply divided over peace
terms, both Prime Ministers Meir and Rabin strove to avoid any serious negotiations which would compel them to come up with specific positions on
the territorial and other issues and to stall for time in an attempt to strengthen
their bargaining position and to convince the Arabs that their only hope of
regaining even part of their lost lands was to negotiate directly, separately,
and primarily on Israeli terms. In an interview in September 1983, former
Foreign Minister Abba Eban said:

> I will be honest: the collapse of Israel's diplomacy began under the
> Labour Government, not under the Likud. In the early '70's, Moshe
> Dayan was regarded as the true voice of Israeli policy. It is true that
> Labour's official line was that the territories were a temporary bargain-
> ing card until peace was attained. But at the same time, Dayan said

"Sharm el-Shaykh is more important than peace," all the more so, the West Bank.

When I examine the national mood at that time, I do not only mean statements issued by the Foreign Ministry, but also those made by the defense establishment, media, etc., anyone who observed us in the years before the Yom Kippur War would have had the impression that we were really not interested in peace—we were a nation content without it. We felt that we held the trump cards in our hands and we were happy to hold them, but as time went on, we grew fond of them, and we were not ready to play them. . . . [Moreover], bringing together the proponents of the Greater Israel camp with those favoring territorial compromise cost that government the ability to maneuver.[44]

In the middle 1970s a number of cabinet ministers opposed Rabin's and Peres' "barren policy" and urged them to make territorial concessions and to negotiate with any Palestinian group which would acknowledge Israel's right to exist and would renounce terrorism.[45] But as Rabin told the World Jewish Congress in February 1975, as long as Israel retained the balance of power in her favor she did not have to make any concessions to the Arabs. Moreover, he was less interested in a long-range settlement based on compromise than on weakening Arab military capability and placing primary emphasis on maintaining Israeli security by retaining large parts of the occupied areas for allegedly security purposes and by maintaining an overwhelming military superiority over all of the Arabs.[46] Therefore, when Rabin came to Washington in January 1976, he rejected American pleas to be more flexible, opposed any new peace initiatives, and kept "stalling" and "dragging" his feet with the expectation that Congress and pro-Israeli domestic pressures would make it unnecessary for him to make any concessions.[47]

When in 1977 President Carter sought to reconvene the Geneva conference, Rabin admitted in his own memoirs that he opposed such a move and sought to "lay the matter of Geneva to rest" because he feared that such a conference would compel Israel to make far greater political and territorial concessions than she was prepared to make even in return for a peace settlement.[48]

In short, all Labor governments after the 1967 war preferred the continuation of the *status quo* to entering a negotiating process which might force them to make distasteful concessions no matter how essential they would be to achieve a lasting peace. While claiming that they would negotiate directly with each frontline Arab state separately as long as there were no Arab preconditions, Labor leaders nevertheless insisted on their own conditions. In the first place, refusing to negotiate unless negotiations were direct ones and without conditions were themselves conditions. Besides, Israel frequently asserted that she would never recognize or negotiate with the PLO, even if it accepted Resolution 242 and Israel's right to exist; never accept a separate Palestinian state; never give up any part of Jerusalem; and never return to any of the pre-1967 borders. For allegedly security reasons—and contrary to the terms of Resolution 242 as understood by virtually all countries in the world—she insisted on retaining large parts of the West Bank, Gaza, Golan, and Sinai areas and maintaining a military presence on the western bank of the Jordan River. These territorial demands not only were completely unacceptable to the Arabs, but, as the Israeli publication *Brief: Middle East Highlights,* conceded in its August 16–31, 1975, issue, they put Israel "in a political confrontation with practically the entire world, which will demand the return of the 1967 frontiers." Moreover, even former Prime Minister David Ben-Gurion, who had been a leading hawk prior to the 1967 war, warned in the spring of 1971: "Peace is more important than real estate. . . . As for security, militarily defensible borders, while desirable, cannot by themselves guarantee our future. *Real* peace with our neighbors—mutual trust and friendships—that is the only true security. . . . In every conflict, there comes a time when to settle is more important than to get everything you want . . . and the time has come to settle."[49] But Ben-Gurion's perceptive advice was ignored.

When Begin and the Likud came to power in 1977, Israel's position on peace hardened still further. Like Labor, the Likud opposed dealing with the PLO in any way, accepting a Palestinian state, and giving up any part of Jerusalem. While Labor claimed substantial parts of the occupied areas on the ground of security, it conceded that Resolution 242 required at least some withdrawal on all fronts. Likud, however, was prepared to withdraw only on the Egyptian front, and then primarily to detach Egypt from the Arab coalition in order to make it easier for Israel to hold on to the rest of the occupied territories. In fact, for religious, historical, and ideological reasons, Begin refused to make any withdrawals from the West Bank, Gaza, and Golan sectors even in return for peace with the Arabs. Consequently, according to Weizman, Carter, Vance and others (as discussed in earlier chapters), following the Egyptian-Israeli treaty Begin opposed any further peace efforts. Whenever these efforts were seriously pressed by the United States or the UN, he did everything he could—such as by speeding up the establishment of new settlements, annexing Jerusalem and the Golan Heights, and reiterating that he would never give up any more territory and never deal with the PLO or accept a Palestinian state—to undermine these efforts. In fact, as many Israelis and others have noted, Begin was more alarmed when Arab and Palestinian leaders took a moderate rather than a hawkish position. As long as they appeared to be militant and inflexible, it was easy for Israel to avoid negotiating while blaming the Arabs for the failure to bring about any negotiations. As *Haretz, Yediot Aharonot,* and the *Jerusalem Post* noted, what Israel 'feared'' most of all was a formally expressed willingness by Hussein and Arafat to enter negotiations, such as under the Reagan plan, thus creating the threat of American pressures on her to make those kinds of territorial and other concessions she did not want to make.[50] *Haretz* held that Israel feared any "sign of PLO moderation" to such an extent that she was "refusing to encourage the trend towards moderation which is emerging in the leadership" of the PLO.[51] A *New Outlook* editorial (February 1984) stated: "The present Israeli government fears Palestinian moderation more than Palestinian terrorism. It would do anything in its power to discourage the former and encourage the latter."

Therefore, whenever the United States appeared to be winning Arab and Palestinian support for a peace process, as discussed in earlier chapters, Israel sought ways to kill it. For example, a former Labor Minister of Justice charged that while Israel claimed she was ready to negotiate peace, "in practice," she ended up "blocking any avenue for the continuation of the peace process" because she refused to give up any more territory.[52] Actual negotiations would have proven embarrassing to Israel not only because they would have quickly and clearly revealed that Israel preferred the *status quo* to making concessions, but also because they would have forced an open debate within Israel on such critical issues as the value of exchanging territory for peace and the need to satisfy in some way Palestinian national rights— issues which seriously divided the Israeli people.

According to the *Jerusalem Post* (February 28, 1984), "In the eyes of the Likud nothing is more desirable than perpetuation of the present impasse, while at the same time voicing pious statements about readiness to negotiate"; but since it refused to give up any territory on the West Bank, Gaza, and Golan sectors and to consider any kind of a Palestinian state the question was what was there to negotiate about? "On keeping the territories?" As noted by a former Labor minister, Israeli opposition to various peace proposals "does not stem from the fear that there is no one to talk to but, rather, from the fear that there is nothing to talk about" since the government was "simply not prepared to make concessions" and negotiations would be "impossible without concessions."[53] The *New York Times* (February 13, 1983) concluded that Begin's "determination never to give" up the West Bank "seems to preclude any profitable negotiations with the Palestinians and King Hussein . . . , even if they agree to talk."

Any meaningful negotiations require giving as well as taking. But if Israel wants recognition, peace treaties, full normalization, security arrangements and the like and yet insists upon giving up either nothing in return (as in the case with Likud) or so little in the way of territory and Palestinian political rights (as in the case of Labor), then neither the Arabs nor the Palestinians can be expected to enter negotiations on that basis and to accept peace terms any less favorable than those supported formally by nearly all nations in the world. General Harkabi, former head of Israeli military intelligence, warned that "the only way to produce a change in Arab positions vis-à-vis Israel is through" agreeing to peace terms "acceptable to world public opinion. The Arabs will not grant Israel demands that the world will not support."[54] He also warned that "the policy adopted by Israel is frustrating any possibility of the emergence in Arab states of a thrust towards a settlement with us. Even the foundations of the peace treaty with Egypt are being steadily eroded. . . . Thus far, at least, Israel's position is reinforcing the doubts in Arab minds that there is any possibility of a relationship with us that is not based on violence."[55] To many Israelis and others, therefore, Israel's unwillingness to make further meaningful concessions "remains the very core of the Middle East stalemate."[56]

Israel's claim that direct negotiations with each Arab state separately was the only acceptable path to peace was apparently prompted primarily by her desire to bypass UN resolutions, to prevent big power pressures on her to make concessions, and to extract the maximum bargaining value from her superior military power—in short, to compel the Arabs to accept a peace settlement largely on Israeli terms. Moreover, she has also insisted that she would negotiate only from a position of great strength. But there are serious drawbacks to these contentions. While under present circumstances Israel's superior power would give her substantial advantages in any direct negotiations, the weaker Arabs and Palestinians would be placed in a disadvantageous position. The problem is that every state wants to negotiate only from a position of strength and no one from a position of weakness. In fact, if today the Arabs were in a position of strength vis-à-vis Israel, the Arabs would be more than happy to negotiate directly, while Israel would be the party to object to it. If both sides insist on negotiating only from a position of superior strength, then there will never be any negotiations because there will always be the weaker party which would object. Just like the Soviets and Americans, neither the Arabs nor the Israelis will negotiate from a position of weakness. That is why the Arabs, the weaker party, logically refuse to negotiate directly until they can rectify the imbalance in their favor.

However, the Arabs are prepared to negotiate within an international conference where UN resolutions favorable to them will play a role and Arab weaknesses could be overcome by attending and negotiating as a single, unified party and by gaining from the presence of the major powers who could help counterbalance the existing power advantage in Israel's favor. Thus, any peace treaty which came out of such a conference would more likely be more balanced and provide a fairer peace settlement for the Arabs than a peace treaty imposed by a militarily superior Israel on each Arab neighbor separately.

There are major, inherent drawbacks to Israeli-imposed peace settlements. Because they would be harsh and one-sided, the Arab states would feel unable to accept them, so direct negotiations could fail to reach any agreement. In the event an imposed settlement was formally accepted for some reason or another, the chances are that the harsh, one-sided treaty would not endure and would, instead, sow the seeds for future war. History reveals many examples of harsh peace treaties which did not last and which ended up creating conditions which led to another war. The Versailles Treaty is a classic example since this imposed treaty helped to bring Hitler to power and to precipitate World War II. On the other hand, magnanimous peace treaties which considered the interests and feelings of the defeated enemy, such as those the Western allies made with Germany, Japan and Italy after World War II, ended up producing real, durable peace, and even friendship and alliances between former bitter enemies. The United States voluntarily gave up strategic Okinawa to prevent the rise of Japanese irredentism.

On the other hand, all Israeli governments have from the beginning insisted on negotiating directly and from a position of great strength not in order to provide magnanimous peace terms but in order to obtain peace treaties with the Arabs which would leave Israel with as much Arab territory as possible, provide demilitarized zones and other restrictions on the national sovereignty of her neighbors, and perpetuate Israeli dominance in the area. Such treaties inevitably would produce dangerous irredentist sentiment, would leave the Palestinian issue unresolved, would leave all of Jerusalem under Israeli rule despite not only Arab but also strong Muslim opposition and resentment, and would leave all Arabs bitter and humiliated. In short, such treaties would be neither fair nor lasting and the Arab-Israeli problem would remain as alive and destabilizing as ever. Even Israel would end up with a large hostile Arab minority, which could become a majority someday through rapid Arab population growth, and with a country which would no longer be truly Jewish or democratic. Surely, as Israeli doves have stressed, Israel would not find lasting peace and security through this path. So why insist on direct negotiations and on imposing tough peace terms when the result would be more harmful than helpful to Israel's real long-term best interests?

Only a just and fair peace which would return virtually all occupied territories and provide for the national rights of the Palestinians would leave no resentful, humiliated, and wholly dissatisfied Arabs and Palestinians and could, instead, promote true reconciliation and a real peace between the peoples who will be living in the same area. Only such a peace would be to the long-term best interests of Israel, as well as of the Arabs and Palestinians and the world as a whole.

In short, whether there will ever be real, lasting peace and security for Israel, as well as for everyone else in the Middle East, will depend not so much on the procedure used (whether by direct negotiations or by an international conference) as on the final terms of the peace treaty itself—on how fair or how harsh these are. Moreover, Israelis must realize that there is no need for everlasting enmity and hostility between peoples. The Germans and French fought three major, costly wars in less than a century before becoming warm friends and allies. Despite the recent holocaust, Israel and West Germany have developed normal and friendly relations. Not long ago, Israelis considered the Egyptians to be their most dangerous and implacable enemy, yet they have negotiated a peace settlement. Therefore, with good will and sound and farsighted policies and attitudes even the bitterest of foes can ultimately become good and trusted friends. Israeli doves are aware of these facts and have been trying to change their government's hardline and short-sighted policies and views, but, so far, with too few favorable results.

Despite Ben-Gurion's warning that "peace is more important than real estate," many Israelis continue to misunderstand the relationship between territory and security. According to *Davar,* in early 1984, Shimon Peres, while still supporting security borders, nevertheless warned that "annexation of occupied territory" would inevitably generate war. "What does distance matter," he asked, "if an intercontinental missile can traverse the distance between Washington and Moscow in thirty minutes, and between countries in this region in two minutes? And what is the use of quantities of arms in the era of atomic, hydrogen—and now the neutron—bomb."[57] In an interview Abba Eban said:

> We should say to them [the Arabs] that if we have peace, then Israel does not have any territorial aspirations beyond . . . minor [territorial] adjustments. . . . Our security would depend on very limited territorial adjustments, plus demilitarization, pus security arrangements, plus, of course, the peace relationship itself, plus the balance of strength which would dissuade aggression, plus as much international support as possible for such an agreement. We should forget the idea of security based on the territorial component.[58]

According to Rabbi Arthur Hertzberg (*Jerusalem Post,* December 9, 1983), "All five chiefs-of-staff before Raful [Rafael Eitan] are agreed that if the occupied territories were forcibly assimilated into the Jewish state, they would become a military liability." General Weizman held that the most important component of Israeli security is not more territory, but "the feasibility of peaceful relations with the Palestinians and with the rest of the region. Our future depends upon it."[59] Secretary of State Shultz warned that living with a lot of occupied territory provided the "prospect of living with perpetual hostility, and the long term threat from advanced weapons technology in many hands'' and with ''the moral burden of the occupation'' which ''could undermine the values on which Israel was founded and can divide society.'' While ''military might and control of territory [have] prevented defeat on the battlefield, true security and peace . . . can come only when Israel has gained the acceptance of its neighbors.''[60]

Abba Eban also stressed that ''not a single country in the world community, including those in favor of Israel, [have been] prepared to support the idea that Israel's security required the imposition of permanent Israeli jurisdiction over a foreign nation''—the Palestinians.[61]

Moreover, as some Israelis and others have pointed out, during the 1973 war such an allegedly ''secure'' border as the Suez Canal did not stop the Egyptian army, and even Israel's control over Sharm el-Sheikh did not prevent the blockade of her port of Elath from Bab-al-Mandeb at the entrance of the Red Sea.

Many Israelis are seriously concerned that the annexation of occupied areas with a large Palestinian population would make Israel a colonial power, undermine Israel as a Jewish and democratic state, further deepen divisions within Israeli society, and further weaken Israel's moral position within the world community. In addition, they fear that annexing over a million hostile Palestinians and Syrian Druze would threaten Israel's security from within and produce dangerous irredentism, which would ensure continued strife, instability, terrorism, and even war—not the lasting peace and security Israel is seeking.

The Golan dispute is one of the most difficult and misunderstood of all territorial issues between the Arabs and Israelis. As indicated on pages 191–96 and 223–24, while Syria had some responsibility for incidents in the Golan-Huleh area prior to the 1967 war, according to virtually all neutral Western observers and even some Israelis, Israel had much greater responsibility. According to Swedish General Carl von Horn, former UNTSO Chief of Staff, Israeli encroachments on Arab lands in the Syrian-Israeli demilitarized zone were ''part of a premeditated Israeli policy to edge east toward the old Palestine border with [Syria] and to get all of the Arabs out of the way by fair means or foul. . . . It is unlikely that these [Syrian guns on the Heights] would ever [have] come into action had it not been for Israeli provocation.''[62] According to *New Outlook* (May 1972), even Israeli Reserve General Mattityahu Peled conceded that ''over 50% of the border incidents . . . were a result of [Israel's] security policy of maximum settlement in the demilitarized areas.''

Although Israel had contended that she needed the Golan Heights to protect her Huleh settlements, shortly after capturing this area she began to establish settlements there, including some close to the new cease-fire lines.

Therefore, according to Aharon Geva, quoted in *Israel Digest,* May 24, 1974: "The Golan was needed as a buffer . . . [but] once communities were established there, it no longer acted as a buffer. The Golan itself then required a buffer." Security on that basis would require a never-ending expansion of territory. Moreover, as General Peled stressed, "The security of Israel is not based on the quality of the border, but on the quality of the army," and not on the height of any particular piece of territory, but on establishing stable relations with her neighbors. The Golan Heights did not save Syria during the 1967 war from superior Israeli forces, and neither it nor any other Arab land will save Israel once the Arab world, with its vastly superior military manpower and resources, sooner or later, attains superior power.[63] With advanced weapons of warfare, Syrian long-range artillery and land-to-land missiles can easily reach the Huleh area from beyond the Golan.

It must also be stressed that whereas Resolution 242 affirmed the "right of every state in the area"—and not only of Israel—"to live . . . within secure borders," whatever added security Israel might achieve by holding on to the Golan Heights would be achieved only at the price of greater insecurity for Syria, whose capital would be within easy striking distance of the Israeli army. There would naturally be risks for Israel to give up the Golan and other occupied lands, but the risks could be minimized by providing for an Israeli withdrawal in reasonable stages, demilitarized and buffer zones manned by UN peacekeeping forces for a period of time, and international guarantees. Israel too often ignores the risks the Arabs will have to take, as well as the greater risks which she would ultimately face if she refused to give up these occupied areas. Such a refusal would lead to never-ending strife, to ever more costly arms races and ever more destructive weapons of warfare and, inevitably, to more wars, thus creating, in time, increasing dangers not only to her security, but, some day, even possibly to her survival. A number of leading Israelis (including Yitzhak Rabin, Ezer Weizman, and Simha Flapan) and others (such as Secretary of State Shultz and Edgar Bronfman, president of the World Jewish Congress) have stressed that the "risks of peace are preferable to the grim certainties that await every nation in war";[64] "the risks contained in a peaceful compromise" would be "infinitely smaller than the risks of war without end";[65] and the risks would be far "greater" if the *status quo* were allowed to continue.[66]

The very concept of attaining perfect and everlasting security, whether through the expansion of borders or through some other traditional means, has been one of mankind's greatest and most persistent delusions. Throughout history, the unstable and unreliable balance of power system has never, on its own, provided permanent security for even the mightiest of empires. Therefore, in the final analysis, Israel's future security will depend not on mere power or territorial size, but on achieving a just and lasting peace and reconciliation with her neighbors.

The Israelis and all Jews naturally have strong feelings about Jerusalem. Israel has not only annexed East Jerusalem despite the opposition of the UN and the United States, but has extended its original boundaries to encompass neighboring Arab villages and areas, moved large numbers of Jews into the Old City while replacing some Arabs, and built many housing complexes and settlements around it. At the same time, as indicated earlier, Arabs and Jews live virtually separate lives in two segregated systems in the Holy City with little integration having yet taken place between them. Therefore, in so far as the peoples living there are concerned, the city is far from being truly united, and discrimination, friction, and hostility persist between the two communities.

At the same time, not only the Arabs but Muslims everywhere also have strong feelings about the Holy City and these feelings have intensified with the rise of Islamic fundamentalism. Therefore, Arabs and even non-Arab Muslims have refused to accept the permanent loss of East Jerusalem containing revered Muslim shrines. In addition, if the Palestinians were ever able to set up their own state in the areas evacuated by Israel, East Jerusalem, or at least the Arab and Muslim parts of it, would be the logical capital.

Actually, Israeli retention of all of Jerusalem is not essential to freedom of movement to and from the Holy Places for all religious groups, as has been contended. It was the lack of a peace settlement before the 1967 war, not the political division of the city *per se,* which caused an interference in this freedom of movement. Many urban centers are split by international borders, such as those on the American-Canadian and American-Mexican borders, and yet freedom of movement exists. It must be stressed that according to the world community and even to the United States, East Jerusalem is considered an occupied area under Resolution 242. The most practical and reasonable compromise solution within the context of peace, and one which would be most consistent with the views of the world community, would be to extend Israel's control to the Wailing Wall and the Jewish sector of the Old City and to establish functional internationalization with international guarantees for the Holy Places and for freedom of access to them. No religious group and no state would really benefit in the long run if, because of the failure of the contending parties to make sufficient concessions, the City of Peace becomes a critical obstacle to peace itself in the Middle East.

No aspect of the Arab-Israeli conflict has divided the Israelis as deeply as the Palestinian issue. Many Israelis agree with virtually the rest of the world that the Palestinian problem is the crux to the Arab-Israeli conflict and there can be no lasting solution to this conflict and, therefore, no lasting peace and security for Israel until the national rights of the Palestinian people have been fairly provided for. Many Israelis, including three former chiefs-of-staff (Yitzhak Rabin, Chaim Bar-Lev, and Mordechai Gur) have publicly declared that there was no "military solution to the Palestinian problem."[67] Increasing numbers of Israelis have concluded that in the long run Israel had virtually nothing to lose and much to gain by involving the PLO in the negotiating process. If moderate PLO leaders, in return for their own state, signed a peace treaty which committed them to accept Israel and to cease all hostile activities against her, then the two peoples could finally open the way to lasting peace and reconciliation. If these leaders refused to accept such a treaty, then Israel could also refuse to accept it and to withdraw from the West Bank and Gaza areas and, at the same time, she could claim that it was the PLO, not Israel, who represented the real obstacle to peace. Israel would not have given up any territory and at the same time would have gained substantially both politically and in the area of public relations.

Sharon and Begin had invaded Lebanon in 1982 partly in the belief that they could destroy the PLO and, thereby, eliminate the need to deal any further with the Palestinian issue. But the invasion did not destroy the PLO. Even if the PLO had been destroyed, Palestinian nationalism and aspirations for an independent state would have remained alive because you cannot kill a nationalist movement or solve a basically political problem by force. As Nadav Safran stressed:

> It seems to me that something like the PLO has become necessary. If it did not exist it would have to be invented; the Palestinians need it . . . [because] it fulfilled a necessary function, and the Palestinians will continue to provide support for any organization that fills that function, whether it is the present PLO or its equivalent. Here there is a partial analogy with the Jewish Agency in Israel's pre-independence period [for there was a need for some Jewish/Zionist organization to act on behalf of the Zionist movement]. This seems to me the case with the Palestinians and with the Palestinian issue. The issue has become so entrenched in the political configuration of the area, as well as in the political consciousness and existence of the Palestinians, that the PLO—or something like it—will continue to exist. The politicization of the Palestinian issue . . . has reached the point where it is irreversible. That politicization requires a political organization.
>
> -. . . It is easier—if avoiding the issue is what you want—to have a rejectionist opponent than a moderate opponent . . . [but] if anyone thinks that [the Israelis] have knocked out the Palestinian national de-

mands, he is kidding himself. . . . But there is no escaping coming
to terms with the issue [the PLO or some other equivalent] organization represents.

. . . You cannot play tricks on reality and history. You have to come
to terms with reality, with history. Your chances of safeguarding your
fundamental interests are much better if you try to come to terms than
if you try to play tricks.[68]

It would, furthermore, be to Israel's advantage to have the PLO participate in the peace negotiations and directly sign a peace treaty under its own
banner, and not just as part of some Jordanian delegation, because only by
doing this would the PLO and the Palestinians feel legally and morally bound
to abide by the treaty. Later, no Palestinians could claim that since they had
been bypassed and had been given no say about the terms of the final treaty,
they had no obligation to abide by it. Mark Heller, a leading Israeli specialist on the Palestinians and military and security matters who was writing under the auspices of the Center for Strategic Studies at Tel Aviv University,
concluded after an exceptionally thorough and able discussion and analysis
from an Israeli perspective of Israel's policy options vis-à-vis the PLO:

Thus the main drawback of a settlement bypassing the PLO is that it
would relieve the PLO mainstream of the necessity to purge itself of
its absolutist ideology, its maximalist goals . . . and its extremist factions, and to confer its imprimatur on a settlement that inevitably requires wide-ranging Palestinian concessions. Within the foreseeable
future, this drawback would appear to outweigh by far the potential
benefit to Israel of attempting to exclude the PLO. In terms of its probable durability and political-strategic value to Israel, a Palestinian settlement without the PLO is therefore less desirable than one that directly implicates the PLO and diminishes its interest in, or capacity
for, revisionism.[69]

In order to alleviate Israel's concerns about her security in the event a
Palestinian state were to be established in the West Bank and Gaza Strip,
many proposals have been made, such as a phased Israeli withdrawal from
these areas; demilitarized zones; UN peacekeeping forces (within recent months
Israel has adopted a more favorable view about the UN peacekeeping role,
particularly in relation to UNIFIL in south Lebanon); UN administration for
a short transitional period; monitoring stations; and big power guarantees.
Mark Heller presents an excellent, detailed study and analysis of various types
of security arrangements which could be provided.[70] Arafat and other moderate Palestinian leaders have expressed a willingness to accept security arrangements. In fact, they have contended that a weak and divided Palestin-

ian state would be far more in need of security measures and guarantees than a much more powerful Israel. Moreover, since it is obvious that whenever a Palestinian state began to pose any kind of threat to Israel, Israeli military forces could and would quickly and easily regain control over the West Bank and Gaza areas. A Palestinian government would have every incentive to do everything in its power to prevent its territory from being used as a base to mount attacks on Israel, for such attacks could lead to the extinction of its state. History, including the history of the Zionist movement, has clearly shown that once a national movement has gained its state, it no longer needs to use terrorism and other acts of force and it finds it wise and beneficial to concentrate on building its own internal political, economic, social, and even security institutions and to behave correctly in its relations with other states, even with former enemies. (This has been the experience of virtually all nationalist movements in Africa and Asia after attaining independence from the colonial powers.) Neighboring Arab states, such as Egypt, Saudi Arabia, Jordan, and even Syria, would apply their own financial and/or political pressures to ensure moderate and peaceful behavior on the part of a Palestinian state because otherwise their own internal and external security interests could be threatened.

When unable to achieve their goals by peaceful means, nationalist movements—including the Zionist, Palestinian, and other movements—feel compelled to resort to armed struggle and terrorism. According to Dan Margolit in *Haaretz* (October 28, 1983), Yitzhak Shamir contended in a 1977 interview with *The Times* (London) that there were cases when terrorism was justified, such as when he and his comrades in the Stern Gang resorted to terrorism against the British in order to force their demands onto the international agenda. Margolit goes on to point out that the Palestinians had resorted to terrorism for the very same reason—to make the world aware that there was a Palestinian political question that had to be dealt with.[71] In July 1984, Shamir indicated that "the fight of our underground in the 30's and 40's was for the creation of a Jewish state" and implied that there was no longer need to fight once the Jewish state was established.[72] In fact, once Israel came into existence the two leading terrorist organizations led by Shamir and Begin were disbanded and turned into normal political movements within Israel. Moderate Palestinian leaders, as well as many Israelis and others, have contended that once the Palestinians have their own state they too would cease armed struggle and terrorism and turn to normal political activities.[73] Yitzhak Rabin has stated that Israel's long experience with terrorism has "proved that terrorism cannot be overcome by purely military means. Only through political solutions can we be sure of putting an end to terrorism once and for all."[74] Israeli writer, Simha Flapan, perceptively pointed out that "in the long run, the eradication of terrorism is possible only by eliminating the conditions that breed it. Palestinian terrorism is a result of statelessness and a refugee existence. Only a political solution that offers the prospect of statehood . . . might put an end to terrorism."[75] In short, the solution to Palestinian terrorism—as it was for Jewish terrorism—is not force, but providing for national rights of self-determination.

After a detailed analysis from Israel's perspective, Mark Heller concluded that "it is most unlikely that a Palestinian state would constitute, in the foreseeable future, a serious independent military threat to Israel." In fact, he effectively demonstrates that Israel would face greater risks to her security by continuing the *status quo* than by agreeing to a comprehensive peace settlement which provided for a weak, divided Palestinian state subject to all kinds of formidable constraints on her ability to pose a realistic threat to Israel.[76] In a final conclusion in which he again carefully and fully weighs the advantages and disadvantages to Israel of the establishment of a Palestinian state, Heller wrote:

> The pursuit of a settlement with the PLO leading to an independent Palestinian state, with appropriate risk-minimizing provisions, would best promote Israel's fundamental strategic objectives of neutralizing the Palestinian issue as a factor in Israeli-Arab relations and reducing the overall Arab threat to Israeli security, while preserving the Jewish, democratic character and vitality of Israeli society. Such a settlement would not be a panacea for all of Israel's problems; it would not provide absolute security or guarantee perpetual peace. But given Israel's historical and geographical circumstances, no conceivable posture is without considerable risks and costs. This one, however, is almost surely the "least of all evils." Rather than avoiding a comprehensive peace settlement with the Palestinians, Israel should therefore pursue the Palestine-state settlement as the primary goal of foreign and security policy. . . . Therefore, a settlement on this basis would probably leave Israel in a better overall position than would a continuing stalemate or any other potential outcome. Furthermore, this goal should be sought on an urgent basis.[77]

Heller and others refute the contention that the Soviet Union would end up controlling a Palestinian state and, thereby, pose a threat to Israel. The Palestinians are first and foremost nationalists who have been making many sacrifices for years to attain their own sovereign state. They—like all nationalist movements in Africa and Asia, including the Zionist movement—do not fight and struggle for their own independent state and then allow its freedom and sovereignty to be undermined by becoming a satellite of some other power. The moderate PLO leaders, who are the ones most likely to accept a compromise peace settlement with Israel, are not Marxist and are much more oriented to Western, than to Soviet, ideologies and cultures. More-over, no Arab neighbor and surely not Israel would condone any develop-ment which could lead to Soviet military and political domination of a Pal-estinian state. A new Palestinian state would badly need financial and economic help from the conservative, oil-rich Arab states who are strongly anti-Com-munist. Even the peace treaty could forbid foreign bases and alliances in-volving outside powers. The PLO sought Soviet military and political help for the same reasons as did many other nationalist movements, including the Zionist movement and the newly independent State of Israel between 1947 and the early 1950s, and for the same reason the United States was allied to the USSR during World War II—out of sheer necessity and not out of ide-ological, political, or other motives.[78] In an editorial (September 8, 1982) the *New York Times* denies there would be a Soviet threat. "That Washing-ton or Amman would let the area become a 'Soviet Base' is disingenuous propaganda. That Israel could thwart such a threat at any time has been made brutally clear, in Lebanon."

The 1982 Lebanese war made more Israelis aware of the limits of power and Israel's inability to solve political problems by military means.[79] The war also strengthened the peace movement in Israel, as indicated by the hundreds of thousands of Israelis who turned out in support of some peace demonstrations and by the fact that some 20 to 30 members of the Knesset have publicly adopted dovish positions on some critical issues. Neverthe-less, the hardliners remain the dominant majority in the country, Knesset, and government and the leaders of Likud and Labor have not basically al-tered their adamant positions. The coalition government itself prevents any flexibility, and it has been clear that Prime Minister Peres, while claiming he was prepared to meet with Hussein, was not truly ready to offer the major territorial and other concessions which alone could provide the basis for any acceptable and meaningful negotiations. Moreover, Peres did not really want to be faced by any United States peace initiative because, among other rea-sons, this would threaten the survival of his fragile coalition government.[80]

The position of the Arab and Palestinian moderates has been weakening and it has become increasingly more difficult for them to convince others—and even themselves—that the diplomatic-political road to a fair, overall peace settlement still remains open. In fact, on the basis of official Israeli policies, actions and even statements, to these moderates the road appears to be firmly closed—at least for the foreseeable future. The stalemated situation can only increase the likelihood of more strife, instability, militancy, and conflict. Even the peace treaty with Egypt could be endangered. Moderate Arabs and Pal-estinians have come a long way toward accepting Israel and being prepared to make a fair and lasting peace settlement with her. Israel's continued fail-ure to exploit this relatively favorable opportunity could cause her to lose the only chance she has of ultimately achieving durable peace and reconciliation with all of her neighbors, which, in turn, will be the only way she could ever attain lasting security.

THE UNITED STATES

After the 1967 war the United States viewed her policies toward the Arab-Israeli conflict as part of a global strategy in which the superpower rivalry was the dominant element. Increasing numbers of American officials and congressmen began to contend that Israel had become a major strategic asset in containing Soviet expansion in the Middle East. Americans also accepted without question Israel's contentions that if Israel was able to acquire overwhelming military power (1) peace and stability could be maintained indefinitely in the Middle East without the need for any active United States involvement; and (2) Israel would then be able to enter future peace talks with the Arabs from a position of great strength, thereby enabling her to win the most favorable peace terms. In addition, American officials believed that the stronger Israel was the more secure she would feel and, therefore, the more likely she would be to make concessions for peace.

These beliefs and contentions led the United States to support the *status quo* in the Middle East—a situation which favored Israel—to give low priority to the Arab-Israeli conflict in the expectation that it would remain quiescent for years to come, and to sit back and wait for the Arabs to make the first moves toward peace negotiations. The United States also committed herself to back Israeli policies and interests, to provide all the economic and military aid Israel needed to maintain her military dominance, and not to use economic and military aid as pressures to elicit concessions. At the same time, little effort was seriously made to question the validity of these beliefs and contentions and to evaluate if they would actually be consistent with American long-term best interests in the area.

In fact, peace and stability did not last long and the Arabs in desperation initiated war in 1973. Moreover, as indicated earlier, the stronger Israel became with American help, (1) the fewer the concessions she was willing to make for peace and the easier it was for her to resist our exhortations for flexibility, to reject our advice, and to disregard our interests in carrying out some of her policies; (2) the more convinced the Arabs were that the United States was primarily concerned about Israel's security and the attainment of peace on her terms; and (3) the more dependent key Arab states became on Soviet military and economic assistance, thereby, in some critical ways, making Israel more of a liability than an asset in preventing the spread of Soviet influence in the Middle East and in strengthening America's position in the Arab world. As President Ford stated in his memoirs, although the United States helped Israel become "stronger militarily than all [her] Arab neighbors combined" in the expectation that she would feel confident enough to be "more flexible and more willing to discuss a lasting peace," her position actually became more intransigent and "peace was no closer than it had ever been."[81]

The 1973 war proved how wrong many American assumptions had been. Despite Israeli military superiority, the Arabs went to war and challenged the *status quo*. Moreover, since the war had led to a dangerous threat of a superpower confrontation and to the use of an oil embargo, American officials finally realized that the Arab-Israeli conflict could no longer be left on the back burner and they now had to play a more active role in trying to resolve the volatile Arab-Israeli problem.

But the United States did not develop any meaningful strategy for resolving the overall Arab-Israeli conflict. Under Henry Kissinger's leadership, the United States initiated a step-by-step diplomacy aimed at dealing with the problem piecemeal, partly in the hope that this procedure would enable the United States to bypass the Soviet Union and establish herself as the key diplomatic broker and partly because Kissinger wished to put off indefinitely having to deal with the Palestinian issue; to reduce pressures on Israel and the United States; and to buy time in order to enable Israel to improve her bargaining position and to convince the Arabs they had no choice but to negotiate peace with Israel largely on Israel's terms. But this step-by-step approach had no sense of a long-term purpose or goal and Kissinger was more concerned with the potential of the immediate situation than with the "contingencies of the future."[82]

After the 1974 Egyptian-Israeli and Syrian-Israeli disengagement agreements had helped to stabilize the situation in the area, some American officials and Middle East experts, including the author, opposed the continuation of the piecemeal approach, but Kissinger insisted on continuing to follow it. Kissinger was warned that making progress on one issue could end up making it even more difficult than ever before to deal later with other much more important issues. Thus, short-term gains could be made only at the expense of broader and more vital long-term goals.

In September 1975, Kissinger helped negotiate a second Egyptian-Israeli agreement (Sinai II) which, while providing some gains for Egypt and Israel, had harmful consequences because it split the Arab world; antagonized Syria, Jordan, the Palestinians, and other Arabs because they considered it to be a separate deal made at their expense; and required the United States to provide Israel with such vast and long-term economic, military, and political commitments that America's leverage over her to obtain future concessions on far more vital territorial and political issues was seriously undermined and Israel was left with much less incentive than before to soften her stand.[83] Therefore, the second Egyptian-Israeli accord actually ended up doing more to impair than to improve the climate and chances for a durable, overall Arab-Israeli peace settlement.

In 1977 Carter went further than any previous president in making a serious study and analysis of the Arab-Israeli problem on its own merits and how best to deal with it to promote American interests. He developed a balanced policy and program aimed at providing a lasting settlement of all major aspects of that problem and he committed himself to give top priority to resolving it. Carter made considerable headway in educating Americans about the importance of a fair and lasting Arab-Israeli peace to United States vital interests and about those basic principles which were deemed necessary for lasting peace in the Middle East. He also made progress in obtaining greater flexibility from key Arab leaders

In the final analysis, however, he, like his predecessors, lacked the political courage to stand up to Israel's defiant attitude and to the pro-Israeli lobby and its supporters in Congress and elsewhere. When he continued to supply Israel with vast military and economic aid with virtually no questions asked or conditions set and when he repeatedly assured Israel that he would not use American economic and military aid as a means to pressure her to make concessions, he left himself with no real leverage to be used to obtain a more flexible Israeli position. On a few occasions he spoke of a possible showdown with Israel, but he never did go through with it, even while complaining bitterly that Israel's deliberately provocative statements and actions were the "main obstacles to peace" and that "we are financing their conquest and they simply defy us in an intransigent fashion and generally make a mockery of our advice and preferences."[84] Some administration officials and even some members of Congress urged a tougher line with Begin, especially on the settlements issue, but Carter did not act. The Israelis clearly continued to believe that Carter would accommodate if pressed by their domestic supporters. Dr. Zbigniew Brzezinski, Carter's National Security Council adviser, had warned Carter "on more than one occasion that there would be no breakthrough to peace without U.S. persuasion of Israel. Israeli internal politics were so stalemated that no Israeli politician could take the responsibility for advocating a genuine compromise unless he could also make the added argument that otherwise U.S.-Israeli relations would suffer."[85] Brzezinski later concluded:

> Perhaps the comprehensive approach never had a chance. However, it is also true that the United States did not apply pressure during the critical summer months to sustain the momentum. . . . The Israelis . . . became more confident that they could resist American pressure,

and their experience with the White House encouraged them in that feeling. In that respect, the first Carter-Begin meeting was probably decisive in conveying the conclusions that the Administration would not force a showdown, and thus Begin could adopt [obstructive tactics to thwart Carter's plans for going to Geneva].[86]

Carter's backing down after the October 1, 1977, United States–Soviet communiqué was also decisive because it further strengthened Israeli conviction that she could always get her way and caused the moderate Arabs and Palestinians, whose hopes of achieving some positive gains as a result of a Geneva conference had been raised by Carter's efforts, to begin to doubt whether they could depend on the United States to play a fair and effective role in the peace process.[87]

The Sadat initiative brought to an end Carter's attempts to work for a comprehensive peace settlement through a reconvened Geneva conference and also revived the piecemeal approach in dealing with the Arab-Israeli conflict. While the Sadat initiative helped produce the Camp David accords, Israel, on the one hand, and Egypt and the United States, on the other hand, held radically different interpretations on the meanings of many major provisions of these accords. Since Carter did not seriously challenge Begin's interpretations, Begin was merely encouraged to continue to disregard American advice and views, as well as important United States interests in the area.[88]

Despite the desires of both Carter and Sadat, the Egyptian-Israeli peace treaty ended up as a separate peace which dealt with only one major aspect of the overall Arab-Israeli problem, which provided no effective ties to progress on other important Arab-Israeli differences, and which, by splitting the Arabs and greatly strengthening Israel's bargaining position, made it more difficult than ever to promote progress on all of the other unresolved Arab-Israeli issues. So, as proven by developments since then, the Camp David accords and the Egyptian-Israeli treaty ended up doing more to obstruct than to promote later efforts to bring about a truly comprehensive and lasting peace settlement.

Believing that the Soviet Union and Communism represented the main threats to American security interests in the Middle East and elsewhere, the Reagan Administration generally ignored the Arab-Israeli problem and naively sought to promote a strategic consensus based on Israel and several key Arab states. Reagan and Secretary of State Haig strongly believed that Israel was the most important strategic asset the United States had against the USSR in the Middle East. They, therefore, continued to back her politically at the UN, to supply her with large amounts of military and economic aid, and to promise not to pressure her to make concessions—thereby virtually ensuring that no concessions would be made.

The Lebanese war caused the administration to realize the urgent need to resolve the Arab-Israeli problem, and, as a result, this problem, for the first time, was given high priority. On September 1, 1977, President Reagan came out with his own plan in the hope that it could restart the peace process. But because Israel rejected it outright and Hussein and Arafat could not agree on a joint formula for getting involved, the Reagan plan never got off the ground and was not seriously pushed.

United States-Israeli relations deteriorated badly following Israel's massive assaults on West Beirut. Although some members of Congress and most of the media began to criticize Israel for the heavy civilian casualties she was causing, Congress not only rejected the suggestions of those few congressmen who urged a cutback of economic aid for the next fiscal year by at least the amount Israel had been spending annually on her harmful settlements program, but, with administration acquiescence, actually substantially increased the amount of aid compared to that given in prior years. Such action did not encourage greater Israeli flexibility or more moderate policies and actions. Moreover, neither the administration nor Congress seriously sought to press Israel to soften her rejection of the Reagan plan. This rejection made it much more difficult to win Arab and Palestinian support for the plan.

The failure of the Israeli-Lebanese withdrawal treaty to come into force, the embarrassing withdrawal of American Marines from Lebanon, and the signing of an American-Israeli strategic agreement further weakened American credibility and position in the Arab world and convinced the Arabs that the United States had become so allied to Israel that she could no longer be depended upon to play the role of honest broker in any peace process. Even moderate Arabs began to call for an international peace conference with the Soviet Union and the major Western powers participating in it. The United States, as well as Israel, however, strongly opposed such a conference and insisted that the only path to peace was through direct negotiations between the parties directly concerned.

Ironically, even while the United States was insisting that the Arabs negotiate directly with Israel, despite their weak bargaining position, Lawrence S. Eagleburger, Undersecretary of State for Political Affairs, told the Governing Board of the World Jewish Congress on February 1, 1983:

> History offers few clear lessons for those who manage our nation's affairs, but one of them surely is that an imbalance of power between two rivals leads to trouble. Where such an imbalance exists for long,

the stronger party talks, while the weaker listens. Soon the stronger makes demands, and the weaker submits.[89]

On August 20, 1984, Secretary of State Shultz stated in an address:

> As your Secretary of State, I can tell you from experience that no diplomacy can succeed . . . from a position of weakness. We know, as surely as we know anything, that negotiations and diplomacy not backed by strength are ineffectual at best, dangerous at worst.[90]

While Eagleburger and Shultz were specifically thinking in terms of negotiating with the Soviet Union, they were nevertheless providing "clear lessons" for negotiations between any and all states.

Using the same reasoning employed by Eagleburger and Shultz, then, the clear lesson for the Arabs is that they should never negotiate from a position of weakness because "soon the stronger demands, and the weaker submits" and this could prove "dangerous" to their interests. Therefore, according to American official reasoning, direct negotiations between parties where a big disparity of power exists between them, as in the case of the Arabs and Israelis, and where the stronger party's main goal in the negotiations is to demand treaty terms most favorable to her, should be the worst way to try to resolve the Arab-Israeli problem. Besides, direct negotiations also have the very serious drawbacks of the piecemeal approach discussed earlier. For example, if Jordan and the Palestinians were to negotiate directly over the West Bank and Gaza Strip, then where would this leave Syria and her chances of ever getting back the Golan Heights? In such a situation, Syria would feel compelled to do everything possible to prevent the Jordanians and Palestinians from negotiating with Israel.

So, unless Israel is prepared to provide the most magnanimous peace terms possible, as the United States did in negotiating peace with her former enemies in World War II—and there is absolutely no indication that the leaders of the major Israeli parties are prepared to do this—then a comprehensive peace settlement brought about by some kind of international conference or joint efforts of the big powers would be the only possible procedure that could elicit those major territorial and/or political concessions from Israel and the Arabs which would take into adequate consideration the basic, legitimate needs and interests of all the parties and which alone could produce lasting reconciliation, peace, and security for all states and peoples in the area. The United States criticizes an international conference as being unrealistic. It is unrealistic only because Israel and the United States object to it—and they object to it only because they are interested primarily in achieving a peace which is based largely on Israel's terms and not on the terms acceptable to the world community. But this position is shortsighted because it ignores the fact that such a peace would not really be in Israel's or our own long-term best interests for it will sow the seeds for more strife and war and will not finally and fully resolve the Arab-Israeli conflict.

For many years the United States has tried many approaches in an effort to promote peace in the Middle East. Yet, the Middle East is no closer to a fair and lasting comprehensive peace settlement than it has ever been. Moreover, even our best Arab friends have been losing hope in the credibility, sincerity, and willingness of the United States to act constructively and decisively in achieving such a settlement. In fact, more and more Arabs have been turning to Moscow not because they want to but because they feel that they have been left with no alternative. Clearly, anti-American feeling in the area has been growing and American position and influence there have weakened.

It is also obvious that the Arabs and Israelis are not capable of bringing peace on their own, whether through direct negotiations or any other format. In fact, for many years only we have had the potential ability to break the impasse. Yet, over the years we—through our massive and virtually unquestioning financial, economic, political, and military support of Israel and assurances that no pressures would be applied on her to influence her policies—have actually contributed to that impasse by encouraging Israel to maintain with impunity her inflexible position on a peace settlement; disregard our advice and pleas; and follow policies and take actions which many of our officials have openly acknowledged as being illegal, major obstacles to peace, and even seriously detrimental to our own national interests in the area. We have also allowed great ignorance about the realities of the Arab-Israel problem, domestic politics, and lack of political courage on the part of our leaders to prevent our government from adopting those policies and taking those actions which many officials and experts both inside and outside the government, as well as among our European allies, have considered and continue to consider indispensable to promoting both peace and Western long-term best interests in the Middle East.

It will be virtually impossible to break the existing deadlock and to make serious progress toward peace unless the administration under the active, well-informed, and determined leadership of the president (1) assumes the peace initiative and plays an active, direct, and balanced role; (2) decides to face squarely the most important root causes of the overall Arab-Israeli dilemma and helps the parties develop a basic framework for a final settlement which will provide a realistic basis for a fair and lasting comprehensive peace in the area; (3) makes every effort possible to promote a considerably better understanding, first among its own top officials, and then in Congress and among Americans at large of the realities of the situation, of the great perils which we, as well as both Arabs and Israelis, will continue to face as long as the Arab-Israeli conflict remains unresolved, and of the farsighted policies which the United States must follow to promote her own long-term best interests; (4) marshals broader and more effective support for these policies, especially in Congress; and (5) resolutely and persistently applies all the essential pressures on the contending parties, especially Israel—even if this produces a confrontation with the more hardline pro-Israeli groups whose self-defeating policies, over the years, have helped both to undermine serious American peace efforts and to work against the ultimate best interests of not only the United States but also Israel.[91]

Sooner or later, these difficult, unpopular, and politically hazardous pressures will have to be resolutely and consistently applied because, in many ways, they provide the key to peace in the Middle East. If the United States does not apply effective pressures, Israel's position will remain intransigent, leaving virtually no hope for peace; the positions of Arab and Palestinian moderates, as well as that of the United States in the Middle East, will be further weakened; and the area will drift into more instability, strife, and conflict.

Many American officials, former officials and diplomats, and specialists on the Middle East have warned for years that words and entreaties alone would not be enough to cause Israel to soften her position and that only resolute, consistent pressures, together with major incentives, could bring about such a change. As one American expert noted, it was ''vain'' to expect Israel to bend unless she is ''subjected to intense American pressures. The entire history of American-Israeli relations illustrate that Israeli concessions will come only under the threat of sanctions.''[92] In the last two chapters, references were made to administrative officials who urged getting tough with Israel, but without success because of presidential disinclinations. *Newsweek* (July 13, 1981) wrote: ''Since they see Begin as an obstacle to peace . . . , some State Department officials argue that the United States should wield its military and economic leverage to force Israel to make concessions.'' The *New York Times* (January 25, 1982) reported that some leaders in the White House and the Pentagon ''are already convinced that Israel must be pushed hard to make some concessions.''[93]

Even many Israelis have sought greater American pressures on their government. Believing that their government's hardline policies and actions would ultimately prove to be disastrous for Israel and knowing that they did not have enough political influence to change these, many Israeli moderates, according to *Yediot Aharonot* (August, 31, 1982) ''have been praying in their hearts that Washington would save Israel from itself'' by applying the necessary pressures to bring about a change in Israel's harsh policies and actions.[94] An editorial in *Davar* (September 20, 1982) held that ''only Reagan's threats of actions can prevail upon'' the Begin government; and an editorial in *Haaretz* (March 20, 1984) said: "In the past bold steps, backed strongly by one of the superpowers, have broken the ice. Today boldness is in short supply. Israel is not ready to make the slightest gesture of goodwill, while the United States" was not willing to take any bold steps. "This is the cause of the stalemate."[95] Yehoshofat Harkabi, a former chief of army intelligence, contended that by failing to apply pressures and by allowing Israel to disregard with impunity American views and interests, the United States had "contributed to the primitivization of Israel's political thinking." He also wrote: "Certainly, Israel is not subservient to the United States and need not always concur with United States policy, but by the same token the United States is entitled to react to and to oppose Israeli policy. Moreover, the United States is not obligated to finance, and thus make possible, an Israeli policy with which it does not agree."[96]

It is wrong to claim as an absolute truth that applying pressures on Israel would not work and would be self-defeating. When presidents went all-out to apply pressures, they did work. The best example is when President Eisenhower made it crystal clear to the Israeli government that he would stop all aid if Israel did not withdraw from the Sinai and Gaza Strip following the 1956 war. Israel, heavily dependent on United States aid then, as well as now, felt it necessary to comply—and she did. Kissinger applied effective pressures to compel Israel to stop her efforts to surround and destroy the Egyptian Third Army during the 1973 war. Carter acted in a tough and determined way after Israeli forces invaded Lebanon in late September 1975 and in June 1978 when he threatened to halt all military aid and to reassess United States-Israeli relations if Israeli forces did not withdraw from Lebanon—and they did withdraw. By educating and winning over the public, President Reagan overcame the Israeli and the American pro-Israeli lobby when they sought to prevent the sale of AWACS planes to Saudi Arabia.

Of course, pressures would not work if (1) you kept reassuring Israel no pressures would be applied no matter what she did; (2) pressures were primarily verbal in nature and applied in a hesitant and inconsistent manner; and (3) Israel was left with the impression that a president would not go all-out and could be forced to retreat when Israel and her friends in the United States applied their own domestic pressures. (Israel has been opposed to United States pressures on herself, but she obviously has never hesitated applying all kinds of pressures on the American government.) But, as one former American ambassador and specialist on the Middle East wrote: "A strong president can override a domestic lobby in the pursuit of broad U.S. national interests if he is determined to do so." The president must go to the American people over the head of the lobby and "stay the course." If he can convince the people what is needed for United States vital interests, the public would rally around him. "A strong president has the capacity to do so" if he has the "will."[97] As a great power the United States has the responsibility to define and then give priority to her own best interests and to act decisively to protect and promote these interests regardless of the views of foreign governments and domestic lobbyists.[98]

Of course, pressures should be applied on any and all parties, not only Israel, if deemed necessary for American interests. The moderate Arabs and Palestinians already face many pressures, such as Israeli military superiority and control over their territories; the pressure of time as Israel continues to establish "facts on the ground" in the occupied areas; and the rise of Islamic fundamentalism and growing pressures to achieve progress on the Jerusalem and Palestinian issues. In fact, because of these and other pressures and the overall realities of the existing situation, the moderate Arabs and Palestinians have finally given up many of their prior demands and have been prepared to accept—and many even desperately want to attain—a comprehensive peace settlement based on principles accepted by virtually the entire world community. For this reason, if such a peace is to have a chance of being negotiated, from a practical point of view most American pressures would have to be applied on Israel because she alone of the parties directly involved still refuses to accept those principles even in exchange for peace.

The United States has vital, economic, political, and security interests at stake in the Middle East which will be either greatly strengthened or gravely endangered, depending on whether she succeeds or fails in bringing about a just and lasting peace between Arabs and Israelis. A failure would (1) undermine our military and political positions and enhance those of the Soviet Union in the strategic Arab world; (2) cause a further split between ourselves and our Western Allies; (3) facilitate the growth and spread of anti-Western nationalist and religious fanaticism throughout the Middle East; (4) weaken the positions of both Arab and Israeli moderates and strengthen those of the hawks on both sides; (5) cost us vast sums of money for unending economic and military aid to Israel; (6) further isolate ourselves, as well as Israel, at the UN and in the world community as a whole; (7) pose a threat to an assured supply of oil which many of our allies have need of; and (8) greatly increase our own insecurity and the chances for a military confrontation with Russia.

There are a number of major problems in the Middle East which are of great concern to the United States: the Soviet presence in Afghanistan; developments within Iran; the war between Iraq and Iran; and the rising force of extreme nationalism and religious fundamentalism which is increasingly anti-American. But none of these is as crucial to American long-term political, economic, and security interests as the Arab-Israeli conflict. That is why a just and comprehensive Arab-Israeli peace is of such crucial importance to us and why we should make every effort and be prepared to take whatever action and assume whatever political risks deemed essential to achieve such a peace.

THE SOVIET UNION

Following the 1967 war, Russia was actively involved in dealing with the Arab-Israeli problem. She helped draw up Resolution 242 and worked with the United States, Britain, and France from 1969 to 1971 in an attempt to bolster UN Special Representative Gunnar Jarring's efforts to implement that resolution. Outside of the UN, however, the United States preferred by-passing Moscow.

Because during the 1973 war the superpowers came close to a military confrontation, they cooperated to end the war and to pass Resolution 338 which called for immediate negotiations between the belligerents in order to implement Resolution 242. Both powers were co-chairmen of a conference held in Geneva in December 1973 to promote these negotiations. But Kissinger quickly had the conference adjourned and did all he could after that to confine the Soviets to the sidelines.

In 1977, the Carter Administration brought the USSR back into the negotiating picture, especially by negotiating the October 1, 1977 communique which was meant to enable the Soviet Union, as co-chairman of any reconvened Geneva conference, to become more fully and directly involved. The Carter-Dayan working paper a few days later, however, undermined the value of the communique; and Sadat's initiative, the Camp David accords, the Egyptian-Israeli treaty, and Palestinian autonomy talks all took place with the deliberate effort to exclude Soviet involvement. Because of ideological inclinations, the Reagan Administration was even more determined to keep Moscow out of any peace process.

The Soviets resented American efforts to bypass their views and security and political interests. Because of the area's importance to Soviet security[99] and because the USSR was a superpower, she contended that she had legitimate interests in the Arab-Israeli conflict which should not be ignored and that she should have co-equal status with the United States in dealing with it. Foreign Minister Andrei Gromyko insisted that the Soviet role would not be "merely that of a passive onlooker"; and another high Soviet official warned that "we will never let ourselves be excluded" from any peace negotiations.[100]

To assert her role, the Soviet Union rebuilt the military power of Syria and developed still closer relations with her; restored full diplomatic relations with Egypt; offered to sell arms to Kuwait and Jordan; and improved her relations with other Arab states. She sent a delegation to Israel to meet with an Israeli peace group and several dovish members of the Knesset, supported Arab peace efforts, and issued peace plans of her own. While she was able to obtain American agreement for talks on the Middle East situation in February, 1985, the talks did not go much beyond an exchange of views.[101] She pressed for an international peace conference which she, as well as the other major powers, could attend; but Israel and the United States opposed such a conference, partly to keep the USSR out of any peace process.

The Soviet Union could probably benefit to some extent from the continuation of limited strife and instability in the Middle East. It is doubtful, however, that she would want the Arab-Israeli dispute to lead to another war, especially because this could undermine her important economic and political relations with Western Europe and could lead to another dangerous confrontation with the United States. Ezer Weizman wrote in his memoirs: "The Soviets operate very cautiously" because they feared such a confrontation;[102] and, according to the *Christian Science Monitor* (February 11, 1984), "even some Israeli analysts, not in the habit of saying nice things about the Syrians and the Soviets, speak of Moscow as a 'moderating' influence in the Syrian-Israeli rivalry." Therefore, while she had been aggressive in Afghanistan, as far as the Arab-Israeli conflict was concerned the Soviet Union sought to moderate the policies of the more extremist Arabs and Palestinians; repeatedly stated that she supported the existence of the State of Israel within her pre-1967 borders; and expressed her willingness to help guarantee the terms of any final peace treaty.

Soviet officials have frankly admitted their conviction that in the long run "matters will move their way" because they would be able to exploit American mistakes. They believed, for example, that American policies would fail to resolve the Palestinian and other major problems, and this failure would cause even pro-American Arab states to eventually become so "tired of American initiatives" which skirt such critical problems that they would become more "receptive to having the Soviet Union play a more important role" in any peace process.[103] In fact, in 1983–1984, even moderate Arabs, having lost faith in American credibility and evenhandedness, began to press for just such a Soviet role through an international peace conference.

While nearly all Arabs have much more in common with the West than with Communist Russia, if the United States and Israel give them no other choice, more and more of them will, as in the past, turn to Moscow in desperation for help. It was largely the unresolved Arab-Israeli problem which enabled the Soviets in 1955 to spread their influence in the Arab world in the first place; and if that problem persists, that influence is bound to grow.

It is clear that while the Soviet Union cannot bring about an Arab-Israeli peace, she can do much to block it as long as she feels that her interests and feelings are being ignored. Therefore, Soviet involvement to some degree and at some stage is essential both to achieve and then to enforce any peace settlement. The USSR would be able to play a more effective role if she restored diplomatic relations with Israel. Obviously, better United States-Soviet relations would also be helpful if not also necessary. Although major differences exist between the United States and the Soviet Union, there is one common interest that can provide a substantial basis for cooperation in finally defusing the explosive situation—namely, the mutual fear that an unwanted military confrontation could lead to a global conflict.

WESTERN EUROPE

Between the 1967 and 1973 wars, Western Europe's role in dealing with the Arab-Israeli problem was a very limited one; and it, like the United States, was not very greatly concerned about the situation. The 1973 war, however, aroused deep concern among the Europeans not only about having reliable access to badly needed Arab oil, but also about the grave political and military consequences that could develop for them in the event of another major Arab-Israeli conflict which might produce another dangerous superpower confrontation. Therefore, European leaders began to take a more active interest in trying to press for a fair and lasting comprehensive Arab-Israeli peace settlement which would provide not only for mutual recognition, security, and territorial withdrawals, but also for the right of national self-determination for the Palestinians. Because moderate Arabs and Palestinians showed increased readiness to make concessions for peace whereas Israel's position, especially after Begin came to power, had actually hardened, Western European states improved their relations with the Arabs and even with the PLO, while European impatience with and criticism of Israel grew.

Serious differences had developed between the Europeans and the Americans over a number of critical Arab-Israeli issues. The Europeans strongly disagreed with the Reagan Administration's efforts to deal with the problems in the Middle East in the context of United States-Soviet rivalry. Moreover, they were convinced that there could be no peace in the Middle East until the Palestinians were provided with the right to national self-determination and the PLO was brought into any peace process. They contended that all-out, unconditional American support of Israel had worked to harden, not soften, Israel's position and that the United States should firmly apply her considerable potential leverage over Israel to ensure greater willingness to make essential concessions for peace. Whenever the EEC sought to take the initiative in trying to promote a peace settlement, the United States strongly objected and even threatened to veto any EEC-sponsored draft Security Council resolution which sought to combine the provisions of Resolution 242 with General Assembly resolutions calling for the right of the Palestinians to national sovereignty. Bowing before American opposition and threats, the EEC confined itself to expressing its support for a peace settlement based on such a combination by means of resolutions passed at its own summit meetings and by statements and votes in the UN General Assembly.

Some Europeans and many Arabs have urged the EEC to play a more active and independent role in the search for peace in the Middle East. Edward Heath, a former British prime minister, held that Western Europe collectively had "considerable influence with the parties . . . and they often had greater flexibility in using their influence than does the United States," whose government, unlike those in Western Europe, had major domestic political constraints to contend with.[104] Israel has considerable trade with EEC countries and has benefited from a free trade agreement with the EEC for industrial products. Thus, the EEC has not been without some leverage. Nevertheless, European leaders have never seriously considered applying major pressures on Israel and have merely convinced themselves that, while substantial movement toward a fair, comprehensive peace was urgently needed, they were helpless to do anything without the leadership of the United States. But since the United States is not providing the leadership they feel is essential, then they apparently are resigned to allow the situation to drift— which will mean that the Middle East is destined to suffer still more instability, strife, and conflict. There is too much at stake for Western Europe and the world to just sit back and allow the situation to drift without making much more determined efforts than have been made so far by Western Europe to constructively influence the situation.

THE UNITED NATIONS

Although the UN has been unable to resolve the Arab-Israeli conflict, it has nevertheless played and will continue to play an important and, in some ways, an indispensable role in dealing with it. After the 1967 war the UN provided, through Resolution 242 and various General Assembly resolutions on the Palestinian issue, clear guidelines for a framework of principles which the overwhelming preponderance of the international community considered essential to lasting peace in the Middle East. During the 1973 war, the UN played a significant role in bringing about and then enforcing cease-fires and in preventing a superpower confrontation. After the war, UN peacekeeping forces were essential to implementing United States–sponsored disengagement agreements, with the peacekeeping force on the Golan Heights still helping to maintain peace in that particular area. In 1978, a UN force (UN-IFIL) was formed to facilitate an Israeli withdrawal from Lebanon and to man a buffer zone between the Palestinians in Lebanon and northern Israel. Although in the past Israel had generally belittled the value of UN peace-keeping activities, including those of UNIFIL, when Israel sought in 1984 and 1985 to arrange for the withdrawal of her troops from south Lebanon, she actually urged an expansion in the size and role of UNIFIL so that it could take over responsibility for policing and preventing Palestinian infil-tration in a substantial part of south Lebanon from which Israel was with-drawing. Therefore, even without peace treaties the UN has played and con-tinues to play a vital peacekeeping role.

Over the years various UN Secretary Generals attempted to provide good offices and/or mediation between the disputing parties, but with little suc-cess. In 1983 the UN General Assembly passed resolutions calling for the convening of a UN-sponsored international conference to negotiate a com-prehensive peace settlement, which would have revived the UN's role in the peace process. But the United States and Israel opposed such a conference, partly in order to bypass the UN and its resolutions.

Virtually the entire world believes that UN resolutions still offer the best and probably the only realistic framework of principles which could provide the basis for durable reconciliation, stability, and peace in the Middle East. It is also widely believed that UN peacekeeping activities and security guar-antees will be essential to the implementation and enforcement of any final peace settlement which might ultimately be achieved.

It must be clearly understood that the UN is not a superstate with powers to act on its own. It is only an instrument established by sovereign states to promote international cooperation and to provide means for the peaceful res-olution of disputes. Therefore, its effectiveness depends upon either the vol-untary compliance of the contending parties or the willingness of the big powers to enforce its will. Nevertheless, in the final analysis, it will not be to any country's real advantage to disregard and work to weaken the UN and the rule of law because only by strengthening and, ultimately, by developing an even more effective world organization and international law can there be any serious hope that someday man will be able to replace the dangerous, unstable, and unreliable balance of power system—which provides greater security for one state *only* at the expense of greater insecurity for the other state—and to provide equal and lasting security and peace for all states in the Middle East and in the world.

CONCLUSION

Over the years the overwhelming preponderance of the countries of the world has indicated, through UN resolutions and other means, what they considered to be the requisites for a just and lasting peace in the Middle

East. For a very brief period most states believed that Resolution 242 provided the best basis for peace. Since then, however, the Palestinian issue came increasingly to the fore and this caused a growing number of countries to conclude that providing for the legitimate national aspirations of the Palestinians was also essential to a just and durable peace.

Today, as indicated by UN General Assembly resolutions and official statements by UN member states, including those from Western Europe, there is overwhelming agreement that the basic framework for peace should include (1) an end to the state of belligerency and all hostile activities; (2) mutual recognition achieved through a formal peace treaty; (3) the right of all states in the Middle East to live in peace and within secure and recognized borders; (4) an Israeli withdrawal from all or nearly all of the occupied areas, including East Jerusalem, with the possibility of limited border rectifications; (5) demilitarized zones and other provisions for the security of all states; (6) the right of the Palestinians to set up their own state in the West Bank and Gaza Strip sectors, with the voluntary option of uniting with Jordan in some way; (7) PLO involvement in the peace process and; (8) a just settlement of the refugee problem.

All of the front-line Arab states (as well as virtually all other Arab states except for Libya) have accepted this entire framework and have generally been prepared to carry out their obligations under it. Arafat and other moderate Palestinian leaders have indicated a willingness to accept this framework. Of course, as is the case in any political issue, there are dissenters. There are militants within the Arab world and among the Palestinians who reject any compromise with Israel, and they would, if they could, sabotage efforts to achieve peace with her. But these militants presently lack the numbers and influence to prevent acceptance of the above framework. However, if the existing stalemate persists, sooner or later more and more moderate Arabs and Palestinians will lose all hope of ever being given the opportunity to attain even their more limited goals by peaceful means and will then conclude that they are left with no alternative to joining the rejectionists and resorting to force, thus creating a new, serious obstacle to peace.

Leaders of the two major parties who control the Israeli government have unequivocally rejected the major territorial, Palestinian, and refugee aspects of this framework, thereby providing the most formidable obstacle to peace. Dissenters in Israel are moderates who have been trying to soften their government's position. They are a minority, however, and do not have the influence to change Israel's hardline stance. Therefore, for the foreseeable future, there is little or no prospect that Israel will on her own initiative move to accept the framework.

In fact, if she acts wisely, courageously, and in time, only the United States can resolve the situation because only she has the potential ability to press Israel to make the concessions so essential to any kind of lasting peace and to support the Israeli doves. It is their contention that a fair, comprehensive peace is, in the long run, far more to Israel's enlightened self interest than either the continuation of the present stalemate, which will lead to more instability, strife, and war, or an imposed peace which will not last and will sow the seeds for more conflict and war. Also, as many Israelis have stressed, the risks and costs involved in a fair, lasting peace settlement will be infinitely smaller than the far greater risks and costs of continued strife and war or the threat of war virtually without end. Of course, the Arabs and Palestinians—and even the Americans—must also take their share of risks and pay some costs for real peace for ultimately all parties will lose and no one will really win if the Arab-Israeli conflict is not fully, fairly, and expeditiously resolved.

But no American initiative can succeed until American leaders first acquire an accurate and complete understanding about the basic roots of the overall Arab-Israeli problem; the real obstacles to resolving it; and the policies which must be firmly and courageously adopted to remove these obstacles and to promote that kind of peace settlement which reasonably takes into consideration the legitimate needs and interests of all the parties. In this manner, all of them will have an incentive to abide by a settlement that provides a firm basis for that degree of reconciliation between the parties so vital to achieving lasting peace and friendship.

Unless the United States can provide the knowledgeable, bold, and effective leadership which is so urgently and desperately needed, the Middle East will continue to face mounting tensions and instabilities and, ultimately, another war. Because of the much more advanced weapons available to all parties, another war in the future would clearly be far more destructive than previous conflicts. Moreover, it could even draw the superpowers in a military confrontation. The question is whether the United States will be able to provide the necessary leadership—before it is too late.

Appendix

A. DOCUMENTS

1. SECOND NOTE FROM SIR HENRY McMAHON TO SHARIF HUSSEIN OF THE HEJAZ, 24 OCTOBER 1915 *(Cmd. 5957, 1939)*

It is with great pleasure that I communicate to you on . . . behalf [of the government of Great Britain] the following statement, which I am confident you will receive with satisfaction—

The two districts of Mersina and Alexandretta and portions of Syria lying to the west of the districts of Damascus, Homs, Hama and Aleppo cannot be said to be purely Arab, and should be excluded from the limits demanded.

With the above modification, and without prejudice of our existing treaties with Arab chiefs, we accept those limits.

As for those regions lying within those frontiers wherein Great Britain is free to act without detriment to the interests of her ally, France, I am empowered in the name of the Government of Great Britain to give the following assurances and make the following reply to your letter—

(1) Subject to the above modifications, Great Britain is prepared to recognize and support the independence of the Arabs in all the regions within the limits demanded by the Sharif of Mecca.

(2) Great Britain will guarantee the Holy Places against all external aggression and will recognize their inviolability.

(3) When the situation admits, Great Britain will give to the Arabs her advice and will assist them to establish what may appear to be the most suitable forms of government in those various territories.

(4) On the other hand, it is understood that the Arabs have decided to seek the advice and guidance of Great Britain only, and that such European advisers and officials as may be required for the formation of a sound form of administration will be British.

. . .

I am convinced that this declaration will assure you beyond all possible doubt of the sympathy of Great Britain towards the aspirations of her friends the Arabs and will result in a firm and lasting alliance, the immediate results of which will be the expulsion of the Turks from the Arab countries and the freeing of the Arab peoples from the Turkish yoke, which for so many years has pressed heavily upon them. . . .

2. THE BRITISH (BALFOUR) DECLARATION, 2 NOVEMBER 1917

(Official Zionist Formula submitted by Baron Lionel Walter Rothschild to the British Government on 18 July 1917)

H. M. Government, after considering the aims of the Zionist Organization, accepts the principle of recognising Palestine as the National Home of the Jewish people and the right of the Jewish people to build up its National life in

Palestine under a protection to be established at the conclusion of Peace, following upon the successful issue of the war.

H. M. Government regards as essential for the realisation of this principle the grant of internal autonomy to the Jewish nationality in Palestine, freedom of immigration for Jews, and the establishment of a Jewish National Colonising Corporation for the re-settlement and economic development of the country.

The conditions and forms of the internal autonomy and a charter for the Jewish National Colonising Corporation should, in the view of H. M. Government, be elaborated in detail and determined with the representatives of the Zionist Organisation.

The Balfour Declaration, 2 November 1917

I have much pleasure in conveying to you, on behalf of his Majesty's Government, the following declaration of sympathy with Jewish Zionist aspirations which has been submitted to and approved by the Cabinet—

His Majesty's Government view with favour the establishment in Palestine of a national home for the Jewish people, and will use their best endeavours to facilitate the achievement of this object, it being clearly understood that nothing shall be done which may prejudice the civil and religious rights of existing non-Jewish communities in Palestine, or the rights and political status enjoyed by Jews in any other country.

I should be grateful if you would bring this declaration to the knowledge of the Zionist Federation.

3. BRITISH AND ANGLO-FRENCH STATEMENTS TO THE ARABS, JANUARY–NOVEMBER, 1918

(Message from Commander D. G. Hogarth of the British Arab Bureau in Cairo to Sharif Hussein in January, 1918. Cmd. 5974, 1939)

(1) The Entente Powers are determined that the Arab race shall be given full opportunity of once again forming a nation in the world. This can only be achieved by the Arabs themselves uniting, and Great Britain and her Allies will pursue a policy with this ultimate unity in view.

(2) So far as Palestine is concerned we are determined that no people shall be subject to another . . .

(3) Since the Jewish opinion of the world is in favour of a return of Jews to Palestine and inasmuch as this opinion must remain a constant factor, and further as His Majesty's Government view with favour the realisation of this aspiration, His Majesty's Government are determined that in so far as is compatible with the freedom of the existing population both economic and political, no obstacle should be put in the way of the realisation of this ideal. . . .

British Declaration to Seven Arab Spokesmen, 16 June 1918

His Majesty's Government have considered the memorial of the seven with the greatest care. His Majesty's Government fully appreciate the reasons why the memorialists desire to retain their anonymity, and the fact that the memorial is anonymous has not in any way detracted from the importance which His Majesty's Government attribute to the document.

The areas mentioned in the memorandum fall into four categories—

1. Areas in Arabia which were free and independent before the outbreak of war;

2. Areas emancipated from Turkish control by the action of the Arabs themselves during the present war;

3. Areas formerly under Ottoman dominion, occupied by the Allied forces during the present war;

4. Areas still under Turkish control.

In regard to the first two categories, His Majesty's Government recognise the complete and sovereign independence of the Arabs inhabiting these areas and support them in their struggle for freedom.

In regard to the areas occupied by Allied forces, His Majesty's Government draw the attention of the memorialists to the texts of the proclamation issued respectively by the General Officers Commanding in Chief on the taking of Baghdad and Jerusalem. These proclamations embody the policy of His Majesty's Government towards the inhabitants of those regions. It is the wish and desire of His Majesty's Government that the future government of these regions should be based upon the principle of the consent of the governed and this policy has and will continue to have the support of His Majesty's Government. . . .

Anglo-French Declaration, 7 November 1918

The object aimed at by France and Great Britain in prosecuting in the East the War let loose by the ambition of Germany is the complete and definite emancipation of the peoples so long oppressed by the Turks and the establishment of national governments and administrations deriving their authority from the initiative and free choice of the indigenous populations.

In order to carry out these intentions France and Great Britain are at one in encouraging and assisting the establishment of indigenous Governments and administrations in Syria and Mesopotamia, now liberated by the Allies, and in the territories the liberation of which they are engaged in securing and recognising these as soon as they are actually established.

Far from wishing to impose on the populations of these regions any particular institutions they are only concerned to ensure by their support and by adequate assistance the regular working of Governments and administrations freely chosen by the populations themselves. . . .

4. THE MANDATE FOR PALESTINE, 24 JULY 1922 (Cmd. 1785, 1922)

. . .

Art. 1. The Mandatory shall have full powers of legislation and of administration, save as they may be limited by the terms of this mandate.

Art. 2. The Mandatory shall be responsible for placing the country under such political, administrative and economic conditions as will secure the establishment of the Jewish national home, as laid down in the preamble, and the development of self-governing institutions, and also for safeguarding the civil and religious rights of all the inhabitants of Palestine, irrespective of race and religion.

Art. 3. The Mandatory shall, so far as circumstances permit, encourage local autonomy.

Art. 4. An appropriate Jewish agency shall be recognised as a public body for the purpose of advising and co-operating with the Administration of Palestine in such economic, social and other matters as may affect the establishment of the Jewish national home and the interests of the Jewish population in Palestine, and, subject always to the control of the Administration, to assist and take part in the development of the country.

The Zionist organisation, so long as its organisation and constitution are in the opinion of the Mandatory appropriate, shall be recognised as such agency. It shall take steps in consultation with His Britannic Majesty's Government to secure the co-operation of all Jews who are willing to assist in the establishment of the Jewish national home. . . .

Art. 6. The Administration of Palestine, while ensuring that the rights and position of other sections of the population are not prejudiced, shall facilitate Jewish immigration under suitable conditions and shall encourage, in co-operation with the Jewish agency referred to in Article 4, close settlement by Jews on the land, including State lands and waste lands not required for public purposes.

Art. 7. The Administration of Palestine shall be responsible for enacting a nationality law. There shall be included in this law provisions framed so as to facilitate the acquisition of Palestinian citizenship by Jews who take up their permanent residence in Palestine. . . .

Art. 11. The Administration of Palestine shall take all necessary measures to safeguard the interests of the community in connection with the development of the country. . . . It shall introduce a land system appropriate to the needs of the country, having regard, among other things, to the desirability of promoting the close settlement and intensive cultivation of the land.

The Administration may arrange with the Jewish agency mentioned in Article 4 to construct or operate, upon fair and equitable terms, any public works, services and utilities, and to develop any of the natural resources of the country, in so far as these matters are not directly undertaken by the Administration. . . .

Art. 15. The Mandatory shall see that complete freedom of conscience and the free exercise of all forms of worship, subject only to the maintenance of public order and morals, are ensured to all. No discrimination of any kind shall be made between the inhabitants of Palestine on the ground of race, religion or language. No person shall be excluded from Palestine on the sole ground of his religious belief.

The right of each community to maintain its own schools for the education of its own members in its own language, while conforming to such educational requirements of a general nature as the Administration may impose, shall not be denied or impaired. . . .

Art. 22. English, Arabic and Hebrew shall be the official languages of Palestine. Any statement or inscription in Arabic on stamps or money in Palestine shall be repeated in Hebrew, and any statement or inscription in Hebrew shall be repeated in Arabic. . . .

5. THE ZIONIST (BILTMORE) PROGRAM, 11 MAY 1942

. . .

4. In our generation, and in particular in the course of the past twenty years, the Jewish people have awakened and transformed their ancient homeland; from 50,000 at the end of the last war their numbers have increased to more than 500,000. They have made the waste places to bear fruit and the desert to blossom.

Their pioneering achievements in agriculture and in industry, embodying new patterns of cooperative endeavor, have written a notable page in the history of colonization.

5. In the new values thus created, their Arab neighbors in Palestine have shared. The Jewish people in its own work of national redemption welcomes the economic, agricultural and national development of the Arab peoples and states. The Conference reaffirms the stand previously adopted at Congresses of the World Zionist Organization, expressing the readiness and the desire of the Jewish people for full cooperation with their Arab neighbors.

6. The Conference calls for the fulfilment of the original purpose of the Balfour Declaration and the Mandate which *"recognizing the historical connection of the Jewish people with Palestine"* was to afford them the opportunity, as stated by President Wilson, to found there a Jewish Commonwealth.

The Conference affirms its unalterable rejection of the White Paper of May 1939 and denies its moral or legal validity. The White Paper seeks to limit, and in fact to nullify Jewish rights to immigration and settlement in Palestine, and, as stated by Mr. Winston Churchill in the House of Commons in May 1939, constitutes "a breach and repudiation of the Balfour Declaration." The Policy of the White Paper is cruel and indefensible in its denial of sanctuary to Jews fleeing from Nazi persecution; and at a time when Palestine has become a focal point in the war front of the United Nations, and Palestine Jewry must provide all available manpower for farm and factory and camp, it is in direct conflict with the interests of the allied war effort.

7. In the struggle against the forces of aggression and tyranny, of which Jews were the earliest victims, and which now menace the Jewish National Home, recognition must be given to the right of the Jews of Palestine to play their full part in the war effort and in the defense of their country, through a Jewish military force fighting under its own flag and under the high command of the United Nations.

8. The Conference declares that the new world order that will follow victory cannot be established on foundations of peace, justice and equality, unless the problem of Jewish homelessness is finally solved.

The Conference urges that the gates of Palestine be opened; that the Jewish Agency be vested with control of immigration into Palestine and with the necessary authority for upbuilding the country, including the development of its unoccupied and uncultivated lands; and that Palestine be established as a Jewish Commonwealth integrated in the structure of the new democratic world.

Then and only then will the age-old wrong to the Jewish people be righted.

6. UN GENERAL ASSEMBLY RESOLUTION NO. 181 (II) OF 29 NOVEMBER 1947—PARTITION OF PALESTINE

A.

The General Assembly:

. . .

Recommends to the United Kingdom, as the mandatory Power for Palestine, and to all other Members of the United Nations the adoption and implementation, with regard to the future Government of Palestine, of the Plan of Partition with Economic Union set out below;

Requests that:

(a) The Security Council take the necessary measures as provided for in the plan for its implementation;

. . .

Calls upon the inhabitants of Palestine to take such steps as may be necessary on their part to put this plan into effect;

Appeals to all Governments and all peoples to refrain from taking any action which might hamper or delay the carrying out of these recommendations.

B.

PLAN OF PARTITION WITH ECONOMIC UNION

PART I—Future Constitution and Government of Palestine

A. TERMINATION OF MANDATE—Partition and Independence.

1. The Mandate for Palestine shall terminate as soon as possible but in any case not later than 1 August 1948.

2. The armed forces of the mandatory Power shall be progressively withdrawn from Palestine, the withdrawal to be completed as soon as possible but in any case not later than 1 August 1948. . . .

3. Independent Arab and Jewish States and the Special International Regime for the City of Jerusalem, set forth in Part III of this Plan, shall come into existence in Palestine two months after the evacuation of the armed forces of the mandatory Power has been completed but in any case not later than 1 October 1948. The boundaries of the Arab State, the Jewish State, and the City of Jerusalem shall be as described in Parts II and III below. . . .

B. STEPS PREPARATORY TO INDEPENDENCE

1. A Commission shall be set up consisting of one representative of each of five Member States. The Members represented on the Commission shall be elected by the General Assembly on as broad a basis, geographically and otherwise, as possible.

. . .

4. The Commission, after consultation with the democratic parties and other public organizations of the Arab and Jewish States, shall select and establish in each State as rapidly as possible a Provisional Council of Government. . . .

9. The Provisional Council of Government of each State shall, not later than two months after the withdrawal of the armed forces of the mandatory Power, hold elections to the Constituent Assembly which shall be conducted on democratic lines. . . .

10. The Constituent Assembly of each State shall draft a democratic constitution for its State and choose a provisional government to succeed the Provisional Council of Government appointed by the Commission. . . .

11. The Commission shall appoint a preparatory economic commission of three members to make whatever arrangements are possible for economic co-operation, with a view to establishing, as soon as practicable, the Economic Union and the Joint Economic Board, as provided in section D below. . . .

D. ECONOMIC UNION AND TRANSIT

1. The Provisional Council of Government of each State shall enter into an undertaking with respect to Economic Union and Transit. . . .

The Economic Union of Palestine

2. The objectives of the Economic Union of Palestine shall be:

(a) A customs union;

(b) A joint currency system providing for a single foreign exchange rate;

(c) Operation in the common interest on a non-discriminatory basis of railways; inter-State highways; postal, telephone and telegraphic services, and ports and airports involved in international trade and commerce;

(d) Joint economic development, especially in respect of irrigation, land reclamation and soil conservation;

(e) Access for both States and for the City of Jerusalem on a non-discriminatory basis to water and power facilities.

3. There shall be established a Joint Economic Board, which shall consist of three representatives of each of the two States and three foreign members appointed by the Economic and Social Council of the United Nations. . . .

4. The functions of the Joint Economic Board shall be to implement either directly or by delegation the measures necessary to realize the objectives of the Economic Union. . . .

PART II—Boundaries

. . .

PART III—City of Jerusalem

A. SPECIAL REGIME

The City of Jerusalem shall be established as a *corpus separatum* under a special international regime and shall be administered by the United Nations. The Trusteeship Council shall be designated to discharge the responsibilities of the Administering Authority on behalf of the United Nations. . . .

C. STATUTE OF THE CITY

The Trusteeship Council shall, within five months of the approval of the present plan, elaborate and approve a detailed statute of the City which shall contain, inter alia, the substance of the following provisions:

1. *Government machinery; special objectives.* The Administering Authority in discharging its administrative obligations shall pursue the following special objectives:

(a) To protect and to preserve the unique spiritual and religious interests located in the city of the three great monotheistic faiths throughout the world, Christian, Jewish and Moslem; to this end to ensure that order and peace, and especially religious peace, reign in Jerusalem; . . .

2. *Governor and administrative staff.* A Governor of the City of Jerusalem shall be appointed by the Trusteeship Council and shall be responsible to it. . . .

4. Security measures.

(a) The City of Jerusalem shall be demilitarized; its neutrality shall be declared and preserved, and no para-military formations, exercises or activities shall be permitted within its borders. . . .

5. *Legislative organization.* A Legislative Council, elected by adult residents of

the city irrespective of nationality on the basis of universal and secret suffrage and proportional representation, shall have powers of legislation and taxation. . . .

13. Holy Places.

. . .

(b) Free access to the Holy Places and religious buildings or sites and the free exercise of worship shall be secured in conformity with existing rights and subject to the requirements of public order and decorum. . . .

7. UN GENERAL ASSEMBLY, RESOLUTION NO. 194 (III) OF 11 DECEMBER 1948—UN CONCILIATION COMMISSION FOR PALESTINE

The General Assembly:
Having considered further the situation in Palestine, . . .

2. *Establishes* a Conciliation Commission consisting of three States Members of the United Nations:

. . .

5. *Calls upon* the Governments and authorities concerned to extend the scope of negotiations provided for in the Security Council's resolution of 16 November 1948 and to seek agreement by negotiations conducted either with the Conciliation Commission or directly, with a view to the final settlement of all questions outstanding between them;

6. *Instructs* the Conciliation Commission to take steps to assist the Governments and authorities concerned to achieve a final settlement of all questions outstanding between them;

7. *Resolves* that the Holy Places—including Nazareth—religious buildings and sites in Palestine should be protected and free access to them assured, in accordance with existing rights and historical practice; . . .

8. . . . *Requests* the Security Council to take further steps to ensure the demilitarization of Jerusalem at the earliest possible date;

Instructs the Commission to present to the fourth regular session of the General Assembly detailed proposals for a permanent international regime for the Jerusalem area which will provide for the maximum local autonomy for distinctive groups consistent with the special international status of the Jerusalem area: . . .

11. *Resolves* that the refugees wishing to return to their homes and live at peace with their neighbours should be permitted to do so at the earliest practicable date, and that compensation should be paid for the property of those choosing not to return and for loss of or damage to property which, under principles of international law or in equity, should be made good by the Governments or authorities responsible;

Instructs the Conciliation Commission to facilitate the repatriation, resettlement and economic and social rehabilitation of the refugees and the payment of compensation, and to maintain close relations with the Director of the United Nations Relief for Palestine Refugees and, through him, with the appropriate organs and agencies of the United Nations; . . .

14. *Calls upon* all Governments and authorities concerned to co-operate with the Conciliation Commission and to take all possible steps to assist in the implementation of the present resolution; . . .

8. JORDAN-ISRAELI GENERAL ARMISTICE AGREEMENT, APRIL 3, 1949 *(Security Council Document S/1302)*

. . .

Article VII

1. The military forces of the Parties to this Agreement shall be limited to defensive forces only in the areas extending ten kilometres from each side of the Armistice Demarcation Lines, except where geographical considerations make this impractical, as at the southernmost tip of Palestine and the coastal strip. . . .

Article VIII

1. A Special Committee, composed of two representatives of each Party designated by the respective Governments, shall be established for the purpose of formulating agreed plans and arrangements designed to enlarge the scope of this Agreement and to effect improvements in its application.

2. The Special Committee shall be organized . . . and shall direct attention to the formulation of agreed plans and arrangements for such matters as either Party may submit to it, which, in any case, shall include the following, on which agreement in principle already exists: free movement of traffic on vital roads, including the Bethlehem and Latrun-Jerusalem roads; resumption of the normal functioning of the cultural and humanitarian institutions on Mount Scopus and free access thereto; free access to the Holy Places and cultural institutions and use of the cemetery on the Mount of Olives; resumption of the Latrun pumping station; provision of electricity for the Old City; and resumption of operation of the railroad to Jerusalem. . . .

Article XII

. . .

2. This Agreement, having been negotiated and concluded in pursuance of the resolution of the Security Council of 16 November 1948 calling for the establishment of an armistice . . ., shall remain in force until a peaceful settlement between the Parties is achieved. . . .

9. UN GENERAL ASSEMBLY, RESOLUTION NO. 273 (III) OF 11 MAY 1949—ADMISSION OF ISRAEL TO UN MEMBERSHIP

Having received the report of the Security Council on the application of Israel for membership in the United Nations,

Noting that, in the judgment of the Security Council, Israel is a peace-loving State and is able and willing to carry out the obligations contained in the Charter,

Noting that the Security Council has recommended to the General Assembly that it admit Israel to membership in the United Nations,

Noting furthermore the declaration by the State of Israel that it "unreservedly accepts the obligations of the United Nations Charter and undertakes to honour them from the day when it becomes a Member of the United Nations,"

Recalling its resolutions of 29 November 1947 and 11 December 1948 and taking note of the declaration and explanations made by the representative of the

Government of Israel before the *Ad Hoc* Political Committee in respect of the implementation of the said resolutions,

The General Assembly:

Acting in discharge of its functions under Article 4 of the Charter and rule 125 of its rules of procedure,

1. *Decides* that Israel is a peace-loving State which accepts the obligations contained in the Charter and is able and willing to carry out those obligations;

2. *Decides* to admit Israel to membership in the United Nations.

10. ISRAEL-SYRIAN GENERAL ARMISTICE AGREEMENT, 20 JULY 1949
(Security Council Document S/1353)

Article I

With a view to promoting the return of permanent peace in Palestine and in recognition of the importance in this regard of mutual assurances concerning the future military operations of the Parties, the following principles, which shall be fully observed by both Parties during the armistice, are hereby affirmed:

1. The injunction of the Security Council against resort to military force in the settlement of the Palestine question shall henceforth be scrupulously respected by both Parties. The establishment of an armistice between their armed forces is accepted as an indispensable step toward the liquidation of armed conflict and the restoration of peace in Palestine.

2. No aggressive action by the armed forces—land, sea, or air—of either Party shall be undertaken, planned or threatened against the people or the armed forces of the other; it being understood that the use of the term planned in this context has no bearing on normal staff planning as generally practised in military organizations.

3. The right of each Party to its security and freedom from fear of attack by the armed forces of the other shall be fully respected.

Article II

With a specific view to the implementation of the resolution of the Security Council of 16 November 1948, the following principles and purposes are affirmed:

1. The principle that no military or political advantage should be gained under the truce ordered by the Security Council is recognized.

2. It is also recognized that no provision of this Agreement shall in any way prejudice the rights, claims and positions of either Party hereto in the ultimate peaceful settlement of the Palestine question, the provisions of this Agreement being dictated exclusively by military, and not by political, considerations.

Article III

1. In pursuance of the foregoing principles and of the resolution of the Security Council of 16 November 1948, a general armistice between the armed forces of the two Parties—land, sea, and air—is hereby established.

2. No element of the land, sea or air, military or para-military, forces of either Party, including non-regular forces, shall commit any warlike or hostile act against the military or para-military forces of the other Party, or against civilians in territory under the control of that Party; or shall advance beyond or pass over for any purpose whatsoever the Armistice Demarcation line set forth in Article V of

this Agreement; or enter into or pass through the air space of the other Party or through the waters within three miles of the coastline of the other Party.

3. No warlike act or act of hostility shall be conducted from territory controlled by one of the Parties to this Agreement against the other Party or against civilians in territory under control of that Party.

Article IV

1. The line described in Article V of this Agreement shall be designated as the Armistice Demarcation Line and is delineated in pursuance of the purpose and intent of the resolution of the Security Council of 16 November 1948.

2. The basic purpose of the Armistice Demarcation Line is to delineate the line beyond which the armed forces of the respective Parties shall not move.

3. Rules and regulations of the armed forces of the Parties, which prohibit civilians from crossing the fighting lines or entering the area between the lines, shall remain in effect after the signing of this Agreement, with application to the Armistice Demarcation Line defined in Article V, subject to the provisions of paragraph 5 of that article.

Article V

1. It is emphasized that the following arrangements for the Armistice Demarcation Line between the Israeli and Syrian armed forces and for the Demilitarized Zone are not to be interpreted as having any relation whatsoever to ultimate territorial arrangements affecting the two Parties to this Agreement.

2. In pursuance of the spirit of the Security Council resolution of 16 November 1948, the Armistice Demarcation Line and the Demilitarized Zone have been defined with a view toward separating the armed forces of the two Parties in such manner as to minimize the possibility of friction and incident, while providing for the gradual restoration of normal civilian life in the area of the Demilitarized Zone, without prejudice to the ultimate settlement.

3. . . . The Armistice Demarcation Line shall follow a line midway between the existing truce lines, as certified by the United Nations Truce Supervision Organization for the Israeli and Syrian forces. Where the existing truce lines run along the international boundary between Syria and Palestine, the Armistice Demarcation Line shall follow the boundary line.

4. The armed forces of the two Parties shall nowhere advance beyond the Armistice Demarcation Line.

5. (a) Where the Armistice Demarcation Line does not correspond to the international boundary between Syria and Palestine, the area between the Armistice Demarcation Line and the boundary, pending final territorial settlement between the Parties, shall be established as a Demilitarized Zone from which the armed forces of both Parties shall be totally excluded, and in which no activities by military or para-military forces shall be permitted. This provision applies to the Ein Gev and Dardara sectors which shall form part of the Demilitarized Zone.

(b) Any advance by the armed forces, military or para-military, of either Party into any part of the Demilitarized Zone, when confirmed by the United Nations representatives referred to in the following sub-paragraph, shall constitute a flagrant violation of this Agreement.

(c) The Chairman of the Mixed Armistice Commission established in Article VII of this Agreement and United Nations observers attached to the Commission shall be responsible for ensuring the full implementation of this article.

(d) The withdrawal of such armed forces as are now found in the Demilitarized Zone shall be in accordance with the schedule of withdrawal annexed to this Agreement (Annex II).

(e) The Chairman of the Mixed Armistice Commission shall be empowered to authorize the return of civilians to villages and settlements in the Demilitarized Zone and the employment of limited numbers of locally recruited civilian police in the zone for internal security purposes, and shall be guided in this regard by the schedule of withdrawal referred to in sub-paragraph (d) of this article.

6. On each side of the Demilitarized Zone there shall be areas, as defined in Annex III to this Agreement, in which defensive forces only shall be maintained, in accordance with the definition of defensive forces set forth in Annex IV to this Agreement.

Article VII

1. The execution of the provisions of this Agreement shall be supervised by a Mixed Armistice Commission composed of five members, of whom each Party to this Agreement shall designate two, and whose Chairman shall be the United Nations Chief of Staff of the Truce Supervision Organization or a senior officer from the observer personnel of that organization designated by him following consultation with both Parties to this Agreement.

2. The Mixed Armistice Commission shall maintain its headquarters at the Customs House near Jisr Banat Ya'qub and at Mahanayim, and shall hold its meetings at such places and at such times as it may deem necessary for the effective conduct of its work.

. . .

4. Decisions of the Mixed Armistice Commission, to the extent possible, shall be based on the principles of unanimity. In the absence of unanimity, decisions shall be taken by majority vote of the members of the Commission present and voting.

5. The Mixed Armistice Commission shall formulate its own rules of procedure. Meetings shall be held only after due notice to the members by the Chairman. The quorum for its meetings shall be a majority of its members.

6. The Commission shall be empowered to employ observers, who may be from among the military organizations of the Parties or from the military personnel of the United Nations Truce Supervision Organization, or from both, in such numbers as may be considered essential to the performance of its functions. In the event United Nations observers should be so employed, they shall remain under the command of the United Nations Chief of Staff of the Truce Supervision Organization. . . .

7. Claims or complaints presented by either Party relating to the application of this Agreement shall be referred immediately to the Mixed Armistice Commission through its Chairman. The Commission shall take such action on all such claims or complaints by means of its observation and investigation machinery as it may deem appropriate, with a view to equitable and mutually satisfactory settlement.

8. Where interpretation of the meaning of a particular provision of this Agreement, other than the preamble and Articles I and II, is at issue, the Commission's interpretation shall prevail. The Commission, in its discretion and as the need arises, may from time to time recommend to the Parties modifications in the provisions of this Agreement.

. . .

10. Members of the Commission and its observers shall be accorded such freedom of movement and access in the area covered by this Agreement as the Commission may determine to be necessary, provided that when such decisions of the

Commission are reached by a majority vote United Nations observers only shall be employed.

. . .

Article VIII

1. The present Agreement is not subject to ratification and shall come into force immediately upon being signed.

2. This Agreement, having been negotiated and concluded in pursuance of the resolution of the Security Council of 16 November 1948, calling for the establishment of an armistice in order to eliminate the threat to the peace in Palestine and to facilitate the transition from the present truce to permanent peace in Palestine, shall remain in force until a peaceful settlement between the Parties is achieved, except as provided in paragraph 3 of this article.

. . .

11. UN SECURITY COUNCIL RESOLUTION NO. 93 (1951) OF 18 MAY 1951—PARTIES TO OBSERVE ARMISTICE AGREEMENTS: SYRIAN-ISRAELI DEMILITARIZED ZONE

The Security Council: . . .

Calls upon the Governments of Israel and Syria to bring before the Mixed Armistice Commission or its Chairman, whichever has the pertinent responsibility under the Armistice Agreement, their complaints and to abide by the decisions resulting therefrom;

Considers that it is inconsistent with the objectives and intent of the Armistice Agreement to refuse to participate in meetings of the Mixed Armistice Commission or to fail to respect requests of the Chairman of the Mixed Armistice Commission as they relate to his obligations under Article V, and calls upon the parties to be represented at all meetings called by the Chairman of the Commission and to respect such requests;

Calls upon the parties to give effect to the following excerpt cited by the Chief of Staff of the Truce Supervision Organization at the 542nd meeting of the Security Council, on 25 April 1951, as being from the summary record of the Israel-Syrian Armistice Conference of 3 July 1949, which was agreed to by the parties as an authoritative comment on Article V of the Armistice Agreement between Israel and Syria:

"The question of civil administration in villages and settlements in the demilitarized zone is provided for, within the framework of an Armistice Agreement, in sub-paragraph 5 (b) and 5 (f) of the draft article. Such civil administration, including policing, will be on a local basis, without raising general questions of administration, jurisdiction, citizenship and sovereignty.

"Where Israel civilians return to or remain in an Israel village or settlement, the civil administration and policing of the village or settlement will be by Israelis. Similarly, where Arab civilians return to or remain in an Arab village, a local Arab administration and police unit will be authorized.

"As civilian life is gradually restored, administration will take shape on a local basis under the general supervision of the Chairman of the Mixed Armistice Commission.

"The Chairman of the Mixed Armistice Commission, in consultation and cooperation with the local communities, will be in a position to authorize all necessary arrangements for the restoration and protection of civilian life. He will not assume responsibility for direct administration of the zone";

Recalls to the Governments of Syria and Israel their obligations under Article 2, paragraph 4, of the Charter of the United Nations and their commitments under the Armistice Agreement not to resort to military force and finds that:

(a) Aerial action taken by the forces of the Government of Israel on 5 April 1951, and

(b) Any aggressive military action by either of the parties in or around the demilitarized zone, which further investigation by the Chief of Staff of the Truce Supervision Organization into the reports and complaints recently submitted to the Council may establish, constitute a violation of the cease-fire provision in Security Council resolution 54 (1948) and are inconsistent with the terms of the Armistice Agreement and the obligations assumed under the Charter;

Noting the complaint with regard to the evacuation of Arab residents from the demilitarized zone.

(a) *Decides* that Arab civilians who have been removed from the demilitarized zone by the Government of Israel should be permitted to return forthwith to their homes and that the Mixed Armistice Commission should supervise their return and rehabilitation in a manner to be determined by the Commission;

(b) *Holds* that no action involving the transfer of persons across international frontiers, armistice lines or within the demilitarized zone should be undertaken without prior decision of the Chairman of the Mixed Armistice Commission;

Noting with concern the refusal on a number of occasions to permit observers and officials of the Truce Supervision Organization to enter localities and areas which are subjects of complaints in order to perform their legitimate functions, considers that the parties should permit such entry at all times whenever this is required, to enable the Truce Supervision Organization to fulfill its functions, and should render every facility which may be requested by the Chairman of the Mixed Armistice Commission for this purpose;

Reminds the parties of their obligations under the Charter of the United Nations to settle their international disputes by peaceful means in such manner that international peace and security are not endangered, and expresses its concern at the failure of the Governments of Israel and Syria to achieve progress pursuant to their commitments under the Armistice Agreement to promote the return to permanent peace in Palestine; . . .

12. UN SECURITY COUNCIL RESOLUTION NO. 95 (1951) OF 1 SEPTEM-BER 1951—PASSAGE OF ISRAELI SHIPPING THROUGH SUEZ CANAL

The Security Council:

Recalling that in its resolution 73 (1949) of 11 August 1949 relating to the conclusion of Armistice Agreements between Israel and the neighbouring Arab States it drew attention to the pledges in these Agreements "against any further acts of hostility between the parties," . . .

Considering that since the armistice regime, which has been in existence for nearly two and a half years, is of a permanent character, neither party can reasonably assert that it is actively a belligerent or requires to exercise the right of visit, search, and seizure for any legitimate purpose of self-defense,

Finds that the maintenance of the practice mentioned in paragraph 4 above is inconsistent with the objectives of a peaceful settlement between the parties and the establishment of a permanent peace in Palestine set forth in the Armistice Agreement between Egypt and Israel;

Finds further that such practice is an abuse of the exercise of the right of visit, search and seizure;

Further finds that that practice cannot in the prevailing circumstances be justified on the ground that it is necessary for self-defense;

And further noting that the restrictions on the passage of goods through the Suez Canal to Israel ports are denying to nations at no time connected with the conflict in Palestine valuable supplies required for their economic reconstruction, and that these restrictions together with sanctions applied by Egypt to certain ships which have visited Israel ports represent unjustified interference with the rights of nations to navigate the seas and to trade freely with one another, including the Arab States and Israel,

Calls upon Egypt to terminate the restrictions on the passage of international commercial shipping and goods through the Suez Canal wherever bound and to cease all interference with such shipping beyond that essential to the safety of shipping in the Canal itself and to the observance of the international conventions in force.

13. UN SECURITY COUNCIL RESOLUTION NO. 106 (1955) OF 29 MARCH 1955—CONDEMNATION OF ISRAEL FOR ATTACK ON GAZA

The Security Council: . . .

Noting that the Egyptian-Israel Mixed Armistice Commission on 6 March 1955 determined that a "prearranged and planned attack ordered by Israel authorities" was "committed by Israel regular army forces against the Egyptian regular army force" in the Gaza Strip on 28 February 1955,

1. *Condemns* this attack as a violation of the cease-fire provisions of Security Council resolution 54 (1948) and as inconsistent with the obligations of the parties under the General Armistice Agreement between Egypt and Israel and under the United Nations Charter;

2. *Calls again upon* Israel to take all necessary measures to prevent such actions;

3. *Expresses* its conviction that the maintenance of the General Armistice Agreement is threatened by any deliberate violation of that Agreement by one of the parties to it, and that no progress towards the return of permanent peace in Palestine can be made unless the parties comply strictly with their obligations under the General Armistice Agreement and the cease-fire provisions of its resolution 54 (1948).

14. UN SECURITY COUNCIL RESOLUTION NO. 237 (1967) OF 14 JUNE 1967—ON THE TREATMENT OF CIVIL POPULATIONS AND PRISONERS OF WAR AND ON THE RETURN OF DISPLACED PERSONS

The Security Council,

Considering the urgent need to spare the civil populations and the prisoners of the war in the area of conflict in the Middle East additional sufferings,

Considering that essential and inalienable human rights should be respected even during the vicissitudes of war,

Considering that all the obligations of the Geneva Convention relative to the Treatment of Prisoners of War of 12 August 1949 should be complied with by the parties involved in the conflict,

1. *Calls upon* the Government of Israel to ensure the safety, welfare and security of the inhabitants of the areas where military operations have taken place and to facilitate the return of those inhabitants who have fled the areas since outbreak of hostilities,

2. *Recommends* to the Governments concerned the scrupulous respect of the humanitarian principles governing the treatment of prisoners of war and the protection of civilian persons in time of war, contained in the Geneva Convention of 12 August 1949:

3. *Requests* the Secretary-General to follow the effective implementation of this resolution and to report to the Security Council.

15. UN GENERAL ASSEMBLY RESOLUTION NO. 2254 (ES-V) OF 14 JULY 1967—ON JERUSALEM

The General Assembly,

Recalling its resolution 2253 (ES-V) of 4 July 1967,

Having received the report submitted by the Secretary General,

Taking note with the deepest regret and concern of the noncompliance by Israel of resolution 2253 (ES-V),

1. *Deplores* the failure of Israel to implement resolution 2253 (ES-V);

2. *Reiterates* its call to Israel in that resolution to rescind all measures already taken and to desist forthwith from taking any action which would alter the status of Jerusalem;

3. *Requests* the Secretary General to report to the Security Council and the General Assembly on the situation and on the implementation of the present resolution.

16. UN SECURITY COUNCIL RESOLUTION NO. 242 (1967) OF 22 NOVEM-BER, 1967—SPECIAL REPRESENTATIVE TO THE MIDDLE EAST

The Security Council

Expressing its continuing concern with the grave situation in the Middle East,

Emphasizing the inadmissibility of the acquisition of territory by war and the need to work for a just and lasting peace in which every state in the area can live in security,

Emphasizing further that all member states in their acceptance of the Charter of the United Nations have undertaken a commitment to act in accordance with Article 2 of the Charter,

1. *Affirms* that the fulfillment of Charter principles requires the establishment of a just and lasting peace in the Middle East which should include the application of both the following principles:

(i) Withdrawal of Israeli armed forces from territories of recent conflict;

(ii) Termination of all claims or states of belligerency and respect for and acknowledgment of the sovereignty, territorial integrity and political independence of every state in the area and their right to live in peace within secure and recognized boundaries free from threats or acts of force;

2. *Affirms Further* the necessity

(a) for guaranteeing freedom of navigation through international waterways in the area;

(b) for achieving a just settlement of the refugee problem;

(c) for guaranteeing the territorial inviolability and political independence of every state in the area, through measures including the establishment of demilitarized zones;

3. *Requests* the Secretary General to designate a special representative to proceed to the Middle East to establish and maintain contacts with the states concerned in order to promote agreement and assist efforts to achieve a peaceful and accepted settlement in accordance with the provisions and principles in this resolution,

4. *Requests* the Secretary General to report to the Security Council on the progress of the efforts of the special representative as soon as possible.

17. UN GENERAL ASSEMBLY RESOLUTION NO. 2341A (XXII) OF 19 DECEMBER 1967—REPORT OF THE COMMISSIONER-GENERAL OF UNRWA FOR PALESTINE REFUGEES IN THE NEAR EAST

The General Assembly,

Recalling its resolutions 194 (III) of 11 December 1948, 302 (IV) of 8 December 1949, 393 (V) and 394 (V) of 2 and 14 December 1950, 512 (VI) and 513 (VI) of 26 January 1952, 614 (VII) of 6 November 1952, 720 (VIII) of 27 November 1953, 818 (IX) of 4 December 1954, 916 (X) of 3 December 1955, 1018 (XI) of 28 February 1957, 1191 (XII) of 12 December 1957, 1315 (XIII) of 12 December 1958, 1456 (XIV) of 9 December 1959, 1604 (XV) of 21 April 1961, 1725 (XVI) of 20 December 1961, 1856 (XVII) of 20 December 1962, 1912 (XVIII) of 3 December 1963, 2002 (XIX) of 10 February 1965 and 2052 (XX) of 15 December 1965, and 2154 (XXI) of 18 November 1966,

Noting the annual report of the Commissioner-General of the United Nations Relief and Works Agency for Palestine Refugees in the Near East, covering the period from 1 July 1966 to 30 June 1967,

1. *Notes with deep regret* that repatriation or compensation of the refugees as provided for in paragraph 11 of General Assembly resolution 194 (III) has not been effected, that no substantial progress has been made in the programme endorsed in paragraph 2 of resolution 513 (VI) for the reintegration of refugees either by repatriation or resettlement and that, therefore, the situation of the refugees continues to be a matter of serious concern;

2. *Expresses its thanks* to the Commissioner-General and the staff of the United Nations Relief and Works Agency for Palestine Refugees in the Near East for their continued faithful efforts to provide essential services for the Palestine refugees, and to the specialized agencies and private organizations for their valuable work in assisting the refugees;

3. *Directs* the Commissioner-General of the United Nations Relief and Works Agency for Palestine Refugees in the Near East to continue his efforts in taking such measures, including rectification of the relief rolls, as to assure, in co-operation with the Governments concerned, the most equitable distribution of relief based on need;

4. *Notes with regret* that the United Nations Conciliation Commission for Palestine was unable to find a means to achieve progress on the implementation of paragraph 11 of General Assembly resolution 194 (III) and requests the United Nations Conciliation Commission for Palestine to exert continued efforts towards the implementation thereof;

5. *Directs attention* to the continuing critical financial position of the United Nations Relief and Works Agency for Palestine Refugees in the Near East, as outlined in the Commissioner-General's reports;

6. *Notes with concern* that, despite the commendable and successful efforts of the Commissioner-General in collecting additional contributions to help relieve the serious budget deficit of the past year, contributions to the United Nations Relief and Works Agency for Palestine Refugees in the Near East continue to fall short of the funds needed to cover essential budget requirements;

7. *Calls upon* all Governments as a matter of urgency to make the most generous efforts possible to meet the anticipated needs of the United Nations Relief and Works Agency for Palestine Refugees in the Near East, particularly in the light of the budgetary deficit projected in the Commissioner-General's report, and, therefore, urges non-contributing Governments to contribute and contributing Governments to consider increasing their contributions.

Notes

Chapter I. The Historical Background of Palestine Through World War I

1. Leonard Stein, *Balfour Declaration* (New York, 1961), 16, 23, 27. Argentina, Cyprus, and the Egyptian Sinai were also considered as possibilities by some Zionists.
2. *Ibid.*, 91 ff; Nahum Sokolow, *History of Zionism* (London, 1919), I, 300 f.
3. Chaim Weizmann, *Trial and Error* (New York, 1949), I, 206; Stein, *op. cit.*, 465–71, 520–32, 543–49, 587–97; John Marlowe, *The Seat of Pilate* (London, 1959), 25f.
4. These letters were published in British Command Papers (Cmd.) 5957, 1939.
5. George E. Kirk, *A Short History of the Middle East* (New York, 1960), 6th ed., 146.
6. Col. A. P. Wavell, *The Palestine Campaign* (London, 1928), 56; Royal Inst. of Internat. Affairs, *The Middle East* (London, 1954), 2nd ed., 24; *War Memoirs of Lloyd George* (Boston, 1934), 75f; E. L. Woodward and R. Butler, eds., *Documents on British Foreign Policy, 1919–39* (London, 1952), IV, 487.
7. Quoted in George Antonius, *The Arab Awakening* (London, 1946), 257, 431f.
8. Hogarth's message quoted, *ibid.*, 268; see also Stein, *op. cit.*, 632f, Julia E. Johnsen, compiler, *Palestine: Jewish Homeland* (New York, 1946), 12; H. W. Temperley, ed., *A History of the Peace Conference of Paris* (London, 1924), VI, 132; William R. Polk, D. M. Stamler, and E. Asfour, *Backdrop to Tragedy* (Boston, 1957), 66.
9. Cmd. 3530, 1930, 127. The Declaration to the Seven quoted in Antonius, *op. cit.*, 433f; reply of Committee of Seven quoted in Johnsen, *op. cit.*, 12.
10. Communiqué quoted in Antonius, *op. cit.*, 435f; see also Temperley, *op. cit.*, 141.
11. Cmd. 3530, 1930, 127; Cmd. 5974, 1939, 45.
12. J. C. Hurewitz, ed., *Diplomacy in the Near and Middle East* (Princeton, 1956), II, 38f; Woodward and Butler, *op. cit.*, 312, 364; Antonius, *op. cit.*, 437f; Weizman, *op. cit.*, 245f; Ben Halpern, *The Idea of the Jewish State* (Cambridge, Mass., 1961), 331, 334.
13. Quoted in Woodward and Butler, *op. cit.*, 345.
14. *Ibid.*, 256ff; Hurewitz, *op. cit.*, 66–74. For a detailed account of the King-Crane Commission, see Harry N. Howard, *The King-Crane Commission* (Beirut, 1963).
15. Woodward and Butler, *op. cit.*, 256ff, 272, 360, 364f, 368, 616; Paul L. Hanna, *British Policy in Palestine* (Washington, 1942), 159; Marlowe, *op. cit.*, 40, 75f, 80.
16. Quoted in Stein, *op. cit.*, 93.
17. *Ibid.*, 629f; Woodward and Butler, *op. cit.*, 364.

Chapter II. The Palestine Mandate, 1922–1948

1. For terms of the Mandatory Agreement see Hurewitz, *op. cit.*, 106–11.
2. J. C. Hurewitz, *The Struggle for Palestine* (New York, 1950), 23.

3. Cmd. 3530, 1930, 101f; Palestine Govt., *A Survey of Palestine* (Palestine, 1946–47), I, 141, 144, 185, 200ff, 373; Hurewitz, *The Struggle*, 30.

4. Hurewitz, *The Struggle*, 29, 36.

5. Cmd. 3692, 1930, 5; Cmd. 1700, 1922, 17–21; Palestine Govt., *op. cit.*, 21; Stein, *op. cit.*, 555f.

6. Cmd. 1700, 28f; Weizmann, *op. cit.*, 290.

7. Cmd. 3530, 106, 111f, 125ff, 139ff; Cmd. 3686, 1930, 41, 50f, 54; Cmd. 5479, 1937, 110ff; Cmd. 5854, 1938, 116; Palestine Govt., *op. cit.*, 38ff.

8. Cmd. 3692; Cmd. 5479, 112; Palestine Govt., *op. cit.*, 28f; Hurewitz, *The Struggle*, 23.

9. Cmd. 5479, 110ff, 292ff, 376; Cmd. 5513, 1937; Cmd. 5854, 1938.

10. Cmd. 6019, 1939.

11. Hurewitz, *The Struggle*, 141.

12. Sumner Welles, *We Need Not Fail* (Boston, 1948), 19; Palestine Govt., *op. cit.*, 39, 63; Hurewitz, *The Struggle*, 164–66; Christopher Sykes, *Cross Roads to Israel* (London, 1965), 294ff.

13. Weizmann, *op. cit.*, II, 436; Johnsen, *op. cit.*, 136; Hurewitz, *The Struggle*, 169ff, 215.

14. Biltmore Declaration, May 11, 1942. See Appendix.

15. American Council for Judaism: Statement of Principles by Non-Zionist Rabbis, *NY Times*, August 30, 1942.

16. *NY Times*, Oct. 19, 1945; William A. Eddy, *F.D.R. Meets Ibn Saud* (New York, 1954), 35f.

17. Samuel Halperin, *The Political World of American Zionism* (Detroit, Mich., 1961), 35f, 247f, 258ff.

18. Harry S. Truman, *Memoirs* (Garden City, N.Y., 1956), II, 135, 148; *NY Times*, Nov. 11, 1946.

19. Elie Wiesel, "Eichmann's Victims and the Unheard Testimony," *Commentary*, XXXII (Dec., 1961), 512f; Truman, *op. cit.*, 132ff; George E. Kirk, *The Middle East (1945–1950)* (New York, 1954), 188ff; Hurewitz, *The Struggle*, 226, 267; H. Bradford Westerfield, *Foreign Policy and Party Politics* (New Haven, 1955), 227f; Palestine Govt., *op cit.*, 80; Halperin, *op. cit.*, 21.

20. Barnett Litvinoff, *Ben-Gurion of Israel* (New York, 1954), 163.

21. *Middle East Opinion*, Vol. I, No. 1 (June 10, 1946), 16f.

22. In a letter to Atlee, Aug. 12, 1946, Truman objected to the plan. Truman, *op. cit.*, 152.

23. *NY Times*, Oct. 5, 1946.

24. Hurewitz, *The Struggle*, 265; *Arab News Bulletin* (London), Nov. 18, 1946, 2.

25. Judah L. Magnes, "Jewish-Arab Cooperation in Palestine," *Political Quarterly* (London, Oct. 1945), 287–307.

26. David Ben-Gurion, *Rebirth and Destiny of Israel* (New York, 1954), 33–37.

27. Sykes, *op. cit.*, 121.

28. Cmd. 3530, 168.

Chapter III. The Palestine Question Before the United Nations

1. Kirk, *The Middle East*, 243f and n 4, 244f.

2. Hurewitz, *The Struggle*, 267–68.

3. UNSCOP, *Report to GA*, (1947), III, 1–113, 204–31.

4. *Ibid.*, Annex A, 243f; IV, Annex B, 34–43.

5. *Ibid.*, 195f.

6. *Ibid.*, IV, 24–41.

7. *Ibid.*, I, 40ff, 59ff.

8. Most authorities support this contention. See Leland Goodrich and Edvard Hambro, *Charter of the United Nations* (Boston, 1946), 47, 93, 96, 98, 104; Hans Kelsen, *The Law of the United Nations* (New York, 1950), 195f; Clyde Eagleton, "Palestine and the Constitutional Law of the United Nations," *American J. of Internat. Law,* XLII (1948), 397ff; Pitman Potter, "The Palestine Problem before the United Nations," *ibid.,* 859ff. On November 28, 1960, Israel's delegate to the UN contended that General Assembly resolutions were only "recommendations." UN, Official Records of the 15th Session of the General Assembly (to be referred to hereafter as UN, OR of the 15th Ses of the GA), Special Political Committee (Spec Pol Com), 209th Meeting, 14.

9. UN, OR of 2nd Ses of the GA, *Ad Hoc* Com, 18th Meeting, Oct. 18, 1947, 122; 3rd, Sept. 29, 5ff; 5th, Oct. 3, 20ff; 6th, Oct. 6, 26ff; 8th, Oct. 8, 44f; 14th, Oct. 15, 90ff; 18th, Oct. 18, 122; 32nd, Nov. 24, 203ff, 213; 126th Plenary Meeting (PM), Nov. 28, 1374f.

10. *Ibid., Ad Hoc* Com, 4th, Oct. 2, 11ff; 17th, Oct. 17, 109ff; 18th, Oct. 18, 123ff; 28th, Nov. 22, 168; 31st, Nov. 24, 197ff.

11. Hurewitz, *The Struggle,* 287, 305ff; UN, OR of 2nd Ses of GA, *Ad Hoc* Com, 12th Meeting, Oct. 13, 1947, 68ff.

12. UN, OR of 2nd Ses of GA, 13th Meeting, Oct. 14, 1947, 81; 125th PM, Nov. 26, 133ff.

13. Truman, *op. cit.,* 133, 140, 149, 162; Walter Millis, ed., *The Forrestal Diaries* (New York, 1951), 360ff, 411.

14. Truman, *op. cit.,* 135ff.

15. *Ibid.,* 157.

16. UN, *Survey of Opinion,* II/40 (Oct. 8, 1947), 12; II/41 (Oct. 14), 1, 10.

17. Truman, *op. cit.,* 158ff; Aba Silver, *Visions of Victory* (New York, 1949), 54ff; Zionist Organization of America, *America's Role in Israel's Independence* (Pamphlet series No. 121, 1949), 3ff; Halperin, *op. cit.,* 21; James Batal, *Zionist Influence on the American Press* (Beirut, 1956), 2ff; Cecil Crabb, *Bi-Partisan Foreign Policy: Myth or Reality* (Evanston, Ill., 1957), 121ff.

18. Millis, *op. cit.,* 360ff.

19. Claire Hollingsworth, *The Arabs and the West* (London, 1952), 150.

20. Sir Zafrullah Khan, *Palestine in the U.N.O.* (Karachi, 1948), 21.

21. Silver, *op. cit.,* 150; Kermit Roosevelt, "The Partition of Palestine," *The Middle East J.,* Jan., 1948, 14f; Weizmann, *op. cit.,* 456ff; *Times* (London), Dec. 1, 1947.

22. UN, OR of 2nd Ses of GA, 126th PM, Nov. 28, 1947, 138ff.

23. *Ibid.,* 127th PM, Nov. 28, 1947, 1402ff; 128th PM, Nov. 29, 1411ff; *Arab News Bulletin* (London), Jan. 16, 1948, 6.

24. UN, OR of 2nd Ses of GA, 124th PM, Nov. 26, 1947, 1319; 125th PM, Nov. 26, 1364f.

25. *Arab News Bulletin* (London), Dec. 12, 1947, 1.

26. Menachem Begin, *The Revolt: Story of the Irgun* (New York, 1951), 335ff.

27. Hurewitz, *The Struggle,* 310; Kirk, *The Middle East,* 247; *NY Times,* Sept. 21, Oct. 14–23, Nov. 9, 12, 30, 1947.

28. Sir Alan Cunningham, "Palestine—The Last Days of the Mandate," *Internat.*

Affairs (London), *XXIV* (Oct., 1948), 488; Maj. R. D. Wilson, *Cordon and Search* (Aldershot, Britain, 1949), 155f; R. M. Graves, *Experiment in Anarchy* (London, 1949), 102f, 106, 120.

29. UN Doc. A/AC.21/9, Feb. 16, 1948, 5.

30. Official Records of Sec. Council (OR of SC), 253rd Meeting, Feb. 24, 1948, 49; 271st, March 19, 29ff; 275th, March 30, 2ff; 283rd, April 19, 41; 287th, April 23, 15ff.

31. Trygve Lie, *In the Cause of Peace* (New York, 1954), 170ff.

32. UN, OR of 2nd Spec. Ses of GA, 1st Com, 130th Meeting, April 28, 1948, 145; 131st, April 29, 155; 128th PM, April 27, 123.

33. *Ibid.*, OR of 2nd Ses of GA, 125th PM, Nov. 26, 1948, 1355.

Chapter IV. The Palestine War and UN Truces

1. Don Peretz, *Israel and the Palestine Arabs* (Washington, 1958), 6f; Edgar O'Ballance, *The Arab-Israeli War, 1948* (New York, 1957), 63f; A/648, Sept. 18, 1948, 24.

2. Kirk, *The Middle East,* 270; Jon and David Kimche, *A Clash of Destinies* (New York, 1960), 110.

3. O'Ballance, *op. cit.,* 80ff; John Bagot Glubb, *A Soldier with the Arabs* (New York, 1958), 94f; J. and D. Kimche, 162; Jon Kimche, *Seven Fallen Pillars* (New York, 1953), 242; Harry Sacher, *Israel and the Establishment of the State* (London, 1952), 207ff; Hurewitz, *The Struggle,* 318; Kirk, *The Middle East,* 270ff; King Abdullah, *My Memoirs Completed* (Washington, 1954), 10; Polk, Stamler, and Asfour, *op. cit.,* 129; Mohammed Neguib, *Egypt's Destiny* (London, 1953), 16ff, 220; Anwar el-Sadat, *Revolt on the Nile* (New York, 1957), 108; *NY Times,* May 15, 20, 21, 23, June 4, July 20, 1948.

4. *NY Times,* May 20, June 4, August 11, 1948; Kirk, *The Middle East,* 279; O'Ballance, *op. cit.,* 60ff; J. and D. Kimche, *op. cit.,* 223; Glubb, *op. cit.,* 95; Neguib, *op. cit.,* 16, 220; Wilton Wynn, *Nasser of Egypt* (Cambridge, Mass., 1959), 34.

5. *Israel Govt Yearbook, 1959/60,* 124, 180; *ibid., 1958,* 124; Ben-Gurion, *op. cit.,* 382; J. and D. Kimche, *op. cit.,* 160; *NY Times,* May 19, 30, 1948.

6. *NY Times,* May 16, 23, June 6, 11, 14, July 1, Oct. 11, 1948; *Israel Govt. Yearbook,* 1958, 118, 123; *Israel Digest* (Jerusalem), II (May 29, 1959), 3; Sacher, *op. cit.,* 276, 290.

7. S/745, May 16; S/760, May 20; S/767, S/768, S/769, S/770, May 22; S/774, S/775, May 24; UN, OR of the SC, 292, May 15, 3, 16ff, 26; 297th, May 20, 12f; 298th, May 20, 20ff; 299th, May 21, 11ff; 301st, May 22, 8; 302nd, May 22, 46f; 309th, May 29, 15f; 310th, May 29, 17ff; 293rd, May 17, 11.

8. *Israel's Struggle for Peace* (Israeli Office of Information, New York, 1960), 45; *NY Times,* May 25, June 1, 6, August 11, 1948; O'Ballance, *op. cit.,* 93f, 99, 118ff, 123; Kirk, *The Middle East,* 271; Glubb, *op. cit.,* 148.

9. J. and D. Kimche, *op. cit.,* 202ff; J. Kimche, *op. cit.,* 261; Sacher, *op. cit.,* 269f, 277; Kenneth W. Bilby, *New Star in the Near East* (Garden City, N.Y., 1950), 42; *NY Times,* August 11, 12, 1948.

10. O'Ballance, *op. cit.,* 124; *Israel Govt Yearbook, 1958,* 119f, 135, 137; Sacher, *op. cit.,* 269; *NY Times,* June 4, 19, August 11, 12, 1948; Moshe Pearlman, *Ben-Gurion Looks Back* (New York, 1965), 140.

11. *NY Times,* June 1, 2, 3, 7, July 4, August 11, 12, 1948; Glubb, *op. cit.,* 150; Kirk, *The Middle East,* 274, 280; King Abdullah, *op. cit.,* 10, 24; S/805, S/810, June 1; S/830, S/833, June 9.

12. J. and D. Kimche, *op. cit.,* 223; *NY Times,* July 8, 10, 11, 1948; Alex Rubner, *The Economy of Israel* (New York, 1960), 19.

13. O'Ballance, *op. cit.,* 139; Sacher, *op. cit.,* 270, 277f, 286; Kirk, *The Middle East,* 276f; J. Kimche, *op. cit.,* 261; Litvinoff, *op. cit.,* 200f, 204, 206; Robert St. John, *Ben-Gurion* (Garden City, N.Y., 1959), 147, 163; *NY Times,* June 11, 12, July 17, August 9, 10, 11, 12, 1948.

14. *NY Times,* July 10, 11, 1948; O'Ballance, *op. cit.,* 137f; J. Kimche, *op. cit.,* 262; J. and D. Kimche, *op. cit.,* 223.

15. *NY Times,* May 23, June 4, 1948; Jan. 6, 1949.

16. UN, OR of SC, 3rd year, 331st, July 7, 1948, 23ff; S/970, July 7, 1948, 27ff.

17. *NY Times,* June 2, 19, July 4, 1948; Westerfield, *op cit.,* 234ff; O'Ballance, *op. cit.,* 139.

18. *NY Times,* July 19, 22, August 11, 12, 1948; O'Ballance, *op. cit.,* 153ff, 162f; Sacher, *op. cit.,* 281ff, 288; Kimche, *op. cit.,* 265.

19. *NY Times,* Sept. 22–26, Oct. 1, 22, 25, 28–30, Nov. 5, 9, 1948.

20. UN, OR of 3rd Ses of GA, 1st Com, 200th, Nov. 15, 640ff; 216th, Nov. 29, 805f.

21. J. and D. Kimche, *op. cit.,* 243, 267; *NY Times,* Nov. 10, Dec. 9, 1948; Jan. 6, 1949; Glubb, *op. cit.,* 195; O'Ballance, *op. cit.,* 169. A Jewish Agency spokesman stated that 60,000 immigrants had arrived in Israel between May 15 and November 1, 1948, and that another 40,000 had arrived by December 8, *NY Times,* Nov. 10, Dec. 9, 1948.

22. A/648, Sept. 18, 17ff, 33; S/961, Aug. 12; S/891, July 13; S/915, July 23; S/1023, Oct. 2.

23. *NY Times,* July 30, Aug. 8, 14, 15, Sept. 17–20, 29, Oct. 3, 15, 20, 22, Nov. 9, 1949; J. Kimche, *op. cit.,* 272ff; Sacher, *op. cit.,* 295; O'Ballance, *op. cit.,* 166, 175; St. John, *op. cit.,* 163, 167; *Time,* Aug. 16, 1948, 25; Bilby, *op. cit.,* 18, 161; Folke Bernadotte, *To Jerusalem* (London, 1951), 60, 158, 222; Rony Gabbay, *A Political Study of the Arab-Jewish Conflict* (Paris, 1959), 155.

24. *NY Times,* Sept. 16, 17, 1948.

25. *Ibid.,* Oct. 15, 16, 1948.

26. Kimche, *op. cit.,* 274; St. John, *op. cit.,* 167; *NY Times,* Oct. 10, 31, 1948.

27. Sacher, *op. cit.,* 295; O'Ballance, *op. cit.,* 177. There were about 25 Jewish settlements with a total of approximately 2,000 persons in the area involved. All of these settlements had been established after 1939 in order to help strengthen Jewish claims to the Negev and also to provide strategic bases, according to Kirk, *The Middle East,* 222, 288.

28. *NY Times,* Oct. 8, 10, 1948.

29. S/1042, Oct. 18, 1948.

30. Sacher, *op. cit.,* 132, 295; St. John, *op. cit.,* 48; J. and D. Kimche, *op. cit.,* 206, 236.

31. S/1042, Oct. 18, 1948, 6; *NY Times,* Oct. 18–20, 1948.

32. O'Ballance, *op. cit.,* 156, 183f; Sacher, *op. cit.,* 263, 297, 299; J. and D. Kimche, *op. cit.,* 245ff; *NY Times,* Oct. 17, 18, 1948.

33. Sacher, *op. cit.,* 263; *NY Times,* Oct. 17–19, 1948.

34. *NY Times,* Oct. 29, 31, 1948; S/1023, Oct. 2; S/1040, Oct. 17; S/1042, Oct. 18; UN, OR of SC, 365th, Oct. 14, 4ff; 367th, Oct. 19, 2ff, 24ff; 374th, Oct. 28, 8f.

35. *NY Times,* October 26, 27, 1948.

36. *NY Times,* Oct. 21, 31, Nov. 13, 1948.

37. *Ibid.,* Oct. 21–31, Nov. 4–17, 1948; Jan. 6, 1949; UN, OR of SC, 374th, Oct. 28, 18ff; 375th, Oct. 29, 12ff; 376th, Nov. 4, 18f; Sacher, *op. cit.,* 303.

38. *NY Times,* October 28–31, 1948.

39. J. and D. Kimche, *op. cit.,* 255f.

40. S/1071, Nov. 6, 1949; *NY Times,* Oct. 31, Nov. 1, 2, 7, 1948.

41. UN, OR of SC, 3rd Year, 381st, Nov. 16, 1948, 8, 28; Sacher, *op. cit.,* 134.

42. *NY Times,* Nov. 14, 1948.

43. Bilby, *op. cit.,* 277.

44. *NY Times,* Dec. 31, 1948; St. John, *op. cit.,* 168f; Sacher, *op. cit.,* 304f.

45. St. John, *op. cit.,* 168f.

46. Bilby, *op. cit.,* 277; Kirk, *The Middle East,* 291f; *NY Times,* Dec. 29, 1948. Jan. 1, 1949.

47. O'Ballance, *op. cit.,* 201; *NY Times,* Jan. 4, 1949.

48. *NY Times,* Dec. 26, 27, 1948, Jan. 4–6, 8, 1949; O'Ballance, *op. cit.,* 198; Kirk, *The Middle East,* 293.

49. UN, OR of SC, 3rd Year, 394th, Dec. 28, 1948, 2ff.

50. J. and D. Kimche, *op. cit.,* 268.

51. *NY Times,* Jan. 6, 1949; Kirk, *The Middle East,* 293.

52. *N.Y. Times,* March 12, 1949; J. and D. Kimche, *op. cit.,* 267.

53. *NY Times,* Jan. 1, March 12, 22, 1949; Kirk, *The Middle East,* 297; J. and D. Kimche, *op. cit.,* 267; Glubb, *op. cit.,* 233f.

54. Glubb, *op. cit.,* 234ff.

55. Kirk, *The Middle East,* 297–99; Glubb, *op.cit.,* 234ff, 241; S/1302, April 4, 1949; J. and D. Kimche, *op. cit.,* 267f; *NY Times,* April 4, 1949; UN, *Survey of Opinion,* IV/20, May 17, 1949, 12; IV/22, May 31, 9.

56. Walter Eytan, *The First Ten Years* (New York, 1958,) 42; S/1353, July 20, 1949; *NY Times,* March 17, April 5, 8, 1949.

57. *NY Times,* Dec. 31, 1948; Carl von Horn, *Soldiering for Peace* (London, 1966), 66ff, 240, 283.

58. Von Horn, *op. cit.,* 61, 80, 126, 283.

59. *Jewish Exponent* (Philadelphia), Sept. 11, 1959, 18; A/PV.897, Oct. 10, 1960, 78ff; A/PV, 899, Oct. 11, 47ff; *NY Times,* May 23, June 4–12, 1948; Jan. 8, 1961; *Israel Digest* (Jerusalem), May 29, 1959, 3; *Israel Govt. Yearbook, 1958,* 135; Ben-Gurion, *op. cit.,* 382; Sacher, *op. cit.,* 278, 297; O'Ballance, *op. cit.,* 57, 80ff; J. and D. Kimche, *op. cit.,* 245ff.

Chapter V. Jerusalem—City of Peace and Source of Conflict

1. See statement by Brazilian delegate, UN, OR of 4th Ses of GA, *Ad Hoc* Pol Com, 45th Meeting, Nov. 25th, 1949, 267.

2. UN Conc. Com for Palestine, A/838, April 19, 1949, 4f; Constantine Rackauskas and the Committee on World Order, *The Internationalization of Jerusalem* (Washington, n.d.), 38, 47ff, 68ff.

3. UN, OR of 4th Ses GA, *Ad Hoc* Pol Com, 44th Meeting, Nov. 25, 1949, 261ff; 49th, Nov. 29, 293ff; 59th, Dec. 6, 352ff; A/939 April 19, 1949, 7ff. James Mac-Donald, The first American ambassador to Israel, wrote in *My Mission in Israel* (New York, 1951), 189, "There were some important Israeli leaders who consid-

ered the strategic vulnerability of Jerusalem and the economic advantages of its internationalization more important than its historical and religious appeal. These 'realists' would, had they dared, have favored a compromise or at any rate a less unyielding attitude than that adopted by Ben-Gurion and his Cabinet. But none of them spoke out, because Israeli public opinion was simply adamant against any form of internationalization of the New City."

4. *Times* (London), Sept. 22, 1949; Kirk, *The Middle East,* 306n.

5. A/838, April 19, 1949, 7ff; A/927, June 21, 1949, 9.

6. UN, OR of 3rd Ses of GA, Part II, 191st PM, April 13, 1949, 38ff; *Ad Hoc* Pol Com, 42nd, May 3, 186f; 45th, May 5, 227ff.

7. *Ibid.,* 217th PM, May 11, 330; *Ad Hoc* Pol Com, 46th, Nov. 26, 1949, 276. Also see statements of Belgium, Australia, and France, *ibid.,* 266; 43rd, Nov. 24, 251, 254.

8. UN, OR of 4th Ses of GA, *Ad Hoc* Pol Com, 44th, Nov. 25, 1949, 261ff; 49th, Nov. 29, 293ff; 59th, Dec. 6, 1949, 352ff.

9. *Ibid.,* 44th, Nov. 25, 257ff; 45th, Nov. 25, 268ff; 46th, Nov. 26, 277ff; 47th, Nov. 28, 279; 48th, Nov. 28, 284–91; 49th, Nov. 29, 292ff, 300; 58th, Dec. 6, 349f; 59th, Dec. 6, 356; 60th, Dec. 7, 359; A/927, 9.

10. UN, *Survey of Opinion,* IV/40, Oct. 4, 1949, 3; IV/42, Oct. 18, 12; IV/43, Oct. 25, 12; Kirk, *The Middle East,* 306; UN, OR of 5th Ses, *Ad Hoc* Pol Com, 46th, Nov. 26, 277; 58th, Dec. 6, 351.

11. *Ibid.,* 43rd, Nov. 24, 243, 247ff; 44th, 260f; 45th, 266, 270; 46th, 271ff; 47th, 280ff; 49th, 293ff; 50th, 302ff; 57th, Dec. 5, 342f; 60th, 361f; 61st, Dec. 7, 367; 274th PM, Dec. 9, 598ff, 605, 607; U.S. *Daily Worker,* Nov. 21, 1949, quoted in UN, *Survey of Opinion,* IV/48, Nov. 29, 1949, 10.

12. St. John, *op. cit.,* 220.

13. Kirk, *The Middle East,* 308; UN, OR of 2nd Spec Ses of Trusteeship Council (TC), 4th Meeting, Dec. 13, 1949, 37ff; 5th, Dec. 15, 47f.

14. UN, OR of 4th Ses of GA, 274th PM, Dec. 9, 1949, 581f, 588f, 594ff; UN, *Survey of Opinion,* IV/50, Dec. 13, 9.

15. UN, OR of 2nd Spec Ses of TC, 7th Meeting, Dec. 19, 1949, 69; UN, OR of 6th Ses of TC, 9th Meeting, Jan. 30, 1950, 48ff; 16th, Feb. 5, 109ff; 18th, Feb. 8, 128f; 20th, Feb. 10, 146ff.

16. *Ibid.,* 81st Meeting, April 4, 1950, 634ff; 78th, March 31, 622.

17. *Ibid.,* 81st. 634, 639f; 7th Ses, 2nd Meeting, June 2, 1950, 7; 8th, June 12, 56f; 10th, June 14, 74f.

18. UN, OR of 5th Ses of GA, *Ad Hoc* Pol Com, 73rd Meeting, Dec. 7, 1950, 469f; 74th, Dec. 8, 471ff; 75th, Dec. 8, 475ff; 76th, Dec. 11, 482; 77th, Dec. 11, 485ff; 78th, Dec. 12, 496ff; 80th, Dec. 13, 518f; 79th, Dec. 12, 506; 81st., Dec. 13, 517ff; 288th PM, Sept. 28, 167; 6th Ses *Ad Hoc* Pol Com, 40th, Jan. 14, 1952, 220; 7th Ses, *Ad Hoc* Pol Com, 30th, Dec. 2, 1952, 175; 400th PM, Dec. 18, 1952, 413ff; 8th Ses, 447th PM, Sept. 28, 1953, 182f; 445th, Sept. 25, 151; 448th, Sept, 28, 195; 9th Ses, 1st Com, 741st, Dec. 6, 1954, 496; 10th Ses, 523rd PM, Sept. 26, 1955, 87; 11th Ses, 595th PM, Nov. 26, 1956, 313.

19. U.S. Dept. State, *American Foreign Policy, 1950–1955: Basic Documents* (Washington, 1957), II, 2254f; *The Middle East J.,* Autumn, 1953, 506, 511f; *Middle East Report,* Sept. 18, 1953, 3; *NY Times,* April 11, 1954.

20. *NY Times,* Dec. 3, 1953; April 11, 1954.

21. *Ibid.,* Nov. 3, 4, 5, 9, 11, 1954; Dec. 15, 1962; *American Foreign Policy,* 2255; *Israel Govt Yearbook,* 1959/60, 308ff; Harry N. Howard, *U.S. Policy in the*

Near East, South Asia and Africa, 1954 (Washington, 1955), 31f. By 1966, twenty states, mostly from Africa and Latin America, had moved their diplomatic establishments to Jerusalem.

22. *NY Times,* Oct. 23, 1962; *Daily Star* (Beirut), Jan. 5, 1964.

23. *Arab News Bulletin* (London), Aug. 9, 1946, 3; *ibid.* (Washington), July 5, 1947, 8; UN, OR of 11th Ses of GA, 588th PM, Nov. 21, 1956; *Middle East Opinion* (Cairo), July 15, 1946, 11; Aug. 19, 1946, 12f; *The Middle East J.,* July, 1947, 313; Jan., 1948, 63; Spring, 1951, 200; *NY Times,* Jan. 3, 6, 1951; Dec. 5, 19, 24, 1963.

24. *Arab News and Views* (Arab Information Center, N.Y.), Sept. 15, 1966, 1; *NY Times,* Aug. 31, Sept. 2, 12, 13, Oct. 4, 1966.

25. *NY Times,* June 15, 1967.

26. *NY Times,* June 29, July 14, 1967.

27. *Ibid.,* June 24, 27, 1967.

28. *Ibid.*

29. *Ibid.,* June 18, 25, 1967.

30. Sanche de Gramont, "Jerusalem: Experiment in Coexistence," *NY Times,* Magazine, July 30, 1967, 14.

31. *NY Times,* June 29, 1967.

32. A/PV., 1529, June 21, 1967, 12, 27; APV. 1542, June 29, 1967.

33. S/8052.

34. *NY Times,* July 12, 1967.

35. *Ibid.,* July 13, 14, 16, 1967; *Evening Bulletin,* July 15, 1967.

36. *NY Times,* July 13, 16, 21, 1967; *Evening Bulletin,* July 13, 1967.

37. In the middle of August, 1967, U Thant appointed Ambassador Thalmann as his personal representative in Jerusalem to gather information needed by the Secretary-General to prepare a report on the Jerusalem situation as required by resolution 2254 (ES-V) passed by the General Assembly on July 14. Because Israel strongly opposed providing Thalmann with broad powers and functions, he was instructed to visit the Holy City in the latter part of August on a fact-finding mission only. Since he made little effort to go much beyond presenting mostly unevaluated data which was submitted to him primarily by Israeli sources, Ambassador Thalmann's report was not very helpful or informative. Besides noting the material and other benefits which the Arabs in the Old City would gain from a united city, he indicated that while the Arabs were generally resigned and willing to cooperate with a regime of military occupation, they "were opposed" to the imposition of Israeli laws and to their "civil incorporation into the Israel state system" and they were fearful of racial and religious discrimination and uneasy about their future, S/8146, September 12, 1967.

38. Information from personal interviews.

39. Sanche de Gramont, *op. cit.,* 18, 20.

40. *NY Times,* Aug. 18, 1967.

41. *Ibid.,* July 25, 1967; S/8093, July 25, 1967; S/8107, Aug. 3; S/8109, Aug. 3; S/8146, Sept. 12, 21ff.

42. Sanche de Gramont, *op. cit.,* 22.

43. *NY Times,* Aug. 21, 1967.

Chapter VI. The Arab Refugees

1. Peretz, *op. cit.,* 6f; A/1905, Sept. 28, 1951, 1; A/648, Part III, Sept. 18, 1948, 1, 24; Hurewitz, *The Struggle,* 313f; Kirk, *The Middle East,* 261, 263; *Israel's*

Struggle for Peace, 90; Gabbay, *op. cit.,* 85f, 96f; Begin, *op. cit.,* 164f; Kimche, *op. cit.,* 227; Lucille W. Pevsner, "The Arab Refugees," *J. of International Affairs* (Columbia University), III, No. 1, 1953, 43; Theodore Huebner and Carl Voss, *This is Israel* (New York, 1956), 91.

2. Erskine B. Childers, a British journalist, made an intensive effort to find some proof of the existence of the alleged orders. He interviewed Arab leaders, checked the monitored records made by official British and American sources of all radio broadcasts made during the months involved, and asked Israeli officials to show him whatever documentary proof they had concerning these claims. After his investigation, Childers reported that he found "not a single order, or appeal, or support about evacuation from Palestine from any Arab nation, inside or outside of Palestine, in 1948." In fact, there was "repeated monitory record of Arab appeals, even flat orders, to the civilians of Palestine to stay put" and not to leave. Childers, "The Other Exodus," *The Spectator,* May 21, 1961. See also letters to the editor in the May 26, June 2, 9, 16, 23, and 30, 1961, issues of this British weekly, and Walid Khalidy, "The Fall of Haifa," *Middle East Forum* (Beirut), Dec., 1959, 24.

3. O'Ballance, *op. cit.,* 147, 150, 171f; Bilby, *op. cit.,* 31; Kirk, *The Middle East,* 281; Glubb, *op. cit.,* 162; Sacher, *op. cit.,* 149; Gabby, *op. cit.,* 108f; Kimche, *op. cit.,* 226f; Hal Lehrman, "The Arabs of Israel," *Commentary,* VIII, No. 6, Dec., 1949, 529f; James Ludlow, *Department of State Bulletin,* XXXIX, No. 1012, Nov. 17, 1958, 775; *NY Times,* Aug. 8, 1948; A/648, Part III, 1. Some 7,000 Jews fled their homes during the earlier phases of the Palestine War. Most of these were women and children temporarily evacuated from the Israeli-held part of Jerusalem because of the heavy fighting and the difficulty involved in keeping Jerusalem supplied with food and other necessities of life. According to the Israeli government, only 1,700 Palestine Jews ultimately became "refugees" as a result of the war, *Israel's Struggle for Peace,* 89.

4. *NY Times,* Oct. 31, Nov. 1, 2, 7, 1948; March 11, 15, 1949; S/1071, Nov. 6, 1948, 4; S/1122, Jan. 26, 1949; S/1286, March 14, 1949; see also Chapter IV.

5. S/1797, Sept. 18, 1950; S/2234, July 8, 1951; S/2300, Aug. 16, 1951.

6. A/648, Part III, 1ff, 17, 23ff, 53.

7. A/838, April 19, 1949, Part I, 1ff, 7; Part II, 7.

8. Gabby, *op. cit.,* 153.

9. Bilby, *op. cit.,* 231, 239; Gabbay, *op. cit.,* 280.

10. MacDonald, *op. cit.,* 175, 181, 184; Peretz, *op. cit.,* 41f; Bilby, *op. cit.,* 239.

11. A/927, June 21, 1949, 4; A/992, Sept. 22, 1949, 1–6; Peretz, *op. cit.,* 43ff; Gabby, *op. cit.,* 244f; Kirk, *The Middle East,* 303; Bilby, *op. cit.,* 240; *UN Survey of Opinion,* IV/28, July 12, 1949, 8.

12. Peretz, *op. cit.,* 64.

13. *Ibid.,* 55; A/992, 4ff, 8; Gabbay, *op. cit.,* 311.

14. A/992, 9, 13; A/1252, Dec. 14, 1949, 2.

15. Gordon Clapp, "An Approach to Economic Development," *International Conciliation,* April, 1950, 211f.

16. A/AC.25/6, Dec. 28, 1949, Part I, 3; A/992, 11; A/1252, 2; Fred J. Khouri, "The Jordan River Controversy," *The Review of Politics,* Jan., 1965, 35.

17. UN, OR of 4th Ses of GA, *Ad Hoc Pol Com,* 51st Meeting, Nov. 30, 1949, 307ff; 52nd, Nov. 30, 311ff; 54th, Dec. 2, 316ff; 55th, Dec. 2, 320ff, 329f; 273rd PM, Dec. 8, 571.

18. A/1255, May 29, 1950, 2; A/1367, Sept. 22, 44; A/1451, Oct. 19, 20.

19. A/1255, 2, 7ff; A/1288, July 17, 1950, 3; A/1367, 43, 60; A/1367/Add 1,

Oct. 24, 5; A/1451, 6, 14f, 31f; UN, OR of 5th Ses of GA, *Ad Hoc* Pol Com, 31st, Nov. 1, 1950, 194f.

20. A/1793, March 22, 1951, 1.

21. *Department of State Bulletin,* XXXIX, No. 1012, Nov. 17, 1958, 778; A/1985, 2ff, 10.

22. UN, OR of 5th Ses of GA, *Ad Hoc* Pol Com, 35th, Nov. 7, 213f; 61st, Nov. 29, 394; 70th, Dec. 5, 454; Peretz, *op. cit.,* 192, 196, 200f; Gabbay, *op. cit.,* 283ff, 368.

23. A/3199, Oct. 4, 1956, 1, 3ff; A/3835, June 18, 1958, 1; A/4225, Sept. 22, 1959, 4ff; A/4225/Add 1, Nov. 12, 1959; A/4573, Nov. 14, 1960, 2; *Israel's Struggle for Peace,* 107; *NY Times,* Sept. 28; Nov. 4, 5, 1954.

24. A/2171, 1952, 2ff; A/2171/Add 1, 1952, 1f; A/2210, 1952, 5; OR of 7th Ses of GA, *Ad Hoc* Pol Com, 3rd, Oct. 23, 1952, 9ff; A/2470, 1953, 1ff; A/2470/Add 1, Oct. 26, 1953, 1ff; UN, OR of 8th Ses of GA, *Ad Hoc* Pol Com, 23rd, Nov. 2, 1953, 113; *UNRWA Reviews: A Background Information Series* (Beirut, 1962), No. 5, 7f; No. 1, 18ff.

25. UNRWA has reported that the total number of refugees had increased from 904,122 in June, 1951, to 1,344,576 as of May 31, 1967. In the same period, full rations had increased from 826,459 to only 845,625 (A/6713, Table 1). From the beginning, Israel, using population statistics provided by the Palestine Mandate authorities, has contended that UNRWA's refugee figures were inaccurate and exaggerated. Actually, the last complete census was taken in Palestine in 1931, and only population estimates were made by British authorities after that date. British officials have admitted that the official population figure given for the rootless Bedouins in 1931 was far below what it should have been. Moreover, this inadequate figure was left unchanged after 1931 despite the fact that there was a natural population increase as a result of a declining death rate and high birth rate. The post-World War II population estimate also ignored the influx of many Arabs from the neighboring areas into Palestine. Then, too, the original census figures did not take into consideration the natural reluctance of many Palestinians to supply true census figures because of their fear that these would be used to assess taxes (Gabbay, *op. cit.,* 6f, 9, 165; A/364/Add 3, 1f). UNRWA has indicated yet another source for error by those Israelis who have used the 1931 census and later British estimates in order to come up with a much smaller figure than UNRWA did for the total number of legitimate refugees. UNRWA pointed out that many Palestine Arabs had moved into such cities as Jerusalem, Jaffa, and Haifa from the rural areas after 1931—as part of a general trend from rural to urban areas— and this brought about a "double source of error into any estimates of the number of persons who could have become refugees, since more people came out of the towns in Israeli-held territory than were registered there and fewer people were actually living in the villages of the area which was later annexed by Jordan." (A/1905, Sept. 28, 1951, 1) Consequently, there is no way of ascertaining exact population and refugee figures. In the final analysis, the exact figures would only affect the extent of the refugee problem, but not its fundamentals.

26. A/2470/Add 1, 1; A/3931, 1958, 2; A/4213, 1959, 5; A/4478, 1960, 1; UN, OR of 14th Ses of GA, Spec Pol Com, 149th, Nov. 10, 1959, 103.

27. A/2978, 1955, 1–6; UN, OR of 11th Ses of GA, Spec Pol Com, 23rd, Feb. 11, 1957, 10; *UNRWA Reviews,* No. 5, 10.

28. *Hearings on the Palestine Refugee Problem before the Senate Subcommittee on the Near East and Africa of the Committee on Foreign Relations* (Washington,

D. C., 1953), 1; A/2171, 1–6; A/2717, 1954, 1–6; A/2712/Add 1, 1954, 1ff; A/2470/Add 1, 1; UN, OR of 9th Ses of GA, *Ad Hoc* Pol Com, 28th, Nov. 16, 1954, 127; OR of 10th Ses, *Ad Hoc* Pol Com, 22nd, Nov. 28, 1955, 93f.

29. A/4478, 1–5; O. Remba, "The Arab Press Reviews the Refugee Dilemma," *Land Reborn,* Dec., 1960, 14.

30. Khouri, *op. cit.,* 40f; St. John, *op. cit.,* 55, 168, 282, 292, 335; Lt. Gen. E. L. M. Burns, *Between Arab and Israeli* (London, 1962), 112f. Also see Chapters VII and VIII for more detailed information about the border conflicts, the arms race, and other topics discussed in the paragraph.

31. A/2978, 9; A/3686, 1957, 1f; A/3931, 1; A/4213, 1959, 2; UN, OR of 11th Ses of GA, Spec Pol Com, 23rd, Feb. 11, 107; 12th Ses, Spec Pol Com, 64th, Nov. 18, 1957, 99; 13th Ses, Spec Pol Com, 101st, Nov. 7, 1958, 65f.

32. 8th Ses, *Ad Hoc* Pol Com, 23rd, Nov. 2, 1953, 113; 11th Ses, Spec Pol Com, 27th, Feb. 19, 1957, 124; 29th, Feb. 20, 136; 12th Ses, Spec Pol Com, 64th, Nov. 18, 1957, 99, 101; 65th, Nov. 19, 103f; 75th, Dec. 3, 148; 76th, Dec. 4, 149; 13th Ses, Spec Pol Com, 101st, Nov. 7, 1958, 66; 14th Ses, Spec Pol Com, 149th, Nov. 10, 1959, 103; A/4478, 2, 5, 8; *Palestine Refugee Program: Background Information for the Study of the Palestine Refugee Program,* Staff Memorandum, Senate Foreign Relations Committee, 1953, 12f; *Palestine Refugee Problem: Report of the Subcommittee on the Near East and Africa,* Senate Foreign Relations Committee, 1953, 4; *NY Times,* Nov. 11, 1958; Nov. 20, 1960; Crabb, *op. cit.,* 135f.

33. See, for a more detailed study of the Johnston Mission, Khouri, *op. cit.,* 38–41. See also Chapter VII.

34. "A Survey of the Arab Refugee Problem." *Department of State Bulletin,* XXX, No. 760, Jan. 18, 1954, 101; *Review of Foreign Policy: Hearings before the Committee on Foreign Relations,* U.S. Senate, 1958, 541.

35. *NY Times,* Aug. 27, 1955; John Beal, *John Foster Dulles* (New York, 1957), 253. See also Chapter IX.

36. UN, OR of 12th Ses of GA, Spec Pol Com, 76th, Dec. 4, 1957, 149; *Hearings on the Palestine Refugee Problem,* 4; G. Lewis Jones, "Mutual Security Program in the Near East and South Asia," *Department of State Bulletin,* XLI, No. 1088, April 18, 1960, 613.

37. *NY Times,* Aug. 19, Oct. 6, 9, 1959; *Arab News and Views* (New York), V, No. 18, Sept. 15, 1959, 1, 6; No. 19, Oct. 1, 1; Izzat Tannous, *Failure of the UN in the Palestine Tragedy* (New York, 1959); *The Israel Digest,* II, No. 25, Dec. 11, 1959, 3; No. 26, Dec. 25, 1959, 3f; UN, OR of 14th Ses of GA, Spec Pol Com, 150th, Nov. 12, 1959, 109f; 162nd, Nov. 30, 163ff.

38. *Ibid.,* 155th, Nov. 20, 125; 171st, Dec. 8, 209; *NY Times,* Dec. 4, 8, 9, 1959.

39. Letter to Jordan quoted in *NY Times,* June 26, 1961; A/4573, 3.

40. *NY Times,* Oct. 3, 1962; *Daily Star* (Beirut), May 29; Oct. 3, 1962; Jan. 14–18, 1964; Joseph E. Johnson, "Arab vs. Israeli: A Persistent Challenge to America," Address given before The American Assembly, Arden House, Harriman, N.Y., Oct. 24, 1963.

41. A/SPC/SR.307, Dec. 5, 1961, 2ff; A/SPC/SR.315, Dec. 12, 2ff; A/SPC/SR.316, Dec. 13, 10ff; *Daily Star,* April 13, June 25, July 5, Aug. 24, Oct. 2, 19, 25, 1962.

42. A/5545, Nov. 1, 1963, 1ff; *Daily Star,* Jan. 30, Nov. 5, 9, Dec. 25, 1963.

43. UN, OR of 14th Ses of GA, Spec Pol Com, 171st, Dec. 8, 1959, 209; A/SPC/SR.313, Dec. 11, 1961, 6; A/SPC/SR.314, Dec. 11, 6ff, 15; A/SPC/SR.365, Dec. 11, 1962, 3; A/SPC/SR.367, Dec. 12, 17.

44. A/SPC/SR.200, Nov. 15, 1960, 4; A/SPC/SR.207, Nov. 24, 1960, 4f; A/SPC/SR.209, Nov. 28, 1; A/SPC/SR.307, Dec. 5, 1961, 9; A/SPC/SR.309, Dec. 6, 1961, 10; A/SPC/SR.370, Dec. 14, 1962, 7.

45. A/SPC/SR.310, Dec. 7, 1961, 8f; A/SPC/SR.316, Dec. 13, 1961, 15, 21; A/SPC/SR.317, Dec. 14, 1961, 9; A/SPC/SR.318, Dec. 15, 1961, 3f; A/SPC/SR.323, Dec. 19, 1961, 6; A/SPC/SR.370, Dec. 14, 1962, 10; A/SPC/SR.371, Dec. 14, 1962, 9.

46. UN, OR of 12th Ses of GA, Spec Pol Com, 66th, Nov. 20, 1957, 110; 728th PM, Dec. 12, 579.

47. NY Times, June 12, 13, 25, 1967; The Economist, June 19, 1967; S/8021, June 29, 1967, Annex I, p. 1.

48. NY Times, June 11, 12, 13, 15, 21, 24, 26, 30; August 10, 24, 27, 1967; Gramont, op. cit., 18, 22, 25; The Times (London), July 27, 1967; S/8001/Add 1, July 4, 1967, 3; S/8013, June 23; S/8117, Aug. 10, 2; S/8123, Aug. 16; A/6713, Oct., 1967, 11; S/8158, Oct. 2, 1967, 9.

49. NY Times, July 3, 1967.

50. Ibid., June 26, Aug. 14, 1967.

51. Ibid., June 13, Aug. 25, 1967.

52. Ibid., June 12, 24, July 6, 1967; The Evening Bulletin, June 11, 24, 1967.

53. Israel Digest, July 14, 1967, 5; The Evening Bulletin, July 3, 1967; NY Times, July 3, 4, Aug. 14, 21, 25, 1967.

54. NY Times, July 5, 6, 1967; The Evening Bulletin, Aug. 8, 1967.

55. Christian Science Monitor, Aug. 1, 1967; The Times (London), July 27, 1967; NY Times, July 15, Aug. 23, Sept. 1, 2, Nov. 28, 1967; A/AC. 132/PV. 1, Dec. 6, 1967, 6f.

56. Quoted in NY Times, August. 8, 1967.

57. Ibid., Aug. 14, 17, 18, 19, 23, 28, Sept. 1, 1967; A/6713, Oct., 1967, 13; The Evening Bulletin, Aug. 13, 18, 19, 1967.

58. The Evening Bulletin, Aug. 25, 29, 1967; S/8032, July 25, 1967; NY Times, Aug. 23, 25, 26, 1967.

59. NY Times, Aug. 24, 30, 31, Sept. 1, 2, 12, 1967.

60. Ibid., June 16; July 2, 3; Aug. 26, 30; Sept. 2, 4, 7, 11, 12; Nov. 28, 1967; A/6713, 21; A/SPC/121, Dec. 13, 1967, 2ff; U.S. News and World Report, Aug. 14, 1967, 82; Israel allowed some trade to continue between Jordan and the occupied west-bank zone. She did this because it helped to relieve the troubled economic situation in the west bank, to make it easier to rule over the Jordanians there, and to keep some lines of communication open with Jordan. Jordan, in turn, hoped to benefit both economically and politically from the continuation of commercial and personal contacts with her people living under Israeli control, NY Times, Jan. 15, 1968.

61. S/8001, June 20, 1967, 1; S/8010, June 23; S/8124, Aug. 15, 5; A/6713, 10ff, 100; UN Weekly News Summary, WS/301, July 7, 1967, 5; WS/305, Aug. 14, 5.

62. A/SPC/SR.588, Dec. 18, 1967, 2ff; A/SPC/SR.594, Dec. 20, 2ff.

63. A/SPC/PV.584, Dec. 13, 1967, 4ff; A/SPC/PV.585, Dec. 12, 7ff; A/SPC/SR.587, Dec. 15, 3ff; A/SPC/SR.588, Dec. 18, 8ff, 16ff; A/SPC/SR.590, Dec. 19, 5ff, 24ff; A/SPC/SR.591, Dec. 19, 4ff, 8ff, 16ff; A/SPC/SR.593, Dec. 20, 3ff; A/SPC/SR.594, Dec. 20, 7ff.

64. A/SPC/PV.584, Dec. 13, 2ff; A/SPC/SR.586, Dec. 15, 2ff; A/SPC/SR.588 Dec. 18, 11ff; A/SPC/SR.590, Dec. 19, 2ff, 17ff, 26, 31; A/SPC/SR.591, Dec. 19,

2ff, 6ff, 11ff; A/SPC/SR.593, Dec. 20, 2, 7ff; A/SPC/SR.594, Dec. 20, 5f; A/PV.1640, Dec. 19, 6ff.

65. UN, OR of 8th Ses of GA, *Ad hoc* Pol Com, 29th, Nov. 11, 1953, 141ff; 9th Ses, *Ad Hoc* Pol Com, 35th, Nov. 26, 1954, 163ff; 38th, Nov. 30, 177; 10th Ses, *Ad Hoc* Pol Com, 17th, Nov. 8, 1955, 65ff; 11th Ses. Spec Pol Com, 28th, Feb. 19, 1957, 127ff; 13th Ses, Spec Pol Com, 106th, Nov. 17, 1958, 82ff; 108th, Nov. 19, 96ff; 111th, Nov. 24, 110f; 113th, Nov. 26, 118; 14th Ses, Spec Pol Com, 105th, Nov. 12, 1959, 109f; 162nd, Nov. 30, 163ff; 15th Ses, Spec Pol Com, A/SPC/SR.209, Nov. 28, 1960, 13ff; A/3199, 3ff; *NY Times,* Nov. 12, 1953; Jan. 10; Oct. 10, 1956; Oct. 6; Dec. 1, 1959; *Israel Digest,* Dec. 25, 1959, 3f.

66. UN, OR of 12th Ses of GA, Spec Pol Com, 70th, Nov. 27, 1957, 128; 14th Ses, Spec Pol Com, 150th, Nov. 12, 1959, 110.

67. A/5813, 8. See also the reports by the Commissioner-General of UNRWA for the years 1964–65 and 1965–66 for the direct contributions made by the host countries to the refugees ($6,646,410 and $7,603,708), as well as the contributions made to UNRWA. A/6013, 6 and table 19, 33f; A/6313, 70, table 19, 58–61.

68. A/5813, 8, 37f; Harry N. Howard, "Arabs: DP's and Hosts," *Issues* (New York), Spring, 1962, 55ff; *UNRWA Reviews,* No. 1, 22f; A/4121, June 15, 1959, 12; A/4213, 1959, 2, 5; A/3686, 7f, 38f; A/3931, 3, 7, 13, 19, 24ff; UN, OR of 12th Ses of GA, Spec Pol Com, 64th, Nov. 18, 1957, 101; 14th Ses, Spec Pol Com, 149th, Nov. 10, 1959, 103; Gabbay, *op. cit.,* 211, 218f; personal interviews with many of the top UNRWA officials in the host states and with Arab officials dealing with the refugees.

69. *U.S. Foreign Policy: Middle East Staff Study Prepared for the Use of the Committee on Foreign Relations,* U.S. Senate, No. 13, June 9, 1960, 38f; Joseph E. Johnson, *op. cit.,* 10; Ludlow, *op. cit.,* 779f; *Hearings on the Palestine Refugee Problem,* 96; Institute for Mediterranean Affairs, *The Palestine Refugee Problem* (New York, 1958); *NY Times,* Oct. 20; Nov. 15, 1955; April 12, 1957; James A. Pike, "Key Piece in the Mideast Puzzle," *NY Times Magazine,* May 19, 1957, 36, 38; Gabbay, *op. cit.,* 308; Michael Adams, *Suez and After* (Boston, 1958), 208; Harry E. Ellis, *Heritage of the Desert* (New York, 1956), 295.

70. Morris Sacks, "Economic Illusions and Reality," *New Outlook,* March–April, 1963, 77; Z.K., "America and the Refugees," *ibid.,* Feb., 1963, 9.

71. Beal, *op. cit.,*

72. UN, OR of 12th Ses of GA, Spec Pol Com, 70th, Nov. 27, 1957, 129; 14th Ses, Spec Pol Com, 162nd, Nov. 30, 1959, 164; A/SPC/SR.318, Dec. 15, 1961, 8.

73. Donald C. Burgus, "Palestine: Focal Point of Tension," *Department of State Bulletin,* XXXIV, No. 874, March 26, 1956, 505.

74. *U.S. Foreign Policy: Middle East,* 38. Words italicized in the original study.

75. *NY Times,* Jan. 22, 1956; Aubrey Hodes, "Signpost to a Solution," *New Outlook,* March–April, 1964, 37f; Meir Grossman, "Solving the Arab Refugee Problem," *ibid.,* July–Aug., 1962, 28; Dr. Ze'ev Katz, *ibid.,* 30f; Simha Flapan, "The Knesset Votes on the Refugee Problem," *ibid.,* Dec. 1961, 9f; Martin Buber, "Statement on Arab Refugee Problem," *ibid.,* Jan., 1962, 8; Shimon Shereskevsky, "Peace—Without a Peace Treaty," *ibid.,* July, 1961, 3–9.

76. A/2978, 8; A/3212, 2, 9; A/3686, 2, 8f; A/3931, 7; A/4213, 3, 6; A/4478, 10; UN, OR of 14th Ses of GA, Spec Pol Com, 149th, Nov. 10, 1959, 103.

77. *U.S. News and World Report;* Don Peretz, "Israel's Administration and Arab Refugees," *Foreign Affairs,* Jan. 1968, 346.

78. UN, OR of 10th Ses, *Ad Hoc* Pol Com, 19th, Nov. 22, 1955, 78; 11th Ses,

Spec Pol Com, 28th, Feb. 18, 1957, 127; 29th Feb. 20, 136; 12th Ses, Spec Pol Com, 69th, Nov. 26, 1957, 121, 124; 13th Ses, 107th, Nov. 18, 1958, 89f; 14th Ses, Spec Pol Com, 155th, Nov. 20, 1959, 126; 159th, Nov. 26, 148ff; 162nd, Nov. 30, 164; 15th Ses, Spec Pol Com, 203rd, Nov. 18, 1960, 131; A/648, Part III, 23ff, 53; A/992, Sept. 22, 1949, 4ff; A/1985, 2ff, 10; *NY Times,* Aug. 27; Nov. 10, 1955; May 19, 1957, *Magazine,* 12, 34, 36, 38; Nov. 8, 1957; Nov. 27, 1959; June 16, 1960; Nov. 20, 1960; June 26, 1961; *Land Reborn,* Dec.–Jan., 1957–58, 10f; Dr. Effan Rees, "Refugees in the Middle East," *The Refugee Problem Today and Tomorrow* (Geneva, 1957), 7; *Institute for Mediterranean Affairs,* 4, 34ff; *The Middle East and Southern Europe; Report of Sen. H. H. Humphrey,* U.S. Senate, 1957, 4f; *Congressional Record, Proceedings and Debates of the 86th Congress Second Session,* Vol. 106, No. 109, June 15, 1960; *U.S. Foreign Policy: Middle East,* 36–41. See also the articles in *New Outlook* mentioned in footnote 75.

Chapter VII. Armistice Complications and the Sinai War

1. *NY Times,* April 5, 1949; UN, OR of SC, 433rd, Aug. 4, 1949, 76, 84; 542nd, April 25, 1951, 10; *Israel Digest,* April 20, 1956, 1.

2. UN, OR of SC, 433rd, 6; *NY Times,* Dec. 25, 1948.

3. S/3596, May 9, 1956, 23f, Annex VIII; S/3319 & Corr. 1, Nov. 16, 1954; S/3373, March 17, 1955; S/3390, April 14, 1955, 7f; S/3393, April 18, 1955; S/1459, Feb. 20, 1950; S/3659, Sept. 27, 1956, 5f; UN, OR of SC, 696th, March 30, 1955, 13f, 23ff; 698th, April 19, 2ff; 700th, Sept. 8, 17f; *NY Times,* Aug. 2, 4; Oct. 18, 1954; March 30; June 9, 13, 29; July 7, 8, 14–16, 21; Aug. 5, 19, 25; Sept. 8, 21, 1955; Feb. 8, 1956; April 22, 1957; Elmo Hutchinson, *Violent Truce* (New York, 1956), 19, 100f.

4. S/3394, April 18, 1955; S/3373, Annex VIII; S/3390, 8; S/3596, p. 23, Annex VIII; *NY Times,* May 11, 1955.

5. S/3596, 21f, Annex VIII; S/3659, 9f; S/3390, 8; UN, OR of SC, 698th, 2ff; 700th, 17f; S/3393; *NY Times,* July 1; Aug. 2; Sept. 27; Oct. 10, 1954; Feb. 8, 17; May 1–3, 24; July 22, 26; Sept. 29, 1956.

6. S/2084, April 12, 1951; S/2388, Nov. 8, 1951, 9; Fred J. Khouri, "The Policy of Retaliation in Arab-Israeli Relations," *Middle East J.,* Autumn, 1966, 436f (see this article for all phases of the problem of retaliation); UN, OR of SC, 542nd, April 25, 1951, 5ff; *NY Times,* April 7, 1951.

7. *Israel Govt Yearbook, 1958,* 136; *Israel and the United Nations* (New York, 1956), 248; St. John, *op. cit.,* 55, 168, 282, 292; Litvinoff, *op. cit.,* 217; Eytan, *op. cit.,* 99f; Ben-Gurion, "Israel's Security and Her International Position," *Israel Govt Yearbook, 1959/60,* 17.

8. *NY Times,* March 30; April 9; July 5, 1954; April 6; June 18; July 31; Nov. 6; Dec. 17, 1955; Jan. 2, 4; Feb. 22; June 18; July 11; Sept. 30, 1956; Feb. 14, 1957; St. John, *op. cit.,* 292; Eliezer Ben-Moshe, "The Peace That Does Not Come," *New Outlook* (Tel Aviv), July, 1961, 22f; Shimon Shereshevsky, "Peace —Wanted a Peace Treaty," *ibid.,* 3ff; Gerda Luft, "Wait and See—A Blind Alley," *ibid.,* May–June, 1961, 10; Litvinoff, *op. cit.,* 217.

9. S/3685, Oct. 18, 1956, 7f.

10. S/3670, Oct. 13, 1956, 7f.

11. Gabbay, *op. cit.,* 325.

12. *NY Times,* Nov. 6, 1955; Feb. 2, 1959.

13. *Ibid.,* Nov. 6, 1955; Feb. 2, 1959; George Lenczowski, *The Middle East in World Affairs* (Ithaca, 1962), 3d ed., 419f; Anthony Nutting, *I Saw for Myself: The Aftermath of Suez* (Garden City, 1958), 91f.

14. S/3139/Rev. 2, Nov. 24, 1953; S/3373, March 17, 1955; S/3378, March 28; S/3390/Add 1, April 18, 7f; S/3538, Jan. 19, 1956; S/3596, 5ff, 15; S/3638, Aug. 21, 1956, Annex 11, 2; S/3670, Oct. 13, 1956, Annex IV, 2; UN, OR of SC, 630th, Oct. 27, 1953, 19ff; 635th, Nov. 9, 26; 695th, March 29, 1955, 5ff; 698th, April 19, 3ff, 15ff; *NY Times,* April 10, 1951; Sept. 27, 1954; Nov. 6; Dec. 14, 15, 17, 29, 1955; Jan. 13, 14, 20, 1956.

15. *NY Times,* Dec. 14, 1955; S/2388, Nov. 8, 1951, 11; S/1631, July 26, 1950; UN, OR of SC, 630th, Oct. 27, 1953, 18.

16. UN, OR of SC, 541st, April 17, 1951, 3ff; 542nd, April 25, 27ff; 544th, May 2, 7ff; 629th, Oct. 27, 1953, 18; 630th, Oct. 27, 14ff; S/PV.1001, April 4, 1962, Annex, 1ff, 7; S/2049, March 21, 1951; S/2067, April 4, 2ff; S/2833, Oct. 30, 1952, 21ff; S/3815, April 23, 1957, 5; S/4270, Feb. 23, 1960, 1f, 5ff, 12ff; Personal interviews with UN and Syrian officials. See also Fred J. Khouri, "Friction and Conflict on the Israeli-Syrian Front," *The Middle East J.,* Winter–Spring, 1963, 14ff.

17. Khouri, *ibid.,* 18; S/3844, July 1, 1957, 47.

18. S/2152/Rev. 2, May 18, 1951; S/3151/Rev. 2, Jan. 20, 1954; S/3530/Rev. 3, Jan. 18, 1956; S/5110/Corr. 1, April 9, 1962; UN, OR of SC, 546th, May 16, 1951, 9ff; 648th, Dec. 16, 1953, 2ff; 650th, Dec. 18, 6, 11ff; S/PV. 782, May 28, 1957, 38; S/PV.845, Jan. 30, 1959, 51ff; S/PV.1003, April 5, 1962, 21f; *NY Times,* Oct. 21, 22, 29, 1953.

19. S/1459, Feb. 20, 1950, 12; S/2084, April 12, 1951; S/2300, Aug. 17, 1951, 8; S/2234, July 9; S/2389, Nov. 8, 1951, 1, 4ff; S/2833, Nov. 4, 1952; S/3596, Annex VII; personal interviews.

20. See Abraham M. Hirsch, "Utilization of International Rivers in the Middle East," *American J. of Internat. Law,* Jan., 1956, 91; *Official Gazette of the Government of Palestine,* No. 115, May 15, 1924, 662ff; No. 161, April 16, 1926, 203ff.

21. S/3516, Dec. 20, 1955, 5f, 11f; S/3122, Oct. 23, 1953, Annex III, 9; S/3558, March 13, 1956, 1ff; S/3596, 25f; S/3659, 9ff, Annex VIII; S/5102, March 26, 1962, 4; UN, OR of SC, 639th, Nov. 18, 1953, 19ff; S/PV.1002, April 5, 1962, 36ff; *NY Times,* Dec. 13, 14, 17, 23, 1955; May 12, 1956; July 17; Aug. 5, 8, 13, 30, 1957.

22. S/4270, Feb. 23, 1950, 1; S/2101, April 24, 1951; S/3516, 4ff; S/3516/Add 1, Dec. 30, 1955, 21; S/3558, 5; *NY Times,* Dec. 14, 1955. Lt. General E. L. Burns, Chief of Staff of UNTSO at the time, believed that the December 10 incident had been provoked "deliberately" by Israel to give her the excuse to attack Syria in order to show Syria Israel's power and to warn her against tying herself too closely to Egypt. Burns, *op. cit.,* 118f.

23. S/3516, 5f, 11f; S/3558, 1ff; S/3596, 25f; S/3659, 9ff, Annex VIII; S/5102, 4; S/PV.1002, 36ff; *NY Times,* Dec. 14, 17, 23, 1955; May 12, 1956; July 17; Aug. 5, 8, 13, 30, 1957.

24. S/3685, Oct. 18, 1956; S/3660, Sept. 27; S/3670, Oct. 13, 3; UN, OR of SC, 744th, Oct. 19, 1956; 745th, Oct. 25; *NY Times,* Oct. 4, 1956.

25. S/4030, June 17, 1958, 39.

26. *Ibid,* 35ff; S/4030/Add 1, July 28, 1958, 2.

27. S/3456, Nov. 3, 1955; S/3596, Annex V; S/3174, Feb. 4, 1954.

28. S/3373, March 17, 1955, 2f; S/3430, Sept. 6, 1955, 1; *NY Times*, June 2, 1955.

29. *NY Times*, Feb. 23, March 29, 1964; July 13, 1963; Jan. 2, Feb. 1, 1961.

30. *Ibid.*, March 4, 6, 1955; Jan. 1, 1961; Gabbay, *op. cit.*, 502.

31. *NY Times*, March 14, 16, 1955; Edgar O'Ballance, *The Sinai Campaign* (London, 1959), 24; Gabbay, *op. cit.*, 414, 421, 426, 503; Wynn, *op. cit.*, 112f.

32. *NY Times*, March 5; Oct. 6, 9, 1955; Feb. 15, 1958; *Life*, Nov. 14, 1955, 127, 130; *U.S. News and World Report*, Nov. 4, 1955, 48, 50; Gabbay, *op. cit.*, 514ff; *The President's Proposals on the Middle East: Hearings Before the Committee on Foreign Relations and the Committee on Armed Services*, U.S. Senate, Part II, 1957, 710f, 714; UN, OR of SC, 693rd, March 17, 1955, 14; John C. Campbell, *Defense of the Middle East* (New York, 1958), 88.

33. *NY Times*, Oct. 9, 1955; Feb. 26, 1956.

34. *Ibid.*, Sept. 26, 27, 28; Oct. 1–6, 9, 17, 19, 21, 25, 29, 30; Nov. 11, 22, 1955; Ian 6; Feb. 26; May 13; June 20; July 3, 5, 7; Sept. 22, 23; Oct. 30; Nov. 3, 1956; *Life*, *loc. cit.*, 127, 130; Gabbay, *op. cit.*, 505f; Beal, *op cit.*, 257, 27; Wynn, *op. cit.*, 117ff; *Israel Govt Yearbook, 1956*, 247; *State Department Bulletin*, XXXII, No. 823, April 4, 1955, 568.

35. Robert W. MacDonald, *The League of Arab States* (Princeton, 1965), 118ff; *NY Times*, Feb. 10, 12; June 2, 9, 1965; April 16; May 23, 1966; *Israel Digest*, June 18, 1965, 6.

36. UN, OR of SC, 550th, Aug. 1, 1951, 3ff; 549th, July 26, 14ff; 661st, March 12, 1954, 21; 686th, Dec. 7, 9; 688th, Jan. 13, 1955, 17ff.

37. UN, OR of SC, 522nd, Nov. 13, 1950, 22ff; 549th, July 28, 1951, 2ff; 658th, Feb. 5, 1954, 1ff; 659th, Feb. 15, 12ff; Shabtai Rosenne, *Israel's Armistice Agreements with the Arab States* (Tel Aviv, 1951), 84; *Israel Digest*, April 20, 1956, 1; *NY Times*, July 13, 17, 20, 1951; Feb. 13, 1954.

38. S/3093, Sept. 10, 1953; S/3153, Dec. 18; S/3168, Jan. 28, 1954; UN, OR of SC, 658th, Feb. 5, 1954, 1ff; 659th, Feb. 15, 1ff, 12ff; 661st, March 12, 5ff, 21ff; 662nd, March 23, 8ff; *NY Times*, Jan. 28; Feb. 13, 1954.

39. UN, OR of SC, 663rd, March 25, 1ff; 664th, March 29, 2, 7ff; *NY Times*, Jan. 28; Feb. 13; March 17, 26, 1954.

40. S/3323, Nov. 25, 1954; S/3309, Oct. 25; S/3310, Oct. 27; S/3326, Dec. 4; S/3335, Dec. 23; S/3420, Aug. 12, 1955; S/3596, 27f; S/3606, June 8, 1956; S/3611, June 28; S/3642, Sept. 5; S/3653, Sept. 20; S/3663, Oct. 4; S/3673, Oct. 13; UN, OR of SC, 682nd, Oct. 14, 1954; 683rd, Nov. 3; 686th, Dec. 7; 688th, Jan. 13, 1955; *NY Times*, Dec. 7, 8, 1954; Jan. 2, 5, 1955; July 11; Aug. 27; Sept. 11; Oct. 9, 14, 1956; *Israel Digest*, March 25, 1957, 2; Moshe Dayan, *Diary of the Sinai Campaign* (New York, 1965), 10f.

41. UN, OR of SC, 659th, Feb. 15, 1954; 661st, March 12, 11ff; UN, OR of GA, 644th PM, Jan. 28, 1957, 973; Charles B. Selak, "A Consideration of the Legal Status of the Gulf of Aqaba," *American J. of Internat. Law*, Oct. 1958, 667f, 679; *NY Times*, March 16, 19, 31; April 13; July 8, 1957; "The Trouble about Aqaba," *Egyptian Economic and Political Rev.* Feb., 1957, Military Section, XI–XII.

42. UN, OR of SC, 659th, p. 10; Selak, *loc. cit.*, 667 (footnote 29), 670; *NY Times*, Feb. 24, 1954; Halford Hoskins, *The Middle East* (New York, 1957), 70.

43. UN, OR of SC, 549th, July 26, 1951, 3ff; S/3168/Add 1, Jan. 29, 1954; OR of SC, 658th, Feb. 5, 1954, 1ff; A/3168, Jan. 28, 1954; Selak, *op. cit.*, 669f, 681; *NY Times*, July 11; Sept. 12, 27, 1955; July 19, 1957.

44. Dayan, *op. cit.*, 12ff.

45. Lenczowski, *op. cit.*, 513.

46. *The Suez Canal: A Selection of Documents Relating to the International Status of the Suez Canal and the Position of the Suez Canal Company* (London, 1956), 41ff.

47. Lenczowski, *op. cit.*, 627; Campbell, *op. cit.*, 100f; Fayez A. Sayegh, *Notes on the Suez Canal Controversy* (New York Arab Information Center, 1956); B. Boutros-Ghali and Youssef Chala, *Le Canal de Suez: 1854–1957* (Alexandria, 1958).

48. Dayan, *op. cit.*, 60.

49. *Ibid.*, 3; Hugh Thomas, *Suez* (New York, 1966), 88, 107f, 112ff.

50. *NY Times,* Oct. 29, 30, 31; Nov. 4, 8, 24, 1956; Jan. 1; March 5, 7; April 3, 1957; Nov. 13, 1959; O'Ballance, *The Sinai Campaign,* 12, 29, 45ff, 67ff, 90; *Israel Digest,* June 10, 1960, 4; Campbell, *op. cit.*, 95; Adams, *op. cit.*, p. 68.

51. Dayan, *op. cit.*, 3, 31f, 60.

52. *NY Times,* Oct. 29, 30, 31; Nov. 11, 1956; March 7, 1957; *Israel Govt Yearbook, 1958,* 118; UN, OR of SC, 749th, Oct. 30, 1956, 8, 10, 15; A/3320, Nov. 8, 1956; O'Ballance, *The Sinai Campaign,* 43ff, 79, 194; Adams, *op. cit.*, 68; Hanson Baldwin, "Middle East in Turmoil," *Headline Series* (Foreign Policy Association), May–June, 1957, 22.

53. *NY Times,* Oct. 30, 31; Nov. 19, 22–25, 1956; Jan. 1, 3, 1957; Nov. 13, 1959; *NY Herald Tribune,* Nov. 23, 1956; *Israel Govt Yearbook, 1956,* 119; Campbell, *op. cit.*, 95, 105ff; Merry and Serge Broomberger, *Secrets of Suez* (London, 1957), 11, 22, 24f, 84, 87, 92; Beal, *op. cit.*, 276; Dayan, *op. cit.*, 30, 47, 62, 68, 112; *Survey of International Affairs* (London, 1962), 48–57; Paul Johnson, *The Suez War* (London, 1957), 81f, 102f, 136ff; Erskine Childers, *Road to Suez* (London, 1962), 227, 241ff, 257; Michael Foot and Mervyn Jones, *Guilty Men, 1957* (London, 1957), 191–201; Benjamin Matovu, "How Zionism Threatened the Peace at Suez," *Issues* (New York, American Council for Judaism), Autumn, 1965, 14ff; Don Peretz, *The Middle East Today* (New York, 1963), 297.

54. *NY Times,* Nov. 11, 15, 1956.

55. *Ibid.,* Nov. 28; Dec. 10, 19, 1956; Jan. 16; Feb. 4, 19, 1957; A/3491, Jan. 10, 1957.

56. O'Ballance, *The Sinai Campaign,* 84ff, 144ff; personal interviews with Egyptian government and military officials. For the best objective account of the Sinai War, see O'Ballance, *The Sinai Campaign.* For the best Israeli account, see Dayan, *op. cit.*

57. Dayan, *op. cit.*, 61, 68, 99, 123f, 146.

58. A/3347, Nov. 21, 1956; A/3389, Nov. 28; A/3412, Dec. 1; A/3457, Dec. 14; A/3478, Dec. 21; UN, OR of 11th Ses of the GA, 600th PM, Nov. 28, 1956, 408ff; A/PV.624, Dec. 18, 1956, pp. 61ff; A/PV.630, Dec. 21, pp. 38ff; A/PV.631, Dec. 21, 58ff; *NY Times,* Oct. 13, 17, 29; Nov. 16; Dec. 13, 1956; Jan. 11; Feb. 19; March 3, 9, 1957.

59. *Israel Digest,* April 24, 1957, p. 3; *Israel and the UN,* 245; *Middle East J.,* Summer, 1959, 298; A/3818 and A/3818/Add 1; A/4132/Add 1, 5; A/3576; UN, OR of 14th Ses of GA, 820 PM, Oct. 5, 1959, 352ff; 11th Ses, 644th PM, Jan. 28, 1957, 973; *UN Review,* May, 1960, 1; S/PV.776, April 26, 1957, 7; *NY Times,* March 9, 10, 11, 16, 29; April 6, 25, 28; May 15, 16, 18, 19, 1957; June 5; July 2, 24, 1959.

60. *NY Times,* March 28, 31; June 4; July 2, 1959; *Israel Govt Yearbook,*

1959/60, 274; *Israel Digest*, April 3, 1959, 1; Jan. 8, 1960, 2; Gamal Abdel Nasser, "Where I Stand and Why," *Life*, Feb. 20, 1959, 107; *Arab News and Views*, July 15, 1959, 1.

61. S/2833, Nov. 4, 1952; S/4030 & Corr. 1, June 17, 1958, 29, 35ff; S/4030/Add 1, July 28, 1958, 2ff; *NY Times*, Nov. 9, 10, 30, 1957.

62. *NY Times*, Jan. 24, 1958; S/3892, Sept. 24, 1957, 1ff, 6; S/3878, Sept. 4; UN, OR of SC, 787th, Sept. 6, 1957, 9ff; 788th, Sept. 6, 2ff; 806th, Nov. 22, 5ff, 22ff; S/PV.809, Jan. 22, 1958, 16ff, 39ff; S/PV.810, Jan. 22, 6ff.

63. S/4270, Feb, 23, 1960.

64. S/5401, Aug. 24, 1963; UN, OR of SC, 1058th, Aug. 26, 2.

65. UN, OR of SC, 1058th, Aug. 28, 1963, 2; 1059th, Aug. 28, 18ff; 1062nd, Aug. 30, 4ff; 1063rd, Sept. 3, 18f; S/5401, Aug. 24, 1963; S/5394, Aug. 21; *Israel Digest*, Aug. 30, 1963, 8; Sept. 13, 4; Sept. 27, 4; *NY Times*, Aug. 24–26, 29; Sept. 1, 4, 1963; ZK, "After the Security Council," *New Outlook*, Oct., 1963, 3, 5.

66. S/5102 and Add 1, March 26, 1962; S/5092, March 17; S/5093, March 19; S/5098, March 21; UN, OR of SC, 999th, March 28; 1003rd, April 5; 1005th, April 6; *NY Times*, March 19; April 5, 7, 8, 1962; *Israel Digest*, March 16, 1962, 4; Khouri, "The Policy of Retaliation," *loc. cit.*, 443.

67. Khouri, "The Jordan River Controversy," *loc. cit.*, 38ff.

68. *Ibid.*, 43f; The League of Arab States Secretariat General, *The Development of the Jordan River* (Cairo, n.d.), 34f; *Arab News and Views* (New York, Arab Information Office), Feb. 1, 1961, 1; *NY Times*, Feb. 6, 1961; Jan. 14, 1964; *Daily Star* (Beirut), April 19, 1962; March 8, 1963; Jan. 14, 1964.

69. Khouri, "The Jordan River Controversy," *loc. cit.*, 43.

70. *NY Times*, Nov. 29, 1964; S/6061, Nov. 24, 1964, pp. 5ff.

71. *NY Times*, Dec. 1, 4, 18, 22, 1964; S/6061, 8ff.

72. S/6061, 5ff; S/6248, March 19, 1965; S/6243, March 17; S/7432, July 26, 1966; *NY Times*, Nov. 15, 29; Dec. 1–4, 18, 22, 1964; March 18; May 22; June 6; July 15, 1965; Jan. 25; April 30, 1966; *Evening Bulletin*, April 14; May 26, 1965; Feb. 3; March 8, 30; April 1, 29, 1966; *Israel Digest*, Dec. 17, 1965, 2; Dec. 31, 3; Feb. 25, 1966, 5; April 8, 8; Khouri, "Policy of Retaliation," *loc. cit.*, 448, n42.

73. Khouri, *ibid.*, 448; *NY Times*, Jan. 20; March 1, 11; May 29, 31; June 3, 1965; July 16, 1966; *Evening Bulletin*, May 29; Dec. 14, 1965; *Israel Digest*, March 12, 1965; *Daily Star*, July 22, 1965; *Middle East J.*, Spring, 1965, 205; Autumn, 1965, 501.

74. S/6208, March 1, 1965; *Israel Digest*, March 12, 1965, 2; June 4, 1; *Middle East J.*, Spring, 1965, 206; Autumn, 1965, 501; *NY Times*, March 14; May 28, 29, 31; June 1, 3, 1965; *Evening Bulletin*, March 1; May 28, 29, 30, 1965; *Arab News and Views*, July 1, 1965, 1.

75. *Israel Digest*, Dec. 31, 1965, 3; *Arab News and Views*, Dec. 1, 1965, 1; *Daily Star*, Oct. 30; Nov. 4, 1965.

76. *Israel Digest*, May 31, 1966; May 6, 3, 8; June 3, 2; *News from Israel*, May 12, 1966, 1; Aug. 31, 1966, 1; S/7275, May 2, 1966; S/7333, June 1.

77. S/7296, May 16, 1967; S/7326, May 31; *Israel Digest*, Feb. 11, 1966, 3; *NY Times*, May 7, 16, 19, 1966. In the early part of 1966 Israel also accused the Syrians of shooting at an Israeli patrol boat on Feb. 2, 1966, of firing on an Israeli fishing vessel on March 7, and of throwing a hand grenade at another Israeli fishing craft on April 3. *Israel Digest*, April 22, 1966, 3; *Evening Bulletin*, Feb. 23, 1966.

78. S/7432, July 26, 1966; S/7433, July 27; S/PV.1293, Aug. 1, 1966, 41ff; S/PV.1295, Aug. 3, 32ff; *Evening Bulletin*, July 18, 19, 25, 1966; *NY Times*, July 16, 17, 18; Aug. 14, 1966. In Feb., 1966, leaders of the militant wing of the Baathist Party came into power in Syria. Their strong anti-Israeli attitude and their desire for a more activist policy helped to aggravate Syrian-Israeli relations. *NY Times*, Jan. 29, 1967.

79. *NY Times*, Aug. 14; Oct. 30; Nov. 20, 27, 1966.

80. *Ibid.*, Aug. 14, 16–23; Sept. 8, 10, 12, 1966; *Evening Bulletin*, Aug. 15, 16, 1966; *News from Israel*, Aug. 31, 1966, 1; *Israel Digest*, Aug. 26, 1966, 1f; Sept. 9, 1966, 8; *UN Weekly News Summary*, WS/255, Aug. 19, 1966, 4; S/7460, Aug. 16; S/7470, Aug. 23; S/7477, Aug. 27, 1966.

81. S/7540, Oct. 12, 1966; S/7544, Oct. 13; *UN Weekly News Summary*, WS/263, Oct. 14, 1966, 19; *Evening Bulletin*, Oct. 5, 10, 19, 1966; *NY Times*, Oct. 13, 15, 19, 1966.

82. S/PV.1307, Oct. 14 through S/PV.1319, Nov. 4, 1966; *UN Weekly News Summary*, WS/264, Oct. 21, 18; WS/265, Oct. 28, 11; WS/266, Nov. 4, 9; WS/267, Nov. 11, 1966, 11; *Arab News and Views*, Nov. 15, 1966, 1; S/7556, Oct. 18, 1966; *Evening Bulletin*, Oct. 24; Nov. 1, 3, 4, 21; Dec. 29, 1966; *NY Times*, Oct. 13, 18, 24; Nov. 5, 7, 17; Dec. 6, 29, 1966.

83. C. L. Sulzberger, *NY Times*, Dec. 23, 1966; Anthony Carthew, "After the Raid on Es Samu," *ibid.*, Dec. 18, 1966, *Magazine*, 31; *Evening Bulletin*, Dec. 27, 1966.

84. S/7536, Oct. 10, 1966; S/7553, Oct. 17; S/7562, Oct. 23; S/7569, Oct. 27; *UN Weekly News Summary*, WS/268, Nov. 18, 12; WS/269, Nov. 25, 1966, 13; S/7584; *Israel Digest*, Nov. 18, 1966, 1f; Dec. 2, 1966, 1; *NY Times*, Sept. 26; Oct. 5, 9, 13, 15, 31; Nov. 13, 16, 20, 26; Dec. 15, 1966; Carthew, *loc. cit.*, 30; *Evening Bulletin*, Oct. 10, 21, Nov. 14, 20, 1966; *Newsweek*, Nov. 28, 1966, 42.

85. S/7586, Nov. 13, 1966; S/7593, Nov. 18; S/7594, Nov. 21; *NY Times*, Nov. 20, 24, 25, 26, 27, 28, 29; Dec. 2, 28, 1966; Jan. 5; Feb. 24, 1967; *Evening Bulletin*, Nov. 26, 28; Dec. 1, 27, 1966; Feb. 5, 9, 1967.

86. *NY Times*, Nov. 30, 1966; Sulzberger, *loc. cit.*; Carthew, *loc. cit.*, 31; *Evening Bulletin*, Dec. 27, 1966.

87. *Evening Bulletin*, Dec. 11, 18, 1966; *NY Times*, Dec. 11, 12, 18, 24, 1966; Jan. 26, 1967.

88. S/PV.1320, Nov. 16, through S/PV.1327, Nov. 24, 1966; *NY Times*, Nov. 17, 20, 22, 25–28, 1966; *Evening Bulletin*, Nov. 17, 1966; S/7586; *UN Weekly News Summary*, WS/268, Nov. 18, 12; WS/269 and WS/269/Add 1, Nov. 25, 13, 2f.

89. *NY Times*, Nov. 19, 20, 21, 22, 28; Dec. 24, 1966; Sulzberger, *loc. cit.*; Carthew, *loc. cit.*, 30, 31, 80, 81; *Newsweek*, *loc. cit.*; *Evening Bulletin*, Dec. 1, 1966.

90. Carthew, *loc. cit.*, 30, 81.

91. *Ibid.*, 30; *Israel Digest*, Dec. 2, 1966, 1; *NY Times*, Nov. 15, 20, 21, 26, 27, 28; Dec. 4, 7, 16, 1966; Feb. 20, 25; March 17, 1967; *Evening Bulletin*, Nov. 26, 1966; Feb. 9, 24; March 13, 14, 16, 1967; *UN Weekly News Summary*, WS/270, Dec. 2, 1966, 7.

92. S/7573, Nov. 2, 1966, 5; S/7668, Jan. 9, 1967; S/7673, Jan. 10; S/7675, Jan. 12; S/7680, Jan. 13; S/7684, Jan. 16; S/7688, Jan. 18; *Israel Digest*, Jan. 27, 1967, 1f, 7; Feb. 27, 1f; *Evening Bulletin*, Dec. 29, 1966; Jan. 27, 1967.

93. *NY Times*, Feb. 2, 1967.

94. S/7683, Jan. 15, 1967; S/7685, Jan. 16; S/7690, Jan. 18; S/7692, Jan. 20; S/7696, Jan. 24; S/7698, Jan. 25; S/7699, Jan. 26; S/7704, Jan. 27; S/7725, Feb. 8; S/7734, Feb. 10; S/7769, Feb. 20; S/7784, Feb. 23; *NY Times*, Jan. 26, 27, 29, 30; Feb. 2, 15, 17, 20, 1967; *Israel Digest*, Feb. 10, 1967, 1f; Feb. 24, 3, 8; *Evening Bulletin*, Jan. 27; Feb. 9, 14; March 3, 1967.

95. UN, OR of SC, 542nd, April 25, 1951, 27ff; 544th, May 2, 7ff; personal interviews with UN officials.

Chapter VIII. The June War

1. S/7843, April 7, 1967.

2. S/7845, April 9, 1967.

3. *NY Times*, April 9, 1967.

4. *Ibid.*, April 8, 1967, *Israel Digest*, April 21, 1967, 2.

5. S/7843, April 7, 1967; S/7845, April 9; S/7853, April 14; S/7880, May 11, Annex, 1; S/7890, May 17; *NY Times*, April 8, 9, 16, May 7, 10, 1967; *Israel Digest*, May 19, 1967, 5.

6. *NY Times*, April 10, 1967; *The Middle East J.*, Summer, 1967, 388; Charles W. Yost, "The Arab-Israeli War: How It Began," *Foreign Affairs*, Jan., 1968, 305f.

7. *NY Times*, April 9; *Evening Bulletin*, April 9, 1967.

8. S/7880, Annex, 1, May 11; *Israel Digest*, May 19, 1967, 5; *NY Times*, May 13, 17, 1967.

9. Yost, *op. cit.*, 307.

10. *Ibid.*; *NY Times*, May 13, 17, 1967; S/7880, Annex, 1. On May 17, *NY Times* also reported, "There is a widely held view in Israel that the threats of force against Syria were intended as much for domestic consumption as they were for distribution abroad." According to Yost, *op. cit.*, "press accounts of these [Israeli] statements . . . seemed so inflammatory to U.S. State Department officers that they expressed concern to Israeli authorities."

11. S/7885, May 15, 1967; *NY Times*, May 16, 17, 21, 1967.

12. *Ibid.*, May 18, 21, 22, 1967; *Evening Bulletin*, May 15, 16, 1967; *Time*, June 2, 1967, 21.

13. *NY Times*, May 18, 21, 22; June 5, 7, 1967; *The Evening Bulletin*, May 15; June 5, 1967; Yost, *loc. cit.*, 306, 308, 310; John Badeau, "The Arabs, 1967," *Atlantic Monthly*, Dec., 1967, 109.

14. Yost, *loc. cit.*, 310, 317; Badeau, *loc. cit.*, 108, 110.

15. *NY Times*, May 21—1967. Even the Israelis had believed that Egypt had not expected UNEF to be pulled out so quickly. The same newspaper reported on June 14 that Secretary of State Dean Rusk held that even the UAR had been surprised at the speed with which her withdrawal request had been met.

16. A/6669, May 18, 1967; S/7906, May 26, 1ff.

17. A/PV.1527, June 20, 1967, 6.

18. *NY Times*, May 21, 23, 1967.

19. *Ibid.*, May 18, 21; *The Evening Bulletin*, May 18, 23, 1967.

20. *NY Times*, May 18–30; June 4, 5, July 24, 1967; *Evening Bulletin*, May 18–29; June 4, 5, 1967; *Time*, June 2, 1967, 21; Badeau, *loc. cit.*, 108, 110; Yost, *loc. cit.*, 317.

21. *NY Times,* June 5, 1967.

22. *Ibid.,* May 17, 18, 21; June 5, 1967; *Evening Bulletin,* May 17, 23, 1967; *Israel Digest,* June 2, 1967, 1, 5, 8. According to *NY Times,* June 5, 1967, some American officials, noting that "only one Israeli vessel had passed through the strait [of Tiran] in the last two years, have argued that this [limited movement of Israel's ships through the Gulf of Aqaba] is a practical concession that Israel could make without much sacrifice."

23. *NY Times,* May 31, June 4, 1967.

24. S/7896, May 19, 1967; S/7906, May 27; *NY Times,* May 21–28, 1967.

25. S/PV.1342, May 24, 1967, 41ff; S/PV.1343, May 29, 62ff.

26. S/PV.1342, May 24, 31ff; S/PV.1343, May 29, 21ff, 112ff; S/PV.1344, May 30, 7ff; S/PV.1345, May 31, 6ff. See letter to the editor from Professor of Law Roger Fisher, of Harvard University, published in *NY Times,* June 11, 1967, relating to the "legality" of the Egyptian "blockade" of the Gulf of Aqaba.

27. S/PV.1342, May 24, 21ff; S/PV.1343, May 29, 82ff; S/PV.1345, May 31, 56ff; S/PV.1346, June 3, 23ff; 67ff; *NY Times,* June 1, 4, 1967.

28. *NY Times,* May 22–30, June 12, 1967.

29. S/PV.1342, May 24, 2ff; S/PV.1343, May 29, 7ff; S/PV.1344, May 30, 52ff; S/PV.1345, May 31, 21ff; *The Evening Bulletin,* June 1, 1967.

30. S/PV.1342, May 24, 31ff; S/PV.1345, May 31, 6ff, 27ff; *The Evening Bulletin,* June 3, 4, 1967.

31. S/PV.1345, May 31; S/PV.1346, June 3; *The Evening Bulletin,* June 4, 1967.

32. *NY Times,* June 5, 1967.

33. *Ibid.,* May 27–30, June 4, July 10, 1967.

34. *Ibid.,* June 2, 3, 12, 1967.

35. *Ibid.,* May 30, June 5, 1967; *The Evening Bulletin,* June 3, 5, 1967.

36. *NY Times,* June 6, 1967.

37. S/PV.1346, June 3, 1967, 6ff; *NY Times,* June 4, 1967.

38. *NY Times,* May 30, June 3, 1967; *Evening Bulletin,* May 23, 1967.

39. *NY Times,* June 6, July 8, 10, 1967; Curtis G. Pepper, "Hawk of Israel," *NY Times* Magazine, July 9, 1967, 48; Edmund Stillman, "The Short and the Long War," *ibid.,* June 18, 1967, 7; *Time,* June 16, 1967, 22.

40. Pepper, *op. cit.; Israel Digest,* June 2, 1967, 8. *NY Times,* May 20, 27, 30, June 2, 4, 8, 12, July 10, 1967. Israel's Chief of Staff Major General Yitzhak Rabin was quoted as having stated in 1965 that if Arab military strength were to grow too rapidly, Israel would have to strike first while she was still able "to disrupt any Arab timetable for war against us." George De Carvahlo, "Desperate Arab-Israeli Struggle for Scarce Water: An Ancient Hatred Builds towards War," *Life,* June 18, 1965, 50.

41. *NY Times,* June 6, 1967.

42. *Ibid.,* June 6–16, 1967; S/PV.1347, June 5, 17ff; *The Evening Bulletin,* June 12, 1967.

43. *NY Times,* June 10, 11, 19, 26; *Time,* June 16, 1967, p. 22; S. T. Marshall, *Swift Sword: The Historical Record of Israel's Victory, June 1967* (1967).

44. Different sources gave the following estimates of the military forces of the combatants: (1) Israel—275,000–300,000 regular troops and reservists when fully mobilized; (2) the UAR—with a fully mobilized potential of some 250,000–300,000 men, but with only from 80,000–90,000 soldiers actually in the Sinai area at the outbreak of the war; (3) Jordon—55,000–80,000 men; and (4) Syria—60,000–

100,000 men. Because of internal security and other reasons, not all the Jordanian and Syrian soldiers were actually used against Israel. Some Iraqi units fought in the war, primarily in Jordan. Other Arab states had agreed to send some of their troops; but, apparently, only a small number of Algerians reached the combat area before the war ended. *Time, loc. cit.*, 28; *NY Times*, May 24, 29, June 6, 7, 8, 10, 24, 1967; A/PV.1529, June 21, 1967, 56 [Abba Eban referred to "90,000 (Egyptian) troops" as being in the Sinai on the eve of the war]; *U.S. News and World Report*, May 29, 1967, 8; *Israel Digest*, June 2, 1967, 2.

45. *NY Times*, May 24; June 6, 7, 8; *Time, loc. cit.; U.S. News and World Report, loc. cit.*

46. *NY Times*, May 24, June 6, 8, 13, 18, 23, 27, July 1, 12, 1967; *Evening Bulletin*, July 10, 13, 1967; *Time, loc. cit.*

47. S/PV.1347, June 5, 1967, 17ff; S/PV.1348, June 6, 71ff; S/PV.1350, June 7, 16ff; S/PV.1351, June 8, 36ff; S/PV.1352, June 9, 70ff; S/PV.1353, June 9, 37ff.

48. S/PV.1347, June 5, 22ff; S/PV.1348, June 6, 51ff, 91ff, 117ff; S/PV.1350, June 7, 11ff; *NY Times*, June 6, 1967.

49. S/PV.1348, June 6, 1967, 6ff, 21ff; S/1351, June 8, 11, 21ff, 58ff; S/PV.1352, June 9, 22ff; *NY Times*, June 7, 8, 9, 1967; *The Economist*, June 17, 1967, 1224.

50. S/PV.1347, June 5, 2ff; S/PV.1348, June 6, 51ff, 91ff, 117ff; S/PV.1350, June 7, 11ff; S/PV.1351, June 8, 67ff; S/7943, S/7945, June 7; S/7947, S/7953, June 8; *NY Times*, June 8, 1967. Because Israel had wanted to gain complete control of the entire Sinai and west-bank areas and because she probably could not have had enough time to occupy all parts of these large areas in the several days of the war, the chances are that the UAR and Jordanian complaints had some validity.

51. S/7958, June 9; S/PV.1353, June 9, 12ff, 32ff, 48ff; S/PV.1354, June 10, 8ff, 21; S/PV.1356, June 10, 88ff; S/PV.1357, June 11, 11ff; S/7973, June 11; *NY Times*, June 9, 10, 11, 12, 19, Aug. 20, 1967; *Time*, June 16, 1967, 28. James Reston wrote in *NY Times*, June 11, 1967, "The United States . . . is asking for a detailed and verified report on 'the facts' in the Israeli-Syrian War, which it knows will give the Israelis time to knock out the Syrian guns and bring the last of the Arab states into line by threatening the capital of Damascus."

52. S/PV.1351, June 8, 21ff; S/PV.1352, June 9, 28ff; S/PV.1353, June 9, 76ff; S/PV.1357, June 11, 17ff; *NY Times*, June 8, 9, 10, 11, 1967; *Evening Bulletin*, June 7, 10, 1967.

53. S/PV.1356, June 10; S/PV.1357, June 11.

54. S/PV.1358, June 13, 6ff; S/PV.1360, 84ff.

55. S/PV.1348, June 6, 11ff, 57ff, 116ff; S/PV.1358, June 13, 42ff.

56. S/PV.1348, June 6, 51ff; S/PV.1350, June 7, 11ff; S/PV.1360, June 14, 101ff.

57. S/PV.1348, June 6, 51ff; S/PV.1357, June 11, 37ff; S/PV.1360, June 14, 101ff; *NY Times*, June 8, 1967. According to *NY Times*, June 12, 1967, "the Johnson Administration appeared content to let the Israelis capitalize on their strength" by not pressing for a cease-fire. "The Administration's greatest pressures to have Israel halt the fighting did not develop until Friday (June 9), while the Israelis were making their final bid to seize high ground in Syria." C. L. Sulzberger wrote on June 7, 1967, "Washington is about as neutral on Palestine as Peking on Vietnam." The same paper, June 29, stated that the United States had given "diplomatic support" to Israel "throughout the recent crisis."

58. S/PV.1348, June 6, 71ff; S/PV.1351, June 8, 42ff; S/PV.1358, June 13, 100ff. *Israel Digest,* June 16, 1967, 7; June 30, 3.

59. *NY Times,* June 24, 1967; *Evening Bulletin,* June 23, 26, 1967.

60. *NY Times,* June 14–16, 22–26, 1967.

61. *Ibid.,* Aug. 10, 21, Sept. 20, Oct. 12, 1967; *Evening Bulletin,* July 8, 9, 28; Sept. 17; *Christian Science Monitor,* July 13, 1967.

62. *NY Times,* June 11–26, July 1, 5, 6, 10, 13, Sept. 3, 1967; *Evening Bulletin,* June 28; July 8, 9, 1967; *Christian Science Monitor,* July 13, 1967.

63. A/PV.1527, June 20, 1967, 8ff; *NY Times,* June 18, July 1, 10, 1967; *The Evening Bulletin,* June 12, 13, 1967.

64. *NY Times,* June 18, 28; July 1, 10, 1967; *Evening Bulletin,* July 1, 17, 1967.

65. A/PV.1544, June 30, 1967, 1ff.

66. *Israel Digest,* Sept. 22, 1967, 1f.

67. A/PV.1526, June 19, 1967, 26ff; A/PV.1528, June 20, 20ff; A/PV.1529, June 21, 56ff; A/PV.1535, June 26, 40ff; A/PV.1541, June 29, 52ff; A/PV.1544, June 30, 11ff.

68. A/PV.1529, June 21, 27ff; A/PV.1530, June 21, 43ff, 48ff; A/PV.1531, June 22, 2ff; A/PV.1533, June 23, 2ff; A/PV.1537, June 27, 12f, 17, 23ff, 28ff; A/PV.1539, June 28, 61; A/PV.1542, June 29, 7ff; A/PV.1543, June 30, 27ff, 36; A/PV.1547, July 4, 48ff.

69. A/PV.1527, June 20, 27, 32; A/PV.1529, June 21, 22; A/PV.1530, June 21, 28, 48ff; A/PV.1536, June 26, 26ff; A/PV.1537, June 27, 21ff; A/PV.1541, June 29, 21; A/PV.1542, June 29, 6; A/PV.1543, June 30, 13ff, 36; A/PV.1545, July 3, 41; A/PV.1547, July 4, 48ff.

70. A/PV.1529, June 21, 5ff; A/PV.1531, June 22, 38ff; *NY Times,* June 22, 24, 1967.

71. A/PV.1531, June 22, 32ff, 37ff; *NY Times,* May 25, 29, June 3, 17, 22, 1967.

72. *NY Times,* July 6, 1967.

73. *Ibid.,* July 21–23, 1967; *Evening Bulletin,* July 22, 1967.

74. S/7930/Add 20, July 4, 1967.

75. S/7930/Add 3, June 11, 1967, 3; S/7930/Add 5, June 12; S/7930/Add 6, June 13.

76. S/8025, July 1, 1967; S/8026, July 1; S/7930/Add 23, July 17; *NY Times,* July 2–16, 1967.

77. S/8053, July 11, 1967; *NY Times,* July 10, 11, 14, 1967.

78. *NY Times,* July 12, 14, 15, 16, 23, 1967; *Evening Bulletin,* July 10.

79. S/7930/Add 23, July 17; S/8053/Add 1, Aug. 10, 1967; *NY Times,* July 10. 15, 16, 17, 23, Aug. 22, 1967; *Evening Bulletin,* July 10, 1967.

80. S/8053/Add 1, Aug. 10, 1967; S/8053/Add 2, Aug. 27; *NY Times,* July 16, 17, 28, Aug. 4, 28, Sept. 5, 6, 7, 13, 19, 1967; *Evening Bulletin,* July 25, Sept. 4, 5, 7, 27, 28, 1967.

81. *NY Times,* June 20, 22, July 16, 1967.

82. *Ibid.,* July 16, 29, 31, Aug. 26, Oct. 5; *Evening Bulletin,* June 20, 1967. Late in Dec., 1967, Egypt expressed a willingness to release the 15 ships trapped in the canal. On Jan. 25, 1968, Israel agreed to a UN proposal to allow obstructions in the southern part of the canal to be removed by Egypt so that the ships could leave. However, after a heavy exchange of fire between Egyptian and Israeli forces had taken place as a result, according to Israel, of Egyptian efforts to sail four launches to the northern part of the canal, Egypt decided to postpone in-

definitely any further effort to clear the canal—*NY Times,* Dec. 28, 29, 1967, Jan. 26, 31, 1968.

83. S/7930/Add 33, Sept. 4; S/7930/Add 34, Sept. 7; S/7930/Add 35, Sept. 12; S/7930/Add 40, Sept. 27; S/7930/Add 43, Oct. 22; S/7930/Add 44, Oct. 24; S/7930/Add 45, Oct. 24; S/7930/Add 46, Oct. 24; S/7930/Add 47, Oct. 25; S/7930/Add 48, Oct. 25; S/7930/Add 49, Oct. 25; S/8140, Sept. 6; S/8145, Sept. 8; S/8163, Sept. 25; S/8169, Sept. 26; S/8173, Sept. 27; S/8183, Oct. 6; S/8203, Oct. 22; S/8204, Oct. 23; S/8205, Oct. 23; S/8207, Oct. 24; S/8208, Oct. 24; S/PV.1369, Oct. 24; S/PV.1370, Oct. 25; S/PV.1371, Oct. 25; *Israel Digest,* Nov. 3, 1967, 1f; *New York Times,* Sept. 21, 22, 26, Oct. 22, Dec. 2, 1967.

84. S/7930/Add 55, Nov. 21, 1967; S/8195, Oct. 16; S/8198, Oct. 18; S/8202, Oct. 20; S/8254, Nov. 21; S/8258, Nov. 22; *NY Times,* Sept. 6; Nov. 21, 22, 1967; Jan. 9, 13, 1968; *Evening Bulletin,* Jan. 14, 1968.

85. S/8171, Sept. 28; S/8178, Oct. 3; S/8181, Oct. 4; S/8194, Oct. 16; *Israel Digest,* Oct. 20, 1967, 3f; Nov. 3, 3; Nov. 17, 3; Dec. 29, 6; *NY Times,* Sept. 22, 26; Oct. 2, 13, 16, 21; Nov. 6, 8, 24, 26, 30; Dec. 13, 14, 1967. *NY Times* reported, January 12, 1968, that: (1) Israeli intelligence and Western diplomatic sources held that President Nasser, who formerly opposed Arab commando raids on the ground they were "counter-productive," had "shifted" his position; (2) Egypt had begun to provide arms, money, and training sites for guerrilla organizations; (3) while Israel claimed to have killed or captured about 600 "terrorists," the "number of guerrillas is believed by some sources to exceed 10,000"; and (4) Israeli officials had become concerned about commando activities and increasingly convinced that they would soon have to launch "strong, though limited, military" reprisals by land and air forces against such countries as Jordan and Syria if guerrilla activities persisted. Until early March, 1968, while Israel had employed air strikes and artillery fire against her neighbors, she had not sent ground units across the cease-fire lines on reprisal actions since the June War.

86. *NY Times,* June 6, 8, 12, 1967; Oct. 15, 1967—American officials were aware that before June 5, 1967, Israel "privately knew that she could outmatch the Arabs militarily despite their superior numbers and equipment."

87. U.S. Dept. of State, *The Digest of International Law* (Washington, 1963), IV, 471f; 1965, IV, 233; S/PV.1350, June 21, 1967, 81; Fisher, *loc. cit.*

88. *Israel Digest,* June 30, 1967, 4.

89. In a speech delivered before the American Council for Judaism, Nov. 2, 1967, Anthony Nutting, former British Minister of State in the Foreign Ministry, suggested that with her control of all parts of former Palestine, Israel was in a position to "recreate a bi-national state in Palestine." However, neither the Arabs nor the Israelis were prepared to accept such a solution with all of its implications. The Arabs wanted, as a minimum, the return of all areas seized by Israel in the June War, and they would strongly oppose any proposal for allowing Israel to retain the Gaza Strip and west bank of the Jordan River areas even if this were done for the alleged purpose of setting up a binational entity. The Israelis, in turn, were still determined to maintain a Jewish nation, and they would not be willing to share it with the Palestine Arabs, especially since these Arabs could become a majority in time.

90. Von Horn, *op. cit.,* 61ff, 67ff, 283. General von Horn, former Chief of Staff of UNTSO, wrote, "There was hardly a man among us [on UNTSO and the four MAC's] who had not originally arrived in the Holy Land with the most positive and sympathetic attitude towards the Israelis and their ambitions for their country.

. . . All of us who went to Israel knew very little about the Arabs, but a great deal about the Jews and their appalling sufferings in the Second World War. . . . Nearly all . . . had arrived with the honest intention to help both parties to the Armistice Agreements, but with a conscious sympathy for the people of 'poor little Israel. . . .' " *Ibid.*, 283. Also personal interviews with UNTSO and MAC officials.

91. *NY Times,* June 13, 15, 27, July 1, 9, 10, 12, Aug. 26, Sept. 29, 1967; *Christian Science Monitor,* July 14, 19, 1967; *The Evening Bulletin,* July 10, Aug. 30, 1967.

Chapter IX. Arab-Israeli Peace

1. See Chapter IV.

2. A/927, June 21, 1949, 7f, 11f; A/1367, 9, 45, 49; Gabbay, *op. cit.,* 241; Peretz, *op. cit.,* 65.

3. MacDonald, *op. cit.,* 181, 184; Peretz, *op. cit.,* 64. Also see Chapter VI.

4. Gabbay, *op. cit.,* 325; *NY Times,* Oct. 15, 1950.

5. MacDonald, *op. cit.,* 212f; Gabbay, *op. cit.,* 318, 339f; Glubb, *op. cit.,* 341; *NY Times,* March 1, 5, 25; Oct. 15; Nov. 28, 1950; Eytan, *op. cit.,* 41; UN, OR of SC, 637th, Nov. 12, 1953, 66; Litvinoff, *op. cit.,* 23.

6. *NY Times,* Feb. 13; March 9, 1950; April 15, 1951; Gabbay, *op. cit.,* 317ff.

7. *Ibid.,* 322.

8. *Ibid.,* 322, 326ff.

9. A/1985, 6f, 9, 21ff; UN, OR of 6th Ses of the GA, *Ad Hoc* Pol Com, 33rd, Jan. 7, 1952, 175ff; 34th, Jan. 8, 181ff; 35th, Jan. 9, 187ff; 36th, Jan. 10, 197ff; 38th, Jan. 11, 211f.

10. A/1985, 7ff; UN, OR of 6th Ses of GA. *Ad Hoc* Pol Com, 35th, 189ff; 40th, Jan. 14, 221; *NY Times,* Sept. 9, 19, 21, 23, 25, 29; Oct. 4, 6, 16, 1951.

11. UN, OR of 6th Ses of GA, *Ad Hoc* Pol Com, 33rd, Jan. 1, 1952, 176ff; 34th, Jan. 8, 181f; 35th, Jan. 9, 187ff; 36th, Jan. 10, 196ff; 38th, Jan. 11, 209ff; 37th, Jan. 11, 201ff; 40th, Jan. 14, 220ff; 364th PM, Jan. 26, 392f; 365th PM, Jan. 26, 402f; A/2216, 1ff; A/2216/Add. 1, 2.

12. *NY Times,* March 4, 11, 12, 15; Nov. 16, 1952; March 28, 30, 1953.

13. UN, OR of 7th Ses of GA, *Ad Hoc* Pol Com, 26th, Nov. 26, 1952, 155; 28th, Nov. 29, 159; 29th, Dec. 1, 171f; 30th, Dec. 1, 173ff; 31st, Dec. 2, 178ff; 32nd, Dec. 3, 185f; 33rd, Dec. 4, 192ff; 36th, Dec. 8, 214; *NY Times,* Dec. 6, 1952.

14. UN, OR of 7th Ses of GA, *Ad Hoc* Pol Com, 29th, Dec. 1, 1952, 165ff; 36th, Dec. 8, 213.

15. *NY Times,* Dec. 8, 15, 1952.

16. UN, OR of 7th Ses of GA, 405th PM, Dec. 18, 1952, 393ff; 406th PM, Dec. 18, 408ff.

17. *Report on the Middle East—Address by the Secretary of State, June 1, 1953,* State Dept. Publication 5088, Middle East Series, 12, June, 1953; *NY Times,* June 2, 1953.

18. *NY Times,* April 29, May 4, 11, 1954.

19. "On Peace and Negotiations," *New Outlook,* Jan., 1963, 51.

20. Beal, *op. cit.,* 252f; Campbell, *op. cit.,* 87f; *NY Times,* March 3; June 2; July 10; Sept. 18; Oct. 9, 1955; UN, OR of SC, 693rd, March 17, 1955, 10.

21. *State Dept. Bulletin*, Sept. 5, 1955, 379; *NY Times*, Aug. 27, 28, 29; Sept. 12, 1955; Jan. 4, 1956; Beal, *op.cit.*, 252f; Campbell, *op. cit.*, 88; Lenczowski, *op. cit.*, 427f.

22. *NY Times*, Nov. 4, 16, 17, 19, 25, 26, 30; Dec. 1, 7, 12, 18, 29; Nov. 14, 28, 1955; Jan. 3, 1956; Ben-Gurion, "Israel's Security . . ," 18, 20f; Wynn, *op. cit.*, 130; Gabbay, *op. cit.*, 518; Childers, *op. cit.*, 141f.

23. *State Dept. Bulletin*, Oct. 10, 1955, 561; *NY Times*, Nov. 30; Dec. 29, 1955; Jan. 8, 20, 24, 1956.

24. *State Dept. Bulletin*, March 12, 1956, 412; Royal Institute of International Affairs, *Documents on International Affairs, 1956* (London, 1959), 57f; Richard P. Stebbins, *The United States in World Affairs, 1956* (New York, 1957), 83–86; Paul E. Zinner, ed., *Documents on American Foreign Relations, 1956* (New York, 1957), No. 31.

25. See Chapter VII.

26. *NY Times*, March 5, 15; July 17, 1957; Feb. 21, 1958.

27. See Chapter VI.

28. *NY Times*, April 1, 22–30, May 1–7, 1960; Jan. 9, 12; Feb. 26; June 26; July 13; Aug. 24, 1961; *Israel Digest*, Sept. 2, 1960, 4; Ze'ev Katz, "Israel's Foreign Policy Stands in One Place," *New Outlook*, Dec., 1961, 16; Ismael, "Month by Month," *ibid.*, May–June, 1961, 60.

29. *NY Times*, June 26, 1961; *Daily Star*, Sept. 22, 1962; A/5545, Nov. 1, 1963, 1ff.

30. *Daily Star*, Jan. 22, 23, 25, 1964; *NY Times*, May 1, 6, 9, 11, 14; Oct. 3, 1963; Jan. 14, 23, 1964; Jan. 17; March 7, 27, 1956; May 14, 19; Nov. 5; Dec. 5, 10, 11, 1966; *Israel Digest*, Jan. 21, 1963, 4; May 24, 1963, 2; May 21, 1965, 2; *The Evening Bulletin*, May 5, 18; Dec. 1, 1966.

31. *NY Times*, Oct. 12, 1961; July 24; Aug. 6, 28, 1962; May 6, 9, 14; Oct. 3, 1963; Oct. 23; Dec. 1, 5, 1966; *Daily Star*, July 24, 26, 1962.

32. *The Evening Bulletin*, Oct. 18; Nov. 6, 29; Dec. 11, 1966; *NY Times*, Oct. 16, 23; Nov. 5, 1965; Nov. 5; Dec. 5, 1966; Jan. 3, 1967.

33. *Israel Digest*, Sept. 22, 1967, 3.

34. S/PV.1351, June 8, 1967, 42ff; A/PV.1544, June 30, 17ff; *Israel Digest*, Sept. 22, 1967, 1, 2, 3; Abba Eban, *Every Item in Israel's Current Policy Conforms with Established International Practice* (New York, Israel Information Services, 1967); *NY Times*, July 18; Sept. 2, 4, 11, 18, 24; Oct. 12, 31, 1967.

35. *NY Times*, June 20; Sept. 4; Oct. 9, 1967.

36. *Ibid.*, Aug. 13, 14, 15, 20, 29, 31; Sept. 1, 2, 6, 1967; *Israel Digest*, Sept. 22, 1967, 1.

37. *NY Times*, June 18, 19; July 10, 11, 16, 17, 19; Sept. 24; Oct. 7, 9, 1967.

38. *Ibid.*, Aug. 26, 28, 1967.

39. *Ibid.*, July 24; Aug. 1, 3, 5, 13, 20, 28, 30, 1967.

40. *Ibid.*, Aug. 30, 31; Sept. 1, 2, 3, 7, 8, 10, 13, 26, 1967; *Arab News and Views*, Sept., 1967, 1, 5.

41. A/PV.1582, Oct. 6, 1967, pp. 18ff; S/PV.1375, Nov. 13, 42; *NY Times*, Sept. 17, 30; Oct. 3, 12, 1967.

42. *NY Times*, Oct. 7, 15, 22; Nov. 1, 1967; *U.S. News and World Report*, Sept. 18, 1967, p. 67; *Corpus Christi Caller* (Texas) (AP), Oct. 16, 1967; *The Brownsville Herald* (Texas) (UPI), Oct. 6, 1967.

43. *NY Times*, Nov. 8, 9, 10, 1967.

44. *Ibid.,* Nov. 6, 7, 8, 10, 11, 16, 1967.

45. S/PV.1373, Nov. 9, 1967; S/PV.1375, Nov. 13; S/PV.1377, Nov. 15; *NY Times,* Oct. 28, 29; Nov. 4, 7, 8, 9, 11, 14, 16, 1967.

46. S/PV.1373, Nov. 9, 1967; S/PV.1375, Nov. 13; S/PV.1377, Nov. 15; S/PV.1379, Nov. 16; S/PV.1381, Nov. 22; S/PV.1382, Nov. 22; *NY Times,* Nov. 4, 25, 29, 1967.

47. *NY Times,* Sept. 20, 1967.

48. UN, OR of 8th Ses of GA, 445th PM, Sept. 25, 1953, 151; 447th PM, Sept. 28, 181; 448th PM, Sept. 28, 195f; 449th PM, Sept. 29, 213f.

49. *Daily Star,* Dec. 28, 1963; April 30; June 19, 1964; *Evening Bulletin,* Nov. 29, 1966. Personal interviews.

50. *NY Times,* Feb. 22, 29; March 1, 2, 3, 4, 8, 9, 10, 1968; *Evening Bulletin,* March 8, 10, 1968.

51. *NY Times,* May 21, 1951; Dec. 20, 1955; Feb. 27; March 27, 1958; June 7, 1959; Oct. 11, 1960; April 30; May 7, 1963; UN, OR of 7th Ses of GA, *Ad Hoc Pol Com,* 29th, Dec. 1, 1952, 165ff; OR of 14th Ses of GA, Spec Pol Com, 162nd, Nov. 30, 1959, 165; Ben-Gurion, "Israel's Security . . . ," 20ff; *Israel Digest,* June 26, 1959, 2; Oct. 11, 1963, 1; May 21, 1965, 2; *News from Israel,* March 31, 1965, 1; Ellis, *op. cit.,* 291.

52. *Israel Digest,* April 17, 1959, 2; May 24, 1963, 2; March 11, 1966, 7; Sept. 23, 1966, 2; *NY Times,* April 17, 1960; May 7, 14, 25, 1963; *Jewish Exponent* (Philadelphia), Aug. 26, 1960, 7; Abba Eban, "The Advocates of Change," *New Outlook,* July, 1961, 16.

53. *NY Times,* Oct. 6, 1955.

54. *Ibid.,* Jan. 4, 1960; Aug. 5, 1961; Feb. 9; April 27; Nov. 18, 1963; *Israel Digest,* Sept. 27, 1963; Z. K., "Federation, the Powers and Israel," *New Outlook,* May, 1963, 3, 6; Charles D. Cremeans, *The Arabs and the World* (New York, 1963), 192.

55. *NY Times,* Jan. 4, 1960; Aug. 5, 1961; April 27, 1963; *Israel Digest,* May 24, 1963, 2; Cremeans, *op. cit.,* 192; Amnon Kapeliuk, "Arab Unity a Fact," *New Outlook,* May, 1963, 14.

56. Aubrey Hodes, "Practical Proposals and Not Resolutions," *New Outlook,* Sept., 1962, 43f.

57. George De Carvalho, "Desperate Arab-Israeli Struggle for Scarce Water," *Life,* June 18, 1965, 58. The Foreign Minister of Jordan was also reported to have stated, "Negotiating with the Israelis is hopeless. They don't give us an inch. We have challenged them a hundred times to implement the UN resolutions, but they have refused." *Ibid.*

58. Simha Flapan, "The Knesset Votes on the Refugee Problem," *New Outlook,* Dec., 1961, 10f; Shimon Shereshevsky, "Peace—Without a Peace Treaty," *ibid.,* July, 1961, 8; Ze'ev Katz, "Leaders for a New Era," *ibid.,* May, 1963, 56; Ernst Simon, "There is Another Way," *ibid.,* May–June, 1961, 4f; Hodes, *op. cit.,* 44.

59. *Israel Digest,* Aug. 2, 1963, 1, 2, 8; Jan. 28, 1966, 2; Abba Eban, *Towards a Peaceful World* (New York, Israel Information Service, 1966), 13; *NY Times,* July 11, 1963; May 18, 1965; Carvalho, *op. cit.,* 58.

60. *NY Times,* Oct. 25; Dec. 30, 1960; Nov. 16, 1963; *Israel Digest,* Feb. 19, 1960, 3; Nov. 11, 1960, 5; Dec. 9, 1960, 2; Nutting, *op. cit.,* 87; Begin, *op. cit.,* 298; Marlowe, *op. cit.,* 112; O'Ballance, *The Sinai Campaign,* 192; Bilby, *op. cit.,*

261f; Ben-Gurion, "Israel's Security . . . ," 62, 68; Cremeans, *op. cit.*, 189f; Yizhak A. Abbody, "Paramount Problem of Foreign Policy," *New Outlook,* July–Aug., 1963, 40f.

61. *Ibid.*, 40ff; Eliezer Livne, "Israel's Path to the Arabs," *New Outlook,* Jan., 1960, 43f; Cohen, *op. cit.*, 10ff; *Israel's Oriental Problem: A Monthly Bulletin of News and Comment* (The Council of the Sephardi Community, Jerusalem), March–April, 1967, 9f.

62. *Israel Digest,* Jan. 29, 1965, 5; Dec. 16, 1966, 6; *NY Times,* Oct. 22, 1963; Jan. 2, 23; April 4; Dec. 1, 1966; Walter Schwartz, *The Arabs in Israel* (London, 1959), 54, 67, 72ff, 164, 169; Oscar Kraines, *Government and Politics in Israel* (Boston, 1961), 169, 192f; Yusef Waschitz, "Arabs in Israeli Politics," *New Outlook,* March–April, 1962, 37. According to *NY Times* of March 9, 1968, the Jewish mayor of Jerusalem, Teddy Kollek, complained that the "national Government had proved itself a failure in the social and psychological" integration of the Arabs in Jerusalem. He "criticized Jewish Jerusalemites for what he termed their unwillingness to accept Arabs in their schools or to work for non-Jewish employers."

63. Kraines, *op. cit.*, Schwartz, *op. cit.*, 54, 67, 164ff; *NY Times,* Feb. 21, 1962; Feb. 21, 1963; Livne, *op. cit.*, 44; Livne, "Fine Words but No Deeds," *New Outlook,* July, 1961, 17; Simha Flapan, "Integrating the Arabs of Israel," *ibid.*, Jan., 1963, 25ff; Nahum Goldman, "The Hope of the Symposium," *ibid.*, 3f; Shmiel Shnitzer, "An Arab Policy That Went Bankrupt," *ibid.*, Dec., 1961, 56ff. *Israel's Oriental Problem,* 5ff.

64. A/PV.1566, Sept. 25, 1967, 56ff; S/PV.1375, Nov. 13, 6ff; *Israel Digest,* Sept. 22, 1967, 1; Oct. 9, 1967, 3, 7; *NY Times,* Sept. 4, 6, 7; Oct. 12, 13, 29, 31; Nov. 8, 9, 1967.

65. Ben-Gurion, *Israel: Years of Challenge* (New York, 1963), 189.

66. *NY Times,* June 13, 19; July 2, 9; Sept. 20, 24; Oct. 14, 1967.

67. *Ibid.*, Feb. 29; March 1, 2, 3, 9, 10, 1968; *The Evening Bulletin,* March 10, 1968.

68. *NY Times,* Nov. 25; Dec. 2, 3, 6, 10, 13, 1967; Jan. 12, 1968; Peretz, "Israel's Administration and Arab Refugees," 340f.

69. *Israel's Oriental Problem,* 1f, 5ff; May, 1967, 1f.

70. A/PV.1562, Sept. 21, 1967, 23ff; *NY Times,* June 8, 18, 20, 24, 27; July 4, 1967.

71. *NY Times,* June 8, 20, 24, 29; July 30, Aug. 21; Sept. 24, 27; Oct. 13; Nov. 3, 1967; Jan. 8, 9, 1968.

72. A/PV.1563, Sept. 22, 1967, 52ff; *NY Times,* Aug. 20; Sept. 23, 27; Oct. 29; Nov. 23; Dec. 3, 13, 14, 15, 1967.

73. S/PV.1373, Nov. 9, 1967, 147ff; A/PV.1571, Sept. 28, 1967, 22ff; *NY Times,* Sept. 1, 29; Nov. 25, 28, 29, 30; Dec. 2, 8, 11, 12, 16, 17, 1967.

74. *NY Times,* Sept. 27; Oct. 15, 16; Nov. 3, 20, 30, 1967; A/PV.1567, Sept. 26, 38ff.

75. *UN Weekly News Summary,* WS/305, Aug. 4, 1967, 3.

76. Simon, *op. cit.*, 7; Schwartz, *op. cit.*, 80; *NY Times,* Aug. 5, 1961; Salah Baransi, "To Face Facts and Confess Faults," *New Outlook,* March–April, 1963, 67.

77. Personal interviews.

Chapter X.

1. *Middle East Intelligence Survey* (Tel Aviv), April 1, 1973, p. 2. Also personal interviews with Palestinians in Beirut during the first week of Aug. 1971.

2. *State Dept. Bulletin,* Aug. 10, 1970, p. 176; *New Middle East* (London), July 1972, p. 5; *New York Times,* Feb. 26, 1971.

3. Yehoshua Arieli, "What Is Realistic Politics?" *New Outlook,* Aug. 1971, pp. 8ff. See also *ibid.,* Jan.–Feb. 1971, p. 42; and Sept. 1971, pp. 3ff, 19ff. In addition, personal interviews with Israelis in Tel Aviv and Jerusalem during the latter part of March 1969.

4. *New York Times,* July 5, 1968.

5. S/10070, Jan. 4, 1971, Annex I, 8; *New Middle East,* Aug. 1971, p. 23; also personal interviews with Jordanian officials in Amman during the first week of Aug. 1969 and the last week of July 1971.

6. *State Dept. Bulletin,* Jan. 5, 1970, pp. 7ff; Michael Brecher, *Decisions in Israel's Foreign Policy* (New Haven: Yale University Press, 1975), pp. 483ff; Malcolm Kerr, ed., *The Elusive Peace in the Middle East* (Albany: State University of New York Press, 1975), pp. 140, 293f.

7. *Middle East Journal,* Summer 1975, p. 329; *Time,* Sept. 11, 1972, p. 22; *Evening Bulletin* (Philadelphia), March 7, 1972; Walter Laqueur, *Confrontation: The Middle East and World Politics* (New York: Quadrangle/New York Times, 1974) p. 33.

8. *New York Times,* July 13, 1975; Simha Flapan, "Middle East Brinkmanship," *New Outlook,* Dec. 1971, p. 4; Michael Brecher, *The Foreign Policy System of Israel* (New Haven: Yale University Press, 1972), pp. 309f; Samuel J. Roberts, *Survival or Hegemony? The Foundations of Israeli Foreign Policy* (Baltimore: John Hopkins Press, 1973), p. 121; Laqueur, *Confrontation,* pp. 43, 254; Insight Team of the London *Sunday Times, The Yom Kippur War* (Garden City, N.Y.: Doubleday, 1974), p. 27.

9. According to Israeli writer Amnon Kapeliuk, "Secretary of State William Rogers had told . . . Sadat that in his opinion Egypt had done everything it was obliged to do in order to promote a Near East Settlement" ("Student Unrest in Egypt," *New Outlook,* Feb. 1972, pp. 29, 31). Former U.S. Ambassador to the UN Charles Yost wrote in *Life,* April 9, 1971: "It has been my strong impression . . . that the Arabs have in fact been ready for a year and a half to make such a peace and undertake such commitments" as were required for peace. See also A/10070/ Add 2, March 5, 1971, 4.

10. For example, see articles by various Israelis in *New Outlook,* Aug. 1971, pp. 8ff; Dec. 1971, p. 4; Jan. 1972, p. 23; and Feb. 1972, p. 9. Israeli professor Yehoshua Arieli stated: "Israel has been less flexible than Egypt in seeking the path to peace" ("What Is Realistic Politics?" *ibid.,* Aug. 1971). *Newsweek* reported on Dec. 6, 1971, that "the Nixon Administration regards Israeli inflexibility as the main cause of the diplomatic stalemate that has afflicted the Middle East for the last four years." Simha Flapan, Israeli writer and editor, wrote in *New Outlook,* Dec. 1971: "Most objective observers of Israeli policy are drawn to the conclusion that Israel is more interested in gaining time than in winning peace." See also Yost, *Life,* April 9, 1971, and the *New York Times,* Feb. 13; April 8, 20; Dec. 1, 1971.

11. Even prior to March 8, 1972, some Syrian officials had privately expressed a willingness to go along with Resolution 242 under these conditions (personal

interviews with Syrian officials in Damascus during the second week of Aug. 1971).

12. Jon Kimche, *There Could Have Been Peace* (New York: Dial, 1973), pp. 311f.

13. See also Laqueur, *Confrontation*, p. 66.

14. In a detailed study of the views of various Israeli leaders, Michael Brecher concluded that Golda Meir was "hawkish and rigid" and totally distrustful of Arab intentions and that she disregarded the views of such Israeli "doves" as Foreign Minister Abba Eban and Secretary-General of the Mapai Party Pinhas Sapir (*The Foreign Policy System*, pp. 310, 316). Walter Laqueur held that her "intransigence had obstructed progress to a settlement"; to Meir and other Israeli leaders "the *status quo* seemed greatly preferable to any agreed settlement"; "Mrs. Meir's government practiced a policy of *immobilisme*"; and it had "no concept for relations with the Arab world" (*Confrontation*, pp. 43, 217, 254).

15. *New York Times*, Dec. 2, 1973.

16. Edward R. F. Sheehan, "How Kissinger Did It: Step By Step In The Middle East," *Foreign Policy*, Spring 1976, pp. 47, 69f; Uri Avneri, "Reflections on Mr. Hammami," *New Outlook*, Jan. 1976, p. 51.

17. *Brief: Middle East Highlights* (Tel Aviv), Oct. 1–15, 1975, p. 2; *New Outlook*, Sept. 1975, p. 10; *Jerusalem Post*, Sept. 12; Nov. 21, 28, 1975; *New York Times*, July 13, 16, 22, 1974; Dec. 27, 1975; Uri Avneri *et al.*, *Israel and the Palestinians: A Different Israeli View* (New York: Breira, 1975).

18. Sheehan, "How Kissinger Did It," pp. 58, 63.

19. *New York Times*, March 3, 1976. As of this writing, American officials have not confirmed that they promised to prevent an Israeli attack on Syria and to insure Palestinian participation in any Middle East settlement.

20. Sheehan quoted Kissinger in "How Kissinger Did It" (p. 52) as telling the Israelis after the breakdown of the March 1975 negotiations: "Our strategy was to save you from dealing with all these pressures all at once. If we wanted the 1967 borders we could do it with all world public opinion and considerable domestic opinion behind us. The strategy was designed to protect you from this. We've avoided drawing up an overall plan for a global settlement. I see pressures building up to force you back to the 1967 borders." These Arabs could interpret this statement, taken from State Department files, as supporting their contention that Kissinger was stalling for time to help Israel.

21. *New York Times*, Oct. 3, 1975; *New Outlook*, July–Aug. 1974, p. 2. A senior Israeli official told *Time* magazine: "Given nonacceptance of Israel by the Arabs, we have been maneuvering since 1967 to gain time and to return as little as possible. The predominant government view has been that stalemates are to our advantage. Our great threat has been the Rogers plan—and American policy to move us back to the [1967] lines. The . . . agreement with Egypt is another nail in the coffin of that policy. We realize that the entire world is against us on the issue of borders and that we are terribly dependent on one nation for sophisticated arms. Nevertheless, we have been successful for the past . . . eight years, and we may have to go on maneuvering for another ten. If the . . . interim agreement [gave] us only six months rather than three years, we would buy it because the alternative is Geneva and . . . more pressure to go back to the 1967 borders. The . . . agreement has delayed Geneva, while . . . assuring us arms, money, a coordinated policy with Washington and quiet in the Sinai. . . . We gave up a little for a lot" (quoted by Sheehan, "How Kissinger Did It," p. 64).

22. *Israel Digest*, Sept. 12, 1975, p. 4; Dec. 5, 1975, p. 4.

23. *Christian Science Monitor*, Feb. 10, 1974; *Jerusalem Post*, Jan. 31, 1975; *Washington Post*, Jan. 29, 1975; Joseph Alsop, *New York Times Magazine*, Dec. 14, 1975.

24. Department of State, *Selected Documents*, "United States Policy in the Middle East: Nov. 1974–Feb. 1976" (1976), pp. 59ff.

25. *Israel Digest*, Feb. 13, 1976, p. 3.

26. *New York Times*, Jan. 26, 1976.

27. Gerald R. Ford, *A Time to Heal: The Autobiography of Gerald R. Ford* (New York: Harper & Row, 1979), pp. 245, 287f. See also Peretz Merhav, "Challenge Facing the Doves," *New Outlook*, April–May, 1976, p. 10.

28. For excerpts from Scranton's statement see *New York Times*, March 25, 1976.

29. *Ibid.*, March 25–27, 1976; *Evening Bulletin* (Philadelphia), March 25, 1976.

30. William Quandt. *Decade of Decisions: American Policy Toward the Arab-Israeli Conflict, 1967–1976* (Berkeley: University of California Press, 1977), pp. 279, 281; *The Middle East and North Africa, 1982–83* (London: Europa Publications, 1982), p. 82; quotations from *Davar*, Oct. 11 and 15 in *Journal of Palestine Studies*, Spring 1977, p. 149.

31. Ford, *A Time to Heal*, p. 245.

32. *UN Monthly Chronicle*, Dec. 1976, pp. 5, 67; *The Middle East and North Africa*, p. 48.

33. Sheehan, "How Kissinger Did It," pp. 203f; Quandt, *Decade of Decisions*, p. 286; Yitzhak Rabin, *The Rabin Memoirs* (Boston: Little, Brown, 1979), p. 201.

34. *Davar* and *Haaretz* quoted in *Journal of Palestine Studies*, Spring 1977, pp. 145f, 150.

35. Kamal S. Salibi, *Cross Roads to Civil War: Lebanon, 1958–1976* (Delmar, N.Y.: Caravan Books, 1976) pp. 9, 89ff; Michael C. Hudson, *The Precarious Republic: Political Modernization in Lebanon* (New York: Random House, 1968), p. 11; P. Edward Haley and Lewis W. Snider, eds., *Lebanon in Crisis: Participants and Issues* (Syracuse: Syracuse University Press, 1979), pp. 161, 165f.

36. Salibi, *Cross Roads to Civil War*, p. 160; *New York Times*, Aug. 13, 1977.

37. *New York Times*, Sept. 22 and 26, 1977; Hudson, *The Precarious Republic*, p. 28; Meir Pail, "In the Region," *New Outlook*, May 1984, p. 26.

38. Quandt, *Decade of Decisions*, p. 282; Aaron David Miller, *The PLO and the Politics of Survival* (New York: Praeger, 1983), pp. 37f; Zeev Schiff, "Dealing with Syria," *Foreign Policy*, Summer 1984, pp. 92, 99.

39. Schiff, "Dealing with Syria," p. 100.

40. *Christian Science Monitor*, Nov. 9, 1976; *New York Times*, Sept. 1, 1977; Haley and Snider, *Lebanon in Crisis*, p. 167.

41. *New York Times*, July 3, 1976. The *Times* reported (Feb. 22, 1984) that "senior American diplomats acknowledge that their embassy could not function without PLO protection." The *Times* also reported (Feb. 28, 1984) that CIA officials indicated that "clandestine CIA contacts have been maintained [with the PLO in Beirut] for security intelligence matters." For example, the PLO helped warn them when threats to the embassy or Americans developed.

42. *New York Times*, Nov. 12, 1976.

43. *The Middle East and North Africa*, p. 82.

Chapter XI. The Carter Administration, Israel, the Arabs, and Palestinians, 1977–1980

1. Zbigniew Brzezinski, *Power and Principle: Memoirs of the National Security Adviser: 1977–1981* (New York: Farrar, Straus, Giroux, 1983) pp. 83ff, 87; Cyrus Vance, *Hard Choices: Critical Years in America's Foreign Policy* (New York: Simon and Schuster, 1983), pp. 163, 166, 179; Rabin, *The Rabin Memoirs*, pp. 293f, 296.

2. Brzezinski, *Power and Principle*, p. 87; Vance, *Hard Choices*, p. 164.

3. *Toward Peace in the Middle East: Report of a Study Group* (Washington: Brookings Institution, 1975); Brzezinski, *Power and Principle*, pp. 91, 194; Vance, *Hard Choices*, pp. 160, 173, 177; Jimmy Carter, *Keeping the Faith: Memoirs of a President* (New York: Bantam Books, 1983) pp. 280f.

4. *Ibid.*, p. 209; Vance, *Hard Choices*, p. 177; Brzezinski, *Power and Principle*, p. 87.

5. Carter wrote in *Keeping the Faith* (p. 288): "After meeting with these key Arab leaders, I was convinced that all of them were ready for a strong move on our part to find solutions to long-standing disputes and that with such solutions would come their recognition of Israel and the right of Israelis to live in peace." Also see Vance, *Hard Choices*, pp. 166f.

6. *New York Times*, Aug. 21, 1977; Ismael Fahmy, *Negotiating for Peace in the Middle East* (Baltimore: Johns Hopkins Press, 1983), pp. 191f. In the first half of November 1977 the author held discussions with top leaders of Jordan and Syria. They indicated their readiness to go to Geneva and to negotiate a fair, comprehensive peace settlement with Israel. Lebanese leaders indicated they would accept whatever the other Arab leaders agreed to at Geneva. The author did not arrive in Egypt until after Sadat's trip to Jerusalem. See note 43.

7. *Ibid.*, pp. 191f; Vance, *Hard Choices*, pp. 166f, 176.

8. Carter, *Keeping the Faith*, p. 280; Vance, *Hard Choices*, pp. 173ff; Brzezinski, *Power and Principle*, pp. 90f. Rabin contended that he was constrained by divisions within his own cabinet and by the forthcoming elections with the hawkish Likud as his primary opponent. Rabin, *The Rabin Memoirs*, pp. 292, 300.

9. *Ibid.*, pp. 263, 293–297. Also see *New York Times*, March 14, 1977. *Haaretz*, Nov. 5, 1976, held that Israel preferred "interim solutions" and "was not particularly interested . . . in the establishment of a full [comprehensive] peace between us and the Arabs." (Quoted by *Journal of Palestine Studies*, Spring 1977, p. 145.)

10. Vance, *Hard Choices*, p. 166; Robert Slater, *Rabin of Israel: A Biography* (London: Robson Books, 1977) p. 239.

11. Carter, *Keeping the Faith*, p. 280; Vance, *Hard Choices*, p. 166; Brzezinski, *Power and Principle*, pp. 90, 92f.

12. Rabin, *The Rabin Memoirs*, pp. 294, 332; Vance, *Hard Choices*, pp. 159f, 169, 170, 184; Slater, *Rabin of Israel*, pp. 233, 236; Moshe Dayan, *Breakthrough: A Personal Account of the Egypt-Israel Peace Negotiations* (New York: Alfred A. Knopf, 1981) p. 57; *New York Times*, Jan. 20, 1977.

13. *The Middle East and North Africa*, p. 50.

14. Amnon Kapeliuk, "To Whom Does the West Bank Belong?" *New Outlook*, Dec. 1977/Jan. 1978, p. 47; Simha Flapan, ed., *When Enemies Dare to Talk: An Israeli-Palestinian Debate* (London: Croom Helm, 1979) p. 42; Simha Flapan, "Begin and the Diaspora," *New Outlook*, June/July 1977, p. 18.

15. In 1970, Begin had left the national unity government, which had been founded during the May 1967 crisis, because that government had accepted Resolution 242. He

declared before the Knesset at the time that the preamble of the resolution, which forbade the annexation of any territory by force of arms, and the provision in the resolution's body which required Israel to withdraw her armed forces from occupied territories were "irrevocably connected." Thus, by his interpretation in 1970, Israel had to withdraw from *all* occupied lands. For a discussion of this see the article "Re-interpreting International Law" by Nathan Feinberg, Professor of International Law, Hebrew University in *New Outlook,* Aug. 1977, p. 20.

16. Haley and Snider, *Lebanon in Crisis,* pp. 96f, 100; *New York Times,* June 28, Sept. 3, 4, 18, 21, 24, 25, 26, 27, Oct. 6, 1977.

17. Carter, *Keeping the Faith,* p. 288.

18. *Ibid.,* p. 185; Brzezinski, *Power and Principle,* pp. 100, 104.

19. *Ibid.,* pp. 96ff.

20. Vance, *Hard Choices,* p. 185.

21. Brzezinski, *Power and Principle,* p. 105; Vance, *Hard Choices,* p. 185. Carter told Foreign Minister Dayan on September 19, that he was "convinced that some of Israel's recent actions were the main obstacle to progress on peace talks" and that "the gratuitous endorsement of a new group of settlements, the recent invasion of Lebanon [Israeli forces entered south Lebanon to fight with right-wing Christians against the Palestinians] and the failure to make reasonable proposals or counterproposals on the question of Palestinian representation were almost insurmountable obstacles" (Carter, *Keeping the Faith,* p. 185).

22. Dayan, *Breakthrough,* p. 59.

23. Brzezinski, *Power and Principle,* p. 105.

24. Dayan, *Breakthrough,* p. 69.

25. Fahmy, *Negotiating for Peace in the Middle East,* pp. 196, 212f.

26. *New York Times,* March 21, Aug. 9, 1977.

27. Brzezinski, *Power and Principle,* p. 94.

28. Vance, *Hard Choices,* p. 188; Dayan, *Breakthrough,* p. 23; Rabin, *The Rabin Memoirs,* p. 319.

29. Brzezinski, *Power and Principle,* p. 103.

30. Helena Cobban, *The Palestine Liberalization Organization: People, Power and Politics* (Cambridge, England: Cambridge University Press, 1984), p. 240. See also: Sabri Jirys, "On Political Settlement in the Middle East," *Journal of Palestine Studies,* Autumn 1977; Mattityahu Peled, "Talking to the PLO," *New Outlook,* March/April 1983; Robert O. Freedman, ed., *World Politics and the Arab-Israel Conflict* (New York: Pergamon Press, 1979), p. 229. The author held discussions with four top PLO officials in Damascus (November 13–16) and Beirut (November 18). They indicated a desire to be invited to a Geneva conference but were unprepared to recognize Resolution 242 and Israel until they received more assurances from the United States about receiving something meaningful in return for giving up their "bargaining card" and taking the risks involved. He found Cobban's evaluation of the situation to be an accurate one.

31. For a convenient source for this and other documents related to the Arab-Israeli conflict for the period 1967–1983 see *The Quest for Peace: Principal U.S. Publications, Statements and Related Documents on the Arab-Israeli Peace Process, 1967–1983,* U.S. Department of State, Publication 9373, Bureau of Public Affairs, Washington, D.C.

32. Vance, *Hard Choices,* pp. 192f; Fahmy, *Negotiating for Peace in the Middle East,* p. 234.

33. Vance, *Hard Choices,* p. 192.

34. *New York Times,* Oct. 5, 1977.

35. Bureau of Public Affairs, Department of State, "Joint U.S.–Israeli Statement, Oct. 5, 1977"; *New York Times,* Oct. 6, 1977.

36. Vance, *Hard Choices,* p. 192; *New York Times,* May 2, 1978; Cobban, *The Palestine Liberation Organization,* p. 90.

37. Brzezinski, *Power and Principle,* pp. 109ff; Vance, *Hard Choices,* p. 193.

38. *Ibid.,* p. 191; Fahmy, *Negotiating for Peace in the Middle East,* pp. 249f.

39. Dayan, *Breakthrough,* pp. 19–22.

40. R. D. McLaurin, Don Peretz, Lewis W. Snider, *Middle East Foreign Policy: Issues and Processes* (New York: Praeger, 1982) p. 161.

41. *New York Times,* Nov. 7, 9, 10, 1977.

42. Fahmy, *Negotiating for Peace in the Middle East,* pp. 230, 279, 283.

43. Anwar el-Sadat, *In Search of Identity* (New York: Harper & Row, 1977) pp. 302f; Hermann Frederick Eilts, "Standing Small in the Middle East," *Middle East Insight,* April/May 1984, p. 10; discussions held by the author with Sadat in Egypt on November 28, 1977, shortly after his return from Jerusalem. In a letter from Sadat to the author he wrote that he was "trying to dispel" the "historical roots of mistrust, fear and hostility."

44. For Sadat's and Begin's addresses before the Knesset see Itmar Rabinovich and Jehuda Reinharz, eds., *Israel in the Middle East: Documents and Readings on Society, Politics, and Foreign Relations* (New York: Oxford University Press, 1984) pp. 321–27.

45. Ezer Weizman, *The Battle for Peace* (New York: Bantam Books, 1981) pp. 151, 190, 234; Vance, *Hard Choices,* p. 197; Brzezinski, *Power and Principle,* pp. 235f.

46. Text of Begin's proposal in Rabinovich and Reinharz, *Israel in the Middle East,* pp. 327f.

47. Weizman, *The Battle for Peace,* pp. 119f, 231. Weizman concluded (p. 151): "Begin's position was clear: he was going to give up the Sinai to protect himself against any eventual concessions in the West Bank."

48. Carter, *Keeping the Faith,* pp. 304, 191.

49. Weizman, *The Battle for Peace,* pp. 137f.

50. Robert O. Freedman, ed., *Israel in the Begin Era* (New York: Praeger, 1982) p. 87; McLaurin, Peretz, and Snider, *Middle East Foreign Policy,* p. 154.

51. Secretary Vance said, after seeing President Assad in mid-December, that Assad was cautious about aligning himself with the rejectionists and remained on the sidelines to see what developed. Vance, *Hard Choices,* p. 197. See also Freedman, *World Politics and the Arab-Israeli Conflict,* p. 105.

52. For Tripoli and Algiers statements see *Journal of Palestine Studies,* Spring, 1978, pp. 188ff, 207.

53. *Ibid.,* Winter 1978, p. 30; Freedman, *World Politics and the Arab-Israeli Conflict,* p. 72.

54. A joint Syrian-Soviet communiqué of February 23, 1978, stated: "The two sides declared their firm intention of continuing joint efforts to reach a compromise and just solution" of the Arab-Israeli question (*Journal of Palestine Studies,* Summer 1978, p. 182). See also the statement made by the Syrian Foreign Minister at the non-aligned conference in Belgrade in July 1978 (*Journal of Palestine Studies,* Autumn, 1978, p. 197).

55. Haley and Snider, *Lebanon in Crisis,* pp. 151, 162; Freedman, *World Politics and the Arab-Israeli Conflict,* p. 230.

56. Rabinovich and Reinharz, *Israel in the Middle East,* p. 32.

57. Brzezinski, *Power and Principle*, p. 253.

58. Brzezinski wrote (*ibid.*, p. 121) that the Israelis "became confident that they could resist American pressures, and their experience with the White House encouraged them in that feeling." Egyptian Foreign Minister Ismael Fahmy claimed that Carter told Sadat in September 1977 that he did not have the political will to stand up to Israel (Fahmy, *Negotiating for Peace in the Middle East*, p. 290).

59. Brzezinski, *Power and Principle*, pp. 254, 273.

60. Carter, *Keeping the Faith*, p. 337.

61. Dayan, *Breakthrough*, p. 167.

62. Brzezinski, *Power and Principle*, p. 273.

63. Carter claimed: "Begin wanted to keep two things: the peace with Egypt and the West Bank . . . [and the Israelis] use the settlements and East Jerusalem issues to prevent the involvement of the Jordanians and the Palestinians" (Carter, *Keeping the Faith*, p. 405). See also Dayan, *Breakthrough*, p. 305.

64. Carter, *Keeping the Faith*, p. 405. Vance held that Begin's statements that he had given nothing new and that the inhabitants of the West Bank and Gaza would be given only limited administrative autonomy "caused untold damage" and weakened the U.S. position when she sought to explain the benefits from the accords to the inhabitants and to elicit their cooperation in the peace process (Vance, *Hard Choices*, p. 237).

65. Brzezinski, *Power and Principle*, pp. 276, 278.

66. Weizman, *The Battle for Peace*, pp. 190f.

67. *London Times*, Sept. 20, 1978; *The Middle East and North Africa*, p. 53; *Washington Post*, Sept. 24; Vance, *Hard Choices*, pp. 229f.

68. For the best Palestinian critical analysis of the Camp David accords see Fayez Sayegh, "The Camp David Agreement and the Palestine Problem," *Journal of Palestine Studies*, Winter 1979, pp. 3–40.

69. Vance, *Hard Choices*, p. 238; Freedman, *World Politics and the Arab-Israeli Conflict*, p. 271.

70. Carter, *Keeping the Faith*, p. 409; Vance, *Hard Choices*, p. 237.

71. Weizman, *The Battle for Peace*, pp. 138, 335, 383f, 386f; Dayan, *Breakthrough*, p. 305; *New York Times*, Oct. 22, 1979; Freedman, *Israel in the Begin Era*, pp. 35f.

72. Weizman, *The Battle for Peace*, pp. 190f; *New York Times*, March 20, 21, 1979.

73. For texts of the treaty and the memorandum of agreement see *Middle East Journal*, Summer, 1979, pp. 327–47.

74. Weizman, *The Battle for Peace*, pp. 383f.

75. *New York Times*, April 29, May 22, Aug. 16, 1979.

76. *New York Times*, June 12, 1979.

77. *Ibid.*, June 21, 19979; *Newsweek*, July 9, 1979, p. 42; *Time*, Nov. 5, 1979, p. 52.

78. *New York Times*, April 20, May 3, 1979.

79. William Quandt, "The Middle East Crisis," *Foreign Affairs: America and the World*, 1979, p. 551.

80. *The Middle East and North Africa*, p. 55; *New York Times*, July 9, 1979; March 13, April 24, 1980.

81. *Ibid.*, July 12, 1980.

82. Carter, *Keeping the Faith*, p. 427; Brzezinski, *Power and Principle*, p. 438.

83. Vance, *Hard Choices*, p. 254.

84. Weizman, *The Battle for Peace*, pp. 119f, 122, 191.

85. Carter, *Keeping the Faith*, p. 494.

86. Freedman, *Israel in the Begin Era*, pp. 35f; *The Middle East and North Africa*, p. 476; *New York Times*, Oct. 22, 1979.

87. *Jerusalem Post*, Dec. 13, 1979.

88. The issue of East Jerusalem will be discussed later.

89. Michael Oren, "Horseshoe in the Glove," *Middle East Review*, Fall 1983, p. 23.

90. *New York Times*, Feb. 7, 1979, Nov. 23, 1981; *Middle East International*, June 6, 1980, p. 13.

91. *Evening Bulletin* (Philadelphia), Dec. 7, 1980.

92. Jewish "terrorist" activities will be discussed later.

93. Oren, "Horseshoe in the Glove," pp. 17–21.

94. *Presidential Documents*, XVI, Oct. 20, 1980, pp. 2194, 2305; Nov. 3, p. 2462.

95. Alfred Atherton, "Arabs, Israelis and America," *Foreign Affairs*, Summer, 1984, p. 1199.

96. Richard P. Stevens, "The Vatican, the Catholic Church and Jerusalem," *Journal of Palestine Studies*, Spring, 1981, pp. 109f. Also see the letter to the editor (*New York Times*, May 12, 1984) from the Director of the Secretariat for Catholic-Jewish Relations, National Council of Bishops for further information about the views of the Vatican on the Jerusalem question.

97. Costa Rica withdrew her embassy, but later returned it to Jerusalem. El Salvador moved her embassy from Tel Aviv to Jerusalem.

98. *New York Times*, Dec. 4, 1980.

99. Meron Benvenisti, *Jerusalem: Study of a Polarized Community*, quoted by *Palestine Congress of North America, PNCA Monthly*, May 1984, pp. 8f; *The Other Israel: Newsletter of the Israel Council for Israeli-Palestinian Peace*, Nos. 6–7, Feb.–March, 1984, p. 6.

100. Brzezinski, *Power and Principle*, p. 442; *Presidential Documents*, XVI, March 17, 1980, p. 460; New York Times, May 1, Oct. 29, 1980.

101. *The Middle East and North Africa*, p. 58; William Safire in the *New York Times*, March 24, 1980.

102. *Ibid.*, April 24, 1980; *Newsweek*, June 23, 1980, p. 39; *The Middle East and North Africa*, p. 57.

103. *New York Times*, June 14, 1980.

104. *Journal of Palestine Studies*, Autumn 1980, pp. 165ff, 194ff.

105. *New York Times*, Feb. 12, Oct. 15, Nov. 6, 10, 12, 1981, April 5, 1982; *Newsweek*, March 9, 1981, p. 2.

Chapter XII. The Reagan Administration, Israel, the Arabs, and Palestinians, January 1981–March 1985

1. William Safire claimed that Carter had assured Arab officials that once he was reelected he would be free to push more vigorously for Palestinian self-determination (*New York Times*, June 19, 1980).

2. *The Middle East and North Africa*, p. 58; *Newsweek*, Feb. 9, 1981, p. 45; *Christian Science Monitor*, Feb. 4, 1981; William Quandt, "Reagan's Lebanon Policy: Trial and Error," *Middle East Journal*, Spring 1984, p. 238.

3. *New York Times,* April 8, 19, 1981.

4. Some Israelis claimed that Begin took a tough stand partly to shift the focus of Israeli public opinion from the worsening economic situation in Israel to security issues in order to help him win the elections in June (*Middle East and North Africa,* p. 59; Freedman, *Israel in the Begin Era,* p. 96).

5. *Middle East and North Africa,* p. 59.

6. *Ibid.; Newsweek,* July 2, 1984, p. 17. Intelligence Chief Yehoshua Saguy had opposed launching the attack on the grounds that it could "serve as a precedent and Israel would expose itself to a similar attack"; it could cause a rift with the United States; and since Iraq needed at least five to ten more years to develop a nuclear device, there was no early threat to Israel (*Davar,* Aug. 18, 1983, quoted in *Israel Press Briefs,* Tel Aviv, Sept. 16, 1983, pp. 13f. *Israel Press Briefs* will be referred to in subsequent footnotes by the abbreviation *IPB*).

7. *Presidential Documents* XVII, June 22, 1981, pp. 633f.

8. *IPB, Background,* March 1984, p. 1; Freedman, *Israel in the Begin Era,* pp. 41, 50, 151; *Middle East and North Africa,* p. 60.

9. Zeev Schiff, "Lebanon: Motivations and Interests in Israel's Policy," *Middle East Journal,* Spring 1984, p. 224.

10. *New York Times,* Nov. 6, 11, 1981.

11. *Middle East and North Africa,* p. 60; *New York Times,* Dec. 1, 1981. Also see op ed article by Claudia Wright, *New York Times,* Dec. 1, 1981.

12. *Ibid.,* Aug. 17, Nov. 22, 29, 1981; *Washington Post,* Dec. 14, 1981; *Time,* Feb. 8, 1982, p. 46; *Journal of Palestine Studies,* Autumn, 1981, pp. 241ff.

13. *New York Times,* Nov. 16, Dec. 1, 16, 1981, Feb. 16, 1982.

14. *Ibid.,* Dec. 31, 1981; Jan. 25, 1982.

15. *Ibid.; Washington Post,* May 5, 1982.

16. *UN, Weekly News Summary,* Oct. 9, 1981, p. 6.

17. *Washington Post,* Dec. 15, 24, 1981.

18. *Ibid.,* Dec. 15, 16, 1981.

19. Moshe Arens, new Israeli ambassador to the United States, said that any further territorial concessions would be "too dangerous"; and Defense Minister Sharon insisted that after the Sinai, Israel would make no more concessions and that in any case Israel was strong enough to resist having to make them (*New York Times,* Jan. 25, 1982; *Washington Post,* April 26, 1982). See also Zeef Schiff, "Dealing with Syria," *Foreign Policy,* Summer 1984, p. 102.

20. *Le Monde Diplomatique,* July 1982, reproduced in *Journal of Palestine Studies,* Summer/Fall 1982, p. 287. See also Abba Eban in *Jerusalem Post,* Feb. 16, 1983; *Christian Science Monitor,* Feb. 19, 1982; *Time,* Feb. 15, 1982, p. 32; Zeef Schiff, "Green Light, Lebanon," *Foreign Policy,* Spring 1983, pp. 78–82.

21. Abba Eban in *Jerusalem Post,* Feb. 13, 1984.

22. Schiff, "Dealing with Syria," p. 101; Kapeliuk, *Journal of Palestine Studies,* p. 288; Adam M. Garfinkle, "Sources of the al-Fatah Mutiny," *Orbis,* Fall, 1983, pp. 614f.

23. Schiff, "Dealing with Syria," p. 108; Kapeliuk, *Journal of Palestine Studies,* p. 289; *Time,* June 21, 1982, p. 15. Sharon and some other Israelis had begun to claim that the Palestinians already had their state—in East Jordan—more than half of whose population was Palestinian. The Israeli Foreign Ministry had issued an English-language booklet entitled *Jordan Is Palestine (Time,* March 1, 1982, p. 24). According to Kapeliuk, in his May trip to the United States, Sharon showed American officials a map showing a "Christian Lebanon, an Israeli West Bank and a Palestinian Jordan"

(*Journal of Palestine Studies*, p. 289). Chief of Staff Rafael Eitan publicly stated on Israeli TV that the invasion should "finish the PLO and finish the Palestinian problem. There will be no more PLO and then you'll be able to dictate terms to the West Bank people" (Quoted by Naomi Joy Weinberger, "Peacekeeping Options in Lebanon," *Middle East Journal*, Summer, 1983, p. 355).

24. Meir Pail, "In the Region: Lebanon, 1984—The Way Out," *New Outlook*, May 1984, p. 27; *Davar*, June 13, 1983, reproduced in *IPB*, Aug. 1983, p. 10; *New York Times*, June 16, 1982; *Jerusalem Post*, June 21, 1982.

25. Schiff, "Green Light, Lebanon," pp. 73ff; Schiff, "Dealing with Syria," p. 101; Kapeliuk, *Journal of Palestine Studies*, p. 288; Garfinkle, "Sources of the al-Fatah Mutiny," pp. 614; *New York Times*, Feb. 26, 1984; *Philadelphia Inquirer*, Jan. 23, 1983. For an excellent study of the entire involvement of Israel in the Lebanon war, see Zeev Schiff and Ehud Yarri, *Israel's Lebanon War* (New York: Simon and Schuster, 1984).

26. *New York Times*, Feb. 26, March 6, April 6, 1982; *Time*, Feb. 15, p. 32; *Newsweek*, March 8, p. 32, May 24, p. 43. According to *Time*, April 26, 1982, p. 30, one Israeli general said, "the coming days will provide the opening Sharon is waiting for."

27. Abba Eban admitted in the *Jerusalem Post* of Feb. 16, 1983, that the borders had been kept quiet by the PLO. See also: *New York Times*, April 4, May 11, 1982; *Haaretz*, June 5, 1984, reproduced in *IPB*, July 1984, p. 6; *Al Hamishmar*, June 1, 1983, quoted in *Journal of Palestine Studies*, Fall 1983, p. 194; Pail, "In the Region," p. 27. According to the *New York Times*, (Dec. 16, 1981) some American officials "were encouraged that the PLO had observed the cease-fire in Lebanon 'even to the point' one official said of killing Syrian-backed Palestinians who opposed the cease fire.'"

28. *Washington Post*, April 22, 1982: *New York Times*, May 10, 11, 13, 16, 1982.

29. *Washington Post*, June 5, 1982.

30. *New York Times*, June 5; Schiff, "Green Light, Lebanon," p. 82; and Kapeliuk, *Journal of Palestine Studies*, p. 287. Even the wounded Israeli ambassador was later to hold that the invasion was unjustified (*Journal of Palestine Studies*, Fall 1983, p. 149); and a former military intelligence chief wrote: "The pretext of initiating the war . . . stands on filmsy grounds" [Yehoshafat Harkabi, *The Bar Kokhba Syndrome: Risk and Realism in International Politics* (Chappaqua, N.Y.: Rossel Books, 1983), p. 184].

31. Schiff, "Dealing with Syria," p. 104; Schiff, "Green Light, Lebanon," p. 83; *Davar*, June 13, 1983, quoted in *Journal of Palestine Studies*, Fall 1983, p. 195.

32. *New York Times*, Nov. 2, 1983, March 1, 1984.

33. Schiff, "Dealing with Syria," p. 105; *New York Times*, Oct. 25, 1982, Feb. 26, 1984; Ehud Yaari, "Israel's Dilemma in Lebanon," *Middle East Insight*, April/May 1984, pp. 19f.

34. Haig press conference at the U.S. Mission to the UN, Department of State, *Bulletin*, July 1982, p. 60.

35. *Washington Post*, April 29, May 5, 11, 1983; *New York Times*, June 22, 23, July 20, 1982; *Newsweek*, June 28, 1982, p. 30; Michael W. Suleiman, "Development of Public Opinion on the Palestine Question," *Journal of Palestine Studies*, Spring 1984, pp. 108ff.

36. Ann Smith, "The European Reaction to Israel's Invasion," *Journal of Palestine Studies*, Summer/Fall 1982, pp. 38–44; *Christian Science Monitor*, June 11, 1982; *New York Times*, June 30, 1982; *Washington Post*, July 28, 1982; *Middle East and North Africa*, p. 63.

37. Department of State, Bureau of Public Affairs, "Lebanon: Plan for the PLO Evacuation from West Beirut," *Current Policy*, No. 415, Aug. 1982, p. 8ff. Cobban, *The Palestine Liberation Organization*, p. 124.

38. The Commission's report is given in *New York Times*, Feb. 9, 1983.

39. Schiff, "Green Light, Lebanon," pp. 74, 83.

40. Editorials in *Davar, Haaretz, Jerusalem Post, Yediot Aharonot,* and *Maariv* reproduced in *IPB*, Feb. 1983. See also: Abba Eban, *The New Diplomacy* (New York: Random House, 1983), p. 232; Yael Yishai, "Dissent in Israeli Opinion on the Lebanese War," *Middle East Review*, Winter 1983, pp. 38ff; *New York Times*, June 1, 1982.

41. Robert G. Neumann, "Assad and the Future of the Middle East," *Foreign Affairs*, Winter 1983/84, pp. 238, 247; Schiff, "Dealing with Syria," p. 95; Gideon Rafael, "Atlantic Conference: A Trilateral Solution," *New Outlook*, Feb. 1984, p. 29; Amnon Rubinstein, *The Zionist Dream Revisited from Herzl to Gush Emunim and Back* (New York: Schoken Books, 1984) p. IX. *New York Times*, Feb. 11, 1983; *Newsweek*, Feb. 20, 1984, p. 47; *Haaretz*, Feb. 17, 1983 reproduced in *IPB*, March 1983, p. 19; Harkabi, *The Bar Kokhba Syndrome*, p. 184.

42. *Davar*, Jan. 13, 1983 in *IPB*, Feb. 1983, p. 8; *New Outlook*, June/July 1983, p. 12; Schiff, *Dealing with Syria," p. 95; New York Times*, Feb. 20, 1983.

43. Eban, *The New Diplomacy*, p. 232; Raphael, "Atlantic Conference," p. 9; *Haaretz*, Jan. 16, 1983, in *IPB*, Feb. 1983, p. 11; *Haaretz*, Oct. 26, 1983, in *IPB*, Nov. 1983, p. 10.

44. Neumann, "Assad and the Future of the Middle East," pp. 237f; Schiff, "Dealing with Syria," p. 111; *New York Times*, Oct. 24, 1984. When the PLO left Beirut, the CIA lost a secretly productive network of sources among the PLO who had provided contacts and information on radical groups and warnings when threats developed to the U.S. embassy and its personnel (*New York Times*, Dec. 6, 1983).

45. Department of State, Current Policy, No. 524, Oct. 1983; Schiff, "Dealing with Syria," p. 107; Hermann F. Eilts, "Standing Small in the Middle East," *Middle East Insight*, April/May 1984, p. 6; *New York Times*, Sept. 2, 1982. For good critical analyses of the Reagan plan see *Wall Street Journal*, April 20, 1983; and Hermann F. Eilts, "President Reagan's Middle East Peace Initiative," *American-Arab Affairs*, Fall 1983, pp. 3ff.

46. For the Fez plan see *Journal of Palestine Studies*, Winter 1983, pp. 202f.

47. *New York Times*, Sept. 15, 16, 1982, March 30, May 20, 1983; Robert O. Freedman, "Moscow, Damascus and the Lebanese Crisis, 1982–84," *Middle East Review*, Fall 1984, p. 26.

48. *Washington Post*, Sept. 3, 11, Nov. 5, 1982; *New York Times*, Dec. 22, 1982; Larry L. Fabian, "The Middle East: War Dangers and Receding Peace Prospects," *Foreign Affairs: America and the World*, 1983, p. 642.

49. *Ibid.*, p. 642; *Washington Post*, Nov. 5, 1982, April 20, 1983; *New York Times*, Dec. 22, 1982, April 13, 1983; *Jerusalem Post*, Oct. 6, 1983.

50. *Christian Science Monitor*, March 23, 1983. According to *Yediot Aharonot*, Jan. 14, 1983, the Israeli government was "alarmed by the positive statements emanating from Baghdad and by rumors of King Hussein's readiness to join the peace talks" (*IPB*, Feb. 1983, p. 11). Some administration officials charged that "Israel had been deliberately delaying talks over Lebanon in order to thwart any prospects for broader peace talks" through the Reagan Plan (*Time*, April 11, 1983, pp. 34f).

51. *New York Times*, Sept. 4, Oct. 13, Dec. 16, 1982; Fabian, "The Middle East," pp. 638f; *Christian Science Monitor*, Feb. 24, 1983.

52. Eric Rouleau, *Le Monde*, Oct. 1, 1982, quoted by *Journal of Palestine Studies*, Winter 1983, p. 192.

53. *Ibid.*, Spring 1983, pp. 253f.

54. Eric Rouleau, *Le Monde*, May 5, 1983 quoted by *ibid.*, Summer 1983, p. 200.

55. *New York Times*, April 12, 1983.

56. Cobban, *The Palestine Liberization Organization*, p. 241; Fabian, "The Middle East," p. 642.

57. Assad's speech quoted by *Journal of Palestine Studies*, Spring 1983, pp. 239f. *Washington Post*, Oct. 12, 1982. See also: *New York Times*, March 30, Dec. 8, 1983; *The Times* (London), May 17, 1983; Schiff, "Dealing with Syria," p. 94.

58. *New York Times*, Dec. 8, 1983; *Philadelphia Inquirer*, Dec. 8, 1983; *Journal of Palestine Studies*, Summer 1983, p. 132.

59. *Ibid.*, p. 132.

60. *New York Times*, Feb. 5, 10, April 1, 1983.

61. *New York Times*, March 15, 1983.

62. *Middle East International*, July 8, 1983; Schiff, "Dealing with Syria," p. 103; Neumann, "Assad and the Future of the Middle East," p. 240.

63. *Ibid.*, p. 239; *New York Times Magazine*, pp. 40f; Eilts, "Standing Small in the Middle East," p. 4.

64. For the texts of the treaty and U.S.-Israeli agreement see *Journal of Palestine Studies*, Summer 1983, p. 146; *Time*, May 16, 1983, p. 25.

65. *New York Times*, Oct. 24, Nov. 28, 1983.

66. *Ibid.*, Nov. 30, 1983, March 1, 1984; *Christian Science Monitor*, Feb. 7, 1984; Schiff, "Green Light, Lebanon," p. 106; Neumann, "Assad and the Future of the Middle East," p. 239.

67. Even after the treaty had been abrogated, the strongly pro-Israeli Lebanese Forces—the military arm of the right-wing Maronites, especially the Phalangists—set up its own liaison office in Jerusalem; and some of its militiamen held joint military exercises in northern Israel with Israeli troops. *Saudi Report* [Washington], July 2, 1984, p. 1.

68. *New York Times*, Oct. 16, 1983, *New York Times Magazine*, April 8, 1984; Neumann, "Assad and the Future of the Middle East," pp. 245ff; *Newsweek*, Sept. 26, 1983, p. 28.

69. *New York Times*, Nov. 5, Dec. 8, 10, 16, 20, 23, 1983.

70. Neumann, "Assad and the Future of the Middle East," p. 238.

71. *New York Times*, Nov. 20, 1983. For good accounts of the situation in south Lebanon see: *Philadelphia Inquirer*, Oct. 9 and Nov. 30, 1983; *New York Times*, Dec. 7, 1983.

72. *Ibid.*, Feb. 7, 10, June 23, 1984: *Al Hamishmar*, Feb. 15, 1984, in *IPB*, March 1984, p. 18; Yaari, "Israel's Dilemma in Lebanon," p. 18.

73. *UN Report of the International Conference on the Question of Palestine*, Geneva, A/Conf. 114/42, pp. 68–75.

74. *UN Chronicle*, Feb. 1984, pp. 81f.

75. *Ibid.*, pp. 83f.

76. *Ibid.*, pp. 83ff.

77. *Ibid.*, p. 88.

78. *New York Times*, July 5, 1984; *UN Weekly Summary*, Press Release, June 15, 1984, p. 3; *Palestine Perspectives*, June/July 1984, p. 13.

79. *Focus* (Washington, National Association of Arab-Americans), Vol. 7, No. 4, May 1984, p. 3.

80. *New York Times*, Nov. 27, 1984.

81. *Philadelphia Inquirer,* Nov. 27, 1983; Department of State, *Bulletin,* Jan. 1984, p. 3; *New York Times,* Nov. 1, 5, 1983.

82. *Ibid.,* Nov. 1, 5, 27, Dec. 4, 5, 1983; *Newsweek,* Dec. 5, 1983, p. 79.

83. Secretary Schultz began to contend that "you get peace and stability out of strength and deterrence" (*Philadelphia Inquirer,* Dec. 3, 1983). See also *ibid.,* Nov. 27; *New York Times,* July 20, 1984.

84. *Ibid.,* December 11, 1983.

85. *Ibid.,* Nov. 30, 1983. On June 24, 1984, the United States and Israel held their first joint military exercise to practice the evacuation of "wounded" servicemen from ships off shore to Israeli hospitals (*ibid.,* June 21, 1984).

86. *Philadelphia Inquirer,* Nov. 30, 1983; *Newsweek,* Dec. 12, 1983, p. 35.

87. *New York Times,* Dec. 5, 6, 1983, July 20, 1984.

88. *Ibid.,* Dec. 8, 1983.

89. *Ibid.,* Nov. 11, 1983; *Philadelphia Inquirer,* Dec. 5, 1983.

90. According to Foreign Minister Shamir, U.S. officials had told Prime Minister Peres during an October 1984 visit to Washington that even the Reagan plan would "not be revived" (*Haaretz,* Oct. 14, 1984 referred to in *Israeli Foreign Affairs,* Oakland, California, Dec. 1984, p. 4). According to *Maariv,* Oct. 18, 1984, Shamir told Likud activists that all forty foreign ministers he spoke to at the UN General Assembly session spoke against the settlements, while "President Reagan did not even mention the issue" (also quoted in *Israeli Foreign Affairs,* p. 4).

91. For example, see *New York Times,* March 14, 19, 23, 30, July 13, 1984. The White House deliberately asked Prime Minister Peres to visit Washington just before the elections to help win support from pro-Israel voters (*Time,* Oct. 22, 1984, p. 62).

92. Statement made by Undersecretary of State Lawrence Eagleburger on Feb. 23, 1984, before the Senate Foreign Relations Committee, quoted by *Mideast Observer* (Washington), March 1, 1984, p. 2.

93. *New York Times,* April 2, 1984.

94. *Saudi Report* (Washington), Nov. 12, 1984, p. 7; *New York Times,* Nov. 9, 1984.

95. *Ibid.,* Nov. 9, 1984.

96. *US News and World Report.* April 16, 1984, p. 47; *Newsweek,* June 11, 1984, p. 52.

97. *UN Division of Palestine Rights,* Vol. VII, Nos. 1–2, Jan./Feb. 1984, p. 2.

98. *Haaretz,* Feb. 20, 1984 in *IPB,* March 1984; pp. 5f. According to *Haaretz,* Oct. 14, 1983, at times settlers even attacked Israeli police and soldiers when they tried to stop settler attacks on the inhabitants (*IPB,* Nov. 1983, pp. 3f).

99. *New York Times,* May 22, 24, 1984.

100. *Ibid.,* June 22, 1984.

101. *Davar,* May 10, 1984 in *IPB,* June, 1984, p. 5. According to *Haaretz,* June 1, 1984 while the Likud government was arresting and trying Jewish terrorists, it held a "state dinner in the Knesset" to commemorate the anniversary of the blowing up of the British Embassy in Rome by the Irgun shortly after the end of World War II (*IPB,* July, 1984, p. 3).

102. *Moment,* Sept. 1983 quoted in *Jews Speak Out: Views From the Diaspora,* No. 3, Nov. 1983 (International Center for Peace in the Middle East, Tel Aviv), p. 8. According to *Davar,* July 27, 1983: "Thus, slowly but surely, the true struggle in the West Bank will become that for the expulsion of the Arabs" (*IPB,* Sept. 1983, p. 2). See also *Hadashot,* May 15, 1984, in *IPB,* June 1984, p. 6; *Davar,* July 29, 1983, quoted in *Journal of Palestine Studies,* Fall 1983, p. 188; *Haaretz,* Aug. 4, 1983, in *IPB,* Sept. 1983, p. 7; *Jerusalem Post,* May 9, 1984.

103. *Time,* July 9, 1984, p. 33; *New York Times,* July 10, 1984.

104. *Jerusalem Post*, May 6, 1984.

105. *Philadelphia Inquirer*, May 22, 1984.

106. *New York Times*, July 10, 1984.

107. *Ibid.*

108. *Ibid.*, July 16, 1984.

109. *Ibid.*, Aug. 28, 1984.

110. *Haaretz*, April 16, 1984 in *IPB: Background*, April 1984.

111. See Labor Party's platform in *New Outlook*, June/July 1984, pp. 24f. Also see *New York Times*, May 3 and June 23, 1984; *Time*, July 9, 1984, p. 32.

112. *New Outlook*, March/April 1983, p. 50.

113. See *New Outlook*, June/July 1984, pp. 26–30.

114. *Philadelphia Inquirer*, July 25, 1984. Grave concern about Kahane was expressed by many leading Israeli newspapers both before and after the elections. For example, the *Jerusalem Post*, July 11, 1984; *Yediot Aharonot*, July 24; *Maariv*, July 26; *Davar*, July 27—all in *IPB*, Aug. 1984, pp. 13ff.

115. *New York Times*, July 26, 29, 1984.

116. *Ibid.*, Dec. 4, 1984; *Philadelphia Inquirer*, December 2, 1984.

117. *Ibid.*, Oct. 29, 1984; *New York Times*, Nov. 4, 9, 1984.

118. *Ibid.*, Nov. 9, 11, 16, 1984; Jan. 16, 1985.

119. *Ibid.*, Jan. 15, 1985.

120. *Ibid.*, Oct. 16, Nov. 8, 1983; *Time*, July 4, 1983, p. 32; *Newsweek*, June 6, 1983, p. 46; *Haaretz*, June 14, 1984 in *IPB*, July 1984, *Special Supplement on the PLO Today*, p. 8.

121. *Ibid.*, pp. 4ff; *Wall Street Journal*, Nov. 10, 1983; *New York Times*, July 31, Nov. 8, 1983.

122. *Ibid.*, Dec. 3, 4, 23, 1983; Jan. 4, 21, 22, 1984; *Philadelphia Inquirer*, Dec. 8, 1983; *Palestine Perspectives*, Feb. 1984, pp. 1f.

123. Garfinkle, "Sources of the al-Fatah Mutiny," pp. 628f. In Dec. 1984, the *Jordan Times* quoted high PLO sources as saying that the PLO had sent a written message to President Reagan through President Mubarak which set two conditions for recognizing Israel: American and Israeli recognition of the legitimate rights of the Palestinians and Israel's acceptance of the principle of the exchange of land for peace (*Philadelphia Inquirer*, Dec. 11, 1984).

124. See the article of Yaacov Shimoni, a former senior Foreign Ministry official, in *Jerusalem Post*, June 12, 1984 and a resolution passed by an Israeli peace group on June 28, 1984, in *IPB: Special Supplement on the PLO Today*. *Newsweek* reported on Jan. 9, 1984, p. 17: "Israeli observers" believe that Arafat, with his military role fading, had "definitely decided to seek a diplomatic solution."

125. *New York Times*, Jan. 4, 1984.

126. *Ibid.*, Nov. 25, 1984.

127. *Ibid.*, Nov. 18, Dec. 4, 1984.

128. *Ibid.*, Nov. 25, 1984; *Philadelphia Inquirer*, Dec. 2, 1984.

129. *Ibid.*, Nov. 29, Dec. 5, 1984; *Saudi Report* (Washington), Nov. 12, 1984, p. 1; *New York Times*, Nov. 20, 25, 1984.

130. *Ibid.*, Nov. 23, Dec. 1, 2, 4, 1984; *Philadelphia Inquirer*, Nov. 23, 25, 30, Dec. 2, 1984.

131. *New York Times Magazine*, Feb. 19, 1984; Neumann, "Assad and the Future of the Middle East," p. 249; Schiff, "Dealing with Syria," p. 99; Aaron David Miller interview in *New Outlook*, Jan. 1984, p. 24; *New York Times*, March 29, 1983, July 2, 12, 1983, Oct. 1, 1983.

132. For example, see William Quandt, *US News and World Report*, Feb. 20, 1984, p. 32; *Time*, Feb. 6, 1984, p. 32; *New York Times*, Feb. 19, 1984, Jan. 22, 1985; *Newsweek*, Dec. 19, 1983, p. 33.

133. *Philadelphia Inquirer*, Nov. 19, 1983.

134. Quandt, *US News and World Report*, p. 32; Schiff, "Dealing with Syria," p. 107; *Time*, Feb. 6, 1984, p. 32. Secretary of State Schultz conceded that Syria had "legitimate security concerns with respect to Lebanon" (State Department *Bulletin*, Nov. 1983, p. 5).

135. Yaari, "Israel's Dilemma in Lebanon," p. 20.

136. *Newsweek*, Dec. 19, 1984, p. 32; *New York Times*, Jan. 11, 1984.

137. *Christian Science Monitor*, April 9, 1983; *Wall Street Journal*, May 2, 1983; *New York Times*, May 20, 1983; Neumann, "Assad and the Future of the Middle East," p. 248.

138. *New York Times*, Dec. 8, 1983.

139. *Newsweek*, Dec. 19, 1983, p. 27.

140. *Philadelphia Inquirer*, Jan. 14, 1984; *New York Times*, Jan. 15, 1984. Syrian officials held they were anxious to meet the United States "more than half way" in resolving the Lebanese and Arab-Israeli conflicts if the United States stopped negotiating separate agreements and followed more even-handed policies (*New York Times*, Feb. 19, 1984).

141. *New York Times*, Jan. 9, 12, 1984; *Philadelphia Inquirer*, Nov. 19, 1983, Jan. 8, 1984.

142. *New York Times*, July 11, 26, 1984.

Chapter XIII. Analyses and Conclusions

1. *New Outlook*, March/April 1983, p. 26.

2. International Center for Peace in the Middle East, *Newsletter*, Dec. 1984, p. 2; Abba Eban, "No Choice but Activism," *Foreign Policy*, Winter, 1984–85, p. 3; Uri Avneri, "1983: Auspicious or Ill Starred?" *New Outlook*, Jan./Feb. 1983, p. 13; *Ibid.*, March 1982, p. 6.

3. The interview was in a Beirut weekly, *Monday Morning*, Sept. 10–16, 1979, quoted in *Journal of Palestine Studies*, Winter 1980, pp. 148f.

4. Department of State, *Current Policy*, No. 475, April 11, 1983, p. 4. Assistant Secretary of State Nicholas Veliotis also stated before a congressional subcommittee that "the moderate Arabs now recognize that the question is not whether to make peace with Israel, but how best to do so" (Department of State, *Current Policy*, No. 490, p. 3).

5. Harold H. Saunders, *The Middle East Problem in the 1980s* (Washington: American Enterprise Institute, 1981), p. 8.

6. Alfred L. Atherton, Jr., "Arabs, Israelis and Americans," *Foreign Affairs*, Summer 1984, p. 1207.

7. See Eric Rouleau interview in *Journal of Palestine Studies*, Winter 1984, pp. 22f; Seth P. Tillman, *The United States in the Middle East: Interests and Obstacles* (Bloomington: Indiana University Press, 1984) p. 108; *New York Times*, June 21, 1984.

8. *Ibid.*, Jan. 21, Feb. 15, Dec. 2, 4, 23, 1984; *Christian Science Monitor*, Feb. 23, 1984; *Philadelphia Inquirer*, Dec. 21, 1984.

9. *New York Times*, Jan. 4, 16, 1985; Muhamed Hakki, "U.S.–Egyptian Relations," *American-Arab Affairs*, Fall 1983, pp. 29f.

10. *Ibid.; New York Times*, July 29, 1984.

11. Hussein's interview with the *New York Times*, March 15, 1984.

12. Crown Prince Hassan Bin Talal, "Return to Geneva," *Foreign Policy*, Winter 1983/84, pp. 1f; *Washington Report on Middle East Affairs*, Nov. 26, 1984, p. 4; *Jordan Newsletter* (Washington), July–Aug. 1984, pp. 1, 6.

13. *Saudi Report*, Nov. 1984, p. 4 quoting from an interview with Hussein. See also *New York Times*, Dec. 2, 4, 1984; *Philadelphia Inquirer*, Dec. 2, 1984.

14. For example, the *New York Times*, Oct. 2, 1984, wrote: "Privately, top aides to Mr. Shultz said he was reluctant to see the United States drawn into another mediation role in the Middle East unless there was virtual certainty that Syria and Lebanon would support the effort and be more forthcoming toward the Israelis."

15. *Ibid.*, Sept. 27, Oct. 12, Nov. 30, 1984; *Philadelphia Inquirer*, Sept. 28, 1984.

16. *New York Times*, Sept. 27, 1984.

17. Vance, *Hard Choices*, pp. 166f.

18. Saunders, *The Middle East Problem in the 1980s*, p. 68.

19. See also: op-ed articles in the *New York Times* by former Undersecretary of State Joseph Sisco, (Oct. 20, 1983); former Ambassador Robert G. Neumann (Dec. 1, 1983); Dimitri Simes (May 20, 1983); Edgar Bronfman, President of the World Jewish Congress (Dec. 9, 1983); Judith Kipper, (Feb. 14, 1984). Editorial in *New Outlook* (Tel Aviv) Jan./Feb. 1982, p. 4; Adeed Dawisha, "Comprehensive Peace in the Middle East and the Comprehension of Arab Politics," *Middle East Journal*, Winter 1983, p. 50; McLaurin, Peretz, and Snider, *Middle East Foreign Policy: Issues and Processes* (New York: Praeger, 1982) p. 273.

20. See also Eban, "No Choice but Activism," p. 5; Dimitri Simes, *New York Times*, May 20, 1983; Quandt, "Reagan's Lebanon Policy," p. 253; Neumann, "Assad and the Future of the Middle East," p. 247; Schiff, "Dealing with Syria," p. 97; interview with Aaron David Miller, State Department analyst, *New Outlook*, Jan. 1984, p. 24; *New York Times*, May 29, 1983, March 18, Dec. 25, 1984; *Philadelphia Inquirer*, Dec. 9, 1984. Even Labor party leaders Shimon Peres and Yitzhak Rabin urged the United States to help Israel to come to terms with Syria over the Lebanese situation (*Philadelphia Inquirer*, Dec. 9, 1984; *New York Times*, Oct. 21, 1983).

21. *Ibid.*, Feb. 14, April 24, 1984; Vance, *Hard Choices*, p. 177; McLaurin, Peretz, and Snider, *Middle East Foreign Policy*, p. 275.

22. See, for example, an interview with Assad in May 1984 in *IPB*, June 1984, p. 13; a statement by the Syrian Minister of State for Foreign Affairs in early February 1984 in *Philadelphia Inquirer*, Feb. 3, 1984; *New York Times*, Feb. 12, 1983; *Christian Science Monitor*, Feb. 21, 1984; McLaurin, Peretz and Snider, *Middle East Foreign Policy*, pp. 268–73.

23. *New York Times*, April 20, May 3, 1979.

24. Schiff, "Dealing with Syria," pp. 107f; Neumann, "Assad and the Future of the Middle East," pp. 246, 248; Vance, *Hard Choices*, p. 176; *Wall Street Journal*, Dec. 8, 1983; *The Times* (London) May 17, 1983; McLaurin, Peretz, and Snider, *Middle East Foreign Policy*, pp. 267, 273; *New York Times*, Jan. 23, July 4, Dec. 25, 1983, Feb. 14, 1984.

25. Quoted by Flora Lewis, *New York Times*, Dec. 25, 1984.

26. Assad has taken the position that only by negotiations for a comprehensive settlement from a position of strength can the Arabs elicit Israeli concessions. He felt that since the Arabs have no leverage, Israel will not give up the Golan Heights and settle

the Palestinian issue. Thus, according to former U.S. ambassador to Syria, Talcott Seelye, Assad was "not ready to negotiate at this time" (Seelye, "Syria's Middle East Role," *The Washington Report on Middle Eastern Affairs*, Sept. 17, 1984, p. 3). Israeli military writer, Zeev Schiff, wrote that Syria was not attempting "unilaterally to balance Israel's military strength." Her "main objective is simply to gain time to put off serious discussions until she rebuilds her military power" ("Dealing with Syria," *Foreign Policy*, Summer 1984, pp. 105, 109); Adeed Dawisha, "The Motives of Syria's Involvement in Lebanon," *Middle East Journal*, Spring 1984, pp. 231f.

27. Seelye, "Syria's Middle East Role," p. 3; McLaurin, Peretz, and Snider, *Middle East Foreign Policy*, p. 283; Paul A. Jureidini and R. D. McLaurin, *Beyond Camp David: Emerging Alignments and Leaders in the Middle East* (Syracuse: Syracuse University Press, 1981), p. 40; *New York Times*, May 20, 1983, Feb. 14, 1984.

28. Judith Kipper, *New York Times*, Feb. 14, 1984. Even Kissinger once said that "no peace is possible without Syria" (*Wall Street Journal*, May 2, 1983).

29. According to Israeli journalist Amnon Kapeliuk, who interviewed George Habbash, leader of the PFLP, in February, 1983, "George Habbash is also ready to agree to compromises, but he . . . does not believe that compromises [because of Israel's intransigent position] are realistic" (*New Outlook*, May 1983, p. 21).

30. See Sabri Jiryis, "On Political Settlement in the Middle East: The Palestinian Dimension," *Journal of Palestine Studies*, Autumn, 1977, p. 20 on the problem involved in PLO charter changes.

31. *Jerusalem Post*, June 12, 1984, reproduced in *IPB: Special Supplement on the PLO Today*, July 1984, p. 1.

32. *Ibid.*

33. *Haaretz*, June 5, 1984, reproduced in *IPB: Special Supplement on the PLO Today*, July 1976, p. 8.

34. *Maariv*, Jan. 1, 1977 quoted in *Change* (Briera), Feb. 1977; *New Outlook*, Feb./March 1976, p. 5.

35. Article in *Moment*, a Jewish monthly quoted by the *New York Times*, June 10, 1979; Abba Eban, "Sadat's Bid," *New Outlook*, Feb. 1975, p. 7.

36. *Ibid.*, Sept. 1979, pp. 8f.

37. Mordechai Bentov, "Israel and Palestine: Siamese Twins," *New Outlook*, March/April 1983, pp. 26f.

38. Mattityahu Peled, "Talking to the PLO," *New Outlook*, March/April 1983, p. 29. See also: Arie Eliav, former Secretary General of the Labor Party, *New Outlook*, Nov./Dec. 1979, p. 42; *Yediot Aharonot*, Jan. 14, 1983, in *IPB*, Feb. 1983, p. 10; Yosi Sarid, Labor Knesset member, *New Outlook*, Sept. 1979, p. 10; Meir Pail, Knesset member, *New Outlook*, Nov. 1969, pp. 33f; *New York Times*, March 21, 1982; Mark Heller, *A Palestinian State: The Implications for Israel* (Cambridge, Mass: Harvard University Press, 1983), pp. 45ff, 153. Simha Flapan, *When Enemies Dare to Talk* (London: Croom Helm, 1979), presents a debate involving over ten noted Israeli scholars and writers who supported a Palestinian state and most of whom called for talks with the PLO. Various peace groups, such as the Israel Council for Israeli-Palestinian Peace and some smaller political parties, the most important being Mapam, also back a two-state solution. *Newsweek* reported in its Dec. 8, 1975, issue that even as early as 1975 "some Israeli Arabists say that a majority of the leaders of the PLO now favor recognizing Israel in exchange for the creation of a Palestine state."

39. See also: *New York Times*, July 10, 1979, March 18, 1980, Oct. 10, 1981, June 9, 1982; *Christian Science Monitor*, Feb. 24, April 15, 1983; Joseph Greene, Philip Klutznik, Harold Saunders, Merle Thorpe, *The Path to Peace: Arab-Israeli Peace and*

the United States (Mt. Kisko, N.Y.: Seven Springs Center, 1981) p. 46; *UN Monthly Chronicle*, Dec. 1982, p. 9.

40. See discussions in prior chapters. The PLO formally accepted the Fez and Brezhnev plans and their peace terms. Also see: *New York Times*, Nov. 20, 22, 1978; Valerie Yorke, "Palestinian Self-Determination and Israel's Security," *Journal of Palestine Studies*, Spring 1979, pp. 5, 14ff.

41. For example, see Eric Rouleau, *Journal of Palestine Studies*, Winter 1984, p. 14.

42. Peled, "Talking to the PLO," p. 29.

43. Abu Iyad (Salah Khalaf) quoted in *Palestine Perspectives*, Feb. 1984, p. 6.

44. Interview with Abba Eban by Yaron London in *Ha'r*, Sept. 23, 1983, reproduced in *IPB*, Oct. 1983, p. 9. During this period Weizman also criticized the Labor government for "sitting with folded arms waiting for the telephone to ring and the Arabs to plead with us to make peace" on Israeli terms instead of taking the initiative to promote a fair and lasting peace (Weizman, *The Battle for Peace*, p. 72).

45. Edward R. F. Sheehan, *The Arabs, Israelis, and Kissinger: A Secret History of American Diplomacy in the Middle East* (New York: Reader's Digest Press, 1976), p. 210.

46. William R. Brown, *The Last Crusade: A Negotiator's Handbook* (Chicago: Nelson-Hall, 1980), pp. 191, 194, 203.

47. *New York Times*, Jan. 26, 29, 1976; *Newsweek*, Feb. 9, 1976; Ford, *A Time to Heal*, pp. 245, 287f.

48. Rabin, *The Rabin Memoirs*, pp. 263, 293, 297.

49. *Saturday Review*, April 3, 1971, pp. 14, 16.

50. *Haaretz*, Dec. 28, 1983 in *IPB*, Jan. 1984, p. 20; *Yediot Aharonot*, Jan. 14, 1983 in *IPB*, Feb. 1983, p. 11; *Jerusalem Post*, Dec. 25, 1983; *New York Times*, May 17, 1982.

51. *Haaretz*, Jan. 26, 1983, in *IPB*, Feb. 1983, p. 2.

52. *Maariv*, Dec. 9, 1983, in *IPB*, Jan. 1984, p. 5.

53. Bentov, "Israel and Palestine," pp. 25f.

54. Harkhabi, *The Bar Kokhba Syndrome*, p. 173.

55. Yehoshafat Harkabi, in *Yediot Aharonot*, Aug. 1, 1983 in *IPB*, Sept. 1983, p. 5.

56. *Time*, April 25, 1983, p. 32. See also the statement by former president Carter in *Moment*, quoted by *Middle East Perspectives*, April 1984, p. 32.

57. *Davar*, Jan. 5, 1984 in *IPB*, Feb. 1984, p. 4.

58. *New Outlook*, Sept. 1975, pp. 8f.

59. Weizman, *The Battle for Peace*, p. 227. See also: Harkabi, *The Bar Kokhba Syndrome*, pp. 107f.

60. State Department, *Bulletin*, Jan. 1984, p. 35.

61. Ebban, *The New Diplomacy*, p. 231.

62. Major General Carl von Horn, *Soldiering for Peace* (New York: David McKay, 1967), pp. 129, 76, 86f, 127–137; Lieutenant-General E. L. M. Burns, *Between Arabs and Israelis* (London: George Harrap, 1962), pp. 113–20; Fred J. Khouri, "Friction and Conflict on the Israel-Syrian Front," *Middle East Journal*, Winter–Spring 1963, pp. 16–23; Fred J. Khouri, "The Golan Heights in Perspective," *Middle East International*, Oct. 1974, pp. 15f.

63. Edgar Bronfman, President of the World Jewish Congress, held that it was an "illusion" to believe that "three million Jews can forever prevail in hostile confrontation with 120 million Arabs" (*Jews Speak Out: Views from the Diaspora*, Center for Peace in the Middle East, Tel Aviv, July 1983, p. 15).

64. Rabin, *The Rabin Memoirs*, p. 337.

65. Simha Flapan, ''Where Do We Go From Here? Return to Geneva or Back to the Brink,'' *New Outlook*, May 1974, p. 5.

66. Secretary Schultz stated this in an address before the United Jewish Appeal, Sept. 12, 1982, Department of State, *Bulletin*, Oct. 1982, pp. 1, 3. Also see: Weizman, *The Battle for Peace*, p. 283; and the views of other Israelis referred to by *Washington Post*, Feb. 2, 1983.

67. *New Outlook*, June/July 1983, p. 13.

68. *Moment*, Sept. 1983, reproduced in *IPB, Jews Speak Out: Voice from the Diaspora*, No. 3 (International Center for Peace in the Middle East, Tel Aviv), 1983, p. 7f. Ariel Yaari wrote in ''The Jordanian Option: A Persistent Illusion,'' *New Outlook*, June/July 1980, p. 34: ''National self-determination and independence have been the dominant phenomenon of the twentieth century, that even great world powers have had to accept, sometimes after prolonged and futile bloodletting. Today it is generally understood that no power on earth can stop a nation from throwing off foreign rule, once it has made up its mind to do so. What better proof than the history of Israel, whose independence was won in circumstances far worse than those faced by the Palestinians today.''

69. Heller, *A Palestine State*, p. 47.

70. *Ibid.*, Chapter 6.

71. *IPB*, Nov. 1983, p. 12.

72. *New York Times*, July 10, 1984.

73. For example, see the *Jerusalem Post*, Jan. 7, 1979.

74. *Yediot Aharonot*, April 27, 1979 in *Journal of Palestine Studies*, Autumn 1979, pp. 153f.

75. *New York Times*, Dec. 4, 1984.

76. Heller, *A Palestinian State*, pp. 32, 37 and Chapter 4.

77. *Ibid.*, pp. 146f, 153f. See also on Palestine state and Israel's security: *Trialogue* (Trilateral Commission), Winter 1983, p. 41.

78. *Ibid.;* Heller, *A Palestine State*, pp. 99ff.

79. *Haaretz*, Oct. 26, 1983 in *IPB*, Nov. 1983, p. 1; Ebban in *Jerusalem Post*, Feb. 13, 1984.

80. *New York Times*, Feb. 21, 1984, Feb. 7, 1985.

81. Ford, *A Time to Heal*, p. 245. Yehoshafat Harkabi wrote: ''If the U.S. officials tried to draw the Israel's government's attention to certain facts of political life, or delimit for them their latitude of action, they did so in a manner that Israeli leaders got the impressions that such advice could be ignored, that the United States would 'always' back Israel come what may, and that Israel's policy would always 'prevail' even when objected to by the United States' (*The Bar Kokhba Syndrome*, p. 178).

82. Brown, *The Last Crusade*, pp. 291, 333, 364.

83. See page 380 in text.

84. Brzezinski, *Power and Principle*, p. 105.

85. *Ibid.*, p. 88; Sheehan, *The Arabs, Israelis, and Kissinger*, p. 188.

86. Brzezinski, *Power and Principle*, p. 121.

87. *Ibid.*, pp. 109f.

88. Harkabi, *The Bar Kokhba Syndrome*, p. 179.

89. Department of State, *Current Policy*, No. 450, ''Review of U.S. Relations with the Soviet Union,'' Feb. 1, 1983, p. 2.

90. *New York Times*, Aug. 21, 1984.

91. Some Israelis and American Jews have criticized these pro-Israeli groups for uncritically supporting Israel's hard-line policies. For example, after visiting the United

States, Reserve General Mattityahu Peled found "the American Jewish community . . . supporting the most intransigent views in Israel on the Arab-Israeli conflict, in the belief that this is expected of it, and oblivious to the fact that Israel is not monolithic politically and that the hard-line taken by the Israeli Government is seriously challenged within Israel. The uncritical acceptance of Israel's official policy and the assessment of any disagreement with, or criticism of, that policy as betrayal and even anti-semitic is unworthy of the liberal tradition of American Jewry" (*New Outlook* May–June, 1975, p. 18). Albert Axelrod, a rabbi at Brandeis University, wrote in *ibid.*, May 1974: "Our Zionist movements tend to treat Israel slavishly, unthinkingly, and never critically: in brief, as a sacred cow. . . . They parrot the line of the Israeli government. . . . This is in marked contrast to the situation in Israel where a more pluralist map exists" (p. 54).

92. Edward Sheehan, "It Changes, It Changes Not," *Journal of Palestine Studies,* Autumn 1977, p. 188. See other specialists and former officials who have dealt with the Arab-Israeli problem extensively: William Quandt, *New York Times,* Aug. 8, 1982; Joseph Sisco, *Christian Science Monitor,* Dec. 9, 1981, Harold Saunders, *New York Times,* Aug. 8 1982; Saunders, *Time,* June 28, 1982, p. 17; Talcott Seelye, "Can the PLO Be Brought to the Negotiating Table?" *American-Arab Affairs,* Summer 1982, pp. 78f.

93. The *US News and World Report,* Aug. 3, 1981, p. 11 wrote: "Every top official but one [in the White House] had come around to the view that Reagan must crack down harder on Begin. The exception, the President himself." See also *New York Times,* Jan. 25, 1982, April 10, June 16, June 23, 1982; *Christian Science Monitor,* Feb. 23, 1983; *Time,* April 14, 1980, p. 50, June 17, 1983, p. 20.

94. *IPB,* Sept. 1982, p. 5. Arthur Hertsberg, vice president of the World Jewish Congress, wrote in the *New York Times,* May 27, 1984, op-ed page: "Israeli moderates know that the Palestinian problem and continued occupation of the West Bank area" were threatening to make Israel into another Northern Ireland. "But only Washington can press Israeli leaders to pay the political price of dealing with these issues." Col. (Reserve) Meir Pail, "Zionism Today: Zionism in Danger of Cancer," *New Outlook,* Jan. 1984, p. 28.

95. *IPB,* Sept. 1982, p. 6; *IPB,* April 1984, p. 12. See also *Jerusalem Post,* editorial, Nov. 7, 1982.

96. Harkabi, *The Bar Kokhba Syndrome,* pp. 178, 180.

97. Seelye, "Can the PLO Be Brought to the Negotiating Table?," pp. 78ff. In the case of the Panama Canal treaty, which had been strongly opposed in both the Senate and American public opinion, President Carter won the battle in the Senate and in public opinion by going all out in educating the public, as well as many senators, as to why the treaty was, in fact, very much to American vital interests. Carter was also doing well in winning over public opinion on the Palestinian and territorial issues during most of 1977 when his administration and he personally went all-out to convince the American people as to why a fair, comprehensive peace settlement was vital not only to our own best interests but even to Israel's best interests as well. It was only the lack of his political courage and "will" which ultimately undermined his efforts, which had made such great progress until he gave way to Israeli and pro-Israeli pressures following the October 1, U.S.–Soviet communiqué. The American public was often readier than Congress to apply pressures on Israel, especially when government leaders were making a serious attempt to make it aware of the realities of the situation (for example, see *US News and World Report,* Aug. 23, 1982, p. 18).

98. Seth P. Tillman, "U.S. Middle East Policy: Theory and Practice," *American-*

Arab Affairs, Spring 1983, p. 2; See also: George Ball, "American Policy on Trial," *Journal of Palestine Studies,* Spring 1978, p. 29; and Seth Tillman, *The United States in the Middle East,* pp. 282f.

99. Former Defense Minister Ezer Weizman wrote: "The Soviet Union needs the Middle East for its own defense because of the region's geopolitical proximity to its borders." Weizman, *The Battle for Peace,* p. 254.

100. *New York Times,* June 17, 1984; *Newsweek,* Jan. 16, 1984, p. 13.

101. *New York Times,* Feb. 20, 21, 22, 1985.

102. Weizman, *The Battle for Peace,* p. 255; *New York Times,* Oct. 16, Nov. 23, 1983.

103. *New York Times,* May 14, 1983; Saunders, *The Middle East in the 1980s,* pp. 14f.

104. *New York Times,* April 11, 1980.

Index

Abdullah, King: Egypt and, 94; Great Britain and, 97; "Greater Syria" and, 70, 106; Husseini and, 78–79; Israel and, 70, 96–97, 99, 107, 284, 294–95; Old City of Jerusalem and, 107, 111–12, 118; Palestine and, 70, 83; Palestine War and, 88; United States and, 97

Abu Nidal group, 429

Abu Rudeis (Sinai), 379

Aden, 7

Afghanistan, 416, 449, 478, 516, 518

Africa: 367, 372; see also Organization of African Unity

Aireli, Yohoshua, 361

Algeria, 211, 258, 280, 289, 343, 357, 462, 468–69

Allen, Richard V., 422

Allon Plan, 455

Allon, Yigal, 377

"All-Palestine Government," 83, 106

Almagor incident, 223–24

American Council for Judaism, 30, 45, 58

American-Israeli Public Affairs Committee, 438

American Jews: financial aid to Israel and, 73, 77; Israeli settlement policy and, 414; Reagan Peace Plan and, 438; United States immigration policy and, 24; World War I and, 5; Zionism and, 29, 32

American public opinion: anti-Arab, 267; anti-Egyptian, 258; Israeli invasion of Lebanon and, 431–32; pro-Israeli, 254, 258, 262, 267; Zionist influence upon, 29–39, 52, 65, 79–91, 138, 213, 253–59, 304, 342

American Zionists: growth in importance of, 44; political influence of, 29, 32, 37, 55, 79, 82, 90, 138, 213, 238, 253, 304, 338, 342; trusteeship proposal and, 61

Amman Conference. See Palestine National Council

Anglo-American Committee of Inquiry, 34–36, 105

Anglo-Egyptian Suez Agreement, 200–201, 207

Anglo-Egyptian Treaty (1936), 94–95

Anglo-French attack on Egypt, 140, 156, 177, 212–19, 253

Anti-Semitism, 3–4, 24

Aqaba, Gulf of: Arabs and, 250, 253; "blockade" of, 182, 208, 249, 257, 262, 287; Egypt and, 208–10, 240, 247–50, 257,

283, 287, 324; Great Britain and, 209, 255, 258; Israel and, 183, 208–10, 218, 248–59, 284, 353, 365; Jordan and, 208; legal controversy over, 283; Nasser and, 247, 255–56, 263, 281; Saudi Arabia and, 208; Sinai War and, 214, 217–18, 248; UNEF and, 218, 246; United States and, 217–18, 253–58; World Court and, 283–84

al-Aqsa, 419, 453

Arab Americans, 32

Arab boycott, 35, 182–83, 204–205, 214

Arab disunity, 19, 69–106, 138–39, 227, 235, 243, 249, 281, 289, 306–307, 310–17, 380, 392, 403–405, 414–15, 471–72, 476, 508–509

Arab Front for Steadfastness and Confrontation, 404–405

Arab Higher Committee: creation of, 24; King Abdullah and, 78; outlawed, 25; trusteeship proposal and, 61; United Nations and, 45, 48, 59

Arab-Israeli Federation: 45, 354–55; see also UNSCOP Minority Plan

Arab League: Arab refugees and, 130; boycott of Israel and, 204–205; headquarters, 411; Information Offices, 32, 57; Jerusalem and, 112; King Abdullah and, 106–107; origin of, 31; partition and, 57; Syrian invasion of Lebanon and, 444

Arab League Pact, 31

Arab Legion, 70, 73, 80, 86, 96–98

Arab Liberation Army, 69–70, 73

Arab Liberation Front, 358, 375, 483–84

Arab nationalism: Great Britain and, 13; growth of, 17, 20–21, 24, 353; King Abdullah and, 98–99, 107; Palestine and, 24; Soviet Union and, 140; World War I and, 6–7; Zionism and, 21; see also Palestinian nationalism

Arab propaganda, 15, 26, 32, 35, 39, 46, 52, 162

Arab refugees: attitude of, 123, 135, 137, 139, 162–64, 179; border incidents and, 183, 197; effect on Arab masses, 69, 139; family reunions of, 128, 155, 162, 166, 326, 328; funds, 158; numbers of, 149, 155–58, 172–74; peace and, 127–31, 139, 160; politics and, 161–62; property of, 128, 133, 147–48, 159–60, 174; resettlement of, 125–81; works projects, 129–35, 141; see also UN Relief and Works Agency for Palestine Refugees

593

THE ARAB-ISRAELI DILEMMA

Third Edition

was composed in 10-point Times Roman and leaded 2 points,
with display type in Times New Roman, by Dix Typesetting Company, Inc.,
and Maple-Vail Book Manufacturing Group, Inc.;
printed sheet-fed offset on 50-pound, acid-free P & S Offset Smooth,
Smythe-sewn, and bound over binder's boards in Joanna Arrestox B,
also adhesive bound with paper covers by Maple-Vail Book Manufacturing Group, Inc.;
with jackets and paper covers printed in two colors by Frank A. West Company, Inc.;
and published by

SYRACUSE UNIVERSITY PRESS

SYRACUSE, NEW YORK 13210